INFORMATION TECHNOLOGY LAW

Information Technology Law

Seventh Edition

IAN J. LLOYD

Senior Research Fellow, ILAWS: The Institute for Law and the Web, Faculty of Business and Law, University of Southampton

OXFORD
UNIVERSITY PRESS

OXFORD
UNIVERSITY PRESS

Great Clarendon Street, Oxford, OX2 6DP,
United Kingdom

Oxford University Press is a department of the University of Oxford.
It furthers the University's objective of excellence in research, scholarship,
and education by publishing worldwide. Oxford is a registered trade mark of
Oxford University Press in the UK and in certain other countries

© Oxford University Press 2014

The moral rights of the author have been asserted

Fourth Edition 2004
Fifth Edition 2008
Sixth Edition 2011

Impression: 1

Published in the United States of America by Oxford University Press
198 Madison Avenue, New York, NY 10016, United States of America

British Library Cataloguing in Publication Data
Data available

Library of Congress Control Number: 2014932447

ISBN 978-0-19-870232-0

Printed in Great Britain by
Ashford Colour Press Ltd, Gosport, Hampshire

Preface

Much is written today about 'big data'. Essentially the term refers to collections of data that are so large that in a previous era they could not have been processed. Today they can be. We live in an age when more and more data is created. One estimate suggests:

In 2012, every day *2.5 quintillion bytes of data* (1 followed by 18 zeros) are created, with 90% of the world's data created in the last two years alone. As a society, we're producing and capturing more data each day than was seen by everyone since the beginning of the earth.[1]

Whether the estimate is correct to a few percentile points is not significant. We all know from experience just how much access to data we have. When I wrote the first edition of this book in 1993 almost all footnote references were to paper-based sources that were available only to readers with access to a substantial library. In this edition, almost all detailed references are to online sources that can be accessed by anyone with an Internet connection.

The incredible amount of data that we can access does creates its own problems. In the body of the text I reflect on the difference between possessing information and knowledge—between being able to access information and understanding what it means. In the Middle Ages we had the notion of the 'Renaissance Man', the educated person who could discourse profoundly (in a range of languages) with colleagues across all artistic and scientific disciplines. Today the pace of progress is such that we all become increasingly specialised. When I wrote the first edition of this book it was quite difficult to find enough material to fill it. Today I struggle to cope with the deluge of new information in every sector. I do often wonder whether the notion of a single author writing on a broad topic is sustainable.

What I have tried to do in this edition is to give some account of the law, to reflect on its current state but also to provide a springboard for readers to pursue issues and topics that intrigue them. The e-book version has, of course, direct hypertext links to sites – although nobody can guarantee that links will work in a year's time. There is also the Online Resource Centre which I will try—given my human tendency towards indolence—to keep updated. One factor that does encourage activity is feedback from readers. One of the problems I have encountered with online sites is the sense that you are speaking to yourself. And that can be very boring! So please do communicate with me—even if only to say this is the worst book ever written.

Blame for the many faults and failings of the work lie with me. Things would be worse without the help of many friends and colleagues. It remains a notable feature of IT law that it is populated by nice people and, in all cases, I am acknowledging the help of friends rather than colleagues. I've known and worked with Steve Saxby for (too) many years and we have established together an LLM course at Southampton, which I contribute to whilst living in Glasgow. I could not bear to be separated from my beloved Celtic whilst Steve owns a number of season tickets at Southampton FC. There are things that are much more important than Law. I also work with and greatly appreciate the advice and friendship of David Mellor, the Chairman of the United Kingdom Telecommunications Academy. It is perhaps not the best-known of organisations but it, and David in particular, do great work in providing education in the sector to students in developing countries. Christopher

---

[1] <http://marciaconner.com/blog/data-on-big-data/>.

Millard and Richard Susskind are also friends of long standing. Richard goes from strength to strength and is undoubtedly the world's leading authority on the impact of IT on the legal profession. Christopher has followed a slightly different career path. From being a partner in major city law firms he has switched very successfully to academic life at the Centre for Commercial Law Studies in Queen Mary University. One of the joys of teaching is to see students developing and, again, to become friends. It is almost insidious to name names but a special word for Neil Brown who has helped a great deal with this book. He has forgotten more than I will ever know about telecommunications. Thanks also to Ray London and John Craparo, former students and now good friends. Finally, people who are not friends. Moira, who I was lucky enough to marry, I love you so much. And our sons Thomas and James. Aged ten and seven, you may not have helped much with the academic content of the book (although James is far more skilled at Nintendo games than I am) but life would be so much poorer without you. The joy and laughter you bring has helped me persevere at times when I might otherwise have abandoned the work. Any worthwhile elements of this book are dedicated to Moira, Thomas, and James with all my love.

Ian Lloyd
2014

New to this Edition

Key revisions to the 7th edition include:

- new introductory sections giving a general overview of the topic to be considered in each part of the book
- a new chapter on electronic money and online gambling
- new sections on expanding topics such as cyberterrorism and cyberwarfare
- commentary on the EU proposals for a data protection regulation and consideration of the revelations relating to monitoring by the NSA and GCHQ
- expanded treatment of issues related to online criminality
- consideration of the new system of Internet domain names introduced by ICANN and national domain registries
- consideration of new cases in all areas of the law.

Outline Contents

Late Developments   xxiii

List of Tables and Figures   xxxii

Table of Cases   xxxiii

Table of Statutes   xxxvii

Table of Statutory Instruments   xlii

Table of European Legislation   xliv

Table of Conventions and Other Enactments   xlvii

PART I Privacy, Anonymity, and Data Protection

1   Privacy, technology, and surveillance   7

2   The emergence of data protection   26

3   The scope of data protection   42

4   Supervisory agencies   62

5   The data protection principles   83

6   Individual rights and remedies   112

7   Sectoral aspects of data protection   138

8   Transborder data flows   167

PART II Computer-Related Crime

9   National and international responses to computer-related crime   197

10   Substantive criminal law provisions   202

11   Computer fraud and forgery   221

12   Virtual criminality   229

13   Detecting and prosecuting computer crime   243

PART III Intellectual Property Issues

14   Key elements of the patent system   263

15   Patents and software   280

16   Copyright protection   309

17   Copyright in the information society   348

18   Protection of databases   372

19   Design rights   392

20   Trade mark and domain-name issues   400

PART IV   E-Commerce

21   International and European initiatives in e-commerce   427

22   Cryptography, electronic signatures, and the Electronic
     Communications Act 2000   442

23   Electronic money and online gambling   459

24   Contractual liability for defective software   469

PART V   Internet-Specific Issues

25   Social networking, defamation, and the Internet   505

26   Internet regulation and domain names   526

Index   535

Detailed Contents

Late Developments   xxiii

List of Tables and Figures   xxxii

Table of Cases   xxxiii

Table of Statutes   xxxvii

Table of Statutory Instruments   xlii

Table of European Legislation   xliv

Table of Conventions and Other Enactments   xlvii

PART I Privacy, Anonymity, and Data Protection

1 Privacy, technology, and surveillance   7

Introduction   7

Smoke and mirrors—from echelon to prism   7

Public and private surveillance   9

Forms of surveillance   11

Living in the surveillance society   12

Surveillance and the law   15

Privacy issues   17
   The post-Second World War expansion of rights to privacy   17

Surveillance-based legislation   20

Privacy and surveillance   22

Conclusions   24

2 The emergence of data protection   26

Introduction   26

Early data protection laws   27

International data protection initiatives   27
   The Council of Europe   28
   The Organisation for Economic Co-operation and Development (OECD)   30
   The Asia-Pacific Privacy Charter initiative   32
   The UN   32

The development of data protection in the United Kingdom   33
   The Committee on Data Protection   34
   The Data Protection Act 1984   35

The European Data Protection Directive and the Data Protection Act 1998   36
   The Data Protection Act 1998   38

Conclusions   39

3 The scope of data protection   42

Introduction   42

The concept of personal data   42
    Sensitive personal data   44

Personal data relating to the data subject   46

Issues of identification   50

The concept of processing   52

Non-automated filing systems   53

Data protection actors   56
    Data controllers   56
    Data processors   57
    Data subjects   58

Jurisdictional issues   58

Conclusions   60

4 Supervisory agencies   62

Introduction   62

Forms of supervisory agencies   62
    Key functions of supervisory agencies   64

The Information Commissioner and the Information Tribunal   65

Procedural requirements for data controllers   66
    From registration to notification   66
    Exemptions from the requirement to notify   67
    The scope of the exemptions   68
    Staff administration   68
    Advertising, marketing, and public relations   69
    Accounts and records   69
    Non-profit-making organisations   70

Independent data protection supervisors   70

Information to be supplied on notification   71

Preliminary assessments   72

The Data Protection Register   72

Enforcement of the legislation   73
    Powers of entry and inspection   73
    Information notices   74
    Enforcement notices   75
    Undertakings   75
    Audits   75
    Monetary penalties   77

General duties of the Information Commissioner   77
    Disseminating information   77
    Codes of practice   78
    International cooperation   79

Professional secrecy 80

Appellate Bodies 80

Other supervisory agencies 81

Conclusions 81

5 **The data protection principles** 83

Introduction 83

Fair and lawful processing 85

Requirements for processing to be fair 85
Information obtained from the data subject 86
Information not obtained from the data subject 86
Unfair processing subsequent to obtaining data 87
The credit reference agency cases 89

Requirements for processing to be lawful 92
Specific factors legitimising processing 92
Subject consent 93
Duration of consent 95

Other factors legitimising processing 95
General data 95
Necessity for concluding or performing a contract with the data subject 95
Necessity for the controller to comply with a legal obligation 96
Necessity to protect the vital interests of the data subject 96
Necessity for the administration of justice, etc. 96
Legitimate interests of the controller 96
Factors legitimising the processing of sensitive data 97
Explicit subject consent 97
Employment-related processing 98
Vital interests 98
Processing by specified bodies 98
Information in the public domain 99
Legal proceedings and the administration of justice 99
Processing for medical purposes 99
Ethnic monitoring 99
Order of the Secretary of State 100
Political data 101

Exceptions to the application of the first data protection principle for law
enforcement and revenue-gathering purposes 101

The second data protection principle—purpose limitation 102

The third data protection principle—relevance 103

The fourth data protection principle—adequacy and timeousness 107

The fifth data protection principle—duration of record-keeping 108

The seventh data protection principle—data security 109

Codes of practice 110

Conclusions 110

6 Individual rights and remedies   112

Introduction   112

Subject access and information rights   112
  Access timetable   115

Exceptions to the subject access provisions   115
  Third-party data   116
  National security   119
  Data held for policing and revenue-gathering purposes   122
  Health data   124
  Education and social-work data   125
  Regulatory activity   126
  Research, history, and statistics   126
  Information required to be made available to the public   126
  Miscellaneous exceptions   126
    Confidential references   127
    Armed forces   127
    Judicial appointments and honours   127
    Crown employment and Crown and ministerial appointments   127
    Management forecasts   127
    Corporate finance   127
    Negotiations   128
    Examination marks and examination scripts   128
    Information about human embryos   128
    Legal professional privilege   129
    Self-incrimination   129

Matters arising subsequent to an access request   129
  Denial of access   129
  Rectification of inaccurate data   130
  Compensation   130

Other subject rights   131
  Right to request an assessment of processing   131
  Right to resist enforced subject access   132
  Right to object to data processing   133
    Direct marketing   133
    Other forms of processing   135
    Automated decision-making   135

Conclusions   136

7 Sectoral aspects of data protection   138

Introduction   138

Data protection and the media   138

Scope of the provisions   140
  Activities covered   140
  Scope of the exemption   141
  Procedural aspects   142

Special information notices   145

Enforcement notices   146

Individual rights and remedies 146

Granting of assistance by the Commissioner 146

Data protection in the electronic communications sector 146

The development of sector-specific legislation 149

The Privacy and Electronic Communications Directive and Regulations 150
  Obligations imposed on network and service providers 150
  Security and confidentiality 151
  Breach notification 152
  Cookies 153
  Traffic and location data 155
  Data retention 157
  Itemised billing 159
  Directory information 160
  Calling and connected line identification 162
  Unsolicited communications 163

Conclusions 166

8 Transborder data flows 167

Introduction 167

Regulating transborder data flows 168

Procedures for determining adequacy 169
  Defining adequacy 170
  Activity in determining adequacy 171
  The 'safe harbor' agreement 172
  Consequences of a finding of adequacy 175

The SWIFT case 176

Air passenger data 178

Transfers when an adequate level of protection is not provided 180
  The role of contract 182
  Binding corporate rules 185

Conclusions 186

PART II Computer-Related Crime

9 National and international responses to computer-related crime 197

Introduction 197

The Council of Europe Cybercrime Convention 198

OECD Guidelines for the Security of Information Systems 199

EU initiatives 200

Conclusions 201

10 Substantive criminal law provisions 202

Introduction 202

Offences against the confidentiality, integrity, and availability of
computer data and systems 202

Illegal access 203
Obtaining or enabling access to computers or data 204
When is access unauthorised? 206
Unauthorised use by authorised users 207

Interception of communications 210

Data and system interference 211
Damage to data 212
Denial-of-service attacks 214
Misuse of devices 216
Malicious communications 217

Conclusions 219

11 Computer fraud and forgery 221

Introduction 221

Computer-related forgery 222

Computer-related fraud 223
Deception of a machine 224
The dishonest obtaining of services 227

Conclusions 228

12 Virtual criminality 229

Introduction 229

Internet pornography 230

The Internet and child pornography 232

Photographs and pseudo-photographs 233

Multimedia products 235

Jurisdictional issues 237

Where next for the criminal law? 239
Revenge pornography 240

Conclusions 242

13 Detecting and prosecuting computer crime 243

Introduction 243

Interception of communications 244
Interception of content and communications data 245
Interception of content 245
Financing interception 246
Communications data 247
Search warrants 248

Computer evidence 250

Jurisdictional issues 251

Extradition 253

PART III Intellectual Property Issues

14 Key elements of the patent system 263

Introduction 263

Patents in the international arena 264

The Patent Co-operation Treaty 265

The European Patent Convention 265

The Unitary Patent 266

Intellectual property in the GATS and WTO 267

Requirements for patentability 268

Novelty 268

Inventive step 269

Capacity for industrial application 270

Matters excluded from patent protection 271

Patenting software 272

The process of obtaining and enforcing a patent 273

The application 273

Specification and statement of claim 273

Preliminary examination 274

Publication of the application 274

Substantive examination 275

Third-party involvement 275

Award of a patent 275

Infringement of patents 276

Remedies for infringement of a patent 277

Revocation of a patent 277

Conclusions 278

15 Patents and software 280

Introduction 280

The Patents Act 1977 and the European Patent Convention 282

The quest for a technical contribution 284

The development of software patent jurisprudence 289

New millennium, new patent law? 292

IBM's Application 292

Pensions benefits 294

Hitachi 295

Microsoft 296

Let a thousand flowers bloom? 296

Schemes for performing mental acts 301

The mobile-phone patent wars 302

Issues of priority 303

Conclusions 305

16 Copyright protection   309

Introduction   309

Copyright basics   309

Obtaining copyright   311

Forms of protected work   311

The requirement of originality   312

Ownership of copyright   313
   Employee-created works   313
   Computer-generated works   313

Infringement of copyright   315

The nature of copying   315
   How temporary is temporary?   316
   Fair and unfair use of an earlier work   319

Other rights belonging to the copyright owner   321
   To issue copies of the work to the public   321
   To perform, show, or play the work in public   322
   To broadcast the work or include it in a cable programme service   322
   To make an adaptation of the work   322

The development of software copyright   323
   Applying copyright principles to software   324
   Software piracy   325
   User rights in respect of software   326
   Fair dealing   326

A use right for software?   327
   Error correction   329
   Back-up copies   329
   Reverse engineering and decompilation   330
   Reverse engineering and computer programs   333

Literal and non-literal copying   335
   The rise and fall of look-and-feel protection   337
   The computerised pharmacist   337
   Agricultural software   339
   Financial markets   340
   Arm's length reproduction   343
   Computer programs as visual works   346

Conclusions   347

17 Copyright in the information society   348

Introduction   348

The Directive on Copyright in the Information Society   349
   Caching   350
   Copy protection and Digital Rights Management (DRM)   351

Private copying in the digital age   353

Copyright enforcement   354
   Norwich Pharmacal orders and threats of litigation   355

The Digital Economy Act 2010 356
   Online infringement of copyright 357
   The initial obligations code 357
   Initial obligations code by OFCOM in the absence of an approved code 358
   Notification reports 359
   Copyright infringement lists 359
   Progress reports 359
   Obligations to limit Internet access 360
   Code by OFCOM about obligations to limit Internet access 360
   Contents of code about obligations to limit Internet access 361
   Legal challenges to the Digital Economy Act 362
   The E-Commerce Directive 362
   Data protection issues 363
   Where now for the Digital Economy Act? 364
   Blocking orders 365

New directions in UK copyright law 367
   Orphan works 367
   Harvesting the Internet 368

Conclusions 369

18 Protection of databases 372

Introduction 372

What is a database? 373
   Examples of databases 373

Databases and new technology 374

Traditional forms of protection for databases 375
   The 'sweat of the brow' doctrine 376

The database regime 378
   Copyright and databases 379
   Licensing and databases 380
   Other copyright changes 381
   The database right 381
   Duration of the right 382

The database right in the courts 383
   Football fixture lists 386
     How much is too much? 387

Conclusions 390

19 Design rights 392

Introduction 392

The development of design right and key legislative instruments 392
   Registered design right protection 394
   Unregistered design right 394

Design rights in tablet computers 395

Conclusions 399

20 Trade mark and domain-name issues   400

Introduction   400

Effect of trade marks   401

Passing off   402

Trade marks and information technology   403

Internet-related trade mark disputes   404
    Domain-name hijacking   404
    Honest concurrent use   408
    Reverse domain-name hijacking   410

The Uniform Dispute Resolution Rules   412

Trade marks and Internet search engines   415

Conclusions   422

PART IV E-Commerce

21 International and European initiatives in e-commerce   427

Introduction   427

International initiatives   427

Key legal instruments   428
    The Distance Selling Directive   429
    The Electronic Commerce Directive and Regulations 431
    Defences provided to Information Service Providers 432
    Substantive provisions in the Directive   435
        When and where is a contract made? 435
        Choice-of-law issues   438
    Alternative dispute resolution   439

Conclusions   440

**22 Cryptography, electronic signatures, and the Electronic
Communications Act 2000**   442

Introduction   442

The nature of encryption   443

Enter trusted third parties   446

Legal approaches   447

Background to the Electronic Communications Act 2000 and
E-Commerce Directive   448
    The basis of requirements for writing   449
    Electronic documents and the requirements for writing 453
    Electronic signatures and the Electronic Communications Act 2000 455
    Electronic signatures   455
    Cryptography service providers   456

Conclusions   457

23 Electronic money and online gambling   459

Introduction   459

E-money 460
  National and European legislation 460
  The nature of e-money 461
  E-money issuers and small e-money issuers 462
  Criteria for admission to the register 462
  Safeguarding arrangements 462
  Passport rights 462
  Virtual currency 462
  Peer-to-peer lending 465

Online gambling 466
  Introduction 466
  The Gambling Act 2005 467
  Licencing of remote gambling activities 467
  Technical standards 468

Conclusions 468

24 Contractual liability for defective software 469

Introduction 469

Forms of liability 470

The nature of software defects 471

Forms of software 472

The legal status of software and software contracts 473

Implied terms in software contracts 475
  Title in software 476
  Description 477
  Quality 477
  Remedies for breach of the implied terms 480

Software quality and the courts 481
  Questions of time 481
  Problems with the Community Charge 484
  Water privatisation 485
  The Monday software package 487
  The dog with an MBA 490

Exclusion or limitation of liability 492

Enforceability of shrink-wrap licences 493
  Consumer contracts 494
  Non-consumer contracts 495

The requirement of reasonableness 497

Conclusions 500

PART V Internet-Specific Issues

25 Social networking, defamation, and the Internet 505

Introduction 505

The nature of defamation 508

The law on defamation 508

Who is liable for defamatory comments?   509
   Employer's liability   513
   Liability of ISPs as publishers   514

Single or multiple publications?   519

Jurisdictional issues   522

ISPs and the Electronic Commerce Directive   523

Conclusions   524

26   Internet regulation and domain names   526

Introduction   526

The emergence of Internet regulation   527

Domain names   529

Regulation of the domain-name system   530
   The domain-name structure   531
   National domain names   532

Conclusions   533

Index   535

Late Developments

Data protection

A Chinese blessing (or curse) expresses the wish that the recipient should live in 'interesting times'. That is certainly the case in the field of data protection. Significant reform proposals were published at the end of 2012 and are making their way through the labyrinth that is the EU legislative process. Initially intended to be adopted by April 2014, it is now hoped that the reform will be adopted by the end of the year. Complicating matters has been the disagreement between the EU and the United States concerning monitoring of communications and ongoing concerns over the functioning of the 'safe harbor' agreement which applies to the transfer of personal data from Europe to US companies.

The EU legislative proposal is for a data protection Regulation that will replace existing national laws with a pan-European legal and supervisory infrastructure. Changes will come into effect twenty-four months after the adoption of the Regulation.

Data protection has, of course, been much in the news recently. It is perhaps fair to say that little of the publicity has been complimentary of the legislation. After a prolonged period of gestation, the European Commission has now published legislative proposals based in some respects on concepts in the recently revised Directive on Privacy in the Electronic Communications Sector that, if adopted, will alter significantly the data protection landscape.

One of the major complaints that has been raised at European level is that the existing Directive has been implemented in significantly different ways across the Member States. In the case of some countries, perhaps especially the UK there is the belief that the implementing legislation is too weak—and legal proceedings alleging a failure to implement fully the Directive have been initiated by the Commission. The range of legislative approaches is also seen as creating difficulties for multinational companies who have to comply with up to twenty-seven different regulatory regimes.

In order to enhance legislative consistency across the Member States, a significant change is proposed with a Regulation (which will be binding in all Member States without the need for any implementing legislation) replacing the current Directive. In some respects it is difficult to see how this might operate in practice, especially at the level of supervisory authorities. In the absence of a single EU supervisory authority—something that would probably be politically unacceptable to many countries—responsibility for establishing and resourcing national authorities remains with the Member States. The Regulation may will the ends but it cannot provide the means.

The IT world has been transformed massively since the original Directive was adopted in 1995. Indeed the Directive itself draws heavily on legal principles dating back to the 1970s. It has been suggested that if a single smart phone had existed in the 1970s it would have been classed as the most powerful computer in the world. OFCOM now reports that there are almost 13 million smart phones in use in the UK. The search engine Google was founded in 1998 and the ubiquitous social-networking site Facebook, in 2004. The list of examples could go on and on but, undoubtedly explaining the increasing publicity afforded to privacy-protection issues, more and more important and indeed sensitive elements of our lives are conducted online. The key question relating to the new legislative proposal is how well can it refine data protection law to meet the demands of the online world? The Commission Communication accompanying the draft Regulation commences:

> The rapid pace of technological change and globalisation have profoundly transformed the way in which an ever-increasing volume of personal data is collected, accessed, used and transferred. New ways of sharing information through social networks and storing large amounts of data remotely have become part of life for many of Europe's 250 million internet users. At the same time, personal data has become an asset for many businesses. Collecting, aggregating and analysing the data of potential customers is often an important part of their economic activities.

Whilst there are some interesting aspects to the new draft Regulation (which is very substantially larger than the current Directive) my initial assessment is that it represents something of a wasted opportunity. Given the size of the new instrument, an early comment cannot be comprehensive but I will try to focus on the points that seem most significant to me.

Plus ça change?

Many of the key definitions survive unchanged from the original Directive. In some respects this is not a surprise but the emergence of cloud computing has raised some novel and serious issues regarding the applicability of concepts of data controller and processor and it is unfortunate that the opportunity has not been taken to attempt to address the issue.

There is a potentially significant change in the definition of consent. The UK approach has traditionally been to accept that the use of 'opt out' approaches is a valid means of securing and evidencing consent. The draft Regulation takes a different approach stating that:

> the data subject's consent' means any freely given specific, informed and explicit indication of his or her wishes by which the data subject, either by a statement or by a clear affirmative action, signifies agreement to personal data relating to them being processed.

It is further provided that 'Consent shall not provide a legal basis for the processing, where there is a significant imbalance between the position of the data subject and the controller.' It is difficult to see how this can be implemented but the effect could be devastating for many data controllers. A passenger seeking to book a railway ticket online is in a weak position compared with the train provider. The choice is between accepting the conditions of carriage or find another mode of transport. It is normal practice for websites to 'offer' to send further promotional mailings if the traveller consents. It seems that this will no longer be possible. This seems draconian, given especially that if there was real evidence of abuse of a dominant position, there could be a challenge on the ground that consent was not freely given. Many consumers might actually value being notified of future offers.

A further change to the notion of consent relates to the processing of data relating to children under the age of thirteen. In such cases it is provided that processing 'shall only be lawful if and to the extent that consent is given or authorised by the child's parent or custodian'. It is difficult to see what problem this provision is seeking to overcome and again the consequences may be undesirable. If a child should be injured and taken to hospital it would appear that it would be unlawful for the hospital to take any X-rays without parental consent. Whilst consent might always be desirable the consequences could be serious in the case of an emergency and where the parent cannot be contacted.

Likewise, perhaps, the data protection principles have remained largely unchanged since the earliest days of data protection legislation. They can fairly be analogised to religious notions such as the Ten Commandments (or mother's apple pie). Few would disagree with the concepts but the devil is always in the detail. The headline change proposed in the Regulation is that there should be a 'right to be forgotten'. As an old-fashioned sort or person, this concerns me. I am old enough to recall the debates in the UK in the context of computer-related fraud about whether the machine could be the victim of deception. The Law Commission's work on fraud seems to have provided compelling reasons why the establishment of criminal offences should be based on other criteria (which can fairly easily be established, as Scots law has shown with the notion of basing criminality on the making a false pretence). By focusing on the intent of the perpetrator this neatly avoids the issue. If computers cannot be subject to the human fallibility of being deceived, neither can they forget. This, however, is exactly what the Regulations proposes. Article 17 is headed 'Right to be forgotten and to erasure'. The first part of this is abject nonsense. Just as a computer cannot be deceived, so it cannot forget. Even placed in a human context, no law can compel forgetfulness—although human frailty may be more effective.

There is no doubt that the emergence of social-networking sites has lured many users into placing sensitive aspects of their lives into a public or semi-public domain. It does seem clear beyond doubt that this data may be used in ways which would not have been conceived of or approved by the individual. Article 17 goes on at some length:

> The data subject shall have the right to obtain from the controller the erasure of personal data relating to them and the abstention from further dissemination of such data, especially in relation to personal data which are made available by the data subject while he or she was a child, where one of the following grounds applies:
>
> (a) the data are no longer necessary in relation to the purposes for which they were collected or otherwise processed;
>
> (b) the data subject withdraws consent on which the processing is based according to point (a) of Article 6(1), or when the storage period consented to has expired, and where there is no other legal ground for the processing of the data;
>
> (c) the data subject objects to the processing of personal data pursuant to Article 19;
>
> (d) the processing of the data does not comply with this Regulation for other reasons.

Whilst certainly well meaning, it is difficult to see what this provision will accomplish that could not have been attained under existing provisions. It has always been the case, for example, that data must be processed fairly and that it must not be retained for longer than is necessary for the controller's legitimate purposes.

There have long been issues whether an individual is aware of the implications of their online conduct but the reality is that once data is put into the public domain it cannot be retrieved. It does appear that responsible social-networking sites have made efforts to inform users and, within their possibilities of control, accede to request that data be deleted. It is hard to see this provision as anything other than an attempt at headline grabbing which takes advantage of vulnerable elements of society. It is wrong to give a headline promise of legislative support that is not worth the paper it is written on.

One of the most impressive legal documents of recent times has been the Hargreaves Report on the digital economy. Covering issues such as the value of software patents and the losses caused by copyright piracy it makes the point again and again that what is needed is an evidence-based approach. In some respects it seems the Commission is falling into the trap of making proposals without evidence. There are certainly tales of individuals being denied employment because a potential employer has viewed their social-networking postings. A recent survey has suggested that 69 per cent of employers have denied an applicant a job on the basis of such a search. That is the bad news. Sixty-eight per cent of employers have indicated that they have offered a job because they have been impressed by online postings. A bigger problem perhaps is the malicious dissemination of personal data. Reference might be made to the recent English case of *AMP v Persons Unknown*. This relates to a sad, but perhaps increasingly common, situation where a teenage girl had used her mobile phone to take intimate photographs of herself. They were intended to be sent to her boyfriend (itself often a source of problems) but the phone was stolen and an unknown person posted copies on the Internet. In this case, the English courts have issued orders compelling any ISPs who can be identified to take steps to block access to the pictures and ordering that the anonymity of the complainant be preserved. It appears, however, that in order to serve an order in the USA on Google, US law requires that the identity of the complainant be disclosed.

Data portability

Linked in some respects to the deletion of data is the issue of portability. The draft Regulation proposes that:

> The data subject shall have the right, where personal data are processed by electronic means and in a structured and commonly used format, to obtain from the controller a copy of data undergoing processing in an electronic and structured format which is commonly used and allows for further use by the data subject.

Concerns have been expressed that data subjects might effectively be locked into online services, perhaps in particular social-networking (or blogging) sites because of the investment in time and effort expended in creating their profiles. It is not clear, however, to what extent competing sites operate in ways that are sufficiently interoperable to make the right of significant value.

Data security breaches

The imposition of requirements to notify supervisory authorities and data subjects of security breaches which may have implications for data subjects was introduced in the Directive on Privacy in Electronic Communications. It is now proposed to extend it to the more general field of data protection with the draft Regulation proposing that:

> In the case of a personal data breach, the controller shall without undue delay and, where feasible, not later than 24 hours after having become aware of it, notify the personal data breach to the supervisory authority.

When the personal data breach is likely to adversely affect the protection of the personal data or privacy of the data subject, the controller shall, after the notification referred to, communicate the personal data breach to the data subject without undue delay.

In an era of 24/7 online businesses there might perhaps be a query whether supervisory authorities are in a position to respond to notifications received between 5 p.m. on Friday and 9 a.m. on Mondays.

It is perhaps strange that the formula for notifying a data subject is less extensive than that for notifying the supervisory authority. Certainly it can be accepted that it is easier to notify one person than perhaps several millions but it is hard to see what constructive purpose is served by such a notification. One of the criticisms made of breach notification requirements (which have been commonplace in the United States for several years) is that the number of notifications required is too great so that there is the danger of notifications of potentially serious breaches being disregarded following a number of trivial notifications. In the event of a potentially serious breach—perhaps involving details of credit cards or bank accounts—there seems no reason why controllers should not be subject to the same 24-hour rule. Many businesses manage to send marketing communications on a daily basis to millions of subjects so there is no valid reason why they should not be as quick to send breach notifications on a similar timescale.

Data protection officers

The notion of in-house supervisory officials has been an established feature of the German data protection scheme. Although it is sanctioned in the Data Protection Act 1988, it does not appear to have been adopted to any significant extent within the UK. The draft Regulation proposes what will be a significant change. Every public authority or private-sector undertaking employing more than 250 persons will have to appoint a data protection officer:

> The controller or processor shall designate the data protection officer on the basis of professional qualities and, in particular, expert knowledge of data protection law and practices and ability to fulfil the tasks referred to in Article 37. The necessary level of expert knowledge shall be determined in particular according to the data processing carried out and the protection required for the personal data processed by the controller or the processor.
>
> The controller or the processor shall ensure that any other professional duties of the data protection officer are compatible with the person's tasks and duties as data protection officer and do not result in a conflict of interests.

The tasks of the data protection officer are stated to be to inform the data controller of the extent of its obligations under the Regulation and to monitor its compliance with its requirements. Data protection officers (who may be an employee of the data controller or an independent subcontractor—possibly a lucrative new source of work for IT Lawyers) are to be appointed on a fixed-term contract of at least two years' duration. Within this period the data protection officer may be dismissed only for a failure to fulfil data protection obligations.

Any legislative move to increase awareness amongst data controllers and their staff as to data protection issues is to be welcomed. In some respects, however, the approach demonstrates some of the weaknesses of the new approach. It specifies that there is to be a data protection officer and what the prime duties are to be. It does not indicate how extensive requirements may be. Is it to be a full-time job or a part-time (how part time?) position? If part-time and the position is held by an employee what is to happen if the person is considered to be guilty of misconduct in other aspects of his or her work sufficient to justify dismissal? There is need for much more detail. In this provision, as with a number of the other Articles, the Regulation provides that the Commission is to have power to make supplementary provision. These will not, however, have legal effect.

Data protection by design and by default

Considerable work has been carried out by the UK's Information Commissioner under the general heading of Privacy by Design.[1] The basic premise is that it is easier and better to take data protection factors into consideration at the earliest stage of designing IT systems than to attempt to include them at a later stage. The draft Regulation endorses this approach proposing that:

1. Having regard to the state of the art and the cost of implementation, the controller shall, both at the time of the determination of the means for processing and at the time of the processing itself, implement appropriate technical and organizational measures and procedures in such a way that the processing will meet the requirements of this Regulation and ensure the protection of the rights of the data subject.

2. The controller shall implement mechanisms for ensuring that, by default, only those personal data are processed which are necessary for each specific purpose of the processing and are especially not collected or retained beyond the minimum necessary for those purposes, both in terms of the amount of the data and the time of their storage. In particular, those mechanisms shall ensure that by default personal data are not made accessible to an indefinite number of individuals.

Such an approach could create difficulties for many websites. The word 'necessary' has featured prominently in many instruments in the field of human rights. It sets a high threshold for data collection. An e-commerce website sending goods to consumers through a postal system will not *need*, for example, details of phone numbers. The same will apply with systems such as airline booking systems. Very often these give customers the option of giving a mobile phone number so that they can be advised of any schedule alterations by SMS. It might be argued that this should be classed as a distinct form of processing, but what is a well-meaning attempt to protect individuals could all too easily turn into a bureaucratic nightmare.

Subject rights

In many respects what has been considered here is intended to protect the interests of data subjects. It has also been a feature of data protection laws that subjects should have the right to object to certain forms of processing. The draft Regulation proposes that:

The data subject shall have the right to object, on grounds relating to their particular situation, at any time to the processing of personal data which is based on points (d), (e) and (f) of Article 6(1), unless the controller demonstrates compelling legitimate grounds for the processing which override the interests or fundamental rights and freedoms of the data subject.

This is a significant and very much welcome change from the current legislation which provides that, except in the case of processing with a view to direct marketing and a few other limited situations, a data subject can object to processing only if he or she can

---

[1] See <http://ico.org.uk/for_organisations/data_protection/topic_guides/privacy_by_design>.

demonstrate that the processing is unlawful (as implemented in the UK, the requirement is to show that the processing would cause substantial and unwarranted damage or distress). It seems entirely appropriate to reverse the burden of proof and after many paragraphs of criticising aspects of the new Regulation, three cheers are in order.

Supervisory authorities

In some respects the provisions regarding the status, powers, and duties of supervisory agencies appear to be based on those contained in the Electronic Communications Privacy Directive. There may well be implications for the UK regime and it is perhaps here where it becomes difficult to identify the basis for a Regulation.

> Each Member State shall provide that one or more public authorities are responsible for monitoring the application of this Regulation and for contributing to its consistent application throughout the Union, in order to protect the fundamental rights and freedoms of natural persons in relation to the processing of their personal data and to facilitate the free flow of personal data within the Union. For these purposes, the supervisory authorities shall co-operate with each other and the Commission.

The Regulation states that supervisory authorities are to be given 'complete independence' and in particular provides that:

> Each Member State shall ensure that the supervisory authority is provided with the adequate human, technical and financial resources, premises and infrastructure necessary for the effective performance of its duties and powers, including those to be carried out in the context of mutual assistance, co-operation and participation with the European Data Protection Board.

Throughout, the terminology of the Regulation appears consistent only with the notion that the supervisory authority should be a multi-membered authority, something which has been recommended by the UK's former Information Commissioner but which has not been adopted as government policy.

In terms of the powers to be afforded to supervisory authorities, the draft Regulation provides that there should be a general auditing power:

> *Each supervisory authority shall have the investigative power to obtain from the controller or the processor:*
>
> (a) *access to all personal data and to all information necessary for the performance of its duties;*
>
> (b) *access to any of its premises, including to any data processing equipment and means, where there are reasonable grounds for presuming that an activity in violation of this Regulation is being carried out there*

Such a power has long been sought by the UK's Information Commissioner.

One further element of the Regulation may have significant implications for data protection in the United Kingdom. At present, the Information Commissioner's office is funded almost entirely through fees paid by data controllers upon notification. The Regulation proposes that responsibility for maintaining the data associated with notification should lie with the data controller and that this should only be supplied to the supervisory authority on specific request. There does not appear to be any possibility of the authority charging fees and it appears that significant change will be required to the UK's funding mechanism.

Given that the section of the Information Commissioner's office which is responsible for the freedom of information legislation is funded directly by the exchequer, it would seem logical to treat data protection in the same way.

Transborder data flows

The attempt to regulate Transborder data flows was one of the most controversial aspects of the Data Protection Directive. With its headline of 'you shall not transfer there unless there is an adequate level of protection', the legislation offered so many hostages to fortune.

There is remarkably little change in the headline provisions of the Regulation. Given the small number of findings of adequacy which have been made in the fourteen years that Directive 95/46 has been in force, it might be questioned whether it serves a particularly useful role. Assuming (perhaps a big assumption) that transfers are lawful there are so many other mechanisms which can be used to confer legitimacy. The notion of adequacy is a complex one and certainly as interpreted by the Commission would not seem to provide a basis which would secure sufficient global acceptance to form part of any wider privacy protection instrument.

Binding corporate rules

The concept of binding corporate rules has emerged through the work of Article 29 Working Party as a potential mechanism for evidencing an adequate level of protection in the case of transborder data flows. The concept has been applied without any specific statutory provision, something which the draft Regulation proposes to rectify although without changing significantly anything in the system as it has been applied.

The European Data Protection Board—and consistency

Since the implementation of Directive 95/46, the Article 29 Working Party has provided a forum for national data protection supervisors to meet and publish opinions and guidance on a wide range of data protection-related issues. The Regulation proposes that it should be replaced by a European Data Protection Board. The membership will be essentially the same but the intention appears to be that it should operate on a more formal basis with the general duty to 'ensure the consistent application of this Regulation'.

The Data Protection Board's powers are, however, limited and legal authority to ensure the consistent operation of the Regulation lies with the Commission. The Regulation establishes a general obligation for supervisory authorities to 'cooperate with each other and with the Commission'. In respect of a range of issues, principally relating to the regulation of transborder data flows, any national proposals are required to be notified to the Commission which, after consulting the European Data Protection Board, may approve the proposal, require modifications, or require that it be withdrawn.

Conclusions

The draft Regulation has been the subject of internal discussion within the Commission and consultation with external parties for a number of years. My initial impression might be summed up by the old aphorism 'the elephant has laboured and given birth to a mouse'.

Few would deny that there have been problems with the implementation of Directive 95/46. These were perhaps inevitable. At the time of its adoption two countries in particular raised concerns. Germany feared that the Directive was too weak and might weaken its own strong data protection regime. The United Kingdom, which abstained in the final vote in the Council, complained that it went too far. Given the normal problems that arise concerning national implementation of a Directive, problems were perhaps inevitable.

Although it does seem to me that there is now greater awareness of the value of data protection in the United Kingdom than was the case in the 1990s, the core problems do remain. The decision to proceed on the basis of a Regulation may overcome some of the problems of inconsistency although the political road to implementation may be a long and tortuous one. Some of the headline elements of the draft Regulation, such as the right to be forgotten, are stronger on style than on substance. It is probably politically inconceivable that a single European Data Protection Supervisory Authority would be acceptable to all the Member States, but in its absence it is unclear how consistency of application will be achieved in practice.

Perhaps the main cause for concern is how reluctant the draft Regulation is to accept that the computer world has moved on from the 1970s. In previous eras, it was important to know what data was held by a data controller. Today the key question is 'what data can be accessed'? Networks and data sharing agreements have transformed the data processing world but this is not reflected in the draft Regulation. It still reads like a twentieth-century piece of legislation. Individuals certainly need more rights but there is also need for a workable regime for data controllers.

As a final point, and perhaps as important as any, we are faced every day with evidence that the Internet operates on a global basis. National borders have not disappeared and we also see continually evidence of nation states trying to flex their muscles in respect of particular activities. As is perhaps emerging in the field of computer crime, there is a need to establish wide consensus. It is not clear that the draft Regulation will assist. Fortress Europe may have some appeal but history tells us that medieval fortresses which were largely resistant to bow and arrows crumbled before the cannon. It is unfortunate that part of the effort which has obviously gone into drafting the new proposals had not been diverted to seeking to find a basis for a wider Convention which might in the medium term better protect the interests of EU citizens.

List of Tables and Figures

Table 1.1   Concerns with issues of social importance   16
Table 3.1   Attitudes towards sensitivity of types of data   45
Figure P2.1 The cost of cyber crime   190

Table of Cases

Actavis UK Ltd v Merck & Co Inc (2008)... 300

Aerotel v Telco Holdings (2006) ... 280, 283, 289, 292, 297–301, 308

A-G's Reference (No. 1 of 1991) (1992) ... 205, 210, 244

AMP v Persons Unknown (2011) ... 219, 241

Aswan Engineering v Lupdine (1987)... 478

Autodesk v Dyson (1992) ... 342

Baker v Secretary of State for the Home Dept (2001) ... 120–2

Barthold v Germany (1985) ... 96

Beecham Group Ltd v Bristol Laboratories Ltd (1978) ... 276

Beechwood House Publishing v Guardian Products Ltd and Precision Direct Marketing Ltd (2011) ... 387

Bernstein v Pamsons Motors (Golders Green) Ltd (1987) ... 480, 481

Bilhofer v Dixon (1990) ... 340

Bravado Merchandising Services Ltd v Mainstream Publishing (Edinburgh) Ltd (1996) ... 407

Brinkibon Ltd v Stahag Stahl und Stahlwarenhandel GMBH (1982) ... 436

British Horseracing Board Ltd, the Jockey Club and Weatherbys Groups Ltd v William Hill Organization Ltd (2001); (2004); (2005) ... 383–7, 389, 390

British Leyland Motor Corpn Ltd v Armstrong Patents Co Ltd (1986) ... 310, 330, 331, 393, 394

British Telecommunications plc, Virgin Enterprises Ltd, J Sainsbury plc, Marks & Spencer plc and Ladbroke Group plc v One in a Million (1998) ... 405, 406, 413

Bryson v Deane (1937)... ... 508

BSkyB v EDS and Others (2010) ... 490–2

Bunt v Tilley and Others (2006) ... 365, 433, 434, 517

Byrne v Deane (1937) ... 518

Campbell v Mirror Group Newspapers (2002); (2004); (2005) ... 16, 29, 38, 60, 142, 143

Canon v Green Cartridge (1997) ... 393

Cantor Fitzgerald International v Tradition UK Ltd (2000) ... 340–2

Catnic Components Ltd v Hill and Smith Ltd (1982) ... 276

CBS Songs Ltd v Amstrad Consumer Electronics plc (1988) ... 311, 351

Census Decision (1984) ... 47

Chambers v DPP (2012) ... 217

Chief Constable of Humberside Police and Others v Information Commissioner (2009) ... 105, 106

Chief Constables of West Yorkshire, South Yorkshire and North Wales Police v The Information Commissioner (2005) ... 105, 106, 133

Common Services Agency v Scottish Information Commissioner (2006); (2008) ... 42, 46, 48, 50

Computer Associates Inc v Altai (1992) ... 338–40

Copland v United Kingdom(2007) ... 19

Data Protection Registrar v Griffin (1993) ... 57

Davies v Flackett (1973) ... 225

Douglas v Hello! (2001); (2005); (2007) ... 2, 16, 29

Dow Jones & Co Inc v Gutnick (2002) ... 520, 521

Dowson v Chief Constable of Northumbria Police (2010) ... 219

DPP v Lennon (2006) ... 215, 216

Duns Licensing Associates' Application (2006) ... 299, 300

Durant v Financial Services Authority (2003) ... 42, 46, 47, 49, 50, 55, 56, 60, 114, 118, 119, 129

Edem v The Information Commissioner and Financial Services Authority (2014) ... 40, 46, 50

Elanco Products Ltd v Mandops Agricultural Specialists Ltd (1980) ... 320, 321

Entores Ltd v Miles Far East Corpn (1955) ... 436

Erven Warnink v Townend (1979) ... 402

Eurodynamic Systems v General Automation Ltd (1988) ... 482

European Parliament v Council of the European Union and Commission of the European Communities (2004) ... 179

Express Newspapers plc v Liverpool Daily Post and Echo plc (1985) ... 313

Exxon Corpn v Exxon Insurance Consultants International Ltd (1982) ... 312, 372

Feist Publications Inc v Rural Telephone Service Co Inc (1991) ... 376–8, 382, 390

Fixtures Marketing v Oy Weikus AB and Others (2004) ... 387

Football Association Premier League Ltd v QC Leisure and Others (2008) ... 319

Football Dataco Ltd and Others v Brittens Pools and Others (2010) . . . 386

Football League Ltd v Littlewoods Pools (1959) . . . 387

Fujitsu's Application, Re [1996]; [1997] . . . 270–2, 297, 298, 306

Gale's Application, Re (1991) . . . 283, 297, 298

Gameaccount Ltd (2007) (EPO) . . . 300

Gaskin v UK (1990) . . . 19, 20, 40, 116–19

Genentech Inc's Patent (1989) . . . 269, 270, 280, 288, 306

Glaxo plc v Glaxowellcome Ltd (1996) . . . 404, 405

Gleeson and Gleeson Shirt Co Ltd v H R Denne Ltd (1975) . . . 332

Godfrey v Demon (1999) . . . 239, 515, 516

Gosling v Secretary of State for the Home Dept . . . 121

Green v Broadcasting Council of New Zealand (1989) . . . 315, 333

Grimme v Scott (2010) . . . 397

Griswold v Connecticut (1965) . . . 17

Gutnick v Dow Jones (2002) . . . 522

Halford v United Kingdom (1997) . . . 19, 514

Halliburton v Comptroller of Patents (2008) . . . 301

Harman Pictures NV v Osborne (1967) . . . 319, 343, 344

Harrods v Lawrie (1997) . . . 404

Harrow Borough Council Case (DA/90 24/49/5) . . . 104

Hatton v United Kingdom (2003) . . . 18

Hitachi's Application, Re (2004) (EPO) . . . 295, 296

Hitchens v Secretary of State for the Home Dept . . . 121, 122

HMA v Davey and Beard (2013) . . . 507

Ibcos Computers v Barclays Mercantile Highland Finance (1994) . . . 339–41

IBM/Computer Related Invention (1990) . . . 291

IBM Corpn/Reading Age (1990) . . . 290

IBM/Data Processor Network (1990) . . . 291, 297

IBM/Semantically Related Expressions (1989) . . . 290, 291

IBM/Text Clarity Processing (T38/86) (1990) . . . 292

IBM/Text Processing (T0115/85) . . . 290, 297

IBM's Application (1999) . . . 292–5

IGT v Commissioner of Patents (2007) . . . 299

Infopaq International A/S v Danske Dagblades Forening ('Infopaq I') (2010) . . . 318

Innovations (Mail Order) Ltd v Data Protection Registrar Case (DA/92 31/49/1) . . . 78, 86, 93, 94, 134, 135

Interflora v Marks & Spencer (2013) . . . 415, 416, 421, 422

International Business Machines Corpn's Application (1980) . . . 281, 282, 287

Jameel (Yousef) v Dow Jones & Co (2005) . . . 518

Jarrold v Houlston (1857) . . . 320

Johnson v Medical Defence Union (2006); (2007) . . . 91, 131

Karen Murphy v Media Protection Services Ltd (2012) . . . 318

Karpov v William Felix Browder and Others (2013) . . . 522, 523

Koch and Sterzel, Re (1988) . . . 286, 287, 289, 290

Ladbroke (Football) Ltd v William Hill (Football) Ltd (1964) . . . 375

Laird v HM Advocate (1984) . . . 252

LB (Plastics) Ltd v Swish Products Ltd (1979) . . . 330, 331, 336

Lee v Griffin (1861) . . . 473, 481

Lindqvist (Criminal proceedings against) Case 101/01 (2003) . . . 42, 45, 46, 52, 53, 60

Linguaphone Institute v Data Protection Registrar (Case DA/94 31/49/1) . . . 93, 94, 135

Lord v Secretary of State (2003) . . . 123

L'Oréal and Others v eBay and Others (2009) . . . 365, 417, 420

Lotus Development Corpn v Paperback Software International and Stephenson Ltd (1990) . . . 306

Loutchansky v Times Newspapers Ltd (2001) . . . 519, 520, 522

Lyngstad v Anabas Products (1977) . . . 413

McAlpine v Bercow (2013) . . . 503, 506

McCrone v Boot Farm Sales (1981) . . . 495

McCulloch v Lewis A May (Produce Distributors) Ltd (1947) . . . 413

MacKenzie Patten v British Olivetti (1985) . . . 479

Marcel v Metropolitan Police Comr (1992) . . . 15

Media CAT v Adams and Others (2011) . . . 356

Meechie v Multi-Media Marketing (1995) . . . 235–7

Merrill Lynch's Application, Re (1989) . . . 287–9, 297, 298

Metropolitan International Schools Ltd v Designtechnica Corporation and Google UK and Google Inc (2009) . . . 432, 434, 511

Microsoft v Stac (1993) . . . 278

Microsoft's Application, Re (2006) (EPO) . . . 296–8

Millars of Falkirk Ltd v Turpie (1976) . . . 482

Mirage Studios v Counter Feat Clothing Co Ltd (1991) . . . 413

National Phonograph Co of Australia v Menck (1911) . . . 327

Navitaire Inc v easyJet Airline Company and
  Bulletproof Technologies Inc (2004) . . . 343,
  345, 347
Norwich Pharmacal Co v Commissioners of
  Customs and Excise (1973) . . . 512, 519
Nova Productions Ltd v Mazoooma Games Ltd
  and Others (2007) . . . 344, 346

Office of Fair Trading v Lloyds TSB Bank Plc and
  Others (2007) . . . 458
Ogden v Association of the United States Army
  (1959) . . . 520

Parliament v Council, see European Parliament v
  Council of the European Union
Pension Benefit Systems Partnership
  (2000) . . . 296, 298
Photo Production Ltd v Securicor Transport Ltd
  (1980) . . . 497
Pitman Training Ltd v Nominet UK (1997) . . . 408,
  409, 412
Plix Products Ltd v Frank M Winstone
  (1986) . . . 331, 332
Pozzoli v BDMO (2007) . . . 305
Prince plc v Prince Sports Group (1998) . . . 409, 410
ProCD v Zeidenberg (1996) . . . 377, 378
Productores de Musica de España (Promusicae)
  v Telefonica de España SAU (2008) . . . 364
Public Relations Consultants Association v The
  Newspaper Licensing Agency Ltd and Others
  (2013) . . . 316–18

Quantel Ltd v Spaceward Microsystems Ltd
  (1990) . . . 268

R (on the application of British Telecommunications
  and others) v BPI (British Recorded Music
  Industry) Ltd and Others (2012) . . . 362
R v Bignell (1997) . . . 207–9
R v Bow Street Magistrates Court, ex p Allison
  (1999) . . . 208–10, 224
R v Brown (1996) . . . 15
R v Fellows (1997) . . . 234, 235
R v Ghosh (1982) . . . 228
R v Gold (1987); (1988) . . . 197, 221–3, 225, 228,
  234, 236, 244, 370
R v Governor of Brixton Prison and Another,
  ex p Levin (1997) . . . 222, 224
R v Graham Waddon (1999) . . . 238
R v R (1992) . . . 92
R v Shepherd (1993) . . . 251
R v Stewart (1988) . . . 521
R v Thompson (1984) . . . 207, 212, 223
R v Whitaker (1993) . . . 213
R v Whiteley (1991) . . . 244
Rechnungshof v Österreichischer Rundfunk
  (2003) . . . 39
Rhondda Borough Council Case (DA/90
  24/49/2) . . . 104
Richardson v Flanders (1993) . . . 337–9

Robinson v Graves (1935) . . . 473, 474, 481
Robinson v Secretary of State for Northern
  Ireland (2002) . . . 144
Roe v Wade (1973) . . . 18
Rogers v Parish (1987) . . . 479
Runnymede Borough Council Case (DA/90
  24/49/3) . . . 104

S v Director of Public Prosecutions (2008) . . . 219
St Albans District Council v ICL (1996) . . . 250,
  474, 475, 484–7, 489, 496, 498, 499
Salvage Association v CAP Financial Services
  (1993) . . . 475, 495, 497
SAM Business Systems Ltd v Hedley & Co (2002)
  . . . 487–90, 499–501
Same Invention (2001) . . . 303
Samsung Electronic Co Lt v Apple Retail UK Ltd
  and Apple Sales International (2012) . . . 302,
  395–9
Saphena v Allied Collection Agencies
  (1995) . . . 472, 474, 482–5, 489
SAS Institute v World Programming Ltd
  (2010) . . . 345
Scottish National Party v Information
  Commissioner (EA/2005/0021) . . . 164
Sheffield Wednesday Football Club Ltd and
  Others v Hargreaves (2007) . . . 512, 517, 523
Shetland Times v Willis (1996) . . . 312, 322, 372
Slee and Harris's Application, Re (1966) . . . 289
Smedleys Ltd v Breed (1974) . . . 471
South Northamptonshire District Council Case
  (DA/90 24/49/4) . . . 104
South West Water Services Ltd v International
  Computers Ltd (1999) . . . 485, 496, 497, 499,
  501
Spiliada Maritime Corpn v Consulex Ltd (1987)
  . . . 523
Steve Jackson Games Inc v United States Secret
  Service (1993); aff'd (1994) . . . 249
Stratton Oakmont v Prodigy (1995) . . . 509
Symbian v Commissioner of Patents (2008) . . . 300,
  301

Tamiz v Google (2013) . . . 517, 518
Taverner Rutledge v Trexpalm (1975) . . . 413
Telnikoff v Matusevitch (1997) . . . 525
Thornton v Shoe Lane Parking (1971) . . . 136, 493
Totalise v Motley Fool Ltd (2001) . . . 510, 512
Twentieth Century Fox Film Corporation and
  Others v Newzbin Ltd (2010) . . . 365, 366

Unilin Beheer v Berry Floor (2004) . . . 303
United States v Thomas (1997) . . . 238, 239
University of London Press Ltd v University
  Tutorial Press Ltd (1916) . . . 312

Valensi v British Radio Corpn Ltd (1973) . . . 270
Vicom Sysems Inc's Application, Re
  (1987) . . . 285, 286, 288–90, 294, 306

Waterlow Publishers v Rose (1995) . . . 376

Watford Electronics Ltd v Sanderson (2001) . . . 499, 501

Wenham Gas Ltd v Champion Gas Lamp Co (1891) . . . 277

Winterson v Hogarth (2000) . . . 413, 414

Wombles Ltd v Wombles Skips Ltd (1977) . . . 413

Wormell v RHM Agriculture (East) Ltd (1987) . . . 321, 475

Table of Statutes

Access to Health Records Act 1990 . . . 54, 124
Access to Personal Files Act 1987 . . . 124
Act of Union 1707 . . . 260
Anti-Terrorism, Crime and Security
   Act 2001 . . . 21, 157
   s 102 . . . 22, 158

Broadcasting Act 1990 . . . 141
Broadcasting Act 1996 . . . 141

Communications Act 2003 . . . 63, 526
   s 127 . . . 217
   134C . . . 526
Computer Misuse Act 1990 . . . 102, 198, 204–15,
   224, 249, 250, 252–4
   s 1 . . . 202, 204, 206–10, 217, 224, 249, 250,
     252, 254
     (1) . . . 205
       (a) . . . 205
   2 . . . 202, 208, 209, 224, 253, 254
     (2) . . . 214
       (a), (b) . . . 208
   3 . . . 202, 206, 209, 212, 214–17, 224, 252, 254
     (2) . . . 212, 214, 215
     (5) . . . 213
   3A . . . 206, 217
   5 . . . 252
   7, 13 . . . 253
   14 . . . 250
   16 . . . 253
   17 . . . 209, 212
     (1) . . . 205
     (5) . . . 206, 210
Consumer Credit Act 1974 . . . 54, 114
   s 75 . . . 458
   83, 84 . . . 458
   158 . . . 114
   160 . . . 114
Consumer Protection Act 1987 . . . 470
Contracts (Rights of Third Parties) Act 1999 . . .
   183
Copyright Act 1911 . . . 310
   s 1(2)(d) . . . 310
Copyright Act 1956 . . . 234, 310
   s 4(2) . . . 313
   14 . . . 310
   48 . . . 234
     (1) . . . 330, 331
Copyright and Design Act 1839 . . . 392
Copyright (Computer Software) Amendment Act
   1985 . . . 254, 310
   s 1 . . . 310

Copyright, Designs and Patents Act 1988 . . . 235,
   249, 310–14, 322–4, 326, 327, 329–31, 346,
   355, 357, 379, 380–2, 392, 393
   s 1 . . . 311
   3 . . . 375, 379
     (1) . . . 323, 379, 380
       (c) . . . 324
   3A . . . 380
     (2) . . . 379
   4(1) . . . 346
     (2) . . . 235, 324, 346
   7 . . . 322
   9 . . . 249
     (3) . . . 314
   10(1), (3) . . . 313
   11(1), (2) . . . 313
   12(1), (3) . . . 315
   13, 15 . . . 315
   16(1)(a)–(e) . . . 315
   17(2) . . . 315
     (3) . . . 316, 392
   21(4) . . . 322
   29 . . . 326
     (4) . . . 327
   50A . . . 328
     (1) . . . 330
     (2) . . . 328
   50B(3)(b), (c) . . . 335
     (4) . . . 335
   50C . . . 328
     (2) . . . 329
   50D . . . 381
   51 . . . 392, 393
   66 . . . 322
   70 . . . 353
   96 . . . 382
   s 97A . . . 366
   107 . . . 354, 355
   s 109 . . . 249
   Chaps VII, VIII . . . 381
   124(3)(b) . . . 358
   124A(9) . . . 359
   124D(2) . . . 358
   124L(2) . . . 362
   178 . . . 314
   213 . . . 394
   213(3) . . . 331
   296 . . . 351
   296A(1)(b) . . . 330
   296ZA, 296ZD, 296ZE, 296ZG . . . 352
   301 . . . 315
   Sch 6 . . . 315

Coroners and Justice Act 2009 . . . 233
   s 62(1), (4)–(7) . . . 23 34
   173 . . . 76
Criminal Damage Act 1971 . . . 197
   s 1 . . . 197
Criminal Justice Act 1972 . . . 205
   s 36 . . . 205
Criminal Justice Act 1988 . . . 233
   160 . . . 233
Criminal Justice Act 2003 . . . 251
Criminal Justice and Police Act
   2001 . . . 218, 249
Criminal Justice and Public Order Act 1994 . . .
   233, 235
   s 84 . . . 233
     (4) . . . 235
Criminal Law Act 1977 . . . 253
   s 1(1A) . . . 253
   13, 16 . . . 253

Data Protection Act 1984 . . . 10, 20, 35–8, 40, 42, 44,
   53, 57–60, 65–7, 69, 70, 73, 75, 77–80, 89, 94, 103,
   114, 116, 119, 120, 126, 127, 129, 136,
   139, 208
   s 1(4) . . . 58
     (8) . . . 127
   3(4), (5) . . . 80
   14(3)–(5) . . . 81
   16 . . . 74
   21(4)(a) . . . 116
   27 . . . 119
   31 . . . 127
     (2) . . . 129
   32, 33 . . . 67
   35 . . . 128
   35A . . . 128
   36(4) . . . 78
   39 . . . 58
Data Protection Act 1998 . . . 35, 36, 38–44,
   46–8, 51, 52, 54–61, 65–7, 70–2, 74, 75, 77, 78,
   81, 84–7, 92, 97, 100, 101, 107, 108, 112–14,
   116–22, 124, 126–30, 132, 133, 135, 137,
   139–43, 145, 146, 151, 152, 157, 161, 162, 169,
   170, 171–2, 181, 182, 362, 510
   s 1(1) . . . 42, 49, 52, 54, 57, 58, 87
   2 . . . 44
   3 . . . 140, 145
   5 . . . 79
     (1) . . . 59
     (2) . . . 86
     (3) . . . 60
   Pt II . . . 112
   7 . . . 113, 115, 123
     (1)(a) . . . 120
      (c) . . . 114
       (i) . . . 114
     (2) . . . 113, 114
     (4) . . . 117, 118
      (b) . . . 118, 130
     (5) . . . 117–19

     (6) . . . 117, 118
     (9) . . . 116, 118, 130
     (10) . . . 115
   8 . . . 113
     (2) . . . 114
     (3) . . . 115
     (5) . . . 113
     (6) . . . 114, 115
   9 . . . 113, 114
   10(1)–(4) . . . 135
   11(1) . . . 135
   12 . . . 92, 141
   13 . . . 58, 107, 144
   13(1) . . . 131, 146
     (2) . . . 131
      (a) . . . 131
   14 . . . 107, 141, 146
     (1)–(3) . . . 130
   16(1) . . . 71
   17 . . . 58
     (1) . . . 67
     (3) . . . 67
   18 . . . 71, 72
     (2) . . . 72
      (b) . . . 71
     (3) . . . 72
   21(8) . . . 129
   22(1) . . . 72
   23 . . . 70
   26(1), (2) . . . 67
   28 . . . 81, 120
     (1) . . . 120
     (2), (5) . . . 120
   29 . . . 96
     (1) . . . 123
     (4) . . . 123, 124
   30(1) . . . 124
   31 . . . 126, 141
   32 . . . 141–3
     (1) . . . 140, 143, 144
     (2), (3) . . . 143, 144
     (4) . . . 142, 144
     (5) . . . 143, 144
   33, 34 . . . 126
   38(1) . . . 126
   40 . . . 75
   41(1), (2) . . . 75
   41A . . . 76
   42 . . . 105, 131, 132, 145
     (1), (7) . . . 74
   43(1) . . . 74
   44 . . . 145
     (6) . . . 145
   45 . . . 142
   46(1), (2) . . . 146
   46(3) . . . 145
   47 . . . 74, 75
   50 . . . 73
   51(1) . . . 77
     (3) . . . 60, 79

(4)(b) . . . 79
(6) . . . 79
(7) . . . 76
(8) . . . 78
(9) . . . 77
52(3) . . . 79
53 . . . 146
  (1)–(4) . . . 146
54(1), (2) . . . 79
  (7) . . . 182
55 . . . 102
56 . . . 132, 133
  (8) . . . 132
57 . . . 132
59(1), (2) . . . 80
64 . . . 13
70(1) . . . 118
  (2) . . . 107
Sch 1 . . . 21, 83, 157
  Pt II, para 1 . . . 85
    para 2(1)(b) . . . 87
    para 2(2) . . . 87
    para 2(3) . . . 86
    para 3(2)(a) . . . 87
    para 7 . . . 108
    paras 11, 12 . . . 58
  Sch 2 . . . 83, 85, 93, 97, 181
    para 6 . . . 96
  Sch 3 . . . 83, 85, 93, 97, 142, 143, 145
    para 2 . . . 98
    para 3(a), (b) . . . 98
    para 4 . . . 98
    paras 5–9 . . . 99
    para 10 . . . 100, 101
  Sch 4 . . . 182
  para 4(2) . . . 181
  paras 8, 9 . . . 182
  Sch 5
    para 2 . . . 65
  Sch 7 . . . 128
    paras 1–4 . . . 127
    paras 7–9 . . . 128
    paras 10, 11 . . . 129
  Sch 9 . . . 73
    para 1(3) . . . 74
    para 2(1)(b)(ii) . . . 74
  Sch 10 . . . 146
Defamation Act 1952 . . . 508
Defamation Act 1996 . . . 435, 508, 514, 516–19
  s 1 . . . 514, 517, 524
    (2) . . . 514
    (3) . . . 515
Defamation Act 2013 . . . 505, 509, 518, 519, 521,
  523
  s 5 . . . 518
  8 . . . 521, 523
Digital Economy Act 2010 . . . 348, 349, 354–6,
  360, 362–7, 526
Dramatic Copyright Act 1833 . . . 309

Electronic Communications Act 2000 . . . 443,
  447–9, 453, 455–7
  Pt I . . . 449, 456
  ss 2, 3 . . . 456
  6 . . . 456
  Pt II . . . 449
  7 . . . 450
    (1), (2) . . . 455
  8 . . . 450, 455
    (2)(c) . . . 455
  Pt III . . . 449
  16 . . . 456
Engraving Copyright Act 1734 . . . 309
Enterprise and Regulatory Reform Act
  2013 . . . 367
European Communities Act 1972 . . . 310
Extradition Act 1870 . . . 253
Extradition Act 2003 . . . 253
  s 137 . . . 254

Financial Services and Markets Act 2000 . . . 460
  s 19 . . . 460
Fine Art Copyright Act 1862 . . . 310
Forgery and Counterfeiting Act 1981 . . . 197,
  222, 225
  s 1 . . . 197, 222
  10 . . . 198
Fraud Act 2006 . . . 191, 224, 226, 228
  s 2 . . . 226, 227
    (1), (2) . . . 226
    (5) . . . 226
  5 . . . 227
  6 . . . 226
  7 . . . 226
    (1) . . . 226
    (8) . . . 227
  11 . . . 227
    (1), (2) . . . 227
Freedom of Information Act 2000 . . . 48, 50, 54,
  56, 65, 66
  s 18 . . . 65
Freedom of Information (Scotland) Act
  2002 . . . 48, 49
  s 38 . . . 49

Gambling Act 2005 . . . 466–8
  s 2 . . . 467
  4 . . . 467
  6(1) . . . 467
  14 . . . 467
  66 . . . 468
  68 . . . 468
  89 . . . 467
  97 . . . 468
Gambling (Licensing and Amendment)
  Act 2014 . . . 466

Human Fertilisation and Embryology Act 1990—
  s 31 . . . 128

Human Rights Act 1998 . . . 40, 510

Interception of Communications Act
  1985 . . . 245
Interpretation Act 1978
  Sch 1 . . . 449

Larceny Act 1916 . . . 224
  s 32(1) . . . 224
Legal Deposit Library Act 2013 . . . 367
Limitation Act 1980 . . . 520
  s 4A . . . 519–21
Local Government Finance Act 1988 . . . 104
  s 6 . . . 104

Malicious Communications Act of 1998 . . . 218,
  219
  s 2 . . . 219

Obscene Publications Act 1959 . . . 234, 235, 238
Obscene Publications Act 1964 . . . 231
Official Secrets Act 1911—
  ss 1, 2 . . . 192

Patent Act 1902 . . . 264, 274
Patents Act 1949 . . . 280, 281, 283, 294, 394
  s 101 . . . 280
Patents Act 1977 . . . 264, 266, 268, 269, 271, 272,
  274–6, 280, 282–5, 298, 303, 306, 307, 310, 344
  s 1(1) . . . 268
    (2) . . . 271, 272, 282, 283, 287, 288
      (c) . . . 289
  3 . . . 269
  4(2) . . . 271
  14(2) . . . 273
  16 . . . 274
  17(2) . . . 274
    (4), (5) . . . 274
  18(1) . . . 275
    (3) . . . 275
  20, 21 . . . 275
  60(1), (2) . . . 276
  72 . . . 277
  91 . . . 283
  130(7) . . . 283
Police Act 1997 . . . 106, 132, 133
Police and Criminal Evidence Act 1984 . . . 239,
  249–51
  s 8 . . . 249
  14, 17 . . . 249
  19(4) . . . 249
  22(4) . . . 249
  68 . . . 250
  69 . . . 251
  116 . . . 249
Police and Justice Act 2006 . . . 202, 204, 206, 215,
  217, 254
  s 35 . . . 204

Protection from Harassment Act 1997 . . . 218,
  241
  s 1 . . . 218
  2–4 . . . 219
Protection of Children Act 1978 . . . 233–35
  s 1 . . . 233
    (1) . . . 234
      (c) . . . 234
    (4)(b) . . . 234
  7(4) . . . 234
    (b) . . . 234
    (7) . . . 233

Registered Designs Act 1949 . . . 392
  s 44 . . . 392
Registration of Political Parties Act 1998 . . . 101
Rehabilitation of Offenders Act 1974 . . . 133
Representation of the People Act 2000—
  s 9 . . . 88
Regulation of Investigatory Powers Act 2000 . . .
  3, 8, 19, 21, 122, 151, 157, 210, 244–8, 513
  s 2 . . . 210, 246
  5 . . . 246
  12 . . . 246
    (2), (9) . . . 246
  14 . . . 246
  22 . . . 21, 157
  Chap 2 . . . 247
  Pt 2 . . . 210
  26, 27 . . . 210
  49 . . . 248
  50(1) . . . 248
  53 . . . 248
  65 . . . 122

Sale and Supply of Goods Act 1994 . . . 476, 478
Sale of Goods Act 1893 . . . 477
Sale of Goods Act 1979 . . . 470, 474–6, 478–80, 494
  s 12 . . . 476, 477
  13 . . . 477
  14 . . . 321, 474, 477, 478
  14(6) . . . 477
  34(1) . . . 480
  35(1) . . . 480
Sculpture Copyright Act 1814 . . . 309
Serious Organised Crime and Police Act
  2005 . . . 218
Statute of Anne 1709 . . . 258, 260, 309, 369, 370
Statute of Monopolies 1623 . . . 264, 369
  s 6 . . . 264
Supply of Goods and Services Act 1982 . . . 474,
  476

Theft Act 1968 . . . 221, 224
  s 15(4) . . . 224
  16 . . . 225
Trade Marks Act 1994 . . . 259, 400
  s 1(1) . . . 400

2 . . . 401
10 . . . 402
   (3) . . . 407
   (4) . . . 406
11(2) . . . 407
21 . . . 410
24(1) . . . 410
   (2)(a), (b) . . . 410
Trade Marks Registration Act 1875 . . . 400
Trading Stamps Act 1964 . . . 463

Unfair Contract Terms Act 1977 . . . 470, 476,
   493–5, 497, 499, 500
   s 2 . . . 494
   3(1) . . . 496
   4(1) . . . 494
   6 . . . 494
   8 . . . 495
   11 . . . 495, 497
   12(1) . . . 494
   24 . . . 495
   Sch 2 . . . 495, 497

Video Recordings Act 1984 . . . 236
   s 1 . . . 236
   (2)(a) . . . 236
   2 . . . 236
   9, 10 . . . 236

Youth Justice and Criminal Evidence Act
   1999 . . . 251
   s 60 . . . 251

Austria

Federal Act Concerning the Protection of
   Personal Data 2000
   s 13 . . . 176

France

Data Protection Act 1978 . . . 136

Germany

Data Protection Act 1990 . . . 66

Sweden

Data Protection Act 1973 . . . 27, 168
   s 11 . . . 168

USA

Computer Fraud and Abuse Act 1984 . . . 197
Constitution . . . 18, 428
Digital Millennium Copyright Act 2000 . . . 370
Federal Trade Commission Act
   s 5 . . . 175
Uniform Commercial Code . . . 428
   Art 2 . . . 428
Uniform Computer Information Transactions
   Act . . . 428
United States Code
   Title 15, s 45(n) . . . 175
   Title 15, Chapter 22, s 1051 (Lanham
     Act) . . . 410
   Title 17, s 102(b) . . . 335
   Title 35 . . . 307
   Pt II, ss 101–3 . . . 307

Table of Statutory Instruments

Companies Act 1985 (Electronic
  Communications) Order 2000, SI 2000/
  3373 . . . 450
Consumer Protection from Unfair Trading
  Regulations 2008, SI 2008/1277 . . . 494
Consumer Transactions (Restrictions on
  Statements) Order 1976, SI 1976/1813 . . . 494
Copyright (Computer Programs) Regulations
  1992, SI 1992/3233 . . . 324, 328, 379, 381
  reg 9 . . . 381
Copyright and Related Rights Regulations 2003,
  SI 2003/2498 . . . 322, 349, 354, 355
  regs 24, 25 . . . 352
  26 . . . 354
Copyright and Rights in Databases Regulations
  1997, SI 1997/3032 . . . 310, 372, 373, 380–2
  reg 3 . . . 373
  6 . . . 379, 380
  13, 14 . . . 381
  16, 18 . . . 382
  20, 23 . . . 382
  25 . . . 381

Data Protection (Corporate Finance Exception)
  Order 2000, SI 2000/184 . . . 128
Data Protection (Crown Appointments) Order
  2000, SI 2000/416 . . . 127
Data Protection (Designated Codes of Practice)
  Order 2000, SI 2000/418 . . . 141
Data Protection (EC Directives) Regulations
  2007, SI 2007/2199 . . . 158
  reg 5 . . . 158
Data Protection (Functions of Designated
  Authority) Order 2000, SI 2000/186 . . . 60, 79
Data Protection (International Co-operation)
  Order 2000, SI 2000/190 . . . 79
  arts 5, 6 . . . 79
Data Protection (Miscellaneous Subject Access
  Exemptions) Order 2000, SI 2000/419 . . . 128
Data Protection (Monetary Penalties) Order
  2010, SI 2010/910 . . . 77
Data Protection (Notification and Notification
  Fees) Regulations 2000, SI 2000/188 . . . 68, 69
  Sch
    para 2 . . . 68
    para 2(d) . . . 69
    para 3(a) . . . 69
    para 4(1)(a) . . . 69
    para 5 . . . 70
Data Protection (Processing of Sensitive Personal
  Data) Order 2000, SI 2000/417 . . . 100, 145
  Sch, para 3 . . . 145

Data Protection (Processing of Sensitive Personal
  Data) (Elected Representatives) Order 2002,
  SI 2002/2905 . . . 101
Data Protection (Subject Access) (Fees and
  Miscellaneous Provisions) Regulations 2000,
  SI 2000/191 . . . 113–15
  regs 2, 3 . . . 113
  4 . . . 114
Data Protection (Subject Access Modification)
  (Education) Order 2000, SI 2000/414 . . . 125
Data Protection (Subject Access Modification)
  (Health) Order 2000, SI 2000/413 . . . 124, 125
  art 2 . . . 124
  5(3) . . . 125
Data Protection (Subject Access Modification)
  (Social Work) Order 2000, SI 2000/415 . . . 125
Data Protection Tribunal (Enforcement Appeals)
  Rules 2000, SI 2000/189 . . . 81
Data Protection Tribunal (National Security
  Appeals) Rules 2000, SI 2000/206 . . . 81
Data Retention (EC Directive) Regulations 2009,
  SI 2009/859 . . . 158
Defamation (Operators of Websites) Regulations
  2013, SI 2013/3028 . . . 509, 519
  Sch . . . 519

Electronic Commerce (EC Directive) Regulations
  2002, SI 2002/2013 . . . 431–3, 524
Electronic Communications (EC Directive)
  Regulations 2009, SI 2009/859 . . . 158, 159
  reg 5 . . . 159
  11 . . . 159
Electronic Money Regulations 2011, SI 2011/99
  . . . 461, 462
  reg 2 . . . 461
    (1) . . . 461
  6 . . . 462
  13 . . . 462
Electronic Money (Miscellaneous Amendments)
  Regulations 2002, SI 2002/765 . . . 460
Extradition Act 2003 (Designation of Part 2
  Territories) Order 2003, SI 2003/3334 . . . 253

Financial Services and Market Rules (Payment
  Services Regulations) 2009, SI 2009/209 . . .
  191
Financial Services and Markets Act 2000
  (Regulated Activities) Order 2001, SI 2001/544
  . . . 460
Financial Services and Markets Act 2000
  (Regulated Activities) (Amendment)
  (No 2) Order 2013, SI 2013/1881 . . . 466

Information Tribunal (Enforcement Appeals)
  Rules 2005, SI 2005/14—
  r 5 . . . 145
Information Tribunal (National Security Appeals)
  Rules 2005, SI 2005/13 . . . 120
Intellectual Property (Enforcement etc.)
  Regulations 2006, SI 2006/1028 . . . 311

Legal Deposit Libraries (Non-Print Work)
  Regulations 2013, SI 2013/777 . . . 367–9
  reg 2 . . . 369
  18 . . . 368

Patent Rules 1995, SI 1995/2093
  r 33 . . . 275
Privacy and Electronic Communications
  (EC Directive) Regulations 2003,
  SI 2003/2426 . . . 149, 310
  reg 6 . . . 154
Privacy and Electronic Communications
  Regulations 2011, SI 2011/1208 . . . 76, 77,
  150–2, 154, 164, 165
  reg 5 . . . 151
    (1), (3) . . . 151

Registered Designs Regulations 2001, SI
  2001/3949 . . . 392, 394
  reg 2 . . . 394
  4 . . . 394
Regulation of Investigatory Powers (Acquisition
  and Disclosure of Communications
  Data: Code of Practice) Order 2007,
  SI 2007/2197 . . . 157, 247
Regulation of Investigatory Powers (Maintenance
  of Interception Capability) Order 2002,
  SI 2002/1931 . . . 247

Regulatory Reform (Registered Designs) Order
  2006, SI 2006/1974 . . . 392
Regulatory Reform (Trading Stamps) Order 2005,
  SI 2005/871 . . . 463
Representation of the People (Amendment)
  Regulations 1990, SI 1990/520 . . . 88
Representation of the People (England and
  Wales) Regulations 2001, SI 2001/341
  reg 110 . . . 88
Representation of the People (England and
  Wales) (Amendment) Regulations 2002,
  SI 2002/1871 . . . 88, 89
  reg 6 . . . 88
Representation of the People (Scotland)
  Regulations 2001, SI 2001/497 . . . 88
Retention of Communications Data (Code of
  Practice) Order 2003, SI 2003/3175 . . . 158

Telecommunications (Data Protection and
  Privacy) (Direct Marketing) Regulations 1998,
  SI 1998/3170 . . . 149
Telecommunications (Data Protection and
  Privacy) Regulations 1999, SI 1999/2093 . . .
  149, 161
  reg 9 . . . 161
Telecommunications (Lawful Business
  Practice) (Interception of Communications)
  Regulations, SI 2000/2699 . . . 19, 151
Telecommunications (Open Network Provision)
  (Voice Telephony) Regulations 1998, SI
  1998/1580 . . . 162

Unfair Terms in Consumer Contracts Regulations
  1999, SI 1999/2083 . . . 493–5
  reg 10 . . . 495
  Sch 2 . . . 494

Table of European Legislation

Charter of Fundamental Rights of the European
   Union 2010 . . . 28
   Art 8 . . . 28, 30

Decisions

EC Decision 276/1999/EC, OJ 1999 L 33/1 . . .
   230
   Art 2 . . . 230
   3 . . . 231
EC Decision 2000/520/EC, OJ 2000 L 215/7 . . .
   173, 175
   Art 1 . . . 173
EC Decision 2001/497/EC, OJ 2001 L 181/19 . . .
   183, 185
   Recital 10 . . . 184
   Art 1 . . . 183
   Annex
      Clauses 2, 3 . . . 183
      Clause 6 . . . 184
   App 1 . . . 183
EC Decision 2002/16/EC, OJ 2002 L 6/52 . . . 183
EC Decision 2004/55/EC, OJ 2004 L 012/47 . . .
   62
EC Decision 2004/915/EC, OJ 2004 L 181/74 . . .
   184
EC Decision 2007/551/CFSP/JHA, OJ 2002
   L 204/16 . . . 179
Framework Decision 2002/584/JHA, OJ 2002
   L 190/1 . . . 253
   Art 3 . . . 253
Framework Decision 2005/222/JHA, OJ 2005
   L 69/67 . . . 206
   Arts 3–7 . . . 206

Directives

EC Directive 85/374, OJ 1985 L 210/29
   (Approximation of the Laws, Regulations and
   Administrative Provisions of the Member
   States Concerning Liability for Defective
   Products) . . . 470
EC Directive 89/104, OJ 1989 L 40/1 (Trade
   Marks) . . . 259, 400
   Art 5 . . . 417
      (1)(a) . . . 414
EC Directive 91/250, OJ 1991 L 122/42 (Software
   Protection) . . . 310, 312, 316, 323, 324,
   328–30, 335, 336, 343–5, 379, 381, 476
   Preamble . . . 312, 328

Art 1(1) . . . 324
   (2) . . . 316, 335, 343
   (3) . . . 312
   4, 5 . . . 328
EC Directive 95/46, OJ 1995 L 281/31 (Data
   Protection) . . . 20, 28, 30, 36–9, 42–9, 51–4,
   56, 57, 59–62, 64, 67, 70, 72, 76, 78–80, 84–6,
   93, 95, 97–100, 103, 108–10, 112, 114, 115,
   130–2, 134–6, 139, 144, 149, 152, 153, 168–70,
   172, 173, 175, 176, 178, 181, 182, 184, 198, 363,
   364
   Recital 15 . . . 53
      26 . . . 49, 50
      27 . . . 54
      37 . . . 139
      41 . . ., 57
      42 . . . 124
      43 . . . 123
      61 . . . 110
      62 . . . 62
   Art 1 . . . 20
      2 . . . 53, 149
      (a) . . . 42, 50
      (b) . . . 52, 53
      (c) . . . 54
      (d) . . . 57
      (h) . . . 93
      3(1) . . . 53
      (2) . . . 179
      6 . . . 83
      (1)(e) . . . 108
      8 . . . 363
      8(1) . . . 45
      (2)(b) . . . 98
      (4) . . . 100
      (5) . . . 99
      (6) . . . 100
      9 . . . 140, 144
      10 . . . 86
      (c) . . . 86
      11 . . . 124
      (a) . . . 132
      13(1) . . . 115, 123, 364
      14 . . . 135
      (b) . . . 134, 135
      15 . . . 136
      (1) . . . 112
      17(1) . . . 109
      18(1) . . . 67
      (2) . . . 67, 70
      19 . . . 176
      20 . . . 64, 72

23 . . . 131
Chap IV . . . 176
25 . . . 169, 170, 181
　(2) . . . 173, 179
　(3) . . . 169
　(4) . . . 170
　(6) . . . 170, 175, 179
26 . . . 170, 181
　(1) . . . 181
　(2) . . . 181, 182, 185
　(3) . . . 182
27 . . . 78, 110
28 . . . 62, 76, 186
　(3), (4) . . . 64
　(6) . . . 59
　(7) . . . 80
29 . . . 78, 93, 144, 148, 169–72, 178
31 . . . 170, 173
EC Directive 96/9, OJ 1996 L 77/20 (Legal
　Protection of Databases) . . . 310, 352, 372,
　373, 375, 378–82, 384, 385, 387, 388, 390, 391
Preamble . . . 373, 380
Recital 1 . . . 375
　17 . . . 391
　19 . . . 380
　40 . . . 384
Art 1 . . . 373. 379
7 . . . 387
　(1) . . . 385
　(5) . . . 383, 386
8(1), (2) . . . 380
9 . . . 382
10(3) . . . 383, 385
16(3) . . . 381
EC Directive 97/7, OJ 1997 L 144 (Distance
　Selling) . . . 428–30, 438
Preamble . . . 429
Recital 4 . . . 429
13 . . . 430
17 . . . 430
Art 2(1) . . . 429
4 . . . 430
　(2), (3) . . . 429
5 . . . 430
6 . . . 430, 438
10(1) . . . 429
　(2) . . . 430
EC Directive 97/66, OJ 1998 L 24/1 (Telecoms
　Data Protection) . . . 37, 38, 149, 150, 155, 156,
　160, 161, 164
2 . . . 160
11 . . . 161
EC Directive 98/48, OJ 1998 L 217/218
　(Amending 98/34) . . . 431
Recital 19 . . . 431
　EC Directive 98/71, OJ 1998 L 289/28 (Legal
　　Protection of Designs) . . . 392
EC Directive 99/93, OJ 2000 L 13/12 (Electronic
　Signatures) . . . 429, 443, 447, 448, 450, 453–7
Art 1 . . . 453

2(1) . . . 453
3(2) . . . 454
　(4) . . . 453
5 . . . 54
Annex 1 . . . 454
2 . . . 454, 457
3 . . . 453
EC Directive 2000/31, OJ 2000 L 178/L
　(Electronic Commerce) . . . 231, 362–4,
　417–20, 429, 431, 432, 435, 437, 439, 440, 447,
　448, 450, 453, 467, 523, 524
Recital 22 . . . 439
42 . . . 418
Art 3 . . . 363
　(3) . . . 363
9 . . . 450
11 . . . 437
　(2) . . . 437
12 . . . 231, 363, 433, 523, 524
　(1) . . . 362
13 . . . 363, 524
14 . . . 363, 523, 524
　(1) . . . 419
15 . . . 524
16 . . . 439
17 . . . 440
Annex . . . 363
EC Directive 2000/46, OJ 2000 L 275/39
　(Electronic Money Institutions) . . . 460
EC Directive 2001/29, OJ 2001 L 167/10
　(Copyright in the Information Society) . . .
　310, 317, 319, 349–52, 363, 366, 370
Recital 5 . . . 350
33 . . . 350
55 . . . 352
Arts 2–5 . . . 350
2 . . . 317
5(1) . . . 317–19
　(5) . . . 318
6 . . . 351
7 . . . 352
EC Directive 2002/58, OJ 2002 L 201/37 (Privacy
　and Electronic Communications) . . . 21, 38,
　62, 93, 94, 149–51, 156, 157, 159–63, 165, 166,
　363, 364
Recital 33 . . . 160
39 . . . 162
40 . . . 165
Art 1(1) . . . 150
　(2) . . . 150
2 . . . 160
　(b) . . . 156
　(h) . . . 152
3(1) . . . 150
5 . . . 151
6(3) . . . 156, 157
7 . . . 159
　(2) . . . 160
8(1) . . . 163
　(2), (4) . . . 163

9 . . . 95
10 . . . 163
13(1), (2), (4) . . . 165
15 . . . 21, 161
  (1) . . . 153, 364
EC Directive 2004/48, OJ L 195/16 (Copyright
  Enforcement) . . . 311, 354, 355, 419, 420
Art 3 . . . 355
EC Directive 2006/24, OJ 2006 L 105/54 (Data
  Retention) . . . 158
Recital 9 . . . 158
Art 5 . . . 158
EC Directive 2009/110, OJ 2009 L 267/77
  (Electronic Money Institutions) . . . 461, 462
EC Directive 2009/136/EC, OJ 2009 L 337/11
  (Citizens' Rights) . . . 38, 43, 150, 152–4, 363,
  442
Art 2 . . . 156
9(2) . . . 157
15 . . . 157
Directive 2011/92/EC, OJ 2011 L 335/1 (Child
  Pornography) . . . 200
Directive 2013/40/EC, OJ 2013 L 218/8 (Attacks
  against Information Systems) . . . 200, 243

Regulations

Commission Regulation 44/2001/EC, OJ 2001
  L 12/1 . . . 439
Art 15 . . . 439
Council Regulation 40/94, OJ 1994 L 11/1
  (Community Trade Mark) . . . 400
Council Regulation 45/2001, OJ 2001 L 8/1
  (Processing of Personal dData) . . . 62
Art 1 . . . 62
Council Regulation 460/2004, OJ 2004 L 7/13
  (Establishing the European Network and
  Information Security Agency) . . . 194, 200
Recital 1 . . . 194
Council Regulation 6/2002, OJ 2002 L 3/1
  (Community Design) . . . 392, 393
Arts 3–6, 10 . . . 396
Council Regulation 1257/2012, OJ 2012 L 361/1
  (Enhanced Co-operation) . . . 267
Council Regulation 1260/2012, OJ 2012 L 361/89
  (Applicable Translation Arrangements) . . .
  267
Council Regulation 526/2013, OJ 2013 L 165/41
  (Online Dispute Resolution) . . . 200

Table of Conventions and Other Enactments

Treaties and Conventions

Agreement between the European Union and the United States of America on the processing and transfer of Passenger Name Record (PNR) data by air carriers to the United States Department of Homeland Security (DHS) (2007 PNR Agreement) OJ 2007 L 204/18 . . . 179, 180

Berne Convention 1886 (1972 revision: Cmnd 5002) . . . 265, 310, 323, 349, 350
Art 9(2) . . . 317

Brussels Convention 1968 . . . 439

Convention for the Protection of Individuals with Regard to the Automatic Processing of Personal Data (Council of Europe, 1981; set out in Annex A to Cmnd 8538) . . . 20, 29–31, 36, 37, 62, 79, 168, 203, 211, 439
Preamble . . . 30
Arts 4, 5 . . . 211
Chapt II . . . 30
Art 12(2) . . . 30, 168
Additional Protocol . . . 29

Convention on the Organisation for Economic Cooperation and Development 1960 . . . 30
Art 7 . . . 31

Council of Europe Convention on Cybercrime 2001 . . . 29, 198, 199, 201–3, 210, 216, 217, 370
Art 2 . . . 203, 216, 217, 221, 229, 230, 232, 233, 242, 243
3 . . . 203, 210, 216, 217
4, 5 . . . 216, 217
6 . . . 216
Title 2 . . . 221
Arts 7, 8 . . . 221
Title 3 . . . 232
Art 9 . . . 232, 233
Additional Protocol . . . 230

European Convention for the Protection of Human Rights and Fundamental Freedoms (ECHR) 1950 . . . 18, 19, 24, 28, 30, 40, 117, 143, 366, 520
Preamble . . . 18
Art 1 . . . 393
8 . . . 18, 19, 20, 40, 85, 92, 117, 143, 507, 520
(1) . . . 19

10 . . . 28, 40, 64, 139, 143, 366, 507, 509
(2) . . . 40

European Community Patent Convention (the Luxembourg Convention) 1975 . . . 267

European Patent Convention 1973 (the Munich Convention) . . . 264–7, 271, 272, 280–4, 287, 293, 298, 299, 307, 344
Art 52 . . . 271, 283, 293, 299, 300
(1) . . . 291, 294–6
(2) . . . 286, 295–9
(c) . . . 286, 295
(3) . . . 285, 299
69 . . . 304
79 . . . 266
87(1) . . . 303

General Agreement on Tariffs and Trade (GATT) . . . 260, 267, 268

General Agreement on Trade in Services (GATS) . . . 260, 267, 354, 467

Madrid Agreement Concerning the International Registration of Marks 1979 . . . 401

OECD Declaration on Transborder Data Flows 1985 . . . 31
Art 7 . . . 31

Paris Convention . . . 265
Art 4 . . . 265

Patent Co-operation Treaty 1970 (Cmnd 7340) . . . 265
Arts 3, 12 . . . 265
15, 31, 33 . . . 265

Rome Convention on the Law Applicable to Contractual Obligations 1980 . . . 439

Statute of Council of Europe—
Art 1 . . . 18

Treaty on the Functioning of the European Union (Treaty Establishing the European Community (Treaty of Rome)) 1950 . . . 37, 179
Art 24 . . . 179
38 . . . 179
95 . . . 179
100a . . . 37
102 (ex 82/86) . . . 331

Treaty of Amsterdam 1997 . . . 62

United Nations Commission on International
    Trade Law (UNCITRAL) Model Law on
    Electronic Commerce . . . 427, 428, 450
    Art 2 . . . 450
    6 . . . 450
United Nations Convention against Transnational
    Organized Crime 2000 . . . 243
United Nations Universal Declaration of Human
    Rights 1948 . . . 18, 24
    Art 12 . . . 18

Vienna Convention on the Law of Treaties 1969—
    Art 31 . . . 299

WIPO Copyright Convention 1955 . . . 323
WIPO Treaty on Copyright and Performances
    and Phonograms 1996 . . . 323, 350
WTO Protocol on Trade Related Aspects of
    Intellectual Property Rights (TRIPS) . . . 260,
    267, 268, 293, 305, 323, 354
    Art 5 . . . 293
    27 . . . 267

PART I

Privacy, Anonymity, and Data Protection

General Introduction to Part 1

During 2013 we saw massive publicity given to disclosures by Edward Snowden indicating the extent to which the United States' National Security Agency (NSA) and the United Kingdom's Government Communications Headquarters (GCHQ) eavesdropped on electronic communications media. These disclosures followed closely upon other leaks publicised by the organisation Wikileaks.

In some respects, although perhaps attracting less publicity even in the United Kingdom, the activities of GCHQ were potentially more intrusive. Largely for historical reasons (the United Kingdom was the leading maritime power when international telecommunications networks were established in the nineteenth century), many of the underwater cables which form the backbone of the global communications network pass through the United Kingdom's territory. GCHQ, it appears, has extensive capabilities to monitor traffic carried over these cables. Most Internet traffic is routed via cable rather than satellite and even recognised mobile providers such as Vodafone are seeking to develop cable networks. *The Guardian* and other media sources have reported that:

> The (Snowden) documents reveal that by last year GCHQ was handling 600m 'telephone events' each day, had tapped more than 200 fibre-optic cables and was able to process data from at least 46 of them at a time.
>
> Each of the cables carries data at a rate of 10 gigabits per second, so the tapped cables had the capacity, in theory, to deliver more than 21 petabytes a day—equivalent to sending all the information in all the books in the British Library 192 times every 24 hours.[1]

It also reported that the intelligence agency is seeking to develop the ability to 'exploit any phone, anywhere, any time'.

It is not, of course only the activities of national security agencies that have attracted attention over the past couple of years. We have also recently had the Leveson Inquiry into phone hacking by or on behalf of elements of the media. In Autumn 2013 the House of Commons Home Affairs Select Committee engaged in a public dispute with the Serious Organised Crime Agency (SOCA) over delays in publishing details of the identity of businesses and individuals identified

---

[1] <http://www.theguardian.com/uk/2013/jun/21/gchq-cables-secret-world-communications-nsa>.

during the course of an Inquiry, Operation Millipede, into the hacking activities of a number of private investigators. A number of solicitors' firms have been reported to use such services. One is reported as commenting that it had used a private investigator to track down an individual who had embezzled £20 million from their client. In part this was necessary, it was argued:

> Solicitors who used private investigators said they were forced to because police cuts had resulted in fewer dedicated anti-fraud teams.
> They claimed the police often said clients would have to use the civil courts to track down money taken through fraud, fuelling the market in potential illegal data access by private investigators.

Linking to another topic covered in this book, the criticism is frequently made that police forces are unwilling to investigate cases of debit or credit card fraud reported by individuals. Home Office Guidance to police forces indicates that:

> Account holders attempting to report cheque, plastic card or online bank account fraud offences at police stations will be asked in the first instance if they have been specifically told to do so by their Financial Institution. If they have, they will be referred to the Action Fraud contact centre. If they have not, they will be told to contact their Financial Institution who will deal with the account holder. It is not necessary to record a crime related incident.[2]

The emergence of privacy

Recent years have seen the acceptance of privacy rights by the United Kingdom courts, albeit using established legal notions such as the doctrine of breach of confidence rather than establishing a specific right to privacy. The area is fraught with legal and practical difficulties and I must admit that I have never managed to develop an overall theory that strikes me as satisfactory. The seminal article 'The Right to Privacy' by Warren and Brandeis is one of the most frequently quoted legal publications. As it has been developed in the United States it has been linked closely to physical property; essentially adopting the notion that 'an Englishman's home is his castle'. The United Kingdom and European approach to privacy protection is rather broader but it is fair to say that most of our cases have involved some degree of interference with private space. Again, the essence of most of the cases has been that personal or private information is being put into the public domain. We will look a little later at the case of *Douglas v Hello!* where unauthorised photos taken at the wedding of the actors Michael Douglas and Catherine Zeta Jones were published. In essence the case was about money as much as reputation. The couple had entered into an exclusive contract (worth $1.55 million) with another magazine for the publication of wedding photos. This perhaps illustrates one of the problems of privacy. Nobody offered me a million pounds for my wedding photos! Most of our lives are of no interest to anyone outside our closest family and friends.

Another fact limiting the extent to which the law can protect privacy—at least in the Warren and Brandeis sense—is that we live much of our lives in public. It is not feasible for me to walk down a city street and expect everyone else to avert their gaze. It may be that the nature of attention may raise legal issues. The civil and criminal offence of harassment, for example, may be committed by a person whose behaviour is likely to upset another person. In most cases, however, we have no direct remedy from the attentions of others. In addition to direct human observation, our actions are frequently recorded on surveillance cameras. It has been

---

[2] <http://www.gov.uk/government/uploads/system/uploads/attachment_data/file/210800/count-fraud-april-2013.pdf>.

estimated that the United Kingdom has some 14 million surveillance cameras: approximately one for every four inhabitants. The accuracy of the figures has been challenged but it does seem clear that there are more cameras per head of population in the United Kingdom than in any other state.

Although systems of image recognition have been trialled, their effectiveness has yet to be established. Effectively in our increasingly urbanised society we have enjoyed a considerable degree of anonymity. Again, of course, different factors may apply to celebrities. Other people may see my actions but they will not know who I am and, human memory being what it is, recollection will soon fade.

It is tempting to suggest that anonymity is no longer what it was, but that is perhaps misleading and indeed some people would suggest that too much anonymity is a bad thing. In previous generations people tended to live in small, close-knit communities. Every act would be seen and commented on by family, friends, and neighbours. Today, there is generally a culture of indifference to the lives of those around us, something which is frequently the subject of media comment when, for example, it is discovered that someone has been lying dead in their house for months without anyone noticing. Anonymity, however, in respect of public transactions is diminishing. It was reported as 'far' back as 2010 that the volume transactions involving credit or debit cards exceeded those using cash. In many situations today—for example purchasing petrol late at night—it may be difficult to pay by cash. Garages may well take the view that it is unsafe for the company and its staff for potentially large amounts of cash to be held on their premises.

Paying by debit or credit card links an individual with a transaction in a way that is not possible with cash. It is not just credit and debit cards of course. Millions of people hold retail 'loyalty cards'. These link the holder to purchases linked to the card. The same applies to transport cards such as London Transport's Oyster card. The system retains a record of all journeys made using a card for eight weeks with data being retained in anonymised format for an indefinite period. One of the issues that is arising with improvements in processing power is whether supposedly anonymous data might be re-linked to an identifiable individual?

Oyster card data has proved a valuable investigative tool for police forces in the investigation crime. It is reported that more than 6,200 requests (around seventeen a day) were made by the Metropolitan Police in 2011. The figure has increased steadily since 2008 and the current figures may well be higher. It is quite common to see evidence led in criminal cases that an accused person's Oyster card was recorded at an underground station in the locale of a crime at around the time the offence was committed. At a wider level as we will discuss later, the Regulation of Investigatory Powers Act 2000 empowers law enforcement and other public authorities to seek access to communications data. This has been one of the cornerstones of the recent NSA/GCHQ issue. In 2011–12 United Kingdom public authorities submitted 494,078 requests for communications data. Only 3,372 requests were made for authorisation to intercept the content of communications—the traditional notion of telephone tapping. One reason for this is certainly the procedures and controls relating to the acquisition of communications data—data relating to the time destination and duration of calls together with location data in the case of calls originating or terminating on mobile phones are much less stringent than those applying to interception of content. It appears that one of the reasons why GCHQ was a welcome participant in some of the NSA's activities is that United Kingdom law relating to acquisition of communications data is less restrictive than its US equivalent

It is difficult to know how to approach such issues. Few would argue that law enforcement agencies should not be allowed to use new technologies. Fingerprints perhaps provide a good illustration and, perhaps more contentious, the use of DNA data. What is perhaps different in information-based tactics is that a trawl for data will inevitably involve intrusions into the lives of large numbers of completely innocent people. There is also, perhaps, a debatable linkage between data and individuals. The temptation is to assume that because my Oyster card indicated I was at a particular underground station at a particular time, that I was with it. Possibly, but all we can really know is that the card was at the location. I may have lent it to a friend.

We (almost) all spend a significant portion of our lives online, whether it be using social-networking sites, engaging in e-commerce, or searching the Internet. Few actions on the Internet go unrecorded and although many sites such as Facebook allow users to select the extent to which their content is available to other persons, default settings often allow unrestricted access and relatively few people take the time to change these.

An old saying is that 'knowledge is power'. Today we tend to say that 'information is power' and that is certainly true. There is a critical distinction between the concepts of knowledge and information. In this book I am trying to transfer my knowledge of information technology law. Knowledge transfer is not an easy task and can seldom, if ever, be completely successful. I will explain some concepts poorly, may well be wrong in some areas, and readers will also misunderstand the meaning of some passages. The words in the book constitute information and the transfer will be a complete success. Every reader will have the same information that I put into the book. We do perhaps rely too much on information as a substitute for knowledge. My Internet browser groans under the weight of hundreds of bookmarked pages. I have the information but must confess that I have not read, let alone understood, many of the pages. An uncritical acceptance of recorded information can be a dangerous thing but more and more decisions that can impact significantly on our lives are made on this basis.

Can the law help to protect us? A lot of emphasis has been put on the enactment of specialised statutes referred to in Europe as data protection laws, and elsewhere as privacy protection. We will discuss the scope of these laws extensively in this section but one of the major problems that law faces is in trying to find an approach that will ensure its core values of stability and predictability in the context of technologies that are developing with incredible speed. To give a simple example, at the time when the United Kingdom government was beginning to think about legislation in the 1970s a White Paper, 'Computers and Privacy' was published that was able to give the very precise figure that there were 13,263 computers installed in the country in 1975.

Defining what is a computer is not a simple task. Mobile phones, especially smart phones, which the telecoms regulator OFCOM estimate make up more than half of the United Kingdom market, would undoubtedly fall into this category. In some respects they may seem innocuous devices, at least so far as individual privacy is concerned, but it has been estimated that if a modern smart phone could be transmitted backwards in time to 1985, it would then have been the most powerful computing device on earth. Staying in the twenty-first century, there are somewhere in the region of 150 million computing devices in the UK. In less than forty years, the number of computers has increased by a factor of 11,300.

One of the early writers in the field of what was then called Computer Law was Alan Westin. He wrote in the 1970s to the effect that 'you do not find computers on street corners or in free nature, you find them in big powerful organisations'. How times have changed! It is unusual to stand at a street corner and not be surrounded by people texting on their mobile phones; the majority of customers in coffee shops seem to be using the free wi-fi to browse the Internet or catch up with emails. It is a requirement of data protection law in the United Kingdom that anyone who processes personal data on a computer has to notify the Information Commissioner of the nature and extent of their activities—and pay an annual fee of £35 for the privilege. At a guesstimate, some 40 million people should be notifying. At the latest count, 370,000 notifications had been made. Failure to notify constitutes a criminal offence.

We also have increasing amounts of computing power incorporated into the most mundane physical objects and one of the developing concepts is that of machine-to-machine communications. My fridge may be able to tell that it is running low on bottles of white wine and place an order with a supermarket for an online delivery. In another context it is reported that:

> The European Commission has adopted two proposals to ensure that, by October 2015, cars will automatically call emergency services in case of a serious crash. The 'eCall' system automatically dials 112—Europe's single emergency number—in the event of a serious accident. It communicates the vehicle's location to emergency services, even if the driver is unconscious or unable to make a phone call. It is estimated that it could save up to 2500 lives a year.
> [<http://www.eubusiness.com/topics/transport/e-call>]

One of the key concepts in data protection law is the notion of data controllers: persons or entities who control the nature and extent of processing. With social networking, cloud computing, and the more general concept of Web 2.0 which involves much more user generated content, it is difficult to determine who is the data controller.

Conclusions

One comment seems very appropriate to this section and, indeed, to almost every part of the book. Old legal models are broken but it is not clear what should replace them. In less than fifty years we have moved from a situation where computers were scarce devices with limited processing power to today's reality of an all-pervasive technology. It is reported that the first telegraph message sent using the (now obsolete) Morse code was 'What hath God wrought?' What, indeed, is the Internet and what will it become? These questions will recur constantly in the book but in the opening section we will focus on its impact on our private lives.

1

Privacy, technology, and surveillance

Introduction

In 2004 Richard Thomas, then the Information Commissioner for the United Kingdom,[1] warned against the dangers of the country 'sleepwalking into a surveillance society'.[2] This theme was developed in a report published by his office in 2006 entitled *A Surveillance Society*.[3] In the foreword to the report he went further claiming that 'we are in fact waking up to a surveillance society that is already all around us'. The massive publicity generated by the recent revelations concerning data monitoring programmes such as Prism and Tampora which are conducted by the NSA in the United States (with assistance from the British agency GCHQ) and GCHQ's own operation Upstream,[4] provides further evidence in support of the Commissioner's argument.

Smoke and mirrors—from echelon to prism

> Imagine a global spying network that can eavesdrop on every single phone call, fax or e-mail, anywhere on the planet.
>
> It sounds like science fiction, but it's true.
>
> <http://news.bbc.co.uk/1/hi/503224.stm>

The summer and autumn of 2013 saw a plethora of media postings concerning revelations about the US government's systems for obtaining access to communications data. The passage quoted above would seem to fit well into these but actually comes from 1999 and relates to the disclosure of a massive surveillance operation, known as project ECHELON which allegedly allowed the US security agencies (and also those from the UK and a number of other countries) to monitor the content of all email traffic over the Internet. For anyone interested, the footnote below provides a link to a report on ECHELON produced by a European Parliamentary Committee.[5] In the world of espionage and national security, little seems to change. There are always more questions than answers.

---

[1] The status and role of the Information Commissioner will be discussed more extensively in subsequent chapters. Essentially, the Commissioner is charged with enforcement of the United Kingdom's data protection (and freedom of information) legislation. Again, this will be considered more fully in later chapters.

[2] <http://news.bbc.co.uk/1/hi/uk_politics/6260153.stm>.

[3] <http://www.ico.gov.uk/upload/documents/library/data_protection/practical_application/surveillance_society_full_report_2006.pdf>.

[4] For an extensive collection of materials relating to these programmes see <http://www.theguardian.com/world/the-nsa-files>.

[5] <http://www.europarl.europa.eu/sides/getDoc.do?pubRef=-//EP//NONSGML+REPORT+A5-2001-0264+0+DOC+PDF+V0//EN&language=EN>.

In early summer 2013 we learned much about two surveillance programmes apparently operated by the United States' NSA and the Federal Bureau of Investigation (FBI). Under the first, the authorities have apparently been granted a secret court order requiring the major US telecommunications company Verizon (which offers fixed-line and mobile telecommunications services as well as broadband Internet access) to transmit on an ongoing basis a wide range of data concerning its users' communications to the NSA and the FBI.[6] In the UK (and the EU more generally) we are not strangers to the notion that communications providers should be required to retain communications data and, under specified circumstances and procedures, transfer it to law enforcement agencies (and indeed to a range of public authorities). The transfer of communications data is authorised under the Regulation of Investigatory Powers Act 2000 and is supervised by the Interception Commissioner. In his most recent report published in July 2012 he indicated that, during the reporting year, public authorities as a whole submitted 494,078 requests for communications data.[7] The intelligence agencies, police forces, and other law enforcement agencies are still the principal users of communications data. It is important to recognise that public authorities often make many requests for communications data in the course of a single investigation, so the total figure does not indicate the number of individuals or addresses targeted. Those numbers are not readily available, but would be much smaller.

This may seem a substantial figure but to put it into some perspective, Verizon have nearly 145 million customers, data on all of whom is required to be submitted on an ongoing basis to the NSA and FBI. It is not known whether other United States communications companies (in particular AT&T which is similar in size to Verizon) have been served with similar court orders but there are suggestions that these networks have been very willing to cooperate with law enforcement.[8] In theory the requirement to obtain a court order is stricter than the UK procedure which requires only approval by a senior member of staff within the public authority. The fact that proceedings are secret and the fact that the US Verizon order became known only through a leak does not inspire confidence.

The second element of US practice that was exposed by the whistleblower Edward Snowden, concerned NSA access to content-related data held by a range of Internet-related companies such as Google, Apple, and Facebook. This data is clearly much more sensitive than the communications data discussed above. As with all aspects of the story there is uncertainty over even basic issues. The claim is that the NSA enjoyed direct access to servers. This has been vehemently denied by a number of the companies involved. A Google statement asserted that:

> Google cares deeply about the security of our users' data. We disclose user data to government in accordance with the law, and we review all such requests carefully. From time to time, people allege that we have created a government 'back door' into our systems, but Google does not have a back door for the government to access private user data.[9]

Google publishes on a regular basis a so-called 'Transparency Report'.[10] This provides data on the number of requests it receives from governments around the world for access to data on the browsing history of individuals. This does not, however, give details of how many requests from the US authorities relate to national security concerns. A number

---

[6] <http://www.guardian.co.uk/world/interactive/2013/jun/06/verizon-telephone-data-court-order>.

[7] <http://www.intelligencecommissioners.com/docs/0496.pdf>.

[8] <http://online.wsj.com/article_email/SB10001424127887324049504578543800240266368-lMyQjAxMTAzMDEwMzExNDMyWj.html>.

[9] <http://www.guardian.co.uk/world/2013/jun/06/us-tech-giants-nsa-data>.

[10] <http://www.google.com/transparencyreport/>

of other Internet companies have produced similar statistics although, again, with very limited data about the proportion of national security requests.[11] At the time of writing, Google and a number of other communications providers are seeking permission from the US authorities to publish more data about the extent of national security-related requests for data.

In the United Kingdom, a draft Communications Data Bill (subsequently dropped following objections from the Deputy Prime Minister) was published in 2012. It was subjected to scrutiny by a joint Parliamentary Committee. In giving evidence to the committee the Home Secretary was asked to comment on the uses made of communications data. Her response was:

> As I say, I do not make any comment about individuals in relation to the security service, or any of the other security and intelligence agencies. It would not be appropriate for me to do so. Everybody who is working on this Bill is doing so because this Government believes that it is important that the police and the other agencies are able to continue to have the powers that they have today to do as we have discussed earlier, which is to save lives, in a new technological environment. I understand that the police estimate they get 30,000 urgent requests for communications data per year, and they estimate that they save lives in 25% to 40% of those cases. I think that matters to the public.[12]

Very large numbers but ones that sit rather uncomfortably with another statistic that a 'mere' 640 murders were committed in the UK during 2012.[13] It does seem hard to credit that between 7,500 to 12,000 lives are saved annually in the United Kingdom because of access to communications data.

Public and private surveillance

There is no doubt that communications data can be a valuable investigative tool for crime detection. In evidence before the Committee the Director General of the Serious and Organised Crime Agency indicated that it was used in 'around 95%' of their investigations. It is very common for information about Internet activity to be led in criminal cases. What we are seeing increasingly—especially as telecommunications networks and services are located squarely in the private sector—is that distinctions between public and private surveillance are becoming blurred. Surveillance systems such as Prism could not operate without the involvement and cooperation, whether voluntary or under legal compulsion, of private companies.

In 2012, the *Daily Telegraph* reported on a murder trial in which the female victim had vanished from her home with her body being found several weeks later. At the trial of the accused, a Dutch engineer named Tabak, prosecution evidence was led on the following lines:

> Lyndsey Farmery, an internet use analyst who assisted police with the investigation, took the jury through Tabak's online activity in the days after killing 25-year-old Miss Yeates.
>
> Web records from work and personal laptops show he researched the Wikipedia page for murder and maximum sentence for manslaughter, she said.
>
> While regularly checking the Avon and Somerset police website and a local news site, the Dutch engineer was also checking body decomposition rates.

[11] <http://www.guardian.co.uk/technology/2013/jun/17/apple-reveals-us-surveillance-requests>.

[12] <http://www.parliament.uk/documents/joint-committees/communications-data/Oral%20Evidence%20Volume.pdf>.

[13] <http://www.citizensreportuk.org/reports/murders-fatal-violence-uk.html>.

Days after killing Miss Yeates at her Clifton flat on December 17, Tabak watched a time-lapse video of a body decomposing, Bristol Crown Court heard.

Tabak—who denies murder but admits manslaughter—also went on Google to look up the definition of sexual assault.[14]

At another level of communication data, a freedom of information request in 2012 revealed that the Metropolitan Police had made 22,000 requests over a four-year period for access to data held by London Transport relating to journeys made using its system of Oyster cards.[15] The data can be used to place a suspect (or a card registered in the suspect's name) in the vicinity of an offence at the appropriate time. In another example of the use of electronic data, a magistrate was convicted of theft.[16] A woman had lost a Rolex watch in a Tesco supermarket. Two years later the watch was handed in to a jeweller's for repair. Its serial number was checked against a list of missing watches and this led to the arrest of the magistrate who had handed it in for repair. His defence that he had bought the watch as a present for his wife in a second-hand shop (whose location he could not remember) was undermined when data relating to use of his Tesco Clubcard placed him in the supermarket at the time the watch went missing.

As the above examples show, communications and location data can constitute crucial evidence in criminal investigations. In the Tesco example, there is an issue as to why the loyalty card data was still available in such detail two years after the event. The Data Protection Act requires that data be retained for no longer than is necessary for the purpose for which it was acquired. It is difficult to see what justification there might be for a supermarket to keep marketing data at this level of detail for two years.

In any matters relating to criminal investigations and even more to issues of national security, there has to be a balance between the legitimate need for secrecy and public accountability. The key issue is perhaps proportionality. We live very large parts of our existence online. OFCOM data indicates that the average UK consumer now sends fifty texts per week—a figure that has more than doubled in four years—with over 150 billion text messages sent in 2011.[17] Almost another ninety minutes per week is spent accessing social-networking sites and email, or using a mobile to access the Internet, while for the first time ever fewer phone calls are being made on both fixed and mobile phones.

We have well-established laws requiring respect for our physical property. Search warrants are required to be issued before law enforcement agencies can enter our houses and it is perhaps time that our virtual houses received similar protection. Another recent tool which has been extremely useful for law enforcement agencies is DNA evidence. There is certainly controversy concerning the circumstances under which DNA is collected and retained but there does not appear to be a strong body of opinion in favour of universal DNA profiling. Effectively, however, that is what appears to be happening with communications data in the United States. UK practice is more restrained but we do need a more evidence-based debate. I mentioned above data relating to the number of requests for access to Oyster card data. There is no data that I have been able to find relating to the number of times it has been used in the course of criminal prosecutions. In the wake of the Prism revelations in the United States, some cases were cited as evidence of the value

---

[14] <http://www.telegraph.co.uk/news/uknews/crime/8836161/Vincent-Tabak-researched-unsolved-murders-after-killing-Joanna-Yeates.html>.

[15] <http://www.theregister.co.uk/2012/02/10/metropolitan_police_asks_for_tfl_data/>.

[16] <http://www.telegraph.co.uk/news/uknews/1482200/Magistrate-fined-for-keeping-lost-Rolex.html>.

[17] <http://media.ofcom.org.uk/2012/07/18/uk-is-now-texting-more-than-talking/>.

of communications data in preventing terrorist offences but other sources have cast doubt on this, suggesting that other and older forms of intelligence gathering deserve the credit.[18]

To finish this introductory section on a lighter note, but one that does perhaps make the point about proportionality, I recall an intellectual exercise intended to identify the best way to reduce casualties in road accidents. We can all think of suggestions, invariably involving additional or improved safety features in cars. The winning suggestion was rather different. Prohibit seat belts and air bags. Instead make it mandatory to have a sharp spike fitted on the steering wheel pointing directly at the driver's heart. I'm sure it would cut the number of accidents but…[19]

Forms of surveillance

In 1971, Alan Westin in his seminal work, *Information Technology in a Democracy*,[20] identified three forms of surveillance that might be conducted by public authorities:

- physical
- psychological
- data.

Physical surveillance, as the name suggests, involves the act of watching or listening to the actions of an individual. Such surveillance, even making use of technology, has tended to be an expensive undertaking capable of being applied only to a limited number of individuals. In investigations subsequent to the 7 July 2005 bombings in London, it emerged that at least one of the bombers had come to the notice of the security services but had not been placed under surveillance. An intelligence source was reported as suggesting that MI5 considered that at the time of the London bombings in 2005, there were in the region of 800 Al Qaeda suspects, a figure which subsequently rose by a further 200. Whilst the security services tried to keep as many people under surveillance as possible, this was an extremely labour-intensive process, with the source suggesting that keeping a person under surveillance for twenty-four hours a day would require a team of between twenty and forty watchers. At the lower estimate, this would require MI5 to have 20,000 operatives. At the time in question, the total staff to cover all aspects of its work was in the region of 2,000.[21] Obviously—and as illustrated by the failure to monitor the actual bombers more closely— only a small proportion of identified suspects could be subjected to physical surveillance.

Examples of *psychological surveillance* include forms of interrogation or the use of personality tests, as favoured by some employers. Once again, logistical and cost constraints have served to limit the use of these techniques. The end-product of any form of surveillance is data or information.

---

[18] <http://www.guardian.co.uk/world/2013/jun/12/nsa-surveillance-data-terror-attack>.

[19] Also in the field of automotive safety, the European Commission has proposed that from 2015 all new cars should be installed with technology enabling them to contact the emergency services automatically in the event that sensors detect that the vehicle has been involved in an accident. It is estimated (on what basis is not clear) that the system, known as 112 eCall, could save 2,500 lives a year by enabling faster response to accidents. See <http://ec.europa.eu/commission_2010-2014/kallas/headlines/news/2013/06/ecall_en.htm>.

[20] Unir Microfilms Int., 1971.

[21] <http://thescotsman.scotsman.com/londonbombings/MI5-spied-on-only-one.5282797.jp>. The Intelligence and Security Committee made the same point in their report on the bombings (available from <http://www.cabinetoffice.gov.uk/publications/reports/intelligence/isc_7july_report.pdf>) although the precise numbers cited above were omitted for reasons of national security.

With both physical and psychological surveillance, an active role is played by the watcher. *Data surveillance* involves a different, more passive approach. Every action by an individual reveals something about the person. Very few actions do not involve individuals in giving out a measure of information about themselves. This may occur directly, for example, in filling out a form, or indirectly, as when goods or services are purchased. The essence of data surveillance lies in the collection and retention of these items of information.

With the ability to digitise any form of information, boundaries between the various forms of surveillance are disappearing with the application of information technology linking surveillance techniques into a near seamless web of surveillance. Developments in data processing suggest that the distinction between informational and physical privacy is becoming more and more flimsy. The reach of systems of physical surveillance has been increased enormously by the involvement of the computer to digitise and process the information received.

Today, the critical distinction between forms of surveillance is perhaps between direct and targeted surveillance of particular individuals and the more general, all pervasive surveillance which permeates all our lives without being specifically directed at any particular purpose. As George Orwell wrote in his famous novel, *1984*:

> There was of course no way of knowing whether you were being watched at any given moment. How often, or on what system, the Thought Police plugged in on any individual wire was guesswork. It was even conceivable that they watched everybody all the time, but at any rate they could plug in your wire whenever they wanted to. You have to live—did live, from habit that became instinct—in the assumption that every sound you made was overheard, and, except in darkness, every movement scrutinized.

This certainly has echoes of much of the debate about current surveillance. When we are directly and personally the subject of scrutiny, there may well be the sense that our privacy is being infringed—and this chapter will continue to consider the extent to which rights of privacy are accepted and protected in the United Kingdom. In other cases, the issue is perhaps more that we are losing the ability to transact anonymously. A famous cartoon by Peter Steiner and first published in the *New York Times* depicts two dogs sitting in front of a computer screen with one captioned as telling the other 'in Cyberspace, no-one knows you're a dog'. The key word here is 'knows'. As will be discussed in later sections of this book, one of the difficulties created for users of social-networking sites (and indeed the Internet generally) is the difficulty in determining whether another person's online persona matches their real-life existence. A forty-year-old paedophile can easily and convincingly masquerade as a sixteen-year-old boy or girl. That is one danger, but for present purposes we might focus on another. Nobody may 'know' who you are, but if the information generated by your actions fits the profile of a dog, you may find yourself treated as one. Many Internet sites make much of their income through selling advertising space linked to particular search requests. Browse the Internet looking at hotels in a particular city and you will almost inevitably find banner adverts relating to those searches appearing when you view other sites such as online newspapers

Living in the surveillance society

In an information-based society, extensive details concerning the most trivial actions undertaken are recorded. In the context of e-commerce, an online bookshop will know, at least once customers have bought goods and accepted the presence of cookies on their computers, the title of every book which is examined and the nature of catalogue searches made. This can be linked to name and address details.

Perhaps the most noticeable and extensive surveillance tool is the closed-circuit television camera (CCTV). It is a rare high street or even shop which does not have one or more cameras. The estimate is frequently cited that there are in the region of 14.2 million CCTVs in the United Kingdom. With a population approaching 60 million, that equates to roughly one camera for every fourteen inhabitants of the country. Two million motorists are fined each year as a result of being caught by speed cameras. In general, it is estimated that the average person can expect to be 'caught' on camera around 300 times a day.[22]

Traditionally, CCTV systems have relied upon images being viewed and assessed by human operators. In at least some instances this is no longer the case. A nationwide system of Automatic Number Plate Recognition cameras is being installed on the United Kingdom's roads. Around 10 million number plates are recorded each day with a total of some 7 billion records stored[23] and compared against records maintained by the Driver and Vehicle Licensing Agency and motor insurance companies to identify vehicles which are not taxed or insured. The system also links with police databases to flag the appearance of any vehicle recorded as being of interest to the police.[24]

Even in the physical environment, trials are being conducted with image-recognition systems linked to CCTV cameras,[25] which can monitor the movements of specific individuals. One of the most extensive systems has been installed in the London Borough of Newham.[26] Here it has been reported that images from 150 cameras are compared against a database of around 100 known offenders maintained by the Council. If a targeted individual is identified by the system, the police are automatically informed. The system, known as 'Mandrake', is claimed to be sufficiently sophisticated to defeat attempts to conceal identity by such tactics as wearing glasses or make-up, or even growing a beard. An accuracy rate of 75 per cent is claimed for the system,[27] although other sources have cast doubt on this figure.[28] The downside, of course, is that 25 per cent of those recorded on the system are innocent people who will be viewed with suspicion because of a false identification. In more recent developments, it has been reported that CCTV systems are being tested which use advanced monitoring techniques to assess the movements and actions of individuals within their range, with the aim of identifying behavioural patterns which might be regarded as suspicious. An example might be of a person who remains on an underground station platform for a considerable period of time, allowing a number of trains to arrive and depart without attempting to board it.[29]

Surveillance devices in the workplace allow employers to monitor the activities and efficiency of individuals. At a potentially extreme level, the United States Patent Office has published an application from Microsoft for a system which will monitor an employee's

---

[22] <http://news.bbc.co.uk/1/hi/uk/6108496.stm>.   [23] <http://www.npia.police.uk/en/10505.htm>.

[24] Details of the system and its possible uses are given in a document, 'ANPR Strategy for the Police Service 2005–8', produced by the Association of Chief Police Officers and available from <http://www.acpo.police.uk/asp/policies/Data/anpr_strat_2005-08_march05_12x04x05.doc>.

[25] As was reported in *The Independent*, 12 January 2004, more than 4 million CCTV cameras are in use in the United Kingdom. At a ratio of one camera to fifteen people, this, it is claimed, makes the United Kingdom the 'most-watched nation in the world'.

[26] <http://www.bbc.co.uk/londonlive/news/july/cctv_170701.shtml>.

[27] *Daily Mail*, 15 October 1998.

[28] *The Guardian* has published claims that the system had never identified a suspected individual. See <http://www.guardian.co.uk/Archive/Article/0,4273,4432506,00.html>.

[29] <http://rinf.com/alt-news/contributions/mick-meaney/20-of-uk-cctv-could-judge-your-beh aviour-within-3-years/614/>.

heart rate, body temperature, blood pressure, and movement. It is claimed that the system will automatically detect signs of stress or illness. Even the Internet and World Wide Web (WWW), which are often touted as the last refuge of individualism, might equally accurately be described as a surveillance system par excellence. An individual browsing the Web leaves electronic trails wherever he or she passes. A software program can transmit a tracer known as a 'cookie'[30] from a website to the user's computer. Cookies can take a variety of forms and may retain details relating to the user's actions, either for the duration of a visit to a site or for a specified and potentially unlimited period of time.[31]

In terms of goods themselves, the ubiquitous barcode which facilitates identification of the product and its price at the checkout may be replaced by radio frequency identification tags (RFID). These are essentially a form of microchip capable of transmitting information, both prior to and after the point of sale. This would, for example, enable the movement of the object to be tracked, both in the store and also externally. One possibility which has been canvassed is that future generations of banknotes will have RFID tags embedded in them in order to enable movements of cash to be tracked with a view to countering money laundering. In respect of motor cars, the European Commission has launched a programme designed to specify standards for electronic vehicle identification (EVI). The programme, it is stated, aims to develop:

> an *electronic, unique identifier for motor vehicles*, which would enable a wealth of applications, many of them of crucial importance for the public authorities to combat congestion, unsafe traffic behaviour and vehicle crime on the European roads. It is clear that such an identifier as well as the communication means to remotely read it should be standardised and *interoperable* all over Europe.[32]

In the United Kingdom, it has been reported in a similar context that plans are being drawn up to fit all cars with a microchip which will monitor driving behaviour and automatically report a range of traffic offences, including speeding, road-tax evasion, and illegal parking.[33]

Examples of thickening information threads and trails are legion. Barely ten years ago, the only records compiled by United Kingdom telephone companies regarding telephone usage concerned the number of units of charge (an amalgam of the time of day when a call is made, its duration, and its identification as local, long distance, or international). Today, it is near universal practice to present users with itemised bills. These may provide considerable assistance to the person (or company) responsible for paying the bill in monitoring and controlling usage but do also provide useful marketing information to the service provider, as well as raising issues concerning the privacy of other persons who might make use of the facility. Recent research conducted on behalf of BT illustrates well the issues involved. It is reported that 15,000 calls an hour are made from work phones to sex or chat telephone lines.[34] With mobile phones, even more data is recorded, with location data enabling the movements of the phone to be tracked with ever greater precision. Again, the widespread use of cash-dispensing machines allows the withdrawals of bank customers to be tracked on a real-time basis, both nationally and internationally.

---

[30] For information about the nature of these devices see <http://www.cookiecentral.com/faq.htm>.

[31] A Report on Privacy on the Internet has been prepared for the European Commission Working Party on Data Protection and gives some interesting insights into the topic. The report is available from <http://ec.europa.eu/justice/policies/privacy/docs/wpdocs/2000/wp37en.pdf>.

[32] <http://www.publications.parliament.uk/pa/cm200304/cmselect/cmtran/319/319we45.htm> (emphasis in original).   [33] *Sunday Times*, 24 August 2003.

[34] Cited on Ceefax (an electronic information service broadcast by the BBC), 21 July 2003.

Surveillance and the law

Concern at these privacy implications of information technology was expressed by Lord Hoffmann when delivering his judgment in the House of Lords in the case of *R v Brown*:

> My Lords, one of the less welcome consequences of the information technology revolution has been the ease with which it has become possible to invade the privacy of the individual. No longer is it necessary to peep through keyholes or listen under the eaves. Instead, more reliable information can be obtained in greater comfort and safety by using the concealed surveillance camera, the telephoto lens, the hidden microphone and the telephone bug. No longer is it necessary to open letters, pry into files or conduct elaborate inquiries to discover the intimate details of a person's business or financial affairs, his health, family, leisure interests or dealings with central or local government. Vast amounts of information about everyone are stored on computers, capable of instant transmission anywhere in the world and accessible at the touch of a keyboard. The right to keep oneself to oneself, to tell other people that certain things are none of their business, is under technological threat.[35]

The potential dangers were further considered by Lord Browne-Wilkinson VC in *Marcel v Metropolitan Police Commissioner*.[36] Documents belonging to the plaintiff had been seized by the police in the course of a criminal investigation. Civil proceedings were also current in respect of the same incidents, and a subpoena was served on behalf of one of the parties to this litigation seeking disclosure of some of these documents. Holding that the subpoena should be set aside, the judge expressed concern that:

> if the information obtained by the police, the Inland Revenue, the social security offices, the health service and other agencies were to be gathered together in one file, the freedom of the individual would be gravely at risk. The dossier of private information is the badge of the totalitarian state.[37]

As indicated in the above passage, an appropriate balance between privacy—classically expressed in terms of the right to be left alone—and surveillance—representing the wish to discover information about another—is difficult to define. Although initially appearing as opposites, privacy and surveillance are linked almost as if they were conjoined twins.

A wide range of surveys of public opinion evidence show strong support for the protection of privacy. Although many of these derive from the United States, in the United Kingdom, the Information Commissioner has commissioned annual surveys of public opinion. In the annual report for 2000, the then Commissioner noted:

> Respondents were read a list of issues and asked to say how important they think each is. The proportion who thought that protecting peoples' rights to personal privacy was very important increased but not significantly from 73% to 75%. In terms of people's hierarchy of priorities the issue remains extremely important. Again only Crime Prevention and Improving Standards of Education are thought to be more important issues by the public.

Subsequent surveys have adopted a different formulation, more closely linked to the Information Commissioner's remit, by asking for respondents' views concerning the importance of protecting personal information. The answers, however, have remained fairly constant. Table 1.1 contains the results from the 2010 survey.[38]

---

[35] [1996] 1 All ER 545 at 555–6.   [36] [1992] Ch 225.

[37] [1992] Ch 225 at 240. This quotation is also of considerable relevance to the emerging practice of data matching, which is considered more fully later.

[38] <http://ico.org.uk/about_us/research/~/media/documents/library/Corporate/Research_and_reports/annual_track_2010_individuals.ashx>.

Table 1.1 Concerns with issues of social importance

Concerned	2004	2005	2010
Preventing crime	85%	88%	93%
The National Health Service	78%	83%	92%
Equal rights for everyone	69%	81%	87%
Protecting people's personal information	70%	83%	92%
National security	71%	78%	85%
Improving standards in education	76%	84%	90%
Protecting freedom of speech	67%	80%	81%
Environmental issues	66%	74%	77%
Unemployment	50%	70%	90%
Access to information held by public authorities	48%	66%	75%

Whilst it would be an exceptional person who placed no value upon privacy, significant difficulties have to be overcome in the attempt to give the concept a concrete legal meaning. First, it is undoubtedly the case that different people and societies have widely varying interpretations as to which matters are private and which reasonably belong in the public arena. Millions of (mainly) younger people place details of their lives on social-networking websites such as 'MySpace'[39] or 'Facebook'.[40] In many cases, the level of detail exposed appears excessive to those of an older generation.[41] Celebrities may court and value a greater degree of attention than the average person would find tolerable although, as cases such as *Campbell v MGN*[42] and *Douglas v Hello!*[43] illustrate, even celebrities draw distinctions between public and private life. Those living in close-knit communities may accept that their every action will be known to and commented upon by others. City-dwellers may expect much more in the way of freedom from observation but this may carry with it the spectre of the lack of interest and concern.

At a societal level, the United Kingdom is noted for attaching great value to privacy in respect of dealings with the tax system. In Sweden, by way of contrast, information about tax returns is a matter of public record. This is reported to have produced problems for the authorities at the time when the pop group Abba was at the height of its fame. Many thousands of fans discovered that they could readily and cheaply obtain copies of their idols' tax returns (which included a photograph). Dealing with the demand for copies is claimed to have brought the system close to meltdown. Even in the age of freedom of information legislation, it is difficult to envisage such a scenario being acceptable to the average British citizen. As perhaps an anecdote, however, whilst traditional forms of publication of financial information caused little stir, the emergence of a website, 'Ratsit. se', pushed even Swedish notions of openness to their limits when it started publishing financial details obtained from the national tax authority on its website, from where they could be accessed by anyone free of charge. The service proved popular, with about 50,000 searches being made each day. Many, it appears, were made by individuals curious to know details about their friends and neighbours. Whilst most might have hesitated to make a personal visit or request to the tax authorities for the data, the anonymity associated with web searches proved attractive. Numerous complaints were made to the Swedish data protection authorities. The tax authorities indicated to the website owners that, whilst Swedish

---

[39] <http://www.myspace.com/>.   [40] <http://www.facebook.com/>.
[41] See e.g. <http://nymag.com/news/features/27341/>.   [42] [2005] UKHL 61.
[43] [2007] UKHL 21.

freedom of information law obliged them to supply tax data, it did not require that it be supplied in electronic form. Provision of the data in paper form would have involved a massive effort to convert documents into electronic formats. Faced with this prospect, the site was reorganised. From June 2007, access could be obtained only upon payment of a fee and, in line with the principles applying in respect of Swedish credit reference agencies, the subject would be informed of the fact that a request had been made and of the identity of the requesting party.

Whilst surveillance is often seen as involving the surreptitious and unwelcome collection of personal data, this is not always the case. Although individuals may claim to value privacy, they frequently appear to do little to protect themselves. Hundreds of thousands of individuals have applied for supermarket 'loyalty cards'. Such cards provide an invaluable point of linkage between details of individual transactions and the more generic stock management computer systems which have long been a feature of retail life. The seller now knows not only what has been bought but also who has bought it, when, in conjunction with what other products, and what form of payment has been tendered. Analysis of the information will reveal much about the individual's habits and lifestyle which may be used as the basis for direct marketing, targeted at the individual customer.[44] Again, many thousands of individuals respond to lifestyle questionnaires which may be delivered either as a mailshot or accompanying a magazine. In return for the chance to win what are often low-value prizes, respondents freely disclose all manner of items of personal information.

Privacy issues

The classical legal definition of privacy is attributed to a United States judge, Judge Cooley, who opined that it consists of 'the right to be left alone'. A considerable number of other definitions have been formulated over the years. A number of these were cited in the *Report of the Committee on Privacy*.[45] The essential component, at least for the purposes of the present book, may be stated in terms that an individual has the right to control the extent to which personal information is disseminated to other people.

This notion, which is often referred to as involving 'informational privacy', has two main components. The first concerns the right to live life free from the attentions of others, effectively to avoid being watched. This is perhaps the essence of privacy as a human condition or state. Once a third party has information, the second element comes into play, with the individual seeking to control the use to which that information is put and, in particular, its range of dissemination.

The post-Second World War expansion of rights to privacy

Notions of a right to privacy have formed a feature of many domestic laws for decades and even centuries. Generally, however, rights to privacy would be rooted in a number of other legal concepts. In the United States, for example, the right of privacy has been seen as emerging from a range of constitutionally guaranteed protections. As was stated by Mr Justice Douglas in the case of *Griswold v Connecticut*:

> Various guarantees create zones of privacy. The right of association contained in the penumbra of the First Amendment is one, as we have seen. The Third Amendment in its prohibition

---

[44] For an excellent collection of links to materials on this topic see <http://www.nocards.org/>.
[45] (1972) Cmnd 5012.

against the quartering of soldiers 'in any house' in time of peace without the consent of the owner is another facet of that privacy. The Fourth Amendment explicitly affirms the 'right of the people to be secure in their persons, houses, papers, and effects, against unreasonable searches and seizures.' The Fifth Amendment in its Self-Incrimination Clause enables the citizen to create a zone of privacy which government may not force him to surrender to his detriment. The Ninth Amendment provides: 'The enumeration in the Constitution, of certain rights, shall not be construed to deny or disparage others retained by the people.'[46]

This expansive basis for the right to privacy has resulted in the doctrine being held applicable to an extensive range of situations, including forming the basis of the seminal Supreme Court ruling in the case of *Roe v Wade*,[47] which established a constitutional right to abortion.

In the aftermath of the Second World War, the concept of human rights began to be recognised at an international level. In 1948, the General Assembly of the United Nations adopted the Universal Declaration of Human Rights. This proclaimed in Article 12 that:

> No one shall be subjected to arbitrary interference with his privacy, family, home or correspondence, nor to attacks upon his honour and reputation. Everyone has the right to the protection of the law against such interference or attacks.

Although influential, the Universal Declaration has no binding legal force. Such a legal instrument was not long delayed. In 1949, the Council of Europe was established by international treaty. Its stated goals include the negotiation of agreements with the aim of securing 'the maintenance and further realisation of human rights and fundamental freedoms'.[48] One of the first actions undertaken within the Council was the negotiation of the Convention for the 'Protection of Fundamental Rights and Fundamental Freedoms' (European Convention on Human Rights, hereafter, 'the Convention'). The Convention was opened for signature in November 1950 and entered into force in September 1953. As its Preamble states, the signatory states reaffirmed:

> their profound belief in those fundamental freedoms which are the foundation of justice and peace in the world and are best maintained on the one hand by an effective political democracy and on the other by a common understanding and observance of the human rights upon which they depend...

Of the many rights conferred by the Convention, Article 8 is of particular relevance in the present context. This provides that:

1. Everyone has the right to respect for his private and family life, his home, and his correspondence.

2. There shall be no interference by a public authority with the exercise of this right except such as is in accordance with the law and is necessary in a democratic society in the interests of national security, public safety or the economic well-being of the country, for the prevention of disorder or crime, for the protection of health or morals, or for the protection of the rights and freedoms of others.

Although the second paragraph of Article 8 is couched in terms relating to interference by public authority, the jurisprudence of the European Court of Human Rights has established that the obligation imposed upon Member States is to ensure that private and family life is protected by law against intrusions by any person or agency, whether within the public or the private sector. In the case of *Hatton v United Kingdom*,[49] the Court referred to the

---

[46] (1965) 381 United States 479 at 484.   [47] 410 United States 113.
[48] Statute of Council of Europe, Art. 1.   [49] (Application No. 36022/97) (2003) 15 BHRC 259.

existence of 'a positive duty on the State to take reasonable and appropriate measures to secure the applicants' rights under Article 8 § 1 of the Convention'.

The term, 'private life', is not defined further in the Convention. As with the United States concept of privacy, the term has been broadly interpreted by the European Court of Human Rights, which was established to supervise the state's compliance with the Convention's requirements. In one important respect, the Convention right goes beyond the United States notion of privacy. In the United States, a critical distinction exists between activities taking place on private property and those in public (or semi-public) places. The European notion of private life is less tied to physical objects, and may protect individuals in respect of their activities in the public arena. In the case of *Halford v United Kingdom*,[50] the European Court of Human Rights held that the protection of Article 8 extended to telephone conversations made by the applicant from her office phone. When her employers monitored the calls in the course of disciplinary proceedings against the applicant, the Court ruled that there had been a breach of Article 8.

The case of *Copland v United Kingdom*[51] is also of considerable significance. Here, the applicant was employed at a college in Wales. The college's Deputy Principal formed a suspicion about her relationship with another individual and believed that the applicant was misusing college facilities for personal purposes. Although there was no direct monitoring of the content of calls, the communications records of both outgoing and incoming telephone calls were analysed. Monitoring and analysis extended also to Internet usage in the form of the locations of the websites viewed, together with the dates and duration of browsing activities. Details of the addresses of email messages were subjected to a similar process.[52] Arguing that there had been no breach of the applicant's rights under Article 8, the United Kingdom government claimed that:

> Although there had been some monitoring of the applicant's telephone calls, e-mails and internet usage prior to November 1999, this did not extend to the interception of telephone calls or the analysis of the content of websites visited by her. The monitoring thus amounted to nothing more than the analysis of automatically generated information to determine whether College facilities had been used for personal purposes which, of itself, did not constitute a failure to respect private life or correspondence.[53]

This contention was rejected by the Court which, referring to its previous decision in *Halford*, held that email messages should be regarded in the same manner as telephone calls. Although in this case there was no monitoring of the content of either telephone calls or emails, the data recorded, it was held, constituted an 'integral element of the communications'.[54] In the absence of any warning having been given to the applicant of the possibility of monitoring, the conduct constituted a breach of Article 8.

In addition to expanding the scope of private life beyond the limits of private property, the jurisprudence of the European Court of Human Rights has shown that the enforcement of the right to respect for private life imposes positive obligations encompassing the grant of access to at least some forms of personal data. In the case of *Gaskin v United Kingdom*,[55] the complainant, whose childhood had been spent in the care of Liverpool City Council, sought access in adulthood to a wide range of social-work and medical records compiled

[50] 1997, 3 BHRC 31.   [51] [2007] ECHR 62617/00.
[52] At the time that the activities occurred (around 1998–9), United Kingdom law made no provision regarding such conduct. The Telecommunications (Lawful Business Practice) Regulations 2000 made under the authority of the Regulation of Investigatory Powers Act 2000 would now apply to this form of activity.
[53] para. 32.   [54] para. 43.   [55] (1990) 12 EHRR 36.

during these years. At the time the request was made, the Data Protection Act 1984 provided a right of subject access only in respect of data held in electronic format. Although the Council took significant steps to assist the complainant—in particular by seeking the consent of all those responsible for creating records to their disclosure—access was denied, except where positive consent had been obtained.[56] Recognising that the grant of access to records containing personal data was an integral part of the requirements of Article 8, the Court held that the United Kingdom was in breach of its obligations by failing to establish an appropriate mechanism for determining the extent to which access should be granted.

As demonstrated in *Gaskin*,[57] although the breadth of Article 8 rights offers benefits for individuals, it also suffers from an inevitable lack of precision, especially in situations where conflict arises between competing claims. Building on the general principles, a trend emerged within Western Europe during the last third of the twentieth century for the introduction of data protection laws concerned specifically with the issues arising from the processing of personal data. One of the major concerns was that the capability of the computer to store, process, and disseminate information posed significant threats to the individual's ability to control the extent to which personal information was disseminated and the uses to which it might be put.

A linkage has frequently been drawn between the general right to privacy and the notion of informational privacy. This is clearly seen, both in the Council of Europe Convention on the Automated Processing of Personal Data and, more recently and extensively, in the text of the EC Directive on the Protection of Individuals with Regard to the Processing of Personal Data and on the Free Movement of Such Data,[58] which makes no fewer than fourteen references to the noun 'privacy'. Article 1 of the Directive is explicit:

> In accordance with this Directive, Member States shall protect the fundamental rights and freedoms of natural persons, and in particular their right to privacy with respect to the processing of personal data.

The scope of these measures will be discussed in more detail in the following chapters.

Surveillance-based legislation

Great and tragic events invariably carry a lasting legacy and aftershocks from the events of September 11, 2001 continue to reverberate around the globe. The perception, true or false, that the Internet and forms of electronic communications are linked with the spread of global terrorism has impacted significantly on governmental attitudes to many of the issues discussed in this chapter and, indeed, throughout the whole of the field of information technology law. Of particular relevance to the present discussion is the extent to which changes have been made—and are being made—to the delicate balance between personal privacy and the interests of the government and also, of course, of society at large, in preventing the commission of terrorist offences. Many of the legislative responses to the threat of global terrorism, especially those within the United Kingdom, have been enacted with great speed, driven by perceived necessity but also carrying with them the risk of creating a chasm between those whose primary interest is in law enforcement and individuals and

---

[56] In some cases, consent was refused but in a majority of cases, the original author either could not be traced or failed to respond to the request. Effectively, silence was regarded as constituting refusal.

[57] *Gaskin v United Kingdom* (1990) 12 EHRR 36.

[58] Directive 95/46/EC, OJ 1995 L 281/31 (the Data Protection Directive).

bodies concerned with the protection and promotion of individual rights and freedoms. Creative tension between different interest groups is inevitable and can produce benefits when there is a degree of acceptance that each group is acting in good faith. When creation turns to destruction, everyone loses and in many respects the present debate between civil libertarian lobbyists and governments has become sterile. Possible consequences are that individuals may lose some of the major elements of the protection introduced and developed over the past decades, whilst governments risk losing popular legitimacy if they are seen as being unconcerned with and threatening towards the rights of citizens.

Many significant legislative moves have been made in order to enhance the powers of law enforcement and national security agencies in the aftermath of September 11. Most of the aspects, such as increased powers of arrest and detention, are outside the scope of this book. For present purposes, the most important changes relate to increased rights of access to personal data.

The starting point of the analysis should be the EC Directive on Privacy and Electronic Communications.[59] As originally drafted, this Directive provides individuals with extensive guarantees of privacy in respect of data pertaining to their electronic communications. At a very late stage in the legislative process, however, and following the events of September 11, an amendment was accepted by the European Parliament permitting EU Member States to 'adopt legislative measures providing for the retention of data for a limited period justified on the grounds laid down in this paragraph'.[60] The grounds referred to include the safeguarding of 'national security . . . defence, public security, and the prevention, investigation, detection and prosecution of criminal offences or of unauthorised use of the electronic communication system'. Even prior to the entry into force of the Directive, this power has been extensively used within the United Kingdom.

Initial legislative provisions date back to the Regulation of Investigatory Powers Act 2000, which empower a senior police officer to require a communications provider to disclose any communications data in its possession where this is considered necessary in the interests of national security, the prevention or detection of crime, or a number of other situations.[61] The term 'communications data' is defined broadly to include traffic and location data, although, as has been stated by the Home Office:

> It is important to identify what communications data does include but equally important to be clear about what it does *not* include. The term communications data in the Act does not include the content of any communication.[62]

The Regulation of Investigatory Powers Act 2000 did not require that providers retain data, although concerns had been expressed that mobile-phone operators were retaining customer records for a period of months and in some cases years.[63] The conformity of this practice with the requirements of the Data Protection Act 1998 that:

> Personal data processed for any purpose or purposes shall not be kept for longer than is necessary for that purpose or those purposes[64]

had been doubted. The passage of the Anti-Terrorism, Crime and Security Act 2001, which was rushed through Parliament in a matter of weeks, provided a legal basis for the retention of data. The Act conferred power on the Secretary of State to draw up a code of practice

---

[59] Directive 2002/58/EC, OJ 2002 L 201–37.　　[60] Art. 15.　　[61] s. 22.

[62] Consultation Paper on a Code of Practice for Voluntary Retention of Communications Data (March 2003).

[63] See e.g. 'Liberties Fear over Mobile Phone Details', *The Guardian*, 27 October 2001, reporting that the mobile network, Virgin, has retained all data from the establishment of its network in 1999.

[64] Sch. 1, fifth data protection principle.

specifying periods of time during which communications providers would be required to retain communications data.[65] Although the Secretary of State was granted legislative power, it was envisaged that a voluntary code would be agreed between government and the communications industry. Negotiations did not produce agreement with industry, concerns centring in large part on the cost implications of retaining large amounts of data. The leading service provider, AOL, for example, has estimated that it would require 36,000 CDs in order to store one year's supply of communications data relating to its customers with set-up costs of £30 million and annual running costs of the same amount.

Initial proposals by the government for the establishment of a code of practice received heavy criticism, both in terms of the period of time within which data might require to be retained and the range of government agencies which might be granted access to this data. An initial draft code was withdrawn in July 2002 and a further draft was published in March 2003.[66] This restricted the range of agencies which might seek access to data but retains the requirement that data be retained for a period of twelve months.

Privacy and surveillance

One of the main ways in which privacy can be threatened is by the act of placing an individual under surveillance. Surveillance can take a variety of forms. Physical surveillance is as old-established as society. At an official level, it might involve placing individuals suspected of criminal conduct under surveillance, whilst at the private level, reference can be made to the nosy neighbour looking at life through the corner of a set of lace curtains. In some instances, the success of surveillance may depend on its existence being unknown to its target. In other cases, the fact that conduct may be watched is itself used as an instrument for social control. As George Orwell described in his novel *1984*, the mere fact that people were aware that their activities might be subject to monitoring by the authorities would cause them to modify their behaviour, regardless of whether they were being watched or not.

There is no doubt that the world we inhabit today has changed and is changing at considerable speed. As well as being a commodity in its own right, data is the motor and fuel which drives the information society. A database with no data is a poor creature indeed and with the development of more and more sophisticated search-engine technologies, the value of a database lies increasingly in the amount of data held rather than the thought which lies behind the selection and organisation of material. The Internet and its use in academic life provides a very apposite example. There is no doubt that it provides teachers and students with access to a massively increased range of data. An author trying to track down a missing citation need often require only to submit a few words to a search engine such as 'Google' to be presented with the answer in seconds. More, however, does not always mean better. Excessive use of electronic resources will cause traditional research skills to atrophy, the availability of one hundred electronic articles saying the same thing adds little to the reader's understanding of a topic—even making the charitable assumption that the articles are accurate in what they say. The tendency is to seek to find the answer before one has understood the question.

Similar issues arise in the wider world. Information is replacing knowledge and the change in terminology also indicates reliance on a more mechanistic- and statistical-based

---

[65] s. 102.   [66] Available from <http://www.homeoffice.gov.uk/docs/consult.pdf>.

view of the world. An example can be seen in the increasing use of DNA technology for crime-detection purposes. In the United Kingdom, aided by a policy of taking and retaining samples from everyone charged and convicted of even the most minor offence, the national police DNA database now contains over 2 million entries. This tool, as with most forms of scientific evidence, is based upon calculations of probability. Recent high-profile cases in the United Kingdom have shown up some of the failings of such an approach and, in particular, that technology is only as effective as those using it. The consequences for those wrongly identified and convicted on the basis of the misunderstanding of statistics has been profound and tragic.

Although we may challenge the efficacy of some of the models, there is no doubt that the underlying principles of data protection matter more today than ever before. With developments in data processing and other forms of technology, there is the potential for every movement we make to be tracked and recorded. There is a well-established tradition of providing for necessary exceptions from the strict application of data protection principles in the context of national security and crime prevention and detection. These have been applied in the context of specific investigations and with the attempt made to secure a reasonable balance between the interests of the state and of individuals. With a move towards reliance upon databases, whether of DNA samples or other forms of information, there has been a significant shift in the nature of policing, from the attempt to find evidence linking an individual with an offence, to one where an individual is sought whose profile fits that of a suspected offender. In many cases, such an approach is justified but, as will be discussed in the final section of this chapter, the perceived and accepted need to defeat terrorism is leading to the removal of some data protection safeguards, with little being put in place to replace these. As with all aspects of design, unless components are included at an early stage, it is more difficult and expensive to incorporate them at a later stage.

Many of the recorded instances of the misuse of information have occurred, not as part of the original design, but as a by-product of the fact that the information is available. The story has been told of how the elaborate population registers maintained by the Dutch authorities prior to the Second World War (no doubt with the best possible motives) were used by the invading Germans to facilitate the deportation of thousands of people.[67] In this case, as in any similar case, it is clear that it was not the information per se that harmed individuals, but rather the use that was made of it. In this sense, information is a tool, but a very flexible tool; and whenever personal information is stored, the subject is to some extent 'a hostage to fortune'. Information which is freely supplied today, and which reflects no discredit in the existing social climate, may be looked upon very differently should circumstances change. It may, of course, be questioned how far any legal safeguards may be effective in the situation of an external invasion or unconstitutional usurpation of power. In discussions on this point in Sweden it has been suggested that:

> Under a threat of occupation there may be reason to remove or destroy computer installations and various registers in order to prevent the installations or important information

---

[67] F. W. Hondius, *Emerging Data Protection in Europe* (Amsterdam, 1975). See also Victor Mayer-Schünberger, *Delete: The Virtue of Forgetting in a Digital Age* (Princeton, 2009). This states fairly precise figures and comments:

> Because of the information contained in the comprehensive Registry, the Nazis were able to identify, deport and murder a much higher percentage (73 percent) of the Dutch Jewish population than in Belgium (40 percent) or France ((25 percent), or any other European nation.

Obviously, all sorts of factors would have affected the scale of Nazi atrocities in different countries but as so often, history is trying to warn us.

from falling into enemy hands. An enemy may, for example, wish to acquire population registers and other records which can assist his war effort. There may be reason to revise the plans as to which data processing systems should be destroyed or removed in a war situation.[68]

Whilst such plans and procedures might appear to afford protection against the possibility of outside intervention, it must be recognised that, in the past, the use of personal information as a weapon against individuals has not been the exclusive province of totalitarian states. Again, during the Second World War, the United States government used information supposedly supplied in confidence during the Census to track down and intern citizens of Japanese ancestry.[69] More recently, it has been reported that the United States Selective Service system purchased a list of 167,000 names of boys who had responded to a promotion organised by a chain of ice-cream parlours offering a free ice cream on the occasion of their eighteenth birthday. This list of names, addresses, and dates of birth was used in order to track down those who had failed to register for military service.[70] Such practices illustrate, first, the ubiquitous nature of personal information and, second, that no clear dividing line can be drawn between public- and private-sector users, as information obtained within one sector may well be transferred to the other.

At a slightly less serious level, it was reported in the United Kingdom that information supplied in the course of the 1971 Census describing the previous occupations of respondents was passed on to health authorities, who used it to contact retired nurses with a view to discovering why they left the profession and to encourage them to consider returning to work.[71] Whilst it may be argued that no harm was caused to the individuals concerned by the use to which this information was put, it provides further evidence of the ubiquitous nature of information, and of the ease with which information supplied for one purpose can be put to another use.

Conclusions

Almost seventy years ago, the world was recovering from the trauma of global conflict. The negotiation of the Universal Declaration and the European Convention on Human Rights was regarded as a major legislative component of the road to recovery. The enhancement of individual rights was seen as the best response to the trauma of global terror. Today, the view appears to be that rights need to be restricted in order to defeat terror. Whilst it may, of course, be argued that a closer parallel is with the enactment of emergency legislation in time of war, the present situation is perhaps more akin to the image portrayed in George Orwell's novel *1984*, where a condition of perpetual and undeclared war existed between three power blocks, with shifting alliances and battles generally fought far from home but used as justification for repressive domestic policies.

Few issues in the field admit of easy answers. Any attempt to strike a balance between competing interests is difficult, especially in a fast-changing environment. Most would agree that law enforcement agencies should be provided with the best possible tools to enable them to perform their vital tasks. Data can constitute an extremely valuable investigative tool but the whole premise of data protection legislation over the decades has been

---

[68] *Transnational Data Report*, 1(5) (1978), p. 17. [69] W. Petersen, *Japanese Americans* (New York, 1971).
[70] *Transnational Data Report*, 10(4) (1987), p. 25.
[71] D. Madgwick and T. Smythe, *The Invasion of Privacy* (London, 1974).

that the potential for misuse is considerable. At least within a United Kingdom context, the main problem is perhaps a lack of awareness. If data were nuclear particles or perhaps even genetically modified foodstuffs, people would be aware of and respectful of the dangers involved in their use and transportation. The danger today is that data flows are invisible and when society becomes aware of the potential for misuse, it may be too late to put this technological genie back in the bottle.

2

The emergence of data protection

Introduction

As discussed in the previous chapter, a range of concerns about the potential use and misuse of computers spawned a widespread call for legislative intervention. Although similar issues were faced by most countries, there has not been a uniform legal response—something which continues to cause problems to the present day. Two main areas of divergence can be identified. Within Europe, as will be discussed in this and the following chapters, omnibus data protection legislation has been the norm, covering all aspects of processing of personal data. In the United States and perhaps the majority of countries in the world, a sectoral approach has been favoured, with a range of so-called privacy protection statutes being enacted to regulate specific forms of information handling. One source[1] identifies more than thirty United States Federal statutes which have privacy protection implications. There is also extensive legislation at state level.

In terms of substantive law, there is little difference between the privacy and data protection models. Both tend, for example, to establish requirements that processing be fair and lawful and provide for data subjects to obtain access to information relating to them. The major divergence exists at the level of enforcement. The European data protection model is based on the premise that there should be dedicated agencies, ready and able to act to secure the interests of individuals. This is very different from the approach adopted in the United States. In support of the European approach, one leading authority, Professor Spiros Simitis, former Data Protection Commissioner for the German state of Hesse, has suggested that:

> data protection presupposes...the establishment of an independent control authority. Experience confirms what was already stated in the earliest debates: It is not enough to trace a mandatory framework for data processing. The legislator must also secure the monitoring of the processing conditions...Even if the data subject is entrusted with a series of rights he remains an outsider, deprived of the necessary information permitting him to analyze and evaluate the activities of the various public and private agencies.[2]

By way of contrast, it has been that suggested that the approach favoured in the United States:

> [is] designed to put the individual in the centre of the action, to let him have a large voice in decisions as to what information will be collected, used and disseminated about him. The Europeans take a paternalistic approach choosing to vest enforcement in bureaucracy.[3]

---

[1] <http://www.informationshield.com/usprivacylaws.html>.

[2] Spiros Simitis, 'Reviewing Privacy in an Information Society', *University of Pennsylvania Law Rev*, 135(3) (March, 1987), pp. 707–46.

[3] L. Hummer, 'Transnational Data Regulation: The Realities', *Online Conferences* (1979).

Both approaches have points in their favour. There is no doubt that supervisory agencies are better placed than individuals to take an overview of processing activities. However, the agencies have to straddle—sometimes uncomfortably—a wide range of roles ranging from consumer ombudsman, through law enforcer, to acting. This has been notable in the United Kingdom in recent years, with the supervisory agency seeking to play a role as a protagonist in the ongoing debate as to the future development of the law in fields such as identity cards and data sharing, where the interests of law enforcement potentially clash with informational privacy.[4]

The purpose of this chapter is to chart the historical development of data protection legislation at both an international level and in the specific context of the United Kingdom.

Early data protection laws

Initial legislative initiatives in the field occurred at the national level with the German state of Hesse adopting the world's first data protection statute in 1970. The first national statute was the Swedish Data Protection Act adopted in 1973. The fact that data protection laws were pioneered in these two countries may not be entirely a matter of coincidence, and also illustrates what might be classed as the positive and negative aspects of the system. In the case of Germany, there had been experience of the misuse of data by totalitarian governments, both under the Nazis and also looking eastward at the time to the Communist regime in the then East Germany. In seeking to place limits on the ability of public and private sector bodies to process personal data, the law can be seen as acting primarily in a defensive manner. The Swedish situation was rather different. In this country there was no background of totalitarianism, but, as referred to in the previous chapter, a more than two-century long tradition of freedom of information, under which almost any item of information held by public bodies was considered to be in the public domain. By conferring rights on individuals to access information held on any computer, data protection could be seen as extending some of the concepts of freedom of information into the private sector. Historically, neither experiences of tyranny nor of openness have featured strongly in the United Kingdom and it is perhaps not surprising that data protection has sometimes seemed to be a peripheral, rootless branch of law. It may be that with the recent Snowden revelations, things may be changing.

International data protection initiatives

From the emergence of the electric telegraph in the nineteenth century, international data transfers have played a major role. Although the first data protection laws were enacted on a national basis, even before this pressure had been exerted for international action in the field.

In the data protection context, two—perhaps contradictory—concerns prompted international action. There were fears that national laws, which tended to have strong controls over the export of data, might have a protectionist effect. Conversely, there were fears by

---

[4] As a personal anecdote, I raised an issue with the Information Commissioners Office in 2010 and received an automated reply indicating that it was taking the office seven weeks to acknowledge (let alone start to deal with) complaints. Given that data controllers are required by law to respond to subject access requests within forty days, this does seem a rather strange situation.

those states that had adopted data protection legislation that national laws and policies could be circumvented by organisations sending data abroad for processing in counties (often referred to as data havens) which imposed few controls over processing activities.

At a more technical level, the 1970s also marked the period where developments in computers and communications technology rendered feasible a massive expansion in multinational organisations. Although these had existed for many years, they tended to be restricted to activities such as car production, where assembly plants in different companies operated largely as independent freedoms. The year 1971 marked the opening of the first McDonald's restaurant in Europe.[5] The essence of this and similar businesses in the service sector is uniformity of product and identity across the globe. Such activities required the application of computer systems able to communicate across national boundaries.

It was quickly recognised that international solutions were required in order to reconcile the interests of individual privacy with commercial interests. It was accepted that impossible burdens could be placed upon multinational enterprises should they be required to comply with differing standards in every country in which they acquired, stored, processed, or even transferred data. This indeed remains a problematic issue, with companies such as Google advocating global data/privacy protection standards in order to simplify their task of complying with laws on a global basis.[6]

From the late 1960s, a range of international agencies have been active in the field of data and privacy protection. At the initial stages, the most prominent actors were the Council of Europe and the Organisation for Economic Co-operation and Development (OECD). The following sections will consider the major activities carried out under the auspices of these organisations. Brief attention will also be paid to work conducted under the auspices of the UN. During the 1990s, much of the focus—at least so far as relates to the impact upon the United Kingdom—switched to work within the EU and the slow progress towards the adoption of the Data Protection Directive.[7]

The Council of Europe

In 1968, the Parliamentary Assembly of the Council of Europe addressed a request to the Committee of Ministers that they consider the extent to which the provisions of the European Convention on Human Rights safeguarded the individual against the abuse of modern technology.[8] The Assembly noted particular concern at the fact that the European Convention, together with its UN predecessor, the Universal Declaration of Human Rights, had been devised before the development and widespread application of the computer.

Whilst identifying the dangers of computer abuse, the Assembly's report also drew attention to a paradox which remains largely unresolved to this day. Data protection seeks to give an individual a greater measure of control over personal information and to place controls over the dissemination of this information. This approach may conflict with another individual's claim to be allowed access to information under the European Convention on Human Rights. Here it is provided that: '[e]veryone has the right to freedom of expression. This shall include freedom to hold opinions and to receive and impart information and ideas without interference by public authority and regardless of frontiers.'[9] The conflict

---

[5] In Zaandam near Amsterdam in the Netherlands.

[6] See e.g. <http://news.bbc.co.uk/1/hi/technology/6994776.stm>.   [7] Directive 95/46/EC.

[8] The linkage between data protection and notions of fundamental human rights remains significant with the recent European Charter of Fundamental Rights adopted in 2007 (but not applicable in the United Kingdom) providing in Art. 8 that 'Everyone has the right to the protection of personal data concerning him or her.'   [9] Art. 10.

is well illustrated in cases such as *Campbell v Mirror Group Newspapers*[10] and *Douglas v Hello!*,[11] where celebrities clashed with newspapers and magazines over the publication of photographs and stories about them. In both cases, the disputes went to the House of Lords, which delivered judgment for the complainants by slender 3:2 majorities.

Acting upon the Assembly's report, two separate resolutions were adopted by the Committee of Ministers, dealing with the private and the public sectors. The differences between the two sets of recommendations are comparatively minor, and for both sectors it was recommended that national laws should ensure that legislation requires that personal data be obtained fairly, accurate and up to date, relevant, and not excessive nor retained for longer than is necessary. The recommendations also provided for controls over the range of disclosure of data, the grant of subject access, and the application of procedures to allow any errors in data to be corrected.[12]

To a very considerable extent, these principles remain at the heart of data protection laws to this day. In some respects, given that consistency is a quality much respected in law, this is a benefit. If consideration is given, however, to developments in computer technology in the three decades since the original recommendations, problems may be identified. The recommendations, and most subsequent data protection law, are based on the notion of a single controller with a single computer holding data. This bears little resemblance to today's networked environment. In particular, reactive controls may not be sufficient. Once inaccurate data has found its way onto the Internet, the damage can never be undone.

The initial Council of Europe resolutions did not attempt to prescribe the means by which Member States should give effect to the principles contained therein. As more and more European countries enacted data protection legislation, so too did the problems resulting from the international trade of information—frequently referred to as transborder data flows—become more acute. In an effort to minimise restrictions on the free flow of information, and in the hope of preventing major discrepancies between the national data protection laws, the Council of Europe moved beyond its earlier recommendations to sponsor the Convention for the Protection of Individuals with Regard to the Automatic Processing of Personal Data (hereafter, 'the Convention'). The Convention was opened for signature in January 1981 and was to enter into force when it was ratified by five Member States of the Council of Europe. This did not occur until October 1985. The Convention has been amended by an additional protocol, 'regarding supervisory agencies and transborder data flows', which was opened for signature in October 2001 and entered into force in July 2004. At the time of writing, forty-two countries have ratified the Convention and twenty-eight an additional protocol which strengthens the original provisions in the areas of transborder data flow. Although the Convention is open for signature by countries who are not members of the Council of Europe, to date, no non-Member State has done so.[13] The view has been expressed by several United States commentators that the provisions of the Convention were motivated more by considerations of commercial expediency and economic protectionism than by a genuine concern for individual privacy. In the course of a meeting of the Committee of Experts, the United States observer contrasted the sectoral approach

---

[10] [2004] UKHL 22 on appeal from [2002] EWCA Civ 1373 and [2002] EWHC 499 (QB).

[11] [2007] UKHL 21 on appeal from [2005] EWCA Civ 106 and [2005] EWCA Civ 595, [2005] EWCA Civ 861.   [12] Resolution (73) 22.

[13] This may be contrasted with the Council of Europe's Convention on Cybercrime (discussed in Ch. 10), which has been signed by Canada, Costa Rica, Mexico, and South Africa, and signed and ratified by Australia, the Dominican Republic, Japan, Mauritius, Panama, and the United States.

adopted in that country with the omnibus data protection legislation envisaged under the Convention, and concluded that:

> the draft convention appears to regulate a function, that is, it appears to regulate automated or electronic data processing and what the automated data processing industry may do with records about individuals. To our mind the draft convention is, in essence, a scheme for the regulation of computer communications technology as it may be applied to personal data record-keeping. The establishment and exercise of individual rights and the privacy of the individual seem to be treated in a secondary fashion. I would note particularly that the word 'privacy' is rarely mentioned in the Convention and is not included in its title.[14]

Such criticism is perhaps unfounded. The Convention, as with much of the Council of Europe's work, is deeply rooted in the human rights context and specifically in the European Convention of Human Rights and, indeed, as noted earlier in this section, Article 8 of the European Union's Charter of Fundamental Rights provides that 'Everyone has the right to the protection of personal data concerning him or her.' There is thus a strong linkage between notions of privacy and data protection.

In its Preamble, the Convention reaffirms the Council of Europe's commitment to freedom of information regardless of frontiers, and proceeds to prohibit the erection of national barriers to information flow on the pretext of protecting individual privacy.[15] This prohibition extends, however, only where the information is to be transferred to another signatory state. Impliedly, therefore, the Convention permits the imposition of sanctions against any non-signatory state, especially one whose domestic law contains inadequate provision regulating the computerised processing of personal data.[16] A recalcitrant state could effectively be placed in data quarantine. The standards required of domestic laws are laid down in Chapter 2 of the Convention, and its requirements will be considered in detail when considering the substantive aspects of data protection.

In addition to the Convention itself, the Council of Europe has adopted a substantial number of recommendations concerning the interpretation and application of the Convention principles in particular sectors, and in processing for the purposes of particular forms of activity such as might be carried out by police authorities or insurance companies.[17] Following an eight-year period of inactivity, a further recommendation on processing for the purposes of profiling was adopted in 2010.

The Organisation for Economic Co-operation and Development (OECD)

At much the same time as the Council of Europe began its work in the field of data protection, the topic also appeared on the agenda of the Organisation for Economic Co-operation and Development (OECD). The OECD was established by international convention in 1960 and, as its title suggests, is primarily concerned with facilitating cooperation between Member States in order to promote economic development. This might be contrasted with the Council of Europe's emphasis on human rights. Unlike other international organisations, the OECD   as something of a Members Club, with states wishing to join being required to satisfy the existing members as to their suitability. The OECD currently has

---

[14] Text of United States Department of State telegram, quoted in *Transnational Data Report*, 1(7) (1978), p. 22.   [15] Art. 12(2).

[16] The additional protocol referred to earlier was drafted to bring the Convention into line with the EU's Data Protection Directive. It provides that data may be transferred to an external state only if that state guarantees an adequate level of protection. These issues will be considered in more detail in Chapter 8 herein.

[17] The text of all these instruments can be obtained from <http://www.coe.int/t/dghl/standardsetting/dataprotection/Legal_instruments_en.asp>.

thirty members almost exclusively from the developed world. Discussions regarding possible membership are ongoing with a number of countries, including Russia and China, and cooperative agreements are in force with about seventy countries,[18] ensuring that the organisation's influence extends far beyond its formal membership. A Council consisting of representatives of all the Member States is 'the body from which all acts of the organization derive'.[19]

The OECD's work in what it has tended to refer to as the privacy protection field began in 1969 when a group of experts was appointed to analyse 'different aspects of the privacy issue, e.g. in relation to digital information, public administration, transborder data flows, and policy implications in general'.[20] A further group was established in 1978 under Mr Justice Kirby, then Chairman of the Australian Law Commission. The United States representatives also played a prominent role in the group's activities and the resulting product in the form of a Recommendation to Member States Concerning Guidelines on the Protection of Privacy and Transborder Data Flows was endorsed by the OECD Council in September 1980.

It was part of the group's remit that its 'work was to be carried out in close cooperation with the Council of Europe and the European Community'.[21] Although covering much the same ground as the Convention, the Guidelines can perhaps be seen as a common law-based approach to the issues, as opposed to the Convention which was drafted very much in line with the civil law tradition. It has been suggested that:

> In the final result, although substantially similar in core principles, the Convention and the Guidelines could be analogised, albeit in a rough fashion, to the civil and common law approaches, respectively. Common law systems proceed pragmatically, formulating the rules of legal behaviour as they acquire experience, while the civil law tradition tends to rely upon codification of rules in advance of action.[22]

Again, whilst the Convention is a legally binding instrument, the Guidelines, as the terminology indicates, have no legal force.

A further Declaration on Transborder Data Flows was adopted by the OECD in April 1985. This made reference to the fact that:

> Flows of computerised data and information are an important consequence of technological advances and are playing an increasing role in national economies. With the growing economic interdependence of Member countries, these flows acquire an international dimension.

It also indicated its signatories' intention to:

1. *Promote* access to data and information and related services, and avoid the creation of unjustified barriers to the international exchange of data and information.

2. *Seek* transparency in regulations and policies relating to information, computer and communications services affecting transborder data flows.

3. *Develop* common approaches for dealing with issues related to transborder data flows and, when appropriate, develop harmonised solutions.

4. *Consider* possible implications for other countries when dealing with issues related to transborder data flows.

---

[18] <http://www.oecd.org/pages/0,3417,en_36734052_36761800_1_1_1_1,00.html>.   [19] Art. 7.

[20] <http://www.oecd.org/document/18/0,3343,en_2649_34255_1815186_1_1_1_1,00.html>.

[21] <http://www.oecd.org/document/18/0,3343,en_2649_34255_1815186_1_1_1_1,00.html>.

[22] Cited in L. Kirsch, *Legal Issues of European Integration* (Amsterdam, 1982), 21 at 45.

It is clear from these objectives that commercial and trading interests provide at least as significant a force for action as do concerns for individual rights. Although the Declaration commits its member countries to conduct further work relating to specific types of trans-border data flows, especially those accompanying international trade, marketed computer services, and computerised information services and intra-corporate data flows, no further measures have been adopted.

In addition to its work in producing legal texts, the OECD has also sponsored the development of what is referred to as a privacy generator. This online package is intended to be used by website developers and others to incorporate procedures and safeguards to ensure that sites operate in conformity with the principles laid down in the Guidelines.[23]

The Asia-Pacific Privacy Charter initiative

At a rather less formal level than has occurred within Europe, considerable work has been carried out by a range of countries in the Asia-Pacific region (including the United States) who have established the Asia-Pacific Privacy Charter Council. Hosted at the Cyberspace Law and Policy Centre of the University of New South Wales, the Council is described as a 'regional expert group' which aims to:

> develop independent standards for privacy protection in the region in order to influence the enactment of privacy laws in the region, and the adoption of regional privacy agreements, in accordance with those standards.[24]

The Council's work draws heavily on the APEC Privacy Framework drawn up by the Asia-Pacific Economic Cooperation organisation, the Preamble to which recognises the need for APEC economies to provide adequate protection for personal data in order to give individuals the confidence necessary to participate in electronic commerce, behaviour which almost of necessity requires the transfer of significant amounts of personal data.[25] Although still at a relatively early stage of development, the work provides further recognition of the global nature of privacy issues and the relationship between the development of electronic commerce and the effective protection of individuals' data.

The UN

On 20 February 1990, the United Nations' Economic and Social Council agreed to the Guidelines Concerning Computerised Personal Data Files.[26] These identify ten principles which, it is stated, represent the 'minimum guarantees that should be provided in national legislation'. The principles follow what might be regarded as the standard model, but there are two features of these Guidelines which justify mention at this point. First, they make provision for the application of the principles by international agencies,[27] bodies which might fall outside of national laws. Secondly, the UN Guidelines provide the option for the extension of the principles, both to manual files and to files held concerning legal persons.[28] In line with the Convention's approach, the UN Guidelines envisage the establishment of a supervisory agency providing that:

[23] <http://www.oecd.org/document/39/0,2340,en_2649_34255_28863271_1_1_1_1,00.html>.
[24] <http://www.bakercyberlawcentre.org/appcc/members.htm>.
[25] <http://www.bakercyberlawcentre.org/ipp/apec_privacy_framework/index.html>.
[26] Available from <http://www.unhcr.org/refworld/publisher,UNGA,THEMGUIDE,3ddcafaac,0.html>.
[27] Part B.   [28] para. 10.

the law of every country shall designate the authority which, in accordance with its domestic legal system, is to be responsible for supervising observance of the principles set forth above. This authority shall offer guarantees of impartiality, independence vis-à-vis persons or agencies responsible for processing and establishing data, and technical competence. In the event of violation of the provisions of the national law implementing the aforementioned principles, criminal or other penalties should be envisaged together with the appropriate individual remedies.[29]

Recent years have seen attempts made to involve the UN more deeply in the data protection field. At the 2009 meeting of data and privacy protection commissioners, a proposal was endorsed encouraging the adoption of:

'International Standards for the Protection of Privacy and Personal Data', allowing the development of a universal, binding legal document, which must be backed by the most extensive institutional and social consensus via the participation of the authorities and institutions guaranteeing data protection and privacy and representatives of both public and private entities and organisations.[30]

In February 2010 the UN rapporteur on human rights made a call for the establishment of global privacy standards.[31] It is unclear when, or if, such an activity might be undertaken. The meeting of data and privacy protection commissioners, as the name implies, is dominated by representatives from countries which endorse the European model of protection with the establishment of dedicated supervisory authorities. As has been discussed, belief in the efficacy of this approach is not shared in other jurisdictions. There is also a gulf between countries which view data protection as essentially rooted in notions of human rights and those which see data protection as having an economic basis. In part this is based on notions of international data flows but at an internal level there is also often the belief that e-commerce and other online activities will flourish only if individuals have confidence that their data will not be misused.

The development of data protection in the United Kingdom

As with many inventions, the United Kingdom can claim credit for some pioneering developments in the field of data protection, failing to develop these, and subsequently having to act in response to external pressures. As early as 1969, a Data Surveillance Bill was introduced in the House of Commons by Kenneth Baker MP. If matters had been different, the United Kingdom would have possessed the world's first data protection law but, in common with most private members' initiatives, this failed to make significant progress. In the following parliamentary session, a further private member's Bill was introduced by Brian Walden MP. This sought to establish a statutory right to privacy. In a manner which . has not changed through a range of governments over the past thirty-four years, ministers expressed reluctance to establish what would necessarily be a rather vague right. An agreement was made with the Bill's sponsor that in return for its withdrawal, the government would establish the Committee on Privacy, chaired by Sir Kenneth Younger.[32]

In its report, the Committee devoted a chapter to the implications of the computer. After receiving evidence as to the nature and scale of processing activities, it concluded that '[w]e cannot on the evidence before us conclude that the computer as used in the private

---

[29] para. 8.   [30] <http://www.privacyconference2009.org/home/index-iden-idweb.html>.
[31] <http://www.theregister.co.uk/2010/01/20/un_terror/>.   [32] Cmnd 5012, 1972.

sector is at present a threat to privacy'.[33] Despite this, the Committee identified the computer's ability to store and process large amounts of personal information, to develop personal profiles, and to allow remote access to databases as factors causing legitimate public concern.

The Committee's report was published in July 1972. Its contents and recommendations were debated in the House of Commons one year later, in July 1973. Speaking in this debate, the Home Secretary studiously avoided expressing any views on the Younger proposals on computers, but announced the publication for later that year, of a White Paper describing computer practices in the public sector and outlining the government's response to the Committee on Privacy's recommendations.[34] In fact, setting a precedent which was to become depressingly familiar, the White Paper, entitled *Computers and Privacy*, was not published until some two and a half years later, in December 1975.[35] As indicated, the White Paper's coverage extended into the public sector, with a supplement detailing the extent of government computer usage.

Whilst the White Paper reiterated the finding that there was little concrete evidence of computer abuse, its conclusion was rather different. The potential dangers were considered so substantial that:

> In the Government's view the time has come when those who use computers to handle personal information can no longer remain the sole judges of whether their own systems adequately safeguard privacy.[36]

Accordingly, it was announced that a Data Protection Committee was to be established, with a remit to make detailed recommendations as to the scope and extent of data protection legislation and as to the form of supervisory mechanism which should be introduced.

The Committee on Data Protection

With hindsight, the publication of the 1975 White Paper can be seen as marking a high-water point in governmental enthusiasm for the concept of data protection. This enthusiasm was certainly matched by that of the Data Protection Committee, which, under the chairmanship of Sir Norman Lindop, presented its voluminous report in June 1978.[37] This remains the most comprehensive and detailed survey of the impact of data processing activities upon the rights and liberties of the individual conducted in the United Kingdom.

The Lindop Committee's report was published towards the end of 1978. In early 1979, a general election saw a change of government, with the arrival of a Conservative Party pledged to reduce bureaucracy. Proposals to establish a new supervisory agency were not received with acclamation. International developments were to bring about a change of mind, however. During the 1970s, the lack of data protection law could be seen as a factor which would make the United Kingdom attractive to companies wishing to establish a European data processing centre. Unlike the situation in other countries, no formal or procedural requirements would limit the nature of the processing which could be conducted. As communications technologies increasingly facilitated the international transfer of data, the possibility that national controls might be evaded was not lost on countries possessing data protection laws and with the adoption of the Council of Europe Convention, the possibility of data sanctions being imposed against the United Kingdom became more significant. More extensive controls over the export of personal data were introduced. In

---

[33] Cmnd 5012, para. 619.   [34] 859 HC Official Report (5th series), col. 1956, 13 July 1973.
[35] Cmnd 6353.   [36] Cmnd 6353, para. 30.   [37] Cmnd 7341.

commending the first Data Protection Bill to the House of Commons, the then Home Secretary commented that it was designed 'to meet public concern, to bring us into step with Europe and to protect our international, commercial and trading interests'.[38] Whilst undoubtedly civil libertarian concerns are fundamental to the concept of data protection—and indeed the 2009 Charter on Fundamental Rights and Freedoms (subject to a United Kingdom opt out) affords data protection the status of a fundamental human right—it is significant that in 1982 these represented only one out of five interests identified and that, at least numerically, commercial and trading factors assumed greater significance. In a manner akin to a stereotype of the British Establishment's way of proceeding, a significant catalyst for action was a letter sent to *The Times* newspaper by a number of leading industrialists lamenting the fact that the lack of data protection legislation was beginning to impact adversely upon overseas trade by causing the United Kingdom to be regarded as an 'offshore data haven'. Although concern was expressed that old-fashioned economic protectionism might lie behind any sanctions ostensibly imposed on data protection grounds, the clear conclusion was that data protection legislation was needed in the nation's commercial interest.[39]

The validity of this observation is demonstrated by several well-documented instances in which British companies had been prevented from carrying out data processing or related activities on behalf of Swedish companies, owing to the Swedish authorities' concern at the lack of legislative safeguards.[40] Commercial interests and lobbying succeeded where civil libertarian concerns had failed, and, in March 1981, the Home Secretary announced that: 'The Government has decided in principle to introduce legislation for this purpose when an opportunity occurs.'[41]

Following a further round of consultations, a further White Paper was published in April 1982.[42] By this time, the Lindop Report was reduced to the status of 'very helpful background information'. A Data Protection Bill based on the provisions of the White Paper was introduced in the House of Lords in November 1982. It successfully passed through that House, but fell at the committee stage in the House of Commons when Parliament was dissolved prior to the 1983 general election. An amended Bill was speedily introduced by the incoming government, receiving the Royal Assent on 12 July of the Orwellian year, 1984.

The Data Protection Act 1984

Given that the Data Protection Act 1984 was replaced in its entirety by the Data Protection Act 1998, detailed consideration of its contents is unnecessary. Many of its provisions do, of course, remain applicable under the current regime and decisions made by the courts and the Data Protection Tribunal, which was established as an appellate body, continue to be cited as valid precedent. A few general comments concerning the 1984 Act and a brief assessment of its impact may be helpful in providing initial comment on the impact and relevance of data protection within a United Kingdom context.

As indicated earlier, the legislation was not introduced out of any genuine enthusiasm by the (Conservative) government of the day. Time after time, *Hansard* reports comments from ministers to the effect that the legislation was being introduced for commercial

---

[38] HC Official Report (6th series), col. 562, 11 April 1983. [39] *The Times*, 3 March 1980.
[40] See e.g. J. Bing in J. Bing and K. S. Selmer (eds.), *A Decade of Computers and Law* (Oslo, 1980), pp. 70–1, describing the loss of contracts involving the processing of financial and medical data because of these concerns.
[41] HC Official Report (6th series), col. 161, 19 March 1981.   [42] Cmnd 8539.

reasons in order to enable the United Kingdom to ratify the Council of Europe Convention. This was to be done at the most minimal level. On every occasion where the Convention prescribed minimal standards but left the way open for signatories to provide additional protection in national legislation, the United Kingdom Data Protection Act 1984 remained conspicuously silent. Moving ahead some fifteen years to the introduction of the Data Protection Act 1998, *Hansard* reports that the debates are replete with comments from (Labour) ministers to the effect that the legislation was being introduced reluctantly in order to comply at a minimal level with European requirements, this time in the form of European Directive 95/46. It is tempting to suggest that the Conservative ministers of the 1980s could have succeeded in an action alleging breach of copyright in their speeches.

Lack of governmental commitment has been a factor which bedevils data protection to this day. A decision that the concept should not impose any financial burdens on the taxpayer led to the introduction of an outdated and bureaucratic system of registration, whereby any-one involved in processing personal data was obliged to register details of their activities and pay a fee. Failure to do so constituted a criminal offence. Beyond providing the supervisory agency's only significant source of revenue, it is difficult to identify any significant benefits arising from the concept. The financial strait jacket imposed in the Data Protection Act 1984 continues under the Data Protection Act 1998 (although the Commissioner's functions in respect of the Freedom of Information Act are publicly funded), with the consequence that, whilst terminology changes from registration to notification and, more recently, there has been the introduction of a two-tiered scale of notification fees with larger users being required to pay higher fees than their smaller counterparts, the requirement to pay what is effectively a tax associated with computer ownership remains.

Incidents such as the attempt by police forces to blame data protection requirements for the failure to pass on information which may have prevented the Soham murders[43] suggests that data protection retains a role as a scapegoat for organisational failings. Given, as was discussed in Chapter 1, the increasing role and importance of information in our everyday lives, it is disappointing and perhaps even dangerous that there should continue to be such limited understanding of what data protection is and is not about.

The European Data Protection Directive and the Data Protection Act 1998

Until the early 1990s, the EU had played a peripheral role in the data protection arena. This could be ascribed to two main causes. First, the limited nature of the legislative competencies conferred by the establishing treaties gave rise to doubts as to whether, and to what extent, the EU was empowered to act in this field. Although the increasing importance of information as a commodity within the Single Market has provided a basis for European action, the exclusion of matters coming within the ambit of national security and, to a partial extent criminal and taxation policy, has served to limit the scope of the EU's intervention.

A second factor influencing work in this field had been a reluctance on the part of the Commission to duplicate work being conducted under the auspices of the Council of

---

[43] This case concerned the murder in Cambridgeshire of two schoolgirls by a person who had been employed as a caretaker at their school. Subsequent to his conviction, it transpired that allegations concerning his behaviour towards young women had been made to the police in a different location some time previously but that these had not been passed on, allegedly, but almost certainly wrongly, because of concerns that this could contravene the data protection principles.

Europe and in 1981, the Commission addressed a Recommendation to Member States that they sign and ratify the Convention.[44] By 1990, the Convention had been signed by all the Member States, but ratified only by six.[45] As will be described, the Convention establishes minimal standards but affords considerable discretion to signatories. A number of Member States, such as Germany and Sweden, had enacted laws which were considerably in advance of the Convention's minimum standards, whilst others, such as the United Kingdom, had openly indicated an intention to do the bare minimum necessary to satisfy obligations under that instrument. By 1990, Commission concern at the effect that discrepancies in the Member States' laws and regulations might have on inter-community trade resulted in proposals being brought forward for a Directive on the Protection of Individuals with Regard to the Processing of Personal Data and on the Free Movement of Such Data.[46] The EU legislation, it was stated, would 'give substance to and amplify' [47] the provisions of the Convention. The objective of the proposal was stated to be to harmonise the data protection laws of the Member States at a 'high level'.[48] This approach was necessary because the Directive was adopted under the authority of Article 100a of the Treaty of Rome. This provides that the Community's law-making bodies may:

> adopt the measures for the approximation of the provisions laid down by law, regulation or administrative action in Member States which have as their object the establishing and functioning of the internal market.

Reliance upon Article 100a has the further significant consequence in that any harmonising measures introduced under its authority have to secure 'a high level of protection'. Effectively, therefore, the Directive has to secure a level of protection equivalent to the highest currently available in the Member States. It is unclear how effective the Directive has been in this regard, with complaints being aired from countries such as Germany that implementation might dilute their existing regimes, especially in respect of transborder data flows. For the United Kingdom, implementation of the Directive required significant change to the Data Protection Act 1984, as well as its expansion. A Consultation Paper was published by the Home Office in March 1996, seeking views on the implementation of the Directive and indicating a preference for a minimalist approach to law reform:

> Over-elaborate data protection threatens competitiveness, and does not necessarily bring additional benefits for individuals. *It follows that the Government intends to go no further in implementing the Directive than is absolutely necessary to satisfy the United Kingdom's obligations in European law. It will consider whether any additional changes to the current data protection regime are needed so as to ensure that it does not go beyond what is required by the Directive and the Council of Europe Convention.*[49]

The Commission's proposal for a general Directive in the area of data protection was accompanied by a further proposal for a Directive 'Concerning the Protection of Personal Data and Privacy in the Context of Public Digital Telecommunications Networks'.[50] Following a five-year journey through the EU's legislative processes, the Data Protection Directive was adopted on 24 October 1995,[51] with a requirement that it be implemented within the Member States by 24 October 1998. The Telecoms Directive—which for a while appeared to have been dropped from the legislative agenda—resurfaced, to be adopted

---

[44] OJ 1981 L 246/31.

[45] Denmark, France, Germany, Luxembourg, Spain, and the United Kingdom.

[46] OJ 1990 C 277/03.   [47] OJ 1990 C 277/03, para. 22.

[48] OJ 1990 C 277/03, Preamble, para. 7.   [49] para. 1.2 (emphasis in original).

[50] OJ 1990 C 277/12.   [51] Directive 95/46/EC, OJ 1995 L 281/31.

in December 1997.[52] It also required to be implemented by October 1998. The Telecoms Data Protection Directive proved to be a somewhat short-lived measure. In conjunction with a much broader reform of the European telecommunications regulatory regime, the Directive was replaced in 2002 by the Directive 'Concerning the Processing of Personal Data and the Protection of Privacy in the Electronic Communications Sector'.[53] This was required to be implemented in the Member States by 31 October 2003. Once again, aspects of the Directive proved short-lived with the adoption of Directive 2009/136/E, generally referred to as the 'Citizens' Rights Directive' in November 2009. This Directive required to be implemented in the Member States by May 2011. The provisions of these sector-specific measures will be discussed in more detail in Chapter 7.

In January 1998 the Data Protection Bill was introduced in the House of Lords. Its progress through Parliament was relatively uncontroversial, with only one division being required throughout its parliamentary passage.[54] The major feature of the Bill's progress was the very large number of amendments tabled by the government—more than 200 in total. The Act received the Royal Assent on 16 July, although its entry into force was delayed pending the drafting of what proved to be seventeen items of secondary legislation and it was not until 1 March 2000 that the new legislation entered into force. In its failure timeously to implement the Data Protection Directive,[55] the United Kingdom was joined by a majority of the Member States. Legal action was raised by the Commission against Denmark, France, Germany, Ireland, Luxembourg, and the Netherlands, alleging a continuing failure to implement the Directive, although in the case of every state except Luxembourg, the belated implementation of the Directive resulted in the legal proceedings being abandoned.[56]

The Data Protection Act 1998

As an initial comment, it may be noted that the Data Protection Act 1998 is considerably larger than the 1984 legislation. The Data Protection Act 1984 has forty-three sections and six Schedules; the 1998 statute has seventy-five sections and sixteen Schedules. To an extent greater than its 1984 precursor, the Act provides only a framework, with significant matters remaining to be determined by statutory instruments. Although this approach will allow easier modification and updating of the legislation than was possible with the 1984 Act, significant issues relating to the identification of those data controllers who may be exempted from the notification requirement are not covered in the Act.

Given that the Data Protection Act 1998 is intended to implement a European Directive,[57] account has to be taken of the provisions of the latter. In *Campbell v MGN Ltd*,[58] Lord Phillips of Worth Matravers MR stated that:

> In interpreting the Act it is appropriate to look to the Directive for assistance. The Act should, if possible, be interpreted in a manner that is consistent with the Directive. Furthermore, because the Act has, in large measure, adopted the wording of the Directive,

---

[52] Directive 97/66/EC Concerning the Protection of Personal Data and Privacy in the Context of Public Digital Telecommunications Networks, OJ 1998 L 24.

[53] Directive 2002/58/EC, OJ 2002 L 201/37 (Privacy and Electronic Communications Directive).

[54] This was in relation to proposals in the Bill to provide ministers with wide-ranging powers to exempt processing activities from the subject access provisions. The House of Lords voted to remove these powers from the b ill. A more closely defined provision was introduced in the House of Commons.

[55] Directive 95/46/EC.

[56] For current information on the status of implementation, see <http://ec.europa.eu/justice/policies/privacy/lawreport/index_en.htm#firstreport>.

[57] Directive 95/46/EC.   [58] [2002] EWCA Civ 1373, [2003] QB 633 at [96].

it is not appropriate to look for the precision in the use of language that is usually to be expected from the parliamentary draftsman. A purposive approach to making sense of the provisions is called for.

The European Court of Justice has also held in *Österreichischer Rundfunk*[59] that at least some of the provisions of the Directive are sufficiently precise to be relied upon directly by individuals within the Member States.

The Data Protection Act 1998 extends significantly the area of the application of the legislation, including regulating some systems of manual records. In the accompanying Explanatory and Financial Memorandum, it was estimated that compliance with the new regime would result in start-up costs to private-sector data-users of some £836 million, with recurring costs of £630 million. The start-up costs for the public and voluntary sectors were estimated at £194 million and £120 million respectively, with recurring costs of £75 million and £37 million. The Home Office Regulatory Appraisal and Compliance Cost Assessment makes it clear that estimates are based upon a very small sample of users. Only four large and three small manufacturers were surveyed, for example, and although much publicity has been given to headline figures of £1 billion costs arising from implementation, the assessment document itself highlights the need to approach these estimates with caution. The Commissioner has also questioned the accuracy of the financial calculations,[60] suggesting that this may have resulted from misunderstandings as to the nature of the Data Protection Directive's requirements.[61]

To date, it does not appear that data protection has had a significant impact on public consciousness. To justify costs of some £20 for every inhabitant of the United Kingdom, it is to be hoped that the new legislation—perhaps coupled with other legislative initiatives in the field of human rights and freedom of information—will provide the basis for enhanced public awareness of the crucial importance of information in modern society, and the need to secure an appropriate balance between those who hold and use data and those who may be affected by such activities.

Conclusions

Within the United Kingdom, from its earliest days, data protection has been seen as a somewhat isolated measure. Things have not changed significantly although in its report on the press, the Leveson Inquiry devoted considerable attention to the role of data protection law. Its conclusions will be referred to throughout Part I of this book, but at the outset we may note its opening comments:

> **1.2** The UK data protection regime suffers from an unenviable reputation, perhaps not wholly merited, but nevertheless important to understand at the outset. To say that it is little known or understood by the public, regarded as a regulatory inconvenience in the business world, and viewed as marginal and technical among legal practitioners (including by our higher courts), might be regarded as a little unfair by the more well-informed, but is perhaps not so far from the truth. And yet the subject-matter of the data protection regime, how personal information about individuals is acquired, used and traded for business purposes,

---

[59] Joined Cases C–465/00, C–138/01, and C–139/01 [2003] ECR I–4989.
[60] Press Release, 28 January 1998.   [61] Directive 95/46/EC.

could hardly be more fundamental to issues of personal integrity, particularly in a world of ever- accelerating information technology capability, nor, on the face of it, more central to the concerns of this Inquiry.[62]

Essentially, although data protection is vitally important to us all, few recognise the fact and it is perhaps a fair criticism that it has become mired in bureaucracy and to an extent has lost sight of its core principles. The Data Protection Act 1998 should be seen as one of a trilogy of measures operating in the same general field. The Human Rights Act 1998 incorporates the European Convention on Human Rights into domestic law. The provisions of Articles 8 and 10 are of particular relevance to data protection. Article 8 provides that 'everyone has the right to respect for his private and family life, his home and his correspondence'. Any interference with such rights by a public authority must be sanctioned by law and be:

> necessary in a democratic society in the interests of national security, public safety or the economic well being of the country, for the prevention of disorder or crime, for the protection of health or morals, or for the protection of the rights and freedoms of others.[63]

In its jurisprudence, the European Court of Human Rights has interpreted Article 8 liberally to include rights of access to personal data. Indeed, following the decision of the court in the case of *Gaskin v United Kingdom*,[64] changes were required to be made to statutory provisions relating to subject access.

Perhaps the most controversial aspect of the interface between the Human Rights Act 1998 and the Data Protection Act 1998 concerns the activities of the media.

A further area where the Data Protection Act 1998 has to relate with other measures is connected with the introduction of freedom of information legislation. A White Paper, *Your Right to Know*, was published in December 1997,[65] and a Bill was introduced in Parliament in 1999, receiving Royal Assent in 2000 but not entering into force until January 2005.[66] There is a clear overlap between the two concepts and the Information Commissioner has responsibility in respect of both statutes. In other countries which have freedom of information legislation, it has been estimated that some 80 per cent of requests relate to the inquirer's own personal data. In respect of this issue, freedom of information legislation may well supplement rights under the Data Protection Act 1998 by extending these to a wider range of manual records, but, with proposals for significant variations in access rights and exceptions thereto, the prospect arises of what the House of Commons Select Committee on Public Administration described as a 'confusing and messy patchwork of different provisions under which one may obtain access to one's own file'.[67] Even more significantly, however, there will be the potential for conflict between the aims and objectives of the statutes where personal data relates to a party other than the inquirer.[68] Here, whilst freedom of information may give priority to openness and accessibility, data protection seeks to protect individual privacy and confidentiality.

In many respects, it might have been desirable had reform to the Data Protection Act proceeded in parallel with the freedom of information legislation. The Select Committee, whilst welcoming the prospect of freedom of information legislation, commented critically on the possibility for overlap and conflict between the two systems. It is perhaps ironic that whilst the prospect of the European Directives adopted was used to justify much-needed

---

[62] Lord Justice Leveson, *An Inquiry into the Culture, Practices and Ethics of the Press*, 4 vols. (London, 2012), III, Pt H.   [63] Art. 10(2).

[64] (1990) 12 EHRR 36.   [65] Cm. 3818.

[66] Separate legislation applies within Scotland.

[67] *Third Report from the Select Committee on Public Administration* (HC Paper 398/1 (1997–8)), para. 17.

[68] See the discussion of the case of *Common Services Agency v Scottish Information Commissioner* in Ch. 3 and more recently the case of *Edem v The Information Commissioner and Financial Services Authority* {2014} EWCA 92.

reform of the United Kingdom system during the first half of the 1990s, the desire to comply with the timetable for its implementation resulted in the 1998 Act being brought forward in isolation rather than as part of a comprehensive and coherent strategy governing access to information. To compound the irony, of course, the delay in formulating necessary items of secondary legislation meant that the United Kingdom ultimately failed to meet the European deadline.

As will be discussed more extensively herein, there is now the prospect of further reform to data protection law with proposals for a European data protection Regulation at a relatively advanced stage. We have also the seemingly endless revelations concerning the extent of surveillance activities by the UK and US security agencies. It may be that data protection's time is coming. Hopefully it will not be a Warholian fifteen minutes of fame.

3

The scope of data protection

Introduction

Dictionaries and definitions seldom make compelling reading, but in the law an appreciation of basic concepts is key to the understanding of a topic. Prior to considering substantive aspects of data protection, this chapter will consider in some detail the core concepts which define the scope of data protection legislation. A number of definitional terms are closely linked to form a knot almost Gordian in its complexity. Any attempt to describe and analyse them is hindered by the fact that appreciation of the scope of one term presupposes to some extent understanding of others. In the absence of a sufficiently sharp sword, the following précis may serve as an introduction. The italicised terms will be subjected to more detailed analysis in the remainder of the chapter:

> Data protection legislation applies where *personal data* (including *sensitive personal data*) *relating* to an *identifiable individual* (*data subject*) is subjected to certain forms of *processing*. The nature and extent of the processing will be determined by a *data controller*, although the actual processing may be carried out by a *data processor* operating under an outsourcing or similar contract with the data controller.

The apparent simplicity of the terms is unfortunately misleading and there has been extensive debate and uncertainty, both as to the scope of the concepts per se and as to the extent to which the United Kingdom's legislation adequately implements the provisions of the Directive. Decisions of the courts also have to be taken into account, with leading authorities being the decision of the English Court of Appeal in *Durant v Financial Services Authority*,[1] the House of Lords in the case of *Common Service Agency v Scottish Information Commissioner*,[2] and the judgment of the European Court of Justice in the case of *Bodil Lindqvist*.[3]

The concept of personal data

The Data Protection Directive defines personal data in relatively simple terms as 'any information relating to an identified or identifiable natural person (data subject)'.[4] The Data Protection Act's approach is rather more complicated and analysis needs to proceed through a number of steps. The legislation initially states that it applies to 'data which, relate to a living individual'.[5] The Act contains a further addition, providing that the term extends 'to any expression of opinion about the individual and any indication of the intentions of the data controller or any other person in respect of the individual'. This represents in large part an unfortunate legacy from the original Act of 1984 which included a widely criticised

---

[1] [2003] EWCA Civ 1746.   [2] [2008] UKHL 47.   [3] C101/01.   [4] Art. 2(a).
[5] s. 1(1).

distinction between statements of opinion—which were classed as personal data—and statements of the data controller's intentions towards the data subject—which were not. The argument put forward by the government of the day was that statements of intention were personal to the data controller rather than to the subject. This is certainly arguable, but the point applies with equal if not greater validity with regard to statements of opinion. Even the then Data Protection Registrar was moved to comment to the effect that he found the distinction unclear and the provision in the Data Protection Act 1998 should perhaps be seen as a measure to remove what had generally been considered an unsatisfactory distinction, rather than a deliberate effort to depart from the requirements of the Directive.

There are, however, significant questions whether the Act's provisions fully meet the requirements of the Directive. The threat of legal action by the European Commission alleging a failure properly to implement the Directive has been looming for a number of years. One perhaps peripheral issue is whether the legislation should apply to data relating to deceased individuals. The Directive, it will be recalled, applies in respect of data relating to a 'natural person'. It is arguable that this state continues after the individual's death. A minority of Member States have, indeed, chosen to extend their national laws to this category of data. Even accepting the validity of the United Kingdom's interpretation of the concept of a 'natural person' as a living individual, there may be circumstances in which data concerning a deceased person may also have implications for living individuals and therefore come within the scope of the legislation. Certain diseases such as haemophilia are hereditary in nature. The son of a woman suffering from the disease in its active form will always inherit the condition. Data indicating the mother's condition will therefore convey information about the medical condition of any male children.

Again, some EU Member States apply at least elements of the legislation to data relating to legal persons. The United Kingdom does not, although it should be noted that legal persons do acquire some protection under the provisions of the communications-specific Directive on Universal Service and Users' Rights Relating to Electronic Communications Networks and Services.[6] The provisions of this Directive and its implementation in the United Kingdom will be discussed in Chapter 7.

Although in its early stages data protection law tended to apply almost exclusively to textual information, developments in technology mean that almost any form of recorded information is likely to come within the ambit of the legislation. In the event that an individual interacts with an automated telephone service by speaking a series of numbers or words to allow a call to be directed to the appropriate department, those recorded words will class as personal data. Again, CCTV or similar camera systems generally fall within the scope of the legislation in respect of the video images recorded. The Information Commissioner has published guidance regarding the application of the Data Protection Act in respect of such data.

Much attention is paid today to the collection and use of biometric data in situations such as the issuance of passports and visas. Although the term does not have a precise definition, it is generally regarded as encompassing two categories of data. The first relates to the physiological characteristic relating to aspects of physical identity. This category would include items such as fingerprints and, perhaps relating to more advanced forms of technology, face and iris recognition. A second category of biometric data relates to what are referred to as behavioural characteristics. As the name suggests, this concerns the manner in which a person acts. A simple and long-established example would relate to the manner in which a person signs his or her name. More technologically advanced versions relate to

---

[6] Directive 2009/136/EC, OJ 2009 L 337/11.

the use of software to monitor the manner in which a particular individual uses a computer keyboard in terms of the speed, accuracy, and force with which keys are depressed.

Biometric data, which forms a cornerstone of modern passports, is clearly an aspect of personal data. Data may be objective or subjective and, indeed, true or false. In an Opinion on the concept of personal data,[7] the Article 29 Working Party suggested that:

> As a result of a neuro-psychiatric test conducted on a girl in the context of a court proceeding about her custody, a drawing made by her representing her family is submitted. The drawing provides information about the girl's mood and what she feels about different members of her family. As such, it could be considered as being 'personal data'. The drawing will indeed reveal information relating to the child (her state of health from a psychiatric point of view) and also about e.g. her father's or mother's behaviour. As a result, the parents in that case may be able to exert their right of access on this specific piece of information.

As indicated in the above example, personal data may relate to more than one person, a topic which will be considered in more detail later.

Sensitive personal data

Any piece of information, however insignificant, might be classed as personal data. The extent to which certain forms of data can be classed as especially sensitive and deserving of special protection has long been a contentious issue. During the passage of the Data Protection Act 1984, the attempt to identify sensitive data was compared, somewhat scornfully, by government ministers with the quest for the unicorn. Both were considered mythical creatures. In the case of personal data, the context in which data was held or used was considered far more important than the data itself. A list of names and addresses, for example, would not normally be considered sensitive, but this view might change if it referred to the movements of prominent persons and was in the hands of a terrorist organisation. Whilst this view is not without merit, it does seek to transform the exceptional into the norm. Almost invariably, however, data protection statutes have recognised that there are certain categories of information which would generally be regarded as possessing a degree of sensitivity and the processing of which should be subjected to more stringent controls than would generally be applicable.

The Data Protection Act provides for special treatment for data relating to:

(a) the racial or ethnic origin of the data subject;

(b) his political opinions;

(c) his religious beliefs or other beliefs of a similar nature;

(d) whether he is a member of a trade union;

(e) his physical or mental health or condition;

(f) his sexual life;

(g) the commission or alleged commission by him of any offence; or

(h) any proceedings for any offence committed or alleged to have been committed by him, the disposal of such proceedings, or the sentence of the court in such proceedings.[8]

With the exception of substituting the term 'other beliefs of a similar nature' for the Directive's 'philosophical beliefs', the Act's terminology mirrors that of the Directive.

---

[7] Available from <http://ec.europa.eu/justice_home/fsj/privacy/docs/wpdocs/2007/wp136_en.pdf>.

[8] s. 2.

Table 3.1 Attitudes towards sensitivity of types of data

	Percentage
Financial data	88.0
Health information	72.0
Personal contact details	68.0
Sexual life information	67.0
Biometric information	63.0
Genetic information	63.0
Criminal records	58.0
Clickstream data	43.0
Political opinions	42.0
Education qualification	42.0
Data concerning race or ethnic origin	41.0
Employment history	41.0
Membership of political party/organisation	38.0
Religious or philosophical beliefs	37.0
Trade-union membership	33.0

This definition is rather broad and undoubtedly reflects diverse attitudes towards issues across the Member States of the European Union. Research conducted for the Information Commissioner in 2006[9] sought views on the extent to which respondents regarded specific types of information as being sensitive. The results are set out in Table 3.1. Interestingly, financial data, which attracted the highest response rate, is not included in the statutory list of sensitive data.

In addition to covering a wide range of categories of information, the scope of particular categories has been broadly interpreted by the courts. In *Bodil Lindqvist*,[10] the European Court of Justice was asked to give a preliminary ruling in response to a number of questions posed by the Swedish courts. Mrs Lindqvist had been convicted of breaches of the Swedish data protection law in respect of her work as a catechist in the Swedish Lutheran Church and preparation of a number of *www* pages which contained information about Mrs Lindqvist and eighteen of her parish colleagues, including brief details of the nature of their work and hobbies. It appears that much of the information was presented in what was intended to be a light-hearted manner. One particular item of information which was the cause of specific investigation was the indication that a named person had injured her foot and as a consequence was able to work only on a part-time basis. Data concerning the subject's health life? Mrs Lindqvist was prosecuted by the Swedish authorities on a number of charges, including one of processing sensitive personal data without having secured authorisation from the data protection authorities. The European Court of Justice was asked to rule on the question of whether the reference to the foot injury of Mrs Lindqvist's colleague constituted sensitive data relating to health. The court's reply was succinct and emphatic:

> In the light of the purpose of the Directive, the expression data concerning health used in Article 8(1) thereof must be given a wide interpretation so as to include information concerning all aspects, both physical and mental, of the health of an individual.

[9] *2006 Annual Tracking Report*, available from <http://www.ico.gov.uk/upload/documents/library/corporate/research_and_reports/2006_annual_tracking_report_individuals_final.pdf>.

[10] Case 101/01, [2004] QB 1014.

In some respects, the decision in *Bodil Lindqvist* illustrates the difficulties surrounding the concept of sensitive data. Once included in a list of sensitive data, it is almost impossible to say that a reference to illness or injury is not included, but as indicated earlier, context is perhaps more important than content. A reference to the fact that an athlete was unable to compete in a race because of a broken leg, for example, does not seem to be possessed of a sufficient degree of sensitivity to justify the imposition of additional controls.

Personal data relating to the data subject

In *Bodil Lindqvist*, there was no doubt that the information about the foot injury related to the individual concerned. In other cases the situation may be more complex. In the example of the child's drawing cited earlier, the data contained might relate in varying degrees to the child and to other family members. Neither the Directive nor the Act provides any definition of when data relates to an individual and this has been a rather contentious issue. The point was discussed extensively in the case of *Durant v Financial Services Authority*,[11] and more recently has been considered in an Opinion of the Article 29 Working Party and in Guidance produced by the United Kingdom's Information Commissioner together with the decision of the House of Lords in the case of *Common Services Agency v Scottish Information Commissioner*[12] and most recently the decision of the Court of Appeal in *Edem v The Information Commissioner and Financial Services Authority*.[13]

In *Durant*, the appellant had been involved in a protracted dispute with Barclays Bank. This had resulted in unsuccessful litigation in 1993 and a continuing course of complaints to the industry regulatory body, the Financial Services Authority (FSA). The present case arose from a request from the appellant for access to a range of records under the ambit of the subject access provisions of the Data Protection Act 1998. Although some information was supplied, access to other records was provided only in partial form through the concealment or redaction of information which it was considered related to third parties. Other records were withheld on the grounds either that the information contained therein did not constitute personal data relating to the appellant, or—as will be discussed later, in the case of a number of records which were maintained in manual filing systems—that the system was not covered by the Data Protection Act.

Although there was no doubt that much, if not all, of the data in question had been generated following complaints from the appellant, the critical issue was whether it related to him. Counsel for Durant argued that the term 'relate to' should be interpreted broadly to encompass any data which might be generated following a search of a database made by reference to an individual's name. Thus, for example, a document describing the action which had been taken in response to a complaint from the appellant would be classed as personal data by virtue merely of the fact that his name would appear within the text. Counsel for the respondent advocated a more restrictive approach, making reference to the *Shorter Oxford English Dictionary*, which contained two definitions of the term, a broad reference to having 'some connection with, be connected to' and a more restrictive notion that there should be reference to or concern with a subject, 'implying, in this context, a more or less direct connection with an individual'.

This more restrictive interpretation was adopted by the Court of Appeal. The purpose of the subject access provisions in the legislation was, it was stated, to enable the data subject to verify that processing did not infringe his or her rights of privacy and to exercise any

---

[11] [2003] EWCA Civ 1746.   [12] [2008] UKHL 47.   [13] [2014] EWCA Civ 92.

available remedies in the event this was considered not to be the case. The purpose of the legislation was not, it was held, to give an automatic right of access to information purely by virtue of the fact that he might be named in a record or have some interest in the matters covered. In particular, it was stated, subject access was not intended:

> to assist him, for example, to obtain discovery of documents that may assist him in litigation or complaints against third parties.

Giving effect to this principle was that the mere fact that a search of a computer's contents by reference to a data subject's name revealed a number of documents did not mean that these documents necessarily constituted personal data relating to the subject. A more sophisticated analysis was required:

> It seems to me that there are two notions that may be of assistance. The first is whether the information is biographical in a significant sense, that is, going beyond the recording of the putative data subject's involvement in a matter or an event that has no personal connotations, a life event in respect of which his privacy could not be said to be compromised. The second is one of focus. The information should have the putative data subject as its focus rather than some other person with whom he may have been involved or some transaction or event in which he may have figured or have had an interest, for example, as in this case, an investigation into some other person's or body's conduct that he may have instigated. In short, it is information that affects his privacy, whether in his personal or family life, business or professional capacity.[14]

This approach adopts, it is suggested, an overly restrictive view of the rationale of data protection laws. Whilst determining the legality of data processing and correcting errors certainly constitute important elements, equally important is the ability to become aware of what data is held. Much of the Data Protection Directive[15] and the Data Protection Act 1998's requirements relating to the factors legitimising data processing stress the importance of the data subject being aware of what is happening with regard to personal data. As was stated by the German Constitutional Court in the 1980s:

> The possibilities of inspection and of gaining influence have increased to a degree hitherto unknown and may influence the individual's behaviour by the psychological pressure exerted by public interest . . . if someone cannot predict with sufficient certainty which information about himself in certain areas is known to his social milieu, and cannot estimate sufficiently the knowledge of parties to whom communication may possibly be made, he is crucially inhibited in his freedom to plan or to decide freely and without being subject to any pressure/influence.[16]

These factors support the adoption of an expansive definition of the scope of personal data. In a case such as *Durant*, it may well be that personal data in the form of an individual's name or other identifying data makes a peripheral appearance in a record. Rather than arguing that the appearance of the data does not come within the scope of the Act, it might be preferable to focus upon the extent of the information which might be supplied. Whilst the court was clearly concerned that the data protection legislation was being invoked in the present case in the attempt to obtain discovery of documents and data that could not be obtained through other legal channels, it might have been preferable to have laid greater stress on the limited nature of the information which would be classed as personal data.

---

[14] *Durant v Financial Services Authority* [2003] EWCA Civ 1746 at paras. 27–8.
[15] Directive 95/46/EC.   [16] 'The Census Decision', *Human Rights Law Journal* 5 (1984), p. 94.

The Information Commissioner has subsequently noted that 'the Court of Appeal was widely understood to have adopted a rather narrower interpretation of personal data ... than most practitioners and experts had followed previously'.[17] The Article 29 Working Party's Opinion provides extensive guidance when data relates to an individual. Referring to its previous work in relation to RFID chip technology, it affirms that 'data relates to an individual if it refers to the identity, characteristics or behaviour of an individual or if such information is used to determine or influence the way in which that person is treated or evaluated'.[18]

The Opinion identifies three elements which may indicate that data relates to a particular individual. These are referred to as content, purpose, and result elements. The distinction between the elements may be complex on occasion but the Working Party stress that only one element needs to be present in order to justify a finding that data relates to a particular individual. The content element will be satisfied when information is about an individual. A medical or personnel record, for example, will fall within this category. The purpose element applies when the data is intended to be used to determine the manner in which an individual is treated. Data may, for example, be recorded by an employer of the websites accessed from workplace computers. The purpose may be to take disciplinary action against employees who violate Internet usage policies. Finally, a result element applies when the use of data, even though not collected originally for that purpose, is likely to have even a minor impact upon an individual's rights and interests. Guidance produced by the United Kingdom's Information Commissioner emphasises similar criteria, suggesting that:

> Data which identifies an individual, even without a name associated with it, may be personal data where it is processed to learn or record something about that individual, or where the processing of that information has an impact upon that individual.

Subsequently, issues of the definition of personal data came before the House of Lords in the case of *Common Services Agency v Scottish Information Commissioner*.[19] The case revolved around what is a complex and sometime difficult relationship between two statutes that are concerned with rather different aspects of information policy. A key tenet of data protection law—and one which is seldom far from the news today—is that information supplied for one purpose should be kept securely and used only for that purpose. The basic element of the Freedom of Information Act, which was enacted in the year 2000, is that information held by public bodies should be disclosed to anyone upon request.

As has been noted, the Data Protection Act was rushed into force in an ultimately unsuccessful attempt to meet the implementation deadline for the European Data Protection Directive. With hindsight, it might have been preferable to have delayed another year and introduced the two statutes co-terminously (or even to have combined them in a single Information Policy Act).

This case was concerned with a request submitted to the appellant agency, a Health Board, under the terms of the Freedom of Information (Scotland) Act 2002[20] for the provision of information relating to instances of childhood cancer within the locality of a

---

[17] Data Protection Technical Guidance, 'Determining What Is Personal Data'. Published by the Office of the Information Commissioner, Wilmslow. Available from <http://ico.org.uk/for_organisations/guidance_index/~/media/documents/library/Data_Protection/Detailed_specialist_guides/PERSONAL_DATA_FLOWCHART_V1_WITH_PREFACE001.ashx>.

[18] Working Party Document No. WP 105: 'Working Document on Data Protection Issues Related to RFID Technology', adopted on 19 January 2005, p. 8.   [19] [2008] UKHL 47.

[20] The Scottish legislation is equivalent in all relevant respects to the Freedom of Information Act 2000 applying in England and Wales.

nuclear power station. Under the terms of the 2002 Act a range of exceptions apply regarding the types of information which may be supplied and, in particular, it is stated that personal data is not to be disclosed where this would be in contravention of any of the data protection principles.[21] Relying on this provision the appellant refused to disclose information. The Scottish Information Commissioner ruled that such a blanket refusal was unlawful. Although the raw data identifying individual patients was undoubtedly personal data disclosure would not be in breach of the data protection principles were to it be processed using a procedure known as 'barnardisation' which would modify statistical elements so that no individual could be identified. The appellant was ordered to conduct such a process. The Commissioner's ruling was upheld by the highest Scottish court, the Court of Session.[22] Applying the approach of the Court of Appeal in *Durant v Financial Services Authority*[23] that 'mere mention of the data subject in a document held by a data controller does not necessarily amount to personal data',[24] the Lord President ruled that:

> Although the underlying information concerns important biographical events of the children involved, by the stage of the compilation of the barnardised table that information has become not only statistical but perturbed to minimise the risk of identification of any individual child. It is no longer, in respect of any child, 'biographical in a significant sense'. The focus has, in my view, also moved away from the individual children to the incidence of disease in particular wards in particular years. The rights to privacy of the individual children are not infringed by the disclosure of the barnardised data.[25]

A further appeal was made to the House of Lords where, delivering the leading judgment, Lord Hope gave detailed consideration to the scope of the definition of personal data—and also of sensitive personal data. In respect of the former he indicated that the Court of Appeal decision in *Durant* should be distinguished as it related to the operation of the subject information provisions rather than the definition of personal data per se. The answer to that issue, he held, 'must be found in the wording of section 1(1) (of the Data Protection Act 1998) read in the light of Council Directive 95/46/EC'.[26] The Act refers to the possibility that an individual might be identified from data 'and other information which is in the possession of the data controller'. As the appellant had the means to recreate data identifying individuals, the barnardised data remained personal data.

Turning to the question whether the data could be disclosed in conformity with the provisions of the Act, Lord Hope cited the provisions of Recital 26 of the Directive to the effect that when data was truly anonymous 'the principles of protection shall not apply to data'. Section 1(1) it was held, gave effect to this provision.

As noted previously, Recital 26 of the Directive states that in making decisions as to whether an individual can be identified 'account should be taken of all the means likely reasonably to be used either by the controller or by any other person to identify the said person'. The appellant clearly had the means to match data to named individuals but the issue in this respect was whether a third party receiving the barnardised data would be able to re-engineer it. The Scottish Information Commissioner, it was held, should have considered more fully this issue and, accordingly, the case was remitted for him to make findings of fact in this respect. Ultimately, the Commissioner issued a further ruling[27] holding that he was not satisfied that anonymity could be guaranteed and on this basis the freedom of access request was denied.

---

[21] s. 38. [22] [2006] CSIH 58. [23] [2003] EWCA Civ 1746. [24] para. 28. [25] para. 23.
[26] para. 20.
[27] Available from <http://www.itspublicknowledge.info/applicationsanddecisions/Decisions/2005/200500298.asp>.

In some respects the decision in *Common Services Agency* might be seen to have limited the application of the Court of Appeal case in *Durant* although the rather opaque way in which it has been done cannot eliminate all scope for confusion. What appears to be the effect of Lord Hope's dicta is that any element of data relating to an individual will be classed as personal data. There will remain the issue of when data relates to a subject who is applying for subject access—a topic that will be considered in more detail in a subsequent chapter.

Most recently, the interaction between the data protection and freedom of information regimes was at issue in the case of *Edem v The Information Commissioner and Financial Services Authority*.[28] The case has some similarities to *Durant*, but following the decision on *Common Information Services* does perhaps continue the process of restricting its scope.

Once again the former Financial Services Authority was at the heart of the litigation with another claimant regarding the handling of a complaint that he had made. A request was made under the Freedom of Information Act for a range of data relating to the handling of the complaint. Included was a request for the names of the individual (and fairly junior) members of staff who had investigated the issue.

Under the Freedom of Information Act, one of the grounds for refusing to supply information is that it would disclose personal data relating to a person other than the applicant. Relying essentially on the decision in *Durant*, it was submitted on behalf of the claimant that details of the names of the employees would not class as personal data.

The Information Commissioner ruled that the data was personal data and that the Financial Services Authority was entitled to withhold it. The First-tier Tribunal disagreed basing its decision largely on the *Durant* case. The Upper Tribunal and the Court of Appeal disagreed. It considered the jurisprudence of the European Court of Justice and concluded:

> A name is personal data unless it is so common that without further information, such as its use in a work context, a person would remain unidentifiable despite its disclosure.[29]

Following from the *Common Information Services* decision it does seem that, although not overruled, *Durant* will be relevant in only limited circumstances where the motivation of an applicant is at issue. Whether this is properly a relevant consideration is perhaps debatable.

Issues of identification

The premise underlying data protection legislation is that the processing of data relating to individuals constitutes a threat to the subject's rights and freedoms. If an individual cannot be identified from the manner in which data is collected, processed, or used, there can be no significant threat to privacy and no justification for the application of legislative controls. The Data Protection Directive provides that:

> an identifiable person is one who can be identified directly or indirectly, in particular by reference to an identification number or to one or more factors specific to his physical, psychological, mental, economic, cultural or social identity.[30]

Also relevant are the provisions of Recital 26 to the Directive. This states that:

> Whereas the principles of protection must apply to any information concerning an identified or identifiable person; whereas, to determine whether a person is identifiable, account

---

[28] [2014] EWCA Civ 92.   [29] At para 20.   [30] Directive 95/46/EC, Art. 2(a).

should be taken of all the means likely reasonably to be used either by the controller or by any other person to identify the said person.

The United Kingdom's Data Protection Act 1998 provides that personal data:

means data which relates to a living individual who can be identified—

(a) from those data; or

(b) from those data and other information which is in the possession of, or is likely to come into the possession of, the data controller.

It will be recognised that the Directive and the Act differ in that the Act restricts its application to information which is or is likely to come into the possession of the data controller. The Directive's application is open-ended, applying whenever anyone might be able to identify an individual. A recent example might illustrate a difference between the two approaches. In 2006, AOL placed on the Internet data relating to search requests made by millions of its subscribers. Although no names were published, in at least some cases it proved possible to identify individuals following analysis of their search history. One case concerned a user allocated the identifying number 4417749. This user had conducted searches on a range of topics, including medical conditions relating to humans and animals, landscape gardening, persons with a particular surname (Arnold), and house sales in a particular area of the United States. Taking this data, researchers focused on a particular individual, Thelma Arnold, who, when read a list of the searches, confirmed that they had been made by her.[31]

Under the United Kingdom approach, it is likely that the data would not have been considered personal data at the point it was compiled by AOL because that organisation would not have possessed the necessary additional information to identify users.[32] Under the Directive's criteria, the material would probably have been classed as personal data, as AOL would have been required to consider the possibility that third parties could perform the task of identification. It is likely that if its disclosure and decoding were to be carried out in the United Kingdom (or any other state of the European Economic Area (EEA)) the person identifying individuals would be classed as a data controller in his or her own right and subject to the same obligations to comply with data protection law. Matters would be much less satisfactory were the decoder to be located outside of the EEA and, of course, dissemination of information via the Internet is global in its nature.

The AOL example undoubtedly represents an extreme case but the issue of identifiability may frequently be an issue. Once again, the Article 29 Opinion on the concept of personal data identifies a wide range of potential situations and provides extensive guidance. Linking data to a name is an obvious form of identification, although especially in the case of a common name such as Smith or McDonald this may not be sufficient. Use of an identification number may aid identification. In other cases, an individual may be identifiable indirectly. The example might be posited of a CCTV operator instructing an undercover police officer to detain the person wearing a Glasgow Rangers' football shirt and carrying a can of lager sitting slumped in the doorway of 27 Hoops Street, Glasgow. No name is given but the individual would be readily identifiable to the police officer. Again, Internet Service Providers (ISPs)

---

[31] <http://www.iht.com/articles/2006/08/09/business/aol.php>.

[32] Given that AOL operates on a subscription service it may be that the company would have possessed the necessary data. The example might be more accurate in the event that it applied to an organisation such as Google, which does not require users to give their names. Indeed, one of the reasons why Google refused to comply with a United States government request for access to search data was because of concerns that individuals might be identified. See <http://news.bbc.co.uk/1/hi/technology/4630694.stm>.

and possibly employers may maintain records of Internet use associated with particular computers and from these to the individuals behind the computers. Identification may not always be possible; the Working Party posit the example of computers used in an Internet café, but stresses that so long as identification is possible in some cases, all processing will be covered by the legislation.

The concept of processing

Much of what has been said to date is predicated on the notion that data is processed. It is now appropriate to consider what forms of activity can be classed as constituting processing. The Directive provides that processing includes:

> any operation or set of operations which is performed upon personal data, whether or not by automatic means, such as collection, recording, organization, storage, adaptation or alteration, retrieval, consultation, use, disclosure by transmission, dissemination or otherwise making available, alignment or combination, blocking, erasure or destruction.[33]

The Act's definition differs slightly in terminology, largely because of the need to make separate provision for the treatment of non-automated or manual processing. It provides that:

> 'processing', in relation to information or data, means obtaining, recording or holding the information or data or carrying out any operation or set of operations on the information or data, including—

(a) organisation, adaptation or alteration of the information or data;

(b) retrieval, consultation or use of the information or data;

(c) disclosure of the information or data by transmission, dissemination or otherwise making available; or

(d) alignment, combination, blocking, erasure or destruction of the information or data.[34]

Linked to this is a definition of the word data:

(a) is being processed by means of equipment operating automatically in response to instructions given for that purpose;

(b) is recorded with the intention that it should be processed by means of such equipment; or

(c) is recorded as part of a relevant filing system or with the intention that it should form part of a relevant filing system.[35]

The term 'relevant filing system' is designed to extend the legislation to certain forms of manual filing systems and will be considered separately in the next section. It will be noted that the scope of the definition is extremely broad. It might be suggested, with little element of exaggeration, that whilst the act of dreaming about data will not constitute processing, any further activities will bring a party within the scope of the legislation.

Although not yet at issue before a United Kingdom court, the question of what acts constitute processing was raised before the European Court in *Bodil Lindqvist*.[36] An initial

---

[33] Art. 2(b).   [34] s. 1(1).   [35] s. 1(1).   [36] Case 101/01, [2004] QB 1014.

issue concerned the question of whether the mention of a person on a web page constituted processing of personal data as defined in the Data Protection Directive.[37] Two issues arose in this context: first, whether the data on Mrs Lindqvist's web page included personal data. The court's reply was unequivocal:

> The term undoubtedly covers the name of a person in conjunction with his telephone coordinates or information about his working conditions or hobbies.[38]

Equally clear and unsurprising was the court's determination that processing had taken place. The Swedish government argued for a broad approach, suggesting that 'as soon as personal data are processed by computer, whether using a word-processing programme or in order to put them on an Internet page, they have been the subject of processing'. Although counsel for Mrs Lindqvist argued that something more was needed beyond compilation of what was effectively a word-processed document and that only meta tags and other technical means used to assist with the compilation of indexes and retrieval of information would suffice, the Court agreed with the Swedish government's submission:

> According to the definition in Article 2(b) of Directive 95/46, the term processing of such data used in Article 3(1) covers any operation or set of operations which is performed upon personal data, whether or not by automatic means.[39]

Although all forms of processing are potentially covered by the Data Protection Directive,[40] the most stringent controls apply in the case of processing by automatic means. It is arguable that any use of a computer to create a document comes within the scope of this criterion, as there is no direct physical link between the author pressing a key and a letter or symbol appearing on the screen. The act of loading a page onto a web server involves a number of operations, some at least of which are performed automatically.

Non-automated filing systems

Under the Data Protection Act 1984, access was strictly limited to data which had been the subject of some form of automated processing. The Data Protection Directive[41] required an extension to certain forms of manual records. Article 2 of the Directive provides that its scope is to extend to any 'personal data filing system' defined in terms of:

> any structured set of personal data which are accessible according to specific criteria, whether centralised, decentralised or dispersed on a functional or geographical basis.

By omitting any reference to automated processing the effect is clearly to encompass manual record-keeping systems. Whilst every automated system is covered by the legislation, reflecting the ease with which modern retrieval systems can perform full text searches of vast collections of data in accordance with criteria determined by a user, not every manual system is to be included. Recital 15 of the Data Protection Directive[42] explains that:

> Whereas the processing of such data is covered by this Directive only if it is automated or if the data processed are contained or are intended to be contained in a filing system structured according to specific criteria relating to individuals, so as to permit easy access to the personal data in question;...

---

[37] Directive 95/46/EC.   [38] Case 101/01, [2004] QB 1014, para. 24.   [39] Case 101/01, para. 25.
[40] Directive 95/46/EC.   [41] Directive 95/46/EC.   [42] Directive 95/46/EC.

Recital 27 continues the story:

> Whereas the protection of individuals must apply as much to automatic processing of data as to manual processing; whereas the scope of this protection must not in effect depend on the techniques used, otherwise this would create a serious risk of circumvention; whereas nonetheless, as regards manual processing, this Directive covers only filing systems, not unstructured files; whereas, in particular, the content of a filing system must be structured according to specific criteria relating to individuals allowing easy access to the personal data; whereas, in line with the definition in Article 2(c), the different criteria for determining the constituents of a structured set of personal data, and different criteria governing access to such a set, may be laid down by each Member State; whereas files or sets of files as well as their cover pages, which are not structured according to specific criteria, shall under no circumstances fall within the scope of the Directive.

This provision clearly leaves considerable scope for Member States to determine the extent to which manual records should be brought within the scope of their implementing legislation. As indicated earlier, the Data Protection Act 1998 utilises the concept of a 'relevant filing system' as the vehicle for this endeavour. The statutory definition is somewhat complex, in large part because the legislation seeks to coexist with a range of earlier statutes which had provided for a right of access to certain medical, educational, social-work, and credit reference files. In its essential element, however, it provides that:

> 'relevant filing system' means any set of information relating to individuals to the extent that, although the information is not processed by means of equipment operating automatically in response to instructions given for that purpose, the set is structured, either by reference to individuals or by reference to criteria relating to individuals, in such a way that specific information relating to a particular individual is readily accessible.[43]

The extension to some forms of manual records has been the cause of considerable controversy, largely concerning the potential costs to organisations of complying with requests for subject access. It should be noted, however, that the Consumer Credit Act 1974 and the Access to Health Records Act 1990 have long provided for access to credit and medical records, irrespective of the format in which these are stored. More recently, the Freedom of Information Act 2000 has provided very extensive rights of access to public-sector information and as the Information Commissioner has commented:

> Experience elsewhere indicates that in practice, in many cases, information provided in response to Freedom of Information requests will relate to the individual making the request.[44]

In determining what manual records will be covered, the question of when information should be considered 'readily accessible' is of critical importance. In the discussion of the extent of the provision in Parliament, it was suggested that it would not be sufficient that information about an individual should be located in a single place, for example, a manila folder containing all of an employee's work records. In order for the records to be covered, it would additionally be required that the information within the folder should be held in a structured format so that individual items might readily be extracted. Speaking during the Bill's report stage in the House of Lords, Lord Williams stated that:

> Our intentions are clear. We do not wish the definition to apply to miscellaneous collections of paper about individuals, even if the collections are assembled in files with the individual's

---

[43] s. 1(1).

[44] Data Protection Registrar. Our Answers. Response to the Consultation Paper on the EC Data Protection Directive 1998, para. 3.8.

name or other unique identifier on the front, if specific data about the individual cannot be readily extracted from that collection. An example might be a personnel file with my name on the front. Let us assume that the file contains every piece of paper or other document about me which the personnel section has collected over the course of my career and those papers are held in the file in date order with no means of readily identifying specific information about me except by looking at every document. The Government's clear intention is that such files should not be caught.[45]

The then Data Protection Registrar, however, commented that:

It has...been put to us that 'particular information' refers to information of a very specific nature. On this analysis information held in a file relating to an immigration application would arguably be covered as all the information in the file will, or should, be directly pertinent to that application. However, it has been argued that information held in a normal personnel file will not be 'particular information' as there will be a range of information concerning such matters as sickness absence, performance, pay, next of kin. We find this distinction unconvincing. The range of information in a personnel file may be wide because there is a wide range of information relevant to an individual's employment. Nevertheless, the information is 'particular' in that it is all information held for, and relevant to, employment.[46]

Some answers (but at least as many questions) to the issues raised can be found in the Court of Appeal decision in *Durant v Financial Services Authority*.[47] In addition to the issue discussed earlier of whether data is classed as personal in its nature, the court gave extensive consideration to the appellant's claim for access to a range of manual records. As described in the judgment, these took a variety of forms and demonstrated differing levels of structure and organisation. In some cases, documents were located in a folder under Mr Michael Durant's name but in other instances the name on the file was that of the bank against which complaints had been made—whether by Mr Durant or by other persons. It was accepted by the FSA that all of these files contained some information which related to the appellant. The degree and level of identification varied, with some files identifying him 'by reference to specific dividers within the file'. Files also contained a range of documents, including copies of telephone attendance notes and:

a report of forensic examination of documents, transcripts of judgments, handwritten notes, internal memoranda, correspondence with Barclays Bank, correspondence with other individuals and correspondence between the FSA and him.[48]

Again taking account of the issue of whether data might be regarded as personal, the court considered the extent to which the records in question could be considered to constitute a relevant file. Again, reference was made to the Act's intention being to protect the privacy of the data subject rather than that of documents. As has been described, it would be a relatively simple task to identify documents but a more complex one to determine whether a document constituted personal data. Consideration was given to the magnitude of the task which a data controller might be faced with in seeking to respond to a request for subject access. The responsibility for the task, it was held, would often fall on administrators who might not have a specialised knowledge of the subject area or documents

[45] 587 HL Official Report (5th series), col. 467, 16 March 1998.
[46] Briefing Note, 29 January 1998.   [47] [2003] EWCA Civ 1746.   [48] para. 17.

involved. In order for the extent of access to be manageable, the obligations could only be applied in respect of manual systems:

> that enable identification of relevant information with a minimum of time and costs, through clear referencing mechanisms within any filing system potentially containing personal data the subject of a request for information. Anything less, which, for example, requires the searcher to leaf through files to see what and whether information qualifying as personal data of the person who has made the request is to be found there, would bear no resemblance to a computerised search.[49]

It is not clear whether this conclusion is necessarily supported by the reality of modern databases. A Google-type search, for example across an organisation's electronic filing systems, might identify a large number of documents in which an applicant's name appeared—as indeed was at issue in the *Durant* case. Whilst certainly there could be no obligation on a data controller to read, or request an administrator to read, every piece of paper in the organisation, the level of structure and organisation required seems excessive.

It is often stated that hard cases make bad laws. It may also be the case that bad cases make hard laws. There is no doubt that the judges in *Durant* were extremely wary of what was regarded as an attempt to invoke the provisions of the Data Protection Act 1998 for purposes beyond those envisaged by the legislature. It might be noted that in many cases, data of the kind sought by Durant could have been obtained under the Freedom of Information Act 2000, although this legislation was not in force at the time his litigation commenced. Given that the Financial Services Authority had identified the material relating to Durant's case in the context of the data protection proceedings, it might be difficult to refuse any future freedom of information request on the basis that the information would be excessively difficult to collect. Perhaps the most intractable problem facing the courts in a case such as this is that there is the clear signal, not least from the Data Protection Directive,[50] that the legislation is concerned with the protection of the right to privacy, yet, as discussed extensively elsewhere, this remains something which is not explicitly protected in the United Kingdom. The content of the right to privacy has long evaded precise definition. The classic formulation, however, refers to the right 'to be left alone', whilst references to the concept of informational privacy lay stress on the more proactive ability to control the storage and dissemination of personal data. If the right to exercise at least a measure of control over the collection and use of personal data is to have any meaning, knowledge of the nature and extent of the information which is held must be a necessary concomitant. In adopting a restrictive view of the scope of relevant filing systems, the court in *Durant* pays insufficient regard to the concept of informational privacy.

Data protection actors

Data controllers

Data controllers are subject to the most extensive forms of control under the Data Protection Act and Directive. The Directive provides that:

> 'controller' shall mean the natural or legal person, public authority, agency or any other body which alone or jointly with others determines the purposes and means of the processing of personal data; where the purposes and means of processing are determined by

---

[49] para. 45.   [50] Directive 95/46/EC.

national or Community laws or regulations, the controller or the specific criteria for his nomination may be designated by national or Community law.[51]

The Data Protection Act provides that a party will be classed as a data controller when it:

(either alone or jointly or in common with other persons) determines the purposes for which and the manner in which personal data are, or are to be processed.[52]

In the case where data are processed only for purposes required by statute, for example the compilation of an electoral roll, the agency charged with conducting the work will be classed as the data controller.

The key element of the above definitions relates, with the exception of the performance of statutory functions, to the ability to determine the nature and extent of the processing which is to be carried out. It is quite possible for persons to be classed as data control-lers even though they do not own a computer. An example might concern the owner of a small business who records details of transactions on pieces of paper which are stored in the archetypal shoebox. Once a year, the shoebox may be collected by an accountant, who transfers the data to computer in order to prepare a set of accounts. Assuming that some of the data in the accounts relate to individual creditors and debtors, all the criteria necessary for the application of the legislation will be satisfied and, doubtless much to their surprise, the business person will be classed as a data controller. In such a situation, the accountant will also be so regarded, the Divisional Court confirming in *Data Protection Registrar v Griffin*,[53] a case brought under the Data Protection Act 1984, that anyone who processed data on behalf of clients would be regarded as a data user (now controller) when he or she possessed any control or discretion concerning the manner in which the processing was carried out.

A similar result is predicted in the Recitals to the Data Protection Directive:

where a message containing personal data is transmitted by means of a telecommunications or electronic mail service, the sole purpose of which is the transmission of such messages, the controller in respect of the personal data contained in the message will normally be con-sidered to be the person from whom the message originates, rather than the person offering the transmission services; whereas, nevertheless, those offering such services will normally be considered controllers in respect of the processing of the additional personal data neces-sary for the operation of the service.[54]

Data processors

As in the example given above, some data controllers may seek to have processing carried out on their behalf by a third party. This was perhaps more prevalent in the early days of computing than is the case today, although one aspect which remains significant is where undertakings make arrangements as part of a disaster recovery plan, to obtain access to external processing facilities in the event of some interruption to service. Mirroring once again the terminology of the Data Protection Directive,[55] the Data Protection Act 1998 utilises the term 'data processor' which encompasses:

any person (other than an employee of the data controller) who processes the data on behalf of the data controller.[56]

---

[51] Art. 2(d).   [52] s. 1(1).   [53] *The Times*, 5 March 1993.
[54] Directive 95/46/EC, Recital 41.   [55] Directive 95/46/EC.
[56] s. 1(1).

The phrase in brackets was included to avoid the possibility that employees engaged in processing in the course of their employment might be regarded as data processors. Given the expanded definition of processing adopted in the 1998 Act, it will be the case that any other person who collects data for the controller—perhaps by conducting market research surveys using pen and paper—will be classed as a processor.

Although a wide range of persons may be classed as data processors, the requirements imposed on them are limited. Data processors will not be subject to the notification require-ments,[57] whilst, in respect of the requirement to maintain appropriate security (now found in the seventh principle), the onus is placed upon the data controller for whom processing is conducted. The controller is responsible for selecting a processor who can provide satis-factory guarantees regarding security.[58] A written contract must also be entered into oblig-ing the processor to act only on instructions from the controller in respect of the processing carried out, and also to comply with the requirements of the seventh principle.[59] Further, it is only the data controller who may be liable to compensate data subjects for losses arising from processing.[60]

Data subjects

A data subject is 'an individual who is the subject of personal data'.[61] It would be a unique individual who is not to be classed as a data subject—many times over. In contrast to the situation with data controllers and processors, where the focus is very much on the obliga-tions imposed under the legislation, for data subjects, the purpose of the statute is to confer rights. The most important right for data subjects is undoubtedly that of obtaining access to data held by controllers and of securing the correction of any errors contained therein.

Jurisdictional issues

The Data Protection Act 1984 'applies to all data users who control the contents and use of personal data from within the United Kingdom'.[62] In part, this approach was necessary in order to comply with the Council of Europe's provisions regarding mutual assistance. In the situation where data is processed in the United Kingdom relating to, for example, French or German data subjects, the Data Protection Act will apply, with the main issue being the identification of the data user. The question of whether an undertaking can be considered resident in the United Kingdom is one which arises in a number of contexts and which may produce different results. As the Commissioner has commented, a company could be regarded as resident in the United Kingdom for the purpose of the Data Protection Act but not for taxation purposes. In the event that the company is not considered resident, it may be that it will be represented in the United Kingdom by a 'servant or agent' who will be classed as a data user for this purpose. It may also be the case that the undertaking which carries out the processing may be regarded as a computer bureau for the purpose of the legislation.

Similar problems arise when data relating to United Kingdom data subjects is pro-cessed abroad. In many instances, the data will remain under the legal control of the United Kingdom-based user, who will therefore be subject to the legislation. The view has

---

[57] s. 17, which provides for notification, refers only to this obligation being imposed upon data controllers.
[58] Sch. 1, Pt 2, para. 11.   [59] Sch. 1, Pt 2, para. 12.   [60] s. 13.
[61] s. 1(1). Section 1(4) contains the equivalent provision in the Data Protection Act 1984.
[62] s. 39.

been taken by the Commissioner that jurisdiction will be claimed even where all aspects of the processing are carried out abroad but where it is intended that the data will be used in the United Kingdom—regardless of the form in which it is imported. The correctness of this interpretation has not been tested before the courts or the Information Tribunal.

In the Data Protection Directive,[63] it is provided that EU Member States are to apply national laws where processing 'is carried out in the context of the activities of an establishment of the controller on the territory of the Member State'. Such a formulation may lead to extraterritorial application of national laws. Article 28(6) provides further that:

> Each supervisory authority is competent, whatever the national law applying to the processing in question, to exercise, on the territory of its own Member State, the powers conferred on it (to investigate suspected violations of the law and to intervene by legal or administrative measures to terminate breaches). Each authority may be requested to exercise its powers by an authority of another Member State.

There is potential for overlapping jurisdiction in the situation where multinational undertakings process personal data in a variety of Member States. In its Consultation Paper, the Home Office asserted that:

> While some of the provisions relating to geographical extent are clear enough, others are obscure and potentially ambiguous. There is, therefore, the potential for inconsistent approaches being adopted in different Member States. The danger is that this could make it possible for the national law of more than one Member State to apply to a single processing operation, or for no Member State's law so to apply.[64]

The multiple jurisdiction situation would appear to be an inevitable consequence of the free movement of data within the EU. Given that a major purpose of the Data Protection Directive[65] is to harmonise the laws of the Member States, such a result should not be excessively burdensome for data users and, indeed, corresponds to the UK Commissioner's interpretation of the existing situation under domestic law. It is difficult to envisage that a reasonable interpretation of the Directive's terms could produce a situation where no national law applied. In implementing the Directive's provisions, the Data Protection Act 1998 will apply where:

(a) the data controller is established in the United Kingdom and the data are processed in the context of that establishment; or

(b) the data controller is established neither in the United Kingdom nor in any other EEA state but uses equipment in the United Kingdom for processing the data otherwise than for the purposes of transit through the United Kingdom.[66]

An example of the latter situation might be where equipment forming part of a computer network, perhaps involving an ISP, is located in the United Kingdom but managed from the United States.

The question of establishment is defined more precisely than under the Data Protection Act 1984. The criteria adopted are that the controller satisfies one of the following criteria:

1. The controller is an individual who is ordinarily resident in the United Kingdom.

2. The controller is a body incorporated under United Kingdom law.

---

[63] Directive 95/46/EC. [64] *Data Protection: The Government's Proposals* (1997), para. 2.27.
[65] Directive 95/46/EC. [66] s. 5(1).

3. The controller is a partnership or unincorporated association subject to United Kingdom law.

4. The controller is a person maintaining an office, branch agency, or regular practice in the United Kingdom.[67]

For multinational companies, it is the case that they will be regarded as established in every country in which they operate. The geographical location of any data processing operation will not be relevant. A company established, for example, in France, Germany, and the United Kingdom will need to comply with the national laws of each of these states. The effect will be that the Information Commissioner would be obliged to assist any inquiries made by the German supervisory authority regarding processing relating to German citizens carried out in the United Kingdom and to apply German law in determining the legality of this processing. The Data Protection Act 1998 provides that an Order may be made by the Secretary of State relating to the manner in which these functions might be exercised.[68]

Conclusions

Given the expanded nature of some of its basic definitions, there is little doubt that the Data Protection Act 1998 governs a greater range of activities than was the case under the Data Protection Act 1984. In addition to legal changes, developments in technology, such as permitting the automatic identification of individuals whose images are captured on video camera or, indeed, car number-plates, will mean that many of these forms of surveillance will also be governed by the legislation. The scope of the legislation has begun to be examined by the courts. In *Bodil Lindqvist*,[69] the European Court adopted an expansive view of the scope of the legislation. In *Durant v Financial Services Authority*,[70] the Court of Appeal took a rather more restrictive approach. It may well be that further decisions of the European Court will be necessary in order to provide a comprehensive and consistent approach to the scope of the Data Protection Directive[71] across the EU Member States.

It is clearly the task of the courts to apply legislative provisions at issue before them. The courts have perhaps been ill-served by the legislature, which has promulgated laws that are rather imprecise. In *Campbell v MGN*,[72] Lord Phillips of Worth Matravers MR said:

> In interpreting the Act it is appropriate to look to the Directive [Data Protection Directive[73]] for assistance. The Act [Data Protection Act 1998] should, if possible, be interpreted in a manner that is consistent with the Directive. Furthermore, because the Act has, in large measure, adopted the wording of the Directive, it is not appropriate to look for the precision in the use of language that is usually to be expected from the parliamentary draftsman. A purposive approach to making sense of the provisions is called for.[74]

Even the most purposive form of interpretation cannot and should not provide an excuse for unfettered judicial decision-making. Beyond issues of ambiguity and lack of

---

[67] Data Protection Act 1998, s 5(3).

[68] s. 51(3). The Data Protection (Functions of Designated Authority) Order 2000, SI 2000/186, makes provisions for the Commissioner to cooperate with, and seek the cooperation of, other Member State supervisory authorities in such matters. This provision is discussed in more detail in Ch. 6.

[69] Case 101/01, [2004] QB 1014.   [70] [2003] EWCA Civ 1746.   [71] Directive 95/46/EC.

[72] [2002] EWCA Civ 1373, [2003] QB 633.   [73] Directive 95/46/EC.

[74] [2002] EWCA Civ 1373, [2003] QB 633 at [96].

precision in the drafting of the legislation, the Directive and the Act are to a considerable extent surviving dinosaurs from the age when computers were free-standing machines, used almost exclusively by businesses and large organisations but with limited networking capabilities. The world has moved on and, whilst the European Court was undoubtedly correct in determining that the development of a web page constituted processing as defined in the legislation, it is difficult to see that this, and a myriad of other pages maintained by individuals effectively by way of a hobby, constitute a sufficiently serious threat to the rights and freedoms of other individuals to justify the imposition of criminal sanctions. As will be discussed in Chapter 6, the legislation does not apply where processing is for social or domestic purposes. The problem, which arises also in the context of copyright infringement, is that what used to be clear-cut distinctions, not least in terms of the scale of activities possible, are no longer applicable. The old models are broken but the form of their replacements has yet to be resolved in a satisfactory manner.

4

Supervisory agencies

Introduction

The establishment of a dedicated supervisory agency has become a defining element of the European approach towards data protection. Much publicity continues to be given to the actions (or inactions) of supervisory agencies in respect of activities such as Google's collection of personal data in the course of its 'Street View' development activities. The Council of Europe data protection Convention made only minimal provision for the appointment of supervisory agencies. The data protection Directive is more expansive. It specifies in Recital 62 that the establishment of independent supervisory authorities is 'an essential component of the protection of individuals with regard to the processing of personal data', and requires under Article 28 that:

> Each Member State shall provide that one or more public authorities are responsible for monitoring the application within its territory of the provisions adopted by the Member States pursuant to this Directive. These authorities shall act with complete independence in exercising the functions entrusted to them.

In all bar one of the European Union States, a single agency has been established. The sole exception is in Germany which, because of the federal nature of its constitution, has around twenty supervisory agencies working in the field of data protection

In addition to national supervisory agencies, the Treaty of Amsterdam—which made significant changes to the treaties establishing the EU—provided that an independent supervisory agency was to be established in respect of the data processing activities of the European institutions. Acting on this, Regulation 45/2001 'on the protection of individuals with regard to the processing of personal data by the Community institutions and bodies and on the free movement of such data'[1] was adopted, entering into force at the end of January 2001. The Regulation provides for the appointment of a European Data Protection Supervisor[2] and contains provisions, equivalent in scope to those contained in the Data Protection and Electronic Communications Privacy Directives, which will apply to processing carried out by the European institutions. A further two years were to elapse before Decision 2004/55[3] announced the appointment of Peter Hustinx as the first Supervisor for a five-year term of office. Mr Hustinx's appointment was continued for a second term in 2009.[4]

Forms of supervisory agencies

Presupposing the existence of a supervisory agency, one of the key issues for law-makers concerns the form that this body should take. Many options are available but the key choice

---

[1] OJ 2001 L 8/1.   [2] Art. 1.   [3] OJ 2004 L 012/47.
[4] See <https://secure.edps.europa.eu/EDPSWEB/edps/EDPS>.

lies perhaps between the appointment of a single regulator, albeit supported by what may be a substantial staff, or vesting authority in a multi-membered commission or authority. The relative merits of single and multiple regulators have been ventilated in many other areas. A single regulator may be able to bring a more focused and consistent approach to regulation, although much will obviously depend upon the personality and abilities of the post holder. Experience within the United Kingdom would suggest that each Information Commissioner has brought his or her own approaches to the post. With a collegiate body there is more potential for internal dissent, but it is also likely that a wider range of interests and expertise may be represented, with the consequence that decisions, when reached, may carry greater weight.

In part, the choice of whether to appoint a single regulator or a commission is influenced by national traditions. Historically, the United Kingdom has favoured the appointment of a single official. Examples include the Information Commissioner, the Director General of Fair Trading, and the regulators for the privatised gas, electricity, and railway industries. More recently, however, the Communications Act 2003 provided for the establishment of the Office of Communications (OFCOM) as a multi-membered regulatory body to take over the functions of five individual regulators in the media and telecommunications sector. In 2008 the *Data Sharing Review*,[5] produced by the Information Commissioner and Dr Mark Walport, the Director of the Wellcome Trust, canvassed the notion that a multi-membered authority might be established. Posing the question whether existing institutional arrangements were the most appropriate, the report commented: 'We have come to the firm conclusion that it is not.'[6] It does not appear, however, that any legislative changes are likely to follow although speaking in 2008, the then Information Commissioner commented that:

> The post is perhaps somewhat anachronistic in some respects as a sole Commissioner. Most of the former Directors General in other areas of regulation were converted to Boards or Commissions some years ago. I would not wish to call myself a dinosaur—indeed there are others who are sole practitioners like myself, such as the Parliamentary Ombudsman—but I do recognise that we are perhaps an unusual species these days.[7]

The issue of the optimal form of supervisory agency was considered in some detail in the Leveson Report on Press Standards. Acting in the specific context of media activities it concluded:

> The evidence before the Inquiry suggested that the constitution of the ICO as a corporation sole may, in at least some of these dimensions, have risked its ability to discharge effectively its functions in relation to the press. Unresolved questions must remain, for example, as to whether:
>
> (a) the informal approach adopted by the ICO to its regulatory functions (partly a matter, perhaps, of presiding over a regime struggling for a profile, also possibly a matter of personal leadership style) has contributed to a reluctance to bring issues to a head through the use of regulatory powers, and has allowed inaction to be an unremarked default within its own structure;
>
> (b) the tendencies of Information Commissioners to see themselves as having a major, even dominant, outward-facing role with a political or campaigning dimension has been at the expense of their ability to provide clear, engaged, understood and

---

[5] Available from <http://www.connectingforhealth.nhs.uk/systemsandservices/infogov/links/datasharin-greview.pdf>. [6] para. 8.71.

[7] <http://www.ico.gov.uk/upload/documents/library/freedom_of_information/notices/cri_lecture_jan08.pdf>.

accountable leadership in the decisions made within their office, to the detriment of the quality of those decisions, and has posed some risk to the regulatory reputation of the ICO, including in relation to its quasi-judicial functions; and

(c) its current constitution leaves the ICO with insufficient strength to match major business sectors with power and influence, such as the press.

In large part, any changes to the nature of the Information Commissioner's role have been put on hold pending the adoption of the European data protection Regulation. The danger of 'regulatory capture' is one that has been widely recognised across a range of sectors and there is no doubt that any agency—whatever its composition—has to make choices whether to work with or in possible conflict with those it is seeking to regulate. The Leveson report recites evidence from the then Information Commisoner:

> **1.27** ... Mr Thomas recalled a conversation within the office around 2007 along the lines:

> *'Thank God we didn't take the journalists to court. They'd have gone all the way to Strasbourg.' In other words, they would have challenged any action we would have taken, we would have gone right to Strasbourg, the Court of Human Rights, Article 10 issues coming in. We'd seen all the material being thrown at us during What Price Privacy? and the Bill.'*

> **1.28** There was a gut instinct that litigation against the press would present the ICO with enormous difficulties. These were evidently perceived to be difficulties over and above the normal litigation issues of accessing and deploying evidence, navigating the law, and the overall strengths and weaknesses of the case.[8]

Key functions of supervisory agencies

In addition to requiring the establishment of an independent agency or agencies, the Data Protection Directive also prescribes the basic powers to be vested in these agencies. These agencies, it is provided, are to be afforded:

- investigative powers, such as powers of access to data forming the subject-matter of processing operations and powers to collect all the information necessary for the performance of its supervisory duties;

- effective powers of intervention, such as, for example, that of delivering opinions before processing operations are carried out, in accordance with Article 20, and ensuring appropriate publication of such opinions, of ordering the blocking, erasure, or destruction of data, of imposing a temporary or definitive ban on processing, of warning or admonishing the controller, or that of referring the matter to national parliaments or other political institutions;

- the power to engage in legal proceedings where the national provisions adopted pursuant to this Directive have been violated or to bring these violations to the attention of the judicial authorities.[9]

It is further provided that:

Each supervisory authority shall hear claims lodged by any person, or by an association representing that person, concerning the protection of his rights and freedoms in regard to the processing of personal data. The person concerned shall be informed of the outcome of the claim.[10]

---

[8] Lord Justice Leveson, *An Inquiry into the Culture, Practices and Ethics of the Press*, 4 vols. (London, 2012), III, Pt H.

[9] Art. 28(3).   [10] Art. 28(4).

The United Kingdom's implementation of these requirements continues to be a matter of controversy with the European Commission issuing a 'reasoned opinion'[11] in July 2010 alleging that a failure to grant the Information Commissioner adequate powers to audit compliance with the legislation meant that the country was in breach of its obligation to implement the Directive. To date, the issue remains unresolved.

The Information Commissioner and the Information Tribunal

Under the Data Protection Act 1984, the office of Data Protection Registrar was created. In addition to the Registrar, the Act provided for the establishment of a Data Protection Tribunal to hear appeals by data users (or computer bureaux) against decisions taken by the Registrar.

In 1996 the then Registrar, Elizabeth France, indicated concern that the title of Registrar placed undue emphasis on one (perceived as a rather bureaucratic) aspect of her role and suggested that with the introduction of a new Data Protection Act there should be a change in nomenclature so that the office should be described as Privacy Protection Commissioner. The United Kingdom government and legislature has traditionally been wary of making specific references to privacy—and still more to rights thereto. The notion of a Privacy Commissioner was rejected but the 1998 Act established the office of Data Protection Commissioner. With the enactment of the Freedom of Information Act 2000, the Commissioner also became responsible for the operation of that legislation. Recognising this fact, there has been a further change in the nomenclature to Information Commissioner.[12] At the same time, the Data Protection Tribunal was renamed as the Information Tribunal, reflecting additional responsibilities placed on it under the Freedom of Information Act.

The Data Protection Act 1998 specifies the terms and conditions under which the Commissioner is to be appointed. This is to be for a fixed term, not exceeding five years. Within this period, the Commissioner might be removed from office only following a resolution passed by both Houses of Parliament, a status equivalent to that of High Court judges. One change made from the 1984 Act is the provision that a Commissioner may only serve for two terms, save where special circumstances make a continuation of appointment 'desirable in the public interest'.[13] Under the 1984 Act, there was no limit on the number of terms which could be served. Concern has been expressed in the past that a government's role in deciding whether to continue an appointment might deter the supervisory agency from investigating public-sector data processing. Although the matter is not likely to be of significance in the near future, it might be considered unfortunate that the default has effectively been switched from the assumption that the Commissioner might continue in the post for more than two terms, to the assumption that this will not be the case.

Logistically, the Information Commissioner's Office is a substantial one. Separate offices, each headed by an Assistant Commissioner have been established for Scotland, Wales, and Northern Ireland. The Commissioner's annual report for 2013[14] indicated that 367 staff were employed although there is not a breakdown between staff responsible for data protection and those working in relation to the Freedom of Information Act. Inevitably, the

---

[11] Service of such a notice is potentially a precursor to the commencement of formal proceedings before the European Court of Justice.   [12] Introduced by s. 18 of the Freedom of Information Act 2000.

[13] Data Protection Act 1998, Sch. 5, para. 2.

[14] Available from <http://www.ico.org.uk/news/latest_news/2013/~/media/documents/library/corporate/research_and_reports/ico-annual-report-201213.ashx>.

operation of such a substantial organisation requires considerable resources and the 2013 report indicates expenditure of almost £21 million. The issue of how the supervisory agency's work should be funded has been at the core of many of the debates about the format of the legislation. Although the Data Protection Act 1998 makes provision for public funds to be used to meet the Commissioner's expenses, it has been the practice that the office should be largely self-financing. This decision drives many others concerning the scope of the Act and the obligations imposed upon data users. The only significant source of income for the Commissioner comes from the fees payable by data controllers in connection with the Act's notification procedures. In 2012–13 these raised some £16 million.[15] Clearly, maximisation of the numbers of those classed as data controllers will have a similar effect upon the income of the Commissioner, whilst any significant reduction in the numbers of those liable to register would have significant implications, either for the financial burdens imposed on those remaining subject to a registration requirement or for the Commissioner's income stream. This again has been a matter where changes have been made with the introduction from 2010 of a two-tier system of fees with larger users being required to pay significantly more by way of notification fees.

Initially, this chapter will focus on the establishment and maintenance of the Data Protection Register and the obligations imposed on data controllers to register details of their activities. Attention will then be paid to the investigative and enforcement powers conferred on the Commissioner, before concluding with an account of the remaining powers and duties imposed on the Commissioner.

Procedural requirements for data controllers

A feature of many of the early data protection statutes was the imposition of a system of licensing of data users. Although terminology in the field is somewhat inconsistent, the procedure might be analogised to the obtaining of a licence for the possession of a gun or the driving of a motor vehicle, with the onus being placed on the applicant to demonstrate fitness to receive the award. With the massive increase in the number of computers since the 1970s, the impossibility of exercising effective control in this manner has been widely recognised. An initial step, which was implemented in the Data Protection Act 1984, saw the introduction of a system of registration of data users. Registration continues to require those wishing to process personal data to seek authorisation and retains qualitative criteria, but switches the onus to the supervisory agency to indicate the cause of an application being rejected. In the fourteen years that the registration system operated, very few applications were formally refused. Thirty-two applications were refused in the year 1994–5, thirty-one in 1995–6, and none in subsequent years.[16] Even at the 'higher' levels, this translated into a refusal rate of one in every 2,650 applications.

From registration to notification

The effectiveness of the registration process adopted in the Data Protection Act 1984 was criticised from the outset. More recent statutes, such as the German Data Protection Act of 1990, moved away from the requirements of universal registration by exempting large

---

[15] Some £4.25 million was paid directly by government in respect of the Commissioner's activities under the Freedom of Information Act.

[16] *Fifteenth Report of the Data Protection Registrar* (1999), ch. 5.

numbers of data controllers from any procedural requirements. Even where users remain subject to a requirement to record details of their processing, systems of declaration or notification have been adopted. Notification, as the terminology suggests, involves the controller giving information about the nature of processing activities but does not give the supervisory agency any power of rejection—although concerns about the activities notified might serve to trigger further enforcement actions. The Data Protection Directive follows this model. It initially provides that:

> Member States shall provide that the controller or his representative, if any, must notify the supervisory agency...before carrying out [processing of personal data].[17]

Having established the principle of notification, the Data Protection Directive[18] continues to provide that simplification or exemption from notification may be offered:

> for categories of processing operations which are unlikely, taking account of the data to be processed, to affect adversely the rights and freedoms of data subjects.

This was subject to conditions being imposed on the kinds of data to be processed, the persons to whom it is to be disclosed, and the length of time the data are to be stored. A range of other possible exemptions are identified in the Directive, some of which are adopted in the Data Protection Act 1998.[19]

Implementing the Directive, the Data Protection Act 1998 imposes a general requirement to notify details of processing:

> Subject to the following provisions of this section, personal data must not be processed unless an entry in respect of the data controller is included in the Register maintained by the Commissioner.[20]

Exemptions from the requirement to notify

Under the Data Protection Act 1984, the list of categories of exempt processing was defined exhaustively in the statute.[21] The 1998 Act adopted a more flexible approach providing that:

> If it appears to the Secretary of State that processing of a particular description is unlikely to prejudice the rights and freedoms of data subjects, notification regulations may provide [for exemption from the requirement to notify].[22]

In initial consultation exercises concerning the extent of exemptions, the then Registrar advocated that extensive use should be made of this provision in order to exclude 'potentially hundreds of thousands of data controllers from notification'. Subsequently, this position changed, in large part because of perceived difficulties in defining the proper scope of any exemptions but perhaps mainly for financial reasons. The fees obtained from those submitting applications for notification constitute virtually the only source of income for the Commissioner. The Data Protection Act 1998 provides that, in fixing the level of fees, 'the Secretary of State shall have regard to the desirability of securing that the fees payable to the Commissioner are sufficient to offset the costs of running the Commissioner and Tribunal's statutory activities'.[23] A significant reduction in the level of those required

---

[17] Directive 95/46/EC, Art. 18(1).   [18] Directive 95/46/EC.   [19] Art. 18(2).
[20] s. 17(1).   [21] ss. 32 and 33.   [22] s. 17(3).
[23] s. 26(2). It was indicated in Parliament that the cumulative deficit on the Registrar's activities since 1986 is some £4.5 million. The Act further provides that account may be taken of the amount of any outstanding deficit when fixing fees. The Act contains a further provision allowing different levels of fees to be charged to different categories of controller (s. 26(1)).

to notify would inevitably increase the level of fees for those remaining subject to the requirement.

The scope of the exemptions

In the event, the Data Protection (Notification and Notification Fees) Regulations 2000[24] (the 'Notification Regulations') provide for a limited number of data controllers to be exempted from the notification requirement. The exemptions can be placed in two categories, the first relating to particular forms of processing and the second to specific categories of data controller. Especially in respect of the first category, it should be noted that whilst some forms of processing need not be notified, in the (likely) event that a controller engages in additional and notifiable forms of processing, a choice will be given, either to notify everything or to include an indication in the Register entry to the effect that:

> This data controller also processes personal data which is exempt from Notification.

The purpose of this is to put data subjects on notice that the entry on the Register will not give a complete picture of the controller's activities.

The Notification Regulations[25] provide for exemption in respect of three forms of processing, involving what has been referred to by the Commissioner as 'core business activities'.[26] It is stressed, however, that the conditions attached to the exemptions are likely to ensure that they will apply only to small businesses. In addition to the purpose-related exemptions, a further exemption applies in respect of certain forms of processing conducted by non-profit-making organisations.

Staff administration

Although the concept of staff administration sounds relatively broad, the scope of the exemption is much more narrowly circumscribed. The activity of staff administration is defined as involving the purposes of:

> Appointments or removals, pay, discipline, superannuation, work management or other personnel matters.[27]

Data held may relate to past, present, or potential employees, or to 'any person, the processing of whose personal data is necessary for the exempt purposes'. This latter category might include, for example, the processing of data relating to the partner of an employee who will be entitled to pension or other benefits in the event of the employee's death. The data may consist of names, addresses, and other identifiers, as well as information relating to:

(i) qualifications, work experience, or pay

(ii) other matters, the processing of which is necessary for the exempt purposes.

Two further requirements will also need to be satisfied for an exemption to be available. First, the data must not be disclosed to third parties, except with the consent of the data

---

[24] SI 2000/188.   [25] SI 2000/188.
[26] *Notification Exemptions: A Self Assessment Guide*, available from <http://www.dpr.gov.uk/notify/self/index.html>.   [27] SI 2000/188, Sch., para. 2.

subject, or where this is necessary for the exempt purposes. An example within the latter category would concern the transfer of data to HM Revenue & Customs for the purpose of operating the system of PAYE. Secondly, the data must not be retained for longer than is necessary for the exempt purposes. In most cases, this might be taken to mean that data may not be retained once an employee has left employment.[28]

The word 'necessary' has been quoted on several occasions in the previous paragraphs and is used extensively throughout the provisions relating to exemption. A *Concise Oxford Dictionary* definition of the adjective 'necessary' refers to concepts such as:

Unavoidable, indispensable, enforced, that which cannot be left out or done without.

The restrictions imposed by these definitions should be borne in mind when considering all of the exemptions. An employer might, quite reasonably, seek to maintain a record of employees' next of kin. This will be of obvious benefit (perhaps not least to the employee) in the event of an accident or illness occurring at work. It is more arguable, however, whether the holding of such data is essential for staff administration purposes.

Advertising, marketing, and public relations

This exemption applies when processing is:

For the purpose of advertising or marketing the data controller's business, activity, goods or services and promoting public relations in respect of that business or activity or those goods or services.[29]

Whilst the purpose is broad, the exemption is subject to limitations largely similar to those described in relation to the nature of the data that may be processed, the range of disclosure, and period of retention. The exemption applies only in respect of the marketing of the controller's own goods or services.

Accounts and records

This exemption is couched in terms very similar to those applying under the Data Protection Act 1984. Exemption is offered in respect of processing conducted:

for the purposes of keeping accounts relating to any business or other activity carried on by the data controller, or deciding whether to accept any person as a customer or supplier, or keeping records of purchases, sales or other transactions for the purpose of ensuring that the requisite payments and deliveries are made or services provided by or to the data controller in respect of those transactions, or for the purpose of making financial or management forecasts to assist him in the conduct of any such business or activity.[30]

Data must be limited to personal identifiers, together with information about the financial standing of the data subject and any other information necessary to conduct the exempt processing.

The exemption is somewhat broader than that previously provided for under the Data Protection Act 1984, but, once again, the requirement to show that data must necessarily be processed will constitute a significant limitation.

---

[28] SI 2000/188, Sch., para. 2(d).   [29] SI 2000/188, Sch., para. 3(a).
[30] SI 2000/188, Sch., para. 4(1)(a).

Non-profit-making organisations

Under the Data Protection Act 1984, exemption was offered in respect of the activities of 'unincorporated members clubs'. This proved to be a difficult concept to define and the Notification Regulations provide for exemption for non-profit-making organisations. The concept is undoubtedly broader than that applying under the 1984 Act but, as with the other exceptions discussed above, only a limited range of activities will be covered. Processing is exempt in so far as it:

(a) is carried out by a data controller which is a body or association which is not established or conducted for profit; and

(b) is for the purposes of establishing or maintaining membership of or support for the body or association, or providing or administering activities for individuals who are either members of the body or association or have regular contact with it.[31]

The data processed may relate only to limited categories of individuals, principally present, past, or prospective members of the organisation and be limited to identifiers, together with such information as is necessary for the purposes of the organisation, for example data relating to subscription records. In common with the other exemptions, the data may be disclosed to third parties only with the consent of the data subject or where this is necessary for the exempt purpose.

Independent data protection supervisors

Under the German data protection law, it is common practice for data controllers to appoint 'in-house' data protection supervisors. Provided that such supervisors possess sufficient independence, this will exempt the controller from the requirement to notify the Federal Data Protection Commissioner. The Data Protection Directive also sanctions the adoption of such an approach,[32] and the Data Protection Act 1998 provides that the Secretary of State may make an order enabling controllers to appoint a data protection supervisor who will 'monitor in an independent manner the data controller's compliance' with the legislation. Any order will also specify the extent to which such action will exempt the controller from the notification requirement.[33]

In debate on this provision, the United Kingdom government pointed out that when such an option had been outlined in the consultation exercise preceding the introduction of the legislation, it had received some expressions of interest but little active support. It was indicated that, given the workload involved in implementing the new legislation, the making of any enabling regulations would not be seen as a priority issue.[34] Sixteen years later, we await any enabling regulations. In a paper published in 2007, *Sharing Personal Information—A New Approach*, the Information Commissioner's Office indicated that a code of practice would be developed which would make provision for in-house data protection supervisors.[35] A draft code was published in August 2007 which made no reference to this possibility.[36] Quite apart from the notification aspect, it does appear that the

---

[31] SI 2000/188, Sch., para. 5.   [32] Directive 95/46/EC, Art. 18(2).   [33] s. 23.
[34] HC Official Report, SC D (Data Protection Bill), cols. 165–6, 19 May 1998.
[35] <http://www.ico.gov.uk/upload/documents/library/data_protection/detailed_specialist_guides/pinfo-framework.pdf>.
[36] <http://www.ico.gov.uk/upload/documents/library/data_protection/practical_application/ico_information_sharing_framework_draft_1008.pdf>.

appointment of internal data protection supervisors might be a practical way of providing reassurance to the public that data protection interests will be taken fully into account in the development of data sharing.

Information to be supplied on notification

The Data Protection Act 1998 specifies the information which must be supplied to the Commissioner.[37] Referred to as the 'registrable particulars', this encompasses:

- the controller's name and address together with that of any nominated representative;
- a description of the personal data to be processed and the categories of data subject to whom it relates;
- a description of the purposes for which the data will be processed;
- a description of the intended recipients or categories of recipient of the data;
- in the event any additional processing is being carried out under the terms of an exemption from the notification requirement, a statement to this effect; and
- details of any countries outside the EEA to which it is intended that the data may be transferred. Controllers have the option either of specifying particular countries or indicating that 'worldwide' transfers are envisaged.[38]

The above information will be made publicly available in the form of the Data Protection Register.

In addition to the information which will appear on the Register, controllers are required to provide:

a general description of measures to be taken for the purpose of complying with the seventh data protection principle.[39]

The seventh principle relates to the requirement to maintain appropriate data security measures. The Commissioner has identified four matters which need to be addressed:

- a statement of information security policy
- control of physical security (restrictions on access to sites and equipment)
- controls on access to information (anti-hacking measures such as the use of passwords and encryption)
- a business continuity plan (disaster recovery).

Specific reference to and endorsement of is made to BS 7799, the British Standard on Information Security Management, and to the certification scheme 'c:cure' associated with it.[40] It should be stressed that this information—which might be of use to potential hackers—will not appear on the publicly accessible register.

---

[37] s. 16(1).

[38] Notification Handbook, available from <http://ico.org.uk/for_organisations/guidance_index/~/media/documents/library/Data_Protection/Detailed_specialist_guides/notification_handbook_final.ashx>.

[39] s. 18(2)(b).

[40] Data Protection Commissioner, *Notification Handbook* (London, 2000), para. 3.2.3, available from <http://www.ico.gov.uk/upload/documents/library/data_protection/detailed_specialist_guides/notification_handbook_final.pdf>.

Preliminary assessments

In most cases, once notification of processing is submitted, processing operations may commence. Certain forms of processing may, however, be subject to additional controls. The Data Protection Directive obliges Member States to:

> Determine the processing operations likely to present specific risks to the rights and freedoms of data subjects and shall check that these processing operations are examined prior to the start thereof.[41]

As implemented in the Data Protection Act 1998, regulatory power is conferred on the Secretary of State to determine categories of processing, referred to as 'assessable processing', which appear particularly likely:

(a) to cause substantial damage or substantial distress to data subjects, or

(b) otherwise significantly to prejudice the rights and freedoms of data subjects.[42]

To date, no order has been made specifying the form of processing which will be subject to preliminary assessment. It has been indicated that few forms of processing will be covered by such regulations. In Parliament, specific reference was made to activities involving data matching, genetic data, and private investigations.[43]

Where processing comes within the ambit of such regulations, the controller may not commence activities until an assessment of its compliance with the data protection principles has been made by the Commissioner. The timetable for the Commissioner to act is a tight one. When receiving notification from any data controller, the Commissioner is to consider whether any of the processing activities described involve assessable processing[44] and, if so, whether the processing is likely to comply with the requirements of the statute. Such notice is to be given within ten days from receipt of the notification. The Commissioner is then required to give notice of his or her opinion to the controller within twenty-eight days from the date of receipt of notification, which period might, in special circumstances, be extended by a further fourteen days.[45] Processing must not be carried on during this period. In the event the Commissioner's assessment is that the processing would be unacceptable, there would not appear to be any mechanism to prevent the controller continuing with the plans, although it might be expected that an enforcement notice would be served in short order should this occur.

The Data Protection Register

The Data Protection Act requires the Commissioner to:

(a) provide facilities for making the information contained in the entries in the Register available for inspection (in visible and legible form) by members of the public at all reasonable hours and free of charge and

(b) provide such other facilities for making the information contained in those entries available to the public free of charge as he considers appropriate.

---

[41] Directive 95/46/EC, Art. 20.   [42] s. 22(1).

[43] HC Official Report, SC D (Data Protection Bill), cols. 160–1, 19 May 1998.

[44] Data Protection Act 1998, s. 18(2).   [45] s. 18(3).

Continuing the practice established under the 1984 Act, the Register can be accessed over the Internet.[46]

It is unclear, however, how valuable the information contained on the Register may be to the average data subject. The Register currently holds some 370,000 entries.[47] In one respect, the size of the Register makes browsing a daunting task for data subjects. The Register can only be searched by reference to the name of a data controller or a registration number. Unless a subject knows that an organisation is likely to hold information about them, the Register will be of very little assistance in a quest to discover who might hold personal information. If a data subject knows of an organisation there may be little need to consult the Register, other perhaps than to confirm contact details for making a request for a copy of the information held.

Although the figure of 370,000 entries may seem large, it is perhaps the case that after more than twenty years of data protection legislation, many data controllers have failed to comply with the notification requirements. On a point of comparison, Jersey which has a population of around 87,000 and a data protection law almost identical to that applying in the United Kingdom has around 3,500 entries on its Data Protection Register. A similar ratio of entries to population would give the United Kingdom a register with almost 2.5 million entries. It is relevant to note that the heavy dependence of Jersey's economy on the financial services sector, with its voracious appetite for personal data, may result in a proportionately higher number of data controllers; nonetheless, it does appear that non-notification is a fact of data protection life in the United Kingdom. As indicated, failure to notify does constitute a criminal offence although very few prosecutions have been brought on this basis. In April 2013 an estate agent was convicted of this offence and fined £300 (the maximum penalty for the offence is a fine of £5,000). This followed a campaign by the Information Commissioner's office to increase the number of agents registering under the Act and three separate individual contacts with the particular individual.[48]

Enforcement of the legislation

Having established a Register of those processing personal data, the ongoing task for the supervisory agency is to seek to ensure that controllers remain within the scope of their entries on the Register and that in general, processing complies with the substantive requirements of the legislation. The nature of these requirements, principally in the form of the data protection principles, will be considered in Chapter 5. Failures on the part of controllers may constitute an offence and will also expose them to a range of sanctions made available to the Commissioner.

Powers of entry and inspection

Section 50 of and Schedule 9 to the Data Protection Act 1998 provide that the Commissioner may approach a circuit judge (or in Scotland, a sheriff) seeking a warrant to enter and search any premises. The warrant will be granted if the judge is satisfied that a data controller is in breach of one or more of the principles or has committed an offence under the

---

[46] <http://www.ico.gov.uk/ESDWebPages/search.asp>.

[47] <http://www.ico.org.uk/what_we_cover/register_of_data_controllers>.

[48] <http://www.ico.org.uk/news/latest_news/2013/ico-praises-estate-agents-commitment-to-data-protection-as-rogue-company-boss-prosecuted-08042013>.

Act, and that evidence to that effect is to be found at the address specified. The warrant will empower the Commissioner or his or her staff to:

> Inspect, examine, operate and test any equipment found there which is intended to be used for the processing of personal data and to inspect or seize any document or other material found there.[49]

Procedures for the award of the warrant are similar to those found in the Data Protection Act 1984, although one significant loophole has been closed. Under the earlier Act, if the Registrar had sought entry to premises and had been granted admission only for the occupier to refuse to cooperate further with inquiries, it was not subsequently possible in England to obtain a search warrant. The Data Protection Act 1998 now provides that a warrant may be sought in the situation where:

> Although entry to the premises was granted, the occupier unreasonably refused to comply with a request by the Commissioner or any of the Commissioner's officers or staff to [perform any of the acts which might be permitted in the execution of a search warrant].[50]

Apart from delaying action, there will be little benefit to a data controller in exercising evasionary tactics of the kind identified.

Information notices

Although the Data Protection Act 1984 empowered the Registrar to seek and execute search warrants in the event a breach of the principles was suspected,[51] that statute conferred no general investigative power and placed data users under no obligation to cooperate with any inquiries made by the Registrar. The Data Protection Act 1998 stops short of providing a general investigative power, but confers a new power on the Commissioner to serve an 'information notice', requiring the supply within a specified time of specified information relating to the matter under investigation.[52] An appeal against service of an information notice will lie to the Information Tribunal and, save in exceptional circumstances, this act will suspend the operation of the notice.[53] Failure to comply with an information notice will constitute an offence, as will the reckless or intentional provision of false information in response to an information notice.[54]

An information notice may be served either on the Commissioner's own initiative, when he or she considers that information is reasonably required in order to determine 'whether the data controller has complied or is complying with the data protection principles',[55] or following a complaint from a data subject. In this latter respect, the Data Protection Act 1998 provides that any person may contact the Commissioner seeking an assessment whether it is likely that personal data has been or is being processed lawfully.[56] The Commissioner is obliged to consider the request and determine an appropriate response taking into account, inter alia, whether the data subject could have obtained the information by means of a request for subject access.[57]

Although the information notice does constitute a new weapon in the Commissioner's armoury, it may be queried as to how useful the power will be in practice. The notice may be served when the Commissioner reasonably requires information to determine whether the principles are being observed, rather than the requirement for service of an enforcement notice that the Commissioner be satisfied that a breach has occurred.

---

[49] Sch. 9, para. 1(3).   [50] Sch. 9, para. 2(1)(b)(ii).   [51] s. 16.   [52] s. 43(1).
[53] s. 43(4)–(5).   [54] s. 47.   [55] s. 43(1).   [56] s. 42(1).   [57] s. 42(7).

Beyond this, however, the appeal procedures are identical. Whilst it may be expected that many controllers will be happy to respond to an information notice in order to clarify what might be a misunderstanding of the nature of their processing activities, the possibility for appeals may persuade less-scrupulous controllers to prevaricate in their response. Even if the Information Tribunal ultimately upholds the information notice and the Commissioner obtains information indicating that a breach of the principles has occurred, no action can be taken until an enforcement notice, with its own appeal procedures, has been served.

Enforcement notices

The Data Protection Act 1998 retains the 1984 Act's concept of enforcement notices.[58] Under these, the Commissioner may serve notice on data controllers where he or she is satisfied that a breach of one or more of the data protection principles has occurred. The notice will identify the act or omission complained of and specify the steps that require to be taken to put matters right. Failure to comply with an enforcement notice constitutes an offence.[59] As with all other forms of notice served by the Commissioner, the recipient data controller may appeal to the Information Tribunal. Save in exceptional circumstances, the lodging of an appeal will suspend the operation of the notice.

Experience under the Data Protection Act 1984 indicated that a period of years might elapse between the initial moves to serve an enforcement notice and the completion of appeal proceedings. To date, there has been no appeal from a Tribunal decision to the courts, a step which would extend the length of the process even further. Little can be done to speed up the process itself, but one of the problems identified under the previous regime was that the passage of time might render all or part of the terms of an enforcement notice of dubious relevance. The Data Protection Act 1998 establishes a more flexible approach, providing that the Commissioner may, if he or she considers that all of its provisions need not be complied with in order to ensure compliance with the principles, vary or cancel an enforcement notice.[60] The recipient controller may also make a written request to the Commissioner for variation or cancellation on the ground that a change of circumstances means that compliance with its terms is not necessary to secure compliance with the principles.[61] In order to avoid the possibility of a double appeal, such a request may only be made after the time available for submitting an appeal to the Tribunal has elapsed.

Undertakings

Although the concept does not have any statutory recognition, the Commissioner has placed considerable reliance upon obtaining formal undertakings from organisations whose processing activities it is considered might contravene the data protection legislation.

Audits

Linked in many respects to the making of assessments of processing is the concept that the Information Commissioner should be able to conduct an audit of an organisation's processing activities. Under the present legislation, as was stated earlier, the Commissioner may act only with the consent of the controller or where there is evidence of breach sufficient

---

[58] s. 40.   [59] s. 47.   [60] s. 41(1).   [61] s. 41(2).

to justify service of an information notice. It is perhaps doubtful whether this approach complies with the provisions of the Data Protection Directive, which requires that national supervisory agencies be granted:

> investigative powers such as powers of access to data forming the subject-matter of processing operations and powers to collect all the information necessary for the performance of its supervisory duties.[62]

For a number of years, successive Commissioners have lobbied to be granted audit powers. In evidence before the House of Commons Justice Committee in December 2007,[63] the Commissioner lamented what he described as a 'bizarre situation' where, unlike almost all other national data protection authorities and, indeed, many other United Kingdom regulatory authorities such as those concerned with health and safety and the financial services sector, the Information Commissioner had no general power of audit.

Some developments have taken place in the aftermath of the loss of child benefit data, with the Prime Minister announcing that the Information Commissioner would be enabled to perform spot checks on public-sector controllers. This was sanctioned as a matter of administrative direction rather than as a legal requirement, but more general audit powers were conferred on the Commissioner by section 173 of the Coroners and Justice Act 2009. This adds a new section 41A to the Data Protection Act and provides that the Commissioner may conduct an audit of public-sector data controllers following service of an 'assessment notice' requiring the recipient to facilitate access by the Commissioner's staff to specified premises to inspect any documents held there and to observe data processing activities. The procedures relating to service of a notice and the conduct of an audit are laid down in a code of practice[64] published by the Commissioner in July 2010. The Commissioner still does not, however, have any specific audit powers in respect of private-sector data controllers, except in respect of activities in the electronic communications sector which fall under the auspices of the Privacy and Electronic Communications Regulations 2011.[65] The Data Protection Act does provide however in section 51(7) that the Commissioner may, with the consent of the relevant data controller conduct an assessment of processing 'for the following of good practice and shall inform the data controller of the results of the assessment'. Some effort has been put into conducting consensual audits of private-sector processing. The Commissioner's annual report for 2013 notes that:

> During the year we conducted 58 audits of data controllers, a 38% increase on last year. In line with ICO priority areas these have included a significant number of local authorities and criminal justice organisations such as police forces and probation trusts. We also followed up on 35 completed audits to ensure that recommendations made have been implemented, a 66% increase on the number conducted last year.
>
> We completed the first full year of our advisory visit programme, aimed at assisting and educating smaller organisations such as charitable and voluntary sector services. We undertook 78 advisory visits which is a 30% increase on the originally projected numbers.[66]

---

[62] Art. 28.

[63] *Protection of Personal Data*, First Report of Session 2007–8, 17 December 2007.

[64] Available from <http://www.ico.gov.uk/upload/documents/library/corporate/detailed_specialist_guides/assessment_notices_code_of_practice.pdf>.

[65] SI 2011 No. 1208. These regulations are discussed in more detail in Ch. 7.   [66] p. 16

Monetary penalties

A criticism that might be made against all of the Commissioner's powers described in this chapter is that they might amount to little more than an admonishment to 'go away and sin no more'. Certainly service of an enforcement notice or the publicity associated with a requirement on a senior manager in a company to proffer a formal undertaking to improve processing standards might have damaging consequences but the Information Commissioner's powers had been contrasted unfavourably with those available to other supervisory agencies. Contrast was particularly made with the powers of the Financial Services Authority (perhaps wrongly in the light of recent developments in that sector). In June 2010, for example, the Nationwide Building Society was fined almost £1 million for failing to maintain adequate security measures in respect of personal data. The case originated with reports of the theft of a laptop from the home of a member of staff. Perhaps the most expensive laptop computer in history!

The Data Protection (Monetary Penalties) Order 2010 gives the Information Commissioner power for the first time to impose financial penalties upon data controllers. The maximum amount of the penalty is £500,000. This is certainly significantly lower than the amounts imposed by the Financial Services Authority although many of the cases of data misuse investigated by the Information Commissioner have concerned public-sector organisations and it may be queried what useful purpose is served by imposing a penalty (the proceeds of which will go to the government) on an organisation within the public sector. The figures involved continue to be substantial with the Commissioner's 2013 report indicating that penalties of £2.6 million were imposed on twenty-three organisations who were found to have committed serious breaches of the Data Protection Act and Privacy and Electronic Communications Regulations. The majority of the penalties have related to breaches of the requirement to keep data securely but one penalty was imposed in 2013 on the Prudential Insurance Company in respect of its unfair processing. As the Commissioner's 2013 report notes:

> Prudential was issued with a penalty of £50,000 after consistently mixing up two customers' accounts, resulting in tens of thousands of pounds ending up in the wrong account.[67]

General duties of the Information Commissioner

Disseminating information

The remaining powers of the Commissioner follow in large part those established under the Data Protection Act 1984. The Commissioner is to disseminate information giving guidance about good practice under the Data Protection Act 1998.[68] Good practice is defined as:

> Such practice in the processing of personal data as appears to the Commissioner to be desirable having regard to the interests of data subjects and others and includes (but is not limited to) compliance with the requirements of this Act.[69]

Under the 1984 Act, a wide range of material was published, perhaps most notably the series of Guidelines giving information about the Registrar's interpretation of the legislation. Members of the Registrar's office were also frequent speakers at conferences. It is likely

---

[67] p. 32.   [68] s. 51(1).   [69] s. 51(9).

that these activities will continue. The 1998 Act does give a new power to the Commissioner to levy fees for any matters concerned with the exercise of her powers.[70] It was indicated in Parliament that income from publications and presentations might account for 10 per cent of the Commissioner's income.[71]

Codes of practice

Provision relating to codes of practice was inserted into the Data Protection Act 1984 at a late stage during its parliamentary passage by a somewhat reluctant government, which pointed to the nebulous legal status of these documents. Under the 1984 regime, the Registrar's role is limited to encouraging 'trade associations or other bodies' to prepare and disseminate codes of practice.[72] The decision of the Data Protection Tribunal in the case of *Innovations (Mail Order) Ltd v Data Protection Registrar*[73] lends support to this view. Here, the Tribunal held that the appellant was in breach of the data protection principle relating to the fair obtaining of data, even though its conduct complied with a relevant industry code of practice.

In spite of doubts concerning their legal status, a considerable number of codes were adopted under the Data Protection Act 1984. The Data Protection Directive also envisages a substantial role for both national and Community codes, providing that:

1. The Member States and the Commission shall encourage the drawing up of codes of conduct intended to contribute to the proper implementation of the national provisions adopted by the Member States pursuant to this Directive, taking account of the specific features of the various sectors.

2. Member States shall make provision for trade associations and other bodies representing other categories of controllers which have drawn up draft national codes or which have the intention of amending or extending existing national codes to be able to submit them to the opinion of the national authority.

3. Member States shall make provision for this authority to ascertain, among other things, whether the drafts submitted to it are in accordance with the national provisions adopted pursuant to this directive. If it sees fit, the authority shall seek the views of data subjects or their representatives.

4. Draft Community codes, and amendments or extensions to existing Community codes, may be submitted to the Working Party referred to in Article 29. This Working Party shall determine, among other things, whether the drafts submitted to it are in accordance with the national provisions adopted pursuant to this Directive. If it sees fit, the authority shall seek the views of data subjects or their representatives. The Commission may ensure appropriate publicity for the codes which have been approved by the Working Party.[74]

The major novelty for the United Kingdom is the provision in the Directive that supervisory agencies should take a view on the conformity of a draft code with statutory requirements. This is coming close to giving an unelected agency law-making powers—a practice which has been traditionally resisted in the United Kingdom.

The Data Protection Act 1998 establishes two roles for the Commissioner in respect of codes of practice. Acting either on his or her own initiative or under the direction of the

---

[70] s. 51(8).   [71] HC Official Report, SC D (Data Protection Bill), col. 253, 2 June 1998.
[72] s. 36(4).   [73] Case DA/92 31/49/1.   [74] Directive 95/46/EC, Art. 27.

Secretary of State, and after consulting with relevant trade associations and representatives of data subjects, the Commissioner may 'prepare and disseminate codes of practice for guidance as to good practice'.[75] Any code of practice prepared following directions from the Secretary of State is to be laid before Parliament, either in its own right or as part of another report by the Commissioner to Parliament.[76]

As with the procedure under the Data Protection Act 1984, the Commissioner is also under a duty to encourage the adoption and dissemination of codes by relevant trade associations. Additionally, however, it is provided that:

> where any trade association submits a code of practice to him for his consideration, consider the code and, after such consultation with data subjects or persons representing data subjects as appears to him to be appropriate, notify the trade association whether in his opinion the code promotes the following of good practice.[77]

In many respects, this provision formalises practice under the 1984 Act, where many of the codes adopted contain a foreword from the Registrar indicating her views on the appropriateness of the code.

International cooperation

As was the case under the Data Protection Act 1984, the Commissioner is the United Kingdom agency responsible for liaison with other data protection agencies under the auspices of the Council of Europe Convention.[78] The Commissioner is also responsible for working with the various Committees and Working Parties established at EU level[79] by the Data Protection Directive.[80] Such bodies have a particularly important role to play in determining whether third countries provide an adequate level of protection for personal data. The Commissioner is charged with the duty of disseminating information about any such findings and seeking to implement these within the United Kingdom.[81]

The Data Protection Directive[82] also contains provisions requiring national supervisory agencies to cooperate with each other. In particular, '[e]ach authority may be requested to exercise its powers by an authority of another Member State'. The Data Protection Act 1998 provides that the Secretary of State may make an order relating to such tasks and specifying, in particular, the approach to be taken when a request for assistance relates to processing which is exempt under the United Kingdom legislation but is included in the national law of the requesting state.[83] The Data Protection (International Co-operation) Order 2000[84] makes appropriate provision. Article 5 applies in the situation where processing is taking place in the United Kingdom but where the provisions of section 5 would normally exclude jurisdiction—principally where the controller is not established in the United Kingdom. Where the processing is subject to the jurisdiction of a supervisory authority from another Member State, the Commissioner may, in responding to a request for assistance from that authority, act as if the processing were subject to the 1998 Act. Article 6 of the Order provides that the Commissioner may make a similar request for assistance to another supervisory authority in respect of processing subject to United Kingdom jurisdiction which is being carried out in another Member State.

---

[75] s. 51(3).   [76] s. 52(3).   [77] Data Protection Act 1998, s. 51(4)(b).
[78] The Data Protection (Functions of Designated Authority) Order 2000, SI 2000/186.
[79] Data Protection Act 1998, s. 54(1).   [80] Directive 95/46/EC.
[81] Data Protection Act 1998, s. 51(6).   [82] Directive 95/46/EC.   [83] s. 54(2).
[84] SI 2000/190.

Professional secrecy

In addition to providing that powers be conferred on supervisory agencies, the Data Protection Directive also requires that:

> Member States shall provide that members and staff of the supervisory authority, even after their employment has ended, are to be subject to a duty of professional secrecy with regard to confidential information to which they have access.[85]

The Data Protection Act 1998's interpretation of this provision was the cause of a degree of controversy, and, indeed, was criticised by the then Commissioner as likely to impede the effective performance of her duties. It is provided that an offence will be committed where information obtained in the course of employment and relating to an 'identified or identifiable individuals or business' is disclosed by past or present Commissioners or members of staff without lawful authority.[86] The term 'lawful authority' is defined as requiring the consent of the individual or the availability of statutory authority, necessity for the performance of functions under the Act, compliance with Community obligations, or in the course of legal proceedings. Finally, and most significantly, it is provided that 'having regard to the rights and freedoms or legitimate interests of any person, the disclosure is necessary in the public interest'.[87]

Although it is clearly reasonable that confidential information relating to a data controller should not be disclosed, the effect of this provision might be, for example, to prevent the Commissioner from publicising the fact that data controllers have been served with enforcement notices. It was indicated in Parliament that the government has 'found it difficult to get the provision right' and that the issue might be revisited in the context of freedom of information legislation.[88] The format finally adopted is less restrictive than that originally proposed, which would have empowered disclosure only when 'necessary for reasons of substantial public interest', but it remains unclear how extensively it might be interpreted. One possible compromise was suggested in Parliament, that notification regulations may require controllers to include information regarding enforcement notices (or other notices) as part of their entry on the Register.[89]

Appellate Bodies

As originally established, the Information Tribunal was a dedicated body responsible for hearing appeals under the Data Protection and Freedom of Information Acts. It now serves as a division, on Information Rights, of the general Regulatory Chamber. The Tribunal's membership consists of a Chairman and a number of Deputy Chairmen.[90] These appointees are to be barristers, advocates, or solicitors of at least seven years' standing.[91] Additionally, a number of other members may be appointed by the Secretary of State representing the interests of data users and of data subjects.[92] A panel of three members will be convened to hear particular appeals.

Under the Data Protection Act 1984, the Tribunal's sole function was to hear appeals brought by data users (or computer bureaux) against decisions by the Registrar adverse to

---

[85] Directive 95/46/EC, Art. 28(7).   [86] s. 59(1).   [87] s. 59(2).

[88] 316 HC Official Report (6th series), cols. 603–4, 2 July 1998.

[89] 316 HC Official Report (6th series), col. 602, 2 July 1998.

[90] The number of deputy chairmen is to be determined at the discretion of the Lord Chancellor.

[91] s. 3(4).   [92] s. 3(5).

their interests. The only notable change introduced by the Data Protection Act 1998 is that in very limited cases concerned with the application of the exemption for data processed for national security purposes, a data subject will, for the first time, have the right to bring a case before the Tribunal.[93] The procedures to be followed before the Tribunal are specified in detail in the Data Protection Tribunal (Enforcement Appeals) Rules 2000.[94] More specialised rules are prescribed for proceedings involving national security. Here, the provisions of the Data Protection Tribunal (National Security Appeals) Rules 2000[95] will apply. The Tribunal may uphold the Registrar's original ruling, reverse it, or, where the Registrar's act involves the exercise of a discretion, substitute its own ruling.[96] First-tier decisions may be appealed on a point of law to the Upper Tribunal and, with consent to the Court of Appeal (or Court of Session).[97]

Other supervisory agencies

Although not part of the formal data protection structure, brief reference should be made to the fact that many data controllers may be subject to other forms of regulation and that a failure to comply with data protection requirements may result in sanctions being imposed by these regulators. Perhaps the best example can be taken from the financial services regulator where the responsible regulator, the Financial Services Authority, has imposed very substantial penalties on organisations in respect of security breaches. In 2007 a fine of £1.26 million was imposed on the insurance company Norwich Union Life for a failure to maintain adequate security in respect of customers' personal data. As the Financial Services (now the Financial Conduct) Authority's press release stated, weaknesses in Norwich Union's systems allowed fraudsters to access the data and commit instances of identity fraud. In addition to accessing confidential data, the criminals were also able to request the surrender of seventy-four insurance policies and receive payments totalling some £3.3 million. Previously, a fine of almost £1 million was imposed on the Nationwide Building Society following the loss of personal data as a consequence of the theft of a laptop computer from a Nationwide employee's home.

Although the penalties might not be as substantial, it might be expected that other regulators such as those in the medical and legal fields would adopt a similar approach in respect of unduly lax data processing practices.

Conclusions

We live in interesting data protection times. And the role of supervisory agencies has become contentious. It is perhaps significant how extensive were the data protection considerations in the report of the Leveson Inquiry and, indeed, how trenchant were some of the criticisms made of the current United Kingdom regime. Certainly the model of a single Commissioner places great reliance on the individual appointed but as important is the level of resources available to the agency. In an era of austerity, this is always likely to be a difficult issue but the almost total reliance for income on fees from a largely discredited notification regime must be a cause for concern. It may be appropriate to conclude this chapter with a personal anecdote which does, however, indicate some of the resource problems. I submitted a data protection subject access request to my local council. As will

---

[93] s. 28.   [94] SI 2000/189.   [95] SI 2000/206.   [96] s. 14(3)–(4).   [97] s. 14(5).

be described in Chapter 6, access requests are by law to be complied with within forty days. Forty days came and went and then a reply from the Council. The schools are on holiday and we can't access data until they get back. A bit, perhaps very, strange. I may have missed something, but don't think any exemption exists from the forty-day period relating to councils responding to access requests refers to school holidays.

I pointed this out and received no response. The Information Commissioner has an online form allowing data subjects to make complaints. I submitted and received an automated reply on 13 August indicating that someone would get in touch with me. A month later and still no response from the council. Perhaps, I thought hopefully, a phone call to the Information Commissioner. One of the phone numbers given in their email did not work. A second one did, and I spoke to a very pleasant person who confirmed that my complaint had been received, but that the office was busy and had to deal with complaints in the order they were received. At that time (13 September) they were starting to deal with complaints received at the beginning of August. It would take another fortnight before my submission was read.

At one level it concerns me that a major local authority should feel that they can ignore the legislation although this does not appear to be an isolated incident. My main concern is different. Data controllers, as I have said, are supposed to respond to access requests within forty days. At a relatively rough calculation, the Information Commissioner's Office is taking sixty days to read complaints, even before possibly taking any action on them. As the old saying goes, 'Quis custodiet ipsos custodes?' Who will guard the guardians?

5

The data protection principles

Introduction

Whilst we have seen significant changes in procedural aspects of data protection over the past thirty years, the formulation of general statements of acceptable processing practice has been a feature of data protection legislation from the earliest days—although the precise number of principles has been a variable commodity. Article 6 of the Data Protection Directive prescribes five 'principles relating to data quality', requiring Member States to ensure that personal data is:

(a) processed fairly and lawfully;

(b) collected for specified, explicit and legitimate purposes and not further processed in a way incompatible with those purposes;

(c) adequate, relevant and not excessive in relation to the purposes for which they are collected and/or further processed;

(d) accurate and where necessary, kept up to date; every reasonable step must be taken to ensure that data which are inaccurate or incomplete, having regard to the purposes for which they were collected or for which they are further processed, are erased or rectified; and

(e) kept in a form which permits identification of data subjects for no longer than is necessary for the purposes for which the data were collected or for which they are further processed.

Adding a degree of inflation, the Data Protection Act 1998 provides a set of eight data protection principles with Schedule 1 requiring that:

1. Personal data shall be processed fairly and lawfully and, in particular, shall not be processed unless—

   (a) at least one of the conditions in Schedule 2 is met; and

   (b) in the case of sensitive personal data, at least one of the conditions in Schedule 3 is also met.

2. Personal data shall be obtained only for one or more specified and lawful purposes, and shall not be further processed in any manner incompatible with that purpose or those purposes.

3. Personal data shall be adequate, relevant and not excessive in relation to the purpose or purposes for which they are processed.

4. Personal data shall be accurate and, where necessary, kept up to date.

5. Personal data processed for any purpose or purposes shall not be kept for longer than is necessary for that purpose or those purposes.

6. Personal data shall be processed in accordance with the rights of data subjects under this Act.

7. Appropriate technical and organisational measures shall be taken against unauthorised or unlawful processing of personal data and against accidental loss or destruction of, or damage to, personal data.

8. Personal data shall not be transferred to a country or territory outside the European Economic Area unless that country or territory ensures an adequate level of protection for the rights and freedoms of data subjects in relation to the processing of personal data.[1]

The scope of the United Kingdom principles is broader than those adopted under Article 6 but the additional topics covered, namely the rights of data subjects, the maintenance of adequate security, and controls over transborder data flows, are dealt with elsewhere in the Directive. On this occasion differences in terminology do not appear to indicate any distinctions of substance.

The data protection principles span the whole continuum of data processing, from the stage when data is first acquired, perhaps using pen and paper, to the time when it is permanently and irretrievably destroyed. A formula frequently used to justify data protection legislation is to the effect that there should be no processing whose very existence is a secret. More expansively, the principles seek to ensure that data subjects are aware who processes data about them and for what purposes; they should feel confident that it will be kept in secure conditions and that they will be able to verify the accuracy and relevance of the data held.

As with all general statements, almost all of the principles require expansion in the context of particular forms of activity. Detailed guidance concerning the application of the principles can be taken from a variety of sources. No fewer than four Schedules to the Data Protection Act 1998 expand upon the interpretation of the principles. This has prompted an expression of concern from the Commission as possibly restricting the scope of the provisions beyond the level required by the Directive.[2] Provisions in the body of the statute make additional provisions, often in the form of providing exceptions from or restrictions to their applications giving priority to other interests, for example, the prevention or detection of crime. As with other statutes, further guidance on issues of interpretation come from decisions of the courts and the Information Tribunal. Finally, a significant role is envisaged for sector-specific codes of practice, with the 1998 Act providing for these to receive an enhanced legal status compared with their 1984 forbears.

For the purposes of the present work, the sixth and the eighth principles dealing with the rights of the data subject and controls over transborder data flows, respectively, will be considered separately. Focusing on the remaining six principles, this chapter will consider to what extent and under what conditions a data controller may lawfully process personal data. Use may take a variety of forms and will include disclosure of data to a third party. Finally, this chapter will consider the operation of the seventh data protection principle, requiring that users adopt appropriate security measures.

---

[1] Sch. 1.

[2] Analysis and impact study on the implementation of Directive 95/46 in Member States, available from <http://ec.europa.eu/justice_home/fsj/privacy/lawreport/index_en.htm>.

Fair and lawful processing

Both Act and Directive require that data be processed 'fairly and lawfully'. This is undoubtedly the key component of the data protection principles and it might be argued that the majority of the remaining principles merely provide specific illustrations as to what might be considered fair processing. Under the Data Protection Act, the first principle imposes three cumulative obligations on data controllers. They are required to process data:

- fairly
- lawfully
- in accordance with at least one of the specific Schedule 2 or 3 conditions.

Failure in any respect may place the controller in breach of the legislation. Processing might be fair and lawful but if it does not come within one of the Schedule 2 or 3 conditions will be in breach of the Data Protection Act. Again, as will be described further in the context of fair processing, it may be lawful but considered to be unfair.

In some respects the determination whether processing is lawful will be one of the simpler aspects of the legislation. Particular reference should be made to the provisions of Schedules 2 and 3. Schedule 2 applies in respect of processing of what might be classed as 'normal' data whilst Schedule 3 applies in respect of the processing of sensitive personal data. The provisions of these schedules will be discussed in more detail later but, essentially, compliance with their provisions or with the requirements of any other statute will render processing lawful. Whether it is also fair raises more complex issues.

Requirements for the processing to be fair

The notion of fair processing is key to the legislation although, as with its application in other areas of the law, it is difficult to provide precise definitions. Two aspects of fair processing are of particular relevance. First, reference is made in the legislation to some specific requirements with regard to the manner in which information is obtained; and, secondly, a number of actions brought by the Commissioner and decisions of the Information Tribunal illustrate how the concept may be applied in respect of particular forms of processing.

In Part II of Schedule 1 of the Data Protection Act, guidance is given concerning the interpretation of a number of the data protection principles. In respect of the act of obtaining information it is provided that:

> regard shall be had to the method by which it was obtained, including in particular whether any person from whom it was obtained was deceived or misled as to the purpose or purposes for which it is to be held, used or disclosed.[3]

Surreptitious and deceptive collection of personal data, perhaps in the form of a photograph, would contravene this requirement but would also be likely to constitute a breach of the data subject's rights under Article 8 of the European Convention on Human Rights and be stigmatised as unlawful. Again seeking information under the guise of market research when it will actually be used to attempt to sell items will constitute unfair processing.

---

[3] Sch. 1, Pt II, para. 1.

It is not enough that the data subject is not misled as to the purpose for which the data is to be used. In order for processing to be fair it is necessary that specific information be given to the data subject about the purposes for which processing will be carried out. Two situations are specified in the Act and the Directive, the first applying where the data is collected directly from the data subject, perhaps through the completion of a form, and the second where data is obtained from some other source.

Information obtained from the data subject

Where data is obtained from the data subject, it is provided that information must be given to or 'made readily available' to the data subject. This formulation differs from that used in the Directive, which requires that information be provided to the subject 'except where he already has it'.[4] It is not clear whether the United Kingdom's approach fully implements the Directive. If a website, for example, provides a prominent link to its data protection policy giving the necessary details, it could be argued that the information is 'readily available', but unless and until the data subject follows the link it cannot be argued that 'he already has it'.

In terms of the information required to be presented to the data subject, the Act requires details as to the identity of the controller (or that of a nominated representative for cases where the controller is not established in the EEA)[5] and also the purposes for which the data are intended to be used, and any intended recipients of the data. The subject must also be supplied with such:

> further information which is necessary, having regard to the specific circumstances in which the data are or are to be processed, to enable processing in respect of the data subject to be fair.[6]

The extent of this requirement is not defined further in the Act. The Data Protection Directive, however, states that subjects must also be informed whether providing answers to any questions is voluntary or compulsory and as to the possible consequences of a failure to reply.[7] This can be seen in operation on many websites such as airline reservation systems where certain details are marked, typically with an asterisk, as being compulsory. A refusal, for example, to give details of name and address will result in a booking being refused. The supply of other pieces of information such as a contact telephone number may be optional. The Directive specifies also that notice must also be given of the right of subject access.

The Act does not indicate when the information is required to be given to the data subject. In a case brought under the 1984 legislation, *Innovations (Mail Order) v Data Protection Registrar*,[8] the Data Protection Tribunal ruled that the requirements must be met at the time the data was collected from the data subject. The Commissioner has expressed the view that the same approach would be followed under the 1998 Act.[9]

Information not obtained from the data subject

In many instances, information about a data subject may be obtained from a source other than the individual himself. An example might be in the situation where a medical

---

[4] Art. 10.   [5] s. 5(2).   [6] Sch. 1, Pt II, para. 2(3).   [7] Directive 95/46/EC, Art. 10(c).

[8] Case DA/92, available from <http://www.informationtribunal.gov.uk/DBFiles/Decision/i163/innovations.pdf>.

[9] *Legal Guidance*, para. 3.1.7.7, available at <http://www.ico.gov.uk/upload/documents/library/data_protection/detailed_specialist_guides/data_protection_act_legal_guidance.pdf>.

practitioner compiles an assessment of a patient's medical condition and passes this on to a third party, such as a potential employer. In such a situation the Act provides for notification—similar in scope and extent to that described above—to be given to the data subject by the third party.[10] Detailed, and somewhat complex, provision is made for the time at which notification is to be given:

If the data is processed by the recipient data controller, notification must be made at that time.

If data is disclosed to a third party, notification must be given at that time.

If it is subsequently determined that data is unlikely to be disclosed, notification must be made at that time.

In any other situation, notification must be given within a reasonable period.[11]

Given the fact that the statutory definition of processing includes the acts of 'obtaining, recording or holding'[12] the data, it is difficult to envisage how any time other than that at which the data is obtained would constitute the moment at which notification may be required.

In some cases, it might be that data concerning particular subjects makes only a peripheral and individually insignificant appearance in a collection of data. An example might be the individual voters listed in the edited version of the Electoral Register, which may be purchased by a data controller. The Act provides that notification need not be given where it would involve a 'disproportionate effort'.[13] No definition is given as to what might constitute 'disproportionate effort'. The Information Commissioner has expressed the view that this will be a question of fact to be determined in each individual case. A balancing act will require to be performed between the costs and workload implications for the controller and the possible prejudicial effect of the data for the interests of the subject. One specific factor identified as being of relevance would be the extent to which the subject may already know about the processing of the personal data. In the example given at the beginning of this section concerning a medical examination, although the issue of disproportionate effect may not arise, the data subject would be likely to be well aware that the results of his medical examination would be forwarded to the potential employer as part of the process of determining whether an offer of employment would be made.

Unfair processing subsequent to obtaining data

In many instances processing of data in the possession of the data controller will be assessed by reference to some of the other data protection principles. Data, for example, must not be retained for longer than is necessary. Other changes to the nature of processing may be more subtle and might be challenged on the ground of fairness. An example of the operation of this concept can be seen in the enforcement notice served by the Commissioner in August 2006 against the operators of a website company B4U.com. The website promoted itself as providing facilities for tracking the location of individuals using the Electoral Roll. As the enforcement notice[14] states:

This website offers 'people searching' facilities and claims to contain 'over 45 million records from the United Kingdom Electoral Roll'. The website further claims that those records are

---

[10] Sch. 1, Pt 2, para. 2(1)(b).   [11] Sch. 1, Pt 2, para. 2(2).   [12] s. 1(1).

[13] Sch. 1, Pt 2, para. 3(2)(a).

[14] Available from <http://www.ico.gov.uk/upload/documents/library/corporate/notices/b4u_enforcement_notice_130706.pdf>.

'from the 2001 roll'. These search facilities are offered free of charge and require no subscription or registration. Users need only enter the surname and rough location of the person they wish to trace for the system to return a list of electoral register entries that match the search criteria.[15]

Use of the Electoral Roll for commercial and other non-voting purposes had long been a cause of controversy. It is perhaps the nearest document in the United Kingdom to a definitive list of the names and addresses of every adult in a particular constituency. Under the terms of the Representation of the People (Amendment) Regulations 1990,[16] Electoral Registration Officers were obliged to supply copies of the register for their area upon request. Prior to the introduction of these regulations, the officers were required to supply copies of the Register only where these were readily available. The consequence was a massive increase in the usage of data from the Electoral Rolls for direct marketing and similar purposes. Following the report of a working group, the Home Secretary reported to Parliament concerns that:

> As the law stands, anyone may buy a copy of the electoral register for any purpose. The Home Office and electoral administrators receive more complaints about that than any other subject. People are unhappy about the large amount of unsolicited mail—junk mail—from companies that have obtained their details from the electoral register.
>
> Perhaps more worryingly, the advent of powerful CD-ROMs compiled from the electoral register, which allow for searching by name, means for example that abusive spouses can trace their former partners with considerable ease using a single CD-Rom. People who feel threatened in that way may simply not dare to register.[17]

The conclusion drawn was that commercial and other non-electoral uses of the Registers should be restricted. Section 9 of the Representation of the People Act 2000 provided for regulations to be made to establish two versions of the Electoral Register. As implemented in the Representation of the People (England and Wales) (Amendment) Regulations 2001,[18] voters are given information regarding the purposes for which data contained in the register might be used and given the opportunity to opt out of having their data disclosed. Registration officers will then be charged with producing two registers. The full register will contain details of all persons eligible to vote, which will be restricted to electoral purposes and a number of closely defined applications. Although this is available for public consultation it is provided in Regulation 6 that:

> A person who inspects the full register and makes a copy of it or records any particulars included in it otherwise than by means of hand-written notes shall be guilty of an offence.

An edited copy excluding the details of those who have opted out will also be produced, which may be supplied[19] and used for commercial purposes.[20]

By 2005 it appears that around 30 per cent of voters had exercised their right to opt out of the commercially available Electoral Register. Such a level would clearly diminish the value of the resource. The data held on the B4U.com website was taken from the 2001 Electoral Roll, the last created before the 2002 Regulations. The use to which the data was put was lawful under the law as it stood at the time that the Electoral Roll was drawn up. However,

---

[15] para. 3.   [16] SI 1990/520.   [17] Official Report (HoC), 30 November 1999, col. 168.
[18] SI 2001/No. 341. Equivalent provisions are made for Scotland by SI 2001/497.
[19] When supplied in electronic format, the charge will be £20 plus an additional £1.50 for each 1,000 names on the register (Reg. 110).   [20] s. 9.

the Information Commissioner determined that the use of the data in 2006 constituted unfair processing. The enforcement notice concluded that:

1. The Commissioner considers that it is inherently unfair for individuals to be compelled to provide personal information on penalty of a criminal conviction only for that information to be subsequently disclosed to commercial organisations without any express restrictions on its use.

2. Given that individuals now have a right to request that they are excluded from the edited register, it is unfair to undermine the express wishes of those who have exercised that right and the 2002 Regulations by continuing to make the relevant data available on the data controller's website.

3. The Commissioner considers that the processing of the relevant data by the data controller is unfair given that a significant proportion of the individuals whose details are contained in the relevant data will have subsequently exercised their right not to have those details included in the edited electoral register.

Accordingly, the website owner was ordered to cease making the data available on its website.[21]

The case can perhaps be seen as a borderline one and it is perhaps unfortunate that the Information Tribunal was not called upon to deliver a determination. If the data was ten years old, could processing still be classed as unfair? Or twenty years old? Original census data is released after one hundred years so we might assume that this would be legitimate also in respect of the electoral register. The difficulty that is perhaps inherent in the notion of fair processing is that, whilst equity would suggest that controllers should be able to assess whether their processing will comply with the requirements of the legislation at least in this area, it is submitted the state of the law is insufficiently precise.

Although Electoral Registers may represent the most extensive record of their kind, similar issues have arisen with other forms of records which are required to be made available to the public. Concern has been expressed on a number of occasions at the use made of lists of company shareholders, particularly in the case of privatised undertakings which might have several hundred thousand shareholders. It may be argued that the purpose of making details of shareholders publicly available is to allow identification of the owners of a limited liability company. Use of this information for the purposes of compiling mailing lists for direct marketing purposes raises different issues, although it is difficult to see how prohibitions might be enforced against the use of publicly available information for such purposes.

The credit reference agency cases

A further aspect of the fair processing requirement was at issue in a number of cases brought before the Data Protection Tribunal under the provisions of the 1984 Act. At issue was the conduct of the then four leading credit reference agencies: CCN, Credit and Data Marketing Services, Equifax, and Infolink, each of which was the recipient of an enforcement notice served by the Registrar.

Although the details of their operations vary, each of the credit reference agencies referred to above holds an extensive collection of data culled from public sources such as the electoral register, postcode data as made available by the Post Office, and also data relating to judgments handed down by the courts in civil disputes.

---

[21] When checked in September 2007, the site posted a notice claiming that its systems were being upgraded and providing a link to a 'sister site' selling electrical goods.

In addition to publicly available information, each agency holds information supplied by its subscribers reporting instances of bad debts and also maintains records of searches made. An indication of the scale of the agencies' operations can be taken from the Data Protection Tribunal's judgments which indicate that the Infolink agency conducted some 30 million searches per year.

The information held by the credit reference agencies and extracted in connection with a particular application for credit might be used in a variety of ways. The established method of operation would be for the agency to supply the information generated to its client, the potential creditor, leaving the determination whether to extend credit facilities entirely to the recipient. All of the credit reference agencies involved in the Tribunal actions operated on this basis. In a number of cases, the agencies also offered more extensive facilities. Instead of supplying a client with raw data, the client's own acceptance criteria might be applied. These might operate at a fairly simple level so as, for example, to reject all applicants who were not home owners. If searches revealed this fact, a recommendation that the application be rejected would be transmitted to the client.

The critical point concerning the agencies' operations, and the aspect to which exception was taken by the Registrar, is that in all cases, searches were conducted by reference to an address rather than a name. Although at first the practice might seem illogical, it was based upon a number of supposedly objective factors. Names constitute a rather inefficient means of identification. A glance at any telephone directory will show that most surnames appear more than once. Even full names are unlikely to be unique and most recipients of 'junk mail' will be aware of the many and various permutations of names and initials that may appear on envelopes. By contrast, addresses tend to be represented in a reasonably static format and, especially with the use of postcodes, the possibility of duplication is limited. However, the consequence of processing by reference to address would inevitably be that a search resulting from an application for credit by one individual, would retrieve information about previous residents at the address given and as to members of family or others who shared the address with the applicant.

The extraction of third-party data in making decisions about an individual applicant was considered by the Registrar to constitute unfair processing of personal data and, as such, contravened the first data protection principle. After discussions with the credit industry failed to provide an acceptable solution, enforcement notices were served on the four major agencies in August 1990. The terms of these notices were virtually identical, requiring the recipients to ensure that:

> personal data relating to the financial status of individuals ceases to be processed by reference to the current or previous address or addresses of the subject of the search whereby there is extracted in addition to information about the subject of the search any information about any other individual who has been recorded as residing at any time at the same or similar current or previous address as the subject of the search.[22]

Appeals were lodged by all the agencies with the Data Protection Tribunal which considered evidence submitted on behalf of the appellant, arguing that depriving them of third-party information would render their operations less effective. The consequence would be either an increase in bad debts or the denial of credit to persons who might otherwise have been accepted. It might even be that certain creditors would cease to operate in the consumer field.

---

[22] para. 18.

The Tribunal accepted that the operation of credit reference agencies provided benefits but held that the prime purpose of the legislation was to protect the rights of the individual. Whilst the interests of the credit industry should not be ignored, primacy must be given to the interests of the individual applicant. On this basis it was considered:

> unfair for a credit reference agency, requested by its customers to supply information by reference to a named individual, so to program the extraction of information as to search for information about all persons associated with a given address or addresses notwithstanding that they may have no links with the individual [who is] the subject of the inquiry or may have no financial relationship with that individual.[23]

It was also argued that much of the information held—for example, judgments from county courts—was public information. It was in the public interest that such data should be readily available. Whilst not disputing this argument, the Tribunal pointed out that they were concerned with a much narrower issue: whether the extraction of this information in connection with a search relating to an unconnected individual could be considered fair. The answer to this must be in the negative.

The key ground of objection in the credit reference case was that decisions about individuals were being made other than on the basis of information about them. A person might, for example, be denied credit because of a debt incurred by a previous occupant of the property. There are, however, cases where account may be taken of factors other than those relating to the individual. A more recent case concerned with the issue of fair processing is *Johnson v Medical Defence Union*.[24] The case centred upon whether the use of a risk assessment policy by the Medical Defence Union could be considered unfair. The claimant applied to the defendant for renewal of his professional liability insurance and was refused. The reason given was that the risk assessment processes took account of the volume of incidents reported involving a particular member and it was an integral element that limited regard was had for the outcome of such cases. The claimant had reported a number is disputes with patients although none had made a formal complaint or brought legal proceedings against him. The view was taken that if a doctor had a significant history of complaints brought against him in the past, this would be a reliable indicator that the trend would continue, regardless of whether the previous complaints had proved to be unfounded. The prediction would be that the Medical Defence Union would be required to incur continuing expenditure in representing the doctor in the future.

Although there was disagreement between the judges on whether processing had taken place, a point discussed in more detail in Chapter 6, there was unanimity on the issue of fairness. At trial, Mr Justice Rimer concluded that:

> there is in principle nothing relevantly unfair about the MDU's risk assessment policy or about the way in which it processed information in applying that policy...the policy is directed at risk management—at preserving the MDU funds against a risk of claims, and the incurring of costs, *in the future*. The MDU experience is that a risk of that nature cannot be measured simply by awaiting the happening of a statistically significant number of occurrences that do in fact cause a drain on its funds.[25]

Such a situation could be distinguished from that applying in the credit reference agency cases, where there was only the most tenuous statistical correlation between data about a

[23] <http://www.informationtribunal.gov.uk/DBFiles/Decision/i233/infolink.pdf> at para. 53.
[24] [2007] EWCA Civ 262.   [25] [2006] EWHC 321 (Ch) at para. 122.

third party and the likelihood that an applicant would default on a credit agreement. In the present case:

> it is not open to this court to hold that the MDU's risk assessment policy was unfair;…and that its operation involved…no unfair processing for the purposes of the first data protection principle.[26]

This conclusion was unanimously upheld by the Court of Appeal. It may be noted that had the risk assessment processes been carried out completely automatically the complainant would have had the right to object under the provisions of section 12 of the Act. This will be discussed in more detail. By providing for some degree of human intervention, the Medical Defence Union processes fell outside the scope of section 12 and, although the result may have been perceived as unfair by one data subject, the evidence presented to the court satisfied it that the process was based upon rational criteria and sought to produce results which were fair to the totality of the data subjects who made up the membership of the Medical Defence Union, and were also compatible with its legitimate and necessary goal of managing its level of exposure to risk.

Requirements for processing to be lawful

As with the requirement of fairness, neither the Act nor the Directive provides any definition of when conduct will be lawful. In the decision of the House of Lords in *R v R*, a case concerned with marital rape, the concept of unlawful conduct was defined by Lord Keith as relating to 'something which is contrary to some law or enactment or is done without lawful justification or excuse'.[27] In *Legal Guidance on the Act*,[28] the Information Commissioner indicated that:

> This means that a data controller must comply with all relevant rules of law whether derived from statute or common law, relating to the purpose and ways in which the data controller processes personal data.

A number of particular areas were identified as being of particular relevance:

(a)   confidentiality arising from the relationship of the data controller with the data subject

(b)   the ultra vires rule and the rule relating to the excess of delegated powers, under which the data controller may only act within the limits of its legal powers

(c)   legitimate expectation—that is, the expectation of the individual as to how the data controller will use the information relating to him

(d)   Article 8 of the European Convention on Human Rights (the right to respect for private and family life, home, and correspondence).

Many of these topics are dealt with in the Data Protection Act itself, although, again, there is evidence of collision between concepts of fairness and lawfulness.

Specific factors legitimising processing

In addition to imposing a general requirement that data be processed fairly and lawfully, the Act places the onus on the data controller to evidence specific justification for processing.

---

[26]   [2006] EWHC 321 (Ch) at para. 124.   [27]   [1992] 1 AC 599.
[28]   Available   from   <http://www.ico.gov.uk/upload/documents/library/data_protection/detailed_specialist_guides/data_protection_act_legal_guidance.pdf>.

In the case of general data, processing will be permitted only where the controller can demonstrate compliance with one of a list of conditions laid down in Schedule 2. For sensitive data, Schedule 3 provides a more restrictive set of qualifying conditions. In both Schedules, the list of legitimising factors begins with the notion of subject consent.

Subject consent

It is a fundamental tenet of contract law that silence cannot constitute acceptance of an offer. Silence, however, can take a variety of forms. Many supermarket transactions may be carried out without the exchange of a single word, let alone one possessing legal significance. Silence coupled with conduct indicating a wish to contract can establish a valid contract.

Over the years, there has been extensive debate on how a data subject may validly give consent to the processing of personal data. Anyone who has entered into almost any form of mail order or online transaction will be familiar with the basic techniques which are used. Typically, as was described in the context of the *Innovations* and *Linguaphone* Tribunal cases discussed later in this section, a note of the data controller's processing intentions will be given on an order form or similar document. Under what is referred to as an 'opt-out' procedure, the data subject will be told that the specified forms of processing will take place unless notice of objection is received. This would normally require that the subject places a mark in an 'opt-out' box. The alternative approach, referred to as 'opting in', is again to give notice of the desired forms of processing but also to ask the data subject to indicate that they are content for this to take place. Typically, data controllers have sought to maximise the use of the former technique, as it is well accepted that this will also maximise the number of persons whose data may be processed. In many cases, data subjects may not read the notice or may be unaware of the full implications of what is being proposed. A typical formulation might be along the lines, 'We would like to share your data with other carefully selected companies whose goods or services we consider may be of interest to you.' A rough translation might be along the lines, 'We will sell your details to anyone who pays us money'! Whilst data subject apathy may help controllers on an opt-out basis, the reverse will be the case where subjects are asked to opt in.

Schedule 2 to the Data Protection Act 1998 provides that processing will be lawful when 'the data subject has given his consent to the processing'. Schedule 3 requires that the subject gives 'explicit consent'. Neither phrase is defined in the Act. The Data Protection Directive is a little more helpful, providing that:

> the data subject's consent shall mean any freely given specific and informed indication of his wishes by which the data subject signifies his agreement to personal data relating to him being processed.[29]

In the context of consent to the processing of data, the Directive requires that consent be given unambiguously. This term is not defined. As interpreted in the United Kingdom, it is generally seen as being compatible with either an opt-out or opt-in approach, with the basic requirement being that the data subject is able readily to give an indication of his wishes. Albeit in a different context, the Article 29 Working Party appears to suggest that an opt-in approach may be needed. In an 'Opinion on unsolicited communications for marketing purposes'[30] it considered the requirement in the Privacy and Electronic Communications

---

[29] Directive 95/46/EC, Art. 2(h).
[30] Opinion 5/2004, available from <http://ec.europa.eu/justice_home/fsj/privacy/docs/wpdocs/2004/wp90_en.pdf>.

Directive that prior consent be obtained before commercial emails are sent to data subjects. It concluded that:

> Implied consent to receive such mails is not compatible with the definition of consent of Directive 95/46/EC and in particular with the requirement of consent being the indication of someone's wishes, including where this would be done 'unless opposition is made' (opt-out). Similarly, pre-ticked boxes, e.g., on websites are not compatible with the definition of the Directive either.

At least pending any court decision either in the United Kingdom or before the European Court of Justice, it appears that an 'opt-out' approach will be accepted in the United Kingdom. A key criterion in determining the acceptability of the technique concerns the clarity of the notification. In *Linguaphone Institute v Data Protection Registrar*,[31] a case brought before the Tribunal under the 1984 Act, the appellant included in its advertisements a notice to the effect that:

> (Please) tick here if you do not wish Linguaphone to make your details available to other companies who may wish to mail you offers of goods or services.

In holding that there was a breach of the data protection principles, the Tribunal expressed concern that:

> the opt-out box appears in minute print at the bottom of the order form. In the Tribunal's view the position, size of print and wording of the opt-out box does not amount to a sufficient indication that the company intends or may wish to hold, use or disclose that personal data provided at the time of enquiry for the purpose of trading in personal data.

Beyond giving information to the data subject, the controller must afford a reasonable opportunity for the subject to express consent (or the lack of it). This was at issue in another case brought before the Data Protection Tribunal under the 1984 Act, *Innovations v Data Protection Registrar*.[32] In this case, the appellant was in the business of mail order sales. Custom was solicited in a variety of ways, including the distribution of catalogues and the placing of advertisements in various media, including newspapers, radio, and television. The appellant's catalogues gave customers notice of use of their data for broking purposes and its order forms offered customers the opportunity to exclude this. Some adverts, especially those appearing on radio or television, did not make mention of the possibility, and in the event that catalogue orders were placed by telephone, no mention would be made of this secondary purpose. An acknowledgement of an order would, however, be sent and this would convey the message:

> For your information. As a service to our customers we occasionally make our customer lists available to carefully screened companies whose products or services we feel may interest you. If you do not wish to receive such mailings please send an exact copy of your address label to...

The Registrar took the view that notification of the intended use came too late in the contractual process and served an enforcement notice alleging a breach of the first data protection principle, which, as formulated under the 1984 Act, required that data be obtained fairly and lawfully.

A number of arguments were put forward by the applicant as justifying their practices. It was suggested that, at the time of placing an order, customers would be concerned primarily with obtaining the goods and that a notice along the lines referred to above would have

---

[31] Case DA/94 31/49/1.

[32] *Innovations (Mail Order) Ltd v Data Protection Registrar*, Case DA/92 31/49/1.

limited impact. Where orders were made by telephone, giving specific notice would increase the length of the call, thereby increasing costs for both the supplier and the customer. It was also pointed out that the details would not be used for list-broking purposes until thirty days from the date the acknowledgement order was sent. This, it was suggested, allowed ample time for the customer to opt out. It was also pointed out that the appellant's practices were in conformity with an industry code of practice and the Council of Europe's Recommendation on the protection of personal data used for the purposes of direct marketing.[33]

Notwithstanding these factors, the Tribunal upheld the Registrar's ruling. Although codes of practice and recommendations might constitute useful guidance, the task for the Tribunal was to interpret the law. Use of the data for list-broking purposes, it was held, was not a purpose which would be obvious to the data subjects involved. Fair obtaining required that the subject be told of the non-obvious purpose before the data was obtained. Whilst a later notification might 'be a commendable way of providing a further warning', it could not stand by itself. Where prior notification might not be practicable, the Tribunal ruled that 'the obligation to obtain the data subject's positive consent for the non-obvious use of their data falls upon the data user'.[34]

Duration of consent

Consent is not a permanent condition. It is open to a data subject to withdraw consent at any time. This point is not specified directly in either the Data Protection Act or the Directive. Article 9 of the Directive on Privacy and Electronic Communications,[35] which refers specifically to the processing of personal data in the electronic communications sector,[36] provides that:

> Users or subscribers shall be given the possibility to withdraw their consent for the processing of location data other than traffic data at any time.

There is no doubt that whilst the withdrawal of consent cannot have retrospective effect, it would serve to render unlawful any future processing which is dependent upon this head of authority.

Other factors legitimising processing

Although the concept of consent has been a high-profile aspect of the new regime, it constitutes only one of a number of grounds, capable of legitimising processing. For both general and sensitive data, a range of grounds are specified which may allow processing to take place without the subject's consent being obtained.[37]

General data

Necessity for concluding or performing a contract with the data subject

Processing may lawfully take place when this is necessary, either for entering into or performing a contract with the subject. Some stress should be placed on the adjective 'necessary'. This frequently appears in instruments such as the European Convention on Human

---

[33] Recommendation 85/20.   [34] para. 31.   [35] Directive 2002/58/EC, *OJ* 2002 L 201/37.
[36] The provisions of this Directive are discussed in Ch. 7.
[37] As will be discussed later, a data subject has the right to object to processing in limited circumstances.

Rights, and the jurisprudence of the European Court of Human Rights—which has been approved by the European Court of Justice—has adopted an interpretation requiring that the practice in question be close to essential for the specified purpose.[38] Clearly, information about a data subject's income may be necessary for a lender to determine whether to grant a loan and information as to address will be vital for a mail order sale, but controllers should take care not to require more information than is strictly necessary for the purpose.

Necessity for the controller to comply with a legal obligation

Similar comments apply to this requirement. A controller may, for example, require information to ensure that credit facilities are not extended to those under the age of eighteen. It would be reasonable for such a controller to require applicants to give an indication that they are over eighteen years of age.

Necessity to protect the vital interests of the data subject

It is easy to envisage situations where the interests of the data subject may require that data be processed in situations where it is not practicable to obtain consent. The limitation to the subject's 'vital interests' might mean, in practice, that the data is likely to be of a kind considered sensitive. The Information Commissioner has indicated support for this view. The only significant exception might be in respect of information relating to a data subject's financial affairs. As was noted earlier, public opinion surveys conducted for the Commissioner indicate that protection of financial data was ranked higher by most respondents than the protection of many of the categories of data designated as sensitive. Processing designed to guard against the dangers of identity theft, for example, might be seen as coming within the scope of this provision, although, as will be discussed later, the first data protection principle does not apply where processing is conducted in connection with the prevention or detection of crime and where compliance with the principle would prejudice the attainment of those purposes.[39]

Necessity for the administration of justice, etc.

Data may be processed lawfully when this is necessary for a range of specified public-sector purposes. In addition to the administration of justice, processing may be carried out when necessary for the exercise of statutory functions, for example in compiling registers of data controllers, in the exercise of governmental functions, or any other functions of a public nature exercised in the public interest. This might include, for example, the operation of systems of educational scholarships.

Legitimate interests of the controller

This final justification for processing is perhaps the most extensive. It sanctions processing where this is:

> necessary for the purposes of legitimate interests pursued by the data controller or by the third party or parties to whom the data are disclosed, except where the processing is unwarranted in any particular case by reason of prejudice to the rights and freedoms or legitimate interests of data subjects.

It is provided that regulations may be made to specify the circumstances in which this provision may or may not be applied.[40] To date, no regulations have been made.

---

[38] See e.g. the case of *Barthold v Germany* (1985) 7 EHRR 383.   [39] s. 29.
[40] Sch. 2, para. 6.

Although many situations might be identified in which it will be useful for a data controller to hold information, the restrictions associated with the adjective 'necessary' must constantly be borne in mind. It would, for example, be useful for an employer to record details of employees' next of kin in the event of accident or illness at work. This would not, however, be essential for the normal purposes of employment.

It should be noted that although all processing activities must come under the scope of a Schedule 2 condition, it is not required that it is always the same condition. In the example given above, the legitimate interest processing may be supplemented by subject consent. In the example cited, it might be assumed that it would be a reasonably straightforward matter to obtain the details from an employee at the stage employment commences under the consent heading (although it might well be the next of kin who should be consenting). Even if consent is not forthcoming, the matter can be handled in a relatively simple manner by, for example, inserting a note to the effect that contact details have been refused. Matters become more complicated when a controller has to overcome an initial failure to seek consent by subsequent actions. The likelihood is that only a small percentage of subjects will respond to a request for retrospective consent, with the low response rate being due as much to indifference as to opposition. As with many aspects of the law, prevention is much easier than cure.

Factors legitimising the processing of sensitive data

Schedule 3 of the Data Protection Act contains a series of conditions legitimising the processing of sensitive data. These are generally similar in scope to the Schedule 2 conditions but associated conditions are stricter. As with Schedule 2, a controller needs to comply with only one condition.

Explicit subject consent

As with general data, the first ground specified as legitimising processing of sensitive personal data is the fact that the subject has given consent. In this case, the requirement is that consent be 'explicit'. Although the term is not defined in either Act or Directive the *Concise Oxford Dictionary* definition refers to it being:

> not implied merely but distinctly: plain in language: outspoken: clear: unreserved.

Although the definition is perhaps not incompatible with an opt-out approach to consent, more may be required of the data controller to ensure that the subject is aware of what is proposed to be done with the data. The Information Commissioner has suggested that:

> The consent of the data subject should be absolutely clear. In appropriate cases it should cover the specific detail of the processing, the particular type of data to be processed (or even the specific information), the purposes of the processing and any special aspects of the processing which may affect the individual, for example disclosures which may be made of the data.[41]

It is difficult to conceive of many circumstances in which anything other than opt in consent would be considered valid where sensitive personal data is concerned.

Beyond the grant of explicit consent to the processing, the Act provides for a range of other grounds legitimising processing. This list has been supplemented by a number of items of secondary legislation.

---

[41] *Legal Guidance*, a. 3.1.5.

Employment-related processing

The processing is necessary for the purposes of exercising or performing any right or obligation which is conferred or imposed by law on the data controller in connection with employment.[42]

It is further provided that the Secretary of State may either exclude the application of this provision in certain cases or impose additional conditions. It may be noted that, in respect of the processing of employment-related data, the Data Protection Directive requires the provision of 'adequate safeguards'.[43] Unless it can be assumed that existing employment law provides adequate safeguards for the data subject, United Kingdom law will not comply with the Directive unless and until the regulations are made.

Vital interests

Processing is necessary to protect the vital interests of the data subject or of another person where the data subject is incapable of giving consent or where the controller cannot reasonably be expected to obtain consent.[44]

Examples of such situations might be where medical data relating to the subject requires to be processed in order to treat the subject who is unconscious in hospital. Again, processing may be justified where the subject is a carrier of an infectious disease and where the data is needed to provide treatment to a third party. It is further provided that processing may take place when this is:

necessary to protect the vital interests of a third party and the subject unreasonably withholds consent.[45]

This situation may well be similar to that discussed above, but with the distinction that the subject has been identified by the controller. An example might be where the subject suffers from an infectious disease but refuses to consent to the disclosure of a list of persons who might have come into contact with the subject and who might require to be contacted to receive treatment.

Processing by specified bodies

The processing is carried out in the course of legitimate activities by a non-profit-making body or association existing for political, philosophical, religious or trade union purposes. In such cases, appropriate safeguards must be provided for the rights and freedoms of data subjects, the data must relate only to members of the association or those in regular contact with it and does not involve disclosure of the data to third parties without the consent of the data subject.[46]

Given the extension of the definition of processing to include the collection of data, this definition may have some unanticipated consequences. It was conceded in Parliament that political canvassing would be covered if the intention were to transfer returns onto a computer system. A similar situation would apply where religious organisations sought to obtain converts through door-to-door visits. For political data, it was indicated that special regulations would be made.[47]

---

[42] Data Protection Act 1998, Sch. 3, para. 2.   [43] Directive 95/46/EC, Art. 8(2)(b).
[44] Data Protection Act 1998, Sch. 3, para. 3(a).   [45] Sch. 3, para. 3(b).
[46] Data Protection Act 1998, Sch. 3, para. 4.
[47] 315 HC Official Report (6th series), col. 613, 2 July 1998.

Information in the public domain

> The information contained in the personal data has been made public as a result of steps deliberately taken by the data subject.[48]

It is significant to note in this context that it will not suffice that the information has come into the public domain; this must have occurred through the deliberate actions of the subject. There is clearly a relationship between this provision and the statutory provisions discussed later relating to the activities of the media.

Legal proceedings and the administration of justice

> The processing is necessary for the purpose of or in connection with legal proceedings (including prospective proceedings), for obtaining legal advice or to establish, exercise or defend legal rights.[49]

This provision was criticised in Parliament as being excessively broad. Certainly, the provision relating to 'prospective proceedings' appears somewhat opaque.

> The processing is necessary for the administration of justice, for the exercise of statutory or governmental functions. Once again, the Secretary of State may exclude the application of this provision in certain situations or require that additional conditions be satisfied.[50]

An obvious example of such a situation would be the maintenance of criminal records. It may be noted that the Data Protection Directive provides that 'a complete register of criminal convictions may be kept only under the control of official authority'.[51]

Processing for medical purposes

> The processing is necessary for medical purposes and is undertaken by a health professional or by a person owing an equivalent duty of confidentiality.[52]

The term 'medical purposes' is defined broadly to include 'preventative medicine, medical diagnosis, medical research, the provision of care and treatment and the management of healthcare services'.[53] It should be stressed that in this case, as with all the exceptions described in the present section, the effect is essentially to free the controller from the requirement to seek explicit consent to processing. The processing must be carried out in accordance with the data protection principles and other requirements of the Act.

Ethnic monitoring

> The processing relates to data indicating racial or ethnic origin but is carried out in order to monitor compliance with equal opportunities legislation. Appropriate safeguards must also be taken for the rights and freedoms of data subjects.[54]

Once again, it is provided that the Secretary of State may define more precisely the activities coming within the scope of this provision. Care will certainly require to be taken to ensure that information supplied for this purpose, for example by an applicant for employment, is used only for monitoring purposes and retained, at least in a form which can identify the subject, for no longer than is necessary.

---

[48] Data Protection Act 1998, Sch. 3, para. 5.   [49] Data Protection Act 1998, Sch. 3, para. 6.
[50] Data Protection Act 1998, Sch. 3, para. 7.   [51] Directive 95/46/EC, Art. 8(5).
[52] Data Protection Act 1998, Sch. 3, para. 8.   [53] Directive 95/46/EC, Art. 8(5).
[54] Data Protection Act 1998, Sch. 3, para. 9.

Order of the Secretary of State

The processing occurs in circumstances specified by the Secretary of State.[55]

This provision confers a wide-ranging power on the Secretary of State to extend the range of exemptions. The Data Protection Directive requires that additional exemptions must be justified by 'reasons of substantial public interest',[56] and must be notified to the Commission.[57]

The regulatory power has been exercised with the making of the Data Protection (Processing of Sensitive Personal Data) Order 2000.[58] This provides no fewer than ten additional grounds justifying the processing of sensitive personal data.

The first two grounds relate to processing for the purposes 'of the prevention or detection of any unlawful act' and the discharge of any functions intended to secure the public against:

(i) dishonesty, malpractice, or other seriously improper conduct by, or the unfitness or incompetence of, any person, or

(ii) mismanagement in the administration of, or failures in services provided by any body or association.

In all cases, it is a requirement that the processing must necessarily be carried out without the explicit consent of the data subject.

A third ground might be seen as a form of whistleblower's charter. It legitimises the disclosure of data relating to crime, dishonesty, or seriously improper conduct or mismanagement when this is with a view to the publication of the information and where the party making the disclosure reasonably believes that the publication will be in the public interest.

Processing may be carried out without explicit subject consent when this is in the public interest in connection with the provision of counselling, support, or other services. The exemption here is not an open-ended one, with the controller being required to demonstrate that it is impracticable, unreasonable, or undesirable to seek to obtain subject consent.

With developments in DNA research and increased awareness of the role of genetic factors in influencing life expectancy, data of this kind is of potential value to insurance companies. A person applying for insurance cover might be required to supply details relating to the health of parents, grandparents, or siblings. In the event that these persons remain alive, the processing of this data might contravene the requirements of the Data Protection Act 1998. The regulations legitimise this form of processing subject to three conditions: that it is not reasonable to obtain explicit consent; that the controller does not have actual knowledge that consent has been withheld; and that the processing is not used as the basis for decisions which will affect the data subjects concerned.

Processing for insurance purposes also benefits from a further transitional exemption covering activities which were underway prior to the commencement of the Data Protection Act 1998. Under the previous regime, the need for consent was less strict and it is provided that, save where there is actual knowledge that the data subject does not consent to processing, this may continue when it is necessary for the purpose and where it is not reasonable to expect the controller to seek explicit consent (or where the processing must necessarily be conducted without consent).

---

[55] Data Protection Act 1998, Sch. 3, para. 10.   [56] Directive 95/46/EC, Art. 8(4).
[57] Directive 95/46/EC, Art. 8(6).   [58] SI 2000/417.

Two further exemptions serve to permit the continuance of activities which are generally considered desirable but which might otherwise contravene the data protection principles. Many employers may, whether required by law or otherwise, seek to process information to monitor the operation of policies relating to equal opportunities with the view to promoting such equality. It is provided that processing may take place where this is not used to support decisions affecting a particular subject and where the processing is not likely to cause substantial damage or distress to the data subject or to any other person.

Political data

One matter which attracted considerable discussion when the Data Protection Act 1998 was before Parliament was the realisation that the restrictions on the processing of sensitive data would serve to restrict the ability of political parties to conduct activities such as the canvassing of voters where this would involve maintaining a record of likely voting intentions. The regulations seek to avoid this prospect by providing that information relating to political opinions may be processed by persons or organisations registered under the Registration of Political Parties Act 1998 to the extent that this is not likely to cause substantial damage or distress. It is further provided that data subjects may give written notice that their personal data is not to be processed for such purpose. The Data Protection (Processing of Sensitive Personal Data) (Elected Representatives) Order 2002[59] makes further provisions regarding the use of such data by elected representatives.

A further exemption applies where data is processed for research purposes. This will apply where the processing is in the substantial public interest, for example as part of a medical research project; will not result in action being taken with regard to the particular data subject without explicit consent; and is not likely to cause substantial damage or distress.

The final exemption is the shortest of all, but carries significant implications. Sensitive data may be processed where this is:

> necessary for the exercise of any functions conferred on a constable by any rule of law.[60]

Given the extensive powers conferred on constables under the common law, this provision might serve to justify many forms of processing.

Exceptions to the application of the first data protection principle for law enforcement and revenue-gathering purposes

A significant exception to the operation of the first data protection principle applies where data is acquired for the purposes of the prevention or detection of crime, the apprehension or prosecution of offenders, or the assessment or collection of any tax or duty and where compliance with the principle would be prejudicial to the attainment of the purpose in question.

The rationale behind the exception lies in the recognition that law enforcement agencies might reasonably acquire information in ways which might normally be regarded as unfair, for example as the result of overhearing—or even eavesdropping on—a conversation. It

---

[59] SI 2002/2905.   [60] Data Protection Act 1998, Sch. 3, para. 10.

might, however, be considered unfortunate that the Commissioner should not be given the power to define the concept of fairness in the light of the particular situation of the user involved rather than by providing a near-complete exception from the requirement to act fairly. It may also be noted that the restriction upon the Commissioner's ability to act exists even where the data has been acquired unlawfully, although here it may be difficult to sustain the argument that observance of the law would prejudice the prevention or detection of crime, the apprehension or prosecution of offenders, or the assessment or collection of any tax or duty.

The second data protection principle—purpose limitation

The second data protection principle requires that:

> Personal data shall be obtained only for one or more specified and lawful purposes and shall not be processed further in any manner incompatible with that purpose or those purposes.

Given the breadth of the definition of processing—which refers specifically to the obtaining of data—it is difficult to identify a real need for the second data protection principle. In interpreting the second principle, the Act provides that the purposes for which data are to be processed may be specified either by the giving of notice to the data subject (as discussed in the context of the first principle) or in the notification made to the Commissioner. It is to be noted, however, that notification by itself will not satisfy the requirements of the first data protection principle.

The more significant element of the second principle concerns what might be regarded as ongoing processing activities. Data may be obtained for one purpose with due notification given to the data subject but changes in circumstance or technical developments may make other forms of activity attractive to the controller. The Commissioner has indicated that a strict view will be taken in determining whether any future forms of processing— whether carried out by the controller or by a third party to whom the data are disclosed— are compatible with those originally notified to the Commissioner or to the data subject.[61]

A further aspect of unlawful obtaining has been much in the news recently with massive publicity about the behaviour of certain sections of the media in seeking to hack into computers and mobile phones of newsworthy people. The behaviour may also be carried out for other commercial purposes. A trio of private investigators were fined sums of up to £10,000[62] for obtaining unauthorised access to mobile-phone data of individuals involved in the dispute between Tottenham Hotspur and West Ham football clubs over which should be given tenancy of the former London Olympic stadium.

In the situation where the investigator obtained direct access to data held on a computer, it would be likely that an offence would be committed under the Computer Misuse Act 1990. In many instances, however, the information would be obtained, either through bribing an employee of the data user or by misleading the user as to identity and entitlement to access the data. In these situations, the investigator would not normally be guilty of any offence. To remedy this situation, section 55 of the Data Protection Act 1998 provides that an offence will be committed by a person who 'knowingly or recklessly, without the consent of the data controller' seeks to obtain or disclose personal data or procure its disclosure to a third party. An exception is provided where the data is obtained in connection with the

---

[61] *Legal Guidance*, para. 3.2.
[62] The case is reported at <http://www.bbc.co.uk/news/uk-england-london-25468278>.

prevention or detection of crime or in pursuance of a court order. A further offence is committed by a person who sells or offers to sell data obtained in contravention of this provision. Both convictions are punishable by a fine of up to £5,000 in the magistrates' court and to a potentially unlimited amount in the Crown Court.

In spite of the prohibition, there is extensive evidence that the trade in unlawfully acquired personal information is continuing. Taking action against those involved in the practice was identified as a priority in the Information Commissioner's Regulatory Strategy published in 2005 and between 2002 and 2007 twenty-eight prosecutions were brought, with a maximum fine of £4,200 being imposed in a case in 2006. This figure was made up of fourteen fines of £300 each, imposed in respect of a number of offences, and the Commissioner expressed disappointment at the generally low level of punishments imposed by the courts.[63] A report published by the Information Commissioner in May 2006 entitled *What Price Privacy?* provides extensive evidence of the techniques and tactics used. Based on information obtained in the course of one investigation into the activities of one private investigator, the report presents a list of the sums charged for obtaining items of personal data; these included £17.50 for checking addresses on the Electoral Roll, £65–£75 for obtaining an ex-directory telephone number, £500 for a criminal records check, and £750 for obtaining data relating to a mobile telephone account. As stated in a follow-up report, *What Price Privacy Now?*[64] published in December 2006:

> Suppliers use two main methods to obtain the information they want: through corruption, or more usually by some form of deception, generally known as 'blagging'. Blaggers pretend to be someone they are not in order to wheedle out the information they are seeking. They are prepared to make several telephone calls to get it. Each call they make takes them a little further towards their goal: obtaining information illegally which they then sell for a specified price.[65]

The Information Commissioner argued for an extension of the penalties provided for the offence to include a maximum term of imprisonment on conviction in the magistrates' court and two years before the Crown Court. Following a consultation exercise conducted by the Department of Constitutional Affairs in the second half of 2006, it was announced in February 2007 that the government had decided to accept the Commissioner's proposals and that legislation to this end would be brought forward when parliamentary time permitted.

The third data protection principle—relevance

The third data protection principle requires that data shall be 'adequate, relevant and not excessive in relation to the purpose or purposes for which they are processed'. The Data Protection Directive[66] uses the same term. No further interpretation is provided in either instrument. The principle is, however, identically worded to one found in the Data Protection Act 1984. This was at issue before the Data Protection Tribunal in the course of proceedings brought against a number of Community Charge Registration Officers.[67]

---

[63] Foreword in *What Price Privacy?*
[64] Available from <http://www.ico.gov.uk/upload/documents/library/corporate/research_and_reports/what_price_privacy_now.pdf>. [65] p. 5.
[66] Directive 95/46/EC.
[67] The officers involved represented Runnymede Borough Council, South Northamptonshire District Council, Harrow Borough Council, and Rhondda Borough Council.

The Community Charge or 'poll tax' proved one of the most controversial forms of taxation introduced in recent times. Although much of the publicity generated concerned its financial aspects, the implementation of the requirement that registers be established of those liable to pay the tax attracted the attention of the Data Protection Registrar, who took issue with the processing proposals indicated by a number of local authorities: Harrow Borough Council,[68] Runnymede Borough Council,[69] Rhondda Borough Council,[70] and South Northamptonshire District Council.[71] Ultimately, registration was refused on the basis that the Registrar was satisfied that the applicants were likely to contravene the fourth data protection principle. Appeals against these decisions were brought before the Data Protection Tribunal.

Under the terms of the Local Government Finance Act 1988, charging authorities were required to compile and maintain a Community Charge Register.[72] It was specifically provided that the register should include details of the name and address of every person liable to pay the Community Charge, which was payable by everyone over the age of eighteen. In some cases, local authorities, including Rhondda Borough Council, requested the date of birth of every member of the household, regardless of whether they were over eighteen or not. Dates of birth are clearly items of personal data.

Objecting to this form of processing the Data Protection Registrar, although accepting that a record would need to be held of those who would reach the age of eighteen and become liable to pay the charge during the course of a tax year, took the view that the date of birth was irrelevant in the case of those who were already of an age to pay the tax. The appellant argued that many inhabitants of the Rhondda shared surnames and forenames. The addition of a note of date of birth would limit the possibility that an individual might escape inclusion on the register because his or her identity was confused with some other person of the same name. It was also argued that the inclusion of the information would assist the Registration Officer in the efficient performance of his or her duties.

These arguments were rejected by the Tribunal. It heard evidence that, nationally, fewer than 1 per cent of households contained persons who shared the same surname and forename. Although it accepted that the figure might be higher in the Rhondda, it did not consider that this justified the appellant's actions. The Tribunal concluded that:

> We find that the information the appellant wishes to hold on database concerning individuals exceeds substantially the minimum amount of information which is required in order for him to fulfil the purpose for which he has sought registration … to fulfil his duty to compile and maintain the Community Charges Register.

Similar issues were involved in the case of the other councils. Each of the appellants held, or proposed to hold, details of the type of property occupied by each subject. Again, information of this type would be classed as personal data and the Registrar raised objection on the ground that its inclusion was, or would be likely to constitute, a breach of the fourth data protection principle. In the case of Harrow and Runnymede Borough Councils, action took the form of a refusal to accept an application for registration. In the case of South Northamptonshire District Council, whose application for registration had previously been accepted, an enforcement notice was served.

In terms of the status of the information relating to type of property, the Tribunal held that whilst there might be justification for holding some information additional to that required under the Local Government Finance Act 1988, the wish to record details of type

---

[68] Case DA/90 24/49/5.　　[69] Case DA/90 24/49/3.　　[70] Case DA/90 24/49/2.
[71] Case DA/90 24/49/4.　　[72] s. 6.

of property in every case was excessive. The Tribunal endorsed the advice given to data users by the Registrar,[73] to the effect that they should seek to identify the minimum amount of personal data which is required in order to enable them to fulfil their purpose. Where additional data might be required in certain cases, these should again be identified and the further information sought or held only in those cases.

More recently, the application of the third (and also the fifth principle requiring that data not be kept for longer than is necessary) data protection principles was at issue before the Information Tribunal in the case of *The Chief Constables of West Yorkshire, South Yorkshire and North Wales Police and the Information Commissioner*.[74] This case started a long-running dispute between the Information Commissioner and police authorities regarding the latter's policies in respect of the retention of data relating to three individuals' criminal convictions. In each case, records were maintained of criminal convictions: in one case, a single offence dating back to 1979; in the second, five offences relating to the taking of motor vehicles, the last conviction also being in 1979; and in the case of the third data subject, five offences ending with a conviction for theft in 1969. In each case, the primary cause for complaint was not that the information had been retained by the police but that it had been disclosed for purposes unconnected with the operation of the criminal record system. In one case this was in connection with the investigation of a complaint made by the data subject in respect of the conduct of a police officer; in another disclosure was made to the United States immigration authorities in respect of a visa application and, in the third, to an employer in connection with an application for employment. Following the receipt of complaints from the data subjects, the Information Commissioner exercised his powers under section 42 of the Act to conduct an assessment of the legitimacy of the processing of the personal data. After extensive correspondence with the police authorities in question, the Commissioner served each with an enforcement notice alleging breaches of the third and fifth data protection principles. The authorities appealed to the Information Tribunal.

In all the cases, data had been retained on the police national computers and it was accepted that it was held in accordance with the latest version of 'Weeding Rules', which had been the subject of discussion, if not agreement, between the Information Commissioner (and his predecessors) and the Association of Chief Police Officers. In essence, these provide for details of relatively minor offences to be retained for thirty years and more serious offences for a period of one hundred years—a period designed to ensure that the data is retained for the lifetime of the offender. It was accepted by the Tribunal that:

> the Weeding Rules in their present form and edition demonstrate that there is some incontestable value in retaining conviction data dependent largely upon the nature of the offence. The Weeding Rules represent a considered exchange between the parties, i.e. the Commissioner on the one hand and ACPO on the other which has in the result forged some form of generalised understanding that after a given data, certain offences should be removed from the PNC. However, the Tribunal finds equally that the Weeding Rules do not and could not conceivably represent an unqualified and rigid code.[75]

The Tribunal drew a distinction between retention and disclosure of the data. Accepting the benefit for policing purposes of retention of data, even at the level of maintaining links

---

[73] Information Commissioner's Office, Guideline Booklet No. 4, *The Data Protection Principles* (Wilmslow, 1998).

[74] Available from <http://www.informationtribunal.gov.uk/DBFiles/Decision/i204/north_wales_police.pdf>.

[75] para. 206.

to fingerprint and DNA samples, it amended the Commissioner's ruling to require that within six months the appellants:

> procure that the Conviction Data relating to (the complainant data subjects) currently held on the PNC database be retained on the PNC subject to the retention rules of any current ACPO Code of Practice or any equivalent thereof and not be open to inspection other than by the data controller or by any other data controller who is or represents a chief officer of police.[76]

The Commissioner returned to the question of the conformity of police data retention in the later case of *Chief Constable of Humberside Police and ors v Information Commissioner*. This marked the first occasion in which a decision of the Information Tribunal[77] was the subject of an appeal to the Court of Appeal.[78]

The *South Yorkshire* case had focused in large part on issues concerned with the disclosure of data for purposes other than those concerned with core policing activities. These were again at issue in the *Humberside* litigation but the prime focus was on the retention of data on the Police National Computer itself.

Following a series of complaints from data subjects, the Commissioner served enforcement notices on five police forces, each relating to records relating to one individual and requiring removal of the data from the Police National Computer. As discussed in relation to the *South Yorkshire* case, access to data might be restricted although at issue in most of the present cases was an act of disclosure to other statutory agencies, generally in connection with the system of extended disclosure certificates introduced under the Police Act 1997. Any person seeking to work with vulnerable individuals such as children is required to obtain such a certificate which will detail any criminal convictions or formal reprimands received by the individual.

In four of the cases forming the basis of the enforcement notices the individuals concerned had been convicted of relatively minor criminal offences some time in the past. One subject, referred to as HP, is perhaps typical. He had been convicted on two counts of shoplifting in 1984 when aged sixteen. No further convictions were recorded against him. The conviction details were listed on an enhanced disclosure certificate which he was required to obtain twenty-two years later when seeking a position with a local authority as a care officer.

Three of the other cases were broadly similar but in the final case a thirteen-year old girl (referred to as SP) had been accused of assault. She had accepted a formal reprimand but was assured that details would be deleted from the Police National Computer when she reached the age of eighteen if she had not committed any further criminal offences. By the time of her eighteenth birthday, police policy had changed and the details were retained, again to appear on an enhanced disclosure certificate obtained in connection with an application for employment as a care worker. In this case the enforcement notice alleged also a breach of the first data protection principle, that the retention of the data in breach of undertakings given constituted unfair processing.

The Tribunal received statistical evidence indicating that where individuals had such long periods without being convicted of any offences, the likelihood of them being convicted in the future was effectively the same as that of a person with no previous criminal conviction. The Tribunal agreed with the Commissioner that the continued presence of the data on the Police National Computer offered no significant operational benefits to the

---

[76] para. 218.   [77] Available from <http://www.informationtribunal.gov.uk/Public/search.aspx>.
[78] [2009] EWCA Civ 1079.

police and upheld the enforcement notice. The police forces concerned appealed against the Tribunal decision and were successful before the Court of Appeal which was highly critical both of the Commissioner's original decision to serve the enforcement notices and of the Tribunal's decision to uphold them. Delivering the leading judgment, Lord Justice Waller quoted the evidence given to the Bichard Inquiry by the then Information Commissioner. This was set up in the wake of a case in which a school caretaker had murdered two young girls. Subsequently evidence came to light that the caretaker was known to other police forces in connection with inappropriate conduct towards girls but that this information had not been passed on to the force in whose area the murders took place. Responding to suggestions by some police authorities that the requirements of data protection legislation had prevented the sharing of information, the then Information Commissioner gave evidence to the Inquiry in the following terms:

> Police judgements about operational needs will not be lightly interfered with by the Information Commissioner. His office 'cannot and should not substitute [their] judgement for that of experienced practitioners'. His office will give considerable latitude to the police in their decision making. If a reasonable and rational basis exists for a decision, 'that should be the end of the story'.[79]

The same principle, Lord Justice Waller held, should apply in the present case, 'If the police say rationally and reasonably that convictions, however old or minor, have a value in the work they do that should, in effect, be the end of the matter.'

Accordingly, the enforcement notices were quashed on this point. The case of SP and the alleged unfair processing did divide the court but by a majority it was held that the processing had not been unfair. The retention of her data was as a result of a general change in policing policy and was not directed specifically at her.

The fourth data protection principle–adequacy and timeousness

The fourth data protection principle requires that: 'personal data shall be accurate and, where necessary, kept up to date'. Data is defined as being inaccurate when it is 'incorrect or misleading as to any matter of fact'.[80] In the event that personal data is inaccurate, a data subject may be entitled to seek its rectification and, in certain cases, compensation for any resultant damage or distress.[81]

Rather like beauty, accuracy may frequently lie in the eye of the beholder. Although many instances are reported of inaccurate data (for example, it has been suggested that data on the Police National Computer was subject to an 86 per cent error rate),[82] the question of whether data is accurate will not always be susceptible of a straightforward answer. In cases where data relates simply to an issue of fact, objective verification may be possible. A record reading 'Joe Bloggs is 75' will be inaccurate if Joe Bloggs is aged only twenty-five. In some cases, however, a record may repeat information supplied by a third party. The statement may be in the format: 'Fred Smith informs us that Joe Bloggs has defaulted on three loan agreements.' If it is assumed that Joe Bloggs is in reality a person of the utmost financial

---

[79] para. 4.45.2. [80] Data Protection Act 1998, s. 70(2).
[81] Data Protection Act 1998, ss. 13–14.
[82] 'Errors Rife in Police Data Files', *Computer Weekly*, 27 April 2000, p. 5.

probity, can it be said that the statement is false? In determining this issue, the fourth data protection principle is interpreted as follows:

> The fourth principle is not to be regarded as being contravened by reason of any inaccuracy in personal data which accurately record information obtained by the data controller from the data subject or a third party in a case where—
>
> (a) having regard to the purpose or purposes for which the data were obtained and further processed, the data controller has taken reasonable steps to ensure the accuracy of the data; and
>
> (b) if the data subject has notified the data controller of the data subject's view that the data are inaccurate, the data indicate that fact.[83]

These requirements are cumulative.

The second element of this principle requires that necessary updating of information shall be carried out. The Data Protection Act 1998 does not expand on this requirement, but it would appear that the question of whether updating is required will be dependent upon the nature of the data and the purpose to which it will be put. If the data is merely a record of a transaction between the data user and the data subject, no updating would be either necessary or justified. Where the information is being used as the basis for continuing decisions and actions, regular updating may be essential. Thus, where information is to be used for assessing an employee's suitability for promotion, an indication of periods of absence would require to be supplemented by any explanations which might subsequently have been provided.

The fifth data protection principle—duration of record-keeping

The issue of data retention is highly contentious and is discussed in more detail elsewhere in this book. Within the general data protection context the key requirement as laid down in the fifth data protection principle is that data should be retained for no longer than is necessary for the purpose for which it is held by the data controller. The Data Protection Directive contains an equivalent provision.[84] Neither instrument provides further interpretative guidance.

In some cases, data users will be under a legal obligation to retain data for a specified period of time, for example solicitor–client data. In more general terms, there would appear justification for retaining data until the expiry of any limitation period for possible legal action. Beyond situations where specific legal rules or regulations may apply, matters may be more difficult to define. It may also be the case that the nature of processing may change. An example might be taken from university or college exam marks. Whilst a student is at the institution it is clear that records of performance will require to be retained in order to determine the level of any degree awarded. Once a student has graduated, the justification for retaining data on this basis disappears. A past student seeking a reference perhaps twenty years in the future might be disappointed if a reply was in terms 'we do not hold

---

[83] Data Protection Act 1998, Sch. 1, Pt II, para. 7. These provisions are substantially similar to those applying to the data subject's claim to compensation for, or rectification of, inaccurate data.

[84] Directive 95/46/EC, Art. 6(1)(e).

any records'. As with so many aspects of the legislation, difficult decisions may require to be made by a data controller.

The seventh data protection principle—data security

Data security is a topic of major concern today. The media is replete with tales of identity fraud and there are major concerns about the use of botnets to effectively hijack personal computers and put them to criminal use. This chapter has previously considered also attempts to obtain illicit access to personal data held by a controller. Under the terms of the seventh data protection principle data controllers and the operators of computer bureaux are obliged to ensure that:

> Appropriate technical and organisational measures shall be taken against unauthorised or unlawful processing of personal data and against accidental loss or destruction of, or damage to, personal data.

Additionally, controllers will be responsible for ensuring that any data processors contracted by them comply with the requirements of the principle.

The comparable requirement in the Data Protection Directive is that, taking account of the state of the art and making an assessment of costs and risks involved:

> the controller must implement appropriate technical and organizational measures to protect personal data against accidental or unlawful destruction or accidental loss, alteration, unauthorized disclosure or access, in particular where the processing involves the transmission of data over a network.[85]

In determining whether security measures are appropriate, account has to be taken both of technical measures—for example, whether passwords are required to access data—and also of the level or training provided to employees and associated control mechanisms. Almost all of the monetary penalties imposed by the Information Commissioner in recent years have related to a breach of the data security principle. A few examples taken from the Information Commissioner's website might illustrate the scope of the provision.

4. ...A thief reached in through an open window and stole his briefcase from a seat in the car. The briefcase contained an external hard drive, some documents and approximately £3,600 in cash.

5. The external hard drive was protected by an 11-character (letters and numbers) password, but it was unencrypted. It contained a complete copy of the data controller's customer database including the details of approximately 250 clients such as their name, address, contact number, date of birth, nationality, passport number, proof of address (utility bills and bank statements) and proof of identity (passports and driving licences).[86]

A penalty of £5,000 was imposed on the data controller. There have been a number of similar cases where laptop computers or memory sticks have been lost whilst in the custody of employees and in general it may be commented that technological developments have permitted storage capabilities that would previously have been the preserve of major

---

[85] Directive 95/46/EC, Art. 17(1).
[86] <http://ico.org.uk/enforcement/~/media/documents/library/Data_Protection/Notices/jala-transport-limited-monetary-penalty-notice.pdf>.

mainframe computers to be held in tiny—and, from personal experience, very easily lost—memory sticks. In other cases penalties have been more severe. The consumer electronics company Sony were penalised to the extent of £250,000 after hackers were able to access its customer database

Codes of practice

One of the most notable features of the data protection principles is their generality. Given the range of applications across which they have to be applied and the multitude of users subjected to regulation, it is difficult to envisage any other approach. In a considerable number of sectors, codes of practice have been adopted by trade associations seeking to give sector-specific guidance as to the interpretation of the principles. One of the major legal issues concerns the status and respect that should be afforded to such codes. It cannot be the case that data controllers can define the scope of their obligations or even that a party such as the Information Commissioner should be able to exercise what would effectively be law-making powers.

The Data Protection Directive envisages a substantial role for codes of practice to operate at both a national and a Community level. The Directive's recitals state that:

> Member States and the Commission in their respective spheres of competence, must encourage the trade associations and other representative organizations concerned to draw up codes of conduct so as to facilitate the operation of this Directive, taking account of the specific circumstances of the processing carried out in certain sectors, and respecting the national provisions adopted for its implementation.[87]

Article 27 of the Directive[88] provides that draft codes are to be submitted to the national supervisory authority, which is to ascertain 'whether the drafts submitted to it are in accordance with the national provisions adopted pursuant to this Directive'. Such a development would also go at least part of the way to meeting the suggestion of the Registrar in his 1989 review of the working of the legislation that upon receipt of the Registrar's endorsement, the provisions of a code should have a status equivalent to the Highway Code—namely, that although breach of its provisions would not itself constitute an offence, this could be taken into account in determining whether any provision of the legislation had been violated.

Conclusions

As was indicated at the beginning of this chapter, the adoption of general statements of acceptable processing practices has been a feature of data (and privacy) protection legislation from the earliest days. In some respects this is non-contentious. Few would challenge the statement that data shall be processed lawfully or fairly. Like other general precepts, however, context is vitally important and few principles can be absolute. Even a seemingly absolute religious commandment such as 'thou shalt not kill' raises issues in contexts such as self-defence and the notion of 'justified war'. In the data protection context, obtaining data following some form of surveillance which might generally be considered unfair might be regarded differently if it is for the purpose of preventing a terrorist attack.

---

[87] Directive 95/46/EC, Recital 61.   [88] Directive 95/46/EC.

At the level of general principles there can be little to object to or criticise in the underlying principles. As always, the devil is in the detail and in some important respects there may be a need to update the definition of concepts in order to better meet the needs of modern data processing realities.

Specific areas where there may be need for more explicit legislative provision might include the requirements imposed on data controllers to inform subjects of the uses to which data might be put. In the case of social-networking sites, for example, this could include clear statements of privacy options and the positive and negative implications of choices which might be made by subjects. Provision might also be made regarding the default settings associated with such sites and data processing in general. It could, for example, be provided that a minimal range of access to or dissemination of data should be provided unless and until subjects make an informed choice to extend these.

6

Individual rights and remedies

Introduction

Previous chapters have focused on the obligations imposed upon data controllers to ensure that processing complies with the data protection principles. The role of ensuring compliance with these requirements is large for supervisory agencies and indeed, as shown by recent incidents such as the 'inadvertent' collection of personal data by Google in the course of its Street View programme, there are significant limits to the extent to which individuals might take effective legal action against parties suspected of infringing data protection legislation. This, indeed, has been one of the major arguments advanced to justify the establishment of data protection authorities. The Google example does perhaps cast some doubt on the validity of the approach with the response of European data protection authorities perhaps falling to be described as vacillating and confusing.

In other instances, however, the individual data subject may take centre stage and in this chapter consideration will be given to the rights that are specifically conferred upon data subjects and to the remedies which may be available in the event of any breach.

The Data Protection Act 1998 provides in the sixth data protection principle that 'Personal data shall be processed in accordance with the rights of data subjects under this Act.' Part II of the Act is entitled 'Rights of Data Subjects and Others' and provides for rights of access, the right to receive certain items of information, and rights either total or qualified to object to certain forms of processing of their personal data.

Subject access and information rights

The concept of subject access is the aspect of data protection which may impact most directly on individuals. The Data Protection Directive requires that:

Member States shall guarantee every data subject the right to obtain from the controller:

(a) without constraint at reasonable intervals and without excessive delay or expense:

- confirmation as to whether or not data relating to him are being processed and information at least as to the purposes of the processing, the categories of data concerned, and the recipients or categories of recipients to whom the data are disclosed,

- communication to him in an intelligible form of the data undergoing processing and of any available information as to their source,

- knowledge of the logic involved in any automatic processing of data concerning him at least in the case of the automated decisions referred to in Article 15 (1).

In implementing this provision, the Act requires that a data controller respond to requests which are made in writing,[1] which contain sufficient information to allow for identification of the data subject and which enclose any fee required by the controller.[2] A maximum fee of £10 may be required before the controller responds to an access request.[3] In terms of the information which is to be provided, it is now stated that:

Subject to the following provisions of this Section and to Sections 8 and 9, an individual is entitled—

(a) to be informed by any data controller whether personal data of which that individual is the data subject are being processed by or on behalf of that data controller;

(b) if that is the case, to be given by the data controller a description of—

(i) the personal data of which that individual is the data subject;

(ii) the purposes for which they are being or are to be processed; and

(iii) the recipients or classes of recipients to whom they are or may be disclosed;

(c) to have communicated to him in an intelligible form—

(i) the information constituting any personal data of which that individual is the data subject; and

(ii) any information available to the data controller as to the source of those data.

(d) where the processing by automatic means of personal data of which that individual is the data subject for the purpose of evaluating matters relating to him such as, for example, his performance at work, his creditworthiness, his reliability or his conduct, has constituted or is likely to constitute the sole basis for any decision significantly affecting him, to be informed by the data controller of the logic involved in that decision-taking.[4]

A request in respect of one of the items of information referred to above is to be taken as extending to most of the other items.[5] A request to be informed, therefore, whether personal data is held is to be taken as extending to a request for the information itself and for the further information specified relating to purposes, etc. The provision relating to information regarding the logic of processing is treated somewhat differently. The extent of the information to be supplied under this heading was the subject of considerable debate in the House of Lords, where concerns were expressed that the controller might be required to supply information which constituted valuable intellectual property.[6] It is provided that the obligation is not to extend to any information which 'constitutes a trade secret' (section 8(5)), but, as was pointed out in Parliament, this concept is an ill-defined one. The Data Protection (Subject Access) (Fees and Miscellaneous Provisions) Regulations 2000 provide that specific request must be made for receipt of this information.[7]

---

[1] s. 64 of the Act provides in respect of the access procedures and a variety of other procedures under the Act that the requirement for writing may be satisfied where a notice is transmitted by electronic means, received in legible form, and is capable of being used for subsequent reference. An email message would seem to satisfy these requirements. [2] s. 7.

[3] The Data Protection (Subject Access) (Fees and Miscellaneous Provisions) Regulations 2000, SI 2000/191, Reg. 3. [4] s. 7(2).

[5] s. 7(2), implemented by the Data Subject (Subject Access) (Fees and Miscellaneous Provisions) Regulations 2000, SI 2000/191.

[6] 586 HL Official Report (5th series), cols. CWH 43–5, 23 February 1998.

[7] SI 2000/191, Reg. 2. Rather strangely, it is also provided that a request for information about the logic employed in processing will not automatically be taken as extending to the other items of information in s. 7.

The traditional approach towards subject access has been to require that a written copy of data be supplied. The Act imposes the requirement that the copy be supplied in 'intelligible form'.[8] With developments in processing technology, it is possible that data may take the form of audio or video clips, and although the provision of written copies may be expected to remain the norm, expansion of the definition is clearly desirable. In terms of the material to be provided, it was stated by the Court of Appeal in *Durant v Financial Services Authority* that:

> The intention of the Directive, faithfully reproduced in the Act [Data Protection Act 1998], is to enable an individual to obtain from a data controller's filing system, whether computerised or manual, his personal data, that is, information about himself. It is not an entitlement to be provided with original or copy documents as such, but, as Section 7(1)(c)(i) and 8(2) provide, with information constituting personal data in intelligible and permanent form. This may be in documentary form prepared for the purpose and/or where it is convenient in the form of copies of original documents.[9]

It is further provided that, although the copy of the information is normally to be provided in permanent form, this requirement may be waived with the consent of the subject or in a case where the supply of such a copy would be either impossible or involve a disproportionate effort.[10] No indication is given of what might constitute a disproportionate effort but the Commissioner has indicated that decisions will have to be made in the light of the circumstances of each case. A significant factor will be the cost implications to the controller of responding to the request. The information supplied must be that which was held at the time the access request was received, except where any subsequent changes 'would have been made regardless of the receipt of the request'.[11]

The concept of subject access was pioneered in the United Kingdom by the Consumer Credit Act 1974, which provided that individuals should be entitled to obtain a copy of information held by a credit reference agency.[12] The 1974 Act's procedures were unaffected by the original Data Protection Act of 1984. Given that the credit sector has historically generated the largest number of complaints to the Commissioner by data subjects, the retention of two separate regimes was considered unsupportable and the 1998 legislation incorporates the provisions for access to data held by credit reference agencies. Provision is made for different fee levels to be fixed by the Secretary of State, and the Data Protection (Subject Access) (Fees and Miscellaneous Provisions) Regulations 2000[13] provides that a fee of £2 will be payable in respect of access to such records.[14] One issue concerning the change did cause discussion in Parliament.[15] Under the 1974 Act, a modified access procedure applies where the subject is a business person.[16] Effectively, this limits the amount of information supplied so that, for example, the applicant would not receive information about adverse credit reports which had been provided by bankers or suppliers. Where the business constitutes a sole trader or partnership, the general access provisions of the Data Protection Act 1998 will replace the specialised provisions. Concern was expressed that the consequence might be that third parties would be reluctant to supply such information in the knowledge that it could be obtained, with the consequence being that small businesses might find it more difficult to obtain credit. Whilst giving an undertaking to keep the matter under review, the government indicated that it was not convinced that the concerns were justified, and a proposal to amend the Bill to retain the current procedures was rejected.[17]

---

[8] s. 7(1)(c).   [9] [2003] EWCA Civ 1746 at [26].   [10] s. 8(2).   [11] s. 8(6).
[12] s. 158.   [13] SI 2000/191.   [14] Reg. 4.   [15] s. 9.   [16] s. 160.
[17] 316 HC Official Report (6th series), cols. 578–9, 2 July 1998.

Access timetable

Valid requests for access must be satisfied within forty days.[18] Where data is held by a credit reference agency, the current shorter time limit of seven days is to apply.[19] The information supplied must generally be that held at the date of receipt of the access request. Account may be taken, however, of any amendments or deletions made subsequently where these would have been made 'regardless of the receipt of the request'.[20] Having satisfied an access request from a data subject, a controller is not obliged to comply with a subsequent identical or similar request until a reasonable interval has elapsed.[21] In making his or her determination, account is to be taken of the nature of the data, the purpose of the processing, and the frequency with which amendments are made.

Exceptions to the subject access provisions

In certain situations, the individual's interest in obtaining access to personal data has to be restricted, either in the subject's own interests or as a result of giving priority to other competing claims. Access to medical data provides an example of the first situation, where it is provided that an access request may be refused where it is considered that this might be prejudicial to the enquiring subject's physical or mental health, whilst restrictions on access to data held for the purpose of crime prevention or detection illustrate how the subject's desire to know what information is held might reasonably be subjugated to the requirements of the data controller or those of society at large.

The Data Protection Directive provides that Member States may provide for exemptions from subject access when this constitutes a necessary measure to safeguard:

(a) national security;

(b) defence;

(c) public security;

(d) the prevention, investigation, detection, and prosecution of criminal offences, or of breaches of ethics for regulated professions;

(e) an important economic or financial interest of a Member State or of the EU, including monetary, budgetary, and taxation matters;

(f) a monitoring, inspection, or regulatory function connected, even occasionally, with the exercise of official authority in cases referred to in (c), (d), and (e); or

(g) the protection of the data subject or of the rights and freedoms of others.[22]

In respect of the various provisions to be discussed, a variety of approaches exist. Where data is held for national security purposes, total exemption is offered from all aspects of the legislation. In the case of data held for historical, research, or statistical purposes, the exemption relates only to subject access and the related supply of information relating to source, processing purpose, and intended disclosures as defined in section 7 of the Data Protection Act 1998. In other cases, however, the exemption is stated as applying also in respect of the requirements of the first data protection principle relating to the fair and lawful processing of personal data. Although in many cases, the application of the exemption

---

[18] Data Protection Act 1998, s. 7(10).

[19] Data Protection (Subject Access) (Fees and Miscellaneous Provisions) Regulations 2000, SI 2000/191, Reg. 4.

[20] Data Protection Act 1998, s. 8(6).   [21] s. 8(3).   [22] Directive 95/46/EC, Art. 13(1).

is limited to instances where it is necessary to avoid prejudicing the purpose for which the data is being processed, its linkage with subject access does mean that provisions which purport to protect data subjects may, in reality, work to their disadvantage.

Prior to considering the circumstances under which a user may legally deny a subject's access request, mention should be made of a problem that may arise whenever the user determines that all or part of a request for access falls within the scope of an exception. Under the Data Protection Act 1998's definitions, personal data is classed as data to which the subject is entitled to have access. Where an exception is properly relied upon, it may be accepted that it is as undesirable from the user's standpoint to inform the subject that they hold data which they are not willing to disclose as it would be to divulge the information. In the event that a subject suspects that personal data has not been supplied pursuant to a request for access, action may be raised before the courts.[23] An alternative course of action will be to make a complaint to the Commissioner. In the event the Commissioner takes action, the onus will be on the user to justify their action. However, dependent upon the circumstances and the nature of the data, it may be that a subject who receives the reply that no relevant personal data is held may accept this at face value and will make no attempt to pursue the matter before the courts or with the Commissioner.

Third-party data

In some cases, as has been discussed earlier, the linkage of data relating to a third party with mention of a data subject may lead to the conclusion that a record does not constitute personal data relating to the data subject. In other cases, there can be no doubt that a record does constitute personal data but that this relates to more than one individual. It may be that data relates to some form of joint activity: transactions, for example, in connection with the operation of a joint bank account. In this situation, where one subject submits an access request, there is unlikely to be a serious issue concerning the identity of the other subject or subjects, but there may be a case for deleting items of data such as cheque or cash-machine withdrawals made under the signature or against the PIN of the other account holder. In a second situation, the data may relate to the enquiring subject but emanate from a third party. An example might see a social-work record recounting an allegation from a named third party that a subject is behaving in a violent manner to other persons. The record could state that 'Fred Smith has reported that Joe Bloggs is mistreating his wife and children.' There is clearly personal data about Joe Bloggs here and it may be desirable to allow the subject to see and possibly refute the allegation of violence. The record also contains personal data relating to Fred Smith as the source of the data. It is likely to be extremely unwelcome to this person if the fact of his report is disclosed to Joe Bloggs. How the balance is to be struck has been a continuing cause of difficulty.

Under the Data Protection Act 1984, a data user was under no obligation to supply information relating to a third party—including the fact that the third party had been the source of information relating to the data subject. No obligation, however, was imposed on the data user to inquire whether the third party would be willing for the information to be transmitted to the subject.[24] A significant change to the extent of access rights required came as a consequence of the decision of the European Court of Human Rights in the case of *Gaskin v United Kingdom*.[25] The applicant in this case had spent much of his childhood in local authority care. In adulthood, he claimed that he had been the subject of ill-treatment and instituted legal proceedings against the local authority. As part of these proceedings,

---

[23] Data Protection Act 1998, s. 7(9).   [24] s. 21(4)(a).   [25] (1990) 12 EHRR 36.

he sought discovery of all documents held by the authority relating to his case. Many of the documents had been compiled by third parties, such as doctors and social workers. Acting in excess of the statutory obligations imposed upon them, the authority contacted the third parties, seeking their approval to disclosure. Whilst the majority agreed to disclosure of the data, a number of parties refused consent and the authority took the view that this was determinative of the issue. Under United Kingdom law as it stood this was undoubtedly the case, but proceedings were raised before the European Court of Human Rights alleging that the failure of the United Kingdom legislation to provide the applicant with a right of access to the data constituted a breach of its obligations under Article 8 of the European Convention on Human Rights requiring respect for private and family life. The European Court of Human Rights held that, whilst the applicant did not have an unqualified right of access to data, the failure to provide an independent review in the event that a third party refused consent constituted a breach of his rights:

> The Court considers…that under such a system the interests of the individual seeking access to records relating to his private and family life must be secured when a contributor to the records either is not available or improperly refuses consent. Such a system is only in conformity with the principle of proportionality if it provides that an independent authority finally decides whether access has to be granted in cases where a contributor fails to answer or withholds consent. No such procedure was available to the applicant in the present case.[26]

In seeking to bring United Kingdom law into conformity with the European Convention on Human Rights, the Data Protection Act 1998 now provides that:

> Where a data controller cannot comply with the request (for information) without disclosing information relating to another individual who can be identified from that information, he is not obliged to comply with the request unless—
>
> (a) the other individual has consented to the disclosure of the information to the person making the request, or
>
> (b) it is reasonable in all the circumstances to comply with the request without the consent of the other individual.[27]

In determining whether it is reasonable for a controller to provide access without the third party's consent the Act provides that account is to be taken in particular of:

> (a) any duty of confidentiality owed to the other individual,
>
> (b) any steps taken by the data controller with a view to seeking the consent of the other individual,
>
> (c) whether the other individual is capable of giving consent, and
>
> (d) any express refusal of consent by the other individual.[28]

It is further provided that 'reference to information relating to another individual includes a reference to information identifying that individual as the source of the information sought by the request'. The provision, however, 'is not to be construed as excusing a data controller from communicating so much of the information sought by the request as can be communicated without disclosing the identity of the other individual concerned, whether by the omission of names or other identifying particulars or otherwise'.[29]

---

[26] (1990) 12 EHRR 36 at 50.   [27] s. 7(4).   [28] s. 7(6).   [29] s. 7(5).

The application of these provisions was at issue in the case of *Durant v Financial Services Authority*.[30] The background to this case has been described earlier under 'Subject access and information rights'. Although some information was supplied, access to other records was provided only in partial form through the concealment or redaction of information which it was considered related to a third party who was an employee of the defendant. The complainant sought access to the names of this person. It appears that the data controller sought the views of the individual who 'had understandably withheld his or her consent because Mr Durant had abused him or her over the telephone'.

One issue which does not appear to have been discussed before the court concerned the status of the individual who it appears was an employee of the Financial Services Authority. The Data Protection Act provides that the term 'third party' does not include any person 'authorised to process data for the data controller'.[31] Employees would undoubtedly fall into this category,[32] although the court in *Durant* made extensive reference to data relating to third parties. However, section 7(5)–(6) refers to data relating to 'another individual' and does not use the term 'third party'. Although, as discussed previously, there may be a question of whether the identity of an employee dealing with a data subject forms part of that subject's personal data, it would appear a strange result if a data controller could reject or respond only in part to an access request on the ground that data related to a member of staff.

Although in this particular case, the data controller had sought consent for disclosure of the data, the court continued to give guidance as to the nature of the consideration that the statute required to be given by a data controller when faced with such an access request. The general criterion, it was stated, was 'whether it is reasonable to *comply* with the request for information notwithstanding that it may disclose information about another, not whether it is reasonable to *refuse* to comply'. The distinction, it was stated:

> may be of importance, depending on who is challenging the data controller's decision, to the meaning of 'reasonable' in this context and to the court's role in examining it. The circumstances going to the reasonableness of such a decision, as I have just noted, include, but are not confined to, those set out in Section 7(6) [of the Data Protection Act 1998], and none of them is determinative. It is important to note that Section 7(4) leaves the data controller with a choice whether to seek consent; it does not oblige him to do so before deciding whether to disclose the personal data sought or, by redaction, to disclose only part of it. However, whether he has sought such consent and, if he has done so, it has been refused, are among the circumstances mentioned in the non-exhaustive list in Section 7(6) going to the reasonableness of any decision under Section 7(4)(b) to disclose, without consent.[33]

It is difficult to conceive of many situations where a data controller should decline to seek the third party's consent and then refuse an access request on the ground that the data would identify a third party. Such a result would conflict sharply with the principles laid down in *Gaskin*. In the event that the third party—as in the present case—was asked to consent, refused, and the controller determined not to disclose the data to the enquiring data subject, the courts, it was held, should be reluctant to routinely:

> 'second-guess' decisions of data controllers, who may be employees of bodies large or small, public or private or be self-employed. To so interpret the legislation would encourage litigation and appellate challenge by way of full rehearing on the merits and, in that manner,

---

[30] [2003] EWCA Civ 1746.   [31] s. 70(1).
[32] Information Commissioner's Office, *Legal Guidance*.   [33] para. 56.

impose disproportionate burdens on them and their employers in their discharge of their many responsibilities under the Act [Data Protection Act 1998].

The judgment continued to observe that:

the right to privacy and other legitimate interests of individuals identified in or identifiable from a data subject's personal data are highly relevant to, but not determinative of, the issue of reasonableness of a decision whether to disclose personal data containing information about someone else where that person's consent has not been sought. The data controller and, if necessary, a court on an application under Section 7(9), should also be entitled to ask what, if any, legitimate interest the data subject has in disclosure of the identity of another individual named in or identifiable from personal data to which he is otherwise entitled...

...Much will depend, on the one hand, on the criticality of the third party information forming part of the data subject's personal data to the legitimate protection of his privacy, and, on the other, to the existence or otherwise of any obligation of confidence to the third party or any other sensitivity of the third party disclosure sought. Where the third party is a recipient or one of a class of recipients who might act on the data to the data subject's disadvantage...his right to protect his privacy may weigh heavily and obligations of confidence to the third party(ies) may be non-existent or of less weight. Equally, where the third party is the source of the information, the data subject may have a strong case for his identification if he needs to take action to correct some damaging inaccuracy, though here countervailing considerations of an obligation of confidentiality to the source or some other sensitivity may have to be weighed in the balance.[34]

A final issue concerns the question of when a third party is to be considered identifiable. A controller is obliged to supply as much information as is possible without disclosing the third party's identity. In particular, it is stated, this might involve the omission of names or other identifying particulars. Account is to be taken of:

any information which in the reasonable belief of the data controller, is likely to be in, or to come into, the possession of the data subject making the request.[35]

In the *Durant* case, this task was relatively straightforward. The data subject did not know the identity of the employee he had been dealing with and a motive behind the access request was to obtain this information. This requirement may cause some difficulties for data controllers. In a case such as *Gaskin*,[36] for example, it may be a very difficult task for a data controller to assess whether the enquiring data subject would have, after the passage of many years, any recollection of the identity of particular doctors or social workers who had been responsible for submitting reports.

National security

Under the Data Protection Act 1984, information held for the purpose of national security was totally exempted from the legislation.[37] Given the increasing involvement of national security agencies such as MI5 in crime-related functions, such as operations against suspected drug dealers, the division between national security and criminal functions is frequently blurred. This has led the Registrar to express concern that exemptions have been claimed on an organisational rather than a task-related basis.[38] Although no changes

---

[34] para. 66.   [35] Data Protection Act 1998, s. 7(5).
[36] *Gaskin v United Kingdom* (1990) 12 EHRR 36.   [37] s. 27.
[38] See e.g. *Sunday Times*, 1 February 1998.

were required to the 1984 Act in this regard, national security falling outwith the ambit of Community law-making competence, the Data Protection Act 1998 does contain significant new provisions. As under the 1984 Act, a certificate may be issued by a minister of the Crown indicating that personal data is held for the purpose of national security.[39] Under the 1984 Act, such a certificate was not open to challenge. It is now provided, however, that it may be challenged before the Information Tribunal by any person 'directly affected'. This may include a data subject who for the first and only time is given a right to initiate proceedings before the Tribunal. Applying 'the principles applied by the court on an application for judicial review', the Tribunal may quash the certificate if it considers that the minister did not have 'reasonable grounds' for issuing it.[40] Detailed provisions for the procedures to be followed in the Tribunal are now found in the Information Tribunal (National Security Appeals) Rules 2005.[41]

With the introduction of the new right of appeal, a number of cases were brought before the Information Tribunal. In the first case, *Norman Baker v Secretary of State for the Home Department*,[42] the claimant, a Liberal Democrat MP, had sought access to records which he believed were held about him by the security services. This prompted a response:

> Under the Data Protection Act 1998 the Security Service intends to notify the Data Protection Commissioner that it processes data for three purposes. These are: staff administration, building security CCTV and commercial agreements. The Security Service has checked its records and holds no data about you in any of these categories.
>
> Any other personal data held by the Security Service is exempt from the notification and subject access provisions of the Data Protection Act 1998 on the ground that such exemption is required for the purpose of safeguarding national security, as provided for in Section 28(1) of the Act. Thus, if it were to be the case that the Service held any data regarding you other than for the purposes set out in paragraph 2 above, the Data Protection Act would not confer a right of access. There is therefore no data to which you are entitled to have access under the Act, but you should not assume from this letter that any such data is held about you.
>
> I would point out that a right of appeal exists under Section 28 of the Act. The Section provides that the exemption described above can be confirmed by a certificate signed by a Minister of the Crown who is a member of the Cabinet, or by the Attorney General. A certificate relating to the work of the Security Service was signed by the Home Secretary on 22 July. Any person directly affected by the issuing of the certificate may appeal . . .[43]

Such an appeal was brought and provided the opportunity for the first sitting of the National Security Appeals Panel of the Information Tribunal. The appellant argued before the Tribunal that he had been given information that the security services had collected information in connection with his past activities in support of an ecological group. Although his involvement with the organisation had now ceased, he indicated that he had been informed that the file remained in existence.

The Tribunal reviewed the certificate which had been issued by the Secretary of State. This, it was stated, 'can fairly be described as a blanket exemption for "any personal data that is processed by the Security Service" in the performance of its statutory functions':[44]

> By exempting the Security Service from the duty under Section 7(1)(a) of the Act [Data Protection Act 1998] to inform the individual making the request whether or not his personal data are being processed, the Certificate authorises the non-committal reply which was given to Mr Baker. This means that both the Certificate and the response gave effect to

---

[39] s. 28(2).   [40] s. 28(5).   [41] SI 2005/13.   [42] [2001] UKHRR 1275.
[43] [2001] UKHRR 1275 at [14].   [44] [2001] UKHRR 1275 at [25].

the policy which is known colloquially as 'neither confirm nor deny' and by the acronym 'NCND'. We have no doubt that they were intended to do so.[45]

The certificate at issue in the present case was typical of all certificates issued in response to requests for access under the Data Protection Act 1998. The case for applying this policy was that a reply indicating that information was held but was not being made available to an applicant could of itself compromise the national security interests for which the information had been collected.

Although such a policy raises major issues relating to access to national security data, the issue before the Tribunal was a more limited one, namely to determine whether the Secretary of State had acted reasonably in formulating a certificate which left the decision of whether and to what extent a request for access should be granted entirely to the security services. As was stated:

> if the NCND response is permitted in all cases then the practical result is that the Service is not obliged to consider each request on its individual merits. That follows if the NCND reply is invariably justified, and we were furnished with no evidence that individual consideration is given to the possible consequences of making a positive response to every request.[46]

The question for the Tribunal was whether such a blanket policy was acceptable or whether the legislation imposed an obligation to give consideration to the individual circumstances of each application.

Discussion of whether the Secretary of State had reasonable grounds for issuing the certificate focused on the question of whether his action constituted a proportionate response to the need to balance the interests of individual rights and state security. After reviewing the principles appropriate to an action for judicial review, the Tribunal recognised that different situations called for different approaches:

> Where the context is national security judges and tribunals should supervise with the lightest touch appropriate; there is no area (foreign affairs apart) where judges have traditionally deferred more to the executive view than that of national security; and for good and sufficient reason. They have no special expertise; and the material upon which they can make decisions is perforce limited. That the touch should be the lightest in comparative terms does not, of course, assist in weighing up how light that should be in absolute terms.[47]

Even on this basis, however, the Tribunal was of the view that the certificate should be quashed. A blanket exemption, as provided for by the certificate, was wider than was necessary to preserve national security. It was clear from the evidence that there were cases where information held by the security services could be disclosed without prejudicing national security and no evidence that the task of sifting these cases from others where the established 'neither confirm nor deny' response was given would impose unreasonable burdens upon the security service. The decision in the *Baker* case[48] was not concerned in any respect with the merits of a decision that access should not be granted. It provides authority for the proposition that each request must be considered on its merits.

In two further cases brought before the National Security Appeals Panel, *Hitchens v Secretary of State for the Home Department* and *Gosling v Secretary of State for the Home Department*,[49] the attempt was made to challenge the merits of decisions to refuse to supply information which the appellants believed was held by the security services concerning

---

[45] [2001] UKHRR 1275 at [30].   [46] [2001] UKHRR 1275 at [32].
[47] [2001] UKHRR 1275 at [76].   [48] [2001] UKHRR 1275.
[49] The transcript of these decisions can be obtained from the Department of Constitutional Affairs website at <http://www.dca.gov.uk/foi/inftrib.htm>.

their past activities. In the former case, the period covered was some thirty years previously when the claimant, who was to become a somewhat right-wing newspaper columnist, was a member of an extreme Marxist group at York University. Whilst he accepted that the security services would have been justified to take an interest in his youthful activities he argued:

> My aim is purely to know what, if anything, is in these records, mainly because I feel I am entitled to know the details of such records as a matter of natural justice. Since I am no longer a revolutionary Marxist, and the politics of this country have been utterly transformed in the intervening period, and it is most unlikely that any individual mentioned in these files still holds a sensitive position of any kind, I can see no argument for withholding these files from me. I would, if asked, be quite happy to co-operate with the Security Service to ensure that no sensitive information was accidentally disclosed. Their response, however, is simple blank refusal…covered by the meaningless and hard-to-justify claim that this is 'safeguarding national security'. I think the Security Service needs to do better than this to justify secrecy over files almost 30 years old concerning my own youthful follies and their attempts to monitor them.

Following the panel's decision in *Baker*, the format of the ministerial certificate had been amended to make it incumbent upon the security service to give individual consideration to each request for access. The focus of argument in this case was on the merits of the individual decision. Here, the Panel was referred to the Investigatory Powers Tribunal, which was established under section 65 of the Regulation of Investigatory Powers Act 2000 to deal with a wide range of complaints that may be made about the exercise of powers under the Act. This tribunal, it was held, had jurisdiction to deal with complaints of the kind brought by the appellant. Furthermore:

> we believe that the Investigatory Powers Tribunal is the body best placed to determine any specific complaint that the Service has applied the provisos to the certificate in a manner that is manifestly unjustified. That Tribunal is presided over by a distinguished senior judge and has the appropriate expertise to investigate a complaint of this nature.[50]

On this basis, the appeal was rejected.

Whilst it is encouraging that another method of appeal should be available to individuals, the result appears indicative of a somewhat confused and confusing approach towards information policy. Whilst it may well be the case that the structure of the Investigatory Powers Tribunal makes it better equipped to deal with arguments on the merits of a particular access request, the question arises as to what is the continuing function of the National Security Appeals Panel. Having quashed the first version of the ministerial certificate in *Baker*, the terms of the revised version were accepted in *Hitchens*. Short of further changes in format, it is difficult to identify any circumstances in which an appeal to the panel would serve any useful purpose.

Data held for policing and revenue-gathering purposes

The Data Protection Act 1998 provides an exception from the subject access provisions where personal data is processed in connection with:

(a) the prevention or detection of crime,

(b) the apprehension or prosecution of offenders, or

---

[50] [2001] UKHRR 1275 at [56].

(c)   the collection or assessment of any tax or duty

to the extent that the grant of access would be prejudicial to the attainment of the purpose in question.[51]

The determination of whether access would be prejudicial to any of the above purposes requires to be made in the context of an individual request for access. In the event that a denial of access is challenged before the Commissioner, the onus will be on the data user to demonstrate a likelihood of prejudice in the circumstances of the particular case. The criteria to be invoked was discussed before the High Court in *Lord v Secretary of State*,[52] an action in which a prisoner was seeking access to reports produced in the course of a prison review to determine whether his status should be reduced from that of a high-risk (category A) inmate. For the authorities it was argued, inter alia, that disclosure would be likely to prejudice the interests of crime prevention. Considering the approach to be adopted, Mr Justice Mumby commented:

> I accept that 'likely' in Section 29(1) does not mean more probable than not. But on the other hand, it must connote a significantly greater degree of probability than merely 'more than fanciful'. A 'real risk' is not enough. I cannot accept that the important rights intended to be conferred by Section 7 are intended to be set at nought by something which measures up only to the minimal requirement of being real, tangible or identifiable rather than merely fanciful. Something much more significant and weighty than that is required. After all, the Directive, to which I must have regard in interpreting Section 29(1), permits restrictions on the data subject's right of access to information about himself only (to quote the language of Recital (43)) 'in so far as they are *necessary* to safeguard' or (to quote the language of Article 13(1)) 'constitute a *necessary* measure to safeguard' the prevention and detection of crime [emphasis added]. The test of necessity is a strict one...In my judgment 'likely' in Section 29(1) connotes a degree of probability where there is a very significant and weighty chance of prejudice to the identified public interests. The degree of risk must be such that there 'may very well' be prejudice to those interests, even if the risk falls short of being more probable than not.[53]

Consideration was also given to the extent to which the decision of whether data should be disclosed should be made solely by reference to the circumstances of the particular applicant, whilst recognising that this does not mean that one can simply ignore the consequential effect that disclosure in the particular case may have on others.[54]

It was held that a blanket policy of non-disclosure failed to satisfy the test and an order was made that the data should be released to the claimant.

A further exception operates at a higher level of generality. This provides that subject access will not be permitted where personal data is processed by a government department, local authority, or other authority administering housing benefit or council tax benefit as part of a system of risk assessment relating to the assessment of collection of tax or duty, the prevention or detection of crime, or the apprehension or prosecution of offenders and:

> where the offence concerned involves any unlawful claim for payment out of, or any unlawful application of, public funds

and reliance on exemption is required in the interests of the operation of the system.[55]

By referring to the operation of the system, the provision obviates the need to show that allowing a particular data subject access would have prejudicial effects. It was explained on

---

[51] s. 29(1).   [52] [2003] EWHC 2073 (Admin).   [53] paras. 99–100.   [54] para. 122.
[55] Data Protection Act 1998, s. 29(4).

behalf of the government that the provision was intended primarily to benefit the Inland Revenue. An example might be that:

> the Inland Revenue's recently introduced self-assessment system uses a range of indicators to identify individual tax returns which justify further inquiries. Subsection 4 will allow an exemption to be made for withholding this critical risk assessment information from data subjects. If it was not withheld, tax experts, if not the individuals concerned, could soon start to compare cases and deduce the revenue's criteria for further inquiry.[56]

It is to be noted that the exemption relates only to the subject access provision and not to the requirements of the first data protection principle that data be obtained and processed fairly and lawfully.

Health data

The Data Protection Act 1984 established the general principle that access should be provided to medical and social-work data. The Access to Personal Files Act 1987 and Access to Health Records Act 1990 extended these rights to manual files with procedures which are now gathered under the umbrella of the Data Protection Act 1998. The 1998 Act confers power on the Secretary of State to make regulations exempting or modifying the subject information provisions in respect of health data.[57] Such an approach is envisaged by the Data Protection Directive which states in Recital 42:

> Member States may, in the interest of the data subject or so as to protect the rights and freedoms of others, restrict rights of access and information; whereas they may, for example, specify that access to medical data may be obtained only through a health professional.

Article 11 provides that measures may be taken to 'restrict the scope' of access rights on a range of grounds including 'the protection of the data subject or of the rights and freedoms of others'. The United Kingdom legislation perhaps stretches the concept of 'restrict' to its limits by providing for access to be excluded. The Data Protection (Subject Access Modification) (Health) Order 2000[58] provides for exemption when, in the opinion of a relevant health professional, the grant of access would 'cause serious harm to the physical or mental health or condition of the data subject or any other person'.

In cases where the data controller concerned is not a health professional, any decision to grant or refuse access may be made only after consultation with an 'appropriate health professional'. This term is defined as:

(a) the health professional who is currently or was most recently responsible for the clinical care of the data subject in connection with the matters to which the information which is the subject of the request relates; or

(b) where there is more than one such health professional, the health professional who is the most suitable to advise on the matters to which the information which is the subject of the request relates.[59]

A request for access may not be denied on the ground that disclosure would identify a health professional as being responsible for the compilation of a record, except where it can be shown that serious harm is likely to be caused to the physical or mental health or condition of the health professional. This is perhaps likely to apply only in the situation where

---

[56] 586 HL Official Report (5th series), col. 505, 16 March 1998.   [57] s. 30(1).
[58] SI 2000/413.   [59] SI 2000/413, Article 2.

there are grounds for suspecting that the data subject might be liable to attack or harass the health professional identified.

Special provision is made for the situation where access is sought, typically by a parent or guardian, on behalf of a child or a person suffering some mental incapacity. In such a case, it is provided that data are exempted from the access rights where it has been:

(a) provided by the data subject in the expectation that it would not be disclosed to the person making the request;

(b) obtained as a result of any examination or investigation to which the data subject consented in the expectation that the information would not be disclosed; or

(c) which the data subject has expressly indicated should not be so disclosed.[60]

By providing that access may be denied only to the extent that this would cause 'serious harm' to the health of the data subject, the Order[61] must be seen as establishing a strong presumption in favour of access. Whilst recognising that circumstances—particularly those connected with psychiatric illness—may exist in which the supply of a copy of a medical record may not be in the best interests of the patient, it may be doubted whether the procedures adopted under the Order are, in themselves, likely to prove any less harmful. In common with the situations arising under other exemptions, a health professional may respond to a request for access with the statement that no relevant personal data is held. To an extent perhaps greater than with the other exceptions, the data subject is likely to be aware of the fact that data is held. The failure to supply data may well be a source of distress in itself, whilst discovery of the fact that the data has been withheld for fear that access would cause serious harm to the patient's health would, in itself, appear inimical to his or her health interests.

Education and social-work data

The basic format of the exemptions in respect of these categories of data is similar to that applying to health records. The relevant statutory instruments are the Data Protection (Subject Access Modification) (Education) Order 2000[62] and the Data Protection (Subject Access Modification) (Social Work) Order 2000.[63] In both cases, access may be denied in situations where its grant 'would be likely to cause serious harm to the physical or mental health or condition of the data subject or any other person'. Unlike the situation with health records, however, there is no requirement that the decision of whether to grant or refuse access should be made by a person possessing appropriate qualifications.

In both sectors, it is provided that a request for access may not be refused on the basis that the data would identify a third party where this would refer to an employee of the data controller responsible for producing a record in the course of employment, again subject to an exception where it can be shown that the grant of access would be likely to result in serious harm to the individuals concerned.

In the case of both categories of records—but especially in the case of educational records—there is a possibility that access may be sought by a third party acting on behalf of a data subject. In addition to the general ground for refusing access, it is provided in the case of educational records that access may be denied in respect of information indicating that the child is, or may be, at risk of child abuse and where the grant of access would not be

---

[60] SI 2000/413, Article 5(3). [61] SI 2000/413. [62] SI 2000/414. [63] SI 2000/415.

in the best interests of the child. In respect of social-work records, the criteria are identical to those described earlier concerning health data.

Regulatory activity

A broad range of statutory agencies engaged in regulatory tasks are provided with exemptions from the subject information provisions to the extent that compliance with these would prejudice the attainment of their purpose.[64] A number of agencies are specifically identified in the Data Protection Act 1998, namely the Parliamentary, Health Service, Local Government, and Northern Irish Assembly, and Complaints Ombudsmen. Exemption is also offered to the Director General of Fair Trading in respect of the discharge of functions in the fields of consumer protection and competition policy. In addition to named agencies, exemption is also offered to those performing 'relevant functions' which are designed to protect against specified risks. The term 'relevant functions' is defined to encompass functions conferred by statute, performed by the Crown, ministers, or government departments, or 'any other function' which is of a 'public nature and is exercised in the public interest'. The activities involved relate to protection against loss due to 'dishonesty, malpractice or other seriously improper conduct' within the financial services, corporate, and professional sectors, or through the conduct of discharged or undischarged bankrupts. Also exempted are functions concerned with the supervision of charities and the protection of health and safety, both for workers and for third parties who might be affected by particular activities.

Research, history, and statistics

Exemption for data of this description continues the approach adopted in the Data Protection Act 1984. Where data are 'not processed to support measures or decisions with regard to particular individuals', and where the processing is not likely to cause substantial damage or distress to any data subject, exemption is offered from the subject access provisions subject to the further condition that the results of processing are not made available in a form permitting identification of data subjects.[65]

Information required to be made available to the public

In many instances, personal data will be contained in some document which is made available to the public. An example would be the Electoral Roll, copies of which may be supplied in electronic format. In the situation where the data made available is the only data held concerning the data subject, there would be little value for the subject in exercising a right of access. Such an exemption previously applied under the Data Protection Act 1984 and continues under the Data Protection Act 1998, however, again, with the additional benefit to the data controller that there will be exemption from the first data protection principle.[66]

Miscellaneous exceptions

Schedule 7 to the Data Protection Act 1998 contains a substantial list of additional exceptions, which list may be supplemented by regulations made by the Secretary of State.[67] As described in the following paragraphs, the extent of the individual exemptions varies,

---

[64] s. 31.   [65] s. 33.   [66] s. 34.   [67] s. 38(1).

ranging from the application of modified access procedures, through to exemption from access, and to exemption from the fair processing requirement.

Confidential references

In many cases under the Data Protection Act 1984, such references would have been excluded from scrutiny under provisions referring to the processing of data purely in order to create the text of a document (the word-processing exemption).[68] This exemption is not retained in the Data Protection Act 1998 and the expanded definition of processing in the 1998 Act will bring such documents within its scope. It is provided that the subject access provisions will not apply to references given in connection with the data subject's education, employment, or appointment to any office, as well as to the provision of any services by the data subject.[69]

Armed forces

The subject information provisions will not apply where their application would be likely to prejudice the combat effectiveness of the armed forces.[70] This is a new provision and it is difficult to identify situations in which it is likely to apply.

Judicial appointments and honours

Under the Data Protection Act 1984, information held for the first of these purposes was exempted from the subject access provisions.[71] The Data Protection Act 1998 extends the scope of the exemption to data processed in connection with the 'conferring by the Crown of any honour'. Such data are exempt from the subject information provisions, regardless of any issue of prejudice.[72]

Crown employment and Crown and ministerial appointments

Regulatory power is conferred on the Secretary of State to exempt data processed for the purpose of assessing a person's suitability for specified appointments. The Data Protection (Crown Appointments) Order 2000[73] provides that this is to apply in respect of the appointment of senior religious figures in the Church of England and a range of other dignitaries, including the Poet Laureate and the Astronomer Royal.

Management forecasts

Personal data processed for this (undefined) purpose benefit from an exemption to the subject information provisions, where compliance would prejudice the attainment of the purpose.[74] Under the Data Protection Act 1984, a data user was not required to give access to information indicating intentions held towards the data subject. This exemption no longer applies but such information might frequently be held in records maintained for career-planning purposes and these may benefit from this provision.

Corporate finance

Extensive provisions are made for exemptions under this heading. The exemption will apply to data processed by 'relevant persons' concerned with the underwriting of share issues or the provision of advice on capital structure, industrial strategy, and acquisitions and mergers, and will apply when the application of the subject information provisions could affect the price of any shares or other instruments. In the situation where this criterion is not

---

[68] s. 1(8).   [69] Sch. 7, para. 1.   [70] Data Protection Act 1998, Sch. 7, para. 2.   [71] s. 31.
[72] Sch. 7, para. 3.   [73] SI 2000/416.   [74] Data Protection Act 1998, Sch. 7, para. 4.

satisfied, it is further provided that exemption may be granted 'for the purpose of safe-guarding an important economic or financial interest of the United Kingdom'. It is provided that the Secretary of State may specify in more detail the circumstances and situations in which this latter exemption is to apply and this power is exercised in the Data Protection (Corporate Finance Exception) Order 2000.[75] This specifies that account is to be taken of the 'inevitable prejudicial effect' on:

(a) the orderly functioning of financial markets, or

(b) the efficient allocation of capital within the economy,

through granting access to data which might affect the decision of any person on whether or how to act within the financial markets or in respect of the conduct of any business activity.

Negotiations

Data processed in relation to negotiations between the controller and subject which record the intentions of the controller are exempt from the subject information provisions where compliance with these would be likely to prejudice those negotiations.[76] An example of such a situation might concern data relating to an employer's business strategy in a situation where an employee who has been identified as critical to the success of the business is seeking to negotiate a pay rise.

Examination marks and examination scripts

The Data Protection Act 1984 made special provision allowing examination authorities to delay responding to requests for access beyond the normal forty-day period.[77] This was considered necessary for large-scale examinations, such as the GCSE, where a period of months might elapse between examination and publication of the results. This approach is continued in the Data Protection Act 1998.[78] One point which should be noted is that where an examination authority relies upon the extended time limits upon receipt of an access request, its response must provide information as to the data held at the time of receipt of the request, at the time the request is complied with, and any further data which was held at any intervening stage. An enquiring subject will, therefore, receive details of any changes made to exam marks during the various stages of the assessment process.

A novel exemption from the subject access provision relates to the materials produced by students during the examination process.[79] Under the Data Protection Act 1984, it is unlikely that these would have been covered by the legislation. With the extension to some forms of manual records and the deletion of the text-processing exemption, the Data Protection Act 1998 may well govern such materials.

Information about human embryos

The Data Protection Act 1998 provides an exemption from the subject information provisions in respect of information indicating that an individual was born following IVF treatment. The Data Protection Act 1984 made a similar provision with regard to the subject access right.[80] An alternative access procedure involving prior counselling is, however, provided under the Human Fertilisation and Embryology Act 1990.[81] These provisions are continued by the Data Protection (Miscellaneous Subject Access Exemptions) Order 2000.[82]

---

[75] SI 2000/184. [76] Data Protection Act 1998, Sch. 7, para. 7. [77] s. 35.
[78] Sch. 7, para. 8. [79] Sch. 7, para. 9. [80] s. 35A. [81] s. 31. [82] SI 2000/419.

Legal professional privilege

Data are exempt from the subject information provisions where they consist of information in respect of which a claim to legal professional privilege (or client–lawyer confidentiality in Scotland) could be maintained in legal proceedings.[83] This provision replaces an equivalent exemption under the Data Protection Act 1984,[84] but once again with an extension from subject access to the subject information provisions.

Self-incrimination

Data controllers need not supply information in response to a request for access when the provision of the information would indicate that an offence might have been committed (other than under the Data Protection Act 1998), thereby exposing them to the risk of criminal prosecution. Any information supplied pursuant to a request for access is not admissible in any proceedings for an offence under the 1998 Act.[85]

Matters arising subsequent to an access request

Denial of access

If the subject's request is not satisfied, an action seeking access may be raised before the court. Here, it is provided that the court may order the grant of access, except where it considers that it would be unreasonable to do so 'because of the frequency with which the applicant has made requests to the data user...or for any other reason'.[86] Use of the word 'may' in the statute implies that the court possesses a measure of discretion on whether to order the grant of access. This point was raised in the case of *Durant v Financial Services Authority*. At first instance, it was indicated by the judge that, even if he were to accept that the claimant had a right of access to the personal data in question, he would not have made an order to this effect for three reasons:

> First, I cannot see that the information could be of any practical value to the appellant. Secondly, the purpose of the legislation...is to ensure that records of an inaccurate nature are not kept about an individual. A citizen needs to know what the record says in order to have an opportunity of remedying an error or false information. In this case the appellant seeks disclosure not to correct an error but to fuel a separate collateral argument that he has either with Barclays Bank or with the FSA, litigation which is in any event doomed to failure. [Thirdly,] I am entirely satisfied on the facts of the case that the FSA have acted at all times in good faith, and indeed there has been no suggestion to the contrary from the appellant; his argument is with Barclays Bank, not with the FSA.[87]

Assuming that a £10 access fee would cover the costs incurred by most users in satisfying access requests, it may be doubted whether this provision will be utilised to any extent. It has also been suggested, however, that a campaign of mass access requests might be used as a part of an industrial or other campaign directed against a data user. In the field of local government, for example, a spokesman for one authority has suggested that a concerted campaign causing several thousands of applications to arrive simultaneously would create major problems in complying with the legislation's time limits.[88]

---

[83] Data Protection Act 1998, Sch. 7, para. 10.   [84] s. 31(2).   [85] Sch. 7, para. 11.
[86] Data Protection Act 1998, s. 21(8).   [87] [2003] EWCA Civ 1746 at para. 69.
[88] *Glasgow Herald*, 28 December 1987.

On behalf of the claimant, it was argued that the Data Protection Directive requires that Member States 'guarantee' the right of access and that the exercise of any discretion to refuse access would apply only where it was considered that one of the exemptions described earlier applies. The Court of Appeal disagreed with Lord Justice Auld, holding that the discretion conferred by section 7(9) was 'general and untrammelled'. It was added, however, that:

> as a corollary to my comment in paragraph 66 on the subject of reasonableness of disclosure of information about a third party under Section 7(4)(b), that it might be difficult for a court to conclude under that provision that it was reasonable to comply with a data subject's request so as to disclose such information, yet exercise its discretion under Section 7(9) against ordering compliance with that aspect of the data subject's request.[89]

Rectification of inaccurate data

Data will be considered inaccurate if they are false or misleading as to any matter of fact. In such an event, the data subject may request the court to order the controller to 'rectify, block, erase or destroy'[90] the data in question.[91] These remedies may also be invoked when the data controller has acted in such a fashion as would give the subject an entitlement to claim compensation under the Data Protection Act 1998. Additionally, the controller may be ordered to amend any statement of opinion which appears to be based on the inaccurate data. Where data constitutes an accurate transcription of information received from a third party, the court may make one of the above orders. Alternatively, it may permit the data to be retained but be supplemented by a further statement of the true facts as determined by the court.[92] Where the court determines that data is inaccurate and requires that it be rectified, blocked, erased, or destroyed, it may, where this is considered reasonably practical, order that the controller notify details of the changes to any third party to whom the data has previously been disclosed.[93] Such a remedy may provide a valuable audit trail, allowing the detrimental consequences of inaccurate data to be minimised.

Compensation

Under the Data Protection Act 1984, data subjects were entitled to claim compensation for damage and distress resulting from inaccuracy in data or from their unauthorised destruction or disclosure. These rights were seldom utilised,[94] the requirement in particular to demonstrate both damage and distress proving a substantial hurdle.

The Data Protection Act 1998 adopts a more extensive approach in terms of the basis for liability. Compensation may be claimed in respect of losses caused through any breach of the legislation. Except, however, in the situation where a claim arises as a result of the processing of data for media purposes (the 'special purposes'), the 1998 Act retains the requirement that damage be demonstrated as a prerequisite to any claim alleging distress. In all cases, the controller will have a defence if it can be shown that reasonable care was taken to avoid the breach.

---

[89] para. 74.

[90] The distinction between erasure and destruction of the data may relate to the nature of the storage medium involved. Manual files may well be destroyed through burning or shredding. With computer records, the concept of erasure is more relevant, given that data may only be completely destroyed following complete reformatting of the storage device.   [91] s. 14(1).

[92] s. 14(2).   [93] s. 14(3).

[94] The *Fourteenth Report of the Data Protection Registrar* (1998) cites one case where a credit reference agency wrongly registered adverse data against the complainant. The mistake continued for some considerable time and the report indicates that, following the Registrar's intervention, 'a substantial ex gratia payment was made' (p. 88).

Although the claim was ultimately rejected, consideration was given by the court of first instance in the case of *Johnson v Medical Defence Union*.[95] The background to the case has been described in Chapter 5. Essentially, the complainant alleged that his personal data had been subject to unfair processing and that this had caused him some pecuniary damage and also distress and damage to his professional reputation.

Considerable discussion took place on the issue of whether the Act fully implements the provisions of the Data Protection Directive which requires in Article 23 that:

1. Member States shall provide that any person who has suffered 'damage as a result of an unlawful processing operation or of an act incompatible with the national provisions adopted pursuant to this Directive' is entitled to receive compensation from the controller for the damage suffered.

The Directive, it was suggested, used the term 'damage' as encompassing any form of damage, whether pecuniary in nature or not. Evidence was presented to the court indicating that the status of implementation of this provision across the EEA was unclear. Some states provided compensation awards limited to pecuniary damage, whilst others took a more liberal approach. Whilst not commenting on the proper interpretation of the Directive, the conclusion was reached that section 13(1) provided an entitlement to compensation only for pecuniary damage. This heading excluded any compensation for general damage to reputation. After examining and rejecting a range of headings of expenditure, the only item potentially accepted by the court related to a sum of £10.50 spent paying for breakfast for an MDU officer who the complainant had been asked to meet. This small sum could have served as the trigger to a more substantial claim for distress under the provisions of section 13(2), although it was noted that:

I also consider, however, that any compensation under that head must be exclusively in respect of any distress associated with the damage for which recovery is in principle recoverable under Section 13(1). In particular, having concluded that Mr Johnson is not entitled to recover general compensation under Section 13(1) for his claimed loss of professional reputation, I would regard it as inconsistent to permit the recovery under Section 13(2)(a) of compensation in respect of the distress claimed to be suffered by reason of Mr Johnson's perception that the non-renewal of his membership had damaged his reputation.[96]

In respect of other forms of distress, the main claim was to the effect that the complainant had been left without insurance cover for a period of some two months following termination of his MDU membership and that this had caused him anxiety and distress. It was indicated that had the substantive elements of the complainant's case been upheld, compensation of £5,000 might have been awarded. Before the Court of Appeal[97] the size of this figure was criticised, although given that the complainant's case had failed, it 'would be an undue use of judicial time to reason the matter out'.[98]

Other subject rights

Right to request an assessment of processing

Section 42 of the Data Protection Act provides that anyone directly affected by processing—typically the data subject—may request the Information Commissioner to conduct an assessment of the processing in order to determine whether it is being conducted in

[95] [2006] EWHC 321 (Ch).   [96] para. 236.   [97] [2007] EWCA Civ 262.   [98] para. 77.

conformity with the requirements of the legislation. It is the practice of the Information Commissioner to treat any complaint received from a data subject as a request under section 42. The complainant is to be informed of the result of the assessment and of any action which has been taken.

Right to resist enforced subject access

The situation whereby access rights imprison rather than empower the data subject has long been the subject of criticism, not least by the Data Protection Registrar. Devising an appropriate method of control has proved more difficult. The major difficulty facing any attempt to control the practice is the imbalance of power typically existing in such situations. If the subject is seeking employment, for example, a request that the information be supplied may carry as much weight as a demand. The initial drafts of the Data Protection Directive provided that data subjects should be entitled:

> to refuse any demand by a third party that he should exercise his right of access in order to communicate the data in question to that third party.

In the final text, the Directive contained the somewhat enigmatic provision that data subjects should be guaranteed the right to exercise access 'without constraint'.[99] Other language versions of the Directive make it clearer that the provision is intended to apply to enforced access, the German text, for example, requiring that access be provided *frei und ungehindert*.

Although the government indicated the intention to act against enforced subject access from the earliest stages of the Data Protection Act 1998's parliamentary passage, finding an appropriate form of prohibition proved a difficult task. A variety of possibilities were considered. Subject access might, for example, be provided only in person rather than in writing. This would, of course, have made a dramatic change to the whole system of subject access and would have caused great inconvenience in the event, for example, that a data subject was located in Glasgow and the data controller in London. An alternative suggestion was that all access requests should be filtered through the Commissioner. Again, practical constraints might make this solution unworkable. Ultimately, however, it was determined that the only feasible approach was to make the practice criminal. The prohibitions apply, however, only in respect of certain forms of records—criminal records, prison records, and Department of Social Security (DSS) records—and in respect of a limited range of situations. A person must not require the provision of information obtained following a request for access (a relevant record) in connection with the recruitment or continued employment of the data subject or with any contract under which the subject is to provide services. Similarly, when the person is concerned with the provision of goods, facilities, or services to members of the public, it is prohibited to require the production of any relevant records as a condition for the provision of such goods, facilities, or services.[100] It is further provided that any contractual terms will be void in so far as they purport to require the production of any medical information obtained pursuant to an access request.[101] Although it is provided that these categories may be extended by statutory instrument,[102] it may be queried whether the provisions comply fully with the Data Protection Directive's requirements.[103]

In this, as in other areas, the provisions of the Data Protection Act 1998 will not operate in isolation. Under the provisions of the Police Act 1997, new arrangements have

---

[99] Directive 95/46/EC, Art. 11.(a).   [100] s. 56.   [101] s. 57.   [102] s. 56(8).
[103] Directive 95/46/EC, Art. 11.(a).

been made for providing access to criminal records. Three categories of access are created. A basic certificate may be sought by any applicant and will reveal details of any convictions which are not spent under the Rehabilitation of Offenders Act 1974. A more extensive 'criminal record certificate', adding details of spent convictions, will be issued upon the joint application of the individual and an organisation which is exempted from the provisions of the 1974 Act. This will include professional organisations, such as the Law Society, in respect of their role in determining whether individuals might be considered suitable for admission to the profession. The most extensive certificate, the 'enhanced criminal record certificate', will include police intelligence data and details of acquittals, and will be reserved for situations where an individual is seeking to work with children or vulnerable adults (or other sensitive positions, such as those related to gambling or judicial appointments).

Given the large numbers of requests for access relating to criminal records, there will clearly be a close relationship between the access provisions of the Police Act 1997 and those of the Data Protection Act 1998. It was stated in Parliament that the provisions of the Data Protection Act 1998 would not be implemented before those of the Police Act 1997. It is unclear when this may happen. In his *Annual Report for 2003*, the Information Commissioner noted:

> Whilst we are keen that Section 56 should be brought into effect as soon as possible there appear to be two obstacles. Firstly, there is the question of Northern Ireland. Although the Criminal Records Bureau (CRB) has been established for England and Wales and a similar arrangement is in place in Scotland, as far as we are aware there are no plans to introduce a comparable system in Northern Ireland. Secondly, it appears likely that as a result of an independent review of the Criminal Record Bureau's strategies and operations the launch of basic disclosures in England and Wales is to be postponed indefinitely. It therefore seems that the day on which the relevant sections of the Police Act 1997 are all in force across the whole of the United Kingdom might never arrive.[104]

It was suggested that the government might bring section 56 into force, even though the prescribed condition had not been met. It was recognised that this might require primary legislation, something which to date has eleven years later still not been forthcoming. It is undoubtedly disappointing that such a significant element of the legislation is still not in force almost a decade after the Act's enactment. As was recognised in the Information Tribunal decision of the *Chief Constables of West Yorkshire, South Yorkshire, and North Wales Police, and the Information Commissioner*,[105] 'the overwhelming majority of the 200,000-odd police subject access requests per year are currently enforced'.[106] Foreign embassies are major 'beneficiaries' of enforced subject access and it was recognised that even the bringing into force of section 56 might have little practical effect, as embassies are not subject to national law.

Right to object to data processing

Direct marketing
It is a little-known fact that those persons who purchase black-ash furniture are twenty times more likely to respond to a fashion promotion than those whose tastes are less exotic.

---

[104] *Annual Report and Accounts 2003*, p. 37.
[105] <http://www.informationtribunal.gov.uk/DBFiles/Decision/i204/north_wales_police.pdf>.
[106] para. 82.

Such nuggets of information may constitute interesting trivia to most people, but to those engaged in the retail industry they can represent the path to fortune. Direct marketing is one of the fastest-growing sectors of the economy. Although it tends to be referred to under the epithet of 'junk mail', each item delivered represents a not inconsiderable investment on the part of the sender. In many instances, retailers will possess information linking an individual to a purchase and may use this in order to attempt to stimulate further sales. The purchaser of a motor vehicle, for example, is likely to receive a communication from the seller around the anniversary of the purchase in the hope that the buyer might be considering buying a new model. The increasing use of store-based credit cards coupled with the utilisation of laser-scanning cash points provides retailers with detailed information about their customers and their purchases. There are few technical barriers in the way of processing data so as to be able to 'talk to every customer in his or her own life style terms'.[107] It has been suggested, for example, that 'intelligent shopping trolleys' might guide customers towards promotions which analysis of their previous purchases suggests might prove alluring.[108] Assuming that the data users involved have registered the fact that they intend to process personal data for sales and marketing purposes, the only legal barrier to such techniques might come from a determination that such processing is unfair.

The use of personal data for purposes of direct marketing has been the cause of some recent controversy. Reference has previously been made to the *Innovations* case[109] and the data protection implications of list broking. Additionally, however, organisations are seeking to exploit their customer databases by entering into agreements to provide mailings on behalf of other companies. This may take a variety of forms. Analysis of, for example, purchases made with a credit card may indicate that an individual frequently stays in hotels. The credit card company may then enter into an agreement with a hotel chain to include a promotional leaflet with its statement of account. In this example, no personal data will be transferred between the companies. In a guidance note relating to direct marketing,[110] the Registrar has indicated that in certain circumstances use of financial data for such purposes might constitute a breach of confidence.[111] More recently, action has been taken against a number of utilities engaging in the practice of cross-selling, with enforcement notices being served against a number of utilities which sent offers of other products and services to their customers. Significantly, the fact that the utilities offered customers the opportunity to opt out of these offers was not considered sufficient, the Registrar arguing that an opt-in system should apply.[112]

Treatment of data obtained and used for the purposes of direct marketing constituted one of the most controversial aspects of the Data Protection Directive.[113] As originally drafted, the legislation would have imposed strict obligations on data controllers to inform subjects whenever data was to be used for such a purpose. The proposals were weakened in subsequent drafts and, as enacted, the Directive offers Member States a choice of control regimes. It may be provided that data subjects be given the right to object to a controller's intention to process or to disclose data for the purposes of direct marketing. No fees are to be charged in this event.[114] It is arguable that this reflects current United Kingdom practice, especially after the decisions of the Data Protection Tribunal in the *Innovations* and

---

[107] Roger Hymas, GE Capital Executive Director, quoted in *Financial Times*, 4 April 1991.

[108] *Financial Times*, 4 April 1991.

[109] *Innovations (Mail Order) Ltd v Data Protection Registrar* Case DA/92 31/49/1 (see Ch. 4).

[110] *Direct Marketing* Information Commissioner's Office. Available from <http://ico.org.uk/~/media/documents/library/Privacy_and_electronic/Practical_application/direct-marketing-guidance.pdf>.

[111] paras. 81–8.   [112] *Thirteenth Report of the Data Protection Registrar* (1997), pp. 26–7.

[113] Directive 95/46/EC.   [114] Art. 14(b).

Linguaphone cases.[115] As an alternative, the Directive provides that controllers might be required to give specific notice to data subjects before data is used by or on behalf of third parties for direct marketing purposes.[116] This is coupled with the requirement that steps be taken to inform data subjects of their rights.

The Data Protection Act 1998 adopts the second of these options, providing that:

> An individual is entitled at any time by notice in writing to a data controller to require the data controller at the end of such period as is reasonable in the circumstances to cease, or not to begin, processing for the purposes of direct marketing personal data of which he is the data subject.[117]

Other forms of processing

In the case of direct marketing data, the subject's wishes are absolute. With other forms of processing, the subject may serve notice requiring the cessation of processing on the basis that this is likely to cause substantial and unwarranted damage or distress. This right will not apply:

- where the subject has previously consented to the processing;
- where the processing is necessary to conclude or perform a contract with the data subject;
- where it is necessary to comply with any legal obligation on the data controller; or
- where the processing is necessary to protect the vital interests of the data subject.[118]

The Secretary of State may specify other situations in which the right to object is to be withdrawn.[119] Upon receipt of such a notice, the controller must respond in writing within twenty-one days, either indicating that the subject's request will be granted or giving reasons why or to what extent this should not be the case.[120] A negative response may be appealed to the courts, which may make such order for ensuring compliance as it thinks fit.[121]

Whilst the principle that the data subject should be entitled to exercise control over the situations in which personal data is processed must be welcomed, the requirement that 'substantial and unwarranted damage or distress' be demonstrated, coupled with the exceptions described earlier, may remove much of the value from the provision. It may be noted that the Data Protection Directive, in providing for the right to object, states that this is to be based on 'compelling legitimate grounds'.[122] Whilst this term is not defined in the legislation, it does seem rather less demanding criteria than those adopted in the Data Protection Act 1998.

Automated decision-making

Increasingly, the results of data processing may trigger further actions affecting the data subject with minimal intervention from any human agency. A trivial example may be taken from the operation of automated cash-dispensing machines. A customer may approach a machine at midnight, insert a bank card, enter a personal identifier number (PIN), and request a sum of money. Details of the customer's account will be checked with the bank's computer system and if the customer is sufficiently in funds, cash will be dispensed. If the

---

[115] *Innovations (Mail Order) Ltd v Data Protection Registrar* Case DA/92 31/49/1; *Linguaphone Institute v Data Protection Registrar* Case DA/94 31/49/1.   [116] Art. 14(b).

[117] s. 11(1).

[118] Data Protection Act 1998, s. 10(1).   [119] s. 10(2).   [120] s. 10(3).   [121] s. 10(4).

[122] Directive 95/46/EC, Art. 14.

customer is not in funds, no money will be issued. There will be no human involvement at any stage of the transaction. In other instances, it is possible that human agents may be reduced to little more than a cipher. An example might be seen in the operation of systems of credit scoring. Here, an applicant for credit is required to fill in a form giving information about matters such as marital status, employment, and housing status, etc. Points are allocated depending on the answers. A married person, for example, may be awarded one point, a single person two, and a divorced person three. The pointage values are based upon an assessment of the risk of default. Each creditor may establish a predetermined acceptance level. If a customer's total falls below this, the application will be rejected.

The operation of credit scoring has been criticised by the Director General of Fair Trading on the basis of perceived unfairness to persons whose profile may not fit the automated model yet whose credit history may be flawless, and the recommendation has been made that those operating the technique should build in an appeals procedure. A similar approach is adopted in the Data Protection Directive which, drawing on provisions in the French Data Protection Act, provides that individuals must be granted the right:

> not to be subject to a decision which produces legal effects concerning him or significantly affects him and which is based solely on automated processing of data intended to evaluate certain personal aspects relating to him, such as his performance at work, creditworthiness, reliability, conduct, etc.[123]

Inevitably, this general statement is subject to exceptions, the Directive continuing to provide that automated decisions are permissible in the course of entering into or performing a contract, so long as the outcome is favourable to the subject or provision is made to safeguard 'legitimate interests'. An appeals procedure such as that referred to earlier, allowing the subject to present additional information, would appear to meet this requirement. It is further provided that other automated decisions may be sanctioned by law, so long as this also contains safeguards for the subject's legitimate interests.

Although there might be debate about how significant any element of human intervention in a decision-making process is required to be, most applications should pose few intractable problems in that a delay in implementing a decision will not cause significant problems for either data controller or subject. The cash-dispensing example cited at the beginning of this section may be a more difficult issue. In the event a customer is denied funds late at night, there seems little doubt that the statutory criteria will be satisfied. It may be doubted whether there is any realistic prospect of providing an immediate right of appeal. In Lord Denning's memorable phrase from *Thornton v Shoe Lane Parking*,[124] the customer 'may protest to the machine, even swear at it; but it will remain unmoved'.

Conclusions

Under the Data Protection Act 1984, the right of access to data, coupled with rights to require the correction of inaccurate data and very restricted rights to compensation, constituted the major innovation from the standpoint of data subjects. By moving to what are described as 'subject information rights', the Data Protection Act 1998 does confer new entitlements on data subjects. The right to object to data processing and to resist attempts to compel the exercise of access rights also constitute significant advances. That said, what the opening paragraphs of a section confer is often removed by the exceptions and

---

[123] Directive 95/46/EC, Art. 15.   [124] [1971] 1 All ER 686.

qualifications which tend to litter subsequent paragraphs. It would not be practicable or desirable to permit a data subject an absolute right to require that data not be processed, otherwise an individual with a long history of bad debts could require that a credit reference agency expunge all records from its files. Nevertheless, the statutory provision appears somewhat mean-spirited. Much the same can be said of the provisions relating to enforced subject access. Certainly, it must be admitted that it will be very difficult to stamp out such practices. In many cases, such as the making of an application for employment, the imbalance in power between an employing data controller and applicant data subject will be such that a mere expression of desire might be sufficient to make the subject feel compelled to comply. Undoubtedly, the data subject is in a stronger position under the Data Protection Act 1998 than has hitherto been the case. The criticism may be that the level of improvement has not been more pronounced.

7

Sectoral aspects of data protection

Introduction

The application of data protection principles to particular sectors of activity can be a difficult task. Notions of fairness, as has already been discussed extensively in earlier chapters, are highly context-dependent. This chapter will consider two topics concerned with the application of data protection principles within the media and electronic communications sectors. In both areas, the operation of data protection principles has been contentious. In the case of the media, we have recently seen the massive publicity surrounding allegations of telephone hacking and the wide-ranging Leveson Inquiry[1] within which data protection issues featured quite prominently. Data protection issues are principally concerned with the application of what might be regarded as 'traditional' data protection principles in the context of activities where different priorities might legitimately be identified. In some respects media processing might be compared with law enforcement agencies. Digging out the truth about the unsavoury activities of powerful elements in society might well require the use of tactics and techniques that would be regarded as unfair in more general contexts.

With the increasing importance of the electronic communications sector—epitomised by the fact that there are now more mobile phones in use in the United Kingdom than there are people[2]—more and more data processing activities are being conducted over some communications network. Apart, of course, from the growth of mobile phone usage for voice and text communications, we have seen the massive increase in Internet access and usage. We all live more and more (and more and more sensitive) aspects of our lives in an online environment. From the 1990s the need has been identified to develop sector-specific interpretations of general data protection laws.

Data protection and the media

The application of data protection provisions in respect of media activities raises a number of complex issues. As illustrated by the Leveson Inquiry, at the stage of gathering information with a view to publication, investigative journalism in particular may involve the use of tactics and techniques which would normally be stigmatised as unfair (if not unlawful). The Information Commissioner's report *What Price Privacy?*[3] contains extensive information regarding the techniques used by journalists—often assisted by private investigators—to

---

[1] <http://www.levesoninquiry.org.uk/>

[2] In its Communications Market Report for 2013 – available at <http://media.ofcom.org.uk/facts/>. OFCOM estimated that there were 82.7 million mobile phone subscriptions active in the UK.

[3] Available from <http://www.ico.org.uk/~/media/documents/library/Corporate/Research_and_reports/WHAT_PRICE_PRIVACY.pdf>.

obtain access to information. At a perhaps extreme end of the scale, a journalist and a private investigator were jailed in 2007 after pleading guilty to intercepting voice-mail messages belonging to members of the royal family.[4] Debate continues whether this was an isolated example or whether the practice is more entrenched in at least some areas of the media and this was, of course, at the centre of the Leveson Inquiry and the ongoing debate about the appropriate form of regulation of press conduct.[5] At almost the other end of the publication spectrum in terms of time, many newspapers and journals now maintain copies of issues in electronic format. These will certainly come within the scope of the Data Protection Act 1998, under whose general provisions a subject would be entitled to require the rectification of any errors, coupled with a reformulation of any resultant statements of opinion. Whilst generally desirable, the rewriting of documents which claim to represent data as published on a certain date calls to mind the operation of George Orwell's Ministry of Truth. This latter topic will be considered in more detail in Chapter 25 in the context of actions for defamation.

The Data Protection Act 1984 made no special provision for the media. In large measure, this approach was justified by the limited use of computer equipment for journalistic purposes, the existence of the text-processing exemption and the limited nature of the definition of processing. Time and technology have moved on. A 1992 study produced for the Council of Europe[6] identified a range of practices within Member States regarding the treatment of media activities within data protection legislation. Some countries, such as the Netherlands and Sweden, provided a total exemption from data protection laws; others provided partial exemption, in the case of Germany, for example, requiring only that media users comply with requirements relating to data security. Other regimes, including that of the United Kingdom, provided no form of special treatment. The study identified a potential conflict between the provisions of the European Convention on Human Rights relating to freedom of expression and the right to seek out and impart information and those concerned with the right to privacy. Identifying problems is normally easy but providing solutions is a more difficult task and the Council of Europe contented itself with a recommendation that the potential conflict should be borne in mind in framing legislation.

The Recitals to the Data Protection Directive,[7] which also recognise the conflicts inherent in the area, state that:

> Whereas the processing of personal data for purposes of journalism or for purposes of literary or artistic expression, in particular in the audiovisual field, should qualify for exemption from the requirements of certain provisions of this Directive in so far as this is necessary to reconcile the fundamental rights of individuals with freedom of information and notably the right to receive and impart information, as guaranteed in particular in Article 10 of the European Convention for the Protection of Human Rights and Fundamental Freedoms.[8]

The Recitals continue to suggest that national laws should provide for alternative measures—such as the submission of reports to the supervisory agency—to ensure that

---

[4] See <http://news.bbc.co.uk/1/hi/6301243.stm>.

[5] See the report of the House of Commons' Culture, Media and Sports Committee on *Press Standards, Privacy and Libel* (February 2010). The report is available from <http://www.publications.parliament.uk/pa/cm/cmcumeds.htm>.

[6] *Data Protection and the Media*, a study prepared by the Committee of Experts on Data Protection.

[7] Directive 95/46/EC.   [8] Recital 37.

data subjects' rights are not abused. In terms of the articles, themselves, the Directive is somewhat imprecise. Article 9 states that:

> Member States shall provide for exemptions or derogations from the provisions of this Chapter, Chapter IV and Chapter VI for the processing of personal data carried out solely for journalistic purposes or the purpose of artistic or literary expression only if they are necessary to reconcile the right to privacy with the rules governing freedom of expression.

It is clear that this formula empowers rather than requires Member States to act, but for the United Kingdom, the decision was taken to include special provisions for these activities, described as the 'special purposes' in the Data Protection Act 1998.

Scope of the provisions

Section 3 of the Data Protection Act 1998 defines the concept of 'special purposes'. These relate to the processing of personal data:

(a) for the purposes of journalism,

(b) artistic purposes, and

(c) literary purposes.

It was stressed in Parliament that no qualitative criteria would be applied to determine whether a work could be classed as artistic, journalistic, or literary. Although much of the debate in Parliament focused on the activities of the media, this definition recognises that literary and artistic works also raise issues of freedom of expression. The prime purpose of the Act's exceptional provisions is to place limits on the ability of data subjects to invoke statutory rights to impede publication of a work. Similar restrictions are placed upon the powers of the Information Commissioner, with modified provisions for the service of information and enforcement notices. Once the work is in the public domain, the provisions of the general law will apply, including the law of defamation, although, as indicated in Chapter 6, the 1998 Act does provide new rights of compensation for distress caused as a result of processing carried out in connection with one of the special purposes.

Activities covered

The Data Protection Act 1998 applies a three-stage test to determine whether processing for a special purpose should benefit from exemption. Personal data must be subject to processing:

(a) ...with a view to the publication by any person of any journalistic, literary or artistic material;

(b) the data controller reasonably believes that, having regard in particular to the special importance of the public interest in freedom of expression, publication would be in the public interest; and

(c) the data controller reasonably believes that, in all the circumstances, compliance with (statutory provisions) is incompatible with the special purposes.[9]

---

[9] s. 32(1).

It was suggested in Parliament that:

> We have deliberately placed on the face of the Bill, I believe for the first time in an Act of Parliament in this country, that the public interest is not the narrow question of whether this is a public interest story in itself but that it relates to the wider public interest, which is an infinitely subtle and more complicated concept.[10]

In determining whether belief that publication is in the public interest might be considered reasonable, it is provided that account is to be taken of any relevant code of practice. Power is conferred on the Secretary of State to designate codes which are to be taken into account in this way. The Data Protection (Designated Codes of Practice) Order 2000[11] lists five codes:

- the Code on Fairness and Privacy issued by the Broadcasting Standards Commission in 1998 under the terms of the Broadcasting Act 1996

- the ITC Programme Code issued by the Independent Television Commission in 1998 under the terms of the Broadcasting Act 1990

- the Press Complaints Commission's Code of Practice published in 1997

- the Producers' Guidelines issued by the British Broadcasting Corporation in 1996

- the Programme Code issued by the Radio Authority in 1998 under the terms of the Broadcasting Act 1990.

Citation of codes in this manner is a novel feature of the Data Protection Act. It may additionally be noted that whilst three of the codes have some form of statutory basis, the remaining two have no such backing.

In respect of the section 32 provisions, the Leveson report has recommended changes to require publishers to demonstrate that the processing of personal data is 'necessary for publication, rather than simply being in fact undertaken with a view to publication' and also that they have reasonable grounds to believe that the publication would be or is in the public interest. Such an assessment should be conducted without the need for a balancing act between individual rights to privacy and those relating to freedom to publish.

Scope of the exemption

Section 31 of the Data Protection Act defines a range of provisions which will not apply where processing is carried out for the special purposes. With the exception of the seventh principle relating to data security, the data protection principles will not operate; neither will the subject access provisions nor those enabling a data subject to object to data being processed. Also excluded are the provisions of section 12, relating to subject rights in respect of automated decision-making, and the general provisions of section 14, relating to the subject's rights to compensation. These latter provisions are substituted, however, by special and more extensive rights.

These exceptions are wide-ranging. One consequence will be that even the unlawful obtaining of personal data will not expose the controller to action under the Data Protection Act—although other criminal sanctions, such as a charge of theft, may be imposed in respect of the offending conduct.

---

[10] 585 HL Official Report (5th series), col. 442, 2 February 1998.   [11] SI 2000/418.

Procedural aspects

The question of whether processing is covered by one of the special-purpose exemptions is likely to arise in the course of legal proceedings. In this regard, it is provided that proceedings must be stayed when the data controller claims, or it appears to the court, that the data are being processed for a special purpose and:

> With a view to publication by any person of any journalistic, literary or artistic material which, at the time twenty-four hours immediately before the relevant time, had not previously been published by the data controller.[12]

The relevant time will be the moment at which the controller makes the claim for protection or the court determines that the processing is for a special purpose.

It will be recognised that there is no requirement that the controller's claim that processing is covered by the special purpose should have any merit. As discussed later, procedures for the lifting of such a stay are complex, and the Commissioner has criticised the situation whereby an unscrupulous party could delay proceedings for a period of months, if not years, with little justification.[13]

Once a court has determined that procedures should be stayed, the focus of attention switches to the Commissioner, who will be required to make a written determination as to whether the processing is being conducted only in connection with one of the special purposes or with a view to the publication of material not previously published by the data controller.[14] In obtaining evidence necessary to reach such a view, the Commissioner may require to exercise powers conferred under the legislation to serve a special information notice. Service of such notice may itself be the subject of an appeal to the Information Tribunal. If the Commissioner determines that the processing is not exempt, this finding may itself be appealed to the Tribunal. It will only be when appeal procedures have been exhausted that the determination will come into effect and the court will be in a position to lift the stay.

The application of the Data Protection Act's provisions relating to media processing was at issue in the case of *Campbell v Mirror Group Newspapers Ltd*. Finding in favour of the claimant in the High Court,[15] Moreland J held that information relating to her drug addiction was sensitive personal data, that the defendant had failed to show that its processing of the data conformed with any of the provisions of Schedule 3 setting out conditions for the lawful processing of personal data or with the Press Complaints Commission code of practice, an instrument which had been designated by the Secretary of State under section 32. In respect of the defence provided by section 32 it was held that, whilst this would operate in order to prevent a claimant from stopping publication, its benefit ceased at this point and did not confer any form of immunity in respect of a subsequent action for damages on the basis that the unfair or unlawful processing had caused distress to the data subject. Damages of £3,500 were awarded in respect both of the contravention of the Data Protection Act 1998 and of the claimant's claim that the publication constituted a breach of confidence.

The judge's findings in respect of the Data Protection Act were overturned by the Court of Appeal.[16] Delivering the judgment of the court, Lord Phillips MR was critical of the structure of the Data Protection Act 1998. Echoing the views of Moreland J, who described

---

[12] Data Protection Act 1998, s. 32(4).   [13] Briefing Note, 'Media Exceptions', 16 February 1998.
[14] Data Protection Act 1998, s. 45.   [15] [2002] EWHC 499 (QB), [2002] All ER (D) 448 (Mar).
[16] *Campbell v Mirror Group Newspapers Ltd* [2002] EWCA Civ 1373, [2003] QB 633.

the interpretative task as akin to 'weaving his way through a thicket', the Act was described as 'a cumbersome and inelegant piece of legislation'.[17]

Before the Court of Appeal, the appellant did not seek to argue that its processing of Ms Campbell's personal data complied with the requirements of Schedule 3 to the Data Protection Act—as was stated, 'much of their argument was founded on the submission that it was virtually impossible for journalists to comply with the requirements of the Act'[18]—but argued that the effect of the section 32 defence was to confer immunity in respect of any action for damages made subsequent to publication. It was argued for the appellant that the result of the High Court's ruling would be that:

> Without the consent of the data subject, a newspaper would hardly ever be entitled to publish any of the information categorised as sensitive without running the risk of having to pay compensation. Indeed, it would be difficult to establish that the conditions for processing any personal information were satisfied. If this were correct, it would follow that the Data Protection Act had created a law of privacy and achieved a fundamental enhancement of Article 8 rights, at the expense of Article 10 rights, extending into all areas of media activity, to the extent that the Act was incompatible with the Human Rights Convention.[19]

Analysing the provisions of the section 32 defence, the Court of Appeal first focused on subsections (4) and (5). These were described as procedural measures designed to provide for the stay of proceedings brought against a publisher until after publication and there was no dispute that 'the purpose of these provisions is to prevent the restriction of freedom of expression that might otherwise result from gagging injunctions'.[20]

The court continued to examine the provisions of section 32(1)–(3) which, it was stated:

> on their face, provide widespread exemption from the duty to comply with the provisions that impose substantive obligations upon the data controller, subject only to the simple conditions that the data controller reasonably believes (i) that publication would be in the public interest and (ii) that compliance with each of the provisions is incompatible with the special purpose—in this case journalism.[21]

It was concluded that:

> If these provisions apply only up to the moment of publication it is impossible to see what purpose they serve, for the data controller will be able to obtain a stay of any proceedings under the provisions of Subsections (4) and (5) without the need to demonstrate compliance with the conditions to which the exemption in Subsections (1) to (3) is subject.[22]
>
> ...For these reasons we have reached the conclusion that, giving the...provisions of the Subsections their natural meaning and the only meaning that makes sense of them, they apply both before and after publication.[23]

Support for this approach was taken from the comments of the responsible government minister as recorded in the *Hansard* report of the debate of the second reading of the Bill. Here it was indicated that:

> Following the meetings to which I referred, we have included in the Bill an exemption which I believe meets the legitimate expectations and requirements of those engaged in journalism, artistic and literacy [sic] activity. The key provision is Clause 31. This ensures

---

[17] [2002] EWCA Civ 1373, [2003] QB 633 at [72].

[18] *Campbell v Mirror Group Newspapers Ltd* [2002] EWCA Civ 1373, [2003] QB 633 at [74].

[19] [2002] EWCA Civ 1373 at [92].

[20] *Campbell v Mirror Group Newspapers Ltd* [2002] EWCA Civ 1373, [2003] QB 633 at [117].

[21] At [118].   [22] [2002] EWCA Civ 1373 at [118].   [23] [2002] EWCA Civ 1373 at [121].

that provided that certain criteria are met, before publication—I stress 'before'—there can be no challenge on data protection grounds to the processing of personal data for the special purposes. The criteria are broadly that the processing is done solely for the special purposes; and that it is done with a view to the publication of unpublished material. Thereafter, there is provision for exemption from the key provisions where the media can show that publication was intended; and that they reasonably believe both that publication would be in the public interest and that compliance with the bill would have been incompatible with the special purposes.[24]

Although it was indicated that the court, mindful of the dicta of Lord Hoffmann in *Robinson v Secretary of State for Northern Ireland* that reference to *Hansard* should be a matter of 'last resort',[25] did not base its decision on this passage, it may be queried whether the comments do fully support the interpretation that the section 32 defence applies totally, pre- and post-publication. As indicated by the court, the section 32 defence is indeed a measure in two parts. Subsections (4) and (5) provide a very straightforward method of protection against gagging orders. Subsections (1)–(3), it is submitted, should swing into action only after publication. In conformity with the Data Protection Directive's strictures that:

> Member States shall provide for exemptions or derogations from the provisions of this Chapter, Chapter IV and Chapter VI for the processing of personal data carried out solely for journalistic purposes or the purpose of artistic or literary expression only if they are necessary to reconcile the right to privacy with the rules governing freedom of expression.[26]

The use of the words 'only' and necessary' must indicate both that exemptions may be provided only when and to the extent strictly necessary to reconcile the competing rights. This may involve allowing publication to take place but cannot, it is submitted, justify a removal of rights to compensation (and rectification) after the event. As was stated by the Article 29 Working Party:

> The Directive[27] requires a balance to be struck between two fundamental freedoms. In order to evaluate whether limitations of the rights and obligations flowing from the Directive are proportionate to the aim of protecting freedom of expression particular attention should be paid to the specific guarantees enjoyed by the individuals in relation to the Media. Limits to the right of access and rectification prior to publication could be proportionate only in so far as individuals enjoy the right to reply or obtain rectification of false information after publication.
>
> Individuals are in any case entitled to adequate forms of redress in case of violation of their rights.[28]

The basis for the individual's claim to compensation is laid down in section 13 of the Act. This provides that compensation is payable for distress caused as a result of processing for the special purposes which is conducted in breach of any of the Act's provisions. It is further provided that:

> In proceedings brought against a person for breach of this Section it is a defence to prove that he had taken such care as in all the circumstances was reasonably required to comply with the requirement concerned.

---

[24] 585 HL Official Report (5th series), col. 442, 2 February 1998.
[25] [2002] UKHL 32, [2002] All ER (D) 364 (Jul) at [40].   [26] Directive 95/46/EC, Art. 9.
[27] 95/46/EC.   [28] Recommendation 1/97, 'Data Protection Law and the Media'.

Perhaps more significantly, the Data Protection (Processing of Sensitive Personal Data) Order 2000,[29] adds to the Schedule 3 list of factors legitimising processing of sensitive personal data in the situation whereby:

(1) The disclosure of personal data—

(a) is in the substantial public interest;

(b) is in connection with—

(i) the commission by any person of any unlawful act (whether alleged or established),

(ii) dishonesty, malpractice, or other seriously improper conduct by, or the unfitness or incompetence of, any person (whether alleged or established), or

(iii) mismanagement in the administration of, or failures in services provided by, any body or association (whether alleged or established);

(c) is for the special purposes as defined in Section 3 of the Act; and

(d) is made with a view to the publication of those data by any person and the data controller reasonably believes that such publication would be in the public interest.[30]

Whilst not conferring immunity upon data controllers, this provision does provide a defence in situations where disclosure can be justified in the public interest.

Special information notices

A modified form of information notice applies where data is being processed for a special purpose. Acting either in response to a request from a data subject for an assessment of whether data is being processed in accordance with the principles,[31] or where there are reasonable grounds for suspecting that a data controller has wrongfully claimed the benefit of the special purpose—for example, to refuse a request for access—the Commissioner may serve a 'special information notice'.[32] The notice will require that the controller supply the Commissioner with specified information to enable the Commissioner to determine whether the processing is being conducted for a special purpose or with a view to publication of new information. The notice must indicate the ground upon which the Commissioner is making the request and give notice of the controller's rights of appeal. The notice will not come into effect until the expiry of the 28-day period allowed for the lodging of appeals.[33] In cases of urgency, it is provided that the notice may require that information be supplied within seven days.[34]

Having received the information required, the Commissioner will make the determination referred to above as to whether processing is being conducted only for the special purposes. If the determination is that this is not the case, the Commissioner may serve the normal form of information notice seeking information to be supplied allowing a determination whether processing is lawful.[35]

---

[29] SI 2000/417.   [30] Sch., para. 3.   [31] s. 42.   [32] s. 44.
[33] The Information Tribunal (Enforcement Appeals) Rules 2005, SI 2005/14, r. 5.   [34] s. 44(6).
[35] s. 46(3).

Enforcement notices

Whether following service of an enforcement notice or otherwise, a determination by the Commissioner that processing is unlawful may be followed by service of an enforcement notice. Once again, different procedures apply in relation to the special purposes. An enforcement notice may only be served with the leave of the court.[36] Leave will only be granted if the court is satisfied that 'the Commissioner has reason to suspect a contravention of the data protection principles which is of substantial public importance', and that 'except where the case is one of urgency', notice has been given to the controller of the Commissioner's intention to apply for leave.[37]

Individual rights and remedies

As discussed in Chapter 6, the Data Protection Act 1998 gives extended rights to data subjects to institute proceedings before the courts seeking compensation for damage and distress resulting from a breach of any of the Act's requirements.[38] In the case of processing for the special purposes, damages may be awarded for distress without the need for any related damage. The data subject may also bring action in the normal manner seeking rectification, blocking, or erasure of inaccurate data.[39] The question of whether and to what extent such remedies are provided is at the discretion of the court, and it may be assumed that account will be taken of the requirements of the special purposes so that, for example, the court will not order the alteration of the contents of a database containing the contents of stories which have been published in a newspaper. Even where a story contains errors, a notice of correction appended to the file would appear a more appropriate course of action.

Granting of assistance by the Commissioner

Section 53 of the Data Protection Act 1998 confers a new power on the Commissioner to provide assistance following an application from a party to proceedings relating to the special purposes.[40] This will include all the forms of proceeding described earlier, with the assistance taking the form of a contribution towards the costs of legal advice and representation and with indemnification against any award of costs to the other party.[41] The criterion for the award of such assistance is that the Commissioner is of the opinion that 'the case involves a matter of substantial public importance'.[42] The Commissioner's decision of whether or not to grant support must be transmitted to the applicant as soon as practicable. If the Commissioner decides not to grant assistance, reasoned notification to this effect must be given.[43]

Data protection in the electronic communications sector

In the early days of the telephone, all calls were connected by human operators. In order to bill customers accurately, the operator would record when the call was connected, the

---

[36] s. 46(1).   [37] s. 46(2).   [38] s. 13(1).   [39] s. 14.   [40] s. 53(1).
[41] Sch. 10.   [42] s. 53(2).   [43] s. 53(3)–(4).

number to which it was made, and when the call terminated. It was not unknown for operators to listen to the conversation itself and indeed the motivation for the invention of the
world's first automated telephone exchange by a funeral director from Kansas named Alvin
Strowger, is reported to have lain in his discovery that the wife of a competitor who was
employed as a telephone operator was monitoring his calls in order to redirect business to
her husband.[44]

Automated dialling took time to be adopted—it was not until 1979 that the UK's last
staffed exchanges were shut down—but the initial system of subscriber trunk dialling
(STD) established what might be regarded as a 'golden age' of communications privacy.
Calls were connected without human intervention, and while each telephone line had its
own meter located in the telephone exchange, the operation of these was analogous to electricity and gas meters in that they merely recorded the number of units of connection time
consumed. If, for whatever reason, the authorities wished to be able to identify details of
the time and duration of specific calls, a special device referred to as a 'call logger' needed
to be attached to an individual line.

From the 1980s the telephone network began a switch from analogue to digital technology, with the last analogue exchanges being closed on 11 March 1998.[45] While the use of
digital technology has brought considerable benefits in terms of quality, reliability, and the
range of services offered, an inevitable by-product is that increased amounts of data are collected about users. A simple example can be seen with the introduction of systems of itemised billing, where customers are presented with a bill describing, at least for long-distance
calls, details of time, duration, and the cost of individual calls.[46]

With the emergence of mobile networks, even more data concerning user behaviour
is generated and retained. Whenever switched on, every mobile phone transmits a signal
every few minutes. All base stations of that network within range respond and through the
use of triangulation techniques the location of phones can be identified. In geographical
terms, the degree of accuracy with which a particular handset can be located will depend
on the number of base stations which are in range. Typically, in an urban area, a 3G phone
can be placed within a range of 15 metres.[47] As well as usage for network purposes, applications such as 'Find my Friends' available on many smartphones allow individuals to track
the location of family and friends, perhaps to arrange to meet a nearby friend for a coffee.
Less happily, data from such systems have featured in a number of divorce cases.

---

[44] Although the first Automatic Switching was rather crude, the first patents were registered by Connolly,
Connolly, and McTighe (US Patent No. 222458, 9 December 1879 and British Patent No. 4114, 13 December
1879). In 1891 Strowger patented a two-motion selector (US Patent No. 447918). This system was adopted
by the British Post Office and was in service for almost 100 years although it remained policy until the 1950s
that all calls of more than 15 miles should be made via an operator rather than dialled directly, J. Atkinson
Telephony, II: *Automatic Exchanges* (London, 1950).

[45] The last analogue exchanges served Leigh on Sea and Selby and were converted to digital on 11
March 1998.

[46] Itemised billing provides a good example of the regulatory conflicts which frequently apply in the electronic communications sector. It provides information which may be valuable to the account holder to enable
the accuracy of a bill to be checked but may also disclose information about calls made by other members of
the account holder's household with potentially adverse implications for their communications privacy. These
issues are discussed in Ch. 7.

[47] A number of systems allow individuals to track the location of mobile phones. Although a voluntary code
of practice drawn up by the Mobile Broadband Group (available from <http://www.mobilebroadbandgroup.
com/documents/UKCoP_location_servs_210706v_pub_clean.pdf>) seeks to protect individuals against the
risk of third parties being able to access their location data, concerns have been expressed how effective the
safeguards are. See <http://news.bbc.co.uk/1/hi/programmes/click_online/4747142.stm>.

This data, referred to in the legislation as 'location data', can be retained almost indefinitely and, as will be discussed in Chapter 13, governments are increasingly taking powers to require that it be retained for periods of years against the eventuality that access may be sought in connection with criminal or national security investigations.

In quantitative and qualitative terms the most extensive source of communications data is the Internet. Every transmission, whether in the form of sending an email or the accessing and browsing of websites, gives out information about the individual user. Details of every web page viewed can be recorded by the site owner and linked to the Internet Protocol (IP) address from which the communication originated.[48] In the context, for example, of an e-commerce site, the data recorded is analogous to that which might be obtained by a physical retailer who follows a customer around the store noting not only what goods are purchased but any others that are looked at during the course of the visit. An important and contentious aspect of this involves the use by websites of what are referred to as cookies. The simple and seemingly innocuous term can encompass a wide range of forms of activity. The Article 29 Working Party established under the European Data Protection Directive has produced an Opinion on the legitimacy of cookies. This identifies a range of possibilities:

> Cookies are often categorized according to the following characteristics:
>
> 1) Whether they are 'session cookies' or 'persistent cookies'.
> 2) Whether they are 'third party cookies' or not.
>
> A 'session cookie' is a cookie that is automatically deleted when the user closes his browser, while a 'persistent cookie' is a cookie that remains stored in the user's terminal device until it reaches a defined expiration date (which can be minutes, days or several years in the future).[49]

Third-party cookies can be experienced frequently when accessing an Internet site associated with, for example, a newspaper where advertisements may be presented (under contract with the site owner) by a third party based on previous visits to other sites. A user who has previously been looking at sites concerned with holiday accommodation may find, when visiting an online news site, banner advertisements for such a facility.

A further area of controversy relates to the handling of email and text messages. Although often regarded by users as akin to voice communications in terms of speed and informality, unlike telephone conversations these electronic communications do not exist only in real time. While any third party wishing to monitor a telephone conversation must do so while the conversation is being conducted, copies of emails and text messages will be made at various stages of the transmission process and may be recovered with relative ease days, months, or even years after their transmission. Especially when, as is increasingly the case, messages are sent from a mobile phone or similar device, location data will also be captured.

The above activities raise specific data protection issues, while other forms of behaviour relating to the use of communication networks fall more naturally into the wider topic of personal privacy. The increasing number of unsolicited calls received by many consumers

---

[48] Two forms of IP (Internet Protocol) addresses exist. Static addresses are typically allocated to specific fixed-line connections. An individual accessing the Internet from home will have a dedicated IP address linked to that location. Mobile networks operate on a different basis. A pool of addresses exists and one will be allocated to a particular connection from any individual user. If a particular user connects to the Internet on 10 occasions, it is likely that each session will be allocated a different IP address.

[49] Opinion 04/2012 on Cookie Consent Exemption.

is frequently seen as an infringement of domestic privacy. Similar considerations apply with faxes and emails and, as will be discussed later, the legislative provisions seeking to regulate the use of these have been highly controversial.

The development of sector-specific legislation

Although all aspects of communications networks are regulated under the general provisions of data protection law, almost from the inception of the general regime the EU identified a need for a more specialised form of regulation, to 'particularise and complement'[50] the general data protection Directive adopted in 1995.[51] The provisions of the general Directive were therefore supplemented by more specific provisions in the form of the Directive of 15 December 1997 'concerning the processing of personal data and the protection of privacy in the telecommunications sector'.[52] This Directive was implemented in the United Kingdom by the Telecommunications (Data Protection and Privacy) (Direct Marketing) Regulations 1998 and the Telecommunications (Data Protection and Privacy) Regulations 1999.[53]

It is testimony to the pace of developments in the sector (and perhaps also of the slow pace of the initial legislative process) that less than two years after the Directive's adoption the 1999 Communications Review commented that:

> The terminology used in the Telecoms Data Protection Directive, which was proposed in 1990, is appropriate for traditional fixed telephony services but less so for new services which have now become available and affordable for a wide public. This creates ambiguities and has led in practice to divergence in national transposition of the Directive. To ensure a consistent application of data protection principles to public telecommunications services and network throughout the EU, the Commission proposes to update and clarify the Directive taking account of technological developments converging markets.

A point which comes out strongly throughout the document is that data relating to communications have become both more extensive and more valuable. It is important that the optimal use should be made of valuable resources but there are increasingly conflicts between the interests of service providers and their users. The establishment of effective legal controls and safeguards was therefore seen as a matter of importance and Directive 2002/58/EC[54] concerning the processing of personal data and the protection of privacy in the electronic communications sector (Directive on Privacy and Electronic Communications) constituted one of the five Directives that made up the 2002 regulatory package. The Directive was implemented in the United Kingdom by the Privacy and Electronic Communications (EC Directive) Regulations 2003.[55]

As so often in the sector, technology and practice soon outpaced aspects of the legislative provisions. The development of data retention legislation in response to terrorist attacks in cities such as London and Madrid tilted the balance between respect for individual privacy and the requirements of law enforcement agencies. Legislation has been adopted, at both UK and EU levels, requiring communications providers to retain communications and location data for up to two years in the interests of law enforcement.

---

[50] Art. 1(2).   [51] Directive 95/46/EC, OJ 1995 L281/31.
[52] Directive 97/66/EC, OJ 1998 L24/01.   [53] SI 1999/2093.   [54] OJ 2002 L201/37.
[55] SI 2003/2426.

Further changes to the European legislation were adopted in 2009 with the European Directive 2009/136 on universal service and users rights (the 'Citizens' Rights Directive')[56] making a number of significant changes to the 2002 Directive. These were implemented in the United Kingdom by the Privacy and Electronic Communications (EC Directive) (Amendment) Regulations 2011.[57] A particularly contentious element of the legislation concerned its provisions regarding the use of cookies. The Directive's provisions in this regard have been widely criticised as being extremely unclear and, although the provisions formally came into effect in May 2011, the Information Commissioner issued guidance to the effect that he would not seek actively to enforce the legislation save in the case of blatant and deliberate infringements for a further year.

The Privacy and Electronic Communications Directive and Regulations

The Privacy and Electronic Communications Directive's proclaimed aim is to harmonise:

> national provisions required to ensure an equivalent level of protection of fundamental rights and freedoms, and in particular the right to privacy and confidentiality, with respect to the processing of personal data in the electronic communication sector and to ensure the free movement of such data and of electronic communication equipment and services in the Community.[58]

As was also the case in respect of the earlier Telecommunications Data Protection Directive, the 2002 measure's stated aim is to 'particularise and complement' the provisions of the general Data Protection Directive.[59] It also expands the scope of this measure in one important respect by providing at least some rights for legal as well as private persons.[60]

The scope of the Communications Data Privacy Directive[61] is defined in Article 3(1) as extending to:

> the processing of personal data in connection with the provision of publicly available electronic communications services in public communications networks in the Community.

In the context of communications-related activities, it may be assumed that individuals will often be identifiable by reference to telephone numbers or email addresses, matched to lists of subscribers maintained by network providers or ISPs. IP addresses[62] allocated to identifiable users will also be classed as personal data. It is difficult to conceive of any communications-related activity which will not involve processing and, save perhaps in the situation where a payphone is used (with, as is increasingly rare, payment made in cash), will not be carried out by reference to an identifiable individual.

Obligations imposed on network and service providers

The Directive and Regulations impose a range of obligations upon network and also service providers in respect of a range of aspects of electronic communications services.

---

[56] OJ 2009, L337/11.   [57] SI 2011/1208.   [58] Art. 1(1) as amended.   [59] Art. 1(2).
[60] Art. 1(2).   [61] Directive 2002/58/EC.
[62] IP (Internet Protocol) addresses provide the mechanism by which the source and destination of email traffic can be identified and are key to the functioning of the Internet.

Security and confidentiality

The first substantive obligation imposed is that the provider of a public communication network or service must 'take appropriate technical and organisational measures' to ensure the security of the network and any messages transmitted over it.[63] The 2011 Regulations expand the requirement providing that:

The measures ... shall at least—

(a) ensure that personal data can be accessed only by authorised personnel for legally authorized purposes;

(b) protect personal data stored or transmitted against accidental or unlawful destruction, accidental loss or alteration, and unauthorised or unlawful storage, processing, access or disclosure; and

(c) ensure the implementation of a security policy with respect to the processing of personal data.

The most obvious, and well-publicised risk will be that of an unauthorised person obtaining access to data being transmitted. Beyond interception of voice traffic, perhaps the most significant and certainly the most high-profile risks associated with modern communications are those associated with the Internet, with concerns frequently being raised about the security of personal and financial data transmitted in the course of an e-commerce transaction. The obligations imposed upon service providers are twofold. First, appropriate security measures must be put in place to protect data[64] and, secondly, customers must be warned of the risks involved and advised about self-help measures such as encryption which may be used and of the likely costs of such measures.[65]

While the Directive's provisions regarding data security are addressed to network and service operators, obligations are imposed upon governments to ensure that legal sanctions may be imposed against those who breach the confidentiality of communications. Legal prohibitions are to be imposed against 'listening, tapping, storage or other kinds of interception or surveillance of communications' other than any measures which are necessary in connection with the transmission of data. Exceptions are sanctioned in cases where interception is necessary in the interests of national security, law enforcement, and 'the unauthorised use of electronic communications systems'.[66] It is also permissible to record commercial communications where this is 'carried out in the course of lawful business practice for the purpose of providing evidence of a commercial transaction'.

For the United Kingdom, the provisions of the Telecommunications (Lawful Business Practice) (Interception of Communications) Regulations[67] are relevant in this situation. Made under the auspices of the Regulation of Investigatory Powers Act 2000, these provide legal authority for the monitoring or recording of a wide range of electronic and voice communications. Examples would include recording of telephone calls received by businesses and the monitoring of employees' telephone and email communications by employers to determine compliance with policies regarding usage of these facilities.

Although the Regulations[68] and Directive[69] do provide legal authority for substantial forms of monitoring, it should be recalled that the general Data Protection Act's requirement is that processing should be both fair and lawful. While employer-directed monitoring of the kind described above may well satisfy the second requirement, the Information

---

[63] Art. 5 and Reg. 5.   [64] Reg. 5(1).   [65] Reg. 5(3).   [66] Art. 15(1).
[67] SI 2000/2699.   [68] SI 2000/2699.   [69] Directive 2002/58/EC.

Commissioner has suggested that processing carried out without giving proper notice to the individuals affected might well be considered unfair.

Breach notification

While prevention is normally the best form of cure, lapses in security can occur and one of the key issues for data protection legislation is how these should be dealt with. The Citizens' Rights Directive introduces a provision which is new to European legislation but which, under the title 'breach notification', has been used in some areas of processing in the United States for some time.[70] The draft European Data Protection Regulation (which it is envisaged will be adopted in 2014 and will replace the current Directive and the Data Protection Act 1998) allows for the introduction of such provisions into general data protection legislation but pending its (possible) adoption the Citizens' Rights Directive marks its only legislative appearance within the EU.

The Directive contains the term 'personal data breach' which is defined in terms:

> a breach of security leading to the accidental or unlawful destruction, loss, alteration, unauthorised disclosure of, or access to, personal data transmitted, stored or otherwise processed in connection with the provision of a publicly available electronic communications service.[71]

In the event a breach occurs, the service provider involved is to notify the appropriate national supervisory authority and, where the breach is likely to affect adversely individual users,[72] to inform those concerned directly. The supervisory authority may independently require a provider to make notification. As implemented in the 2011 Regulations it is provided that:

(2) If a personal data breach occurs, the service provider shall, without undue delay, notify that breach to the Information Commissioner.

(3) Subject to paragraph (6), if a personal data breach is likely to adversely affect the personal data or privacy of a subscriber or user, the service provider shall also, without undue delay, notify that breach to the subscriber or user concerned.

(4) The notification referred to in paragraph (2) shall contain at least a description of—

    (a) the nature of the breach;

    (b) the consequences of the breach; and

    (c) the measures taken or proposed to be taken by the provider to address the breach.

(5) The notification referred to [sic] the paragraph (3) shall contain at least—

    (a) a description of the nature of the breach;

    (b) information about contact points within the service provider's organisation from which more information may be obtained; and

    (c) recommendations of measures to allow the subscriber to mitigate the possible adverse impacts of the breach.

---

[70] For useful information on developments in the USA, see <http://www.csoonline.com/article/221322/cso-disclosure-series-data-breach-notification-laws-state-by-state>.

[71] Art. 2(c) adding a new para. (h) to Art. 2 of the 2002 Directive.

[72] The obligation to notify individuals will not arise if the data has been stored in a form in which it will be unintelligible to unauthorised parties—effectively that it has been encrypted using a strong form of protection.

(6) The notification referred to in paragraph (3) is not required if the service provider has demonstrated, to the satisfaction of the Information Commissioner that—

    (a) it has implemented appropriate technological protection measures which render the data unintelligible to any person who is not authorised to access it,[73] and

    (b) that those measures were applied to the data concerned in that breach.

Cookies

As indicated previously, cookies are frequently used by Internet sites. In the case, for example, of a website, they may be used to identify the fact that a particular machine (and often by inference a particular individual) has accessed the site previously and may be used to customise the pages presented according to previous activities. Typically, an e-commerce site may present a user with a list of recommended buys based on an analysis of that person's purchasing history.

Such practices may be welcomed in many instances. Cookies may also be used to relieve a user of the need to supply full details of name, address, and credit cards whenever making a purchase from a website. There are however, also implications for the privacy and anonymity of Internet users. The Citizens' Rights Directive provides that:

(1) Member States shall ensure the confidentiality of communications and the related traffic data by means of a public communications network and publicly available electronic communications services, through national legislation. In particular, they shall prohibit listening, tapping, storage or other kinds of interception or surveillance of communications and the related traffic data by persons other than users, without the consent of the users concerned, except when legally authorised to do so in accordance with Article 15(1). This paragraph shall not prevent technical storage which is necessary for the conveyance of a communication without prejudice to the principle of confidentiality.

   ...

(3) Member States shall ensure that the storing of information, or the gaining of access to information already stored, in the terminal equipment of a subscriber or user is only allowed on condition that the subscriber or user concerned has given his or her consent, having been provided with clear and comprehensive information, in accordance with Directive 95/46/EC, inter alia about the purposes of the processing. This shall not prevent any technical storage or access for the sole purpose of carrying out the transmission of a communication over an electronic communications network, or as strictly necessary in order for the provider of an information society service explicitly requested by the subscriber or user to provide the service.

This formulation raises a number of issues and points of uncertainty. There has been a long-standing and largely unresolved issue between the United Kingdom government and the European Commission concerning the manner in which user consent to online actions should be obtained. The key question is whether consent needs to be obtained expressly (often referred to as 'opt in') or whether it may be implied from the fact that the user, having been provided with information about intended activities, has not exercised an opportunity to object ('opt out').

---

[73] Typically, this might require that the data have been encrypted in a manner which makes it highly unlikely that any third party will be able to access the contents.

In the context of cookies, there are issues and controversies about how explicit the level of notification need be. A common formulation used by website owners is along the lines of 'we use cookies to enhance your browsing experience'. A rather vague formulation! Another issue relates to the extent to which a user may legitimately be put into a situation where the choice is between accepting cookies or eschewing access to the website. The United Kingdom's Information Commissioner's website informs users, for example, that if they do not accept cookies, they will not be able to access all the features of the site. The Directive provides that cookies are legitimate when they 'are strictly necessary in order for the provider of an information society service explicitly requested by the subscriber or user to provide the service'. This is a stringent requirement and one of the major issues is how it should be applied in relation to what might be referred to as 'legacy' websites—those developed before the adoption of the 2009 Directive? For a good many years, cookies have been used because they are helpful (not least to website owners) rather than because they are 'strictly necessary'.

The Directive's provisions have been implemented in the United Kingdom by the Privacy and Electronic Communications (EC Directive) (Amendment) Regulations 2011.[74] This inserts amendments to Regulation 6 of the 2003 Regulations to provide that:

(1)   Subject to paragraph (4), a person shall not [store or] gain access to information stored, in the terminal equipment of a subscriber or user unless the requirements of paragraph (2) are met.

(2)   The requirements are that the subscriber or user of that terminal equipment—

(a)   is provided with clear and comprehensive information about the purposes of the storage of, or access to, that information; and

[(b)   has given his or her consent].

(3)   Where an electronic communications network is used by the same person to store or access information in the terminal equipment of a subscriber or user on more than one occasion, it is sufficient for the purposes of this regulation that the requirements of paragraph (2) are met in respect of the initial use.

[(3A) For the purposes of paragraph (2), consent may be signified by a subscriber who amends or sets controls on the internet browser which the subscriber uses or by using another application or program to signify consent.]

(4)   Paragraph (1) shall not apply to the technical storage of, or access to, information—

(a)   for the sole purpose of carrying out…the transmission of a communication over an electronic communications network; or

(b)   where such storage or access is strictly necessary for the provision of an information society service requested by the subscriber or user.

The Information Commissioner has published an extensive guidance note on the operation of the new provisions.[75] The major problem area, it suggests, is to modify existing systems to cope with the new requirements:

Implementing these rules requires considerable work in the short term but compliance will get significantly easier with time. The initial effort is where the challenge lies—auditing of

---

[74] SI 2011/1208.
[75] Available at <http://www.ico.gov.uk/for_organisations/privacy_and_electronic_communications/the_guide/cookies.aspx>.

cookies, resolving problems with reliance on cookies built into existing systems and websites, making sure the information provided to users is clear and putting in place specific measures to obtain consent. This work takes place in the context of limited consumer awareness and understanding of what cookies do. In time a number of factors are likely to make compliance much more straightforward. New sites and systems and upgrades to existing systems can be designed to facilitate compliance with the rules, those operating websites will be more aware about how they choose to use cookies and enhanced browser options will increasingly allow websites to rely on browser settings to help to satisfy themselves they have consent to set cookies.[76]

While the Commissioner indicates that obtaining explicit consent to the use of cookies from users would secure 'regulatory certainty' the guidance note states:

Early reporting on the new rule led some to believe that an explicit, opt-in style consent would be required for every cookie each time it was set. The Information Commissioner's guidance made it clear that although an explicit opt-in mechanism might provide regulatory certainty it was not the only means of gaining consent. In some circumstances those seeking consent might consider implied consent as an option that was perhaps more practical than the explicit opt-in model.

... consent (whether it is implied or express) has to be a freely given, specific and informed indication of the individual's wishes. For implied consent to work there has to be some action taken by the consenting individual from which their consent can be inferred. This might for example be visiting a website, moving from one page to another or clicking on a particular button. The key point, however, is that when taking this action the individual has to have a reasonable understanding that by doing so they are agreeing to cookies being set.[77]

One approach that is widely used is to display a message on the opening screen of a website indicating that cookies are being used, giving a general description of their purpose and indicating that if the user proceeds to use the site further, consent to their use will be assumed.

Traffic and location data

The term 'traffic data' encompasses any data processed in connection with the transmission of signals over a communication network. It will include data relating to the point of origin of a communication, its destination, and the duration of the communication. In the case of a fixed-line telephone, the point of origin will be obvious. With mobile communications, as has been referred to previously, the location of the user may constantly be changing. Data transmitted periodically from the mobile phone will allow the network to remain aware of the phone's location. This is clearly necessary in order to be able to make and receive calls but the retention and processing of location data raises serious issues for the individual's right to privacy.

Undoubtedly reflecting its origins in the era when mobile phones constituted a niche rather than a mass market, the Telecoms Data Protection Directive[78] referred only to traffic data and provided that it might be processed subsequent to a communication only for billing purposes, or—with the consent of the customer—limited items of data might be processed by the telecommunications service provider for marketing purposes.[79]

---

[76] pp. 3–4.   [77] pp. 6–7.   [78] Directive 97/66/EC.
[79] The Annex to the Directive contained a list of the types of data which might be processed. This included data relating to the volume of calls but not the destination or duration of individual calls.

The term traffic data was not defined in the Telecoms Data Protection Directive.[80] The Communications Data Privacy Directive, however, provides that it is to consist of 'any data processed for the purpose of the conveyance of a communication on an electronic communications network or for the billing thereof'.[81] This will encompass both data relating to use of a telephone and any data which might be processed by an Internet Service Provider (ISP) concerned with Internet usage.

The Directive retains the basic prohibition against processing but extends the range of permissible uses. Article 6 provides that:

> For the purpose of marketing electronic communications services or for the provision of value added services, the provider of a publicly available electronic communications service may process the (traffic) data... to the extent and for the duration necessary for such services or marketing, if the subscriber or user to whom the data relate has given his or her prior consent. Users or subscribers shall be given the possibility to withdraw their consent for the processing of traffic data at any time.[82]

'Value added services' are defined as communication services requiring the processing of data 'beyond what is necessary for the transmission of a communication or the billing thereof'.[83] This would include services such as the downloading of ringtones for mobile phones or the provision of information services. User consent is required and must be given on the same basis as that needed in the Data Protection Directive, which demands a 'freely given, specific and informed indication of his wishes by which the data subject signifies his agreement to personal data relating to him being processed'.[84] The key requirement is that the subject be informed of the uses proposed. In this eventuality, it is acceptable for the processing to take place, unless the subject actively indicates objection (opting out). Consent can be withdrawn at any time.

Additionally, the Communications Data Privacy Directive makes provision for the handling of location data, defined as:

> any data processed in an electronic communications network, indicating the geographic position of the terminal equipment of a user of a publicly available electronic communications service.[85]

Beyond use for the purpose of network operation, location data may be processed only when it is rendered anonymous or, with user consent, for the provision of a value added service. Information must be provided to the user of the type of data which will be processed, the purposes for which it will be used, the duration of any further use, and whether this will involve a transfer to third parties.

Although this provision may seem at first glance to provide considerable assistance to users, it is likely that the information may be provided in a relatively lengthy and complex list of standard conditions associated with provision of the overall communications service. Admittedly, prior to the implementation of the Communications Data Privacy Directive, one of the major mobile networks used a clause empowering them to:

> Contact you or allow carefully selected third parties to contact you with information about products and services by post, telephone, mobile text message or email (subject to any preferences expressed by you).

---

[80] Directive 97/66/EC.   [81] Directive 2002/58/EC, Art. 2(b).
[82] Art. 6(3) as amended by the Citizens' Rights Directive, Art. 2.
[83] Art. 6(3) as amended by the Citizens' Rights Directive, Art. 2.
[84] Art. 6(3) as amended by the Citizens' Rights Directive, Art. 2.
[85] Art. 6(3) as amended by the Citizens' Rights Directive, Art. 2.

Given that the processing of data will take place in real time and be associated with the movements and location of the user, the processing might be considered rather more sensitive than is the case where traffic data is used for marketing purposes. It is perhaps unfortunate that the requirement is not that the provider seek a positive indication of consent (opt in).

In addition to providing users with the right to opt out of such uses of their data, the Communications Data Privacy Directive requires that users must be given the possibility 'of temporarily refusing the processing of such data for each connection to the network or for each transmission of a communication.'[86] It is likely that this right could be exercised in a manner similar to that currently applying in relation to the use of systems of 'caller id', where prefixing a number with 141 will prevent details of the caller's number being made available to the recipient.

Data retention

Significant inroads on the level of protection conferred by the Communications Data Privacy Directive came with the inclusion at a late stage in the legislative process of the acceptance by the European Parliament of an amendment permitting Member States to 'adopt legislative measures providing for the retention of data for a limited period justified on the grounds laid down in this paragraph.'[87] The grounds referred to include the safeguarding of 'national security, defence, public security, and the prevention, investigation, detection and prosecution of criminal offences or of unauthorised use of the electronic communication system'.

In the United Kingdom, the provisions of the Regulation of Investigatory Powers Act 2000 empower a senior police officer to require a communications provider to disclose any communications data in its possession where this is considered necessary in the interests of national security, the prevention or detection of crime, or a number of other situations.[88] The term 'communications data' is defined broadly to include traffic and location data, although as was stated by the Home Office:

> It is important to identify what communications data does include but equally important to be clear about what it does *not* include. The term communications data in the Act does not include the content of any communication.[89]

The procedures to be followed in requesting or requiring disclosure are laid down in a Code of Practice on the Acquisition and Disclosure of Communications Data, which was brought into force by the Regulation of Investigatory Powers (Acquisition and Disclosure of Communications Data: Code of Practice) Order 2007.[90]

The Regulation of Investigatory Powers Act 2000 did not require that providers retain data, although data protection concerns had been expressed that mobile phone operators were retaining data for a period of months, and in some cases years. The conformity of this practice with the requirements of the Data Protection Act 1998, that 'Personal data processed for any purpose or purposes shall not be kept for longer than is necessary for that purpose or those purposes',[91] had been doubted. The passage of the Anti-Terrorism, Crime and Security Act 2001 provided a legal basis for the retention of data. The Act

---

[86] Art. 6(3) as amended by the Citizens' Rights Directive, Art. 9(2).
[87] Art. 6(3) as amended by the Citizens' Rights Directive, Art. 15.   [88] s. 22.
[89] Consultation Paper on a Code of Practice for Voluntary Retention of Communications Data, March 2003.
[90] SI 2007/2197.   [91] Sch. 1, fifth data protection principle.

conferred power on the Secretary of State to draw up a code of practice, specifying periods of time during which communications providers would be required to retain communications data.[92] Although the Secretary of State is granted legislative power, it was envisaged that a voluntary code would be agreed between the government and the communications industry.

Initial proposals by the government for the establishment of a code of practice received heavy criticism, both in terms of the period of time within which data might be required to be retained and in terms of the range of government agencies which might be granted access to this data. An initial draft code was withdrawn in July 2002, and a further draft was published in September 2003[93] and entered into force on 5 December 2003, pursuant to the provisions of the Retention of Communications Data (Code of Practice) Order 2003.[94] The code provides authority for the retention of communications data in the interests of national security or the detection or prevention of crime for periods after the business case for retention might have expired up to a maximum period of twelve months.

Compliance with the 2003 code was voluntary. This situation changed upon the implementation of the European Directive 'on the retention of data generated or processed in connection with the provision of publicly available electronic communications services or of public communications networks'[95] (the Data Retention Directive). This Directive, which was introduced in the aftermath of the Madrid and London bombings in 2004 and 2005 respectively, amends the provisions of Directive 2002/58 concerned with privacy in electronic communications networks. Recital 9 to the Directive explains:

> Because retention of data has proved to be such a necessary and effective investigative tool for law enforcement in several Member States, and in particular concerning serious matters such as organised crime and terrorism, it is necessary to ensure that retained data are made available to law enforcement authorities for a certain period, subject to the conditions provided for in this Directive.

Article 5 of the Directive specifies a very wide range of items of communications data relating to the source and destination of telephone calls, emails, and Internet access.

The periods for which items of data are to be retained are to be specified by Member States within the range of six months to two years. The Directive was implemented in the United Kingdom by the Data Protection (EC Directive) Regulations 2007,[96] which entered into force on 1 October 2007. Initially these Regulations did not require retention of Internet data but The Data Retention (EC Directive) Regulations 2009 provided for this. Rather than the voluntary retention scheme applying under the Code, Regulation 5 requires that data must be retained relating to:

(a) the telephone number from which the telephone call was made and the name and address of the subscriber and registered user of that telephone;

(b) the telephone number dialled and, in cases involving supplementary services such as call forwarding or call transfer, any telephone number to which the call is forwarded or transferred, and the name and address of the subscriber and registered user of such telephone;

---

[92] s. 102.   [93] Available from <http://www.opsi.gov.uk/si/si2003/draft/5b.pdf>.
[94] SI 2003/3175.   [95] Directive 2006/24/EC, OJ 2006 No. L105/54.
[96] SI 2007/2199. These regulations were replaced by the Electronic Communications (EC Directive) Regulations 2009 SI 2009/859. The 2007 Regulations had applied only to the telephone sector but the 2009 Regulations extend the scope of the retention requirements to Internet and email traffic.

    (c) the date and time of the start and end of the call; and

    (d) the telephone service used.

Additional information is required to be retained in respect of mobile calls:

    (a) the International Mobile Subscriber Identity (IMSI) and the International Mobile Equipment Identity (IMEI) of the telephone from which a telephone call is made;

    (b) the IMSI and the IMEI of the telephone dialled;

    (c) in the case of pre-paid anonymous services, the date and time of the initial activation of the service and the cell ID from which the service was activated;

    (d) the cell ID at the start of the communication; and

    (e) data identifying the geographic location of cells by reference to their cell ID.

In respect of Internet and email communications, the key retention requirements relate to:

    11.—(1) The user ID allocated.

        (2) The user ID and telephone number allocated to the communication entering the public telephone network.

        (3) The name and address of the subscriber or registered user to whom an IP address, user ID or telephone number was allocated at the time of the communication.

Data is also required to be retained relating to the destination of any communications and as to the date and time at which communications were made. In all cases the data must be retained for a period of twelve months.[97]

Data retention is not a cost-free activity. Capital and running costs have been estimated at around £46 million over an eight-year period.[98] Under the Regulations, the government is empowered rather than obliged to compensate providers for the costs involved.[99] It has been suggested that payments of £18.5 million have been made to date to cover a five-year period.[100]

Itemised billing

The issue of itemised billing is rather less contentious than that of data retention but does serve to illustrate some of the changes which have occurred in the communications sector over the past decade and also some potential conflicts between rights to privacy and to information.

The initial provision of the Communications Data Privacy Directive may appear somewhat strange. Subscribers, it is provided, 'will have the right to receive non-itemised bills'.[101] While few people may want to exercise the option, the rationale lies perhaps in the fact that it has become very much the norm for individuals to receive itemised bills and indeed the Universal Service Directive provides for the right of users to receive itemised bills.[102] In this situation, given that the Directive is seeking to provide for exceptions, the logical approach is to assume the provision of itemised bills and confer a right to refuse these.

---

[97] The Electronic Communications (EC Directive) Regulations 2009 S1 2009/859, Reg. 5.

[98] <http://webarchive.nationalarchives.gov.uk/20100418065544/http://www.homeoffice.gov.uk/documents/cons-2008-transposition-dir/index.html>.   [99] Reg. 11.

[100] <http://www.out-law.com/page-9350>.   [101] Directive 2002/58/EC, Art. 7.

[102] See para. 9–032.

While it is almost inevitably the case that the person responsible for a communications bill would be interested in information regarding the calls made, other persons may have different preferences. The Communications Data Privacy Directive uses two terms—'subscriber' and 'user'. The term 'subscriber' is not defined in the Directive,[103] although it appears that it must refer to the party who has contracted for the provision of services. Perhaps rather inconsistently, the Directive does provide a definition of the term 'user' as 'any natural person using a publicly available electronic communications service, for private or business purposes, without necessarily having subscribed to this service'.[104]

In a household, it will be common for one member to be classed as the subscriber but for other family members to use the equipment. While the subscriber may wish to be able to analyse what calls have been made, the latter may have an interest in maintaining the privacy of their communications. In many cases it may be accepted that the wishes and interests of the subscriber should prevail, but there may be instances, for example where calls have been made to counselling or support agencies, perhaps arising from the behaviour of the subscriber towards the user. The Communications Data Privacy Directive requires that national implementing measures should seek to reconcile the interests of the parties involved 'by ensuring that sufficient alternative privacy enhancing methods of communications or payments are available to such users and subscribers'.[105]

Even by the general standards of EU Directives, this formulation is opaque. In the United Kingdom, there are some 750,000 payphones and it might be argued that this provides sufficient access to telecommunications for users who do not want details of their calls made available to third-party subscribers. The Recitals to the Communications Data Privacy Directive also recommend that Member States:

> encourage the development of electronic communication service options such as alternative payment facilities which allow anonymous or strictly private access to publicly available electronic communications services, for example calling cards and facilities for payment by credit card.[106]

A further possibility canvassed is that itemised bills may delete 'a certain number of digits' from the lists of called numbers. This might well prove useful in the situation, for example, that calls are made to a medical or emotional support helpline. Again, however, it is difficult to see why such an option would be attractive to subscribers and in the event that only certain numbers were censored, the presence of these might in itself be a cause for suspicion. One reasonable option, however, would appear to be to ensure that calls made to Freephone numbers (0800) should not appear on bills. These are frequently provided by support agencies. Given that such calls do not involve any cost implications for the subscriber, the balance of interests may be seen as lying with potential users.

Directory information

When the 1997 Directive was adopted, virtually the only form of communications directories were telephone directories published by major telecommunications operators. In the past fifteen years, there has been a massive increase in the number of telephones in use due to the continuing growth in the mobile market. Tens of millions of individuals have also acquired email addresses as this form of electronic communication has expanded,

---

[103] The Telecoms Data Protection Directive (Directive 97/66/EC) did define the term as 'any natural or legal person who or which is party to a contract with the provider of publicly available telecommunications services for the supply of such services' (Art. 2).   [104] Directive 2002/58/EC, Art. 2.
[105] Directive 2002/58/EC, Art. 7(2).   [106] Directive 2002/58/EC, Recital 33.

to the extent that the volume of email communications dwarfs that carried by the postal networks. Beyond an increase in the range of materials which might be contained in communications directories there has been a similar growth in the level of sophistication of directory services. Increasingly provided in electronic form, directories may include facilities such as reverse searching. While a traditional directory can be searched only in the manner structured by the compiler, typically by alphabetical order, an electronic directory might, for example, allow a user to enter a telephone number and be presented with the name and physical and email address of the person to whom it has been allocated.

The Telecoms Data Protection Directive provided that the information contained in public directories should be limited to that necessary to identify particular customers, that there should be a right to require that details be withheld from the directory, and also that customers should be able to indicate:

> that his or her personal data may not be used for the purpose of direct marketing, to have his or her address omitted in part and not to have a reference revealing his or her sex, where this is applicable linguistically.[107]

The first element of this requirement was met through the establishment of the telephone preference service, which enabled customers to indicate their wish not to receive calls for marketing purposes.[108] Under the Telecommunications (Data Protection and Privacy) Regulations 1999,[109] it is provided that marketing-related communications must not be made to a telephone number which appears on a list maintained by the Director General of Telecommunications of subscribers who have indicated objection to this practice.[110] Breach of this requirement will constitute a contravention of the Data Protection Act 1998 and may entitle the subscriber to compensation for any damage caused. To date, it does not appear that any party has obtained compensation for burnt meals caused by unwarranted interruptions by telephone marketers. In 1999, the Director entered into a contract with the Telephone Preference Service for the compilation and maintenance of the list. Effect was given to the remaining requirements of the Directive by the Telecommunications (Data Protection and Privacy) Regulations 1999.[111] Over 1 million subscribers have now registered with the service.

The Communications Data Privacy Directive adopts a somewhat different approach. Subscribers are to be informed of the nature and purposes of the information which will be made available in a public directory or directory information service and 'of any further usage possibilities based on search functions embedded in electronic versions of the directory'. This information must be supplied prior to publication of the directory.[112] Having been informed of the purposes envisaged, subscribers are to have the right to require that their details be removed in whole or in part. No charge is to be made for this or for compliance with the subscriber's request that errors be corrected.

Especially with electronic directories, it is possible that third parties may seek to copy significant amounts of information and use these for their own purposes. The body of the Communications Data Privacy Directive makes no provision in this respect, although the Recitals indicate that:

> Where the data may be transmitted to one or more third parties, the subscriber should be informed of this possibility and of the recipient or the categories of possible recipients. Any transmission should be subject to the condition that the data may not be used for other purposes than those for which they were collected. If the party collecting the data from the subscriber or

---

[107] Directive 97/66/EC, Art. 11.   [108] <http://www.tpsonline.org.uk/tpsr/html/default.asp>.
[109] SI 1999/2093.   [110] Reg. 9.   [111] SI 1999/2093.
[112] Directive 2002/58/EC, Art. 12.

any third party to whom the data have been transmitted wishes to use the data for an additional purpose, the renewed consent of the subscriber is to be obtained either by the initial party collecting the data or by the third party to whom the data have been transmitted.[113]

Although not a direct legal requirement, the Telecommunications Directory Information Fair Processing Code, drawn up by the then Data Protection Registrar in 1998, is likely to be very relevant. This provides, inter alia, that controllers should take steps to prevent information being misused. Bulk copying might be inhibited by technical measures designed to limit the number of records which can be accessed and copied by a single search. It is also suggested that encryption techniques might be used and, perhaps now outdated, that there should be no online interface to directories. Encryption of data might also be used to prevent reverse searching.

Although not legally binding, a failure to comply with the Code may be regarded as constituting unfair processing under the Data Protection Act 1998 and result in the service of an enforcement notice by the Information Commissioner. Under the Telecommunications (Open Network Provision) (Voice Telephony) Regulations,[114] an undertaking required BT (effectively), when providing directory information to a third party, to obtain an undertaking that the recipient would comply with the Code. Any breach of the undertaking would render the third party's processing unfair. A similar effect is now provided by condition 22 of the General Conditions of Entitlement. This provides that every communications provider is obliged to supply details of its subscribers to any other provider upon reasonable request. This obligation is expressly stated to be 'subject to the requirements of relevant data protection legislation'.

Calling and connected line identification

Systems of calling line identification, often referred to as 'caller id', allow a user to identify the number from which a call originates prior to answering the call. A related system allows a user to discover details of the last call made to the telephone by dialling 1471. As with itemised billing, the systems offer major benefits to individuals, not least as a means of deterring the making of hoax or malicious calls, but there may also be good reason why a party making a call may not wish details to be available to a called party. At a trivial level, a husband may not wish his wife to be aware that rather than a call originating from the office where work demands are requiring a late departure, it is coming from a local pub. Following the break-up of a relationship, one party may wish to contact the other but not to allow the possibility of the call being returned or—especially in an era of reverse searchable directories—to allow their physical location to be discovered. Caller id is also used extensively for commercial purposes. Some companies use systems linked to a database of customers so that the caller's identity is known at the time the call is answered. Many taxi companies use such systems to simplify the task of despatching vehicles and also to provide some check against the making of hoax calls. Less desirable, perhaps, is the situation where a company 'captures' phone numbers from persons calling to inquire about goods or services and uses these for subsequent marketing activities.[115] The situation may therefore arise where subscribers may wish to know who is calling them but, at least in certain situations, may not want their telephone number to be made available to the party they are calling.

---

[113] Directive 2002/58/EC, Recital 39.   [114] SI 1998/1580.

[115] Such processing may, of course, be considered unfair under the provisions of the Data Protection Act 1998.

As well as presenting the called party with information about the origin of a call, the same technology—referred to in this case as connected line information—allows the caller to see the actual number at which the call is answered. Although in the majority of cases this will be the number which was dialled, it may also be the case that calls are forwarded to another number. While in the vast majority of cases the practice will be unobjectionable, there may be situations where the called party is reluctant for this to happen. Out-of-hours calls to a doctor's surgery may be forwarded to the physician's home number, and there may be reluctance to allow patients to know this number.

In respect of caller id, the Communications Data Privacy Directive requires that subscribers and users be presented with a range of options. Users are to be offered the option, free of charge, of blocking the presentation of the number from which they are making a call. In the United Kingdom, this is normally accomplished by prefixing '141' to the telephone number called. Users should also be offered the option of blocking the display of information on a permanent basis, although a charge may be levied for this.[116]

While callers will be entitled to block presentation of their identity, the Communications Data Privacy Directive sets the scene for what might almost be regarded as a battle of the systems by providing that subscribers are to be offered the option to reject incoming calls where the caller has chosen to prevent display of his or her number.[117] One limitation of this approach is that identification details may be withheld either by the deliberate act of the caller or—as typically happens in a work environment—because outgoing calls will be routed through a central switchboard. Even though each instrument may have its own number which can be dialled directly by callers from outside the premises, the identification details will be stripped out in respect of outgoing calls.

In exceptional cases, it may be provided that attempts by callers to conceal details of the number from which a communication originates can be overridden. This may take place on a temporary basis in the event that a subscriber requests the assistance of the service provider in tracing the origin of malicious or nuisance calls and permanently in respect of lines used by the emergency services.[118]

Broadly similar provisions apply in respect of connected line identification. Here, subscribers must be offered the possibility 'using a simple means and free of charge of preventing the presentation of the connected line information'.[119]

Unsolicited communications

For many persons, receipt of unsolicited commercial communications, whether by post, telephone, fax, or email, is a major cause of annoyance. BT estimated in 2005 that almost half of domestic phone users chose to remove their details from telephone directories. A high proportion, it is suggested, do so in order to minimise the numbers of unsolicited marketing calls.[120] Proposals in 2009[121] by a directory enquiry service, '118 800' to establish a directory of mobile numbers attracted significant objections and implementation of the facility was temporarily suspended. More than three years later, the service is still not available. As indicated, very considerable numbers of persons have signed up to the telephone and fax preference service. Currently, much publicity is given to the use of the Internet for

---

[116] Directive 2002/58/EC, Art. 8(1).
[117] Directive 2002/58/EC, Art. 8(2). BT currently charges £3.33 per month for use of this facility.
[118] Directive 2002/58/EC, Art. 10.   [119] Directive 2002/58/EC, Art. 8(4).
[120] Directory Information. <http://www.oftel.gov.uk/publications/1995_98/consumer/dqchap.htm>.
[121] <http://news.bbc.co.uk/1/hi/programmes/working_lunch/8091621.stm>.

unsolicited or junk emails, generally referred to as spam; one respected source estimates that 92 per cent of all Internet-based emails are spam.[122] According to a recent Harris poll, 80 per cent of Internet users claimed to be 'very annoyed' about spam with 74 per cent of those surveyed favouring a legal ban.[123]

A further tactic, which was the subject of an enforcement notice served by the Information Commissioner in the United Kingdom, concerns the use of automated calling systems. With these, numbers are dialled automatically and when the call is answered, a recorded message is played to the recipient. Beyond any nuisance value, these systems have been implicated in at least one fatality in Canada, where a fire broke out in a property just at the moment an automated call was received. Although the householder attempted to terminate the call so that the emergency services might be summoned, the message continued to be transmitted with the result that the user was unable to make an outgoing call. In the case of *Scottish National Party v Information Commissioner*,[124] the political party in question had made use of automated systems during the course of the 2005 general election campaign. It appears that it was not alone in making use of the technology but was perhaps less careful than others in consulting the registers of those who had opted out of receiving unsolicited marketing calls and the Commissioner served an enforcement notice requiring it to desist from what he considered to be processing in breach of the Privacy and Electronic Communications Regulations. On appeal to the Information Tribunal, the Scottish National Party argued principally that as a political party, its communications did not fall into the category of 'marketing'. The Tribunal disagreed and upheld the enforcement notice. Marketing, it was held, was concerned with seeking to influence the way people acted and the fact that in the present case there was no commercial motive was of no relevance. The Scottish National Party was seeking to persuade people to vote for it in preference to other political parties and this, it was held, was no different in principle from one manufacturer or retailer seeking to persuade consumers to deal with them rather than a competitor.

A similar 'opt in' approach was adopted in respect of the use of fax machines for the purposes of unsolicited marketing. The rationale for treating fax transmissions more restrictively than voice communications was an economic one. While receipt of a telephone call does not have any cost implications for the subscriber, paper and ink will need to be used to print out the contents of a fax. This was undoubtedly a more significant consideration in 1990 when the Telecoms Data Protection Directive was initially drafted, as at that time fax machines had to use special and very expensive paper and, given the developments in technology, it is perhaps surprising that it should have continued.

Perhaps unsurprisingly, the original Telecoms Data Protection Directive[125] made no reference to email. Both with the growth in Internet usage and with the expansion in the scope of the legislation, inclusion of provisions concerning email has been a major and contentious feature of the new legislation. As originally introduced, the explanatory memorandum accompanying the draft Communications Data Privacy Directive indicated that:

> Four Member States already have bans on unsolicited commercial e-mail and another is about to adopt one. In most of the other Member States opt-out systems exist. From an internal market perspective, this is not satisfactory. Direct marketers in opt-in countries may not target e-mail addresses within their own country but they can still continue to send

---

[122] <http://www.symantec.com/connect/blogs/spam-and-phishing-landscape-september-2010>.
[123] <http://news.zdnet.co.uk/story/0,t269-s2128193,00.html>.
[124] Case number EA/2005/0021. Available via <http://www.informationtribunal.gov.uk/Public/search.aspx>.
[125] Case number EA/2005/0021. Available via <http://www.informationtribunal.gov.uk/Public/search.aspx>.

unsolicited commercial e-mail to countries with an opt-out system. Moreover, since e-mail addresses very often give no indication of the country of residence of the recipients, a system of divergent regimes within the internal market is unworkable in practice. A harmonised opt-in approach solves this problem.

Accordingly, a prohibition was proposed except in respect of individuals who had indicated the wish to receive commercial emails. This approach was highly controversial and in October 2001 the European Parliament voted in favour of an 'opt out' system. In December 2001, however, the Council voted to reinstate the opt-in approach and the Communications Data Privacy Directive was finally adopted with this format, the Directive providing that the sending of 'electronic mail for the purposes of direct marketing may only be allowed in respect of subscribers who have given their prior consent'.[126]

Although the term 'prior consent' might appear compatible with the use of an opt-out approach where failure on the part of a user to indicate a preference would equate to consent, the Recitals make reference to the need to ensure that the 'prior explicit consent of the recipients is obtained before such communications are addressed to them'.[127] Use of the adjective 'explicit' clearly imposes a heavier burden upon persons wishing to send emails.

The Communications Data Privacy Directive provides for one situation where commercial emails can be sent without prior consent. This applies where there has been a previous commercial relationship between the parties and:

> a natural or legal person obtains from its customers their electronic contact details for electronic mail, in the context of the sale of a product or a service—the same natural or legal person may use these electronic contact details for direct marketing of its own similar products or services provided that customers clearly and distinctly are given the opportunity to object, free of charge and in an easy manner, to such use of electronic contact details when they are collected and on the occasion of each message in case the customer has not initially refused such use.[128]

Use of a hypertext link in the emails allowing recipients to 'click here to unsubscribe from mailings' would suffice to meet with this requirement.

Even where consent has been given to the transmission of commercial emails or where the email is sent to a previous customer, the Directive imposes a final requirement that commercial emails should be clearly identifiable as such and that they should always use a valid return address.[129] In many cases, it may be obvious from the heading of the email that its subject is commercial. A trawl through the author's mailbox reveals subjects such as:

Need a NEW Computer? No Credit—No Problem

Earn $75/hr with Your Own Home Based Business Processing

Sample the weight loss patch—on us!

Nothing more need be done in these situations. Other spammers, perhaps aware that messages with obviously commercial headings may be deleted unread, make use of headings such as:

---

[126] Directive 2002/58/EC, Art. 13(1).   [127] Directive 2002/58/EC, Recital 40.
[128] Directive 2002/58/EC, Art. 13(2).
[129] Directive 2002/58/EC, Art. 13(4). Many spammers attempt to conceal the genuine address from which the message is sent to avoid possible action by the ISP involved, which may well have an anti-spam condition in its contract of supply.

Please get back to me

Re your enquiry

Hello

Headers such as this are now unlawful under the Communications Data Privacy Directive.

While well-meaning, it is uncertain how effective the Directive's approach will be. A very considerable percentage of commercial email originates from the United States or from other countries outside the EU. Unless and until these legal systems adopt a similar approach, there will be little that can practically be done to bring proceedings against spammers. Even within the EU, given the ease with which persons can set up email accounts, the task of tracking down offenders will be a difficult one.

Conclusions

Those using communications services justifiably have an expectancy that the privacy of their communications will be respected. There are, of course, significant issues concerned with the intrinsic security of certain forms of communication. Transmitting an email has been seen as analogous, for example, with using a postcard to send a communication by post. Although the Communications Data Privacy Directive[130] is relevant in respect of these issues, perhaps its most important role relates to the use of traffic data generated as a consequence of the use of networks. Although subject to the inevitable exceptions in the interests of national security and law enforcement, these will provide a reasonable degree of protection.

Undoubtedly, the most publicised provisions in the Communications Data Privacy Directive[131] are those dealing with the processing of junk mail and other forms of unsolicited commercial communications. While likely to be welcomed by the majority of users, it may be questioned as to how effective the prohibition against unsolicited email communications is likely to be. Although estimates as to the costs incurred by industry in dealing with email spam are legion,[132] it is doubtful whether these stand serious comparison with losses due to improper or wasteful use of other resources, such as telephones, stationery, or even heating and lighting. It is difficult to justify the adoption of an opt-in approach for this specific sector while other forms of unsolicited communication using media such as the mail or telephone can continue to operate on an opt-out basis.

---

[130] Directive 2002/58/EC.   [131] Directive 2002/58/EC.

[132] One estimate puts the global cost at $9 billion per year: see <http://news.bbc.co.uk/1/hi/technology/2983157.stm>.

8

Transborder data flows

Introduction

For centuries governments have sought to control channels of communication both internally and also, perhaps more extensively, in respect of transfers to and from other countries. Historically, arrangements for the transfer of messages between states relied upon bilateral treaties and the very real possibility of inspecting messages at the point that they crossed national borders. The emergence of the electric telegraph, well described as the 'Victorian Internet',[1] brought massive changes. For the first time, a communications network was being created which could transmit messages almost instantaneously and almost irrespective of distance.

Direct international transfers using the telegraph required interconnection between national telegraph networks, something which many governments were initially reluctant to permit. National security concerns are not a twenty-first century phenomenon and the 1850s and 1860s, when telegraph technology was developing at speed, was a period of considerable political and social upheaval across the continent of Europe.

After a number of failed initiatives—failure caused in no small measure by British intransigence towards its European neighbours—the International Telegraph Union (ITU) (now the International Telecommunications Union) was established in 1865. It is a sign of the international nature of electronic communications that the ITU is classed as the world's first international organisation (other than in the field of religion), with its establishment preceding by a decade the Universal Postal Union which plays a similar harmonising role in respect of postal traffic. The ITU provided a set of rules relating to the international transfer of telegraph messages and required that governments allowed free passage to messages which complied with those rules.

In keeping with history's tendency to repeat itself, as the computer developed and became linked to communication networks, concerns at the implications of transborder data flows have evolved, paralleling the development of national data protection statutes. Typically, the fear is expressed that an absence of control may result in the evasion of national controls. As has been stated:

> protective provisions will be undermined if there are no restrictions on the removal of data to other jurisdictions for processing or storage. Just as money tends to gravitate towards tax havens, so sensitive personal data will be transferred to countries with the most lax, or no data protection standards. There is thus a possibility that some jurisdictions will become 'data havens' or 'data sanctuaries' for the processing or 'data vaults' for the storage of sensitive information.[2]

---

[1] See the book of that name by Tom Standage (London, 1998).
[2] C. Millard, *Legal Protection of Computer Programs and Data* (London, 1985), p. 211.

Controls over transborder data flows have been a feature of almost all national data protection statutes, with restrictions being justified on the basis of safeguarding the position of individuals. In the pioneering Swedish Data Act of 1973, it was provided that personal data might be transferred abroad only with the prior consent of the Swedish Data Inspection Board. Section 11 of the law provided that:

> If there is reason to assume that personal data will be used for automatic data processing abroad, the data may be disclosed only after permission from the Data Inspection Board. Such permission may be given only if it may be assumed that the disclosure of the data will not involve undue encroachment upon personal privacy.

As concern at the impact of national controls over telegraphic and then voice traffic led to the establishment of the ITU, so international initiatives have sought to establish what are effectively free-trade zones in respect of personal data. In 1980, the Organisation for Economic Co-operation and Development (OECD) adopted 'Guidelines on the Protection of Privacy and Transborder Flows of Personal Data'. These Guidelines were supplemented by a Declaration on Transborder Data Flows, adopted in 1995, which declared its signatories' intention to 'avoid the creation of unjustified barriers to the international exchange of data and information'. As discussed, the Council of Europe Convention on the Automated Processing of Personal Data was the first legally binding international instrument. The Convention states that:

> A Party shall not, for the sole purpose of the protection of privacy, prohibit or subject to special authorisation transborder flows of personal data going to the territory of another Party.[3]

As in other areas of the topic, there is inevitable tension between competing interests: the desirability of encouraging free communications and the desire to ensure that data protection laws are not circumvented.

Regulating transborder data flows

The Council of Europe Convention was shaped by the experiences and practices of the Western European states which have adopted data protection legislation in the late 1970s and early 1980s. Such legislation has three major features: first, it applies to all sectors of automated data processing; secondly, it contains substantive provisions regulating the forms of processing which can take place and the rights and remedies available to individuals; and, finally, it provides for the establishment of some form of supervisory agency. As indicated earlier, a different approach has prevailed in other countries, notably the United States.

Initially, the discrepancies in approach between Europe and the rest of the world were of limited practical significance. The Council of Europe Convention, as originally adopted,[4] makes no explicit reference to the imposition of controls over data to non-signatory states. Although some states such as Sweden required some form of prior approval, others, such as the United Kingdom, provided only a power for the supervisory agency to block a transfer if it was satisfied that a proposed transfer was likely to result in a contravention of the data protection principles. In the decade-and-a-half that the 1984 legislation was in force, this

---

[3] Art. 12(2).
[4] An additional protocol was adopted in 2001 and entered into force in 2004 effectively restating the provisions of the European Data Protection Directive with regard to controls over transborder data flows.

power was invoked only once.[5] The Data Protection Directive adopts a different and significantly more rigorous approach. Although recognising that:

cross-border flows of personal data are necessary to the expansion of international trade; whereas the protection of individuals guaranteed in the Community by this Directive does not stand in the way of transfers of personal data to third countries which ensure an adequate level of protection; whereas the adequacy of the level of protection afforded by a third country must be assessed in the light of all the circumstances surrounding the transfer operation or set of transfer operations.

Article 25 of the Directive lays down as a basic principle the requirement that:

The Member States shall provide that the transfer to a third country of personal data which are undergoing processing or are intended for processing after transfer may take place only if, without prejudice to compliance with the national provisions adopted pursuant to the other provisions of this Directive, the third country in question ensures an adequate level of protection.

Effect is given to this provision by the Data Protection Act 1998's eighth data protection principle which provides that:

Personal data shall not be transferred to a country or territory outside the European Economic Area unless that country or territory ensures an adequate level of protection for the rights and freedoms of data subjects in relation to the processing of personal data.

By including the matter in the principles, it follows that any breach, or anticipated breach, can be answered by service of an enforcement notice. The need, therefore, for an additional transfer prohibition notice disappeared. Controllers intending to transfer personal data outside the EEA are required to indicate this fact in their notification. If transfer to ten or fewer countries is envisaged the names of these countries must be notified; where more extensive transfers are planned notification should be given that transfers may take place on a 'worldwide' basis.[6]

Procedures for determining adequacy

The uniform application of the Data Protection Directive would clearly be threatened if the decision on whether third countries offered an adequate level of protection was to be made by each Member State. It is provided, therefore, that the Member States and the Commission are to inform each other of any cases where they feel that a third country does not provide an adequate level of protection.[7] In practice, general decisions regarding formal findings of adequacy will be made at a Community level with a key role being played by the Article 29 Working Party. Article 29 of the Directive provides specifically that

---

[5] A transfer prohibition notice was served in 1990, requiring the cessation of the transfer of personal data in the form of names and addresses to a variety of United States organisations bearing such titles as the 'Astrology Society of America', 'Lourdes Water Cross Incorporated', and 'Win With Palmer Incorporated'. These companies, which had been involved in the promotion of horoscopes, religious trinkets, and other products in the United Kingdom, were the subject of investigations by the United States postal authorities, alleging wire fraud and a variety of other unsavoury trading practices.

[6] *Notification Handbook*, available from <http://www.ico.gov.uk/upload/documents/library/data_protection/detailed_specialist_guides/notification_handbook_final.pdf>. [7] Art. 25(3).

the Working Party is to give the Commission an opinion on the level of protection in the Community and in third countries.

The Directive provides further that should the Working Party determine that a third country does not provide an adequate level of protection, a report is to be made to a committee established under its Article 31.[8] Consisting of representatives of the Member States and chaired by the Commission, the Committee will consider a proposal from the Commission for action on the basis of the Working Party's findings and deliver an opinion. The Commission may then adopt legal measures. If these are in accord with the Committee's opinion, the measures will take immediate effect. If there is any variation, application will be deferred for three months, within which time the Council of Ministers may adopt a different decision. Member States are obliged to take any measures necessary to prevent data transfers to the country involved.[9]

To date, no country has been specifically identified as failing to provide an adequate level of protection. Given the reference in the Directive to the role of 'sectoral rules', 'professional rules and security measures', it is perhaps unlikely that there will ever be 'black listings' affecting all data processing activities in a particular jurisdiction. More significantly, the Directive also provides for the procedures described above to be used to identify countries which do provide an adequate level of protection[10] and there has been extensive activity in this respect.

Defining adequacy

Although, as will be discussed later, a range of exemptions are provided, determination as to whether a third country provides an adequate level of protection is a key issue and effectively opens the way for data transfers to and from that country. Given different approaches globally to issues of data or privacy protection, it is obviously essential to establish a mechanism through which decisions as to adequacy can be made. A first attempt to define criteria was made in the Article 29 Working Party's Working Paper 4, 'First Orientations on Transfers of Personal Data to Third Countries—Possible Ways Forward in Assessing Adequacy', published in 1987.[11] The ideas raised in this document were presented in an expanded form in Working Paper 12, 'Transfers of Personal Data to Third Countries: Applying Articles 25 and 26 of the EU Data Protection Directive', which was published in July 1998,[12] and remains the most significant document in the field. In terms of the general approach, it is suggested that:

> Using directive 95/46/EC as a starting point, and bearing in mind the provisions of other international data protection texts, it should be possible to arrive at a 'core' of data protection 'content' principles and 'procedural/enforcement' requirements, compliance with which could be seen as a minimum requirement for protection to be considered adequate.

In terms of substantive legal requirements, the Working Party identifies five core principles which reflect very closely the provisions of the Data Protection Directive:

> 1) the purpose limitation principle—data should be processed for a specific purpose and subsequently used or further communicated only insofar as this is not incompatible with the purpose of the transfer...

---

[8] Directive 95/46/EC.   [9] Art. 25(4).   [10] Art. 25(6).

[11] Available from <http://ec.europa.eu/justice_home/fsj/privacy/docs/wpdocs/1997/wp4_en.pdf>.

[12] Available from <http://ec.europa.eu/justice_home/fsj/privacy/docs/wpdocs/1998/wp12_en.pdf>.

2) the data quality and proportionality principle—data should be accurate and, where necessary, kept up to date. The data should be adequate, relevant and not excessive in relation to the purposes for which they are transferred or further processed.

3) the transparency principle—individuals should be provided with information as to the purpose of the processing and the identity of the data controller in the third country, and other information insofar as this is necessary to ensure fairness...

4) the security principle—technical and organisational security measures should be taken by the data controller that are appropriate to the risks presented by the processing. Any person acting under the authority of the data controller, including a processor, must not process data except on instructions from the controller.

5) the rights of access, rectification, and opposition—the data subject should have a right to obtain a copy of all data relating to him/her that are processed, and a right to rectification of those data where they are shown to be inaccurate. In certain situations he/she should also be able to object to the processing of the data relating to him/her...

6) restrictions on onward transfers—further transfers of the personal data by the recipient of the original data transfer should be permitted only where the second recipient (i.e. the recipient of the onward transfer) is also subject to rules affording an adequate level of protection.[13]

In terms of procedural requirements, the key requirements are that the agencies established in the third country should be in a position:

1) To deliver a good level of compliance with the rules.

2) To provide support and help to individual data subjects in the exercise of their rights.

3) To provide appropriate redress to the injured party where rules are not complied with.[14]

Activity in determining adequacy

To date, the Article 29 Working Party has published opinions indicating that an adequate level of protection is provided under the regimes operating in Andorra, Argentina, Canada, the Faeroe Islands, Guernsey, the Isle of Man, Israel, Jersey, New Zealand, Switzerland, and Eastern Uruguay. The Hungarian regime was also accepted as being adequate, although Hungary's subsequent membership of the European Union has made this finding otiose as the adequacy procedures apply only to transfers to or from non-Member States. A further opinion indicated that the regime in Australia did not provide a sufficient level of protection to justify a finding of adequacy. Commission decisions[15] subsequently gave legal effect to the Working Party's positive findings in respect of all these countries.

It is clear from the above listing that only a small proportion of the world's near 200 states are included in the list. A majority of the countries receiving a finding of adequacy have close legal and political links with Member States and the data protection laws in Guernsey, Jersey, and the Isle of Man are effectively identical in scope to the United Kingdom's Data

---

[13] p. 5.   [14] p. 7.
[15] <http://ec.europa.eu/justice/data-protection/document/international-transfers/adequacy/index_en.htm>.

Protection Act 1998. In other cases, decisions and recommendations have been more finely balanced. Initially, it appeared that the Article 29 Working Party adopted a strict approach, effectively equating adequacy with equivalence. It does not appear that many dictionaries would support such a definition and more recent findings have been more tolerant of differences in approach. In respect of the law in Jersey, for example, the Working Party concluded:

> While there may be some doubt that Jersey Law would fully meet the requirements imposed upon the Member States by the Data Protection Directive, the Working Party recalls, though, that adequacy does not mean complete equivalence with the level of protection set by the Directive. Some concerns exist in the areas of definitions of personal data and other concepts; transparency; and powers of the Commissioner but, after taking into account the explanations and assurances given by the Jersey Authorities the Working Party does not consider that these are significant in relation to the protection provided for personal data transferred from EU member states to Jersey.[16]

Warning signals for the United Kingdom might be identified in this somewhat lukewarm acceptance. In its most recent report, concerning the adequacy of the law in Uruguay, the Working Party, after describing in some details relevant legal and procedural safeguards, contents itself with a simple statement that it considers the Uruguay provisions to be adequate.

Given its mistrust of the value of supervisory agencies, it is unlikely that the United States law would ever be considered to provide an adequate level of protection. Clearly, however, data transfers between Europe and the United States are of massive economic significance and it was recognised from the early days of the Directive that mechanisms would have to be established to facilitate lawful data transfers across the Atlantic. The so-called 'safe harbor' agreement represents one significant step in this direction.

The 'safe harbor' agreement

Following the adoption of the Data Protection Directive, discussions took place between the Commission and the United States Department of Commerce with a view to devising mechanisms to avoid the prospect of a transatlantic data war. The discussions centred on the quest to agree to a set of conditions, generally referred to as the 'safe harbor' principles, observance of which by United States-based companies would be accepted by the Commission as ensuring conformity with European data protection requirements.

Throughout the negotiations between the Commission and the Department of Commerce, the Article 29 Working Party issued a number of documents concerned with the proposed agreement.[17] These demonstrated a significantly greater degree of scepticism concerning the effectiveness of enforcement mechanisms than was exhibited by the Commission. In Opinion 7/99, published in December 1999, the Working Party indicated the view that the then version of the principles did not constitute a satisfactory basis for action. Referring to previous reports, it stated that:

> The Working Party notes that some progress has been made but deplores that most of the comments made in its previous position papers do not seem to be addressed in the latest version of the US documents. The Working Party therefore confirms its general concerns.

---

[16] p. 11.   [17] See Documents WP15, WP19, WP21, and WP23.

The Working Party's major concerns centred on the limitations of a system of self-certification and also concerns that the jurisdiction of the Federal Trade Commission is restricted to activities 'in or affecting commerce', with the consequence that:

> This seems to exclude most of the data processed in connection with an employment relationship (FAQ 9) as well as the data processed without any commercial purpose (e.g.: non-profit, research).

The nebulous nature of the assertion that other Federal and State laws might be applicable in certain situations was also criticised.

In a further Opinion[18] on the topic delivered in May 2000, the Working Party, whilst recognising that the negotiating process had resulted in significant improvements to the documents, expressed reservations about a considerable number of points. The proposals were subsequently approved by the Article 31 Committee consisting of representatives of the Member States, although in July 2000 the European Parliament passed a resolution indicating that it felt that the principles required to be strengthened before they could be considered acceptable. In spite of this view, the Commission issued a decision on 27 July,[19] stating that:

1. For the purposes of Article 25(2) of Directive 95/46/EC, for all the activities falling within the scope of that Directive, the 'Safe Harbor Privacy Principles' (hereinafter 'the Principles'), as set out in Annex I to this Decision, implemented in accordance with the guidance provided by the frequently asked questions (hereinafter 'the FAQs') issued by the United States Department of Commerce on 21 July 2000 as set out in Annex II to this Decision are considered to ensure an adequate level of protection for personal data transferred from the Community to organisations established in the United States, having regard to the following documents issued by the United States Department of Commerce:

   (a) the safe harbour enforcement overview set out in Annex III;

   (b) a memorandum on damages for breaches of privacy and explicit authorisations in United States law set out in Annex IV;

   (c) a letter from the Federal Trade Commission set out in Annex V;

   (d) a letter from the United States Department of Transportation set out in Annex VI.[20]

The safe harbor principles basically encapsulate the contents of the Data Protection Directive's[21] principles relating to data quality. They require that notice must be given of the fact that data is held and the purposes for which it will be processed, and relevant 'opt-out' opportunities must be given where it is intended that data will be used or disclosed for purposes other than envisaged or notified at the time of collection. Requirements relating to data security and integrity must also be accepted, as must the principle of subject access.[22] Supplementing the principles are a set of fifteen Frequently Asked Questions (FAQs), which provide detailed guidance on the interpretation of a range of issues, such as the scope of the concept of sensitive data and the manner in which subject access should be provided.

---

[18] Opinion 4/2000.   [19] Decision 2000/520/EC OJ 2000 L 215/7.   [20] Art. 1.

[21] Directive 95/46/EC.

[22] Copies of the safe harbor documents, together with much useful background material can be found on the United States Department of Commerce website at <http://www.export.gov/safeharbor/>.

The principles are very much compatible with the contents of the OECD Guidelines. Given the extensive involvement of the United States in the work of this organisation, it is not surprising that discussions with the EU on the principles themselves did not prove particularly contentious. Most of the difficulty centred on the issue of enforcement. As has been discussed, the United States has tended to reject the concept of specialised supervisory agencies, which is integral to the European data protection model. In respect of enforcement, the principles state that:

> Effective privacy protection must include mechanisms for assuring compliance with the principles, recourse for individuals to whom the data relate affected by non-compliance with the principles, and consequences for the organization when the principles are not followed. At a minimum, such mechanisms must include (a) readily available and affordable independent recourse mechanisms by which each individual's complaints and disputes are investigated and resolved by reference to the principles and damages awarded where the applicable law or private sector initiatives so provide; (b) follow up procedures for verifying that the attestations and assertions businesses make about their privacy practices are true and that privacy practices have been implemented as presented; and (c) obligations to remedy problems arising out of failure to comply with the principles by organizations announcing their adherence to them and consequences for such organizations. Sanctions must be sufficiently rigorous to ensure compliance by organizations.

The FAQ indicate that points (a) and (c) in this paragraph may be satisfied by the organisation indicating a willingness to cooperate with European Data Protection Authorities. Under the terms of FAQ 5, a Data Protection Panel has been established as an 'informal grouping' of seven European data protection authorities (including the United Kingdom's Information Commissioner),[23] which will provide advice to United States organisations ('harborites') concerning the operation of the scheme and investigate and seek to resolve disputes between European data subjects and such organisations. In the case where human-resource data is transferred, FAQ 9 provides that there should be direct cooperation with the data protection authority from the Member State(s) concerned where these authorities have indicated agreement so to act. Only five supervisory authorities, again including the Information Commissioner, have signed up to this obligation.

In order to participate in safe harbor, United States-based organisations self-certify their intention to observe the safe harbor principles. This is done by means of a letter to the Department of Commerce, indicating as a minimum the:

1. name of organization, mailing address, email address, telephone, and fax numbers;

2. description of the activities of the organization with respect to personal information received from the EU;

3. description of the organization's privacy policy for such personal information, including:

   (a) where it is available for viewing by the public,

   (b) its effective date of implementation,

   (c) a contact person for the handling of complaints, access requests, and any other issues arising under the safe harbor,

   (d) the specific statutory body that has jurisdiction to hear any claims against the organization regarding possible unfair or deceptive practices and violations of laws or regulations governing privacy,

---

[23] <http://circa.europa.eu/Public/irc/secureida/safeharbor/home>.

(e) name of any privacy programs in which the organization is a member,

(f) method of verification (e.g. in-house, third party) [footnote omitted], and

(g) the independent recourse mechanism that is available to investigate unre-solved complaints.[24]

Breach of the terms of such a letter may expose the organisation either to action by the Federal Trade Commission under section 5 of the Federal Trade Commission Act which under 15 USC section 45(n) prohibits unfair practices in or affecting commerce, a concept defined in terms of a likelihood to cause 'substantial injury to consumers which is not rea-sonably avoidable by consumers themselves and not outweighed by countervailing benefits to consumers or to competition'.

In accordance with the establishing Commission decision,[25] the operation of the safe harbor arrangements were to be closely monitored by the Commission. A first report was published in 2002 and a second in 2004. Both reports identified similar strengths and weaknesses in the functioning of the system. The 2002 report commented that:

> Compared with the situation before it was available, the framework is providing a simplify-ing effect for those exporting personal data to organisations in the Safe Harbour and reduces uncertainty for US organisations interested in importing data from the EU by identifying a standard that corresponds to the adequate protection required by the [Data Protection] Directive.[26]

Concerns were expressed in both reports, supported by a research report produced under contract to the Commission, that a number of organisations which had signed up to the principles did not have or did not publish privacy policies in conformity with its requirements. Concern was also expressed at the lack of enforcement action by the Federal Trade Commission (FTC) and also at the fact that not a single case had been referred to the European Union's Data Protection Panel. It was also noted that around 30 per cent of harborites were engaging in the transfer of human-resource data concerning employ-ees and that this form of processing was outside the remit of the FTC. It was also noted that, although the FTC claimed that the breach of undertakings regarding privacy policies would be actionable, this had not been affirmed by the courts.

Initially, take-up of the safe harbor scheme was limited and at the time the Commission's 2004 report was published, around 400 organisations had signed up to the principles. At the time of writing, around 2,500 United States companies had signed up to the safe harbor principles, although not all entries on the safe harbor list are current.[27] Although in com-parison with figures of those notifying details of processing in Europe—where the United Kingdom has 297,000 notifications and France 700,000—these figures are tiny, there does seem to be an increased awareness of the concept following the accession to the principles by a number of major companies: Microsoft, Intel, Hewlett-Packard, and Procter & Gamble.

Consequences of a finding of adequacy

In the event a finding of adequacy is made, the Member States must allow transfers to the third country.[28] The laws of a number of Member States continues to require, however, that

---

[24] <http://export.gov/safeharbor/eu/eg_main_018388.asp>.   [25] 520/2000/EC of 26 July 2000.
[26] Directive 95/46/EC.
[27] The list of companies which have signed up to the safe harbor principles can be accessed at <http://web. ita.doc.gov/safeharbor/shlist.nsf/webPages/safe+harbor+list>.   [28] Art. 25(6).

prior permission must be sought from the data protection authorities, an approach which has been criticised by the Commission on the grounds of inconsistency:

> with Chapter IV of the Directive, which aims at guaranteeing both adequate protection and flows of personal data to third countries without unnecessary burdens. Notifications to national supervisory authorities may be required under Article 19, but notifications cannot be turned into de facto authorisations in those cases where the transfer to a third country is clearly permitted either in all cases or in the situation where the law of recipient country does not guarantee an adequate level of protection.[29]

Of the thirty states which are members of the European Economic Area, fifteen—Austria, Bulgaria, Cyprus, Estonia, France, Greece, Iceland, Latvia, Lichtenstein, Lithuania, Malta, the Netherlands, Romania, Slovenia, and Spain—require some degree of prior notification.[30] The controls vary significantly in extent. In some states such as Austria, it is provided that prior permission must be sought from the data protection authorities for all data flows outwith the EEA.[31] In other countries, there may be a requirement to notify the supervisory authority, whilst in others, such as the United Kingdom, there are no procedural requirements to notify the Information Commissioner.

The discrepancy between national approaches has been the cause of criticism of national laws by the European Commission, which has argued that this results in 'an inability to audit compliance with the principles relating to transborder data flows':[32]

> An overly lax attitude in some Member States—in addition to being in contravention of the Directive—risks weakening protection in the EU as a whole, because with the free movement guaranteed by the Directive, data flows are likely to switch to the 'least burdensome' point of export. An overly strict approach, on the other hand, would fail to respect the legitimate needs of international trade and the reality of global telecommunications networks and risks creating a gap between law and practice which is damaging for the credibility of the Directive and for Community law in general.

It has been commented further that:

> it would appear that pending such a formal determination, individual controllers can make this assessment for themselves, and can therefore decide to transfer data to third countries with regard to which there is no formal domestic or European finding of adequacy, if they have come to the conclusion that the country in question ensures an adequate level of protection.[33]

This certainly appears to be an accurate portrait of the system operating in the United Kingdom.

The SWIFT case

The activities of financial services companies (and transportation companies) are excluded from the remit of the FTC. A very major issue arose between Europe and the United

---

[29] As defined by the Commission of the European Communities and discussed more extensively later.
[30] Commission Staff Working Document SEC (2006) 95. Available from <http://ec.europa.eu/justice/policies/privacy/docs/modelcontracts/sec_2006_95_en.pdf>.
[31] s. 13 of the Federal Act Concerning the Processing of Personal Data.
[32] Commission Staff Working Document SEC (2006) 95. Available from <http://ec.europa.eu/justice/policies/privacy/docs/modelcontracts/sec_2006_95_en.pdf>.
[33] Analysis and impact study on the implementation of Directive EC 95/46 in Member States, available from <http://ec.europa.eu/justice_home/fsj/privacy/docs/lawreport/consultation/technical-annex_en.pdf>.

States in the course of 2006, involving the activity of the Society for Worldwide Interbank Financial Telecommunications (SWIFT). SWIFT is a Belgian-based cooperative which processes financial messages for nearly 8,000 financial institutions around the world. SWIFT processes around 2.5 billion messages every year, some two-thirds of which are related to transactions involving parties located in Europe. It has two operating centres, one in Europe and one in the United States, which act as mirror sites for each other. Copies of all messages are retained for 124 days.

Around June 2006, media reports indicated that SWIFT had been providing substantial amounts of data to United States authorities for terrorism investigation purposes since 2001. This data was supplied under the terms of sixty-four administrative subpoenas served on SWIFT in the intervening years in connection with the Treasury's Terrorist Financing Tracking Program (TFTP). When the fact of the transfers came to light, great concerns were expressed within the EU institutions and the Article 29 Working Party launched an immediate investigation. The Working Party's report was published in November 2006,[34] and concluded that the transfers had placed SWIFT and the financial institutions making up its membership in major and continuing breach of its obligations under the Data Protection Directive and the Belgian data protection law to which its operations were subject. As was stated:

> the hidden, systematic, massive and long-term transfer of personal data by SWIFT to the UST in a confidential, non-transparent and systematic manner for years without effective legal grounds and without the possibility of independent control by public data protection supervisory authorities constitutes a violation of fundamental European principles as regards data protection and is not in accordance with Belgian and European law. An existing international framework is already available with regard to the fight against terrorism. The possibilities already offered there should be exploited while ensuring the required level of protection of fundamental rights.

Following negotiations between the Commission and the United States Department of the Treasury, the United States offered a number of undertakings regarding the controls which would be imposed over the use of any data obtained from SWIFT.[35] These included the statements that:

> The program contains multiple, overlapping layers of governmental and independent controls to ensure that the data, which are limited in nature, are searched only for counterterrorism purposes and that all data are maintained in a secure environment and properly handled.
>
> ...
>
> The SWIFT data are maintained in a secure physical environment, stored separately from any other data, and the computer systems have high-level intrusion controls and other protections to limit access to the data solely as described herein. No copies of SWIFT data are made, other than for disaster recovery back-up purposes. Access to the data and the computer equipment are limited to persons with appropriate security clearances. Even among such persons, access to the SWIFT data is on a read-only basis and is limited through the TFTP on a strict need-to-know basis to analysts dedicated to the investigation of terrorism and to persons involved in the technical support, management, and oversight of the TFTP.

---

[34] Opinion 10/2006 'On the Processing of Personal Data by the Society for Worldwide Interbank Financial Telecommunication (SWIFT)', available from <http://ec.europa.eu/justice_home/fsj/privacy/docs/wpdocs/2006/wp128_en.pdf>.   [35] OJ 2007 C166/18.

In order to allay European concerns it was suggested that:

As a sign of our commitment and partnership in combating global terrorism, an eminent European person will be appointed to confirm that the program is implemented consistent with these Representations for the purpose of verifying the protection of EU-originating personal data. In particular, the eminent person will monitor that processes for deletion of non-extracted data have been carried out.

Subsequently, steps were taken to put the agreement on a more formal basis and negotiations took place between the US and European authorities. Following these, a draft agreement was approved by the Council of Ministers although significantly a number of states, including Germany and Austria which have perhaps the strongest domestic data protection legislation, abstained. The German minister was quoted as saying of the decision, 'a not completely-satisfying agreement in this field of data exchange combating terrorism is—in the interest of European and also German data protection—better than no agreement'.

The European Parliament, however, disagreed and flexing newly acquired muscles to reject agreements of this nature did so in February 2010 largely, it would appear, based on concerns about the lack of data protection provisions in the agreement. Following further negotiations a further agreement was submitted to Parliament and approved in July 2010. Significantly, although not perhaps surprisingly, the Article 29 Working Party indicated continuing concerns. The Article 29 Working Party is essentially concerned with the purity of data protection law whilst more politically oriented institutions within the European Union do have to take wider issues into account. The final agreement makes provision for the transfer of data to the United States in connection with its 'Terrorist Finance Tracking' programme. Although the agreement is stated to operate for a five-year term, the intention appears to be that a European programme, equivalent to the United States tracking programme will be established and that this will enable data transfers to be applied on a 'push'—namely, initiated by the European authorities or supplied in response to a specific request—rather than the current 'pull' basis where data will be collected by the United States authorities with the terms of the agreement operating to control the use which may be made of the data.

Air passenger data

The handling of data relating to airline passengers was included in the safe harbor agreement and provides a basis for the transfer of passenger information for the purposes of transportation.[36] It has subsequently been the subject of a further agreement between the EU and the United States in the context of transfers of passenger name record (PNR) data to the United States Department of Homeland Security in connection with its anti-terrorism activities. The basis for the agreement lay in a decision by the United States that it would refuse to allow aircraft to enter its airspace unless information concerning all passengers had previously been made available to its authorities. Such data would invariably be classed as personal data under the Data Protection Directive and, in so far as it could relate to dietary requirements or the need for medical assistance, could be classed as sensitive personal data. Such transfers would not be sanctioned under the Directive.

Following extensive political negotiations, two Commission decisions were published in May 2004: the first declaring that an agreement had been reached on the transfer of PNR

---

[36] FAQ 13.

data and describing its terms; and the second declaring that in the light of undertakings provided by the Department of Homeland Security:

> For the purposes of Article 25(2) of Directive 95/46/EC, the United States' Bureau of Customs and Border Protection (hereinafter referred to as CBP) is considered to ensure an adequate level of protection for PNR data transferred from the Community concerning flights to or from the United States, in accordance with the Undertakings set out in the Annex.[37]

Promulgation of the decisions was controversial within Europe. The Article 29 Working Party had issued a number of critical opinions, although recognising that 'ultimately political judgements will be needed'.[38] Parliament had also expressed opposition, and upon the decisions being adopted, raised proceedings before the European Court of Justice, seeking the annulment of both measures. In June 2006, the Court handed down its judgment in *Parliament v Council*.[39] This declared the decision to be invalid on the grounds that it had been adopted under an inappropriate article of the Treaty of Rome. The treaty justification for the measure was stated to lie in Article 95, which refers to the functioning of the internal market, an argument which was accepted by the court. In respect of the decision relating to the finding of adequacy, this was grounded in Article 25(6) of the Data Protection Directive but it was held that the subject matter of the decision was outside the Directive's scope, Article 3(2) declaring that the measure did not extend to processing:

> in the course of an activity which falls outside the scope of Community law, such as those provided for by Titles V and VI of the Treaty on European Union and in any case to processing operations concerning public security, defence, State security (including the economic well-being of the State when the processing operation relates to State security matters) and the activities of the State in areas of criminal law.

Again, the finding was that the decision should be annulled on the grounds of a lack of legislative competence.

Although the court found in favour of the Parliament, it ruled that 'it appears justified, for reasons of legal certainty and in order to protect the persons concerned, to preserve the effect of the decision on adequacy' for the period of time that would have been required were the EU to have given notice of termination. This continued the validity of the agreement until the end of September 2006. A further short-term agreement was reached in October 2006 to cover the period up until July 2007. On 23 July 2007, a further agreement between the European Union and the United States of America on the processing and transfer of Passenger Name Record (PNR) data by air carriers to the United States Department of Homeland Security (DHS) (2007 PNR Agreement),[40] was signed. This indicated that:

> For the application of this Agreement, DHS is deemed to ensure an adequate level of protection for PNR data transferred from the European Union.

On the same day, Council Decision 2007/551/CFSP/JHA[41] was adopted. Based now on Articles 24 and 38 of the Treaty of Rome, this provided that the terms of the Agreement were to enter into force.

As with previous agreements, provision is made for the United States authorities to access a range of items of passenger data relating to identity and itinerary, together with

---

[37] Art. 1.

[38] Opinion 4/2003. 'On the Level of Protection ensured in the United States for the Transfer of Passengers' Data', available from <http://ec.europa.eu/justice_home/fsj/privacy/docs/wpdocs/2003/wp78_en.pdf>.

[39] Joined Cases C-317/04 and C-318/04.   [40] OJ 2007 L204/18.   [41] OJ 2007 L204/16.

information as to frequent-flier status and details of the method of payment, including details of any credit cards used. As originally agreed, this data would be collected on what is referred to as a 'pull system', whereby the United States authorities are enabled to access the airline's computer systems and collect the required information. This approach has been the cause of criticism within Europe and the 2007 agreement provides that the:

> DHS will immediately transition to a push system for the transmission of data by such air carriers no later than 1 January 2008 for all such air carriers that have implemented such a system that complies with DHS's technical requirements. For those air carriers that do not implement such a system, the current systems shall remain in effect until the carriers have implemented a system that complies with DHS's technical requirements. Accordingly, DHS will electronically access the PNR from air carriers' reservation systems located within the territory of the Member States of the European Union until there is a satisfactory system in place allowing for the transmission of such data by the air carriers.

The 2007 agreement seems likely to be no less controversial than its predecessors. It has been subjected to perhaps unprecedented criticism by the Article 29 Working Party. Although the Working Party was not consulted prior to the conclusion of the agreement, in an Opinion published in August 2007,[42] it expressed dissatisfaction:

> that the opportunity to have adopted a more balanced approach based upon real need has been missed. While there has been much comment on the new agreement, the Working Party would have wished for a different outcome of the EU–US negotiations and feels that the new agreement does not strike the right balance to uphold the fundamental rights of citizens as regards data protection.

It concluded that:

> the new PNR agreement contains some minor improvements in comparison with the previous accord but it is clearly disappointed at the inadequate data protection standard of the new PNR agreement. The new agreement does not even preserve the level of privacy protection of the previous agreement which was already considered weak by the Working Party in its previous opinions.
>
> The new PNR agreement as analysed in this opinion does not compare favourably with accepted data protection standards, such as those of Convention 108 and of the Directive. It will cause understandable concern for all transatlantic travellers who are worried about their privacy rights.

It may be noted that a less extensive agreement[43] on the transfer of PNR data to the Canadian Authorities received a positive Opinion from the Article 29 Working Party.[44]

Transfers when an adequate level of protection is not provided

Even allowing for the inclusion of those organisations from the United States, which are party to 'safe harbor', only a very small number of countries have been determined to

---

[42] Opinion 5/2007 on the follow-up agreement between the European Union and the United States of America on the processing and transfer of passenger name record (PNR) data by air carriers to the United States Department of Homeland Security concluded in July 2007, available from <http://ec.europa.eu/justice_home/fsj/privacy/docs/wpdocs/2007/wp138_en.pdf>.   [43] OJ 2006 L 91/49.

[44] Opinion 1 of 2005, available from OJ 2005 L 82/14.

provide an adequate level of protection. Alternative mechanisms require to be found therefore to legitimise data transfers with the rest of the world, whilst ensuring that the interests of European data subjects are safeguarded. Having laid down a prohibition against data transfers in Article 25, the Directive's Article 26 is headed 'Derogations' and proceeds to lay down a number of situations in which Member States must permit transfers and a further set of situations in which the Member States may authorise transfers. In respect of the first situation, it is provided that transfers are to be permitted when:

(a)   the data subject has given his consent unambiguously to the proposed transfer; or

(b)   the transfer is necessary for the performance of a contract between the data subject and the controller or the implementation of pre-contractual measures taken in response to the data subject's request; or

(c)   the transfer is necessary for the conclusion or performance of a contract concluded in the interest of the data subject between the controller and a third party; or

(d)   the transfer is necessary or legally required on important public interest grounds, or for the establishment, exercise or defence of legal claims; or

(e)   the transfer is necessary in order to protect the vital interests of the data subject; or

(f)   the transfer is made from a register which according to laws or regulations is intended to provide information to the public and which is open to consultation either by the public in general or by any person who can demonstrate legitimate interest to the extent that the conditions laid down in law for consultation are fulfilled in the particular case.[45]

In the main, the Act's wording follows that of the Data Protection Directive, but there is a divergence in respect of the exception relating to subject consent. Whilst the Directive requires unambiguous consent, the Act refers merely to the fact that 'the data subject has given his consent to the transfer'.[46] The Act also confers regulatory power on the Secretary of State to define more closely the circumstances under which transfers may, or may not, take place 'for reasons of substantial public interest'.[47]

Substantial guidance concerning the interpretation of the Article 26(1) exceptions has been provided by the Article 29 Working Party in its 'Working Document on a Common Interpretation of Article 26(1)'.[48] This confirms that the provisions of Article 26(1) constitute exceptions from the general principle that data can be transferred only under conditions that will ensure adequacy. As exceptions, they are to be construed narrowly. Referring to the possibilities for providing adequate protection listed in Article 26(2), the Working Party comments:

> The Working Party would find it regrettable that a multinational company or a public authority would plan to make significant transfers of data to a third country without providing an appropriate framework for the transfer, when it has the practical means of providing such protection.

Particularly relevant in this context are the use of contractual provisions and, a more recent development, the concept of adopting binding corporate rules.

---

[45]   Art. 26(1).

[46]   The nature of these provisions is similar to those of the Sch. 2 conditions legitimising the processing of personal data.   [47]   Sch. 4, para. 4(2).

[48]   WP114, available from <http://ec.europa.eu/justice_home/fsj/privacy/docs/wpdocs/2005/wp114_en.pdf>.

The role of contract

The Data Protection Directive provides that:

> a Member State may authorize a transfer or a set of transfers or personal data to a third coun-
> try which does not ensure an adequate level of protection—where the controller adduces
> adequate safeguards with respect to the protection of the privacy and fundamental rights
> and freedoms of individuals and as regards the exercise of the corresponding rights; such
> safeguards may in particular result from appropriate contractual clauses.[49]

Any exercise of this power must be reported to the Commission and the other Member
States. If any party so informed objects 'on justified measures involving the protection of
the privacy and the fundamental rights and freedoms of individuals', a proposal for action
may be tabled before the Committee by the Commission and, if approved, will require the
Member State involved to take necessary measures to conform.[50]

In implementing this provision, the Data Protection Act 1998 provides in Schedule 4
that transfers will be acceptable when they are:

- made on terms which are of a kind approved by the Commissioner as ensuring adequate safeguards for the rights and freedoms of data subjects[51]
- authorized by the Commissioner as being made in such a manner as to ensure adequate safeguards for the rights and freedoms of data subjects[52]

Although the Act provides[53] for notification of approvals to be transmitted to the
Commission, this has not happened to any extent. In its first report on the implementation
of the Data Protection Directive,[54] the Commission comments:

> National authorities are supposed to notify the Commission when they authorise transfers
> under Article 26 (2) of the Directive. Since the Directive came into operation in 1998, the
> Commission has received only a very limited number of such notifications. Although there
> are other legal transfer routes apart from Article 26 (2), this number is derisory by compari-
> son with what might reasonably be expected. Combined with other evidence pointing in the
> same direction, this suggests that many unauthorised and possibly illegal transfers are being
> made to destinations or recipients not guaranteeing adequate protection. Yet there is little or
> no sign of enforcement actions by the supervisory authorities.

In spite of a Commission Notice sent to the Member States in 2003 urging more extensive notification, matters do not seem to have changed significantly. In 2006, a Commission
Staff Working Document noted that:

> the number of notifications received by the Commission services pursuant to Article 26 (3)
> of the Directive over the last four years is extremely limited: only 78 notifications from seven
> Member States (the Netherlands (34), Spain (20), Germany (14), Finland (5), Portugal (2),
> Austria (2) and Belgium (1)). In addition, most of these notifications concern the use of
> standard contractual clauses which, as outlined above, are not covered by the notifying
> obligation.
>   Since the Directive entered into force in October 1998, the Commission has not received
> any notifications from the United Kingdom, France, Italy, Ireland, Greece, Sweden or

---

[49] Directive 95/46/EC, Art. 26(2).   [50] Art. 26(3).   [51] Sch. 4, para. 8.
[52] Sch. 4, para. 9.   [53] s. 54(7).
[54] COM/2003/0265 final, available from <http://eur-lex.europa.eu/LexUriServ/LexUriServ.do?uri=CELEX:
52003DC0265:EN:NOT>.

Luxembourg. None of the new ten Member States has yet notified the use of contractual clauses or other adequate safeguards to the Commission.[55]

Authorisation may be given under the above provisions on an individual basis, but may also make reference to the controller's adherence to model contractual terms and conditions. There appears to be a general acceptance that the volume of transborder data flows is such that it is undesirable for decisions as to acceptability to require to be made in the context of individual transfers, and that more general provisions should be laid down.

The Article 29 Working Party produced a report in April 1998, outlining its 'preliminary views on the use of contractual terms in the context of transfers of personal data to third countries'.[56] This document identified a number of elements that must be found in any relevant contract. The contract must provide for observance of the data protection principles. Whilst it was recognised that no system could provide a total assurance of compliance, it would be required that the provisions should provide a reasonable level of assurance, should provide support and assistance for data subjects, and appropriate forms of redress.

Subsequent to the report of the Working Party, proposals for decisions on two sets of contracts, one for transfers between two data controllers and one for transfers between European data controllers and external data processors, were brought forward by the Commission. These were the subject of further Article 29 Working Party opinions in 2001;[57] two decisions were adopted by the Commission in 2001 and 2002, and Decision 2001/497/EC on Standard Contractual Clauses for the transfer of personal data to controllers in third countries was adopted in June 2001.[58] This required Member States to accept transfers conducted under its terms (i.e. using the standard form contract within the decision) as satisfying the requirements of adequacy.[59] Decision 2002/16/EC[60] contained standard contract terms relevant to the situation where an EU-based data controller wishes to transfer data to a processor established in a third country.

The annex to both decisions lays out a set of standard terms. Beyond customisation with the identifying details of the parties, these may not be changed or amended in any way whatsoever. This has been regarded in some quarters as an overly prescriptive approach but in common with any legal documents, it may be virtually impossible to know whether any change might have major or minor implications.

Clause 2 provides for identification of the parties and the nature of the transfer, and Appendix 1 provides a form in which these details may be provided. Clause 3 provides that third parties are to be able to enforce the contract—possibly assisted by a consumer protection agency. The possibility of third-party enforcement of contractual obligations had long been a stumbling block for the use of such contracts under English law. The Contracts (Rights of Third Parties) Act 1999 now provides a mechanism for such enforcement.

The model contract lays down in some detail the nature and extent of the obligations which are to be accepted by the data exporter and importer. The former is to warrant that the data has been processed in accordance with any relevant European data protection law up until the time the export takes place. If the data constitutes sensitive personal data, the subject is to be informed, before the transfer, of the fact that the legal system of the importer might not guarantee an adequate level of protection. Copies of the contract clauses are to

---

[55] SEC (2006) 95, available from <http://ec.europa.eu/justice_home/fsj/privacy/docs/modelcontracts/sec_2006_95_en.pdf>.

[56] WP 9, available from <http://ec.europa.eu/justice_home/fsj/privacy/docs/wpdocs/1998/wp9_en.pdf>.

[57] Opinion 1/2001 and 7/2001, available from <http://ec.europa.eu/justice_home/fsj/privacy/workinggroup/wpdocs/2001_en.htm>.   [58] OJ 2001 L 181/19.

[59] Art. 1.   [60] OJ 2002 L6/52.

be made available to data subjects and the exporter is to respond to any reasonable requests from its supervisory agency or from a data subject concerning the processing to be carried out on the data.

For the importing controller, it is required that an undertaking be given that the controller has no knowledge that any provisions of its domestic law will prevent fulfilment of obligations accepted under the contract. The processing is to be carried out in accordance with a set of mandatory data protection principles specified in the model contract. These effectively provide for measures equivalent to those found in the Directive (and also the Article 29 Working Party's WP12 on assessing adequacy), regarding matters such as limitations on the purpose of processing, the accuracy and up-to-date nature of data, the availability of subject access, etc. The importer undertakes to cooperate with requests for information from data subjects and relevant European supervisory agencies and also to submit its facilities for audit by the data exporter or a professionally qualified inspection agency selected by the exporter.

One of the most contentious provisions in the model contract is Clause 6, which provides that the parties are to accept joint and several liability for any breaches of the contract. The effect of this is that a data subject could choose to take action, either against the contracting parties jointly or hold either party solely liable. Given the problems of raising legal proceedings in a foreign jurisdiction or against a foreign party, the consequence might be that the data exporter may well be targeted by an aggrieved data subject as the sole object of any claim for compensation, even though any culpability might lie with the data importer.

The initial model contracts were criticised by some business interests as being cumbersome, inflexible, and out of touch with business needs. Recital 10 of the decision states that:

> The Commission will also consider in the future whether standard contractual clauses submitted by business organisations or other interested parties offer adequate safeguards in accordance with Directive 95/46/EC.

A new set of standard contractual clauses for data transfers was proposed by seven international business associations: the American Chamber of Commerce to the European Union in Brussels (AmCham EU), the Confederation of British Industry (CBI), the European Information and Communications Technology Association (EICTA), the Federation of European Direct and Interactive Marketing (FEDMA), the International Chamber of Commerce (ICC), the International Communication Round Table (ICRT), and the Japan Business Council in Europe (JBCE).

Following negotiations between these associations and the Commission Working Party, a new set of model contracts was approved by the Commission by Decision 2004/915. These sit alongside the initial contracts, with businesses being offered a choice between the two formulations. Welcoming the new decision the then Single Market Commissioner, Charlie McCreevy, was quoted as saying:

> This is a good example of regulating in cooperation with business. The business community has shown a serious commitment towards data protection and the Commission has carefully listened to business needs. That is good for EU citizens, whose privacy is better protected, and for our companies, whose competitiveness is reinforced.

Commenting on an earlier draft of the terms,[61] the Article 29 Working Party was perhaps less enthusiastic, although still broadly supportive of the initiative:

---

[61] Opinion 8/2003, available from <http://ec.europa.eu/justice_home/fsj/privacy/docs/wpdocs/2003/wp84_en.pdf>.

The Working Party has doubts that the current proposals satisfy these conditions fully. It also has doubts that these clauses are easier to use by economic operators. The same business associations that criticised the Commission's standard contractual clauses in 2001 as 'unworkable' do not seem to have found better wording for many clauses and when the proposals deviate from Decision 497/2001/CE, the result is not necessarily clearer but rather more uncertain in legal terms.

In a set of frequently asked questions on the Model Contracts, the Commission suggests that:

Both sets of clauses provide for a similar level of data protection, in other words, individuals are similarly protected by both sets on the basis of the same (adequate) data protection standards and principles. Differences between both sets are mainly of a technical nature (for example, the conditions under which a data protection authority may carry out an audit in the data importer's premises) or related to the differences in the system of liability already explained above.

Perhaps the major variation between the contracts is in respect of the issue of liability. The 2004 contracts state that:

(a) Each party shall be liable to the other parties for damages it causes by any breach of these clauses...Each party shall be liable to data subjects for damages it causes by any breach of third party rights under these clauses. This does not affect the liability of the data exporter under its data protection law.

(b) ...In cases involving allegations of breach by the data importer, the data subject must first request the data exporter to take appropriate action to enforce his rights against the data importer; if the data exporter does not take such action within a reasonable period (which under normal circumstances would be one month), the data subject may then enforce his rights against the data importer directly. A data subject is entitled to proceed directly against a data exporter that has failed to use reasonable efforts to determine that the data importer is able to satisfy its legal obligations under these clauses (the data exporter shall have the burden to prove that it took reasonable efforts).

Although certainly more favourable towards the business parties involved, it is difficult to see that the provision affords the same level of protection to data subjects as that provided for under the 2001 contract.

Binding corporate rules

Whilst the conclusion of contracts, whether using the Commission's model contracts or a formulation devised by the parties themselves may provide an appropriate solution to the requirements of many data controllers, difficulties have been identified in the situation where multinational organisations operate in a wide range of countries and are required to exchange personal data between the legal entities operating in the different countries. A contractual solution here might create a spaghetti forest of agreements between all possible permutations of national legal entities. Although it is possible under the contractual approach to have a single master agreement which is signed by a range of parties, this approach, with a requirement that details of all transfers be recorded, would be difficult to apply in what may well be an organisation subject to continual change and development.

In response to this situation, the Article 29 Working Party has developed the concept of binding corporate rules as an alternative mechanism for demonstrating that data will receive an adequate level of protection. Working Paper 74, applying Article 26(2) of the EU

Data Protection Directive to Binding Corporate Rules for International Data Transfers,[62] was published in 2003 and lays down the basic principles which should be found in such rules. The Working Paper is supplemented by a Checklist published in 2004[63] and Recommendation 1 of 2007 containing a 'Standard Application for Approval of Binding Corporate Rules for the Transfer of Personal Data'.[64] As with all methods for ensuring adequacy, the notion of binding corporate rules seeks to ensure that processing takes place under conditions broadly equivalent to those laid down in the data protection principles. In terms of procedural aspects, the requirement is that one member of the undertaking should be given powers and responsibilities to ensure that the rules are observed throughout the organisation. This member must be located in the EU and will be responsible for seeking approval of the rules from a relevant supervisory agency. In many cases, multinational corporations will be operating in a wide range of EU states, and the Working Paper suggests that supervisory agencies should make use of the cooperation procedures established under Article 28 of the Data Protection Directive to enable a request for approval to be made to only one supervisory agency and, if granted, to be valid throughout all Member States.

Conclusions

The activities described indicate perhaps how complex is the task of applying national or regional rules regarding data protection in a situation where processing may take place anywhere on the planet. In February 2007, it was widely reported that Google, the world's most widely used search engine, was calling upon the UN to intervene to help protect the privacy of web users.[65]

Given much recent controversy concerning aspects of Google's own practices, including its data retention policy and the publication on 'Google Street View'[66] of images of individuals taken without their knowledge or consent, this may seem a classic instance of a poacher turning gamekeeper. As the discussions concerning the concept of binding corporate rules does indicate, organisations operating on a global basis may find it easier to work on the basis of consistent global standards, even though these may place restrictions on their ability to process data in an unrestricted manner. To date, the UN's involvement in the data/privacy protection field has been somewhat peripheral. The Google plea for activity was also addressed to the OECD and certainly this agency has been much more active in the field. In a Ministerial Declaration on the Protection of Privacy on Global Networks on this, the ministers reaffirmed:

> their commitment to the protection of privacy on global networks in order to ensure the respect of important rights, build confidence in global networks, and to prevent unnecessary restrictions on transborder flows of personal data.
>
> They will work to build bridges between the different approaches adopted by Member countries to ensure privacy protection on global networks based on the OECD Guidelines.[67]

---

[62] Available from <http://ec.europa.eu/justice_home/fsj/privacy/docs/wpdocs/2003/wp74_en.pdf>.
[63] Available from <http://ec.europa.eu/justice_home/fsj/privacy/docs/wpdocs/2004/wp101_en.pdf>.
[64] Available from <http://ec.europa.eu/justice_home/fsj/privacy/workinggroup/wpdocs/2007_en.htm>.
[65] See e.g. <http://www.guardian.co.uk/technology/2007/sep/14/news.google>.
[66] <http://maps.google.com/help/maps/streetview/>.
[67] Available from <http://www.oecd.org/internet/ieconomy/1840065.pdf>.

In June 2007, the OECD adopted a Recommendation on Cross-border Co-operation in the Enforcement of Laws Protecting Privacy.[68] In its introductory sections, the Recommendation indicates why action was considered necessary:

> When personal information moves across borders it may put at increased risk the ability of individuals to exercise privacy rights to protect themselves from the unlawful use or disclosure of that information. At the same time, the authorities charged with enforcing privacy laws may find that they are unable to pursue complaints or conduct investigations relating to the activities of organisations outside their borders. Their efforts to work together in the cross-border context may also be hampered by insufficient preventative or remedial powers, inconsistent legal regimes, and practical obstacles like resource constraints. In this context, a consensus has emerged on the need to promote closer co-operation among privacy law enforcement authorities to help them exchange information and carry out investigations with their foreign counterparts.

The Recommendation continues to indicate that Member States should act to ensure that 'Privacy Enforcement Authorities' are both empowered and obliged to cooperate with other national authorities. It is suggested that a national point of contact should be established in each Member State to facilitate cross-border requests for assistance.

Initially, international transfers generally took the form of couriering or posting packages containing disks or tapes. In the modern networked world, online transfers are the norm. With modern forms of electronic communications, national or even supranational boundaries are of limited significance and the European Union's attempt to control the flow of data has drawn comparison with the early English King Canute's attempt to order the incoming tide to retreat. The Canute legend, of course, is susceptible of at least two explanations. One refers to the folly of a monarch who believed that he could control the forces of nature and was surprised when he got his feet wet. A second, and more complex explanation, sees the exercise as a considered attempt to demonstrate to over-deferential subjects the limits of what human authority can and cannot do. In this second case, any folly lies more with those who seek to ascribe human agencies with almighty powers and are disappointed when perfection proves to be an unattainable goal. The fact that data protection legislation cannot prevent all forms of malpractice is no reason for not attempting to prevent some. Fear of the consequences of data havens was a motivating force behind much data protection legislation. Where the European model might perhaps be criticised is in substituting the notion of a European data protection haven. The tale is sometimes told of a discussion between proponents of Rolls Royce motor cars and those of Ford (or any other mass-produced models). The former can point to the quality of build, the levels of comfort, refinement, and reliability. Whilst conceding these points, the opposing case may be that mass-produced cars offer acceptable (adequate) levels of comfort, refinement, and reliability, with the additional fact that they can be afforded by most of the population. If some reduction in standards is the price to be paid for global acceptance of the importance of the need for data protection, the price may be one that is well worth paying.

---

[68] Available from <http://www.oecd.org/dataoecd/43/28/38770483.pdf>.

PART II

Computer-Related Crime

Introduction

I recall viewing (too) many years ago a BBC television series called 'Connections'. It sought to explain how apparently unrelated developments were in fact linked. Fascinating! I don't think it featured in that programme but, in the 1960s, the United Kingdom embarked on a major motorway-building programme. Also in the 1960s there was a substantial increase in the number of burglaries in rural villages. What was the connection?

Essentially city-based burglars realised that by using the new motorways they could travel perhaps sixty miles in an hour rather than thirty. They could expand the range of their operations and, of course, village householders would be likely to be less security-conscious than their urban counterparts.

It does appear to be a feature of history that criminals have proved to be early and skilled adopters of new forms of technology. The computer has proved to be no exception to the rule. As the scope of the technology has expanded so has the range of criminal conduct. As with many aspects of our subject, terminology has tended to evolve. Initially we talked about computer crime (or computer-related crime). Today the talk is more in terms of e-crime or perhaps cyber-crime. I'm not sure that any label is better than the others although, showing my age, I tend to refer to computer crime. Rather than worrying about terminology it is, I think, more important to focus on particular forms of behaviour and consider how these may be challenged by particular forms of criminal law. Following the theme of connections, it does seem that as computer technologies have evolved, so new criminal (or potentially criminal) outlets have developed.

Computer fraud

When the computer began to emerge from research laboratories into the commercial world, early users were in the banking and financial services sectors. Perhaps not surprising. Early computers were effectively calculating machines and banks need to keep track of the movements of large numbers of pounds. Unsurprisingly, the first linkage between the computer and criminal conduct was in the context of computer fraud. This obviously continues to be a topic of interest and there are perhaps two issues of special significance. The first is the attempt to penetrate computer systems to cause the unauthorised transfer of large amounts of money. A case was reported widely in September 2013 of an attempt to steal £1.2 million from the Bank of Santander. Perhaps by coincidence, in the same month the consumer magazine *Which?* reported that this bank had the worst security measures to protect online banking of all the major UK operators. To be fair to the Bank of Santander, the attempt was blocked and similar tactics have been employed against other High Street banks, with Barclays apparently losing a similar sum.

The National Fraud Authority publish an Annual Fraud Indicator.[1] The 2012 report estimates that fraud costs United Kingdom organisations and individuals around £73 billion. The 2012 report claims to have improved its methodology and sources to produce a more accurate (and much higher) figure than presented in its previous studies. It is difficult to extrapolate from the figures, however, how much of this amount involved computers. Identity fraud, for example is estimated to cause losses of £1.2 billion. This activity is often linked with online activities such as 'phishing attacks' where the fraudster tries to persuade the recipient of an email to supply details of their bank accounts which will then be raided. Identity fraud could also involve read-ing a paper bank statement discarded in a dustbin.

The data is now somewhat dated but a study produced by the credit reference agency Experian in 2002 involved searching through 400 household dustbins. In 20 per cent of cases data was found giving name, address, credit card number, and expiry date. Many sites now, of course, require a customer to know also a security number printed on the back of a card—which in my experience becomes almost illegible after a very short period of use. In general what we see is a constant technological war between financial institutions and fraudsters.

A more specific study was produced in 2011 for the Cabinet Office entitled 'The Cost of Cyber Crime: A Detica Report in Partnership with the Office of Cyber Security and Information Assurance in the Cabinet Office' and estimated the annual cost of cybercrime at £27 billion. This is actually more than the National Fraud Authority's 2011 estimate for all forms of fraud in the UK. Definition, as always, is critical, and the Cabinet Office report's single largest category of crime is 'intellectual property fraud' which is estimated to cost £9 billion. Second is espionage at around £7.5 billion. Neither perhaps falls into what might be considered classic categories of computer crime and, indeed, in both categories the distinction between civil and criminal liabilities is not clear cut. Figure P2.1 depicts the full results of the 2011 study.

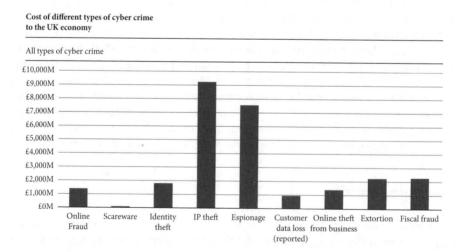

Figure P2.1 The cost of cyber crime

Source: 'The Cost of Cyber Crime: A Detica Report in Partnership with the Office of Cyber Security and Information Assurance in the Cabinet Office' (2011), 2011 Detica Limited, <https://www.gov.uk/government/uploads/system/uploads/attachment_data/file/60943/the-cost-of-cyber-crime-full-report.pdf>.

---

[1] Available at <http://www.homeoffice.gov.uk/publications/agencies-public-bodies/nfa/annual-fraud-indicator/>.

Beyond uncertainties as to statistics, issues of loss, fraud, and the involvement of law enforce-ment agencies are all somewhat problematic issues. Following changes to English law intro-duced in the Fraud Act of 2006, there appears to be reluctance on the part of law enforcement agencies to accept crime reports from individuals and to require that issues be raised with a bank or other financial institution. The police will accept complaints only from (or at the request of) such a body and concerns have been expressed that instances may not be reported thereby skewing statistics as to the scale of the problem. More positively, the organisation 'Action Fraud'[2] has been established to serve as a single point to collate reports of fraud from members of the public.

Questions have also arisen about the manner in which individuals are treated where there are disputes concerning the use or misuse of credit or debit cards that are protected by PIN num-bers. The Financial Services and Market Rules (Payment Services Regulations) of 2009 state that a consumer is to be held liable for fraudulent use of a card (above a limit of £50) only where gross negligence can be established. There has been a long-standing debate concerning the security of this system of protection. Banks have argued successfully before the courts, admittedly at only the County Court level, that cards, at least when using the current Chip and PIN level of security, can be used only if the PIN had been disclosed by the holder. Other techniques can, of course, also be employed. Cameras can be placed by ATM machines to capture PIN numbers with the cards subsequently being stolen. So-called 'shoulder surfing' can be as effective with the criminal looking over the user's shoulder to observe what numbers are being pressed.

Media depictions of computer fraudsters and computer criminals generally tend to depict some form of computer genius. Reality is often rather more down to earth and, in many cases, the techniques are fairly basic. In respect of the Santander and Barclays attacks the device used is known as a keyboard video mouse (KVM). This gadget, which fit into the back of a machine, can cost as little as £10 and is widely available in computer stores or online.

It is, however, testimony to the ease with which money can be transferred electronically that such a simple and cheap device could be capable of facilitating the theft of sums of money far beyond the dreams of most traditional bank robbers.

Computer hacking

Much the same story might be told in respect of the next generation of computer crimes. From around the 1970s, telephone networks began to automate their operations and we also saw the introduction of the first networked services such as Compuserve and AOL. Inevitably we also saw the rise of hacking. Initially often referred to as 'phreaking', proponents sought to manipu-late the dialling codes used by telephone networks to obtain free calls. The technology is now obsolete, but the early networks relied upon audio signals transmitted at specific frequencies to handle traffic. Sometimes technologies were basic. One phreaker discovered that a toy whistle distributed as a gift in a box of breakfast cereals—aimed at a childs' market, mimicked precisely the frequencies of major United States telecommunications networks. Effectively, blowing a series of notes down a telephone line would allow free access to the global telecommunica-tions network.

With the emergence of computer networks around forty years ago we saw the emergence of computer hacking. One of the most famous (or notorious) groups in the field is the Chaos Computer Club which was formed in Germany in 1981. Perhaps anticipating recent leaks of government information, its manifesto pronounced it to be 'a galactic community of life forms,

---

[2] <http://www.actionfraud.police.uk/>.

independent of age, sex, race or societal orientation, which strives across borders for freedom of information...'

To a greater extent in the 1980s than today, there was a range of views about the ethical and legal acceptability of hacking. Reference was sometimes made to the light and to the dark sides of the practice. Light-side, or good, hackers were interested solely in the technical challenge of obtaining access to computer systems and, it was argued, might be able to alert operators to vulnerabilities in their systems. The question of whether such conduct should be criminalised has been at the core of much of the debate in the field. I have mentioned the estimate that losses due to computer espionage cost the UK about £7 billion in 2011. But generally, as was explained by Professor Glanville Williams:

> It is absurd and disgraceful that we should still be making do without any legislation specifically designed to discourage this modern form of commercial piracy. Abstracting or divulging an official secret is an offence under the Official Secrets Act 1911, sections 1 and 2; but Leviathan is not much concerned to protect the secret and immensely valuable know-how of its subjects.[3]

Some thirty years on, that remains very much the legal reality in the physical world. As we will discuss, the online world has been regulated in different ways but the fundamental point remains significant. Discounting any peripheral offences that might be involved, if I am legitimately in a building, walk into an unlocked office, and photograph papers left lying on a desk, I will not have committed any offence. Put simply, the argument with computer crime legislation is whether any different result should pertain if I access data on a computer that has effectively been left unlocked? The question 'what is an effective lock?' raises other issues!

A point which continually arises in the field is 'what is a computer?' Most smartphones have apps which allow individuals to identify where friends or partners are at any point in time. Consent to being tracked will invariably need to be given in the phone's settings but this is a simple procedure. You might consider the following report which related to the Apple iPhone 'FindmyFriends' app:

> The lovely thing about this app is that you can follow people only if they're happy to you to have you follow them. In this particular case, the poster—with the handle 'ThomasMetz'—claims that he had suspicions about the happiness of his marriage. He had a few suspicions about his wife's loyalty and activities. So he allegedly installed the app without happening to mention it.
> In his words: 'I got my wife a new 4S and loaded up find my friends without her knowing. She told me she was at her friends [sic] house in the east village. I've had suspicions about her meeting this guy who live uptown. Lo and behold, Find my Friends has her right there.'[4]

Effectively such applications cause the target phone to transmit location data on request. Is this hacking? It appears that the technology is also used by parents to keep track of their child's movements—or to monitor a typically older person suffering from some form of memory loss. Again, is this hacking and what might be the issues of ownership and/or consent?

The notion and fear of computer hacking remains very prevalent today and a whole new topic is developing with notions of cyberterrorism and cyberwarfare. I'll say more about this later but that conduct essentially relates to the third main strand of computer crime involving attempts to modify or delete programs or data held on a computer.

The conduct is sometimes related to hacking and as such would represent what is referred to as the dark side of the practice. Essentially unauthorised access is a precursor to conduct that damages the intangible elements of a computer system. The distinction between tangible and intangible damage has occupied courts and legislatures for a good number of years. We might

---

[3] *Textbook of Criminal Law*, 2nd edn (London, 1983), p. 739.
[4] <http://news.cnet.com/8301-17852_3-20121104-71/apples-new-find-my-friends-app-finds-wife-cheating/>.

consider an incident whereby somebody sprays paint onto the walls of a building. Leaving aside any issues of the aesthetic value of the finished work, it would generally be assumed that the structure has been damaged although it would not be the case that it is any more likely to fall down than it was before the incident. If data is corrupted on some form of computer storage device, there will be no direct physical evidence of the fact and the object will continue to be usable. You might think of a situation where all the contents of a computer are moved to the recycle bin and deleted. Discounting the use of very expensive data-recovery services, the material has gone. The impact on the owner may be devastating but there is still a perfectly serviceable computer.

The story of how the law has come to deal with these issues is a fascinating one. In many countries, including the United Kingdom, we have seen the enactment of specific computer-crime statutes. Given the all-pervasive nature of computer applications today, it is arguable that there is the need to adjust general principles of criminal law to cope with the realities of the computer age rather than treating the device as an isolated creature.

From cybercrime to cyberwarfare

In its early stages, attention regarding unlawful activities involving computers focused on the activities of what might be regarded as traditional criminals. Over the past decade, paralleling developments in the real world, there has been increasing emphasis on the use of computer systems as a weapon either by terrorists or, and perhaps the other side of the coin, as a form of warfare by states. In its own turn, the distinction between cyberwarfare and cyberterrorism may be tenuous. Conduct is generally classified in the eyes of the beholder. As in the real world, the distinction between criminal conduct and terrorism may be difficult to define and in some respects the focus of discussion relates more to the scale and impact of conduct rather than the nature or motives of the perpetrators. Especially in the era of privatised utilities, attacks on private companies pose as substantial a threat to society as attacks on government installations.

In 2010 the United Kingdom government published its National Security Strategy. As developed by the National Security Council, this sought to identify the risks facing the country and place them into three tiers of severity. The threats in tier one were defined as being 'of highest priority for UK national security looking ahead, taking account of both likelihood and impact' and encompassed:

- international terrorism affecting the UK or its interests, including a chemical, biological, radiological, or nuclear attack by terrorists; and/or a significant increase in the levels of terrorism relating to Northern Ireland
- hostile attacks upon UK cyberspace by other states and large-scale cybercrime
- a major accident or natural hazard which requires a national response, such as severe coastal flooding affecting three or more regions of the UK, or an influenza pandemic
- an international military crisis between states, drawing in the UK, and its allies as well as other states and non-state actors.

A budget of £650 million (over a four-year period) was allocated to improve the country's 'cyberdefences'. This resulted in the adoption in November 2011 by the Cabinet Office of a National Cybercrime Strategy. This referred to the increasing importance of the Internet in all aspects of life and noted that:

> The digital architecture on which we now rely was built to be efficient and interoperable. When the internet first started to grow, security was less of a consideration. However, as we put more

of our lives online, this matters more and more. People want to be confident that the networks that support our national security, our economic prosperity, and our own private lives as individuals are safe and resilient.[para. 2.2]

Concerns about security have been growing for some time. In the global environment there is obvious need for international cooperation and within the EU, the European Network and Information Security Agency (ENISA) was established in 2004. The European Commission commented:

ENISA is the EU's response to these cyber security issues of the European Union. As such, it is the 'pace-setter' for Information Security in Europe, and a centre of expertise.

The objective is to make ENISA's web site the European 'hub' for exchange of information, best practices and knowledge in the field of Information Security.[5]

ENISA was established under Regulation (EC) No. 460/2004 of the European Parliament and of the Council[6]. The Regulation recites that:

Communication networks and information systems have become an essential factor in economic and societal development. Computing and networking are now becoming ubiquitous utilities in the same way as electricity or water supply already are. The security of communication networks and information systems, in particular their availability, is therefore of increasing concern to society not least because of the possibility of problems in key information systems, due to system complexity, accidents, mistakes and attacks, that may have consequences for the physical infrastructures which deliver services critical to the well-being of EU citizens. [Recital 1]

Within the UK the Centre for the Protection of the National Infrastructure (CPNI)[7] was established in 2007 following from the merger of the National Infrastructure Security Co-ordination Centre (NISCC) and a part of MI5 (the UK's Security Service), the National Security Advice Centre (NSAC). The National Infrastructure has been defined as encompassing:

those facilities, systems, sites and networks necessary for the functioning of the country and the delivery of the essential services upon which daily life in the UK depends.[8]

It is categorised into nine sectors:

- communications
- emergency services
- energy
- financial services
- food
- government
- health
- transport
- water

The CPNI note that:

The UK is facing an ongoing, persistent threat of cyber attack from other states, terrorists and criminals operating in cyberspace.

---

[5] <http://www.enisa.europa.eu/about-enisa>.
[6] <http://eur-lex.europa.eu/LexUriServ/LexUriServ.do?uri=CELEX:32004R0460:EN:HTML>.
[7] <http://www.cpni.gov.uk/>.   [8] <http://www.cpni.gov.uk/about/cni/>

They go on to explain that:

Cyberspace lies at the heart of modern society; it impacts our personal lives, our businesses and our essential services. Cyber security embraces both the public and the private sector and spans a broad range of issues related to national security, whether through terrorism, crime or industrial espionage.

E-crime, or cyber crime, whether relating to theft, hacking or denial of service to vital systems, has become a fact of life. The risk of industrial cyber espionage, in which one company makes active attacks on another, through cyberspace, to acquire high value information is also very real.[9]

Terrorists are identified as a potential threat but increasingly, states are seeking to utilise cyberwarfare strategies as an alternative to more traditional military actions. As *The Guardian* commented in July 2011:

Hostile foreign states have used cyberwarfare to attack and map the networks that are part of the country's critical national infrastructure, the government has admitted.

Though officials refused to say what had been hit, the systems that provide the UK with its gas, water, and electricity supplies are all likely to have been targeted, raising the stakes in the battle to stop foreign powers, criminals and hackers from stealing information that could lead to services being disrupted or brought to a standstill.

The counterside of cyberterrorism is the attempt by states to use cyber-based activities as a weapon in their own right. It has, for example, been reported that British intelligence agents hacked into an al-Qaeda online magazine and replaced bomb-making instructions with a recipe for cupcakes. In 2010, Iran's nuclear programme was severely disrupted by the so-called Stuxnet virus. The virus apparently infected computers which controlled the operation of centrifuges which play an essential role in processing nuclear material to make it suitable for use for military purposes. The centrifuges were reprogrammed to spin at excessive speed resulting in major physical damage to their components. This is considered to be one of, if not the, most sophisticated and extensive viruses and the first which specifically targeted infrastructure. It has been widely reported that the virus was created by the United States and Israeli security services.

---

[9] <http://www.cpni.gov.uk/threats/other-threats/>.

9

National and international responses to computer-related crime

Introduction

In considering the application of the criminal law to instances of computer-related conduct, a variety of issues arise. In the early days of computer-related conduct, any criminal charge was required to be brought under traditional legal headings. Incidents where damage was caused to the contents of a computer, either directly or by causing it to be infected by a computer virus, were successfully prosecuted as a species of criminal damage under the Criminal Damage Act 1971.[1]

Starting in the 1980s, a trend began for the adoption of computer-specific statutes. Perhaps the first was the United States Computer Fraud and Abuse Act, enacted in 1984. Within the United Kingdom, the Law Commissions published consultative papers and reports in the 1980s.[2] Although the initial reports identified a case for the introduction of reform, considerable additional impetus came with the failure of the prosecution in the case of *R v Gold*.[3] The defendant in this case, together with another accused, had obtained password details, through the simple expediency of watching closely as an engineer typed in these details at a computer exhibition. He was then able to access an online database without paying the charges which would normally be levied in respect of such usage. The most relevant criminal offence would appear to have been that of obtaining services by deception. As will be discussed in more detail later, there was considerable uncertainty as to whether this offence could be committed when the 'victim' was a machine, and the decision was taken to bring the prosecution under the terms of the Forgery and Counterfeiting Act 1981. The Act provides that:

> A person is guilty of forgery if he makes a false instrument, with the intention that he or another shall use it to induce somebody to accept it as genuine, and by reason of so accepting it to do or not do some act to his own or any other person's prejudice.[4]

---

[1] See e.g. *R v Whitely* (1991) Cr App Rep 25. In this case, the appellant had obtained unauthorised access to a number of computer systems and caused significant amounts of data to be deleted. Upholding his conviction on a charge of criminal damage, the Court of Appeal accepted that no physical damage had been caused to any element of the network but held that '[w]hat the Act requires to be proved is that tangible property has been damaged, not necessarily that the damage itself is tangible. There can be no doubt that the magnetic particles upon the metal discs were a part of the discs and if the appellant was proved to have intentionally and without lawful excuse altered the particles in such a way as to cause an impairment of the value or usefulness of the disc to the owner, there would be damage within the meaning of Section 1 [of the Criminal Damage Act 1971]' (p. 28).

[2] The Law Commission published a consultation paper, *Computer Misuse*, in 1988 (No. 110) and a report of the same title in 1989 (No. 186). Slightly earlier, the Scottish Law Commission had published a consultative memorandum, *Computer Crime* in 1986 (No. 68) and a report in 1987 (No. 106).

[3] [1988] 1 AC 1063.   [4] s. 1.

The problems identified earlier relating to the possibility, or impossibility, of deceiving a machine are overcome in this statute, with section 10 providing that attempts to induce a machine to accept the instrument are to be equated with attempts so to induce a person.

The defendants were convicted at trial but their appeals were accepted unanimously, initially by the Court of Appeal and subsequently by the House of Lords. Delivering his judgment in the Court of Appeal, the Lord Chief Justice concluded:

> We have accordingly come to the conclusion that the language of the Act was not intended to apply to the situation which was shown to exist in this case...It is a conclusion which we reach without regret. The Procrustean attempt to force these facts into the language of an Act not designed to fit them produced grave difficulties for both judge and jury which we would not wish to see repeated. The appellants' conduct amounted in essence...to dishonestly obtaining access to the relevant Prestel data bank by a trick. That is not a criminal offence. If it is thought desirable to do so that is a matter for the legislature rather than the courts. We express no view on the matter.[5]

Rightly or wrongly, the decision was widely seen as conferring a form of legal immunity on hackers. When the government failed to include proposals for legislation in its legislative programme for the following parliamentary session, a Bill was introduced as a private member's measure and, receiving a good measure of governmental support, received the Royal Assent in 1990 as the Computer Misuse Act. This remains the cornerstone of United Kingdom law in the field.

Traditionally, criminal law has been seen as the province of national authorities. As developments in technology gathered pace, it became increasingly apparent that national legislation might be of limited effectiveness. Rather, as was the concern in the field of data protection, the existence of computer crime havens might threaten the effectiveness of national computer crime statutes. Beginning with the Council of Europe Cybercime Convention, which was opened for signature in 2001,[6] there have been a number of international initiatives with the European Union also becoming increasingly active in the field. As well as making provision for harmonising substantive criminal offences, there have been moves to enhance cooperation between law enforcement agencies at a procedural level.

The Council of Europe Cybercrime Convention

The Council of Europe Convention is a substantial document. Its drafting was a lengthy process, occupying some four years and more than fifty meetings of the Committee of Experts on Crime in Cyberspace. The Convention contains a mix of substantive and procedural aspects. In a manner similar to that adopted in the Council's Data Protection Convention, the instrument specifies attributes which must be found in the national laws of its signatory states. It will then be a matter for each state to implement the provisions in domestic law. Although many aspects of the Convention are rather technical and non-contentious, procedural provisions relating to interception and retention of communications data did cause more controversy. The civil rights organisation, 'Treatywatch', for example, commented that:

> The Cybercrime Treaty is an international agreement created for the ostensible purpose of helping police cooperate on crimes that take place on the Internet. Unfortunately, the treaty,

---

[5] [1987] 3 WLR 803 at 809–10.

[6] The United Kingdom signed the Convention in 2001 but did not complete ratification until 2011.

which was drafted with very little public input, requires signatory nations to cooperate with foreign dictatorships and give invasive new surveillance powers to law enforcement. It also lacks protections for privacy or other civil liberties, and applies far more broadly than to just the Internet.[7]

Although concluded under the auspices of the Council of Europe, the Convention (as is the case with the data protection convention) is open for signature and ratification by non-Member States. To date, forty-five countries have signed the Convention, including the non-Member States of Australia, Canada, the Dominican Republic, Japan, the United States, and South Africa. To date thirty-six European states and four non-European (all signatories apart from South Africa) have ratified it and it is becoming a model for legislation in the sector.

OECD Guidelines for the Security of Information Systems

Also active in the field of computer crime has been the Organisation for Economic Co-operation and Development (OECD). As far back as 1986, the organisation published a report on *Computer-Related Crime: Analysis of Legal Policy*. This identified a range of actions relating to computers which it was suggested should attract criminal sanctions.

In 1992, the Council of the OECD adopted a Recommendation Concerning Guidelines for the Security of Information Systems. These guidelines were replaced by a further set of Guidelines 'For the Security of Information Systems and Networks'.[8] Addressed to all players in the sector, the Guidelines recognise that:

> Participants depend upon interconnected local and global information systems and networks and should understand their responsibility for the security of those information systems and networks. They should be accountable in a manner appropriate to their individual roles. Participants should review their own policies, practices, measures, and procedures regularly and assess whether these are appropriate to their environment.

Recognition that all parties share responsibility for developing and maintaining a culture of security perhaps highlights the close existence between concepts of data protection and computer crime. Many of the Guidelines are aimed primarily at computer users, including advice in matters such as ensuring that virus-checking software is installed and up to date and that any security patches issued by software developers are implemented.

An Implementation Plan for the Guidelines was published in 2003.[9] This recommended that governments should be:

- enacting a comprehensive set of substantive criminal, procedural, and mutual assistance legal measures to combat cybercrime and ensure cross-borders cooperation, which should be at least as comprehensive as, and consistent with, the Council of Europe Convention on Cybercrime
- identifying national cybercrime units and international high-technology assistance points of contact and creating such capabilities to the extent they do not already exist
- establishing institutions that exchange threat and vulnerability assessments, such as national CERTs (Computer Emergency Response Teams)
- developing closer cooperation between government and business in the fields of information security and fighting cybercrime.

---

[7] <http://www.treatywatch.org/>.
[8] Available from <http://www.oecd.org/dataoecd/16/22/15582260.pdf>.
[9] Available from <http://www.oecd.org/dataoecd/23/11/31670189.pdf>.

The Guidelines were further supplemented in 2005 with the publication by the Working Party on Information Security and Privacy of a report on *The Promotion of a Culture of Security for Information Systems and Networks in OECD Countries*. This includes a comprehensive account of national measures intended to implement the Guidelines.

EU initiatives

Within Europe, the EU has limited legislative competence in the criminal field and although, it has been active in respect of Internet content, this has primarily taken the form of encouraging the development of schemes to categorise the contents of websites and of filtering mechanisms which can be used to restrict the range of sites which may be accessed from a particular computer. Typically, parents would be able to restrict their children's access to sites which displayed sexual or violent material. The EU has also adopted a Directive on combating the sexual abuse and sexual exploitation of children and child pornography.[10] A more general Directive on Attacks against Information Systems was adopted in August 2013.[11] These measures replace the 2004 Framework Decision on Attacks against Information Systems.[12] In a Communication published in February 2013[13] entitled 'An Open, Safe and Secure Cyberspace', the Commission outlined its legislative priorities indicating that:

> Information and communications technology has become the backbone of our economic growth and is a critical resource which all economic sectors rely on. It now underpins the complex systems which keep our economies running in key sectors such as finance, health, energy and transport; while many business models are built on the uninterrupted availability of the Internet and the smooth functioning of information systems.

A number of action lines were identified as having a high priority:

- achieving cyber resilience
- drastically reducing cybercrime
- developing cyberdefence policy and capabilities related to the Common Security and Defence Policy (CSDP)
- developing the industrial and technological resources for cybersecurity
- establishing a coherent international cyberspace policy for the European Union and promote core EU values.

In respect of substantive legal measures, the Directives referred to constitute the main EU legislation. Also to be noted, however, is the establishment of the European Union Agency for Network and Information Security (ENISA)[14] in 2004. The legal basis for ENISA is now found in the Regulation 'Concerning the European Union Agency for Network and Information Security (ENISA) and Repealing Regulation (EC) No 460/2004'.[15] The Recitals to the Regulation state that the goal of the agency, which is based in Heraklion in Greece, is to contribute:

> to the goals of ensuring a high level of network and information security within the Union and developing a culture of network and information security for the benefit of citizens, consumers, enterprises and public administrations.

---

[10] Directive 2011/92/EC, OJ 2011 L335/1.   [11] Directive 2013/40/EC, OJ 2013 L218/8.
[12] COM (2002) 173 final.   [13] JOIN (2013) 1 final.   [14] <http://www.enisa.europa.eu/>.
[15] Regulation 526/2013, OJ 2013 L165/41.

Effectively, ENISA is intended to be a source of information and advice for all parts of the EU as to emerging threats in the fields of cybercrime and security and as to techniques and procedures through which they may be countered.

At a perhaps more practical level, the European Cybercrime Centre (EC3)[16] has been established since January 2013 as a component of the European Police Agency, Europol. It is indicated that:

> The Centre will be the focal point in the EU's fight against cybercrime, contributing to faster reactions in the event of online crimes. It will support Member States and the European Union's institutions in building operational and analytical capacity for investigations and cooperation with international partners.
>
> . . .
>
> The purpose of EC3 Strategy & Prevention is to make the citizens and businesses of the EU safer through increased insight, knowledge and awareness raising. The EC3 analyses large amounts of data from a variety of sources—both crime data and open sources—to understand how cybercriminals, child sex offenders and fraudsters think and operate. What we learn not only helps law enforcement target its operations more effectively: it also informs changes in policy and legislation and, most important of all, is the basis for our advice to citizens and businesses on how to protect themselves from online threats.[17]

Conclusions

The topic of computer crime has occupied much legislative time around the world. In some respects, the early instances of computer viruses such as the 'I Love You' version, which infected millions of computers globally, served to provide a wake-up call for many governments, who had to come to terms with the existence of gaps in the coverage of national laws.[18] It did not take the Philippine authorities long to enact computer misuse legislation. The widespread adoption of the Council of Europe Convention on Cybercrime—certainly compared with the non-existent adoption of its data protection Convention outwith the ranks of the Council's Member States—indicates perhaps that this initiative has struck a chord. The provisions of this Convention, together with the manner in which these are implemented in the United Kingdom, will be considered in more detail in the following chapters.

---

[16] <http://www.europol.europa.eu/ec3>.   [17] <https://www.europol.europa.eu/ec3/strategy>.

[18] Dating from 2000, 'I Love You' was perhaps the first computer virus to attract widespread attention. The name relates to the subject matter of a message sent to millions of users which invited them to click on an attachment, with dire consequences for their computers' health. A useful account of the virus can be found at <http://news.bbc.co.uk/1/hi/uk/736080.stm>.

10

Substantive criminal law provisions

Introduction

As discussed in the previous chapter, the Council of Europe's Convention on Cybercrime has become accepted as the leading international instrument in the field. Its provisions, which are largely replicated in the EU's Directives, will be used in this chapter to indicate the major headings under which computer-related conduct might be prosecuted and to analyse the effectiveness of United Kingdom legislation in the field. In its provisions, the Convention defines four categories of conduct which it requires to be the subject of criminal offences:

- offences against the confidentiality, integrity, and availability of computer data and systems—this essentially refers to computer hacking and to attempts to impair the operation of computer systems through interception of communications, the promulgation of viruses or the launching of denial of service attacks
- computer-related offences—this category relates essentially to issues of computer fraud, whether through targeting computers directly or engaging in conduct intended to obtain personal data with a view to securing financial advantage, something generally referred to as identity fraud
- content-related offences—as defined in the Convention, this relates to conduct involving the production, dissemination, or possession of child pornography
- offences related to infringements of copyright and related rights.

The first three of these will be considered, respectively, in this and the following two chapters, whilst the fourth will be examined later when considering the general operation of intellectual property law. The Convention and EU legislation also contains extensive procedural provisions and these will be described and discussed in Chapter 14.

Offences against the confidentiality, integrity, and availability of computer data and systems

Under this heading, the Convention sets out the parameters of offences relating to illegal access, often involving hacking, illegal interception of data in the course of its transmission over a communications network, and also the concept of data and system interference, which may typically result from the promulgation of viruses or the use of denial-of-service attacks. The provisions of sections 1, 2, and 3 of the Computer Misuse Act, as amended by the Police and Justice Act of 2006, provide the major United Kingdom input in this regard.

Illegal access

Article 2 of the Convention requires that:

Each Party shall adopt such legislative and other measures as may be necessary to establish as criminal offences under its domestic law, when committed intentionally, the access to the whole or any part of a computer system without right. A Party may require that the offence be committed by infringing security measures, with the intent of obtaining computer data or other dishonest intent, or in relation to a computer system that is connected to another computer system.

Article 3 of the European Directive provides that:

Member States shall take the necessary measures to ensure that, when committed intentionally, the access without right, to the whole or to any part of an information system, is punishable as a criminal offence where committed by infringing a security measure, at least for cases which are not minor.

There are differences between the two approaches although the EU measures provide a minimal set of conditions. Member States may adopt more punitive provisions.

The Council of Europe formulation confers considerable discretion upon signatory states, an approach that is repeated throughout its provisions. Largely, no doubt because it is dealing with provisions of criminal law which tend to be guarded jealously by national legislatures, the Cybercrime Convention provides for a much lower degree of harmonisation than was achieved by the Council's earlier Data Protection Convention. Article 2 provides an excellent example of the approach. There are three elements in its definition which allow states the option how to proceed. The core element of the offence is that conduct be carried out intentionally, something that will be discussed later, but there are also options for states to require the overcoming of security measures, the presence of dishonest intent, or—what might be referred to as the essence of hacking—the use of one computer to connect to and access data on another computer.

The issue of whether criminality should be dependent upon access having been obtained through overcoming security devices has been debated extensively. Adopting such an approach would be compatible with legal provisions in respect of many other areas of activity. If a person obtains entry to premises by overcoming some security system—such as a lock on the door—an offence will generally be committed at that moment in time. If, however, the door has been left open by the property owner, the mere act of entering premises will not normally be unlawful unless and until the individual engages in further aggravating conduct such as damaging or removing objects. Although the Scottish Law Commission in its *Report on Computer Crime* had proposed that commission of an unauthorised access offence should be contingent upon an intention either to secure a benefit for the perpetrator or to cause loss to the computer owner, the Law Commission argued that the mere fact of obtaining unauthorised access should suffice:

because of the possibility that any attempted entrant may have had password access to important levels of authority, sometimes to a level which has enabled him to delete records of his activities from the system, any successful unauthorised access must be taken very seriously. Substantial costs are therefore incurred in (i) taking security steps against unauthorised entry … and (ii) investigating any case, however trivial, where unauthorised activity does in fact occur.[1]

---

[1] Law Commission No. 186 at para. 1.29.

Significantly, however, the Law Commission recommended that the offence should be regarded as a relatively minor one, attracting a maximum penalty of three months' imprisonment. As enacted, the Computer Misuse Act provided for a maximum sentence of six months' imprisonment, a period which was increased to two years with the entry into force of the Police and Justice Act of 2006.[2]

Although in terms of its penalties, the unauthorised access offence (generally referred to as the 'basic offence') is the least significant of the Computer Misuse Act's provisions, its linkage with other provisions makes it in many ways the most critical element of the legislation. The offence is defined in section 1 of the Computer Misuse Act 1990, which, as amended by section 35 of the Police and Justice Act 2006, provides that:

1. A person is guilty of an offence if—

    (a) he causes a computer to perform any function with intent to secure access to any program or data held in any computer or to enable any such access to be secured;

    (b) the access he intends to secure or to enable to be secured, is unauthorised; and

    (c) he knows at the time when he causes the computer to perform the function that that is the case.

In common with other statutes in the field, no attempt is made to define the word 'computer'. This may lead to problems given the increasingly ubiquitous presence of microprocessors. Many modern appliances such as washing machines and motor cars make extensive use of these to control their functioning. In such a situation, it might be argued that a person who, without receiving the owner's permission, switched on a washing machine would be guilty of the unauthorised access offence. Again, a car thief might also face prosecution under section 1 of the Computer Misuse Act. Such a prospect was identified in Parliament, where the prospect was welcomed by at least one MP who, in opposing proposals to amend the offence to restrict its scope, argued:

> This is a computer misuse Bill. It seeks to tackle unauthorised access to computers which may well include electronic locks...Someone breaking into a car using an electronic key to operate the lock may not be caught under the present legislation if a policeman puts his hand on his shoulder before he gets in and tries to drive away. We are attempting to make it an offence for people to gain unauthorised access to an electronic system. The clause is properly drafted.[3]

Although the scope of the offence is broad, a number of conditions require to be established to secure a conviction. Three elements call for detailed consideration. The concept of access raises a number of issues and the scope of the definitions are extremely broad. Next comes the question of whether access is authorised. Finally, it must be established by the prosecution that an accused knew that access was being sought without authority.

Obtaining or enabling access to computers or data

The key step in the commission of the offence will consist of causing a computer 'to perform any function with intent to secure access to any program or data held in any computer'. A variety of elements from this definition call for further discussion and comment.

---

[2] In cases where the prosecution is on a summary basis, the maximum sentence is twelve months' imprisonment in England and Wales, but only six months' for Scotland.

[3] HC Official Report, SC C (Computer Misuse Bill), col. 9, 14 March 1990.

The Act provides that access will be secured to a program or data when the user, by causing the computer to operate in any manner:

(a) alters or erases the program or data;

(b) copies or moves it to any storage medium other than that in which it is held or to a different location in the storage medium in which it is held;

(c) uses it; or

(d) has it output from the computer in which it is held (whether by having it displayed or in any other manner).[4]

Although these provisions are somewhat tortuous (and are themselves subject to further definition in the Act), most actions whereby a user makes contact with a computer system will come within its ambit. The simple act of switching on a computer will cause start-up programs to function and cause various messages to be displayed on the screen.

The popular image of a computer hacker is of someone who accesses computer systems by making a connection from their own computer. This perception caused considerable problems in the first prosecution brought under the Computer Misuse Act 1990 and resulted in the accused being acquitted of charges under the Act on the direction of the judge. The case was referred to the Court of Appeal by the Attorney General, where it is reported as *A-G's Reference (No. 1 of 1991)*.[5] The defendant in this case had been employed as a sales assistant by a wholesale locksmith. He left their employ, but subsequently returned to the premises indicating the intention to purchase an item of equipment. Details of sales transactions were entered into a computer terminal. The defendant was familiar with the use of the system and, taking advantage of a moment when the terminal was left unattended, entered a code into the system. The effect of this was to instruct the computer to give a 70 per cent discount on the sale. The invoice which was subsequently generated charged the sum of £204.76 instead of the normal price of £710.96. Upon these facts coming to light, the defendant was arrested and charged with an offence under the Computer Misuse Act 1990. At trial, the judge dismissed the charge, holding that the phrase in section 1(1)(a) referring to obtaining access to 'any program or data held in any computer' required that one computer should be used to obtain access to a program or data held on another computer.

Given evidence from many computer crime surveys that most instances of computer misuse are perpetrated by 'insiders', such a restriction would severely limit the application of the statute. The Attorney General, acting under the authority of the Criminal Justice Act 1972,[6] sought the opinion of the Court of Appeal on the question whether:

In order for a person to commit an offence under Section 1(1) of the Computer Misuse Act 1990 does the computer which the person causes to perform any function with the required intent have to be a different computer from the one into which he intends to secure unauthorised access to any program or data held therein?

Delivering the judgment of the court, the Lord Chief Justice answered this question in the negative. There were, he ruled:

no grounds whatsoever for implying or importing the word 'other' between 'any' and 'computer', or excepting the computer which is actually used by the offender from the phrase 'any computer'.[7]

---

[4] s. 17(1). [5] [1992] 3 WLR 432. [6] s. 36.
[7] *A-G's Reference (No. 1 of 1991)* [1992] 3 WLR 432 at 437.

Such a view, which is undoubtedly correct but a misunderstanding of the scope of the Act's provisions, has been a recurring theme over the years and perhaps indicates a lack of precision in the drafting of the offences.

As originally enacted, the Computer Misuse Act criminalised only the direct attempt to obtain access to a computer. The European Union Framework Decision (now replaced by the 2012 Directive) required that Member States also criminalise conduct which is intended to aid and abet those committing offences. It provides in Article 7 that:

> Member States shall take the necessary measures to ensure that the intentional production, sale, procurement for use, import, distribution or otherwise making available, of one of the following tools, without right and with the intention that it be used to commit any of the offences referred to in Articles 3 to 6, is punishable as a criminal offence, at least for cases which are not minor:
>
> (a) a computer programme, designed or adapted primarily for the purpose of committing any of the offences referred to in Articles 3 to 6;
>
> (b) a computer password, access code, or similar data by which the whole or any part of an information system is capable of being accessed.

The Police and Justice Act of 2006 adds a new section 3A to the Computer Misuse Act providing that:

> (1) A person is guilty of an offence if he makes, adapts, supplies or offers to supply any article intending it to be used to commit, or to assist in the commission of, an offence under section 1 or 3.
>
> (2) A person is guilty of an offence if he supplies or offers to supply any article believing that it is likely to be used to commit, or to assist in the commission of, an offence under section 1 or 3.
>
> (3) A person is guilty of an offence if he obtains any article with a view to its being supplied for use to commit, or to assist in the commission of, an offence under section 1 or 3.
>
> (4) In this section "article" includes any program or data held in electronic form.

This provision would have the effect of criminalisng websites which provided details of passwords that could then be used to obtain unauthorized access to other sites. Many tools, however, can be categorised as 'dual use' and the extent to which their creators or suppliers may be caught by the prohibition is unclear. Software packages are marketed that can, for example, generate enormous numbers of passwords. These can be used by network operators to check the effectiveness of their own security but can also be used by hackers seeking to obtain unauthorised access.

When is access unauthorised?

Access is held to be unauthorised when the user:

(a) is not him or herself entitled to control access of the kind in question to the program or data; and

(b) he or she does not have the consent to access of the kind in question to the program or data from any person who is so entitled.[8]

---

[8] Computer Misuse Act 1990, s. 17(5).

In many cases, the person entitled to control access will be the owner of the computer system itself. In other cases, a computer system may serve as a 'host', providing storage space and access facilities for programs or data controlled by other parties. In this situation, the question of who has the right to consent to access may be more complex. Most university computer systems provide illustrations of this form of activity. Here, the fact that a student is granted rights of access does not confer any entitlement to transfer these on to a third party.

In many cases, the initial act of making contact with a computer system will not suffice to demonstrate knowledge that access is unauthorised. Even though a hacker contacting computer systems at random (or making use of details supplied by a fellow enthusiast) may well suspect that their attentions may not be welcome, and indeed be reckless whether this would be the case, it may be very difficult to establish that they had actual knowledge that access was unauthorised at the point of initial contact. The dividing line between reckless and intentional conduct may well be crossed once contact is made. Typically, websites which intend to restrict access to authorised users will display a message on their home screen to the effect that 'Unauthorised access to this system is ILLEGAL under the provisions of the Computer Misuse Act 1990'. The mere presence of such a notice might be sufficient to justify the assumption that any further attempts to operate or access the contents of the system will be conducted in the knowledge that this is unauthorised. The installation of a security system, typically allocating authorised users with passwords and requiring these to be entered at the stage of initial contact, would undoubtedly reinforce this position.

Unauthorised use by authorised users

This is one of the most difficult aspects of the unauthorised access offence and the case law illustrates well the problems that have been faced in formulating laws to deal with technology. The Computer Misuse Act prohibits unauthorised access. In the case where an individual has no entitlement to access material, the application of the provision is relatively straightforward. Difficulties have, however, arisen in the situation where an individual is entitled to access information but uses this for an unauthorised purpose. An example might be taken from the case of *R v Thompson* discussed more fully in the following chapter, where a dishonest programmer used his access to his employer's computer to perpetrate a theft. Similar, although perhaps less extreme, conduct was at issue in the case of *R v Bignell*.[9] Here, two police officers obtained access to data held on the police national computer in order to identify the owner of a number of motor vehicles. The information was sought for the officers' personal interest and was not connected with their duties as police officers. The conduct being discovered, they were charged under section 1 and convicted at trial. On appeal, although it was not contended that the use to which the data was put was authorised, the Divisional Court accepted submissions to the effect that:

> the primary purpose of the Computer Misuse Act was to protect the integrity of computer systems rather that the integrity of information stored on the computers ... a person who causes a computer to perform a function to secure access to information held at a level to which the person was entitled to gain access does not commit an offence under S.1 even if he intends to secure access for an unauthorised purpose because it is only where the level of unauthorised access has been knowingly and intentionally exceeded that an offence is committed, provided the person knows of that unauthorised level of access.

[9] *The Times*, 6 June 1997.

The court held that no offence had been committed under the Computer Misuse Act, although it was suggested that charges might have been brought under the Data Protection Act 1984. As discussed more extensively elsewhere, under the provisions of this Act, any obtaining, holding, disclosure, or international transfer of data by a servant or agent of a data user which contravenes the terms of the latter's entry on the Register will render the individual concerned liable under both criminal and civil law.[10]

The decision in *Bignell*[11] was widely criticised and was reconsidered in the later case of *R v Bow Street Magistrates' Court, ex p Allison*.[12] This case concerned an application by the United States authorities for the extradition of the applicant to face charges of, inter alia, securing unauthorised access to the American Express computer system with the intent to commit offences of theft and forgery. The issue before the court was whether the conduct alleged, had it taken place in the United Kingdom, would have constituted a breach of section 2 of the Computer Misuse Act which established what is referred to as the ulterior intent offence. This provides that:

1. A person is guilty of an offence under this Section if he commits an offence under Section 1 above ('the unauthorised access offence') with intent—

   (a) to commit an offence to which this Section applies; or

   (b) to facilitate the commission of such an offence (whether by himself or by any other person).[13]

The offences referred to in the above passage are defined as being those for which the sentence is prescribed by law[14]—effectively the offence of murder or those for which a person with no previous criminal record might, upon conviction, be sentenced to a term of imprisonment of five years or more.[15] The maximum sentence for commission of the section 2 offence is itself a term of five years' imprisonment.

The declared intent behind the ulterior-intent offence was to bring forward in time the moment at which a serious criminal offence is committed. The issues will be discussed in more detail in the next chapter looking at computer fraud, but essentially general provisions of criminal law draw a distinction between conduct which is preparatory to the commission of an offence and that which is part (successful or not) of its perpetration. The Law Commission, in its report, identified a number of problems which might arise in the computer field creating circumstances where conduct might not constitute an attempt under the general provisions of criminal law, but which was felt to justify special treatment within the computer context.[16] One example cited concerned a hacker who secured access to a bank's computer system, the system being used for electronic fund transfers. In order to accomplish a transfer, a password would have to be transmitted. The Law Commission hypothesised that the hacker might attempt to transmit a large number of combinations in the hope of finding the correct one. In the event that the password was discovered, used, and a transfer of funds accomplished, the Law Commission was in no doubt that the offence of theft would be committed. The act of transmitting combinations of numbers and letters in the attempt to discover a valid password would not, it considered, be regarded as more than conduct preparatory to the commission of a crime. As such, it would not constitute a criminal attempt, especially in the event that further steps would be required in order to complete the transfer. Reference has previously been made to the speed at which vast sums

---

[10] s. 5(3).   [11] (1998) 1 Cr App Rep 1.
[12] [1999] 4 All ER 1. The decision of the Divisional Court is reported at [1999] QB 847.   [13] s. 2.
[14] s. 2(2)(a).   [15] s. 2(2)(b).   [16] Law Commission No. 186 (1989) at paras. 3.52–3.53.

of money may be transferred using the electronic fund transfer system. In terms of time, it seems clear that the gap between conduct preparatory of a crime and its perpetration may be very short where this form of conduct is at issue.

In *Allison*, the defendant had allegedly conspired with another party, Jean Ojomo, who had been employed by American Express. In the course of her work, she was instructed to access specific accounts but once online could access other account information. This was passed on to Allison, who was able to use it to encode credit cards, obtain personal identification numbers, and make withdrawals from automatic teller machines. Allison was arrested in England in possession of forged cards, having been photographed using such a card to make a cash withdrawal. The conduct at issue, it was alleged, would have constituted a breach of sections 1, 2, and 3 of the Computer Misuse Act 1990.[17] Following the decision in *Bignell*,[18] it was held by the Divisional Court that the section 1 offence had not been committed and therefore there could be no question of a section 2 offence being committed.

The consequences of the Divisional Court's decisions in *Bignell*[19] and *Allison*[20] for the operation of the Computer Misuse Act 1990 were potentially significant. As stated above, most instances of computer fraud (and perhaps fraud in general) are committed by insiders. The decisions, therefore, were seen as conferring a degree of immunity upon such actors. An appeal was made in the case of *Allison* and resulted in a robust rejection by the House of Lords of the notion that the misuse of access rights could not incur criminal sanctions. Delivering the judgment of the House, Lord Hobhouse quoted from the provisions of section 17, which define the concept of access and authorisation. This provides that access is unauthorised if a person:

(a) is not himself entitled to control access of the kind in question to the program or data; and

(b) he does not have consent to access by him of the kind in question to the program or data from any person who is so entitled.

In both situations, it was held, account had to be taken of the use to which access was put rather than merely to the data which was accessed. The section, it was held:

> makes clear that the authority must relate not simply to the data or programme but also to the actual kind of access secured. Similarly, it is plain that it is not using the word 'control' in a physical sense of the ability to operate or manipulate the computer and that it is not derogating from the requirement that for access to be authorised it must be authorised to the relevant data or relevant programme or part of a programme. It does not introduce any concept that authority to access one piece of data should be treated as authority to access other pieces of data 'of the same kind' notwithstanding that the relevant person did not in fact have authority to access that piece of data. Section 1 [of the Computer Misuse Act 1990] refers to the intent to secure unauthorised access to any programme or data. These plain words leave no room for any suggestion that the relevant person may say: 'Yes, I know that I was not authorised to access that data but I was authorised to access other data of the same kind.'[21]

---

[17] ss. 2 and 3 are considered later. Section 2 creates what is referred to as the 'ulterior intent' offence. This involves securing unauthorised access to programs of data with the intention of using the access to facilitate the commission of a further serious offence. Although extradition could only be authorised for an s. 2 offence, the penalties for breach of s. 1 being too low to warrant this process, it was necessary for the prosecution to establish commission of the unauthorised access offence as a prerequisite for liability under s. 2.

[18] *R v Bignell* [1998] 1 Cr App Rep 1.   [19] *R v Bignell* [1998] 1 Cr App Rep 1.

[20] *R v Bow Street Magistrates' Court, ex p Allison* [1999] 4 All ER 1.

[21] *R v Bow Street Magistrates' Court, ex p Allison* [1999] 4 All ER 1 at 7.

In terms which are reflective of the first decision under the Computer Misuse Act 1990, *A-G's Reference (No. 1 of 1991)*,[22] the Divisional Court was criticised for importing words into the statute. The Act, it was held was not concerned with access to 'kinds' of data. It looked rather at the entitlement to access particular programs or items of data. The decision of Kennedy J in the Divisional Court, it was held:

> treats the phrase 'entitlement to control' as if it related to the control of the computer as opposed to the entitlement to authorise operators to access to programs and data. He adopts the extraneous idea of an authorised level of access without considering whether, on the facts of the case, it corresponds to the relevant person's authority to access the data in fact accessed. He confines s. 1 of the Act to the 'hacking' of computer systems as opposed to the use of a computer to secure unauthorised access to programs or data. Upon a misreading of s. 17(5) [of the Computer Misuse Act 1990], he fails to give effect to the plain words of s.1. The meaning of the statute is clear and unambiguous.[23]

The decision in *Allison*[24] undoubtedly closed a significant loophole that had arisen with the Computer Misuse Act 1990. It is now clear that the statute is much more than an 'anti-hacking' measure and that misuse of facilities by authorised users will expose them to the risk of criminal prosecution.

Interception of communications

Article 3 of the Cybercrime Convention provides that Member States are to ensure that national laws prohibit the intentional interception:

> without right, made by technical means, of non-public transmissions of computer data to, from or within a computer system, including electromagnetic emissions from a computer system carrying such computer data. A Party may require that the offence be committed with dishonest intent, or in relation to a computer system that is connected to another computer system.

The provisions of the Regulation of Investigatory Powers Act 2000, provide in section 2 that an offence will be committed by a person who, without obtaining a warrant, intercepts any communication transmitted over a public or private communications system. Part 2 of the Act applies to surveillance and by section 27 provides that intrusive surveillance will be unlawful unless authorised under the legislation. Section 26 provides that:

> surveillance which—
>
> (a) is carried out by means of a surveillance device in relation to anything taking place on any residential premises or in any private vehicle, but
>
> (b) is carried out without that device being present on the premises or in the vehicle, is not intrusive unless the device is such that it consistently provides information of the same quality and detail as might be expected to be obtained from a device actually present on the premises or in the vehicle.

Attempts to identify the data being processed on a computer by detecting electromagnetic emissions could well fall foul of this provision.

---

[22] [1992] 3 WLR 432.

[23] [1999] 4 All ER 1 at 9.   [24] *R v Bow Street Magistrates' Court, ex p Allison* [1999] 4 All ER 1.

In the above situation, it is likely that an offence would be committed under section 1 of the Computer Misuse Act, as the perpetrator will be causing equipment to perform a function in order to secure access to data on the victim's computer. Although there are no direct precedents, a not dissimilar scenario would see a party attempting to make unauthorised use of a wireless computer network. This appears to be a growing practice, although there appears little doubt that the conduct does constitute an offence under the Computer Misuse Act. In the first case of its kind, a party who accessed a wireless network from his laptop whilst sitting in a car outside the network owner's premises was fined £500.[25]

Data and system interference

The Council of Europe Convention contains two articles prohibiting respectively data and system interference. Data interference, which is the subject of Article 4, criminalises the intentional 'damaging, deletion, deterioration, alteration or suppression of computer data without right'. Article 5 refers to the 'the serious hindering without right of the functioning of a computer system by inputting, transmitting, damaging, deleting, deteriorating, altering or suppressing computer data'.

There are close similarities between the offences. The concept of damage to data is one of the original forms of computer misuse and can be epitomised by reference to the dissemination of computer viruses. System interference is perhaps a more recent concept and would apply to incidents such as denial of service attacks. These can take a range of forms and are generally referred to as either denial of service or distributed denial of service attacks. A typical approach may be to direct so much spurious traffic to an e-commerce website that bona fide customers are unable to access it. No physical damage will be caused and no data may be deleted but the economic impact may be substantial. Such tactics may be carried out using a single computer—in an example discussed later, an individual used an email-generating package running on his PC to send many thousands of copies of an email to his former employer. Distributed attacks are somewhat more sophisticated and involve the use of a network of computers. In many instances, this will involve the perpetrators taking over control of machines belonging to unsuspecting indivuduals. Such networks, generally referred to as botnets, can be established by infecting the computers with malicious software or malware. The magazine PC World reported, in 2009 for example:

> As fireworks boomed on the Fourth of July, thousands of compromised computers attacked U.S. government Web sites. A botnet of more than 200,000 computers, infected with a strain of 2004's MyDoom virus, attempted to deny legitimate access to sites such as those of the Federal Trade Commission and the White House. [26]

As with the Internet itself, networks of infected computers do not respect national borders, something which renders difficult the work of law enforcement agencies in seeking to counter and prevent attacks. In 2013 it was reported by the Financial Times that:

> A vast network of hijacked computers responsible for more than $500 billion in bank fraud has been taken offline by an assault involving Microsoft and the American Federal Bureau of Investigation.[27]

---

[25] <http://news.bbc.co.uk/1/hi/technology/4721723.stm>.
[26] <http://www.pcworld.com/article/170546/how_to_clean_bots.html>.
[27] <http://www.ft.com/cms/s/0/50448d3a-ce50-11e2-8313-00144feab7de.html#ixzz2lBZmELrP>.

About 1,400 botnets have been created by the Citadel malware, which first emerged in early 2012. Microsoft said the Citadel kit could be bought from underground web forums for about $2,400. It added that more than 5 million people had been affected by the malware in as many as ninety countries, including the US and Australia. In this case it is reported that the malware has been used to commit frauds estimated at $500 million.[28]

Damage to data

Anyone possessing a degree of familiarity with computers and their method of operation will be only too well aware how fragile is the hold on its electronic life of any piece of data. The accidental depression of a key can speedily consign data to electronic oblivion. To the risks of accidental damage must be added those of deliberate sabotage.

The vulnerability of computer users to such events is not questioned. Once again, our concern must be with the legal consequences that may follow from such behaviour. The basic scenario involves a party altering or deleting data held on a computer system, such action taking place without the consent of the system owner. Within this, a wide range of activities can be identified. At the most basic level, the perpetrator may use 'delete' or 'reformat' commands or even bring a magnet into close proximity to a computer storage device. Amendment of data may be made for a variety of motives. In some cases, such as that at issue in *R v Thompson*, amendment of data may be a component of a scheme of fraud. Other actions may be driven by the intent to cause disruption to the computer owner's activities. This might involve the manipulation of computer programs through, for example, the insertion of logic bombs, which cause a computer to function in a manner desired by the perpetrator rather than its owner, whilst an ever-expanding range of computer viruses present a continual threat to the well-being of computer owners.

As enacted, section 3 of the Computer Misuse Act provided that it would be a criminal offence—punishable by a maximum sentence of ten years' imprisonment—to knowingly perform an unauthorised act in respect of the contents of any computer. The concept of an unauthorised act encompasses both the addition of data or its alteration or erasure. A modification will be regarded as unauthorised if the person causing it is not authorised so to act or does not possess the consent of a person who is so entitled.[29] Again, the possibility of different categories of rights and privileges attaching to different users must be borne in mind. Typically, an employee or a student may be entitled to use the facilities of a computer system but will not be entitled to delete any portions or to add any programs.

The effect of the unauthorised act must be:

  (a) to impair the operation of any computer;

  (b) to prevent or hinder access to any program or data held in any computer;

  (c) to impair the operation of any such program or the reliability of any such data; or

  (d) to enable any of the things mentioned in paragraphs (a) to (c) above to be done.[30]

The 1990 Act provided that, as with the unauthorised access offence, the prosecution would have to demonstrate that an accused person had acted intentionally. The 2006 modifications reduce the burden somewhat in requiring that conduct may be either intentional or reckless as to whether impairment will be caused.

---

[28] <http://www.ft.com/cms/s/0/50448d3a-ce50-11e2-8313-00144feab7de.html#axzz2lBZTGul2>.
[29] Computer Misuse Act 1990, s. 17.   [30] s. 3(2).

At the most basic level of activity, this provision would apply in the situation where a user intentionally causes the deletion of programs or data held on a computer. The manner in which this is accomplished will be immaterial. At the simplest level, the user may operate delete functions so as to remove programs or data.[31] In the first prosecution brought under this provision of the Computer Misuse Act 1990, the accused had installed a security package on a computer belonging to a firm which he claimed owed some £2,000 in fees. The effect of the installation was to prevent the computer being used unless a password was entered. As this was not disclosed, the computer was effectively rendered unusable for several days, with resultant losses estimated at some £36,000. The accused was convicted and fined £1,650.[32]

An offence may also be committed when data is added to a computer system. One instance of this, which will be discussed later, occurs when a computer is infected with a virus. The offence will also be committed where logic bombs or other programs are added to the computer system with the intent that these will operate so as to cause inconvenience to the computer user. In one instance, an IT manager added a program to his employer's system which had the effect of encrypting incoming data. The data would automatically be decrypted when it was subsequently accessed. The manager left his employment following a disagreement and some time later the decryption function ceased to operate. Once again, the effect was to render the computer unusable. Despite claims that the encryption function was intended as a security device and that the failure of the decryption facility was an unforeseen error, the manager was convicted of an offence under the Computer Misuse Act 1990.[33]

A further case brought under the legislation concerned a contract for the supply of bespoke software. The customer was late in making payment for the software and shortly afterwards the software stopped working. It transpired that the supplier, anticipating possible problems with payment, had inserted a timelock function. Unless removed by the supplier upon receipt of payment, the software would stop working from a specified date. This conduct resulted in prosecution and conviction under the unauthorised modification offence.[34]

The issues raised in this case are undoubtedly less clear-cut than in a number of the other prosecutions brought under the Computer Misuse Act. It was argued that the use of such timelocks was a legitimate response to the failure of the customer to meet the contractual obligation to pay for the software. A further point which does not appear to have been raised was whether the supplier would retain sufficient intellectual property rights in the software to be entitled to control its continued use. It could also be argued that the action would have been lawful had notice been given to the customer of the fact that the software would stop working if payment was not made timeously.

It may be that the drafting of the offence is sufficiently broad to make the mere act of unauthorised use illegal. An example might concern an employee who types a private letter using their employer's computer. As section 3(5) of the Computer Misuse Act states

---

[31] The use of such commands may well remove details of the programs or data from any directories. The program or data will not be removed at that stage, the effect of the command being to render it liable to being overwritten as further programs or data are added to the computer. Such conduct will constitute the unauthorised modification offence, even though the 'damage' may be recoverable.

[32] *R v Whitaker* (1993) Scunthorpe Magistrates' Court. Details of this and a range of other prosecutions under the Computer Misuse Act 1990 are reported in R. Battcock, 'Prosecutions under the Computer Misuse Act', *Computers and Law* 6 (1996), p. 22.

[33] Battcock 'Prosecutions under the Computer Misuse Act', p. 22.

[34] Battcock 'Prosecutions under the Computer Misuse Act', p. 22.

that the fact whether a modification is permanent or temporary is immaterial, it would not even appear that there is a necessity for the text of the letter to be stored on the computer. In the event that a portion of text is stored on a computer's hard disk, utilising only a minuscule fraction of the disk's storage capacity, any degree of impairment of the computer's capabilities will be similarly minute. The Act, however, does not require that the degree of impairment be substantial or significant. Such conditions would add further levels of complexity and uncertainty to the task of defining the scope of the legislation. It is to be recognised, however, that the act of making an unauthorised act constitutes only one element of the offence and that the prosecution is required, additionally, to establish that the party responsible intended to impair the operation of the computer or was reckless as to whether impairment was caused.[35] In addition to proscribing acts impairing the operation of a computer, the unauthorised act offence may be committed when data held on a computer is modified in a fashion which may affect its reliability. A possible scenario might involve an individual giving false information with a view to causing the modification of an unfavourable entry on a credit reference agency's files. This might render unreliable the data held on the computer and, as such, may constitute an offence under section 3.

Taking the concept of an unauthorised modification as a whole, it would seem clear that the offence might be committed by a person who creates a computer virus and sends it out into the world with the intention that it will infect other computers. The Computer Misuse Act provides in this respect that:

1. The intent need not be directed at—

    (a) any particular computer;

    (b) any particular program or data or a program or data of any particular kind; or

    (c) any particular modification or a modification of any particular kind.[36]

A virus creator will therefore cause the modification of any computer which is infected, even though they may not be directly responsible for the infection of any particular machine, this being brought about by an unsuspecting (or even reckless) authorised user. To this extent, the phrase 'to cause' must be interpreted in two senses: in respect of the act which causes the effect and also of the act which is proximately responsible for its occurrence.

One of the early and extensively publicised cases brought under the Computer Misuse Act involved the prosecution of Christopher Pile. Using the pseudonym 'Black Baron', the accused was reported as having told detectives that 'he had wanted to create a British virus which would match the worst of those from overseas'. A number of viruses were created by Pile and concealed in seemingly innocuous programs which he published on the Internet; from there they would infect any computer onto which they were downloaded. It was estimated that the effects of the virus cost companies in the region of £500,000 and Pile secured the dubious distinction of being the first virus writer convicted under the Act, being sentenced to a term of eighteen months' imprisonment.[37]

Denial-of-service attacks

Whilst there was no doubt that the original section 3 offence was an effective tool against those disseminating viruses, conduct involving denial-of-service attacks was widely

---

[35] s. 2(2).   [36] s. 3(3).   [37] M2 Presswire, 24 March 1997.

perceived as more problematic. The All Party Internet Group in its report on the Computer Misuse Act[38] reported that:

> Almost every respondent from industry told us that the CMA is not adequate for dealing with DoS and DDoS (Distributed Denial of Service) attacks, though very few gave any detailed analysis of why they believed this to be so. We understand that this widespread opinion is based on some 2002 advice by the Crown Prosecution Service (CPS) that s 3 might not stretch to including all DoS activity.
>
> In contrast the Government, many academic lawyers and also, we understand, the NHTCU (National High Technology Crime Unit), believe that s 3 is sufficiently broad to cover DoS attacks. In April 2003 the Internet Crime Forum (ICF) Legal Subgroup pointed out that s 3 did not require unauthorised access, merely unauthorised 'modification of the contents of any computer'. They expressed the opinion that the test applied would be whether the attack had rendered unreliable the data stored on a computer or impaired its operation.[39]

The revised wording introduced by the Police and Justice Act by referring to conduct intended to impair or enable the impairment of the operation of any computer is intended to make it clear that denial-of-service attacks are unlawful. In a manner similar to the applicability of the offence of criminal damage, as the 2006 Act was proceeding through Parliament, the Divisional Court declared unequivocally in the case of *DPP v Lennon*[40] that denial-of-service attacks were caught by the original offence. The respondent in the case had admitted downloading a mail-bombing program called Avalanche from the Internet and using this to bombard his former employers with emails. The program has been promoted in the following terms:

> Avalanche is a Windows 3.x and Windows 95/NT based mail-bombing program that was developed by *H-Master*. Unlike the other bombers, Avalanche comes with a number of configuration files that permits the attacker to customize, create, and select random mail headers and messages. Using a sophisticated GUI, the bomber can select the number of mail messages to send or can force the program to send messages continuously until explicitly stopped. For anonymity, Avalanche *'features'* fake mail headers with several built-in anonymous SMTP servers. Avalanche is distributed with over 20 pages of documentation consisting of a detailed user's guide, a *Tips for Bombing* tutorial, and an *Addon Implementation Guide*. The Addon support functionality is a unique feature of Avalanche, which permits the bomber to add new attacks and functionality to the tool without recompiling the source code. Also similar to KaBoom and Up Yours, Avalanche can be used to subscribe Internet citizens to numerous mailing lists without their knowledge.[41]

Over the course of a weekend, around 5 million emails were sent, the majority of which purported to come from the company's human-resource manager who had been responsible for dismissing the respondent. Charges were brought under section 3 of the 1990 Act but the trial judge expressed the view that:

1. Section 3 was intended to deal with the sending of malicious material such as viruses, worms and Trojan horses which corrupt or change data, but not the sending of emails;

---

[38] Formerly available from <http://www.apcomms.org.uk/apig/archive/activities-2004/computer-misuse-inquiry/CMAReportFinalVersion1.pdf>.   [39] paras. 60–1.
[40] [2006] EWHC 1201 (Admin).   [41] < http://www.thecepblog.com/papers/html/bomb/node21.html>.

2. as D&G's servers were configured to receive emails, each modification occurring on the receipt of an email sent by Mr Lennon was unauthorized.[42]

It appears that the report of the case is in error on this point and that the judge was in fact holding that each modification was authorised. Accordingly, he held that there was no case to answer. The prosecutor appealed against this ruling and the Divisional Court was unequivocally of the view that denial-of-service attacks were covered by section 3. Delivering the leading judgment, Mr Justice Jack held that although a party with an email address must give some consent to receipt of emails and for any consequential addition of data to the computer system involved, this:

> plainly does not cover emails which are not sent for the purpose of communication with the owner, but are sent for the purpose of interrupting the proper operation and use of his system. That was the plain intent of Mr Lennon in using the Avalanche program. The difference can be demonstrated in this way. If Mr Lennon had telephoned Ms Rhodes and requested consent to send her an email raising a point about the termination of his employment, she would have been puzzled as to why he bothered to ask and said that of course he might. If he had asked if he might send the half million emails he did send, he would have got a quite different answer. In short the purpose of Mr Lennon in sending the half million emails was an unauthorised purpose and the use made of D&G's email facility was an unauthorised use.

Accordingly, the case was remitted back for trial with the suggestion that:

> One test which the District Judge might consider applying is the answer which Mr Lennon would have expected had he asked D&G whether he might start Avalanche—a point I have referred to in paragraph 9 above. I mention that because it seems to me that it points to the reality of the situation, something which, I consider, has been rather missed in this case thus far.

The respondent was subsequently convicted and sentenced to a two-month period of electronic curfew.

Misuse of devices

As indicated in the *Lennon* case, a wide range of devices may be used in connection with criminal conduct aimed at computers. A market also exists for trading in user names and passwords. Article 6 of the Cybercrime Convention seeks to deter such activities by providing that:

> Each Party shall adopt such legislative and other measures as may be necessary to establish as criminal offences under its domestic law, when committed intentionally and without right:
>
> (a) the production, sale, procurement for use, import, distribution or otherwise making available of:
>
>> (i) a device, including a computer program, designed or adapted primarily for the purpose of committing any of the offences established in accordance with the above Articles 2 through 5;
>>
>> (ii) a computer password, access code, or similar data by which the whole or any part of a computer system is capable of being accessed,
>
> with intent that it be used for the purpose of committing any of the offences established in Articles 2 through 5; and

---

[42] para. 7.

(b) the possession of an item referred to in paragraphs a.i or ii above, with intent that it be used for the purpose of committing any of the offences established in Articles 2 through 5. A Party may require by law that a number of such items be possessed before criminal liability attaches.

The Police and Justice Act 2006 adds a new section 3A to the Computer Misuse Act, providing that:

1. A person is guilty of an offence if he makes, adapts, supplies or offers to supply any article intending it to be used to commit, or to assist in the commission of, an offence under Section 1 or 3.

2. A person is guilty of an offence if he supplies or offers to supply any article believing that it is likely to be used to commit, or to assist in the commission of, an offence under Section 1 or 3.

3. A person is guilty of an offence if he obtains any article with a view to its being supplied for use to commit, or to assist in the commission of, an offence under Section 1 or 3.

4. In this Section 'article' includes any program or data held in electronic form.

In summary proceedings, the offence attracts a maximum penalty of twelve months' imprisonment (six in Scotland) or two years' following conviction on indictment.

Although there has been general support for the principles behind the measure, the manner of its implementation was subjected to extensive criticism in Parliament. The perceived problem lay in the fact that those developing and supplying tools used legitimately for checking computer security know that there is a very strong likelihood that the devices will also prove attractive to those whose intentions are more malign. The United Kingdom approach is perhaps somewhat stricter than that required by the Convention, which refers to articles 'primarily' used for criminal purposes. It is suggested, however, that liability will (or should) arise only in the event that a developer or distributor supplies articles, knowing that it is likely that the particular acquirer will use them for criminal purposes.

Malicious communications

Considerable publicity has been given to the use of social-media sites to disseminate communications which might be regarded as threatening to other people. The case of *Chambers v DPP*[43] is a significant authority. In this case the appellant had been annoyed when a flight from his local airport to take him to visit his girl friend was cancelled because of bad weather. He posted a message via his Twitter account:

Crap! Robin Hood Airport is closed. You've got a week and a bit to get your shit together otherwise I am blowing the airport sky high!!

The message came to the attention of airport employees who reported the posting to the police. The appellant was subsequently charged with and convicted of an offence under section 127 of the Communications Act 2003. This provides that an offence is committed by a person who uses a public communications network to send (or causes to be sent) 'a message or other matter that is grossly offensive or of an indecent, obscene or menacing character'. It is also unlawful under the provision if the message is intended to cause 'annoyance,

---

[43] [2012] EWHC 2157.

inconvenience or needless anxiety to another' either by virtue of its contents or by reason of the frequency with which communications are sent. The offence can be punished by a term of imprisonment of up to six months.

The appellant's defence was that the post was intended as a joke. This view received some support in the initial police report on the case which noted that:

> Male detained re making threats to Doncaster Robin Hood Airport. The male in question has been bailed and his phone/computer has been seized—there is no evidence at this stage to suggest that there is anything other than a foolish comment posted on 'Twitter' as a joke for only his close friends to see.

The Crown Court, however, ruled that the message was of such a nature as to be considered 'menacing' per se. Some emphasis was put on the fact that the message had been seen by security services at the airport and reported to the police. It subsequently transpired that this was due less to genuine apprehension on their part than to a legal obligation to report any possible threat, however trivial it might appear, and convicted the appellant on the basis that he must either have intended the message to be regarded in this way or, at the least, been aware that it might have been so regarded by a recipient.

The High Court, overturning the conviction, disagreed with the approach adopted by the Crown Court. The key element of its decision was the finding that the message could not properly be regarded as menacing. Such a conclusion had to be reached after a thorough consideration of all of the circumstances of the case. The High Court commented:

> Before concluding that a message is criminal on the basis that it represents a menace, its precise terms, and any inferences to be drawn from its precise terms, need to be examined in the context in and the means by which the message was sent.

Whilst recognizing the high level of concern relating to the possibility of terrorist attacks, the message, it was ruled, did not contain any menace. Whilst criminals and terrorists can behave in as stupid a manner as anyone else, it would be an incredibly stupid individual who posted a genuine threat on Twitter under his own name.

> Much more significantly, although it purports to address 'you', meaning those responsible for the airport, it was not sent to anyone at the airport or anyone responsible for airport security, or indeed any form of public security. The grievance addressed by the message is that the airport is closed when the writer wants it to be open. The language and punctuation are inconsistent with the writer intending it to be or to be taken as a serious warning. [para. 31]

Having determined that the message was not of a menacing nature, the appellant's conviction was quashed. The court went on, however to give some consideration to the issue of mens rea. It pointed out that the statutory formulation referring to a person sending (or causing to be sent) a malicious message, referred exclusively to the state of mind of the sender. If it could be established that the message was intended 'as a joke, even if a poor joke in bad taste, it is unlikely that the mens rea required before conviction for the offence of sending a message of a menacing character will be established' (at para. 38).

Also relevant in this context are the Protection from Harassment Act 1997 (amended in part by the Serious Organised Crime and Police Act 2005) and the the Malicious Communications Act of 1998 (which was amended by the Criminal Justice and Police Act 2001). The 1997 Act provides in section 1 that a person must not pursue a course of harassment. In determining what forms of conduct will constitute harassment the Act provides that it is to be determined by reference to 'a reasonable person in possession of the same information would think the course of conduct amounted to harassment of the other' (person). A 'course of harassment' requires that conduct occur on at least two occasions. The conduct may be directed against a single person or a group of individuals. In the case of *Dowson v Chief Constable of Northumbria Police*[44] six elements were set out as being relevant to the question of whether conduct might amount to harassment:

1. There must be conduct which occurs on at least two occasions,

2. which is targeted at the claimant,

3. which is calculated in an objective sense to cause alarm or distress, and

4. which is objectively judged to be oppressive and unacceptable.

5. What is oppressive and unacceptable may depend on the social or working context in which the conduct occurs.

6. A line is to be drawn between conduct which is unattractive and unreasonable and conduct which has been described in various ways: 'torment' of the victim, 'of an order which would sustain criminal liability' (at para. 142).

It is not necessary that the messages be seen by their target. See *S v Director of Public Prosecutions*.[45]

In most cases, the penalty for the offence of harassment is a sentence of up to six months' imprisonment (section 2). Where the conduct conveys a threat of violence this increases to a maximum term of five years' imprisonment (section 4). In addition to the initial criminal offence, the Act provides in section 3 that a victim may seek a civil court order prohibiting continuance of the conduct. Any breach of such an order can be punishable by up to five years' imprisonment. An example of such an action can be seen in the case of *AMP v Persons Unknown*.[46] In this case the claimant, whose identity was concealed, had her mobile phone either stolen or lost. On it were a number of sexually explicit photos that she had taken to send to her boyfriend. Shortly afterwards copies of the photos were uploaded to a website. The claimant was able to persuade the website to delete them but was faced with messages from a person threatening to publish them more widely online unless she agreed to become a Facebook friend with him (or her). An action was brought before the High Court seeking, inter alia, the making of an order under section 3 of the 1997 Act. Considering the dicta in *Dowson v Chief Constable of Northumbria Police*, the court granted an order effective against any person within the court's jurisdiction prohibiting the publication of the images in question.

The Malicious Communications Act provides in section 2 that an offence (punishable by a sentence of up to six months' imprisonment) is committed by a person who sends to another person any electronic communication which is indecent or grossly offensive, threatening, or—to the knowledge of the sender—false. The offence will be committed when it is established that the sender's purpose (or one of his purposes) was to cause distress or anxiety to the intended recipient or recipients.

Conclusions

Nearly twenty years of computer crime legislation has seen perhaps more than its share of ups and downs. Although a number of judgments limiting the scope of the Computer Misuse Act 1990 have been overturned by the higher courts, it is tempting to recall the

---

[44] [2010] EWHC 2621(QB).   [45] [2008] 1 WLR 2847.   [46] [2011] EWHC 3454 (TCC).

words of the Law Commission, arguing that 'There is recurrent (and understandable) difficulty in explaining to judges, magistrates and juries how the facts fit in with the present law of criminal damage', and reflect that perhaps rather little has changed.

The 2006 changes expand substantially the scope and complexity of the legislation and it may be excessively optimistic to predict an untroubled future.

11

Computer fraud and forgery

Introduction

As indicated in the previous chapter, computer fraud was probably the first form of computer-related conduct to attract the attention of the criminal law. The concept of fraud has, of course, featured in the criminal law for many centuries and in the case where the perpetrator seeks to secure direct and umnmerited financial gain the fact that a computer is involved makes no signicant impact. If a person obtains a debit card and PIN number and withdraws money from a cash machine without the consent of the account holder an offence is committed. One area where there may be issues, especially with global financial networks, is when and where an offence is committed. More complex legal issues arise where the pecuniary advantage gained takes the form of avoiding charges that would otherwise have to be paid. A simple example from the non-computer world might be the attempt to make a train journey without purchasing a ticket.

As discussed previously in the context of the case of *R v Gold*, problems have been identified in identifying what offence might be committed in cases where a perpetrator interacts only with a machine. Traditionally, English law offences were based on the notion that the perpetrator had made a false pretence. The Theft Act 1968 introduced the new notion of obtaining goods or services by deception. The change was justified on the ground that it focused attention on the impact of the conduct on the victim. This is perhaps a questionable approach in any event. In the train example given above it is perhaps hard to see a train-operating company as a human victim. It does, of course, also raise the metaphysical point whether a machine can be deceived.

Along with the notion of computer fraud we have another well-established criminal offence, that of forgery. In previous eras we had forged banknotes and coins. Today we may have forged (or cloned) debit and credit cards. As with fraud, in many cases there will be no doubt that an offence has been committed but evidential and jurisdictional difficulties in securing a conviction.

As with other aspects of the topic, the provisions of the Council of Europe's Cybercrime Convention have significantly influenced United Kingdom law in the field. Title 2 is headed Computer-related Offences and Articles 7 and 8 call for the criminalisation of computer-related forgery and computer-related fraud, providing that:

> Each Party shall adopt such legislative and other measures as may be necessary to establish as criminal offences under its domestic law, when committed intentionally and without right, the input, alteration, deletion, or suppression of computer data, resulting in inauthentic data with the intent that it be considered or acted upon for legal purposes as if it were authentic, regardless whether or not the data is directly readable and intelligible. A Party may require an intent to defraud, or similar dishonest intent, before criminal liability attaches.

Each Party shall adopt such legislative and other measures as may be necessary to establish as criminal offences under its domestic law, when committed intentionally and without right, the causing of a loss of property to another person by:

(a) any input, alteration, deletion or suppression of computer data,

(b) any interference with the functioning of a computer system,

with fraudulent or dishonest intent of procuring, without right, an economic benefit for oneself or for another person.

Computer-related forgery

Although its application proved somewhat disastrous in the case of *R v Gold*,[1] there is no doubt that the provisions of the Forgery and Counterfeiting Act 1981 could successfully be applied to most instances of computer-related forgery. Perhaps the leading authority on the point is the case *of R v Governor of Brixton Prison and anor, ex p Levin*.[2] This case concerned extradition proceedings, following a partially successful attempt by a number of computer hackers based in Russia to access customer account details on computers belonging to Citibank in the United States and to transfer balances to accounts controlled by members of the conspiracy. Although the balances were transferred and some sums of money withdrawn, the conduct was discovered. Some of the conspirators were arrested in the United States and the applicant was arrested by the United Kingdom authorities when he arrived at Stansted Airport, reportedly en route to a computer exhibition in London. The United States applied for him to be extradited to stand trial there. In line with normal provisions of extradition law, this request could be granted only if the conduct alleged would consititute an offence in the place where the individual was being held—England. Attention focused on the provisions of the Forgery and Counterfeiting Act 1981. Section 1 of the Act provides that:

A person is guilty of forgery if he makes a false instrument, with the intention to induce somebody to accept it as genuine to his own or any other person's prejudice.

As in *R v Gold*, the issue before the court concerned the identity of the false instrument. The applicant's conduct had caused modifications to be made to the data held on computer storage devices within Citibank. That constituted an instrument and in response to the issue of whether it should be classed as 'false', the court ruled that:

We consider the disk embraces the information stored as well as the medium on which it is stored, just as a document consists both of the paper and the printing upon it. Thus by entering false instructions onto the disk it was in our opinion falsified.[3]

Repelling arguments advanced by counsel for the applicant that the House of Lords decision in *R v Gold* indicated that such a disk could not be an instrument, the court referred to Lord Brandon's judgment in the House of Lords and his approval of the comments of the Law Commission, whose *Report on Forgery and Counterfeit Currency*[4] stated that a forged document contained two messages: one as to the nature of the document, and the second relating to the words intended to be acted upon. In the present case it was concluded, unlike

---

[1] [1988] 1 AC 1063.   [2] [1997] QB 65.   [3] [1997] QB 65 at 79.
[4] Law Commission No. 55, 1973.

the situation in *R v Gold* where data was held in the victim computer only momentarily, the data:

> were inserted onto the disk with the purpose that they should be recorded, stored and acted upon. The instructions purported to be authorised instructions given by Bank Artha Graha to Citibank. They were not authorised and in our view the disk with the instructions recorded and stored on it amounted to a false instrument.[5]

Computer-related fraud

Fraud is a somewhat complex area of the law and is capable of encompassing a wide range of forms of conduct. The simplest, in many respects, is where a perpetrator seeks to obtain money belonging to someone else by means of some form of trick or unauthorised conduct. In respect of this form of conduct, there will be little doubt concerning its criminality of conduct. Both Law Commissions, for example, expressed the view that 'when a computer is manipulated in order dishonestly to obtain money or other property, a charge of theft or attempted theft will generally lie'.[6]

If there is little doubt concerning the fact that once another person's property has been obtained, an offence will be committed, one matter which assumes some significance is the question of when the offence is committed. In this respect, the case of *R v Thompson*[7] furnishes a helpful illustration.

Thompson was employed as a computer programmer by a bank in Kuwait. Details of customers' accounts were maintained on the bank's computer system and, in the course of his work, Thompson was able to obtain information about these. Having identified five target accounts, Thompson opened an equal number of accounts in his own name at various branches of the bank. In what might be regarded as a classic form of computer fraud, he compiled a program which instructed the computer to transfer sums from these accounts to accounts which he had opened with the bank. In an effort to reduce further the risks of detection, the program did not come into effect until Thompson had left the bank's employ to return to England. The program was also intended to erase itself and all records of the transactions once this task had been accomplished. Although the law report does not go into detail on this matter, the fact that Thompson stood trial for his actions might indicate that this part of the scheme was not successful.

On his arrival in England, Thompson opened a number of accounts with English banks and wrote to the manager of the Kuwaiti bank, instructing him to arrange for the transfer of the balances from Kuwait to his new English accounts. This was done. Subsequently, his conduct was discovered and charges of obtaining property by deception were brought against him and a conviction secured at trial. An appeal was lodged on the basis that the English courts had no jurisdiction in the matter, as any offence would have been committed in Kuwait.

This plea did not commend itself to the Court of Appeal, which held that the offence was committed at the moment when the Kuwaiti manager read and acted upon Thompson's letter. At this stage, Thompson was subject to the jurisdiction of the English courts. Delivering the judgment of the court, May LJ stated:

> Discard for the moment the modern sophistication of computers and programmes [*sic*] and consider the old days when bank books were kept in manuscript in large ledgers. In

---

[5] [1997] QB 65 at 80.   [6] Law Commission Working Paper No. 110 (1988), para. 3.4.
[7] [1984] 3 All ER 565.

effect all that was done by the appellant through the modern computer in the present case was to take a pen and debit each of the five accounts in the ledger with the relevant sums and then credit each of his own five savings accounts in the ledger with corresponding amounts. On the face of it his savings accounts would then have appeared to have in them substantially more than in truth they did have, as the result of his forgeries; but we do not think that by those forgeries any bank clerk in the days before computers would in law have thus brought into being a chose in action capable of being stolen or of being obtained by deception.[8]

The conclusion that no offence involving theft or the fraudulent obtaining of property had been committed at the stage of making the false entry on the computer does not entail that no offence would have been involved. Thompson's conduct, had it taken place in the United Kingdom, might have constituted forgery under the terms of the Forgery and Counterfeiting Act. It is also likely that, following the decision in *Allison*, discussed in the previous chapter, and in *Levin*, discussed earlier in this one, the appellant would have committed offences under sections 1, 2, and 3 of the Computer Misuse Act, with the section 3 offence now attracting a maximum jail term of ten years. More recent reform has come with the enactment of the Fraud Act 2006, following the Law Commission's *Report on Fraud* published in 2002.[9]

Deception of a machine

In part, this issue can be seen as having arisen through a well-meaning, though perhaps short-sighted, incident of law reform. Under the provisions of the Larceny Act 1916,[10] conduct involving a machine might have been prosecuted on the ground of obtaining services by means of a false pretence. This remains the basis of liability in Scots law, and, in its Consultative Memorandum,[11] the Scottish Law Commission expressed the view that in determining whether this offence has been committed, attention should be paid to the conduct of the perpetrator. If the intention is to obtain services dishonestly, the offence will be committed and the fact of whether the conduct operates upon a human or a machine is irrelevant.

In England, the *Eighth Report of the Criminal Law Revision Committee* recommended a shift from false pretence to deception, on the basis that the word deception:

> has the advantage of directing attention to the effect that the offender deliberately produced on the mind of the person deceived, whereas 'false pretence' makes one think of what exactly the offender did in order to deceive.[12]

This report was published in 1966, long before the problems of the computer had fully penetrated general legal consciousness. Its recommendations were adopted in the Theft Act 1968, which defines the concept of 'deception' as involving:

> any deception (whether deliberate or reckless) by words or conduct as to fact or as to law, including a deception as to the present intentions of the person using the deception or any other person.[13]

---

[8] *R v Thompson* [1984] 3 All ER 565 at 569. The decision in *Thompson* has been strongly criticised by T. Smith in *Property Offences* (London, 1994), paras. 325–6, on the basis that if the transaction in Kuwait had been a nullity, its transfer to the United Kingdom could not become the theft of a 'chose in action'.

[9] Law Commission No. 276.   [10] s. 32(1).

[11] Sc Law Commission Consultative Memorandum No. 68 (1986), para. 3.9.

[12] 'Theft and Related Offences', Cmnd 2977 (1966), para. 87.   [13] s. 15(4).

Although the point was never definitively settled, it was widely assumed that only a human being could be the victim of deception. In the case of *Davies v Flackett*,[14] a motorist was charged with obtaining car-parking services by deception. The car park in question had an automatic barrier control at its exit. Upon a motorist inserting payment of 5p into a machine, the barrier would be raised, allowing egress. The appellant approached the exit barrier, only to discover passengers from the preceding car forcibly lifting the barrier to allow that car to leave. Considerately, they remained holding the barrier and invited the appellant to follow. This conduct was observed by the police, who proved less charitably disposed, charging the appellant (and presumably the other actors in the drama) with dishonestly obtaining a pecuniary advantage by deception, contrary to section 16 of the Theft Act 1968. The charge against the appellant was dismissed by the justices on the basis that a machine had no mind and therefore could not constitute the victim of a deception. The prosecution appealed, seeking the opinion of the Divisional Court on the question of whether 'an act of deception directed towards a machine in the absence of any human agent is sufficient to support a prima facie case in the preferred information'.[15]

The Divisional Court agreed with the justices that the defendant should be acquitted, but expressed the view that the major flaw in the charge lay in the absence of any evidence that the defendant intended to evade payment. The evidence, it was held, indicated that the defendant had intended to pay when he entered the car park and remained of this intention until the very last moment, when the opportunity to avoid payment was presented to him. The question whether a machine could be deceived was treated very much as a subsidiary question, and differing views were expressed by the judges. Bridge J indicated doubt that this might be the case, commenting 'even if it is possible for a deception to be practised so as to establish that ingredient of the offence under Section 16 [of the Theft Act 1968] without there being a human mind to deceive (though for myself I doubt it)',[16] whilst Acker J, after holding that the case was not properly to be regarded as one involving deception of a machine, stated:

> Nothing which I say expressing my agreement that this appeal should be dismissed in any way suggests that an offence cannot be committed where there is any mishandling of a machine, and thereby an advantage is incurred.[17]

Rather like a ticking time bomb, the comments in *Davies* were to lie dormant for a period of years but ultimately produced explosive results when, rather than seeking a definitive ruling on the point, the decision was taken to bring the prosecution in the case of *R v Gold*[18] under the terms of the Forgery and Counterfeiting Act 1981. The acquittal of the Prestel hackers gave considerable impetus to the move to introduce computer-specific legislation.

In 2002, the Law Commission published a *Report on Fraud*.[19] This gave extensive attention to the question of whether a machine might constitute the victim in a scheme of deception. Initially, it was commented that:

> A machine has no mind, so it cannot believe a proposition to be true or false, and therefore cannot be deceived. A person who dishonestly obtains a benefit by giving false information to a computer or machine is not guilty of any deception offence. Where the benefit obtained is property, he or she will normally be guilty of theft, but where it is something other than property (such as a service), there may be no offence at all.[20]

---

[14] [1973] RTR 8. [15] [1973] RTR 8 at 10. [16] *Davies v Flackett* [1973] RTR 8 at 11.
[17] [1973] RTR 8 at 11. [18] [1988] 1 AC 1063. [19] Law Commission No. 276.
[20] Law Commission No. 276, para. 3.34.

Although consideration was given to the possibility that reform should provide that a machine could be deceived, it was concluded that this form of conduct should be criminalised under a new offence of dishonestly obtaining services. This offence will be considered later. In respect of the general law of fraud, it was proposed that there should be a shift from reliance upon the concept of deception to revert to a focus on the behaviour and intentions of the perpetrator. Accepting the Law Commission's recommendations, the Fraud Act was adopted. This provides in section 2 that:

(1) A person is in breach of this Section if he—

    (a) dishonestly makes a false representation, and

    (b) intends, by making the representation—

        (i) to make a gain for himself or another, or

        (ii) to cause loss to another or to expose another to a risk of loss.

(2) A representation is false if—

    (a) it is untrue or misleading, and

    (b) the person making it knows that it is, or might be, untrue or misleading.

The Law Commission had considered that this provision would have been sufficient to deal with the situation where a person's contact was only (or largely) with a machine. An example might be where a party obtains a credit card and PIN number belonging to someone else and uses this to obtain goods, either over the Internet or by using a chip and PIN machine in a shop. The government argued, however, that:

> We do not want law enforcers to face unreasonably technical choices in making charges and we consider therefore that the Bill should make it clear that a false representation should be an offence whether made to a machine or to a person. This is done by making amendments to provide expressly that representations may be implied and that a representation may be regarded as being made where it or anything implying it is submitted to any system or device, the aim being to clarify, for example, that the entering of a number into a chip-and-pin machine is a representation.[21]

Accordingly, a further subsection was introduced, providing that:

(5) For the purposes of this Section a representation may be regarded as made if it (or anything implying it) is submitted in any form to any system or device designed to receive, convey or respond to communications (with or without human intervention).

In line with developments in the field of computer crime generally, further provision is made to criminalise various forms of dealings in respect of materials that may be used to facilitate a scheme of fraud. Section 6 of the Act provides that possession of an article for use in the commission of a fraud will itself constitute an offence, whilst section 7 provides that:

(1) A person is guilty of an offence if he makes, adapts, supplies or offers to supply any article—

    (a) knowing that it is designed or adapted for use in the course of or in connection with fraud, or

    (b) intending it to be used to commit, or assist in the commission of, fraud.

---

[21] HL Official Report, vol. 679, col. 1106, 14 March 2006.

By section 8, it is provided that '"article" includes any program or data held in electronic form'. Lists of passwords or PIN numbers would come within the scope of this definition.

The dishonest obtaining of services

Money is not the only thing of value in the world. Increasingly, information may be the most significant asset of many businesses. It has long been the case that where information is linked to some tangible object, the informational content may be taken into account in determining the gravity of any offence. In terms of physical components—paper and ink—there will be virtually no difference between a £5 and a £50 note, but theft of the latter will be a more serious matter than theft of the former. It is well established, however, that information taken in isolation will not constitute property which may serve as the subject matter for an offence of theft.

A vast market exists for the provision of electronic information services. In the legal field, information services such as 'Lexis' and 'Westlaw' offer their wares to the legal world—at a price. In a typical scenario, a person wishing to make use of an information service will enter into an agreement with the service provider, and be provided with a password or other identifier, allowing access to all or part of the contents of the database in return for an agreement to make specified payments.

In the event that a party manages to secure unauthorised access to such a database, either by dishonestly obtaining password details or by finding a way to bypass the security system, information will be obtained without proper payment being made. The provisions of section 2 of the Fraud Act described above will not be applicable to the situation where services are involved as it is provided that the terms 'gain' and 'loss' 'extend only to gain or loss in money or other property'.[22] Services cannot come within the scope of this definition.

Recognising that it is more and more common for services to be supplied in situations where a party's only contact is with a computer or some other form of machine, the Law Commission recommended the establishment of a new offence involving the dishonest obtaining of services. Whilst falling short of providing that information could constitute the subject matter of theft, the offence is described as being 'theft-like' in nature. It was accordingly recommended that:

Any person who by any dishonest act obtains services in respect of which payment is required, with intent to avoid payment, should be guilty of an offence of obtaining services dishonestly.[23]

Acting upon this recommendation, the Fraud Act provides in section 11 that:

(1) A person is guilty of an offence under this Section if he obtains services for himself or another—

    (a) by a dishonest act, and

    (b) in breach of Subsection 2.

(2) A person obtains services in breach of this Subsection if—

    (a) they are made available on the basis that payment has been, is being or will be made for or in respect of them,

    (b) he obtains them without any payment having been made for or in respect of them or without payment having been made in full, and

---

[22] s. 5.   [23] Law Commission Report 276, para. 8.13.

(c) when he obtains them, he knows—

(i) that they are being made available on the basis described in paragraph (a), or

(ii) that they might be,

but intends that payment will not be made, or will not be made in full.

In line with general practice, the Act does not provide a definition of the term 'dishonest'. The case of *Ghosh*[24] laid down a two-stage test which is generally accepted as identifying the most appropriate criteria. First, it has to be determined whether conduct would be regarded as dishonest 'according to the ordinary standards of reasonable and honest people'. If that question is answered in the affirmative, it then has to be determined whether the defendant must also have realised that the conduct was dishonest. Although such questions will be a matter for the jury in any particular case, it is difficult to imagine that conduct of the kind at issue in *R v Gold*,[25] involving the surreptitious acquisition and use of a password, would not be classed as dishonest.

Conclusions

In many respects, although of obvious practical importance, issues of computer fraud raise relatively few issues of legal significance. Taking someone else's money without justification will always constitute some form of criminal offence, the exact nature of which will vary dependent upon the nature of the conduct. The situation has been more difficult when the conduct involves evading the charges which would normally be levied in return for the provision of a service. The provisions of the Fraud Act 2006 should serve to close a loophole which had existed in English law since the move in the 1960s to reliance upon the notion of deception as the basis for this form of offence.

---

[24] [1982] QB 1053.   [25] [1988] 1 AC 1063.

12

Virtual criminality

Introduction

Previous chapters in Part II have considered how traditional crimes such as fraud and criminal damage might be committed in an online environment. In essence, the conduct at issue involves attempting either to secure pecuniary advantage or to cause some form of pecuniary loss to the victim.

Issues such as computer fraud and damage to data can be regarded, perhaps, as the first steps in the legal response to computer-related conduct. The Internet has become much more pervasive and is impacting on almost every aspect of our lives. Talk today is of the 'Internet of Things' where previously mundane devices such as fridges will have Internet connectivity to enable them to interact with supermarket systems to automatically reorder food as stock levels drop. More relevant to the aims of the present chapter, the Internet is impacting on the qualitative (and quantitative) aspects of our lives in a major fashion. OFCOM data indicates that the average UK citizen spends around thirty-five hours a month on line.[1] The growth in the use of social-networking sites over the past decade has been phenomenal.

Change seems to be an inevitable element of the online world. Perhaps five years ago much of the discussion was centred on notions of virtual worlds. Probably the best known site was 'Second Life'[2] which created much publicity. Many organsiations rushed to develop a virtual presence in this environment. Today its impact seems much reduced whilst sites such as Facebook and Twitter have come to dominate the market—for now. Essentially all social-networking sites are about communications and interaction. As in the real world, relationships can be good or bad. There is much talk today of cyberstalking or cyberbullying. In some respects these are difficult issues to discuss from a legal perspective. Many aspects of the law remain rooted in the physical world. Bullying may (not always) leave physical scars. How can this concept be transferred to an online environment where the parties do not come into any form of physical conduct?

A very high-profile aspect of the topic relates to the use of the Internet to disseminate offensive material. This is a very broad notion and in itself illustrates one of the key legislative challenges in the sector. The Council of Europe's Cybercrime Convention has a section entitled 'Content Related Offinces'. In spite of the use of the plural in its heading, the section refers only to conduct relating to child pornography. The clue to the result perhaps lies in the additional protocol to the Convention 'concerning the criminalisation of acts of a racist and xenophobic nature committed through computer systems'.[3] The need for the protocol arose because even a group of developed countries could not agree on any form of audio or visual content that should be criminalised other than child pornoraphy. We will consider aspects of that conduct later, but essentially the attempt to extend the scope of the

---

[1] <http://stakeholders.ofcom.org.uk/binaries/research/cmr/cmr13/UK_4.pdf>.
[2] <http://secondlife.com/>.   [3] <http://conventions.coe.int/Treaty/en/Treaties/Html/189.htm>.

Convention was defeated by the refusal of the United States to sign up to provisions that might well be struck down by its courts as breaching constitutional guarantees to freedom of expression—however distasteful the expressions might be. The compromise solution was to restrict the Convention to the most minimalistic level and to include other conduct in an additional Protocol—to which the UK is also not a signatory.

Internet pornography

From its earliest days, the Internet has been used for the display and transfer of pornographic and other forms of unsavoury material. Its status as a communication channel largely outside existing schemes of broadcasting and publishing regulation has made it attractive to those whose activities operate on or beyond the edges of legality. The amount of pornographic materials is a source of some contention. One widely cited source from 2010 suggested that 37 per cent of the Internet was made up of pornographic material. Intuitively, this figure does seem excessive and even the original authors have indicated that they would no longer rely on it.[4] Other estimates put the figure as low as 4 per cent. As with estimates of computer crime generally, the most accurate answer is that nobody knows. In this context also there is great uncertainty what content is unlawful with definititions varying widely between different countries.

A number of instances of successful prosecutions will be described later. Problems may, however, arise in two areas. First, there is the problem of defining or categorising the Internet. Different forms of regulation have tended to apply to different storage media and means of delivery. In part, this has been dictated by the accessibility of material. A television broadcast, for example, is more accessible than a film in a cinema and is subject to more stringent regulation. Likewise, a greater degree of tolerance has tended to be given to printed works than to photographic materials. As has and will be discussed, the Internet does not fall easily into existing categories of communications media. A second problem may prove even less soluble. The Internet is a global network. Material may be placed on a server anywhere in the world and accessed anywhere else. In theory, this means that the Internet is perhaps the most heavily regulated sphere of activity in existence, as any country may claim jurisdiction in respect of material accessible from its territory. Claiming jurisdiction is very different from being able to enforce it in any meaningful manner. If material is lawful in the country from which it originates, there may be little that any other jurisdiction can do to regulate it. In a report on the work of the United Kingdom's Internet Watch Foundation, it was suggested that of 453 reports made concerning the presence of pornographic material, in only sixty-seven cases was the material held on a United Kingdom-based server. The bulk of the material was held in the United States with, rather more surprisingly, Japan constituting the second largest host country.

Concern at the possibilities for misuse inherent in the Internet has spawned a number of international, governmental, and industry-based initiatives. In January 1999, the European Commission adopted an 'Action Plan on Promoting Safe Use of the Internet'.[5] This claims as its objective:

> promoting safer use of the Internet and of encouraging, at European level, an environment favourable to the development of the Internet industry.[6]

---

[4] <http://www.bbc.co.uk/news/technology-23030090>.
[5] Decision 276/1999, available from <http://eur-lex.europa.eu/LexUriServ/LexUriServ.do?uri=OJ:L:1999:0 33:0001:0011:EN:PDF>.   [6] Art. 2.

In order to attain this, provision was made for funding to be provided to encourage work to be conducted in the Member States, under the guidance of the Commission, in specific fields. Particular reference was made to:

- the promotion of industry self-regulation and content-monitoring schemes (for example, dealing with content such as child pornography or content which incites hatred on grounds of race, sex, religion, nationality or ethnic origin);

- encouraging industry to provide filtering tools and rating systems, which allow parents or teachers to select content appropriate for children in their care while allowing adults to decide what legal content they wish to access, and which take account of linguistic and cultural diversity;

- increasing awareness of services provided by industry among users, in particular parents, teachers, and children, so that they can better understand and take advantage of the opportunities of the Internet;

- support actions such as assessment of legal implications; and

- activities fostering international cooperation in the areas enumerated above.[7]

The 'Safer Internet Programme' was originally scheduled to run for a three-year period between 2004 and 2007, with some €38 million of funding. This was extended initially for a further two years, and a further four-year extension with a budget of €55 million was established for the period 2009–13 under the title 'Safer Internet *Plus*'.[8]

Much of the EU-funded work has concerned matters such as the development of net filters and the promotion of industry self-regulation. Within the United Kingdom, the Internet Watch Foundation was established by a number of the largest Internet Service Providers (ISPs) in 1996.[9] In part, this was a response by the industry to suggestions made by the Metropolitan Police that prosecutions might be brought against ISPs unless the industry took steps to regulate material accessible through its servers. As a number of recent cases have demonstrated, possession of material classed as child pornography is unlawful, whilst ISPs could also be classed as publishers and subject to prosecution under statutes such as the Obscene Publications Act 1964.

The Internet Watch Foundation's activities can be divided into two categories. It seeks to encourage the use of systems of content rating. A number of systems exist, such as PICS (Platform for Internet Content Selection) and RSACi, devised by the Recreational Software Advisory Council.[10] The Foundation also acts to report instances of potentially illegal material to the appropriate ISP and law enforcement agencies. To date, its efforts in seeking to prevent prosecutions being brought against service providers appear to have been successful, although it has been stressed by law enforcement agencies that no guarantee of immunity has been given. Implementation of the EU's Directive on Certain Legal Aspects of Information Society Services, in Particular Electronic Commerce, in the Internal Market[11] might reduce the liabilities of ISPs as a matter of law. Discussed in more detail in Chapter 22, this provides in Article 12 that service providers will not be liable (other than to an injunction regarding future behaviour) where the provider:

(a) does not initiate the transmission;

(b) does not select the receiver of the transmission; and

(c) does not select or modify the information contained in the transmission.

---

[7] Art. 3.   [8] <http://www.saferinternet.org/>.   [9] <http://www.iwf.org.uk/>.
[10] For information on rating schemes and a demonstration of their use, see <http://www.icra.org/>.
[11] Directive 2000/31/EC (the Electronic Commerce Directive).

The Internet and child pornography

Whilst initial concern tended to relate to pornography per se, with relatively conservative countries such as the United Kingdom fearing that national controls might be overwhelmed, attention has tended to become more and more focused on the specific topic of the use of the Internet as a vehicle for disseminating paedophilic material. Incidents such as 'Operation Ore', where the United Kingdom police forces are engaged in an ongoing investigation of several thousand United Kingdom citizens whose credit cards were used to pay for access to paedophilic sites based in the United States,[12] mean that the topic is seldom out of the news. It is perhaps testimony to the extent of public concerns that the Council of Europe's Convention on Cybercrime contains only one provision in its Title 3 Section headed 'Content Related Offences'. This provides that:

1. Each Party shall adopt such legislative and other measures as may be necessary to establish as criminal offences under its domestic law, when committed intentionally and without right, the following conduct:

   (a) producing child pornography for the purpose of its distribution through a computer system;

   (b) offering or making available child pornography through a computer system;

   (c) distributing or transmitting child pornography through a computer system;

   (d) procuring child pornography through a computer system for oneself or for another;

   (e) possessing child pornography in a computer system or on a computer-data storage medium.

2. For the purpose of paragraph 1 above 'child pornography' shall include pornographic material that visually depicts:

   (a) a minor engaged in sexually explicit conduct;

   (b) a person appearing to be a minor engaged in sexually explicit conduct;

   (c) realistic images representing a minor engaged in sexually explicit conduct.

3. For the purpose of paragraph 2 above, the term 'minor' shall include all persons under 18 years of age. A Party may, however, require a lower age-limit, which shall be not less than 16 years.

4. Each Party may reserve the right not to apply, in whole or in part, paragraph 1(d) and 1(e), and 2(b) and 2(c).[13]

The inclusion of this provision in what is intended to be a template for computer crime legislation at a global level highlights the point that there is near-universal legislative condemnation of child pornography. The Convention on Cybercrime provides no definitions

---

[12] An indication of the global scale of pornographic activity can be taken from the fact that the United States Postal Inspection Service, a federal agency charged with investigating online paedophile activity, seized records of credit card payments by some 250,000 persons, of whom around 7,000 were resident in the United Kingdom. More than two years after the details were passed to the United Kingdom authorities, although 1,230 individuals have been convicted of offences (only one prosecution having been unsuccessful) with the longest sentence being that of 12 years' imprisonment, 1,300 cases are still under investigation: <http://news.bbc.co.uk/1/hi/uk/3625603.stm>. The organiser of the original website was sentenced to 1,335 years' imprisonment.   [13] Art. 9.

of any of the terms used in Article 9. The explanatory memorandum accompanying the Convention is rather more explicit, although even here, elements of uncertainty persist. It is provided, for example, that:

The term 'pornographic material' in paragraph 2 is governed by national standards pertaining to the classification of materials as obscene, inconsistent with public morals or similarly corrupt. Therefore, material having an artistic, medical, scientific or similar merit may be considered not to be pornographic. The visual depiction includes data stored on computer diskette or on other electronic means of storage, which are capable of conversion into a visual image.

It is noteworthy that although there is absolute condemnation of those involved in the production, sale, or distribution of material, the Convention on Cybercrime leaves it open to signatory states to determine whether and to what extent the acts of obtaining or possessing material should be considered unlawful. Even in this context, international consensus is limited.

For the United Kingdom, the provisions of the Convention on Cybercrime do no more than restate existing legal provisions. The Protection of Children Act 1978 established a number of offences involving the making of photographic images of children.

Following the report of the Bryon Review, *Safer Children in a Digital World* in 2008,[14] a range of offences were established under the Coroners and Justice Act 2009 with the statute providing that it will be an offence for a person to be in possession of what is referred to as a 'prohibited image' of a child.[15] This is defined in terms of an image showing any form of sexual activity either involving a child or being carried out in the presence of a child.[16] The term 'image' includes:

(a) a moving or still image (produced by any means); or

(b) data (stored by any means) which is capable of conversion into an image within paragraph (a).

It is further provided that the term is not to include a photograph or pseudo-photograph. Effectively, it will apply to computer-generated images or to data which can be viewed on a computer.

Photographs and pseudo-photographs

In the Criminal Justice and Public Order Act 1994,[17] provisions were included to extend the ambit of the Criminal Justice Act 1988[18] and the Protection of Children Act 1978[19] to prohibit the possession or distribution of what are referred to as 'pseudo-photographs', where what appears to be an indecent image of a child is made up of a collage of images, modified by the use of computer painting packages, none of the elements of which is indecent in itself. It is now provided that an offence will be committed where:

If the impression created by a pseudo-photograph is that the person shown is a child, the pseudo-photograph shall be treated for all the purposes of this Act as showing a child and so shall a pseudo-photograph where the predominant image conveyed is that the person shown is a child notwithstanding that some of the physical characteristics shown are those of an adult.[20]

---

[14] <http://www.dcsf.gov.uk/byronreview/>.   [15] s. 62(1)   [16] s. 62(4)–(7).   [17] s. 84.
[18] s. 160.   [19] s. 1.   [20] Protection of Children Act 1978, s. 7(7).

The definition of a photograph extends to 'data stored on a computer disc or by other electronic means'.[21] Although this will certainly cover the situation where images are held on a computer disk on a permanent basis, the case of *R v Gold*[22] discussed earlier may be relevant as suggesting that a more transitory storage will not suffice. Given the development of communications technologies, possession of data or software is becoming of less importance than the knowledge that it can be accessed whenever desired.

Under the terms of the Protection of Children Act 1978, an offence is committed by a person who distributes such a photograph or who has 'in his possession such photographs or pseudo-photographs with a view to their being distributed or shown by others'.[23] The fact that possession may be a basis for conviction should give service providers cause for concern. A defence is provided that an accused 'had not himself seen the photographs or pseudo-photographs and did not know, nor had any cause to suspect, them to be indecent'.[24] In the situation where users of a service are responsible for loading images, the service provider may be able to make use of this defence. As with other areas of potential liability, it is unclear to what extent a service provider may be entitled to turn a blind eye to activities on the system. The phrase 'nor have any cause to suspect' might impose a higher standard in this area than is the case with liability for defamatory statements or conduct constituting a breach of copyright.

An indication of the conduct which would now be prosecuted under the Criminal Justice and Public Order Act 1994 can be seen in the case of *R v Fellows*.[25] The appellant, who was at the time employed by Birmingham University, had, without its knowledge or consent, compiled a large database of pornographic images of children. The database was maintained on an Internet-linked computer belonging to the university. The conduct in question occurred before the entry into force of the provisions of the 1994 Act. Given these changes to the law, it is now significant in only two respects. First, it appears to have been the first case in which the word 'Internet' appears in the judgment of an English court. Secondly, it provides an indication of the judicial response to the situation where new technology enables forms of behaviour which could not have been foreseen when statutory provisions were enacted.

Under the Protection of Children Act 1978, an offence is committed by a person possessing an indecent photograph of a child.[26] It is provided that 'references to a photograph...include the negative as well as the positive'.[27] The question before the Court of Appeal in *R v Fellows*[28] was whether images stored on a computer disk could be classed as photographs.

Answering this question in the affirmative, two issues addressed by the Court of Appeal call for comment. First, whether graphical files held on a computer fell within the statutory definition of a copy of a photograph for the purposes of the Protection of Children Act 1978, and, secondly, whether a computer hard disk containing these files could be classed as an 'article' for the purposes of the Obscene Publications Act 1959.

Although aspects of the noun 'photograph' are defined in Protection of Children Act 1978—for example, that 'references to a photograph include the positive as well as the negative version'—there is no general definition. In the Copyright Act 1956, 'photograph' was defined as 'any product of photography or of any process akin to photography'.[29] The trial judge and Evans LJ both made reference to dictionary definitions of the term as 'a picture or other image obtained by the chemical action of light or other radiation on specially

[21] Protection of Children Act 1978, s. 7(4)(b).
[22] [1988] AC 1063.   [23] s. 1(1).   [24] s. 1(4)(b).   [25] [1997] 2 All ER 548.
[26] s. 1(1)(c).   [27] s. 7(4).   [28] [1997] 2 All ER 548.   [29] s. 48.

sensitised material such as film or glass'.[30] On this basis, the data stored on the computer's hard disk could not be classed as a photograph. The statutory prohibitions, however, extended to 'a copy of a photograph'. The computerised images had been produced by scanning 'conventional' photographs and it was held that nothing in the 1978 Act required that the copy of a photograph should itself be a photograph.[31] Given the copyright status of a photograph as an artistic work and the broad definitions of copying applying to such works, there can be little ground to challenge such a finding.

Although this approach sufficed in the particular case, many cameras now record images directly onto disk rather than film. The contents of the disk may then be transferred directly to a computer and the image viewed on screen. There need never be any 'traditional' photograph to act as an original. In such a situation, it may be doubted whether even the most purposive interpretation of the Protection of Children Act 1978 could have sustained a conviction.

The Copyright, Designs and Patents Act 1988 adopted a new definition of photograph as 'a recording of light or other radiation on any medium on which an image is produced or from which an image may by any means be produced, and which is not part of a film'.[32] This marks a significant move away from the dictionary definition referred to earlier. In 1994, the Criminal Justice and Public Order Act 1994 adopted a different approach, providing that references to a photograph should include 'data stored on a computer disc or by other electronic means which is capable of conversion into a photograph'.[33] Juxtaposition of the two definitions can produce a sense of giddiness, but this aspect of changing technology does justify the need for reform of the Protection of Children Act 1978's provisions. Indeed, as is seen by the introduction of the new concept of a 'pseudo-photograph' in the 1994 Act, it may be queried whether the concept of a photograph remains apposite in the digital age. On this point, there is obiter comment by Evans LJ suggesting that the definition 'seems to us to be concerned with images created by computer processes rather than the storage and transmission by computers of images created originally by photography'.[34] Such a view appears unduly restrictive, and leaves open to question whether it would cover the situation where an original photograph was manipulated electronically so as to change the nature of the image.

Both the Obscene Publications Act 1959 and the Protection of Children Act 1978 were enacted before the impact of computers had permeated the legislature's consciousness. The Court of Appeal's judgment indicates that, providing basic concepts are robust, a purposive interpretation can maintain the relevance of statutory formulations so long as electronic activities retain a connection with tangible acts or items.[35] More substantial problems occur when electronic signals constitute the original record rather than a reproduction of a physical object. Here, law reform will often be required. It is somewhat ironic, however, that in a number of cases concerned with computer-oriented statutes, the purposive interpretative techniques adopted in the present case appear to have been replaced by a much more literal and restrictive approach.

Multimedia products

A further case concerned with the application of obscenity law to computer-related material is that of *Meechie v Multi-Media Marketing*.[36] The defendant company established

---

[30] *R v Fellows* [1997] 2 All ER 548 at 556.   [31] [1997] 2 All ER 548 at 557.   [32] s. 4(2).
[33] s. 84(4).   [34] *R v Fellows* [1997] 2 All ER 548 at 557–8.   [35] *R v Fellows* [1997] 2 All ER 548.
[36] (1995) 94 LGR 474.

a club, 'The Interactive Girls Club', described as being an 'organisation dedicated to the production of erotic computer entertainment for broad-minded adults'. One product presented users with a short game. Successful completion of this would cause the display of a series of erotic images. A knowledgeable user would have been able to isolate the game element, moving directly to the erotic display.

Under the provisions of the Video Recordings Act 1984, introduced to control the distribution of so-called 'video nasties', it is an offence to supply video recordings which have not been issued with a classification certificate. No certificate had been sought or issued for the particular game and charges were brought under sections 9 and 10 of the Act, alleging, respectively, supply and possession with a view to the supply of infringing recordings.

These charges were dismissed before the magistrates, who held that the product in question did not come within the scope of the legislation. Section 1 of the Video Recordings Act 1984 defines a 'video work' as:

any series of visual images (with or without sound)—

(a) produced electronically by the use of information contained on any disc or magnetic tape; and

(b) shown as a moving picture.

Although it was accepted that the disk in question satisfied the requirements of section 1(2)(a) of the Video Recordings Act 1984, it was held that the images did not constitute a 'moving picture' by reason both of their brevity and of the staccato nature of the presentation, which appeared more akin to a series of still images. It was further held by the magistrates that the work in question was excluded from the legislation by the provisions of section 2, which provides that a video game is not to be subject to the classification requirements.

Both of these findings were reversed by the Divisional Court.[37] In a finding which may be contrasted with the dicta of the House of Lords in *R v Gold*[38] to the effect that the term 'recording' required storage for a more than transient period of time, it was held that the short duration of the images in no way prevented their being regarded as a 'moving picture'. A significant development arising from the advent of fast and powerful personal computers has been the linkage between text, sound, and graphics. In the present case, this relates to a computer game and picture sequences, but the same could be said of most multimedia products. It would appear arguable following the decision of the Divisional Court that many multimedia products could also be classed as video recordings, and hence be required to seek classification under the regulatory schema. Although there may be an argument in favour of such an approach, it would be difficult to explain to average computer users that their multimedia encyclopaedias are in reality video recordings.

The exemptions under the legislation apply to computer games and to works 'designed to inform, educate or instruct'. In the present case,[39] the court was able to separate the picture sequences from the game-playing element and so remove the former from the scope of the exemption. It must be likely that in the future there will be instances where video images are integrated more fully with the elements of a game, thereby making the classification more difficult. This will almost inevitably be the case with multimedia products. The court's dicta, which must be seen as affording a very restricted scope to the exemption, may make

---

[37] *Meechie v Multi-Media Marketing* (1995) 94 LGR 474.   [38] [1988] AC 1063.

[39] *Meechie v Multi-Media Marketing* (1995) 94 LGR 474.

this of limited significance, and it would be arguable that many examples of multimedia products dealing with medical or artistic topics would be taken outside its scope.

A further point which may be a cause for future difficulty concerns the definition of a moving picture. Although the finding of the court to the effect that the duration of a recording is of minimal significance in determining whether it is to be classed as a 'moving picture', there cannot have been many traditional recordings with a running time of less than thirty seconds. In the present case,[40] the images could be analogised to a more traditional cinematographic recording. In other computer-related products, the duration of individual picture sequences may be very much shorter. Even more problematically, a user may be afforded the opportunity to select particular aspects of an image for expansion or, perhaps, to manipulate the form of the still image. Such activities may present the impression of movement, but it is not clear how they should be regarded for the purpose of the legislation.

Jurisdictional issues

A further, and perhaps more significant, issue concerns the difficulty of applying localised concepts of obscenity, which are dictated by cultural, religious, and societal values in the global environment of the Internet. Attempts by Nottingham County Council to prevent publication on the Internet of a copy of a summary of a report into the handling by social-work officials of a case of alleged Satanic abuse illustrate graphically the near impossibility of such an endeavour.[41] Following publication of a copy of the report on a United Kingdom-based website, the Council obtained a High Court injunction preventing publication of the report on the basis that its reproduction infringed its copyright. It was stated that the order extended to any hypertext links to other sites maintaining copies of the report. Although the order was observed within the United Kingdom, by the time it was issued, copies of the report were also to be found on a number of other websites around the world. A letter from Nottinghamshire's County Solicitor to the operator of a United States website threatening legal proceedings unless its copy was removed drew a somewhat stinging response. Admitting to the presence of a copy of a report, it was pointed out that the Council:

> ignore the fact that I and my website are located in Cleveland, Ohio, in the United States of America, a locus where the writs of the courts of the United Kingdom have never run.

Numerous other instances could be cited of the failure of attempts to impose national controls. In the so-called *Homulka* case in Canada, a husband and wife were accused of committing a horrendous double murder and were to be the subject of separate trials—the wife tendering a plea of 'guilty' to the charge of manslaughter. An order was made prohibiting the publication in Canada of any report of the hearings involving the wife until the husband's trial had been concluded. Once again, the ban was of some effect where traditional media were concerned, but served to prompt the establishment of a number of Usenet newsgroups, which carried full details of the case.

Other developments in the United States raise a further issue which is of wider significance. The individual states retain the power to determine what constitutes obscene material. This has raised questions of whether the operators of online services may be subjected to the most restrictive laws of the range of jurisdictions where the service is made available. Whilst this may be the

---

[40] *Meechie v Multi-Media Marketing* (1995) 94 LGR 474.

[41] For a comprehensive collection of material on the case, see <http://www.users.globalnet.co.uk/~dlheb/jetrepor.htm>.

case in the situation where a service provider has a physical point of presence in a particular locality, in other instances, a perceived danger is that there might be a 'race to the bottom' as countries
compete to attract online business by offering a minimum set of regulatory requirements.

Against this argument, however, the case of *United States v Thomas*[42] illustrates that parties
located within one jurisdiction but offering services or facilities over the Internet may find
themselves subject to the most restrictive legal regime reached by their activities. In this case,
the defendants operated a computer bulletin board allowing subscribers to download pornographic images (which appear to have been placed on the system in breach of copyright in
the original pictures). Subscribers, who were required to submit a written application giving
details of name and address, could also order videos which would be delivered by post. Under
United States law, a federal statute provides that an offence is committed by a person who:

> knowingly transports in interstate or foreign commerce for the purpose of sale or distribu-
> tion, or knowingly travels in interstate commerce, or uses a facility or means of interstate
> commerce for the purpose of transporting obscene material in interstate or foreign com-
> merce, any obscene, lewd, lascivious, or filthy book, pamphlet, picture, film, paper, letter,
> writing, print, silhouette, drawing, figure, image, cast, photograph, recording, electrical
> transcription or other article capable of producing sound or any other matter of indecent
> or immoral character.[43]

The interpretation of this provision may vary between states, the Supreme Court having
accepted that the determination of whether material is obscene is to be made having regard
to 'contemporary community standards'. The material in question was considered lawful
in California.

Following a number of complaints, a postal inspector in Tennessee subscribed to the
bulletin board under an assumed name. In return for a fee of $55, he was able to download a
number of images. The defendants were charged and convicted before the Tennessee courts
of breach of the federal statute cited above. Appealing against conviction, it was argued that
material had not been transported by the defendants. Alternatively, it was contended that
the trial court had erred in applying Tennessee standards of morality. Both arguments are
clearly significant in the context of World Wide Web activities.

The argument against transportation is essentially a simple one. The material in question remained on the defendants' bulletin board. All that was transmitted was a series of
intangible electrical impulses, whilst the terms of the statute related to tangible objects.
This argument was rejected by the Court of Appeal:

> Defendants focus on the means by which the GIF files were transferred rather than the fact
> that the transmissions began with computer-generated images in California and ended with
> computer-generated images in Tennessee. The manner in which the images moved does
> not affect their ability to be viewed on a computer screen in Tennessee or their ability to be
> printed in hard copy in that distant location.[44]

A similar approach would appear to apply in the United Kingdom. In July 1999, an individual pleaded guilty to several specimen charges of publishing obscene materials contrary
to the provisions of the Obscene Publications Act 1959.[45] The pornographic materials in
question were stored on computers in the United States but could be accessed by customers
in the United Kingdom (or anywhere else in the world) upon payment of a fee of around
£20 per month.

---

[42] 1997 United States App LEXIS 12998.   [43] Title 18 USC 1465.
[44] *United States v Thomas*, 1997 United States App LEXIS 12998.
[45] *R v Graham Waddon* (1999, Southwark Crown Court, unreported).

Two contentions were critical to the defendant's case. First, it was argued that publication of the material took place in the United States. This argument was dismissed, with the judge ruling that publication took place whenever the images were downloaded onto a computer in the United Kingdom.[46] A further claim related to evidential requirements. As will be discussed in Chapter 13, the Police and Criminal Evidence Act 1984 requires that evidence be led indicating that a computer whose output is relied upon was operating properly at the relevant time. It was argued that this would have obliged the prosecution to lead information relating to the operation of the servers in the United States. Once again, the judge ruled against the defence, holding that the requirement was limited to demonstrating the reliability of the computer used to access the materials in the United Kingdom.

Although of limited precedential value, the case, coupled with the United States decision in *Thomas*,[47] provides useful evidence that the 'lowest common denominator' standard will not always prevail. The prosecutions, however, could only succeed because the defendants were or could be brought within the court's jurisdiction. Where service provider and user are located in different jurisdictions, enforcement will become much more problematic. Invariably, extradition will only be sanctioned by national authorities where the conduct complained of would constitute an offence if committed on its own territory. If the service providers had been resident in the United States and had not made the mistake of entering the United Kingdom, it is unlikely that any prosecution could have been brought. In the Press Association report of the case, it was noted that:

> Vice Officers are increasingly finding that porn sites siphon subscription money through companies based in countries such as Costa Rica to avoid the attentions of authorities in Britain and the States. And while Internet Service Providers in Britain shut down sites after they are contacted by the police, Scotland Yard's appeals to American companies have fallen on deaf ears in a country where adult porn, however base, remains legal in some states.[48]

With the development of Internet banking, it is a relatively simple matter for accounts to be opened and maintained in offshore locations. Location is becoming an irrelevant consideration for e-commerce and in this, as in many other fields of activity, the prospects for effective national control are limited. As has been seen with Operation Ore, however, where the United States authorities passed on details of credit card payments to their United Kingdom counterparts, there is evidence that international cooperation is increasing in this respect.

Where next for the criminal law?

Historically, the criminal law has been founded on notions of offences against the person and against property. Although in some civil law countries defamation, which might be loosely defined as causing injury to a victim's feelings, the common law has generally restricted in scope to conduct that causes actual or, as in the case of statutes such as the Protection from Harassment Act—anticipated physical harm to the person.

A constant theme throughout this book has been that we live more and more (and more and more significant) aspects of our lives in an online context. Actions occurring online can impact very significantly on our physical existence. A number of cases have been reported where, so-called, cyber-bullying has resulted in the victim attempting suicide.

---

[46] See also the ruling in the defamation case of *Godfrey v Demon* [1999] EMLR 542.

[47] *United States v Thomas*, 1997 United States App LEXIS 12998.

[48] *Press Association Newsfile*, 30 July 1999.

In some instances there is little doubt that criminal offences will be associated with conduct. In one case that was reported in 2013,[49] a teenager had emailed explicit photos of himself in the belief that he was communicating with a fellow teenager of the opposite sex. He then received demands for payment of money failing which the photos would be passed on to family and friends. He committed suicide by jumping of the Forth bridge.

The demand for money in such circumstances must be regarded as a classic form of blackmail and the perpetrator could have faced prosecution on this basis. One complicating factor, of course, is that in the Internet era, that individual could be located anywhere in the world.

> What raises more complex legal issues is that it appears that the victim had posted details of the threat on a social networking website based in Latvia 'ask.fm'. The website allows users to post questions and other users to respond anonymously. In this instance (and also in a number of other reported cases) advice to the question 'what should the poster do?' included the suggestion that the individual should kill himself. Unsavoury behaviour but is it criminal? In the 1970s the American TV show MASH was massively popular. A dark comedy set in the horrors of the Korean war, its theme tune contained lines.
>
> Suicide is painless, it brings on many changes
>
> . . .
>
> The game of life is hard to play, I'm going to lose it anyway.

Doubtless many other examples could be found in popular music but it is inconceivable that the lyricist, Michael Altman, could be held liable for the death of anyone who committed suicide after listening to the song.

What might be the difference? The obvious answer is the sense of intimate contact that we can experience on social networking sites. It can bring many advantages but there are also dangers. There is, I feel, a tendency in some quarters to expect too much of the Internet and, indeed of the criminal law. We do hear much of cyber-bullying and the cases referred to above might be seen as examples. Bullying, however, has been a feature of life probably since the dawn of humanity. It is incredibly difficult to prevent in spite of a paper mountain of anti-bullying policies adopted by schools and similar institutions. In part problems may lie in the sense of intimacy when there is remoteness. In a heated argument I may tell an adversary to 'go jump in the river'. Matters might seem different if the other person was standing on the parapet of a bridge and I was to shout the same phrase.[50] As has been quoted in at least one report,[51] it is unlikely that even in such a case an offence would have been committed. It can be argued that the law should be changed in this regard, but the Internet is not the only culprit.

Revenge pornography

In recent years the topic of 'sexting' has attracted a good deal of media attention. This has emerged essentially in the era of smart phones and the linkage between mobile phones, digital cameras, and Internet connectivity. People have always wanted to communicate and share intimate secrets with those they love. Many love letters have been explicit in their

---

[49] <http://www.bbc.co.uk/news/uk-scotland-edinburgh-east-fife-23712000>.

[50] This report <http://www.dailymail.co.uk/news/article-2205519/Crowd-encourage-suicidal-man-jump-50ft-building-post-video-YouTube.html> illustrates a juxtaposition between the virtual and physical worlds.

[51] <http://www.telegraph.co.uk/news/uknews/3108987/Suicide-teenager-urged-to-jump-by-baying-crowd.html>.

sexual nature and we might consider historical precedents such as the Song of Solomon in the Bible and many of the poems of John Donne. From letters there was a move to telephones although it was only with the emergence of mobile phones that most young people could communicate with any degree of privacy. In most houses in the UK, the (one) phone tended to be located in the living room and any conversation could be overheard by any other member of the family.

We now live in the smart phone era and our mobiles are incredibly powerful devices. Beyond voice or even text communications they invariably include cameras of a level of sophistication that would have been barely credible a few decades ago. The first digital camera was invented in 1975 and could capture images (black and white) at the scale of 1 megapixel. It also weighed 4kg. Today smart phones weigh a few tens of grams and incorporate cameras capable of recording at up to 15 megapixels. The smart phone of today can capture photos at a level of detail that a professional of only a few decades ago could only have dreamed of.

With digitisation we also potentially reduce cost issues. In the analogue era, a roll of film was effectively useless until it was developed. A time-consuming and expensive process. Developing a film would for most people mean putting it in the hands of a professional developer who would inevitably see the contents of the photographs. A good number of cases have been reported where parents have been threatened with prosecution of the loss of custody of their children after handing photos of them in their bath for developing.[52]

In the era of digital photos, there is less call for the services of developers. Many people retain images purely in digital form or can print out a hard copy on their own printer. We hear much of 'selfies'—the act of using a mobile phone to take one's own picture. There is also the notion of 'sexting' when explicit images are sent as text or email attachments to a girl or boyfriend. As has been discussed elsewhere in this book, technology has always been put to a wide range of uses. In some respects, today's sexting might be compared with history's use of a quill pen to express erotic desires and feelings. What is different of course, is the range of dissemination that is possible over the Internet and the phenomenon of reverse pornography attracts a good deal of publicity. Normally following the end of a relationship, this sees a former partner posting intimate photos on the Internet. A number of websites exist that actively promote and facilitate the practice.[53]

There is no doubt that this form of conduct can cause extreme distress to individuals affected. There may certainly be remedies available under civil law.[54] A more difficult question that is attracting a deal of legislative attention around the world[55] is whether the conduct should also be classed as criminal. In some case, for example when the subject of the photo is a minor, this will certainly be the case. In other situations this may not be the case. The issues are complex but provide another illustration of how important our digital

---

[52] See, for example, <http://www.dailymail.co.uk/news/article-2290682/Walmart-Lisa-Anthony-Demaree-lost-custody-children-month-employee-called-police-bath-time-pictures.html>.

[53] See, for example, this report at <http://www.huffingtonpost.com/2014/01/23/hunter-moore-arrested_n_4653733.html>.

[54] See, for example, the case of *AMP v Persons Unknown* [2011] EWHC 3454 (TCC).

[55] See, for example, the story reported at <http://www.theguardian.com/commentisfree/2013/nov/19/revenge-porn-victim-maryland-law-change>. It concerned a US college professor whose ex-partner sought to auction eBay nude photos that she had allowed him to take. He also placed them on pornographic web sites with details of her identity and place of work. The police in the United States were powerless to intervene and it is likely that the result would be the same in the United Kingdom. Under copyright law, a photographer will generally own copyright in images and it does not appear that they would be classed as obscene publications.

identity is and how it may impact on our physical lives. The issue extends far beyond the fields of sexting and revenge pornography. What, for example, should happen to a social networking page when its author dies—and who should have the right to make decisions? The draft European Data protection Regulation refers to a right to be forgotten. Can this ever be possible in our networked world?

Conclusions

From media coverage, it is tempting to believe that Internet pornography poses massive challenges to the law. This is perhaps misleading. What has become clear over the past two decades is that it is difficult for nation states to enforce their own policies regarding what is or is not acceptable. There is no doubt that a computer user in the United Kingdom can readily access material which could not lawfully be purchased over (or under) the counter in a shop. There is very little that law enforcement agencies can do in this situation. Matters assume a different perspective when there is a commonality of approach between the jurisdiction where material is hosted and where it is accessed. In this, as in many other respects, the Council of Europe Convention on Cybercrime is a significant, albeit limited, development.

13

Detecting and prosecuting computer crime

Introduction

The preceding chapters have considered a variety of forms of conduct that may affect adversely the interests of computer users. Assuming that the fact of damage may be established, a variety of practical and legal problems may face the task of establishing the identity of the wrongdoer and obtaining sufficient evidence to support a criminal conviction. Issues of jurisdiction will also be of considerable significance in the situation where access is obtained to a computer system by means of some telecommunications link. In this situation, it is very possible that the perpetrator may be located in one jurisdiction and the victim in another. As was stated in the *Explanatory Report to the Council of Europe's Convention on Cybercrime*:

> One of the major challenges in combating crime in the networked environment is the difficulty in identifying the perpetrator and assessing the extent and impact of the criminal act. A further problem is caused by the volatility of electronic data, which may be altered, moved or deleted in seconds. For example, a user who is in control of the data may use the computer system to erase the data that is the subject of a criminal investigation, thereby destroying the evidence. Speed and, sometimes, secrecy are often vital for the success of an investigation.[1]

The Convention contains extensive provisions relating to procedural matters concerned with the detection of computer-related crime and elements of international cooperation. Also relevant at a more general level is the UN Convention against Transnational Organized Crime and its Protocols,[2] which was opened for signature in 2000 and entered into force in 2003, whilst at the political level extensive work has been carried out under the auspices of the G8, which established the so-called Lyon Group of Senior Experts on Transnational Organized Crime.[3]

Within the EU, the establishment of Europol[4] provides a basis for cooperation between law enforcement agencies and the 2013 Directive on Attacks against Information Systems[5] also contains some provisions relating to procedural aspects. Proposals are under consideration which would strengthen both the Directive and the role of Europol and an agreement was reached in June 2010 for the establishment of a Europol Cybercrime Task Force. In the United Kingdom the Office of Cyber Security and Information Assurance was

---

[1] para. 133. [2] Available from <http://www.unodc.org/unodc/en/treaties/CTOC/index.html>.
[3] For a useful account of the G8's work, see <http://www.g8.utoronto.ca/adhoc/crime99.htm>.
[4] <http://www.europol.europa.eu/>.
[5] Directive 2013/40, OJ 2013 L 208/8. The Directive requires to be implemented in the Member States by 4 September 2015.

established in 2009 to provide 'strategic direction' and to coordinate actions across government departments to tackle what is described as an 'ongoing, persistent threat from other states, terrorists and criminals operating in cyberspace'.[6] Also active is the Centre for the Protection of the National Infrastructure (CPNI)[7] which is established as an expert agency to offer advice on protecting vital assets such as transport and power networks against criminal and terrorist threats. Its remit includes cyber security.

Interception of communications

In the situation where the conduct occurs entirely on the premises of the victim, as in the case of *A-G's Reference (No. 1 of 1991)*,[8] no particular problems may be anticipated in the acquisition of evidence. All matters will be within the control of the computer user and, assuming their willingness to cooperate, there are no legal problems facing the acquisition of evidence.

Greater difficulties arise where access is obtained remotely. The cases of *R v Gold*[9] and *R v Whiteley*[10] might be taken as illustrative of such situations. In both instances, the intruders obtained access to computer systems from their own homes. Certainly, in such a situation, it is open to the victim to make available to the police and prosecution authorities any evidence within their control. This might include details of the time at which access was obtained to the computer system and details of activities undertaken in respect of the system.

In other cases, as has received massive publicity with the revelations about electronic eavesdropping by the National Security Agency (NSA) and Government Communication's Headquarters (GCHQ), communications may be intercepted in the course of their transmission over a public (or private) communications network. The Cybercrime Convention provides that:

> Each Party shall adopt such legislative and other measures as may be necessary, in relation to a range of serious offences to be determined by domestic law, to empower its competent authorities to:
>
> (a) collect or record through the application of technical means on the territory of that Party, and
>
> (b) compel a service provider, within its existing technical capability:
>
> > i.   to collect or record through the application of technical means on the territory of that Party, or
> >
> > ii. to co-operate and assist the competent authorities in the collection or recording of, content data, in real-time, of specified communications in its territory transmitted by means of a computer system.

The Regulation of Investigatory Powers Act 2000 is the major United Kingdom statute setting out the circumstances under which a range of communications data might legitimately be intercepted. This statute has been citicised in some quarters as being out of date and certainly the electronic communications world today is very different from the time

---

[6] <http://www.cabinetoffice.gov.uk/content/cyber-security>.   [7] <http://www.cpni.gov.uk/>.
[8] [1992] 3 WLR 432. In this case the accused was alleged to have physically accessed a computer on his former employers premises and inputted data.   [9] [1988] 1 AC 1063.
[10] (1991) 93 Cr App Rep 25.

the legislation was adopted. The 2000 Act replaced the Interception of Communications Act 1985, which itself marked a somewhat belated attempt to bring the United Kingdom's laws into conformity with the requirements of the European Convention on Human Rights. The provisions of the earlier statute had been designed to regulate situations where voice-telephony messages were intercepted in the course of their transmission over a telecommunications network. This statute had certainly been overtaken by developments in technology. A particular factor has been the explosion in data communications and the switch from traditional circuit-based telecommunications to the packet-switching system that forms the backbone of the Internet. Unlike traditional messages, that are transmitted and require to be intercepted in real time, the use of packet-switching techniques, by which messages are split into a large number of segments, each of which may find its way to its destination by a different route, it will only be at this final stage that the whole message will be reassembled. Interception in the course of transmission will be almost impossible. With the increasing use of packet-switching techniques for voice data, similar problems are going to arise increasingly with attempts to intercept voice traffic. More positively for the authorities, copies of messages will normally be held on equipment belonging to an Internet Service Provider, even after they have been read by the designated recipient.[11] Such factors render easier the task of discovering the contents of email messages. Against this, however, the emergence of systems of cryptography as a tool which can be used by the average person means that interception of a message may reveal no useful or usable information.

Interception of content and communications data

The Regulation of Investigatory Powers Act provides mechanisms for authorising two distinct forms of data content and communications. The former effectively involves the attempt to discover the actual messages exchanged between suspects. In a previous era of telecommunications technology it was colloquially referred to as 'telephone tapping'. This has been regarded as a very intrusive form of surveillance and has been subject to substantial legal and procedural requirements—although it is not clear these have been complied with in the light of the ongoing NSA and GCHQ revelations. The 2012 Report of the Office of Interceptions Commissioner,[12] an independent official with the remit to oversee the operation of the legislation, indicates that in that year 3,372 warrants were issued throughout the UK.

In many instances, the actual content of communications will be of limited interest or significance. Law enforcement and national security agencies may be more concerned with who is talking with whom, at what times, and how often. This is referred to as communications data. A total of 570,135 requests were made for access to communications data in the same period.

Interception of content

The Regulation of Investigatory Powers Act 2000 retains the basic structure introduced by the Interception of Communications Act 1985 whereby warrants for the interception of

---

[11] See also the provisions about data retention, discussed in Ch. 7, which will require ISPs and others involved in the provision of electronic communications services to retain selected items of data for periods of 12 months.

[12] <http://www.iocco-uk.info/docs/2012%20Annual%20Report%20of%20the%20Interception%20of%20 Communications%20Commissioner%20WEB.pdf>.

content[13] must be authorised by the Secretary of State in situations where it is considered to be necessary:

    (a) in the interests of national security;

    (b) for the purpose of preventing or detecting serious crime;

    (c) for the purpose of safeguarding the economic well-being of the United Kingdom; or

    (d) for giving effect to international mutual assistance agreements in connection with the prevention or detection of serious crime.[14]

Financing interception

Until the 1980s interception was carried out on an administrative basis between the police and the then Post Office. With the emergence of competition in the sector, different issues arise. Maintaining a capability to intercept communications is a potentially expensive undertaking for network providers and beyond appealing to sense of civic responsibility—not always present in corporate life—the question arises how interception is to be financed. In this respect the Act provides that:

1.   The Secretary of State may by order provide for the imposition by him on persons who—

    (a) are providing public postal services or public telecommunications services; or

    (b) are proposing to do so

of such obligations as it appears to him reasonable to impose for the purpose of securing that it is and remains practicable for requirements to provide assistance in relation to interception warrants to be imposed and complied with.[15]

Such obligations are only to be imposed following a system of statutory consultation[16] and are subject to parliamentary approval.[17] It is provided that grants are to be given to ISPs to cover additional costs incurred in providing the interceptory capabilities required under the Act.[18]

These provisions were the subject of extensive parliamentary debate and controversy. Concerns were expressed that the requirement to maintain an interceptory capacity in systems would create a ready-made opening for hackers. Additionally, concerns were raised that the cost implications of introducing such facilities would impose a substantial burden upon United Kingdom-based ISPs and would therefore conflict with the government's oft-stated intention of making the country the world's most e-commerce-friendly environment. Against this, the argument was put by the government that obligations to

---

[13] The term interception is defined in s. 2:

    a person intercepts a communication in the course of its transmission by means of a telecommunication system if, and only if, he—

    (a) so modifies or interferes with the system, or its operation,

    (b) so monitors transmissions made by means of the system, or

    (c) so monitors transmissions made by wireless telegraphy to or from apparatus comprised in the system,

    as to make some or all of the contents of the communication available, while being transmitted, to a person other than the sender or intended recipient of the communication.

[14] s. 5.   [15] s. 12.   [16] s. 12(9).   [17] s. 12(2).   [18] s. 14.

provide for interception of communications have traditionally been imposed upon telecommunications companies and that ISPs are licensed under the same regime. Whilst correct, it may be noted that there are very significantly more small and medium-sized ISPs than there are telecommunications companies. It was suggested in Committee[19] that such providers would be compensated for marginal costs incurred in providing the necessary facilities. Implementing the provisions of the Regulation of Investigatory Powers Act 2000, the Regulation of Investigatory Powers (Maintenance of Interception Capability) Order 2002[20] applies to companies that provide a public telecommunications service to more than 10,000 customers. This will include mobile phone companies and ISPs. Such companies may be required by the Secretary of State to maintain a capability to intercept communications at a level permitting the simultaneous interception and transmission to law enforcement agencies of transmissions in a ratio of 1 for every 10,000 users. Responses are to be provided within one working day of receipt of a request for interception.

Communications data

More discussion surrounded the provisions of Chapter 2 of the Regulation of Investigatory Powers Act 2000, which provides for law enforcement agencies to seek access to communications data. Such access may be sought under less restrictive conditions than those required to authorise interception of communications. With modern communications systems, especially mobile networks, data of the kind at issue might be used to track the movements of subscribers, whilst the detailed records of calls made and received could allow a detailed picture to be developed concerning the activities and relationships of individuals. The Regulation of Investigatory Powers (Acquisition and Disclosure of Communications Data: Code of Practice) Order 2007 approves such a code, which specifies the procedures under which a request for access may be made.

The final provision of the Regulation of Investigatory Powers Act 2000 which should be commented on in the context of information technology law concerns its provisions regarding encryption. The use of encryption is widely seen as providing a weapon to criminals to enable their plans to be communicated with minimal risk that, even if the communication is intercepted, its content could be deciphered. Various suggestions have been made by law enforcement agencies as to how the use of encryption might be regulated. The Act provides that where encrypted material has been intercepted in accordance with its provisions and there are reasonable grounds to believe:

(a) that a key to the protected information is in the possession of any person;

(b) that the imposition of a disclosure requirement in respect of the protected information is—

    i. necessary on grounds falling within Subsection (3); or

    ii. necessary for the purpose of securing the effective exercise or proper performance by any public authority of any statutory power or statutory duty;

(c) that the imposition of such a requirement is proportionate to what is sought to be achieved by its imposition; and

[19] HC Official Report, SC F (Regulation of Investigatory Powers Bill), 28 March 2000 (morning).
[20] SI 2002/1931.

(d) that it is not reasonably practicable for the person with the appropriate permission to obtain possession of the protected information in an intelligible form without the giving of a notice under this Section,

the person with that permission may, by notice to the person whom he believes to have possession of the key, require a disclosure requirement in respect of the protected information.[21]

Notices under this heading may be served, either on the owner of the key or on any third party who holds a copy. As an alternative to disclosing the cryptographic key, a copy of the information in decrypted format may be supplied.[22] A deliberate failure to comply with such a notice will constitute an offence.[23] A code of practice for the investigation of protected electronic information was approved by Parliament in October 2007,[24] specifying the procedures and circumstances under which these powers might be invoked.

It remains uncertain how effective, or indeed how intrusive, the provisions of the Regulation of Investigatory Powers Act 2000 will be. There is no doubt that there is concern at the extent to which new communications technologies are threatening the effectiveness of traditional forms of law enforcement. As was said by the Minister of State at the Home Office in Committee:

> I should emphasise what the Home Secretary stated on Second Reading: we expect law enforcement to suffer as a result of the development of new technologies. That is a fact of life. That applies not only to encryption, which has been widely discussed, but to more fundamental developments in communications technology. We are trying to preserve as much as we can of valuable intelligence, while always focusing on the key purposes set out in clause 5 and remaining consistent with our e-commerce objectives. We should not adopt—and the Hon. Gentleman is not proposing—a philosophy of despair, of saying that we can do nothing about the matter or make any progress. However, we acknowledge that law enforcement will suffer from the development of new technology. Communications will be missed. We cannot establish a system that is totally rigid.[25]

The challenge for any new legislation in this field is to provide for effective systems of crime prevention and detection without affecting adversely the rights of the vast majority of totally innocent individuals. It does seem clear that as more and more personal information is recorded in electronic format, so the balance will have to be struck between protecting personal privacy and making use of what can be a valuable intelligence resource for law enforcement agencies.

Search warrants

A significant mechanism for obtaining evidence relating to criminal conduct is for law enforcement agencies to enter premises and search their contents under the authority of a search warrant. In the field of computer-related crime, a number of statutes establish the legal regime for the grant of warrants.

---

[21] s. 49.   [22] s. 50(1).   [23] s. 53.

[24] Available from <https://www.gov.uk/government/publications/code-of-practice-for-investigation-of-protected-electronic-information>.

[25] HC Official Report SC F (Regulation of Investigatory Powers Bill), 28 March 2000 (morning).

The Computer Misuse Act provides procedures for the grant of search warrants in cases where a breach of the section 1 unauthorised access offence is suspected. Section 14 provides that:

(1) Where a circuit judge or a District Judge (Magistrates' Courts) is satisfied by information on oath given by a constable that there are reasonable grounds for believing—

(a) that an offence under section 1 above has been or is about to be committed in any premises; and

(b) that evidence that such an offence has been or is about to be committed is in those premises;

he may issue a warrant authorising a constable to enter and search the premises, using such reasonable force as is necessary.

...

(4) In executing a warrant issued under this section a constable may seize an article if he reasonably believes that it is evidence that an offence under section 1 above has been or is about to be committed.

Also relevant, and perhaps increasingly so, are the provisions of the Copyright, Designs and Patents Act 1988 in respect of activities suspected of constituting criminal infringement of copyright. Section 109 of the Act provides for the grant of a warrant under terms very similar to those laid down in the Computer Misuse Act.

The most general provisions relating to the grant of search warrants are contained in the Police and Criminal Evidence Act 1984[26] and, in respect of the basic unauthorised access offence, in the Computer Misuse Act 1990 itself. The provisions of the Copyright, Designs and Patents Act 1988[27] may also be relevant in respect of cases where software piracy is suspected.

The offences under sections 2 and 3 of the Computer Misuse Act 1990 are classed as serious arrestable offences for the purposes of the 1984 Act.[28] In this event, an application may be made for a search warrant to a justice of the peace who, if satisfied that a serious arrestable offence has been committed and that evidence relevant to the case is likely to be found on specified premises, may issue a search warrant.[29] Such a warrant will, with the exception of specified material,[30] empower the seizure of any item of property which is reasonably considered to relate to the offence under investigation. In addition, it is provided that where information is contained in a computer, the constable exercising the warrant may require that a printout be taken of that information if it is considered 'necessary to do so in order to prevent it being concealed, lost, tampered with or destroyed'.[31]

In the United States, seizure of computers and software was at issue in the celebrated *Steve Jackson* case, where the prolonged detention of the equipment was held by the courts to violate the constitutional guarantees of free speech.[32] Although the submission of the Association of Chief Police Officers suggests that innocent service providers should not be penalised for the actions of their users, there have been suggestions that extensive use has been made of the power of search and seizure. Under the provisions of the Police and Criminal Evidence Act 1984, it is provided that: 'Nothing may be retained...if a photograph or copy would be sufficient for that purpose.'[33] One barrister has been quoted as

---

[26] As amended by the Criminal Justice and Police Act 2001.   [27] s. 9.   [28] s. 116.

[29] s. 8. In certain cases, as prescribed in s. 17, a search may take place without a warrant.

[30] s. 14.   [31] s. 19(4).

[32] *Steve Jackson Games Inc v United States Secret Service*, 816 F Supp 432 (1993); affirmed 36 F 3d 457 (1994).

[33] s. 22(4).

saying that more extensive and prolonged seizures have been justified on the basis that the equipment itself is needed as evidence at the trial.[34]

In respect of the basic offence, the Law Commission's recommendation was that there should be no provision for the issuing of a search warrant. In parliamentary debate, the case was argued that such a facility would be needed if there were to be any realistic possibility of the Computer Misuse Act 1990, section 1 offence being enforced. Particular reference was made to the situation where premises were subject to multiple entry. Although search warrants are not generally made available in respect of summary offences, the Minister of State accepted that:

> the basic hacking offence...is not untypically committed in a private house, remote from public gaze and with no one else present. I am not saying that this is a unique offence, but I cannot immediately think of many others that are committed in private houses to which the police have no access and that do not involve some party other than the offender.[35]

An amendment was accordingly made to the Bill, providing that a search warrant might be issued by a circuit judge where there are 'reasonable grounds for believing' that a Computer Misuse Act 1990, section 1 offence has been or is about to be committed in the premises identified in the application.[36] This provision does not extend to Scotland, it being stated in Parliament that equivalent powers already existed in Scotland, where applications for a warrant would be made to a Sheriff.

Computer evidence

The extent to which computer evidence might be admitted in criminal cases has been a somewhat contentious issue. The law of evidence is a somewhat complex and substantial branch of the legal system. Specific provision for computer generated evidence was made in the Police and Criminal Evidence Act of 1984. As seems so often to have been the case, the attempt to introduce technologically specific legislation was not a conspicuous success. Section 68 of the Act provided that:

> (1) In any proceedings, a statement in a document produced by a computer shall not be admissible as evidence of any fact stated therein unless it is shown—
>
>   (a) that there are no reasonable grounds for believing that the statement is inaccurate because of improper use of the computer;
>
>   (b) that at all material times the computer was operating properly, or if not, that any respect in which it was not operating properly or was out of operation was not such as to affect the production of the document or the accuracy of its contents

It is a general requirement that when evidence is led that is generated by a machine there may be a challenge by the other party to its accuracy and reliability. This provision placed the onus on the prosecution to establish that a computer was operating properly. As every computer user knows, the machines are not infallible and where a defect has occurred it may, as happened in the case of *St Albans District Council v ICL*.[37] be impossible subsequently to replicate the combination of hardware, software, and user input that caused the

---

[34] Alistair Kelman, quoted in 'Privacy: The Strong Arm of the Law', *The Guardian*, 22 September 1994.
[35] HC Official Report, SC C (Computer Misuse Bill), col. 65, 28 March 1990.   [36] s. 14.
[37] [1996] 4 All ER 481.

problem. One of the best-known publishing misprints in history occurred in a copy of the Bible published in 1631 which informed its readers that the Commandments instructed that 'Thou shalt commit adultery'. In the era of computerised typesetting it might be difficult to establish—to the criminal standard of proof—that the blame lay with a human finger rather than a glitch in the software. Although not generally used in word-processing software most of us have probably sent text messages without realising that predictive spell checking has altered the meaning of our message.

Ultimately the Youth Justice and Criminal Evidence Act 1999 repealed[38] section 69 of the 1984 Act. The effect is to place computer-generated evidence in the same position as any other form of evidence. It may be admitted and the presumption will be that it is valid unless and until evidence to the contrary is led.

A further issue that may arise in respect of computer-generated evidence relates to the 'hearsay' rule. It is a general precept of the law of evidence that it must relate to actual knowledge rather than what a witness (whether human or a machine) has been told by someone else. The Criminal Justice Act 2003 provides that:

(1) Where a representation of any fact—

  (a) is made otherwise than by a person, but

  (b) depends for its accuracy on information supplied (directly or indirectly) by a person,

  the representation is not admissible in criminal proceedings as evidence of the fact unless it is proved that the information was accurate.

(2) Subsection (1) does not affect the operation of the presumption that a mechanical device has been properly set or calibrated

This could conceivably have been a very heavy standard of proof although the decision of the House of Lords in the case of *R v Shephard*[39] went some way to minimise the requirements. In this case the defendant was accused of stealing goods from a shop. Evidence was given by a store detective who had examined computerised till receipts corresponding to the time of the alleged theft. These indicated, it was stated, that no combination of the goods found in the defendant's possession had been purchased. Counsel for the defendant argued that section 69 required that evidence be given by someone with specialised knowledge of the working of the computer system. The House of Lords disagreed holding that what was required was that evidence be given by someone who was familiar with the function that the computer was required to perform and could indicate that there was nothing in the nature of particular output to give cause to doubt its accuracy.

Jurisdictional issues

A practical problem relating to the prosecution of computer crime has previously been identified, in as much as the perpetrator of the conduct and the victim computer may be located within different jurisdictions. This is not, of course, an issue which is peculiar to instances of computer crime, but may occur in respect of many instances of fraud. A very simple example might see a person resident in Liverpool ordering goods from a

---

[38] In s. 60.   [39] [1993] AC 380.

mail-order firm based in Edinburgh tendering in payment a cheque which is known to be worthless.

In both England and Scotland, the status of the law relating to jurisdiction is widely regarded as being unclear. The Law Commission has called for urgent reform in the area, arguing that:

> International fraud is a serious problem…It is essential that persons who commit frauds related to this country should not be able to avoid the jurisdiction of this country's courts simply on outdated or technical ground, or because of the form in which they cloak the substance of their fraud.[40]

The Scottish Law Commission indicated that the approach of the Scottish courts has been to claim jurisdiction in the event that the 'main act' of the offence occurred within Scotland.[41] Until recently, the view has been taken that the 'main act' occurs when the fraud produces its result. In the example given, this would happen in Edinburgh when the goods were posted to the customer. A somewhat different approach is evident in the recent case of *Laird v HM Advocate*.[42] This concerned a complex case of fraud in which individuals resident in Scotland fraudulently induced other parties to enter into a contract for the sale of a quantity of steel, the steel to be supplied from England. In this situation, the application of the 'main act' test would appear to dictate that the Scottish courts would not be entitled to claim jurisdiction. In the event, criminal proceedings were instituted and convictions secured in Scotland. An appeal against conviction based on the lack of jurisdiction was rejected by the High Court. Two main points can be identified in the decision of the Lord Justice Clerk (Wheatley). First, it was suggested, where a 'continuous crime' is involved there may be dual jurisdiction within both countries concerned. In terms of the circumstances under which the Scottish courts might claim jurisdiction, he commented:

> where a crime is of such a nature that it has to originate with the forming of a fraudulent scheme, and that thereafter various steps have to be taken to bring that fraudulent plan to fruition, if some of these subsequent steps take place in one jurisdiction and some in another, then if the totality of the events in one country plays a material part in the operation and fulfilment of the fraudulent scheme as a whole there should be jurisdiction in that country.[43]

The concept of joint jurisdiction is one which the Scottish Law Commission recommended should be adopted in respect of any new statutory offences which might result from their deliberations. In similar vein, the Law Commission recommended that the English courts should enjoy jurisdiction when either the perpetrator or the victim computer was located within England.[44] This approach has been adopted in the Computer Misuse Act 1990, although the enabling provisions are somewhat tortuous. Separate provision is made for Scotland, England and Wales, and Northern Ireland.

The basis for any court to claim jurisdiction will be the existence of a 'significant link' with the country in question.[45] In this respect, the provisions relating to jurisdiction can be divided into two categories with the Computer Misuse Act 1990, section 1 and section 3 offences being considered together. In respect of these, a domestic court will have jurisdiction if either the accused person was located in the territory at the time the conduct

---

[40] *Jurisdiction over Fraud Offences with a Foreign Element* (1989), Law Commission No. 180, para. 2.7.
[41] Sc Law Consultative Memorandum No. 68 (1986), para. 7.1.e.   [42] 1984 SCCR 469.
[43] 1984 SCCR 469 at 472.   [44] Law Commission Report No. 186 (1989), para. 4.2.   [45] s. 5.

complained of occurred or the computer to which access was obtained or whose data or programs were modified was so located.

The provisions relating to Computer Misuse Act 1990, section 2 offences are considerably more complicated. Under these, a domestic court may claim jurisdiction in three circumstances:[46]

1. All aspects of the conduct take place in that country.

2. The further offence referred to in section 2 is intended to take place in that country, regardless of whether the 'significant link' required for the establishment of the unauthorised access component of the offence can be established. Effectively, this means that the victim computer will be located in the territory.

3. The 'significant link' requirement can be satisfied in respect of the domestic country and the further offence will be committed (either wholly or in part) in a country (or countries) which recognises such conduct as constituting an offence. In this event, it will also be necessary for the further conduct to satisfy the section 2 requirements of seriousness.

Extradition

The basis for the United Kingdom's laws relating to extradition is currently found in the Extradition Act of 2003, which replaced a series of statutes dating back to the Extradition Act of 1870. The Explanatory Notes to the 2003 Act[47] state that:

> Crime, particularly serious crime, is becoming increasingly international in nature and criminals can flee justice by crossing borders with increasing ease. Improved judicial co-operation between nations is needed to tackle this development. The reform of the United Kingdom's extradition law is designed to contribute to that process.[48]

As was commented by the then Home Secretary, in a foreword to the Home Office document presenting the Extradition Bill, the existing extradition laws:

> date from an age when suspicion and distrust characterised relationships between European nations and the courts saw their role as to protect those fleeing from despotic regimes.[49]

For the purposes of the Act, the world is effectively divided into two categories. Within the EU, the Act gives effect to the Framework Decision on the European Arrest Warrant,[50] creating a fast-track extradition arrangement with Member States of the EU and Gibraltar (Category 1). It includes in Article 3 a list of offences which will be covered. This includes 'computer related crime', albeit subject to a requirement that the offence should carry a penalty of twelve months' imprisonment. For the remainder of the world, power is conferred upon the Secretary of State to place countries in a Category 2 list; the Extradition Act 2003 (Designation of Part 2 Territories) Order 2003[51] gives initial effect to this power. The basic criterion for extradition is that the accused is charged with commission of an 'extradition offence'. This occurs when, inter alia:

---

[46] See s. 7 (adding a new s. 1(1A) to the Criminal Law Act 1977 for England and Wales, s. 13 for Scotland, and s. 16 for Northern Ireland).
[47] Available from <http://www.uk-legislation.hmso.gov.uk/acts/en2003/2003en41.htm>.   [48] para. 6.
[49] <http://www.cejiss.org/assets/pdf/articles/vol3–1/Bures-European_Arrest_Warrant.pdf>.
[50] OJ 2002 L 190/1.   [51] SI 2003/3334.

the conduct would constitute an offence under the law of the relevant part of the United Kingdom punishable with imprisonment or another form of detention for a term of 12 months or a greater punishment if it occurred in that part of the United Kingdom.[52]

With the extension of the Act's penalties in the Police and Justice Act 2006, this will now encompass conduct which could be prosecuted under sections 1, 2, or 3 of the Computer Misuse Act were it to have occurred in the United Kingdom.

---

[52] s. 137.

PART III

Intellectual Property Issues

Introduction

Systems of intellectual property law date back around 700 years. In that sense they can certainly count as established areas of law. Initially some branches, particularly that of copyright, were highly contentious and copyright played an important role in the political and religious struggles of the Middle Ages, as the emergence of the printing press and the feasibility of making multiple copies of political and religious tracts threatened existing authorities.

From around the eighteenth century, the topic largely disappeared from the legal mainstream. I recall my own legal education in the 1970s where our entire exposure to intellectual property law was a half lecture in a course on property law that concentrated otherwise on rights in lands and buildings.

We live in changed days and, in our information-based societies, issues of rights in respect of information assume critical importance and intellectual property law is very much back in the legal mainstream. We have seen numerous examples of companies being purchased by competitors not because of the value of their physical assets but because of the perceived value of their intellectual property. In 2012 Google paid more than $12.5 billion for the technology company Motorola, in large part because of the 17,000 IT-related patents that the company owned.

There is a range of forms of intellectual property law. This Part will consider initially the law of patents, then copyright before looking at more recent systems such as design right, a notion that was at the core of a major UK dispute between Apple and Samsung concerning the question of whether Samsung's Galaxy tablet computer had copied Apple's iPad design. It was eventually held the Galaxy did not infringe although perhaps the sting in the tale was the trial judges comment that the Galaxy was 'not as cool' as its rival. Intellectual property law, on the other hand, is certainly a hot topic today.

Patents

Probably the oldest form of intellectual property right is the notion of a patent. Dating back to the fourteenth century, this effectively confers a monopoly on its owner in respect of the product or process specified. Patents may be awarded in respect of inventions but the difficult question is 'what is an invention?' Did Einstein, for example, 'invent' the theory of relativity? Essentially the answer is 'no'. It was simply a theory. Patents used to be referred to as an industrial (rather than intellectual) property law and this perhaps gives an indication as to its key features. You might get a patent for something that works. A term very frequently used by the courts is that it should produce a technical effect. We can think of devices such as the telephone that made its inventor, Alexander Graham Bell and his successors, massive fortunes, largely because the inventor was able to secure effective patent protection.

A perhaps pivotal move in the patent system came with its application to pharmaceutical products. Pharmaceutical companies invest billions of pounds each year in trying to develop new drugs and have been very successful in securing patent protection in many cases. But we have to ask where is the element of invention—or a technical effect? It is more an issue of dis-covering—often after massive investment in skill, effort, and money—that a particular chemical compound produces beneficial results in treating a particular condition.

A feature of pharmaceutical products, which is shared with software and other digital prod-ucts, is that they can be very expensive to develop but once the formula is established the end-product can be reproduced easily and cheaply. To give one example, one of the most effective drugs for treating patients with AIDS cost $15,000 a year as supplied by the original developer. A pharmaceutical company in India was able to sell a copy for less than $300. The AIDS example has been massively controversial, but the reason why the original developer was able to claim such a high price (which they would, of course, argue was necessary to recoup their research and development costs) was because they had secured a patent and thereby a monopoly over the sale of the drug. It might be, and is, argued that without this level of protection companies would be unwilling to engage in research and development activities.

The process of innovation is a very complex, lengthy and it has been estimated that:

- Only one in 5,000–10,000 compounds tested eventually reach consumers.
- Only two out of every ten compounds that enter clinical testing reach the market.
- Only three out of ten drugs that reach the market ever earn back enough money to match or exceed the average R&D cost of getting them to the marketplace.[1]

There has been significant progress in making drugs legally available to Third World patients at costs which reflect those of production rather than including R&D costs. One difficulty that these efforts face is the ever-increasing impact of globalisation. In previous eras it was quite fea-sible for companies to separate markets. It was generally the case, for example, that an Indian edition of a textbook could be sold for a much lower price than that charged in the UK market with little chance that these copies would find their way back to the UK market and undercut the publisher's price. With global transport networks and especially in the case of digital works with the emergence of the Internet and e-commerce, the possibility of segregating markets is much diminished. Whether this is for good or for bad is an interesting question.

As with pharmaceutical products, software appears also to suffer from a high attrition rate with some 70 per cent of projects being reported as failing to deliver the expected benefits. For both pharmaceutical products and software therefore the legal protection conferred by the patent system is highly valued as a means for protecting investment in those projects that do prove to be successful. I'm not aware of statistics for standard software packages but the failure of these is likely to result in the disappearance of the company from the market place. As individuals live longer, companies do seem to be suffering from a reduction in life expectancy. It has been reported that:

> The average lifespan of a company listed in the S&P 500 index of leading US companies has decreased by more than 50 years in the last century, from 67 years in the 1920s to just 15 years today, according to Professor Richard Foster from Yale University.[2]

---

[1] <http://www.innovation.org/documents/File/Pharmaceutical_Patents.pdf>.
[2] <http://www.bbc.co.uk/news/business-16611040>.

I have seen statistics[3] indicating that the failure rate for information-related companies is higher than in any other sector of the economy. Only 37 per cent of start-up companies, it is reported, are still in operation four years later. The nearest failing sector is transport and utilities with a 45 per cent survival rate.

The key criterion for the award of a patent is that the product is novel and involves an inventive step. This means that the concept and implementation of the product would not be an obvious step. There is the famous saying attributed to Henry Ford to the effect that customers could have their car in any colour so long as it was black. I don't think that the idea of a white car would be patentable because it would be such an obvious and technically trivial task to substitute one colour for another.

We will consider patents and their application in the software context in much more detail in the following chapters. What I would emphasise at this introductory stage is the strength of the protection afforded. A patent is effectively a monopoly. Returning to the telephone, the name Alexander Graham Bell is universally known. That of Elisha Grey, the American electrical engineer, less so. Elisha also invented a telephone and applied for patent protection. The official version of history is that Bell's application arrived at the United States Patent Office a matter of hours before Grey's. Other versions tell a tale of skulduggery and switching of files, with the insinuation being that Grey submitted first and was effectively cheated of the patent. Regardless which version is correct, the undeniable fact is that Bell is famous and Grey (who happily went on to achieve success in other fields, for example as the father of the modern music synthesiser) is essentially a footnote in history.

As we will discuss, the application of the patent system to software has been controversial. One of the major complaints is that patents have been awarded for technologies that are not truly novel. In such a fast-moving field, it is nigh on impossible for any patent examiner to be fully aware of what is referred to as the 'state of the art'. In one sense, any patent is valid only until it is challenged but we might also consider the perhaps less authoritative legal maxim that possession is nine points of the law. In the United States, and it seems to a much lesser extent in the rest of the world, we are seeing the emergence of what are referred to as patent trolls. Named after mythical and rapacious Norwegian monsters, the essence of a troll is that it buys up patents with no intention of exploiting them for its own purpose but as a bargaining tool to be used to persuade other companies to take out (at cost) a licence to use the technology. Such techniques are widely frowned upon although, in the light of the acquisitions of other companies by organisations such as Google, Microsoft, and Apple on account of their patent portfolios, it is perhaps unfair to see this as just a small-company phenomenon. Especially from the United States we are seeing a seemingly endless series of disputes, often referred to as 'patent wars'. Few if any have reached the stage of definitive legal rulings and this is perhaps one of the key issues. It is difficult to separate hype from reality.

Copyright

Whilst the application of the patent system to software is debatable (and contentious), that of copyright has been less so. It is fair to say that every piece of software will qualify for copyright protection. Issues of its proper scope and the techniques that can be used to enforce copyright, however, have been and remain very contentious. In previous generations, copyright infringement on a commercial scale required significant investment in terms of equipment. You might think of this book. Producing unauthorised (pirate) copies is not cheap. A person could photocopy every page of this book but the cost of that would almost certainly exceed

---

[3] <http://www.statisticbrain.com/startup-failure-by-industry/>.

the cover price of the book and the quality of the reproduction would be very much lower than the original. It can be done and I am aware of one pirated copy of a previous edition but it needs printing presses and binding facilities. What the Internet and peer-to-peer websites have done is to put mass copying capabilities into the hands of billions of Internet users. But how did we get here?

Copyright essentially originated in the fifteenth and sixteenth centuries in conjunction with the invention (or at least its appearance in Europe) of the printing press by Gutenburg in the fifteenth century. It does not appear that this invention was ever awarded a patent: not because the basic technology had been applied by the Chinese centuries before and was therefore part of the state of the art, but because at that time the award of patents was very much at the discretion of the monarch (government) and the potential availability of multiple copies of seditious works was a cause for great concern to governments. By not awarding a patent, dissemination of the techniques for manufacturing printing presses en masse was thereby inhibited.

In England, after a period of alternating between censorship and the freedom of the press, the compromise was reached whereby a private corporation, 'The Stationers' Company' was appointed as guardian of the technology. Books could, upon pain of civil and criminal penalties, be published only with its permission. Essentially the industry was asked to police itself and there are clear parallels with current developments whereby Internet Service Providers (ISPs) are being asked to shoulder responsibility for the online activities of their customers.

The Statute of Anne, variously dated to 1709 or 1710 is generally regarded as the world's first copyright statute although it essentially codified common law doctrine in many respects. Originally copyright was restricted to literary works, but as technologies have developed it has been extended to cover a range of other works including photographs, films, and radio and television broadcasts. From 1985 and the Copyright (Computer Programs) (Amendment) Act, it has been specifically provided that computer programs (software) are protected under the category of literary works.

The classification of software as a literary work was undoubtedly influenced by the technology of the time. Programs were essentially functional and essentially text-based. Whether the same approach would be taken today is an interesting question. Software is typically much, much more graphically intensive and certainly a modern computer game resembles a cinema film far more than it does a book. The latest edition of the popular computer game 'Grand Theft Auto' is reported to have cost £170 million to develop, a figure that would make it one of the most expensive films in history—yet also one of the most profitable. Many 'traditional' films, of course, also make extensive use of computer animation and it is, I think, fair to say that traditional boundaries between forms of work are becoming blurred. A term that is generally used is 'convergence' and there will be more discussion of that in the coming chapters.

Whilst there is no doubt that essentially every piece of software will benefit from copyright protection there is uncertainty how extensive the protection is. There is no doubt that the act of copying software without the consent of the copyright owner—often referred to as piracy—is unlawful. What is less clear is the extent to which a rival may lawfully reproduce what used to be referred to as the 'look and feel' of an original program. In cases where copyright infringement is alleged, a court will generally ask two questions: has the alleged copyist had access to the original work and are the two pieces of work substantially similar? The on-screen appearance and functionality of one program can be reproduced in another without the second party having any knowledge of the underlying code and it is debatable today whether copyright in software is effective against anything other than direct copying. It is certainly possible that artistic copyright might be claimed in an on-screen image such as the well-known computer game character 'SuperMario' although this perhaps belongs more in the area of trade mark law.

Other forms of intellectual property right

Intellectual property law has many strands and it is often the case, especially with games, that aspects of characters will be protected by trade mark law. This allows for the protection of names, images, and other attributes. A popular series of computer games features the cartoon character 'SuperMario' and this is protected by a substantial number of trade marks. Also relevant in this context is the common law notion of 'passing off' which resembles in some respects the civil law doctrine of unfair competition. At a typically more hardware-related level, the law of registered (and unregistered) design rights has been at issue in high-profile disputes between, for example, Apple and Samsung.

If copyright and patents can be seen as overlapping to some extent, the role of trade mark law is significantly different. The role of a trade mark is to serve to distinguish the goods or services offered by one party from those of anyone else. The current United Kingdom law concerning trade marks is to be found in the Trade Marks Act 1994, which itself seeks to implement the EU Directive to approximate the laws of the Member States relating to trade marks.[4] Also relevant is the common law doctrine of 'passing off'. As the name suggests, this operates to prevent a party using names or other indicators which are likely to mislead third parties as to the true identity of the person with whom they are dealing. Typically, the impression will be given that a person is connected with some well-known and regarded organisation.

A trade mark may consist of anything which may be recorded in graphical format. Traditionally, marks have tended to take the forms of names or logos, but the scope is increasing, with sounds and even smells forming the subject matter of trade mark applications. For the present purpose, attention can be restricted to the use of names. Given the increasing commercialisation of the Internet, organisations frequently seek the registration of a domain name which creates an obvious link with their real-life activities. The software company Microsoft, for example, can be found at <http://microsoft.com>. In many cases indeed, firms have obtained trade mark registration for their domain name as such. Amazon.com, for example, is a registered trade mark in the United States.

Also relevant in an information technology context is the concept of design rights. The regime is in some respects analogous to the patent system in that eligibility for protection is dependent upon meeting criteria of novelty. Especially as the scope of copyright protection has narrowed, attention has been paid to the role that design right might play in protecting aspects of the look and feel of IT products.

As will be discussed in the following chapters, the task of fitting software and software-related applications into traditional forms of intellectual property law has not been a simple one. In some areas, the attempt has been made to develop new, specialised forms of protection. The two main areas in which this has been attempted have been in the fields of database and semiconductor chip design protection. In both areas, the impetus for reform in the United Kingdom has lain in EU Directives. Whilst providing specialised or *sui generis* forms of protection, both regimes draw heavily on the principles and policies of copyright law.

Conclusions

In our fast-changing societies, it is tempting to conclude that history has few lessons to teach us. Much depends, perhaps, on whether we see change as evolutionary or revolutionary. Prior to considering where and how intellectual property should develop, it is perhaps useful to look

---

[4] Directive 89/104/EEC (the Trade Mark Directive), OJ 1998 L 40/1.

260 INTELLECTUAL PROPERTY ISSUES

back to consider how and why the systems developed. The first intellectual property statutes were motivated very much by economic and trade considerations. In the English patent system, for example, invention took second place to the need to overcome by force of law the obstacles placed by local tradesmen against those seeking to apply techniques and technologies established in other countries but novel in England.

A similar trend can be mapped in respect of the copyright system. Essentially a product of the invention of the printing press, this seeks to protect a range of interests. The world's first copyright statute was the United Kingdom's Statute of Anne, enacted in 1709. The date of the Act's passage is significant. Although the notion of copyright had been developed under the English common law, it had not featured significantly in Scots law. Under the Act of Union between Scotland and England in 1707, an eighteenth-century equivalent of the European Single Market was established, with Scottish producers enjoying access to the economically stronger English market. Scots law was retained under the Act of Union and Scottish publishers discovered a useful source of income by producing what today would be regarded as 'pirate' copies of leading English literary works. One of the motives of the Statute of Anne was to introduce copyright notions into Scots law and prevent what was seen as a form of unfair competition.

Matters have not, perhaps, changed greatly over the past three centuries. In 1707, a relatively poor country saw little benefit in systems of intellectual property law and some advantage in their absence. Its richer, more powerful neighbour used economic and political muscle to cause the introduction of intellectual property laws. Today, it is not self-evidently to the benefit of the developing world to enforce intellectual property rights, which primarily benefit First World owners. The price of entry to the World Trade Organization (WTO) and access to First World market under the General Agreement on Tariffs and Trade (GATT) and General Agreement on Trade and Services (GATS) treaties is, however, that they accept the WTO Protocol on Trade Related Aspects of Intellectual Property Rights (TRIPS). This obliges signatories to recognise intellectual property rights and to provide enforcement mechanisms in the event rights are not observed. This obligation has been the cause of considerable controversy, most notably perhaps in relation to the production and distribution of anti-AIDS drugs, which are invariably protected by patent rights.

Perhaps surprisingly, almost no empirical evidence exists whether the patent system is effective in either economic terms or in ensuring that information regarding technical innovations enters into the public domain. Some studies have suggested that small and medium-sized enterprises make little or no use of patent specifications as a source of information regarding developments in their field of activity. In cases such as DNA research, it may be argued whether the publication of details of an end-product adds anything to the sum of human knowledge and, as such, whether the award of a patent adequately advances the aims of the patent system. A recent study conducted for the Commission on *The Economic Impact of Patentability of Computer Programs*[5] considered the literature on the economics of the patent system before concluding:

> The economics literature does not show that the balance of positive and negative effects lies with the negative. All it says is that there are grounds for supposing that the negative forces are stronger relative to the positive forces in this area than in some others and that any move to strengthen IP protection in the software industry cannot claim to rest on solid economic evidence.

---

[5] Study Contract ETD/99/B5–3000/E/106, available from <http://ec.europa.eu/internal_market/indprop/docs/comp/study_en.pdf>.

In fields such as software and with projects such as the mapping of the human genome, it may be questioned how far the award of patents serves the end of encouraging further innovation. As in the example cited involving Elisha Grey and Alexander Graham Bell, different people may be working independently on the same idea simultaneously. It may be a matter of chance who stumbles on a practical method of implementation first. It may be questioned whether the interests of society in the development of technology are likely to be best served by the grant of a monopoly to one person or whether the existence of at least one competitor might have served as a spur to more rapid developments.

14

Key elements of the patent system

Introduction

The history of the patent system has been a convoluted and complex one and the concept featured in some of the major political upheavals in the late Middle Ages, testimony to the fact that the element of monopoly conferred upon the holder of a patent has at least the potential to provide very significant economic benefits. This chapter will consider in general terms the nature and manner of operation of the patent system, whilst the following chapter will focus upon the somewhat complex manner in which the system has operated in respect of so-called software-related inventions.

The first recorded patent was issued in Florence in the fifteenth century. We are told that:

> Filippo Brunelleschi, the architect of Florence's remarkable cathedral, won the world's first patent for a technical invention in 1421. Brunelleschi...claimed he had invented a new means of conveying goods up the Arno River (he was intentionally vague on details), which he refused to develop unless the state kept others from copying his design. Florence complied, and Brunelleschi walked away with the right to exclude all new means of transport on the Arno for three years.[1]

As adopted in England, the purpose of the patent system was somewhat different. In the early Middle Ages, each town would have its guilds of craftsmen, who would guard access to the various trades jealously. Only a member of the appropriate guild could, for example, act as a butcher or carpenter. One of the major weaknesses of such an approach was that the guilds stifled innovation. Recognising that the country was lagging behind its Continental rivals in terms of technology, the practice began whereby the sovereign would encourage foreigners to come to England, bringing with them their advanced technical skills. To overcome the objections of the craft guilds, letters patent would be issued. Signed with the royal seal, these would command any citizen to refrain from interfering with the bearer in the exercise of the technical skills referred to in the letter. The first recorded English patent of this kind was issued in 1449 to a Flemish glazier, John of Utyman who came to the country to install stained-glass windows in Eton College. Unlike Brunelleschi's patent, the technology covered by the patent was new to the country rather than new in itself.

In the sixteenth and seventeenth centuries the system fell increasingly into disrepute. Although some patents were granted in respect of what might be regarded as inventions (the first recorded patent of this kind being awarded to an Italian émigré, Annoni, who developed a novel system of fortification, used to safeguard the town of Berwick against the Scots invaders), the system was all too often used to boost the royal revenues by conferring a monopoly in respect of basic commodities in return for a fee. In 1602, the courts declared

---

[1] R. King, *Brunelleschi's Dome: The Story of the Great Cathedral of Florence* (London, 2001), p. 3.

unlawful a royal monopoly relating to the manufacture of playing cards and in 1623 the Statute of Monopolies rendered illegal all monopolies except those:

> for the term of 14 years or under hereafter to be made of the sole working or making of any manner of new manufactures within this Realm to the true and first inventor … [monopolies should not be] contrary to the law nor mischievous to the State by raising prices of commodities at home or hurt of trade.[2]

It was almost another hundred years, however, before it was settled that in return for the award of a patent, the inventor was required to specify details of the manner in which the invention functioned, and not until the enactment of the Patent Act 1902 that even a rudimentary form of examination of patent applications was made with a view to establishing novelty.

In recent United Kingdom statutes, it has been made absolutely clear that the element of invention is critical for any award and that a balance is to be struck whereby in return for putting details of the manner in which the invention functions into the public arena, the inventor is to receive a temporary monopoly in respect of its exploitation. An oft-quoted description of the modern system explains that:

> The basic theory of the patent system is simple and reasonable. It is desirable in the public interest that industrial techniques should be improved. In order to encourage improvement, and to encourage the disclosure of improvements in preference to their use in secret, any person devising an improvement in a manufactured article, or in machinery or methods for making it, may upon disclosure of the improvement at the Patent Office demand to be given a monopoly in the use for a period of years. After that period it passes into the public domain; and the temporary monopoly is not objectionable, for if it had not been for the inventor who devised and disclosed the improvement nobody would have been able to use it at that or any other time, since nobody would have known about it.[3]

Today, the United Kingdom's patent system is based primarily on the Patents Act 1977. This statute was enacted in part to reform and update the United Kingdom law relating to patents but also in order to bring domestic law into conformity with the provisions of the European Patent Convention, opened for signature in 1973, which, as will be discussed later, provides for a measure of harmonisation in matters of substance and procedure amongst signatory states.

Whilst there is no doubt that inventiveness is a key requirement of the patent system, what has been more debatable has been the application of the system to software-related inventions—innovations where novelty resides primarily or exclusively in software components. Concern has tended to focus on two elements: first, whether software developments fit conceptually into the industrial nature of the system and, secondly, whether the library and related resources exist to allow claim to novelty to be adequately assessed. This remains the most problematic aspect of the subject and will be discussed in more detail later.

Patents in the international arena

Until recent times, patent systems tended to be found only in the developed world. The advent of the WTO has resulted in many more countries introducing systems of patent protection. Although there is some element of harmonisation, this is at a lower level than

---

[2] s. 6.

[3] T. A. Blanco White, *Patents for Inventions* (London, 1983), p. 1. For a good description of the history of the United Kingdom patent system, see the Patent Office website at <http://www.ipo.gov.uk/types/patent/p-about.htm>.

provided for under the Berne Copyright Convention, which provides for almost world-wide protection to be conferred automatically on literary, dramatic, and musical works. A United Kingdom patent will be valid within the United Kingdom and of no effect in Japan or the United States, and vice versa. A person wishing to secure widespread patent protection for an invention will have to undergo the time-consuming and expensive process of seeking to obtain a patent from each country where protection is desired.

The oldest international instrument which seeks to ease the task of inventors in securing patent protection on a multi-jurisdictional level is the Paris Convention (an instrument signed by ninety-six states, including all of the major industrial states).[4] This provides that the submission of an application for patent protection in one signatory state will serve to establish priority for the applicant in the event that equivalent applications are submitted in other signatory states within twelve months.[5] Although such a facility is of considerable value for inventors, the practical problems involved in obtaining patent protection on anything like a worldwide basis are immense, and a number of subsequent agreements have sought to ease the task facing applicants.

The Patent Co-operation Treaty

The Patent Co-operation Treaty, which was opened for signature in 1970, prescribes basic features which are to be found in the national laws of signatory states. Under the provisions of the Patent Co-operation Treaty, an application may be directed to the patent authorities in any state and will indicate the countries within which patent protection is sought.[6] The national authority will then transmit the application to an International Searching Authority (the national patent offices of Austria, Australia, Japan, Russia, Sweden, and the United States, together with the European Patent Office).[7] The procedure to be adopted subsequently will depend upon the extent to which the state in question adheres to the Treaty. At the most basic level, the International Searching Authority will carry out a prior art search and submit reports to the designated national authorities.[8] Signatory states are given the option to adhere to a more significant regime which will permit the searching authority to conduct a preliminary examination.[9] Once again, reports will be sent to the designated national authorities. The Patent Co-operation Treaty does not contain any specific prohibition against the award of patents for computer programs,[10] but does state that an International Searching Authority is not to be obliged to conduct a search of the prior art in respect of a computer program 'to the extent that the International Searching Authority is not equipped to search prior art concerning such programs'.

The operation of the Patent Co-operation Treaty serves to eliminate a measure of the duplication of searches and examinations which would otherwise face an international applicant. Ultimately, however, the decision as to whether to grant or refuse a particular application is one for the national authorities.

The European Patent Convention

More extensive rationalisation of the patent system has been carried out within Europe with the adoption of the European Patent Convention. This Convention was opened for signature in 1973, and has been ratified by all of the EU states and also by a number of

---

[4] The Convention was first opened for signature on 20 March 1883, with the most recent revision occurring in Stockholm in 1968.

[5] Art. 4.   [6] Art. 3.   [7] Art. 12.   [8] Art. 15.   [9] Art. 31.

[10] Art. 33 provides that the subject matter of a patent may be anything that can be made or used.

non-Member States such as Norway, Switzerland, and Turkey. The Convention establishes the European Patent Office (located in Munich) and the concept of a European Patent. The title, however, is something of a misnomer. An applicant is required to specify those countries in which it is intended that the patent will apply and, assuming the application is successful, the end-product will be the award of a basket of national patents. Effectively, the role of the Convention and the European Patent Office is to centralise the process for the award of national patents, with the costs to applicants rising in line with the number of countries in which protection is sought. As the European Commission has commented, one consequence of this process has been that 'the additional costs of protection for each designated country are prompting businesses to be selective in their choice of countries, with effects that run counter to the aims of the single market'.[11]

Applications for patent protection may be addressed to the European Patent Office. Once again, the applicant must indicate those countries to which they wish the patent to extend.[12] Subsequently, all the examining procedures will be conducted by the European Patent Office, which will then also proceed to make the decision on whether to grant the patent. Although some differences of procedure and style can be identified between the practice of the United Kingdom Patent Office and its European counterparts, the principles which will be applied are virtually identical. The UK law relating to patents is to be found today in the Patents Act 1977. This statute was introduced in part to update domestic law, but principally to enable the United Kingdom to ratify the European Patent Convention. The Act provides that judicial notice is to be taken of decisions of the European Patent Office authorities and, as will be discussed later, decisions made within the European Patent Office have proved extremely influential in the domestic system. In one of the leading United Kingdom cases, the view was strongly expressed that:

> It would be absurd if, on the issue of patentability, a patent application should suffer a different fate according to whether it was made in the United Kingdom under the Act or was made in Munich for a European Parliament (United Kingdom) under the Convention.[13]

As will be discussed later, the absurd has become very close to becoming the rule.

The unitary patent

For many years the European Union has sought to establish a patent system that would mean that a single patent could be issued covering all of the Member States. One of the major obstacles has been the linguistic one. Under the European Patent Office system a translation of the patent documents must be provided by the applicant for every country to which the patent extends. Translation costs are high and an Impact Assessment published by the European Commission[14] in 2011 noted that:

> Direct and indirect translation costs can add up to about 40% of the overall costs of patenting in Europe. It has been estimated that a European patent validated in 13 countries is more than ten times more expensive than a patent in the US or Japan . . . Specialised translators are needed to translate the technical text contained in patents. On average, EUR 85 is charged per page. The number of pages to be translated depends on the specific patent: a patent of typical length contains 15 pages of description, 4 pages of claims and 1 page of drawings.

---

[11] Green Paper, *Community Patent and the Patent System in Europe* (1997), available from <http://europa.eu/documents/comm/green_papers/pdf/com97_314_en.pdf>.   [12] Art. 79.

[13] Per Nicholls J in *Gale's Application* [1991] RPC 305.

[14] SEC(2011) 482 final. Available from <http://ec.europa.eu/internal_market/indprop/docs/patent/sec2011-482-final_en.pdf>.

Additionally, it was suggested, fees of up to €600 per country might have to be paid to national agents to facilitate the filing of translations with national patent offices. As a result, it was argued in a statement by Commissioner Barnier:

> The figures speak for themselves. In the United States, in 2011, 224 000 patents were granted, in China 172 000 while here in Europe only 62 000 European patents were delivered. One of the reasons for this difference is without a doubt the prohibitive cost and the complexity of obtaining patent protection throughout the single market.[15]

Commenting on the prolonged gestation period for the EU system he noted 'Since the 1960s, this project has been put forward, with successive failures. When I took up office, I said that I would not be the first Commissioner to work on the file but that I hoped to be the last.'

The new European regime, which is expected to enter into force in 2014[16] is based on two Regulations, one detailing the mechanics of the system[17] and the other concerning the arrangements for translation.[18] In terms of substance there is no change from the provisions of the European Patent Convention. Applications will continue to be made to the European Patent Office but applications will require to be submitted only in English, French and German[19] but any patent awarded will be valid in the twenty-five participating EU states.

The major structural change will be the introduction of a Unified Patent Court as part of the EU's institutions. The Court will consist of an appellate body which will be based in Luxembourg and a Court of First Instance which will be based in Paris with branches in London and Munich. The Court of First Instance will deal with cases alleging infringement in specific sectors. London will deal with issues involving pharmaceutical products and Munich with mechanical engineering. All other cases, which will include those concerning software-related patents will be determined in Paris. All cases concerned with the validity of patents will also be dealt with in Paris.

For cases at first instance, a panel of three judges will sit. Two will be legally qualified and one technically qualified (in respect of the nature of the patent under scrutiny). The Court of Appeal will sit as a panel of five, with three legally and two technically qualified judges.

Intellectual property in the GATS and WTO

Introduced shortly after the end of the Second World War, the General Agreement on Tariffs and Trade has provided a legal mechanism to regulate and promote international trade. Reform to the system in the 1990s brought services into the international agreement for the first time through the adoption of the General Agreement on Trade in Services (GATS) and also introduced provisions relating to intellectual property rights. The Trade-Related Aspects of Intellectual Property Rights (TRIPS) Protocol[20] to the GATTs requires signatories to make patents:

> available for any inventions, whether products or processes, in all fields of technology, provided that they are new, involve an inventive step and are capable of industrial application…patents shall be available and patent rights enjoyable without discrimination as to the place of invention, the field of technology and whether products are imported or locally produced.[21]

[15] <http://europa.eu/rapid/press-release_MEMO-12-971_en.htm?locale=en>.

[16] Spain and Italy are not participating in the new scheme, largely because of concerns that their national languages will not be recognised.

[17] Regulation (EU) No. 1257/2012 of the European Parliament and of the Council of 17 December 2012 implementing enhanced cooperation in the area of the creation of unitary patent protection, OJ 2012 L 361/1.

[18] Council Regulation (EU) No. 1260/2012 of 17 December 2012 implementing enhanced cooperation in the area of the creation of unitary patent protection with regard to the applicable translation arrangements, OJ 2012 L361/89.

[19] Provision is made for small and medium-sized enterprises to be reimbursed for translation costs.

[20] Adopted in 1994, entering into force on 1 January 1995. The text of TRIPS is available from <http://www.wto.org/english/docs_e/legal_e/27-trips.pdf>.   [21] Art. 27.

This provision was included at the behest of the developed world, and was prompted by concern that companies were suffering losses through audio, software, and video piracy in developing countries, with little legal recourse because concepts of intellectual property law were not recognised by national laws. Effectively, TRIPS requires these states to intro- duce intellectual property statutes as the price for benefiting from the free trade provisions of the GATT. Although not technically binding on either the EU or the European Patent Office, there is no doubt that its provisions requiring that patents be made available 'for any inventions' have proved highly influential in an ongoing debate concerning the patentabilty of software-related inventions.

Requirements for patentability

A patent may be awarded in respect of an invention. The invention may relate either to a new product or to a novel process. The Patents Act 1977 does not define the word 'inven- tion', but it does specify attributes that any invention must possess. These require that:

(a) the invention is new;

(b) it involves an inventive step;

(c) it is capable of industrial exploitation; and

(d) the grant of a patent for it is not excluded.[22]

As will be discussed extensively in Chapter 15, the categories of excluded subject matter are of great significance in the case of software-related inventions. Initially, however, atten- tion will be paid to the positive attributes which must be possessed in order for a product or a process to be considered patentable.

Novelty

The question of novelty is assessed against the existing state of human knowledge. Account will be taken of any material within the public domain which might indicate that the concept of the claimed invention did not originate with the particular applicant. It is not necessary that all the details of the alleged invention should have previously appeared in a single document. The test which will be applied is sometimes referred to as the 'mosaic' test. The analogy might also be drawn with a jigsaw puzzle. This consists of a number of pieces. Once completed, the subject matter will be readily identifiable, as will the manner in which the constituent pieces fit together. Such a result might not have been apparent to someone who merely saw a pile of unassembled pieces.

An indication of the complexity of the task of determining whether a claimed invention is novel or whether key elements have been anticipated in earlier products or publications can be taken from the case of *Quantel Ltd v Spaceward Microsystems Ltd.*[23] This concerned a challenge to the validity of a patent awarded in respect of a computer-based device permit- ting the production of graphical images for display on television screens. The end-products of the system can be viewed every day in the captions and graphical montages which appear on almost all television programmes.

A competing product having been placed on the market, proceedings were instituted alleging breach of patent. In defending this action, the defenders alleged, inter alia, that the patent had been incorrectly awarded to a development that was not novel. A variety of

---

[22] s. 1(1).   [23] [1990] RPC 83.

material was presented in support of this contention, including a thesis submitted by an American student and deposited in the library of Cornell University. Although the validity of the patent was ultimately upheld by the court, when account is taken of the number of such works produced each year and the very limited publicity afforded to them, the incident demonstrates the magnitude of the task of determining whether an alleged invention is truly novel. The case also provides an excellent illustration of the fact that the grant of a patent may be only the first step for the inventor, who may be faced with a challenge to its validity in the course of any subsequent legal proceedings.

A further aspect of novelty concerns the question of whether details of the alleged invention might previously have been brought into the public domain by the applicant. Any significant disclosure of the features of an invention prior to the submission of an application for a patent will lead to its rejection. The Patent Office advises inventors:

> If you are thinking of applying for a patent you should not publicly disclose the invention before you file an application because this could be counted as prior publication of your invention. Any type of disclosure (whether by word of mouth, demonstration, advertisement or article in a journal), by the applicant or anyone acting for them, could prevent the applicant from getting a patent. It could also be a reason for having the patent revoked if one was obtained. It is essential that the applicant only makes any disclosure under conditions of strict confidence.[24]

Inventive step

The application of this test is as much a matter of art as of science and is linked to a considerable extent with the criteria of novelty. The Patents Act 1977 states that an invention:

> shall be taken to involve an inventive step if it is not obvious to a person skilled in the art, having regard to any matter which forms part of the state of the art.[25]

It is very much a question of fact whether the advance involved in a particular invention would have been 'obvious'. Again, the attempt has to be made to apply the test without engaging in the use of hindsight, but by reference to the state of the art at the time the invention was made.

An excellent example of a situation where the requirement of an inventive step was not satisfied can be seen in the case of *Genentech Inc's Patent*.[26] A research programme conducted by Genentech resulted in the identification and mapping of elements of DNA (one of the basic building blocks of life). The research furthered the knowledge of this basic structure and could be used as the basis for the production of anti-coagulant drugs. Genentech sought to patent the results of its efforts, the application ultimately failing when the Court of Appeal held that the work did not involve an inventive step. Mustill LJ referred to Genentech's activities in the following way:

> they won the race. The goal was known and others were trying to reach it. Genentech got there first.[27]

Whilst the achievement of a goal (equivalent, perhaps, to setting a new world record in a sporting event) would constitute evidence of novelty, if the target was widely known, winning the race might tell no more than that the winner was richer or more determined or luckier than others working in the same area. To this extent, therefore, the expenditure

---

[24] <http://www.ipo.gov.uk/types/patent/p-applying/p-apply/p-cda.htm>.
[25] s. 3.   [26] [1989] RPC 147.   [27] [1989] RPC 147 at 251.

of time and effort in making a breakthrough will not, of itself, be conclusive evidence of the existence of an inventive step.[28]

Such arguments are of considerable relevance in the information technology field, where vast sums of money are being expended by large research units throughout the world, all pursuing the goal of faster, more powerful computing devices. A distinction can be drawn between this situation, where the goal can be expressed only in abstract terms, and that applying in *Genentech*,[29] where the target of the research was much more precisely defined. Even on this restricted analysis, the situation appears a little inequitable. The achievement of the goal of running a mile in less than three minutes might not be inventive, but would certainly be meritorious and deserving of recognition. The problem will be encountered in a number of areas and the traditional precepts of intellectual property may not fit well with developments in information technology, yet the effect of denying access to intellectual property rights is to deny any form of legal recognition and protection for the work in question.

Also at issue in the *Genentech*[30] litigation was the identification of the notional persons 'skilled in the art'—those persons to whom the making of the steps leading to the claimed invention would have been 'obvious'. It was recognised that, in respect of advanced areas of technology, the collected knowledge of a team of researchers might be the relevant factor rather than the knowledge possessed by any particular individual. The question also arises of whether the person or persons 'skilled in the art' should themselves be credited with possessing any inventive qualities. In the case of *Valensi v British Radio Corpn Ltd*,[31] it was stated that:

> the hypothetical addressee is not a person of exceptional skill and knowledge, that he is not to be expected to exercise any invention nor any prolonged research, inquiry or experiment. He must, however, be prepared to display a reasonable degree of skill and common knowledge of the art in making trials and to correct obvious errors in the specification if a means of correcting them can readily be found.[32]

A more expansive view of the abilities of the skilled person was adopted by Mustill LJ in *Genentech*. In a comment which is especially relevant in relation to developments in information technology, he held that:

> Where the art by its nature involves intellectual gifts and ingenuity of approach, it would, I believe, be wrong to assume that the hypothetical person is devoid of those gifts.[33]

Capacity for industrial application

The final requirement which must be satisfied in order for a patent application to proceed is that the invention involved should be capable of industrial application. This requirement is, in many respects, at the heart of the patent system. However novel an idea might be, it will be of little practical benefit if it cannot usefully be applied. Application may take two forms, with the subject matter of the patent application referring to a product or a process (sometimes referred to as apparatus and means). In many instances, applications will combine the two elements. A helpful illustration is provided in Laddie J's judgment in the case of *Fujitsu Ltd's Application*:[34]

> it may be useful to consider what the position would be in a case where someone had invented a new way of mowing grass which involved designing a new type of motor with

---

[28] [1989] RPC 147 at 278.   [29] *Genentech Inc's Patent* [1989] RPC 147.
[30] *Genentech Inc's Patent* [1989] RPC 147.   [31] [1973] RPC 337.   [32] [1973] RPC 337 at 377.
[33] *Genentech Inc's Patent* [1989] RPC 147 at 280.   [34] [1996] RPC 511.

micro sensors and blade adjustment motors on it, the sensors being used to determine both the softness of the grass to be cut and the height of it above the ground and then produced an output which operated the motors so as to adjust the height of the cut, the angle of the blades and the speed at which they rotated . . . considerations of novelty aside, such a device would be patentable and, so it seems to me, would be the mowing method itself.

In a software context, the claim may often be that the equipment operating in accordance with the program's instructions constitutes a novel product, whilst the algorithmic steps prescribed by the implementing programs represent a novel process. Virtually any product will be capable of being sold or otherwise disposed of and, in this respect, will satisfy the applicability test. With a process, slightly different considerations will apply. If the end result of the application of the process will be a product, it is likely that the process will be considered capable of industrial application. An illustration of the kind of development which will be excluded from patent protection can be found in the provisions of the Patents Act 1977, which states that:

> an invention of a method of treatment of the human or animal body by surgery or therapy or of diagnosis practised on the human or animal body shall not be taken to be capable of industrial application.[35]

Thus, the intangible concept is not patentable. In the event, however, that new surgical tools or equipment are invented to facilitate the application of the new techniques, these will, assuming the other statutory criteria are complied with, be regarded as patentable.

Matters excluded from patent protection

In addition to defining the elements that must be found in an invention, the Patents Act 1977 lists a number of features which will not qualify for the grant of a patent. Section 1(2) (which mirrors Article 52 of the European Patent Convention) provides that patents are not to be awarded for:

(a) a discovery, scientific theory or mathematical method;

(b) a literary, dramatic, musical, or artistic work or any other aesthetic creation whatsoever;

(c) a scheme, rule or method for performing a mental act, playing a game or doing business, or a program for a computer; or

(d) the presentation of information.

Given the appearance of the phrase 'a program for a computer' in this listing, it may appear surprising that the topic should be of any significance in a text on information technology law. Matters, however, are not so straightforward. After reciting the list of prohibited subject matter, both the Patents Act 1977 and the European Patent Convention continue:

> but the foregoing provision shall prevent anything from being treated as an invention for the purposes of this Act only to the extent that a patent or an application for a patent relates to that thing *as such* [emphasis added].

In his judgment in *Fujitsu Ltd's Application*,[36] which was subsequently affirmed by the Court of Appeal,[37] Mr Justice Laddie analysed the rationale behind a number of the

---

[35] s. 4(2).   [36] [1996] RPC 511.   [37] *The Times*, 14 March 1997.

statutory exceptions. The prohibition against the grant of a patent to a discovery illustrates perfectly the problems inherent in this area. The obvious objection to awarding a patent for a discovery, for example, of a new mineral, is that there is no discernible inventive step. However, as was pointed out in the judgment:

> most inventions are based on what would be regarded by many people as discoveries. Large numbers of highly successful and important patents in the pharmaceutical field have been and continue to be based upon the discovery of new strains of micro-organisms which exist naturally in the wild.[38]

Recognising this fact, the statutory prohibition against the grant of a patent is restricted to the case where the application relates to the discovery 'as such'.[39]

In principle, such an approach must be correct. Its practical application has proved more difficult, with particular problems surrounding the treatment of what are frequently referred to as 'software-related inventions'. In part, the problem may lie with the fact that both the Patents Act 1977 and the European Patent Convention were enacted in the 1970s. At that time, it was considered that computer programs could be separated from the hardware components and should be excluded from the patent system. Both the report of the Banks Committee in the United Kingdom and the initial Guidelines for Examiners produced by the European Patent Office make this point clearly. Over the last twenty-odd years, the nature of computer programs has changed and expanded, and the division between software and hardware has become a matter of choice as much as one of technology.

To complicate matters further, as the relevance of the obvious prohibition has declined, so it has also become apparent that software-related inventions are vulnerable to challenge under a range of the statutory exceptions. Applications have been rejected on the basis that they relate to a mathematical method, a method of doing business, the presentation of information, and a method for performing a mental act, all of which are excluded from the award of a patent. It is difficult to think of any other form of technology whose nature and range of application is sufficiently chameleon as to bring it within so many of the statutory prohibitions. Not unnaturally, those seeking patent protection for software-related inventions have sought to lay as much emphasis as possible on the task performed by the invention, and as little as possible on the contribution made by computer programs. The criterion applied by both the European Patent Office and the United Kingdom authorities is to require that the claimed invention produced a 'technical contribution' to the state of the art (also referred to as a 'technical effect' or 'technical application'). The next question, of course, is whether the mere presence of a technical contribution can outweigh the explicit prohibition against patentability.

Patenting software

Notwithstanding the present prohibitions, there is no doubt that software-related inventions can be patented. In the United Kingdom, approximately one hundred patent applications in their name are published each year. In proceedings before the European Patent Office, this figure rises to one hundred per month.[40] The report of the Parliamentary Office of Science and Technology on *Patents, Research and Technology*[41] indicates that 'in the last

---

[38] [1996] RPC 511 at 523. [39] Patents Act 1977, s. 1(2).
[40] I am grateful to Mr J. Houston, Intellectual Property Rights Officer of the University of Strathclyde, for the provision of these statistics. [41] March 1996.

ten years the EPO has granted around 10,000 patents for software-related inventions, and has refused only one hundred applications'.[42] In 2003, it was estimated that up to 30,000 software patents had been issued by the European Patent Office;[43] although, in part because the existence of the statutory prohibitions requires that software-related inventions be catalogued by reference to their field of application rather than the software component, any calculation is a somewhat subjective assessment. Even more substantial figures are quoted for the number of patents awarded in the United States, and there is no doubt that patents have a significant role to play in the field of information technology.

The process of obtaining and enforcing a patent

The application

The act of making an invention will confer no rights upon an inventor. A person wishing to secure protection is required to make an application for a patent and to pursue this through all the stages of the patent procedure.[44] The key components of the process are described in the following paragraphs.

Specification and statement of claim

The key elements of any patent application are the provision of a specification and a statement of claim(s).[45] The specification consists, essentially, of a description of the invention. It will describe the state of the technical art in the field and indicate the improvements which the invention makes and the manner in which this is accomplished. The specification should be formulated in such a manner as to permit the product to be made or the process operated by 'a person skilled in the art'.

The specification serves to indicate what may be regarded as the inventor's opinion regarding the optimum embodiment of its principles. Beyond this, claims for protection may be made regarding the functioning of the product or process—effectively, what the invention does. The drafting of these claims is critical to the success of a patent. Any claim alleging infringement of a patent will relate to the claims rather than to the specification. If the claims are drawn too broadly, the patent application may be rejected on the grounds that the applicant is seeking protection, either for matters which have not been disclosed in the specification or for matters which are not novel or inventive. If the claims are drawn more narrowly, the patent may well be awarded, but prove worthless, as competitors evade its scope by making minor changes to the design of the invention. In many cases, an applicant will submit a considerable number of claims, commencing with extremely broad references to the technology at issue, with subsequent claims narrowing down the level of protection, ending with a claim to protection for the invention 'substantially as described'.

An example of a failure in this regard has been reported concerning the patents granted to what has become the market-leading telephone modem. Modems play a vital role in the transfer of data between computers.[46] Just as with human telephone conversations, a basic requirement of data transmissions is the ability to identify when a communication has

---

[42] p. 31. The Follow-up to the Green Paper on the Community Patent refers to the existence of 13,000 patents in Europe. [43] <http://eupat.ffii.org/>.

[44] Where an invention is made in the course of employment, the employer will be regarded as the inventor for the purpose of making a patent application. [45] s. 14(2).

[46] *The Guardian*, 9 February 1989.

been completed and thereupon terminate the connection. This is referred to as the escape sequence. A particular sequence had been developed in which the initiating modem would transmit three + signs. Such a transmission would be most unlikely to occur in the course of a message and would signal to a compatible receiving modem that the communication had concluded. In this, as in many other areas of the intellectual property field, the question of compatibility is critical. Although it was not selected at random, the 3+s message possessed no unique qualities. The commercial success of the modem produced consumer demand for modems which transmitted and recognised this sequence. In laying claim to a patent for the modem design, the developers failed to claim in respect of the specific escape sequence. This proved a costly error. The resulting patent protection certainly prevented competitors from copying the specific design features of the modem, but the same effect, that of transmitting and receiving data communications, could readily be achieved using alternative and non-infringing means. Having done this, the absence of a claim in respect of the escape sequence left competitors free to utilise this, thereby acquiring compatibility with the market-leading product to their own commercial advantage.

The lodging of an application with the Patent Office serves to initiate the procedures leading to the grant of a patent. Until the Patent Act 1902, although substantial procedural requirements had to be observed, a patent would be awarded without the invention being subjected to any form of scrutiny. From 1902, increasingly stringent procedures have been introduced, whereby an application will be examined with a view to making a determination on whether it complies with the statutory criteria. Under the Patents Act 1977, a two-stage process operates, with applications being subjected to preliminary and substantive examinations.

Preliminary examination

The first purpose of the preliminary examination is to ensure that the application complies with all the formal requirements of the legislation.[47] If this is the case, the examiner will turn to consider the merits of the application. At the stage of the preliminary examination, the examiner's main task is to identify those documents and information sources which it is considered are likely to prove of assistance in applying the criteria of novelty and inventiveness. Having identified relevant documents, the examiner is to scrutinise the documents to such extent as is considered will serve a purpose in determining the application.[48] The results of the preliminary investigation are to be reported to the Comptroller of Patents and to the applicant.[49]

This initial report will be non-judgmental. It may indicate grounds for objecting to or refusing the grant of a patent. In such circumstances, it might become apparent to an applicant that the chances of the application being granted are minimal and the decision taken to withdraw the application.

Publication of the application

Unless notice of withdrawal is given, details of the specification and claims will be published 'as soon as possible' after the expiry of eighteen months from the date of application.[50] In most cases, an applicant will receive the report of the preliminary examination before the application is due to be published. Whilst publication will have no detrimental effect in the event that the patent is ultimately granted, if the application is unsuccessful, the consequence

---

[47] Patents Act 1977, s. 17(2).   [48] s. 17(4)–(5).   [49] s. 17(2).   [50] Patents Act 1977, s. 16.

will be that the inventor will have disclosed information to the public without securing any benefit in return. Equally seriously, publication may adversely affect the prospects of any modified application which the inventor might wish to make. Under the present United States system, no details of an application are published until the patent is ultimately awarded. Although this may seem fairer to the applicant, problems have been encountered with what are referred to as 'submarine patents'. Even assuming a relatively straightforward application, it will be quite normal for the process to take two to three years. With more complex cases, perhaps including modification of the original application, this period may increase to ten years, or even longer. The essence of a submarine patent is that, originally describing what has been described as 'science fiction technology', it lurks unseen in the patent office awaiting the widespread application of the technology by third parties (perhaps being modified better to describe their applications). At this time, the patent surfaces with claims of patent infringement being fired at any users.

Substantive examination

In the event that the applicant wishes the process to continue, a request must be made for a substantive examination.[51] It is at this stage that the examiner will make a full study of whether the claimed invention is novel, involves an inventive step, is capable of industrial application, and does not fall within one of the prohibited categories. The request for a substantive examination must be made within six months of the date of publication.[52]

Although, as has been said, the determination of whether an invention is novel has to be made by reference to any material in the public domain, it would be unreasonable to expect patent examiners to be aware of every book or article deposited in any library anywhere in the world. The basic tool for examiners will be collections of patents previously awarded in the world's major patent offices.

It is at the stage of the substantive examination that a decision will be made regarding the patentability or otherwise of the invention. The examiner will make a report to the Comptroller of Patents. In the event that this report makes objection to aspects of the application, the applicant must be afforded the opportunity to make observations or to amend the application so as to take account of the examiner's objections. In the event of the applicant's failure adequately so to do, the Comptroller may refuse the application.[53]

Third-party involvement

The Patents Act 1977 contains no provisions for the formal involvement of third parties in the processes leading to the grant or refusal of a patent. It is provided, however, that in any interval between publication of the application and the decision on grant, a third party may submit written observations to the Comptroller, who must take these into account in reaching a decision.[54]

Award of a patent

In the event that a patent is awarded, the Comptroller is required to cause a notice to this effect to be published in the *Official Journal (Patents)*. The maximum term of validity of a patent is twenty years, commencing from the date when the application is first submitted.[55]

---

[51] Patents Act 1977, s. 18(1).   [52] Patents Rules 1995, SI 1995/2093, r. 33.

[53] Patents Act 1977, s. 18(3).   [54] s. 21.   [55] s. 20.

It should be noted, however, that a patent is not awarded for such a period. Protection will be awarded for an initial period of four years; thereafter annual applications will require to be made (accompanied by a fee) to retain the patent's validity. Only a small percentage of patents remain in force for the full twenty-year period, the average lifespan of a patent being in the region of eight years.[56] By this time, it will have become apparent either that the patent has been overtaken by newer technologies or that the invention is of limited practical utility.

Infringement of patents

The definition of infringement is of critical importance. Under the terms of the Patents Act 1977, infringement may be either direct or indirect. Direct infringement occurs when a party, without the consent, express or implied, of the proprietor of the patent 'makes, disposes or offers to dispose of, uses, keeps, or imports' a product constituting the subject matter of the patent. Similar prohibitions apply in the event that the patent covers a process.[57]

Indirect infringement occurs where a party supplies or offers to supply any equipment which constitutes an essential part of the invention in the knowledge (or having reasonable grounds to believe) that infringement will result.[58]

The question of whether a subsequent product infringes the provisions of a patent is essentially one of fact. It will seldom be the case that the subsequent product is an exact copy of a patented object. In the event that any infringement is innocent, with the product being the result of the competitor's own researches, it is unlikely that every detail of the original will be replicated. Should the subsequent producer have been aware of and seek to evade the provisions of the patent, it is again likely that differences of detail will be introduced in an effort to conceal the fact of infringement.

In the event that products are not identical, the task for the court is to examine the patent specification and statement of claim in order to identify the essential features or integers possessed by the patented product. These are then compared with those of the competing product. If the latter replicates the essential elements, infringement may be established even though the product may differ in other respects. An example of the operation of this principle can be seen in the case of *Beecham Group Ltd v Bristol Laboratories Ltd.*[59] Here, the plaintiffs held a patent for a pharmaceutical product possessing a particular chemical structure. The defendant company produced a product possessing a slightly different structure, but the evidence established that the latter product became converted to the patented product upon being absorbed into the bloodstream. In these circumstances, it was held that there was a patent infringement.

In the case of *Catnic Components Ltd v Hill and Smith Ltd,*[60] the plaintiffs had been granted a patent in respect of a design of lintel. The patent made specific reference to the fact that the support member was to be vertical. The defendants subsequently produced a lintel possessing most of the features of the original design, but with the change that the support was angled slightly from the vertical. The alteration made the design slightly less effective, although the difference was of no practical significance. It was held that the similarity between the two designs was sufficient for infringement to be established.

The fact that the addition of further integers increases the efficiency of the product will not necessarily defeat a claim of infringement. As was stated by Bower LJ in the case of

---

[56] For an excellent analysis of the lifespan of patents, see J. Phillips and A. Firth, *An Introduction to Intellectual Property Law*, 3rd edn (London, 2001).   [57] Patents Act 1977, s. 60(1).
[58] s. 60(2).   [59] [1978] RPC 153.   [60] [1982] RPC 183.

Wenham Gas Co Ltd v Champion Gas Lamp Co Ltd,[61] 'the superadding of ingenuity to a robbery does not make the operation justifiable'. More difficult issues may arise in the event that the subsequent product substitutes or modifies some of the essential integers of the patented product. Here, the determination of whether there is any infringement will be strongly influenced by any expert evidence presented by the parties. If it can be established that it would have been obvious to the mythical 'workman, skilled in the art', presented with details of the modification at the date of publication of the patent, that the substitution of one feature for another would not have had a significant effect on the operation of the patented invention, infringement may be established.

Remedies for infringement of a patent

Four basic forms of remedy may be available to the holder of a patent. At the initial stage of legal proceedings, an injunction may be sought to prevent the defendant continuing with the alleged infringement. When the dispute comes to trial, three further remedies may be applicable. An order may be sought requiring the delivery up to the patentee of any infringing copies. In terms of financial compensation, the patentee may seek either an accounting of profits from the infringer or an award of damages.

Revocation of a patent

A patent may be revoked by the court or the Comptroller on the application of any person if it is established:

1. that the invention is not a patentable invention;

2. that the patent was granted to a person or persons who were not the only persons qualified to obtain such a grant. Such an action may only be brought by a person or persons who would have been entitled to be granted the patent or to have shared in such a grant. The action must be brought within two years from the date of the patent grant unless it is established that the patent holder was aware that he or she was not entitled to the proprietorship of the patent;

3. the specification does not disclose the invention sufficiently clearly and completely for it to be performed by a person reasonably skilled in the art;

4. the matter disclosed in the patent specification is more extensive than that disclosed in the patent application; or

5. the protection conferred under the patent has been extended by an amendment which should not have been allowed.[62]

Although it is possible that a challenge to the validity of a patent may be brought in isolation, it will more commonly be raised as an issue in the course of proceedings by the patent holder alleging infringement. Effectively, therefore, the trial may provide the forum for reconsideration of the question of whether the application for patent protection should be granted.

This possibility is particularly relevant in the information technology sector, where substantial criticism has been made of the abilities of patent offices to identify all materials relevant to determinations of novelty and inventiveness. To this extent, acquisition of a patent may mark only the first stage in a continuing battle to establish its validity and enforce its terms.

---

[61] [1891] 9 RPC 49.   [62] Patents Act 1977, s. 72.

Conclusions

The processes for obtaining a patent are frequently lengthy and expensive. Although the United Kingdom Patent Office introduced a 'fast track' process in 1995, which aimed to make a decision on the patentability of an application within twelve months,[63] the patent process will normally occupy a period in excess of two years. Fees must be paid at all stages of the patent process.[64] In addition, the complexity of the processes may compel applications to make use of the services of patent agents—something which is recommended by the Patent Office.

Faced with these factors, coupled with the requirement in the European and United Kingdom systems that details of an invention be published prior to the decision being taken on whether to award a patent, it might be queried where the value of the patent system lies for those working in the software field. Given the pace of technical development, it will certainly be the case that, for many applications, the technology will be rendered obsolete before the patent is awarded. The United States case of *Microsoft v Stac* provides perhaps the best example of the value of the patent system.[65]

At issue in the case was a patent describing novel techniques for the practice of data compression. As the name suggests, this technique is used to reduce the amount of storage space necessary to hold data. A recent application of compression technology can be seen with the MP3 system. MP3 is an audio compression format that enables audio files to be stored and transferred on a computer with relatively small file size. Typically, three minutes of music recorded in digital format would require some 30MB of storage space. Use of the MP3 mathematical techniques, which are themselves patented in the United States[66] and the source of potential litigation, reduces the space required to about 3MB. Such a reduction makes it feasible to place musical tracks on, and download from, the Internet.

In the particular case, Stac held two United States patents for a compression system which was sold under the name 'Stacker'. Interestingly, especially given the controversy which has existed concerning the eligibility of software-related inventions for patentability within the United Kingdom, one of the patents was originally issued in the United Kingdom to a British company, Ferranti, and was subsequently assigned to Stac. Microsoft wished to incorporate a compression system in a new version of its operating system. Negotiations followed with Stac but these proved unsuccessful, largely because Microsoft was unwilling to offer any payment for the use of the Stac system.[67] When the new version of the operating system appeared on the market, it did contain a compression system. It transpired that it was based on the Stac system. Microsoft's claim was that this had been used initially, but it had subsequently devised it's own code. In copyright law, as will be discussed later,[68] this claim may well have succeeded and might at least have resulted in extensive litigation. As the techniques were protected by patents, all that Stac had to establish was that Microsoft had used these. In a jury trial, Stac was awarded $120 million in compensation.[69]

---

[63] <http://www.ipo.gov.uk/press-release-20070404.htm>.

[64] For current details, see <http://www.ipo.gov.uk/types/patent/p-formsfees.htm>.

[65] For details of the case, see <http://www.msversus.org/archive/stac.html>.

[66] See <http://www.mp3.com/news/095.html>.

[67] For details of Stac's claim, see <http://en.swpat.org/wiki/I4i_v._Microsoft_(2009,_USA)>.

[68] See discussion of *Computer Associates v Altai*, 982 F 2d 693 (1992).

[69] Ultimately, the two companies signed a cross-licensing agreement. Stac received $43 million in cash from Microsoft and Microsoft invested $39.9 million in non-voting Stac stock (about 15 per cent of the company's shares)—a total payout of $83 million.

The litigation brought by Stac marked—at least until the anti-trust litigation brought by the United States authorities—the most significant legal finding against Microsoft. As such, it is eloquent testimony to the strength of a patent. Software patents have been, and remain, an extremely controversial subject, especially in the United States. Objections appear to be based on a number of grounds. The system, it is argued, is inequitable in the situation where different people are working independently in the same field. The first one to obtain a patent is then in a position to stop others exploiting their own work. As can be seen from the example of Alexander Graham Bell and Elisha Grey cited earlier, this is not a new phenomenon. A further ground of objection is founded in the perception that the inability of the Patent Offices to make comprehensive searches in the field has resulted in the award of patents in respect of technology which is not truly novel or inventive. This is a more difficult ground to assess. It may be noted that examination is a relatively novel feature of the patent system. Until the twentieth century, the system was effectively one of registration. The fact that a patent is granted is not conclusive evidence of its validity. It may be challenged at any time. Against this, it should be stated that the onus of proving a patent to be invalid lies with the challenger, and patent litigation can be prolonged and expensive. These issues will be considered in more detail in the following chapter, which will consider the manner in which patent law has evolved in relation to patents for software-related inventions.

15

Patents and software

Introduction

Given the apparently clear prohibition against the grant of patents for computer programs in both the Patents Act and the European Patent Convention, it might appear that the topic should be of little significance. This is far from the case and—rather as was said by Humpty Dumpty in the well-known legal authority, *Alice in Wonderland*, 'when I use a word it means exactly what I want it to mean'—judges in both the United Kingdom and the European Patent Office have been forced to engage in word gymnastics when attempting to reconcile the words of the Act and Convention with the realities of a world in which software patents have become a reality. Tensions have been exacerbated because of significant differences in interpretative approaches between the two systems. The judges in the European Patent Office seek in many respects to determine what the drafters of the Convention would have intended had they been aware of the manner in which technologies might develop. United Kingdom courts, of course, are restricted to interpreting the words used in a statute.

Although the patent system has traditionally been based on national or regional instruments, the increasing move towards globalisation is adding additional pressures. The global picture was well described by Lord Justice Jacob in the case of *Aerotel v Telco*[1] when he suggested that, in large part because of the willingness of the United States authorities to grant patents for software-related inventions, '[a]n arms race in which the weapons are patents has set in.'[2] Beyond conflicts between states, patents have become a major weapon in the arsenals of information technology and telecommunications manufacturers. Scarcely a day seems to go by without reports of a new piece of litigation between the likes of Apple and Samsung in some country. On occasion the sums of money involved are eye watering—more than $800 million in one US dispute although it does seem that relatively few cases are ever definitively resolved within the legal system.

The first United Kingdom cases involving the eligibility of software-related inventions for patent protection arose under the Patents Act 1949. Not surprisingly given the time the Act was enacted, there is no mention of the words computer, programs, or software. The Act provided rather more simply that patents might be awarded for 'any manner of new manufacture'[3] without seeking to define the concept further. Although some commentators have expressed the view that the categories of qualifying and prohibited subject matter introduced in the 1977 Act represented a codification of existing precedent, it was stated by Purchas LJ in *Genentech Inc's Patent*[4] that the 1977 Act must be 'viewed in the context of a departure from much of the authority and usage of previous patent law'. What is perhaps clear and worthy of note is that cases brought under the 1949 Act appear to demonstrate a move from initial judicial hostility to acceptance of the need for and desirability of bringing the embryonic software industry within the scope of the patent system. It is again perhaps noteworthy that in the United States—generally regarded as the jurisdiction most friendly towards issuing

---

[1] [2006] EWCA Civ 1371.   [2] para. 18.   [3] s. 101.   [4] [1989] RPC 147.

patents for software-related inventions—the patent law in force dates back to 1952 and is based upon principles very similar to those found in the United Kingdom's Act of 1949.

In the final case decided under the Patents Act 1949, that of *International Business Machines Corpn's Application*,[5] a patent had been awarded and the proceedings related to a challenge by the applicants to its validity. After surveying all of the previous United Kingdom authorities and considering the first United States cases concerned with software-related inventions to reach the level of the Supreme Court, the Patent Appeals Tribunal concluded that although the only novelty in the application lay in the software components, the protection claimed was as:

> a manner of new manufacture is a method involving operating or controlling a computer in which, so far as the contested claims are concerned, the computer is programmed in a particular way or programmes in physical form to control a computer so that it will operate in accordance with his method.

The application, it was concluded, should be accepted on the basis that:

> an inventive concept, if novel, can be patented to the extent that claims can be framed directed to an embodiment of the concept in some apparatus or process of manufacture.[6]

The essential distinction drawn is one which continues to be at issue today—between a program for a computer and a computer programmed to operate in a particular manner.

Towards the end of the 1960s, it became clear that reform would be needed to the United Kingdom's patent system, both for internal purposes and, perhaps more significantly, to ensure that the country was in a position to participate in the nascent European Patent Convention, in whose drafting process the United Kingdom had been heavily involved. As indicated in the previous chapter, the Banks Committee, was established with the remit to consider the patent system, and make recommendations for reform. The Committee's report was published in 1970, with a chapter being devoted to an examination of the position of computer programs.[7] This concluded that the situation was characterised by considerable uncertainty, but indicated that the majority of the evidence submitted to the Committee was hostile to the notion that programs should qualify for patent protection.[8] This view was endorsed by the Committee, which put forward reasons of both principle and utility for denying protection. In terms of principle, it was argued that no significant distinction existed between programs and methods of mathematical calculation, which had always been excluded from protection. Practical problems were also identified, the Committee commenting:

> were programs to be patentable, very real and substantial difficulties would be experienced by the Patent Office in searching applications for program patents even were the search material available in suitably classified form. The issues of novelty and obviousness would be so difficult of determination that patents of doubtful validity would be likely to issue.[9]

Although this comment might appear at odds with much of the case law under the 1949 Act, in almost all of the cases, the legal argument was restricted to the question of whether the subject matter of the application was entitled to be considered for the award of a patent. The cases were not concerned with the question of whether the software developments were truly novel. As will be discussed, one of the major arguments advanced against the application of the patent system to software-related inventions has concerned the difficulty in establishing the true state of the technical art. Especially in the United States, a number of

---

[5] [1980] FSR 564. [6] [1980] FSR 564 at 573. [7] Cmnd 4407 (1970), ch. 17.
[8] Ch. 17, para. 479. [9] Ch. 17, para. 483.

fairly high-profile patent awards have been subject to heavy criticism—in at least one case resulting in the revocation of the patent—on the ground that the technology described was well-known to those working in the field. Thirty years of advances in database technology do not appear to have done much to resolve the concerns voiced by the Banks Committee.

In the event, the final recommendation of the Banks Committee was that:

> A computer program, that is: a set of instructions for controlling the sequence of operations of a data processing system, in whatever form the invention is presented e.g. a method of programming computers, a computer when programmed in a certain way and where the novelty or alleged novelty lies only in the program, should not be patentable.[10]

Such a view clearly conflicts with the judgment of the Patent Appeals Tribunal in the *International Business Machines Corpn's Application* decision,[11] and represents a hardening of attitudes towards the award of patents for software-related inventions. It was not considered, however, that the presence of software components in an otherwise qualifying invention should exclude the latter from patent protection. The report drew a distinction between:

> applications for programs *per se* and for inventions of the kind claimed at a computer controlled steelworks…which involve the use of a program. The invention should then be patentable if it does not reside merely in the details of the program.[12]

Although such a distinction may be supported, once again the seeds of doubt as to the application of patent protection have been planted. Two propositions can be culled from the report of the Banks Committee. A program *per se* should never, at least under the United Kingdom and European regimes, be accepted as the basis for a patent. Equally, an invention that would otherwise be considered patentable is not to be barred from protection merely because a program is utilised somewhere in its operations. Inevitably, problems arise at the margins, and especially in the situation where the product functions in a novel and inventive manner, but where this is due in large measure to the operation of the programs contained therein.

The Patents Act 1977 and the European Patent Convention

As indicated in Chapter 14, after specifying the positive attributes which must be evidenced in a patent application, the Patents Act 1977 provides that:

> the following (among other things) are not inventions for the purposes of this Act, that is to say anything which consists of—
>
> (a) a discovery, scientific theory or mathematical method;
>
> (b) a literary, dramatic, musical or artistic work or any other aesthetic creation whatsoever;
>
> (c) a scheme, rule or method for performing a mental act, playing a game or doing business, or a program for a computer; or
>
> (d) the presentation of information.[13]

Although the first draft of the European Patent Convention was silent on the point, as the result of representations made by the United Kingdom delegation the final text contains a very similar list of prohibited subject matter, providing that:

> 1. European patents shall be granted for any inventions which are susceptible of industrial application, which are new and which involve an inventive step.

---

[10] Cmnd 4407 (1970), ch. 17, para. 487.   [11] [1980] FSR 564 at 573.
[12] Cmnd 4407 (1970), ch. 17, para. 486.   [13] s. 1(2).

2. The following in particular shall not be regarded as inventions within the meaning of paragraph 1:

   (a) discoveries, scientific theories and mathematical methods;

   (b) aesthetic creations;

   (c) schemes, rules and methods for performing mental acts, playing games or doing business, and programs for computers;

   (d) presentations of information.

3. The provisions of paragraph 2 shall exclude patentability of the subject-matter or activities referred to in that provision only to the extent to which a European patent application or European patent relates to such subject-matter or activities as such.[14]

The minor discrepancy in terminology between the Convention and Act has drawn some judicial criticism, Lord Justice Jacob commenting in the case of *Aerotel v Telco* that:

Although s. 1(2) pointlessly uses somewhat different wording from the EPC no-one suggests that it has any different meaning. So we, like the parties before us, work directly from the source.[15]

In both the Act and the Convention, the list of non-qualifying subject matter is followed by the proviso that the prohibition applies only to the extent that the application relates to that item 'as such'. It is the interpretation of this latter provision that has been at the heart of litigation in this area. Typically, as in the cases brought under the Patents Act 1949, the claim has been made that what should be protected is the end-product of the program's operation—namely, what the software plus hardware components accomplish rather than the manner in which this is done.

To complicate matters further, it has become apparent that software-related inventions are vulnerable to challenge under a range of the statutory exceptions. Applications have been rejected on the basis that they relate to a mathematical method, a method of doing business, the presentation of information and a method for performing a mental act, all of which are excluded from the award of a patent. It is difficult to think of any other form of technology whose nature and range of application is so chameleon-like as to bring it within so many of the statutory prohibitions.

As indicated earlier, the Patents Act 1977 was enacted in large part in order to enable the United Kingdom to ratify the European Patent Convention and provides, most unusually, that judicial notice is to be taken of decisions of the European authorities.[16] It is further provided that:

the following provisions of this Act . . . are so framed as to have, as nearly as practicable, the same effects in the United Kingdom as the corresponding provisions of the European Patent Convention . . .[17]

Given this, it is not surprising that it should be stated by Nicholls LJ in *Gale's Application*:[18]

It would be absurd if, on the issue of patentability, a patent application should suffer a different fate according to whether it was made in the United Kingdom under the Act or was made in Munich for a European Patent (United Kingdom) under the Convention.[19]

In spite of this recognition, concerns have been raised that software-related applications have been treated more harshly before the United Kingdom courts than their European counterparts. Such a matter is difficult to determine with any degree of certainty. In recent

---

[14] Art. 52.   [15] [2006] EWCA Civ 1371 at para. 6.   [16] s. 91.
[17] s. 130(7).   [18] [1991] RPC 305.   [19] [1991] RPC 305 at 323.

years matters have become ever more complex. Whilst in the 1990s, the question was whether the United Kingdom authorities were applying the same criteria as the European Patent Office Boards of Appeal, differently composed Boards of Appeal have adopted significantly different criteria in determining applications before them to the extent that it has proved impossible for national courts to determine a single line of authority to follow.

The quest for a technical contribution

Although the term 'technical contribution' (or technical effect) does not appear in either the Patents Act 1977 or the European Patent Convention, it has achieved pivotal significance in the field of software-related inventions since being introduced in Guidelines for Examiners drawn up by the European Patent Office. Originally these stated:

> If the contribution to the known art resides solely in a computer program then the subject matter is not patentable in whatever form it might be presented in those claims. For example, a claim to a computer characterised by having the particular program stored in its memory or to a process for operating a computer under control of the program would be as objectionable as a claim to the program *per se* or the program when recorded on magnetic tape.[20]

By 1985 in view of the increasing importance of computer programs, it was considered desirable to offer more precise guidance, both to inventors and to the examiners in the European Patent Office. To this extent, new Guidelines[21] were promulgated which seek to make it clear that the essential prerequisite for the grant of a patent is the making of a 'technical' invention, namely a requirement that there be some tangible end-product. Thus, although the revised Guidelines provided that:

> A computer program claimed by itself or as a record on a carrier is unpatentable irrespective of its content. The situation is not normally changed when the computer program is loaded into a known computer[22]

it was recognised also that inventions in which a computer program constitutes an essential element might qualify for patent protection, subject to the application of the Convention's general rules. The Guidelines continued:

> If, however, the subject matter as claimed makes a technical contribution to the known art, patentability should not be denied merely on the ground that a computer program is involved in its implementation. This means, for example, that program controlled machines and program controlled manufacturing and control processes should normally be regarded as a patentable subject matter. It follows also that, where the claimed subject matter is concerned only with the program controlled internal working of a known computer, the subject matter could be patentable if it produced a technical effect.

The aim of the new approach, it was stated, was to produce a workable system from the standpoint of the European Patent Office (particularly in relation to the search and examination requirements) whilst 'responding to the reasonable desires of industry for a somewhat more liberal line than that adopted in the past'.

The first significant case following from the adoption of the new European Patent Office Guidelines was the decision of the European Patent Office Technical Board of Appeal in the

---

[20] OJ 1/1978.

[21] The current guidelines were published in 2007 and are available from <http://www.european-patent-office.org/legal/gui_lines/index.htm>.

[22] para. 22.

case of *Vicom/Computer-Related Inventions* in July 1986.[23] This ruling has been of pivotal importance, being cited in virtually every subsequent European Patent Office and United Kingdom decision. Discussion of the question of how far software-related inventions might be patentable under the Patents Act 1977 must therefore commence with discussion of this case.

The *Vicom* application sought a patent for the use of a computer for image-processing purposes. Data representing the image in the form of electrical signals would be processed by the computer so as to enhance the quality of the image as displayed on a monitor. It was accepted by the applicant that the process could be operated using a standard computer. This application was initially rejected by the examiner in the European Patent Office on two grounds, first that it sought protection for a computer program and, secondly, that it related to a mathematical method. The electrical signal, it was argued, could be represented in mathematical terms, likewise the processed signal.

Appealing against this refusal, the applicants claimed that their invention made a novel technical contribution resulting from the novel manner in which data was processed. This, it was argued, produced a direct technical benefit as it allowed data to be processed more speedily than had hitherto been possible. The invention, it was argued:

> made a new and valuable contribution to the stock of human knowledge and patent protec-
> tion for this contribution cannot be denied merely on the basis that the manner in which the
> invention is defined would appear to bring it within the exclusions of Article 52(3) EPC.[24]

Acting on a suggestion from the examiner, amended claims relating both to the apparatus required and the methods of processing utilised were submitted for consideration by the Board of Appeal. This held that the claims referred to patentable subject-matter. In respect of the program objection it was held that:

> Generally, claims which can be considered as being directed to a computer set up to operate in
> accordance with a specified program (whether by means of hardware or software) for control-
> ling or carrying out a technical process cannot be regarded as relating to a computer program...
>
> Generally speaking, an invention which would be patentable in accordance with conven-
> tional patentability criteria should not be excluded from protection by the mere fact that for
> its implementation modern technical means in the form of a computer program are used.
> Decisive is what technical contribution the invention as defined in the claim when consid-
> ered as a whole makes to the known art.[25]

It was further recognised that whilst a mathematical method could not be protected directly, different considerations arose when the formula was applied:

> if a mathematical method is used in a technical process, that process is carried out on a
> physical entity...by some technical means implementing the method and provides as its
> end result a certain change in that entity. The technical means might include a computer
> comprising suitable hardware or an appropriately programmed general purpose computer.[26]

What was required was that the mathematical method should be applied within a specific technical context which, being capable of industrial application, would qualify for patent protection. In this event, the mathematical methods could freely be used by third parties for any purpose other than the specified form of image processing. Such an approach overcomes one of the major concerns which has been expressed by opponents of software patents—especially in the United States—that a patent could be infringed by a party working out calculations with pen and paper.

---

[23] *Vicom Systems Inc's Application* [1987] 2 EPOR 74.   [24] At 77–8.   [25] At 80–1.
[26] At 79.

In respect of the claims relating to the apparatus, it was conceded that the process could be conducted using conventional computing equipment. The Board of Appeal held, however, that:

> a claim directed to a technical process which process is carried out under the control of a program (be this implemented in hardware or in software), cannot be regarded as relating to a computer program as such within the meaning of Article 52(3) EPC [European Patent Convention], as it is the application of the program for determining the sequence of steps in the process for which in effect protection is sought. Consequently, such a claim is allowable under Article 52(2)(c) and (3) EPC.

As technology has developed it is frequently open to developers to determine whether applications should be implemented by dedicated hardware or through software running on multipurpose computers. A simple example can be seen with satellite navigation systems. Initially, these tended to be marketed as stand-alone devices but with the emergence of smart phones it is increasingly common for users to download a software application and use their phone as a navigation device. Commenting on this technical possibility, the Board of Appeal stated:

> In arriving at this conclusion, the Board has additionally considered that making a distinction between embodiments of the same invention carried out in hardware or in software is inappropriate as it can fairly be said that the choice between these two possibilities is not of an essential nature but is based on technical and economical considerations which bear no relationship to the inventive concept as such.
>
> Generally speaking, an invention which would be patentable in accordance with conventional patentability criteria should not be excluded from protection by the mere fact that for its implementation modern technical means in the form of a computer program are used. Decisive is what technical contribution the invention as defined in the claim when considered as a whole makes to the known art.[27]

A number of significant features can be identified from the decision in *Vicom*. The applicants' argument might well be noted that they had made 'a new and valuable contribution to the stock of human knowledge'. Protecting such work is at the core of the patent system. In terms of the decision of the Board of Appeal, there is recognition that what an invention does is more important than the manner in which it is achieved. As was stated in the decision, and as is increasingly the case, the distinction between hardware and software implementation of a concept is a matter of choice.

Software-related inventions returned to the European Patent Office Board of Appeal in 1987 in the case of *Koch and Sterzel*.[28] Here, a patent had been awarded in respect of a 'diagnostic X-ray system operative in response to control signals from a stored program digital computer to generate an X-ray beam and to produce an image of the object through which the X-ray beam passes'.[29] The validity of the patent was challenged by two competitor companies, which argued that its subject matter differed from the state of the art only through the involvement of a novel computer program. The decision in *Vicom*,[30] it was suggested, was erroneous in that an application should not be accepted where the elements of novelty and inventiveness lay only in prohibited subject matter—in this case a computer program. Support for this contention was found in a decision of the German courts, to the effect that:

> a teaching is not technical if in its essence it states a rule that can be carried out without employing controllable natural forces other than human brainpower, even if the use of

---

[27] At 79.   [28] [1988] EPOR 72.   [29] EP0001640.
[30] *Vicom Systems Inc's Application* [1987] 2 EPOR 74.

technical means appears expedient or indeed the only sensible and hence the necessary procedure, and even if reference is made to these technical means in the claims or description.[31]

We will return to this concept in discussing the impact of the prohibition against patenting schemes or rules for performing a mental act. In *Koch and Sterzel*, the Board of Appeal rejected the German approach, holding that:

> an invention must be assessed as a whole. If it makes use of both technical and non-technical means, the use of non-technical means does not detract from the technical character of the overall teaching. The European Patent Convention does not ask that a patentable invention be exclusively or largely of a technical nature; in other words, it does not prohibit the patenting of inventions consisting of a mix of technical and non-technical elements.[32]

The alternative approach, it was suggested, could result in a situation where technical aspects of an invention, which were themselves novel and inventive, would be denied patent protection because they were connected with non-technical aspects such as computer programs.

The question of where novelty is required to reside was a key issue in the next authority to be considered, the United Kingdom case of *Merrill Lynch's Application*.[33] Just as *Vicom*[34] constitutes a landmark decision under the European Patent Convention, so the decision in *Merrill Lynch's Application*[35] has played this role in United Kingdom patent law.

The factual content of this case was very similar to that at issue in *International Business Machines Corpn's Application*.[36] Merrill Lynch had developed what was referred to as 'a data processing system for making a trading market in securities and for executing orders for securities transactions'. The application of computerised trading systems in stocks and shares has proved controversial in a number of areas. Some of the blame for the 'crash' of stock exchanges in times of financial crisis has been apportioned to the operation of systems whereby a fall in share prices automatically triggers the sale of shares which produces a further drop in prices, more selling, and a continuation of a downward spiral. Such considerations were not at issue in the present case, which was concerned solely with the question of whether a patent might be awarded in respect of one such system.

The patent claimed by Merrill Lynch related to a business system which:

> retrieves and stores the best current bid and asked prices; qualifies customers' buy/sell orders for execution; executes the orders; and reports the trade particulars to customers and to national stock price reporting systems. The system apparatus also determines and monitors stock inventory and profit for the market maker.[37]

The specification went on to state that the programs involved could be implemented on a wide range of data-processing equipment. Effectively, what the application was claiming was that a general-purpose computer could operate the computer programs to produce novel effects.

The application was rejected within the Patent Office on the basis that the subject matter of the alleged invention fell within the prohibition of section 1(2) of the Patents Act 1977. The principal patent examiner held that the effect of this section was such that it would prevent the award of a patent in the situation where the program was incorporated in some other object (the computer) but where the novelty and inventive step resided in the elements of the program rather than in any of the other attributes of the subject matter.

---

[31] [1988] EPOR 72 at 74.   [32] [1988] EPOR 72 at 74.

[33] [1989] RPC 561, reported at first instance at [1988] RPC 1.   [34] [1987] 2 EPOR 74.

[35] [1989] RPC 561, reported at first instance at [1988] RPC 1.   [36] [1980] FSR 564.

[37] *Merrill Lynch's Application* [1989] RPC 561 at 569.

This reasoning, which was upheld by Falconer J in the Patents Court, was challenged before the Court of Appeal. The critical issue concerned the interpretation of the concluding passage of section 1(2) of the Patents Act 1977, stating that the prohibitions against patentability extended only 'to the extent that a patent or application for a patent relates to that thing as such'. It was the applicant's contention that the claim related to apparatus operating in accordance with the requirements of the program and, therefore, to more than the program as such.

Subsequent to the decision at first instance,[38] the Court of Appeal delivered its judgment in the case of *Genentech Inc's Patent*,[39] which also took account of the decision of the European Patent Office Board of Appeal in the case of *Vicom's Application*.[40] Although the subject matter of this case concerned developments in genetic engineering, the issue of the extent of the prohibition against patentability was also discussed, in this case in the context of a discovery.

As described in the previous chapter, Genentech had identified elements of DNA and obtained patents for applications based upon this research. These patents were revoked by order of Whitford J sitting in the Patents Court on the ground that, inter alia, the identification of the make-up of the DNA was in the nature of a discovery. Having made the discovery, its application was obvious. The only novelty, therefore, lay in the act of discovery. As discoveries cannot be patented, the patent was invalid.

This interpretation of the legislation was rejected by the Court of Appeal. Although the decision to revoke the patent was upheld on other grounds, it was acknowledged that many developments in the pharmaceutical field could be regarded in the same light. Once it is discovered, for example, that a particular drug has a beneficial effect on stomach ulcers, its application is very obvious. Dillon LJ commented:

> Such a conclusion, when applied to a discovery, would seem to mean that the application of the discovery is only patentable if the application is itself novel and not obvious, altogether apart from the novelty of the discovery. That would have a very drastic effect on the patenting of new drugs and medicinal or microbiological processes.[41]

The Court of Appeal in *Genentech*[42] was referred to the decision of Falconer J in *Merrill Lynch*.[43] Indicating its disagreement with the particular reasoning applied (although concurring with the ultimate result of the case), the court held that so long as the subject matter of the application as a whole satisfied the requirements for patentability, it did not matter that the requisite novelty and inventiveness resided in non-qualifying elements. Effectively, the criterion is what an invention does, as opposed to the manner in which this is accomplished.

Applying the reasoning of the *Genentech* decision[44] and that of the European Patent Offices Technical Board of Appeal in *Vicom*,[45] the Court of Appeal affirmed that an invention could be patentable where the novel or inventive elements lay entirely in a computer program. However, the decision of the Patent Office to refuse Merrill Lynch's application was upheld on another ground. Even though the incorporation of the program in the computer equipment might serve to take it outwith the prohibition against the grant of patents for computer programs, attention had to be paid to the nature of the resulting application. In the present case, the result:

> whatever the technical advance may be, is simply the production of a trading system. It is a data processing system for doing a specific business, that is to say making a trading

[38] *Merrill Lynch's Application* [1988] RPC 1.   [39] [1989] RPC 147.
[40] *Vicom Systems Inc's Application* [1987] 2 EPOR 74.
[41] *Genentech Inc's Patent* [1989] RPC 147 at 239–40.   [42] At 239–40.
[43] *Merrill Lynch's Application* [1988] RPC 1.   [44] *Genentech Inc's Patent* [1989] RPC 147.
[45] *Vicom Systems Inc's Application* [1987] 2 EPOR 74.

market in securities. The end result, therefore, is simply 'a method... of doing business', and is excluded by section 1(2)(c) [of the Patents Act 1977]... A data processing system operating to produce a novel technical result would normally be patentable. But it cannot, it seems to me, be patentable if the result itself is a prohibited item under section 1(2). In the present case it is such a prohibited item.[46]

It may be noted that Merrill Lynch subsequently obtained a patent for broadly the same application from the United States Patent Office.[47] The case demonstrates that, not only must the invention produce some technical contribution—in itself no easy thing to define—but the end-product must not constitute prohibited subject matter. In cases such as *Koch and Stertzel*,[48] where the programs control the operation of some product, this test is fairly easily established. In the situation where the effects are either internal or affect information—echoing back to the debate in *Slee and Harris*[49] on whether information can constitute a product—the prognosis for the grant of a patent is much less favourable.

The following sections will consider the recent development of case law in the United Kingdom and before the European Patent Office. In spite of repeated comments to the desirability of securing uniformity of treatment of applications between the United Kingdom and European patent authorities, it does appear that significant divisions have emerged both between the United Kingdom and Europe and also internally within the European Patent Office, with differently composed Boards of Appeal producing incompatible decisions. In the case of *Aerotel v Telco Holdings*[50] which came before the Court of Appeal in 2006 and is discussed extensively later in this chapter, the court declared that in the face of conflicting European authorities, the United Kingdom would follow its own precedents.

The development of software patent jurisprudence

At one level, the distinction between *Vicom* and *Merrill Lynch* is obvious. Vicom received a patent and Merrill Lynch did not. In terms of legal analysis, however, the two decisions are very much in line and established the principle that software-related inventions were capable of being brought within the ambit of the patent system. During the remainder of the twentieth century and into the first decade of the current century a significant number of software-related cases reached the High Court and Court of Appeal in the United Kingdom and the Board of Appeal in the European Patent Office.

For most of this period, although there was perhaps a sense that the United Kingdom authorities were less enthusiastic about awarding patents for software-related inventions than their European Patent Office counterparts, the jurisprudence of both systems remained very much in line with the phrases 'technical contribution' and 'technical effect' assuming the status almost of a judicial mantra. The concepts, however, are complicated to apply, especially given the pace of technical development. As the US Supreme Court justice Potter Stewart once commented in respect of pornography, 'I don't know what it is, but I know it when I see it', so developing precise definitions proved difficult with different judges adopting seemingly different formulations. This was perhaps most notably the case within the European Patent Office where a number of differently composed Boards of Appeal laid stress on different aspects of the notion.

---

[46] *Merrill Lynch's Application* [1989] RPC 561 at 569.
[47] This patent survived a challenge in the United States courts.   [48] [1988] EPOR 72.
[49] *Slee and Harris's Application* [1966] RPC 194.   [50] [2006] EWCA 1371.

The clear message from cases such as *Vicom*[51] is that in determining whether a software-related invention is patentable, a critical determinant will be what the application achieves. In a case such as *Koch and Sterzel*,[52] this may be relatively easy to identify. The end-product in this case could be classed as a better X-ray machine. It is often suggested that the person who invents a better mousetrap will find the world waiting to pay a fortune for the device. It must surely be of little significance if the improved mousetrap relies on a computer program rather than a piece of cheese. More difficult cases arise when it is difficult to identify tangible elements as resulting from the operation of the program. A number of cases decided before the European Patent Office involving the computer company IBM illustrate the problem. In *IBM/Text Processing*,[53] the application referred to a novel method for correcting homophone errors in a document, for example, the use of the word 'where' when the context of the document required 'wear'. Such a facility is an important feature of speech recognition systems, but is also a process which is carried out (often imperfectly) within the brain of an author. The application, it was held, related only to known and standard apparatus, and was described in functional terms corresponding to the mental steps which would be carried out by a human performing the same text processing operations. Holding it unpatentable, the Board of Appeal ruled that:

> Since the only conceivable use for a computer program is the running of it on a computer, the exclusion from patentability of programs for computers would be effectively undermined if it could be circumvented by including in the claim a reference to conventional hardware features, such as processor, memory, keyboard and display, which in practice are indispensable if the program is to be used at all. In the opinion of the Board, in such cases, patentability must depend on whether the operations performed involve an inventive step in a field not excluded from patentability.[54]

A further decision relating to an application from IBM, *IBM Corpn/Reading Age*,[55] is more explicit. This application concerned a system for checking automatically the text of a document in order to highlight words having a reading age higher than that specified for its readers. The system would go on to present a list of alternative formulations which would meet the appropriate age requirements. Again, the equipment could be seen as replicating functions traditionally carried out by human editors. Although the particular application was rejected, the Board of Appeal held that such a development might be patentable if the technical manner in which the process was conducted involved an advance on the state of the art 'even though' (emphasis added) the steps taken might correspond to those performed in the mind of a human.

IBM/Semantically Related Expressions[56] involved an application by IBM, who sought to patent a system for automatically generating a list of expressions semantically related to an input linguistic expression, together with a method for displaying such a list, namely a form of thesaurus. The actions of the computer in this case were considered to operate in the field of linguistics rather than to produce a technical contribution to the known art.

The computer's functions were all conventional, described as consisting of:

> storing data; comparing input data with an index for finding an address location; storing the address; accessing it with a memory; decoding the addressed data; utilising the decoded data as an address for accessing another memory; displaying the addressed data.[57]

Beyond the technicalities of its performance, all that the computer did was to compare data, in the form of a word, with other data already programmed into a segment of its memory and display the results of any matches. To this extent, its operations were comparable with

---

[51] *Vicom Systems Inc's Application* [1987] 2 EPOR 74.   [52] [1988] EPOR 72.
[53] [1990] EPOR 181.   [54] [1990] EPOR 181 at 183.   [55] [1990] OJEPO 384.
[56] [1989] EPOR 454.   [57] *IBM/Semantically Related Expressions* [1989] EPOR 454 at 458.

a person 'searching' his or her memory for an alternative form of expression. The Board of Appeal concluded:

> It remains, of course, true that internally a computer functions technically and this applies also to its display device. However, the effect of this function, namely the resulting information about the existence of semantically related expressions, is a purely linguistic, that is, non-technical result. The appellant agrees that the claimed system can be implemented by pure software and this implementation is the only one described and preferred. No new reconfigured hardware has been shown to be used in this case. As said before, the two memories can be different sections of a single (conventional) memory. In the opinion of the Board, this new reconfiguration by software is not a technical contribution here.[58]

In a further case, *IBM/Data Processor Network*,[59] the application involved the interconnection of a series of computers in such a manner as to facilitate communications between programs and data held in the various computers. Obviously, the basis for the claimed invention lay in the computer programs which controlled these operations. It was accepted that:

> The proposed improved communication facilities between programs and files held at different processors within the known network do not involve any changes in the physical structure of the processors or the transmission network. The necessary control functions for this purpose, referred to as 'mirror transaction' in the description of the present application, are effected by appropriate software.[60]

In spite of this, it was the opinion of the Board of Appeal that:

> an invention relating to the coordination and control of the internal communication between programs and data files held at different processors in a data processing system...and the features of which are not concerned with the nature of the data and the way in which a particular application program operates on them, is to be regarded as solving a problem which is essentially technical. Such an invention therefore is to be regarded as an invention within the meaning of Article 52(1) EPC [European Patent Convention].[61]

In yet another application involving IBM, *IBM/Computer Related Invention*,[62] an application was accepted which referred to a method for causing a computer to display automatically one of a number of predetermined messages relating to the machine's status. The view was taken that:

> giving visual indications automatically about conditions prevailing in the apparatus or system is basically a technical problem.

The application proposed a solution to a specific problem of this kind, namely providing a visual indication about events occurring in the input/output device of a text processor. The solution included the use of a computer program and certain tables stored in a memory to build up the phrases to be displayed.[63]

The distinction between this successful application and the unsuccessful claim in *IBM/ Semantically-Related Expressions*[64] appears slight. The Board of Appeal was of the view that the present application was more than a computer program, but it is not clear why a development which automatically displays information regarding a computer system's state of health should be so regarded whilst a development which automatically displays the synonyms of a word inputted by a user should be rejected.

---

[58] *IBM/Semantically Related Expressions* [1989] EPOR 454 at 460.   [59] [1990] EPOR 91.
[60] [1990] EPOR 91 at 94.   [61] 1990] EPOR 91 at 95.   [62] [1990] EPOR 107.
[63] [1990] EPOR 107 at 110.
[64] *IBM/Semantically-Related Expressions* [1989] EPOR 454.

Final reference will be made to another IBM application, this time involving a development in what is referred to as text clarity.[65] This consisted of a method by which a computer program would scan text in order to identify incomprehensible or obscure linguistic expressions and suggest alternative formulations. Many authors could benefit greatly from such a facility.

Once again, the Board of Examiners sought to identify whether the claimed invention produced any technical effect. It used, it was held, technical means to substitute for human intellectual acts, but once the steps required to perform the act have been identified, their implementation involved 'no more than the straightforward application of standard techniques'[66] which would be obvious to a person skilled in the technical art. On this basis, there was no inventive step. The Board of Examiners concluded:

> Since the only conceivable use for a computer program is the running of it on a computer, the exclusion from patentability of computer programs would be effectively undermined if it could be circumvented by including in the claim a reference to conventional hardware features... which in practice are indispensable if the program is to be used at all.[67]

Although the case law of the European Patent Office as discussed above does not appear totally consistent, the number of successful applications, coupled with some of the dicta of the Board of Examiners, created a sense that the criteria were being applied more flexibly. This was the case, not just in respect of the prohibition against the award of patents for computer programs, but also in respect of the prohibition against the award of a patent in respect of a scheme or method for performing a mental act. Given that the effect of many computer programs is to automate processes which would previously have required human intervention, this can be a substantial obstacle to the award of a patent.

New millennium, new patent law?

Although it is always possible to identify points of difference between judgments, until the end of the twentieth century there was very considerable similarity in terminological approach both between the United Kingdom and the European authorities and also internally between differently composed Boards of Appeal within the European Patent Office. All authorities shared the view that any patent application required to demonstrate some technical contribution—although what constitutes a technical contribution is sometimes far from clear. Starting with the decision in *IBM's Application*, matters have become more confusing within the European Patent Office, although for the United Kingdom, the decision of the Court of Appeal in *Aerotel v Telco*[68] brings at least a measure of clarity to the situation.

IBM's Application

At issue in this case was an application for a patent for developments in relation to the use of 'windows' as a means for presenting information on a computer monitor. The advantage of IBM's programs, it was claimed, was that it rearranged the information held in one window so that it remained visible even when another window was opened on top of it. The application was rejected by the examiner on the ground that it related to a program *per se* and an appeal was made to the Board of Appeal.

---

[65] *IBM/Text Clarity Processing (T38/86)* [1990] EPOR 606.
[66] *IBM/Text Clarity Processing (T38/86)* [1990] EPOR 606 at 611.
[67] *IBM/Text Clarity Processing (T38/86)* [1990] EPOR 606 at 613.   [68] [2006] EWCA Civ 1371.

IBM's appeal was based on a number of grounds. It was argued that:

the reason for the exclusion of computer programs as such from patent protection under the European Patent Convention was because there was already adequate and clear protection in the form of copyright, but that if the claims sought to protect something which would not attract copyright protection then the objection to patentability must fall. It was also argued that this approach was consistent with the Trade Related Aspects of Intellectual Property Rights (TRIPS). The appellants further argued that since the European Patent Office allowed a claim defining an invention by way of a technical feature, even if that feature was embodied in a computer program, once such an intellectual construction had been accepted as an invention, the provisions of Article 52 of the EPC were satisfied and would no longer justify constraining the applicant as to how to claim the invention.[69]

The issue concerning the availability of copyright for developments such as the IBM software was not pursued by the Board of Appeal. Whilst there is no doubt that computer programs are protected by copyright, this does not extend to the underlying concepts.

As discussed previously, the TRIPS agreement provides that computer programs are to be protected by copyright. However, it requires also that 'patents shall be available for any inventions, whether products or processes, in all fields of technology, provided they are new, involve an inventive step and are capable of industrial application'.[70] There is no equivalent to the European Patent Convention's list of prohibited subject matter.

It is national states (and the EU) who are signatories to TRIPS. The Agreement, therefore, is not binding upon international organisations such as the European Patent Office. The Board of Appeal held, however, that its provisions should be taken into account:

since it is aimed at setting common standards and principles concerning the availability, scope and use of trade-related intellectual property rights, and therefore of patent rights. Thus TRIPS gives a clear indication of current trends.[71]

Reference was made also to developments in the United States and Japanese Patent Offices, which had both adopted a more liberal approach towards the granting of patents for software-related inventions. Whilst recognising that these offices worked under legal provisions different from those applying in Europe, the developments, it was considered, 'represent a useful indication of modern trends' which 'may contribute to the further highly desirable (worldwide) harmonisation of patent law'. The clear implication would appear to be that the European Patent Office was out of step with other major offices in its treatment of software-related inventions.

Turning to the substance of the particular application, reference was made to the fact that computer programs were excluded only to the extent that the invention related to the program 'as such'. This formulation, it was held, indicated that the 'legislators did not want to exclude from patentability all programs for computers'. In previous decisions, the European Patent Office had laid stress on the requirement for a technical contribution. In the present case, attention focused on the interpretation of the phrase 'as such'. This phrase, it was held, had to be construed as meaning that excluded programs were merely abstract creations which did not possess any technical character. 'As such' they could not be considered an invention as this term necessarily implied some technical character. It was held, however, that where programs demonstrated a technical character, they had to be considered eligible for protection.[72]

The question, therefore, was to determine when a computer program constituted more than an abstract creation and exhibited a technical character in its own right, independent

[69] Case T0935/97 [1999] RPC 861 at 862.   [70] Art. 5.   [71] Case T0935/97 [1999] RPC 861 at 868.
[72] Case T0935/97 [1999] RPC 861 at 870.

of linkage with tangible objects. What was required was that the program should have the potential to cause the occurrence of a technical effect. A patent might be granted where a computer program operates to cause a computer to control some industrial process or the operation of a piece of machinery. Additionally, it was held, a patent may be granted when the computer program constituted a necessary part of the device for which protection was sought, even though the technical effect was achieved purely by means of the internal functioning of the computer. Consequently, it was held that:

> on condition that they are able to produce a technical effect in the above sense, all computer programs must be considered as inventions within the meaning of Article 52(1) of the EPC [European Patent Convention], and may be the subject-matter of a patent if the other requirements provided for by the EPC are satisfied.[73]

It was recognised that the Guidelines for Examiners stated that a 'computer program claimed by itself or as a record on a carrier is not patentable'. For the future, however, the Board's decision was that:

> a computer program claimed by itself is not excluded from patentability if the program, when running on a computer or loaded into a computer, brings about, or is capable of bringing about, a technical effect which goes beyond the 'normal' physical interactions between the program (software) and the computer (hardware) on which it is run.[74]

The decision in *IBM's Application* might be seen as marking the culmination of a line of authority stretching back directly to *Vicom*. In very large measure, it might be seen as restating the law as laid down by the United Kingdom authorities in the final years of the 1949 Patents Act. Subsequently, three further decisions have been issued by the European Patent Office, which mark divergences in the approach which should be adopted in determining issues of technical contribution.

Pensions benefits

In a decision[75] handed down in September 2000, the Board of Examiners considered an appeal against the rejection of a patent application for a system designed to manage pension benefit programmes. It was claimed that the combination of hardware and software specified in the application was 'radically different' from existing pension management programmes:

> reducing the financial and administrative burdens for both sides, the employers and the employees, and achieving significant advantages over the former pension systems.

Criticising the decision of the patent examiner that the application fell to be classed as a method of doing business and demonstrated insufficient technical character it was argued that:

> relying on the 'technical character' of inventions was not justified, since such a criterion was not set up by the European Patent Convention as a requirement for patentability.

Reference was also made to the fact that the exclusion of business methods from patentability had been abandoned in many non-European jurisdictions, with specific reference made to the United States.

In its decision, the Board of Appeal accepted that the application was, prima facie, eligible for protection.

---

[73] Case T0935/97 [1999] RPC 861 at 871.   [74] Case T0935/97 [1999] RPC 861 at 877.
[75] Case T0931/95.

In the Board's view a computer system suitably programmed for use in a particular field, even if that is the field of business and economy, has the character of a concrete apparatus in the sense of a physical entity, man-made for a utilitarian purpose and is thus an invention within the meaning of Article 52(1) EPC.

This distinction with regard patentability between a method for doing business and an apparatus suited to perform such a method is justified in the light of the wording of Article 52(2)(c) EPC, according to which 'schemes, rules and methods' are non-patentable categories in the field of economy and business, but the category of 'apparatus' in the sense of 'physical entity' or 'product' is not mentioned in Article 52(2) EPC. This means that, if a claim is directed to such an entity, the formal category of such a claim does in fact imply physical features of the claimed subject-matter which may qualify as technical features of the invention concerned and thus be relevant for its patentability. Therefore the Board concludes that:

An apparatus constituting a physical entity or concrete product suitable for performing or supporting an economic activity, is an invention within the meaning of Article 52(1) EPC.

Although the Board held that a computer programmed to operate in a particular way was not barred from patentability *per se*, the application was ultimately rejected on the basis that the programs used to bring about the desired effects were themselves not inventive.

Hitachi

The decision in *Hitachi*[76] concerned an application for a patent in respect of a method for conducting electronic auctions requiring minimal intervention on the part of bidders. As is described in the report:

The auction starts with preliminary steps of data exchange between the client computers and the server computer in order to collect bids from the participants. Each bid comprises two prices, a 'desired price' and a 'maximum price in competitive state'. After this initial phase the auction is automatic and does not require that the bidders follow the auction on-line. An auction price is set and successively lowered (which is typical for so-called Dutch auctions) until it reaches the level of the highest bid or bids as determined by the 'desired price'. In case of several identical bids the price is increased until only the bidder having offered the highest 'maximum price' is left. He is declared successful.

Therefore, taking into account both that a mix of technical and non-technical features may be regarded as an invention within the meaning of Article 52(1) EPC and that prior art should not be considered when deciding whether claimed subject-matter is such an invention, a compelling reason for not refusing under Article 52(2) EPC subject-matter consisting of technical and non-technical features is simply that the technical features may in themselves turn out to fulfill all requirements of Article 52(1) EPC.

[3.7] For these reasons the Board holds that, contrary to the examining division's assessment, the apparatus of claim 3 is an invention within the meaning of Article 52(1) EPC since it comprises clearly technical features such as a 'server computer', 'client computers' and a 'network'.

[4.6] The Board is aware that its comparatively broad interpretation of the term 'invention' in Article 52(1) EPC will include activities which are so familiar that their technical character tends to be overlooked, such as the act of writing using pen and paper. Needless to say, however, this does not imply that all methods involving the use of technical means are patentable. They still have to be new, represent a non-obvious technical solution to a technical problem, and be susceptible of industrial application.

---

[76] Case T0258/03.

Determining the technical contribution an invention achieves with respect to the prior art is therefore more appropriate for the purpose of examining novelty and inventive step than for deciding on possible exclusion under Article 52(2) and (3).

Microsoft

The most radical decision of the European Patent Office came with the decision in respect of an application by Microsoft[77] for a new form of clipboard operation which, used in its Windows operating system, would enable data held in one format (for example, a graphic) to be copied into another application which is using a different format (for example, text). An application for the grant of a patent was rejected by the examiner on the grounds of lack of novelty and inventiveness. The Board of Examiners disagreed. Initially it was confirmed that:

> Claim 1 relates to a method implemented in a computer system. T 258/03—*Auction method/ Hitachi* (OJ EPO 2004, 575) states that a method using technical means is an invention within the meaning of Article 52(1) EPC. A computer system including a memory (clipboard) is a technical means, and consequently the claimed method has technical character in accordance with established case law.
>
> Moreover, the Board would like to emphasise that a method implemented in a computer system represents a sequence of steps actually performed and achieving an effect, and not a sequence of computer-executable instructions (i.e. a computer program) which just have the potential of achieving such an effect when loaded into, and run on, a computer. Thus, the Board holds that the claim category of a computer-implemented method is distinguished from that of a computer program. Even though a method, in particular a method of operating a computer, may be put into practice with the help of a computer program, a claim relating to such a method does not claim a computer program in the category of a computer program.

The Board next considered the issues of novelty and inventiveness. In *Pensions benefits* and *Hitachi*, these requirements had proved an insurmountable obstacle, with the Board holding that the novel computer program should be regarded as if it constituted part of the prior art. No trace of this holding is to be found in *Microsoft*, with the Board accepting that the previous version of Windows (Windows 3.1) constituted the most relevant prior art. Compared to the features found in this, the new clipboard was considered novel and inventive and the case was remitted to the examiner with the instruction that a patent should be awarded.

Let a thousand flowers bloom?

The phrase, 'let a thousand [or in some sources, a hundred] flowers bloom, let a hundred ideas compete', is attributed to the legendary Chinese leader Chairman Mao. In his case, the application of the principle proved problematic and when individuals took him at his word and put forward ideas critical of current policy the response took the form of the so-called Cultural Revolution, which sought to clamp down ruthlessly on any blossoms other than those expressly approved by authority. Whilst not predicting similar consequences, the varying approaches of the European Patent Office Boards of Appeal may bring confusion

---

[77] Case T0424/03.

rather than enlightenment. The situation has caused difficulties and perhaps a measure of irritation amongst national courts. This was clearly expressed in the United Kingdom in the case of *Aerotel v Telco*, the outcome of which might perhaps be seen as declaring a measure of conditional independence from the internal disagreements within the European Patent Office.

The facts in *Aerotel* can be relatively briefly stated. Aerotel had developed and sought a patent for a method for making telephone calls from phones without using cash. A user would deposit funds with the provider in advance and establish a credit balance. Upon dialling a particular code, the call would be routed to a special exchange. Upon entering a PIN number, the user would have calls connected up to the level of his credit. Although it is not specified in the report, the system could be used by indirect telephone service providers who might, especially for international calls, purchase capacity from BT and sell this on to customers. As with mobile phones, the pay-as-you-go approach would obviate the need for complex contractual and billing procedures.

Aerotel was awarded a patent for the system and subsequently sued a competitor for infringement. The other party counterclaimed, alleging that the patent was invalid as relating to nothing more than a program for a computer, a claim which was upheld by the trial judge. Although the case was settled, Aerotel appealed to the Court of Appeal, seeking reinstatement of the patent.

Delivering the judgment of the Court of Appeal, Lord Justice Jacob provided an extensive survey of the development of the law relating to software-related patents. The approaches adopted within the United Kingdom and before the European Patent Office were summarised succinctly:

(1) The contribution approach

Ask whether the inventive step resides only in the contribution of excluded matter—if yes, Article 52(2) applies.

This approach was supported by Falconer J in *Merrill Lynch* but expressly rejected by this Court.

(2) The technical effect approach

Ask whether the invention as defined in the claim makes a technical contribution to the known art—if no, Article 52(2) applies. A possible clarification (at least by way of exclusion) of this approach is to add the rider that novel or inventive purely excluded matter does not count as a 'technical contribution'.

This is the approach (with the rider) adopted by this Court in *Merrill Lynch*. It has been followed in the subsequent decisions of this Court, *Gale* and *Fujitsu*. The approach (without the rider as an express caution) was that first adopted by the EPO Boards of Appeal, see *Vicom, IBM/Text processing* and *IBM/Data processor network*.

(3) The 'any hardware' approach

Ask whether the claim involves the use of or is to a piece of physical hardware, however mundane (whether a computer or a pencil and paper). If yes, Article 52(2) does not apply. This approach was adopted in three cases, *Pensions Benefits, Hitachi*, and *Microsoft/Data transfer* (the 'trio'). It was specifically rejected by this Court in *Gale*.

However, there are variants of the 'any hardware' approach:

> (3)(i) *Where a claim is to a method which consists of an excluded category, it is excluded by Article 52(2) even if hardware is used to carry out the method. But a claim to the apparatus itself, being 'concrete' is not so excluded. The apparatus claim is nonetheless bad for obviousness because the notional skilled man must be taken to know about the improved, excluded, method.*

This is the *Pensions Benefits* approach.

(3)(ii)   A claim to hardware necessarily is not caught by Article 52(2). A claim to a method of using that hardware is likewise not excluded even if that method as such is excluded matter. Either type of claim is nonetheless bad for obviousness for the same reason as above.

This is *Hitachi*, expressly disagreeing with *Pensions Benefits* about method claims.

(3)(iii) Simply ask whether there is a claim to something 'concrete' e.g. an apparatus. If yes, Article 52(2) does not apply. Then examine for patentability on conventional grounds— do not treat the notional skilled man as knowing about any improved excluded method.

This is *Microsoft/Data Transfer*.[78]

Faced with such a baffling range of authorities, it was considered that, although it was a requirement to place great weight on decisions of the European Patent Office Board of Appeal, the contradictory nature of the jurisprudence made it impossible to do so. Rather than relying on European Patent Office authority, reference was made to the decisions of the Court of Appeal in *Gale*, *Merrill Lynch*, and *Fujitsu's Applications*.[79] These, it was held, adopted the technical effect approach, with the additional qualification or rider that novelty could not lie only in the otherwise excluded subject matter.

Turning to the manner in which this principle should be applied, Lord Justice Jacob accepted a submission by counsel for the Commissioner of Patents which required the decision-maker to:

1. *Properly construe the claim.*

   This is a basic step for any patent application and requires identification of the nature and scope of the subject matter of the patent and the extent of the monopoly which is sought.

2. *Identify the actual contribution.*

   This involves an assessment of the problem which the applicant claims to have solved, the manner in which the invention works, and the advantages which it claims to offer over existing technologies. Lord Justice Jacob summarised the requirement in the following terms '[w]hat has the inventor really added to human knowledge?'

3. *Ask whether it falls solely within the excluded subject-matter.*

   This relates to the provision in the Act and Convention that inventions containing excluded subject matter are ineligible for patent protection only to the extent that they contain nothing more than excluded subject matter.

4. *Check whether the actual or alleged contribution is actually technical in nature.*

   In many cases, it was suggested, the answer to this question would be obvious from that of the previous one.[80]

The four-stage test, it was stated, was a reformulation of the approach followed by the Court of Appeal in *Fujitsu*.

Applying these tests, the *Aerotel application*, it was held, was patentable. The system specified was novel in itself and not merely because of its application to the handling of telephone calls. This meant that it satisfied the second and third criteria. The system required the use of hardware components and so was technical in nature.

---

[78] [2006] EWCA Civ 1371 at para. 26.   [79] [2006] EWCA Civ 1371.
[80] [2006] EWCA Civ 1371 at para. 40.

Following the decision in *Aerotel*, the Patent Office stated that the case:

must be treated as a definitive statement of how the law on patentable subject matter is now to be applied in the United Kingdom (UK). It should therefore rarely be necessary to refer back to previous United Kingdom or EPO case law.[81]

In the subsequent case of *IGT v Commisioner of Patents*,[82] the *Aerotel* approach was adopted, albeit with comment to the effect that:

The Court of Appeal has recently developed the approach which the courts should adopt to the correct interpretation of Article 52(2) and (3). Whether or not the application of the Article is now more or less straightforward, or clear, than it was before is perhaps a matter on which minds may differ.

Following his concerns at the range of approaches adopted by the European Patent Office, Lord Justice Jacob, with the support of the United Kingdom Patent Office, made a request to the President of the European Patent Office that an extended Board of Appeal be convened and asked to determine:

1. What is the correct approach to adopt in determining whether an invention relates to subject matter that is excluded under Article 52?

2. How should those elements of a claim that relate to excluded subject matter be treated when assessing whether an invention is novel and inventive under Articles 54 and 56?

3. And specifically:

   (a) Is an operative computer program loaded onto a medium such as a chip or hard drive of a computer excluded by Article 52(2) unless it produces a technical effect, if so what is meant by 'technical effect'?

   (b) What are the key characteristics of the method of doing business exclusion?

The request, however, was declined. Subsequently, disagreements between the European Patent Office and the Court of Appeal became even more pronounced. In the case of *Duns Licensing Associates' Application*,[83] the Board of Appeal—whilst rejecting an application for a patent in respect of method for estimating sales activities at outlets in the absence of actual returns (effectively by compiling a database allowing comparison to be made with other sales outlets of similar size and in similar locations) on the basis that it related only to a method for doing business—was highly critical of the decisions in *Aerotel v Telco*. The Court of Appeal's adoption of the 'technical effect approach (with rider)' criterion, it was claimed, was 'irreconcilable with the European Patent Convention'[84] and 'inconsistent with a good-faith interpretation of the European Patent Convention in accordance with Article 31 of the Vienna Convention on the Law of Treaties.'[85]

A request by the applicant in *Duns Licensing Associates* for a referral to an Enlarged Board of Appeal was rejected. Referral, it was held, could be justified only in order to ensure uniform application of the law or if an important point of law could be identified. The Rules of Procedure established under the European Patent Convention provided for a referral if a Board of Appeal proposed to deviate from a previous decision of an enlarged board.

---

[81] See 'Patents Act 1977: Patentable Subject Matter', available from <http://www.ipo.gov.uk/pro-types/pro-patent/p-law/p-pn/p-pn-subjectmatter.htm>. [82] [2007] EWHC 1341 Pat.

[83] Case T 0154/04.   [84] para. 13.

[85] para. 12. Article 31 of the Vienna Convention lays down principles to be used in interpreting treaties providing, inter alia, that: 'A treaty shall be interpreted in good faith in accordance with the ordinary meaning to be given to the terms of the treaty in their context and in the light of its object and purpose.'

Disagreements between differently composed Boards of Appeal or with national authorities were not of themselves reasons for making a referral. Hence, it was held:

> the legal system of the European Patent Convention gives room for evolution of the jurisprudence (which is thus not 'case law' in the strict Anglo-Saxon meaning of the term) and leaves it to the discretion of the boards whether to give reasons in any decision deviating from other decisions or to refer a point of law to the Enlarged Board.[86]

This perhaps is the crux of the issue and the disagreements. The European Patent Office, in common with the approach in civil law jurisdictions, has less respect for precedent than the United Kingdom courts, and has tended to modify its interpretation of the Convention in the light of developments in technologies and circumstances. As was said by Lord Justice Jacobs in *Aerotel*, 'An arms race in which the weapons are patents has set in.'[87] As will be discussed later, given a considerable willingness on the part of the United States authorities to grant patents for software-related inventions, and given the importance of that country within the world's software industry, it is perhaps not surprising that the European Patent Office should modify its approach. It is not surprising either that—given the strength of the doctrine of precedent and an approach to statutory interpretation which pays respect to the words used in a legal instrument rather than seeking to determine what its framers would have intended had the measure been redrafted in the light of changing circumstances—the United Kingdom courts should adopt a more conservative approach. Differences may exist only at the margins and it is noteworthy that the appellant in *Duns Licensing Associates* cited the decision in *Aerotel* in support of his application, in apparent contradiction of the received wisdom that the European Patent Office is more receptive to software patents.

More recent developments appear to have at least cooled the level of disagreements between the United Kingdom and European authorities. In the case of *Symbian v Commissioner of Patents*,[88] the applicant sought a patent for what was claimed to be a better method for accessing data held on a computing device. As with all inventions in this field, the technologies are daunting but the key argument was that a computing device would 'avoid the difficulties and potential unreliability, and therefore the malfunctioning, of the prior art' and would have 'application to a wide range of electrical devices including any form of computer, various forms of cameras and communication devices such as mobile phones . . . and other products which combine communications, image recording and computer functionality within a single device.'[89]

The application was rejected in the Patent Office with the examiner ruling that as the effect was to make the computing device work more efficiently, this did not constitute a technical effect as required under the *Aerotel* test. This decision was overturned by Mr Justice Patten in the High Court[90] whose decision was upheld by the Court of Appeal. Reference was made to a 2007 decision of the European Patent Office Board of Appeal, *Gameaccount Ltd*,[91] which, it was suggested, adopted an approach more in line with the *Aerotel* approach than older European Patent Office decisions.

As in previous decisions, the court surveyed extensively the jurisprudence of the English and European courts. The Court of Appeal was, it was held, bound by its own previous decisions unless there was evidence that a contrary and consistent line of jurisprudence had been developed before the European Patent Office.[92] This was not, it was held, the case here. Whilst recognising, as has indeed been described throughout this chapter, that the

---

[86] para. 2.   [87] [2006] EWCA Civ 1371 at para. 18.   [88] [2008] EWCA Civ 1066.
[89] para. 3.   [90] [2008] EWHC 518 (Pat).
[91] T 1543/06.   [92] See *Actavis UK Ltd v Merck & Co Inc* [2008] EWCA Civ 444.

inclusion of software within the patent system was 'rather imprecise and arbitrary',[93] the court was clear that it should follow the *Aerotel* tests. Applying these it was held that:

> not only will a computer containing the instructions in question 'be a better computer',...it can also be said that the instructions 'solve a 'technical' problem lying with the computer itself'. Indeed, the effect of the instant alleged invention is not merely within the computer programmed with the relevant instructions. The beneficial consequences of those instructions will feed into the cameras and other devices and products, which...include such computer systems.[94]

Following the decision in *Symbian* a request was made by the President of the European Patent Office that an enlarged Board of Appeal should consider four questions relating to the Board of Appeal practice and jurisprudence in respect of the patentability of software-related inventions.[95] The enlarged Board surveyed the European Patent Office jurisprudence but ultimately came to the conclusion that the referral was inadmissible as, in the opinion of the enlarged Board, there was no fundamental inconsistency within the jurisprudence. It seems that Lewis Carroll lives and thrives in Strasbourg.

Schemes for performing mental acts

Although at the level only of a High Court decision, the case of *Halliburton v Comptroller of Patents*[96] provides a helpful and lucid account of the current legal state of the art.

The case centred on a patent application for a method of designing drill bits for use in oil exploration taking account of the geological conditions in which the equipment was intended to operate. Interestingly, the claim stopped at the design stage and did not extend to the process of manufacturing a drill bit. It was conceded that such a claim would be patentable but it was indicated that a 'claim limited in that way would not give his client realistic commercial protection for their invention'.

Before the Patent Office the claim was rejected on the ground that it constituted a scheme or method for performing a mental act. Applying the four-step test laid down in *Aerotel* it was ruled that the claimed invention had no elements that would take it outside the scope of the prohibited category. The applicant argued before the High Court that this was taking too broad an interpretation of the prohibition. As the judge, Mr Justice Birss stated:

> There are essentially two possible interpretations of this exclusion, a wide one and a narrow one. The wide construction is that a method is 'a scheme, rule or method for performing a mental act' if it is capable of being performed mentally regardless of whether, as claimed, it is in fact performed mentally...So a claim to a computer programmed to carry out a method of performing a calculation (say a square root), would not only be caught by the computer program and mathematical method exclusions but would also be excluded by the mental act exclusion because calculations are the kind of thing which are capable of being performed mentally.[97]

By way of contrast, the narrow prohibition would apply only where activities are actually carried out mentally.

> The narrow construction is that the exclusion only excludes acts carried out mentally. On this basis 'a claim to a calculation carried out on a computer could never be caught by the

---

[93] para. 26.   [94] para. 54

[95] Case Number G 0003/08. The text of the opinion is available from <http://www.epo.org/topics/issues/computer-implemented-inventions/referral.html>.   [96] [2011] EWHC 2508 (Pat).

[97] para. 42

mental act exclusion because the claim does not encompass carrying out the calculation mentally. The fact that calculations in general are the kinds of thing which are capable of being performed as mental acts is irrelevant.'[98]

After considering a range of authorities in the course of a clear and lucid judgment Mr Justice Birss concluded that the predominance of authority was in favour of the narrow approach. The evil that it sought to guard against was the possibility that a patent could be infringed merely through a thought process. If however, a claim can be 'tethered' to a manufacturing step it can be accepted. Reference was made to the European Patent Office's approach in VLSI Chip Design.[99] There, although 'a claim to a method of designing a silicon chip was not allowed, the patentability problem was solved simply by adding the words "and materially producing the chip so designed" at the end of the claim'.

In the present case this problem could be cured by an amendment of a similar type such as adding the words 'and making the drill bit so designed'. The appeal was allowed and the case remitted to the Comptroller of Patents for further consideration.

The mobile-phone patent wars

Although there are tentative signs of moves towards a peace treaty, the technology giants Apple and Samsung have been engaged in a series of patent disputes in a range of countries. The High Court in London delivered judgments in respect of two disputes in March 2012— making some reference to decisions of the German courts in identical litigation. The two cases are *Samsung Electronic Co Lt v Apple Retail UK Ltd and Apple Sales International* [2013] EWHC 467 (Pat) and a second case of the same name reported at [2013] EWHC 468 (Pat). The former contains the most detailed legal analysis.

The background to the dispute is technical and I must confess to understanding around one word in ten in the technical sections of the judgments. I think the essential dispute is relatively simple. Samsung had been granted patents for elements of technology used to enable mobile phones to connect to mobile networks. These had come to form the basis of international standards for GMS and LTE mobile telephony (effectively 3G and 4G systems).

Where patented technology is used as the basis for international standards it is a condition that the patent holder licence its use to any party upon fair and reasonable terms. Samsung were willing to allow Apple to use its technology in return for a royalty payment amounting to 2.4 per cent of its income from iPhone sales. Such tactics are fairly common in patent litigation. Microsoft own patents in respect of technology used in Android phones and it has been estimated[100] that companies such as HTC and Samsung which manufacture these phones pay royalties of between $10–12 per phone. The income for Microsoft from these two companies alone is around $3 billion per annum. Given Microsoft had an income of around $70 billion in 2012, the benefits are clear and illustrate why companies such as Apple and Microsoft and Google are willing to pay massive amounts of money to buy patent portfolios from technically innovative but financially challenged companies such as Kodak and Motorola.

There was no doubt that Samsung owned patents and the judge made it clear in both cases that the iPhone infringed them. But, and it proved to be a very big but, the validity

---

[98] para. 43. Punctuation as per the original.   [99] T 0453/91 of 31 May 1994.
[100] <http://blogs.computerworld.com/windows/20792/microsofts-haul-mobile-800-million-andr oid-royalties-one-quarter-still-only-relative-trickle-windows-phone>.

of any patent can be challenged at any time. Apple claimed that the Samsung patents were invalid.

Timing is always important in patent matters—as illustrated famously by the telephone patent example of Alexander Graham Bell and Elisha Gray. In the present litigation Samsung had been awarded a number of European patents whose validity extended to the UK. These patents were derived from (the technical term is claimed priority from) earlier patents awarded to Samsung in South Korea. The Patent Cooperation Treaty provides that patent applicants have a period of twelve months from the date of submitting an application in one signatory state to submit elsewhere and claim the benefit of the earlier date. Submission in different states and in different languages can and does cause linguistic problems. In this case the judge (Mr Justice Floyd) commented:

> Neither the 726 patent, nor the document from which it claims priority is a well drafted document. Not only have they both suffered in translation, but there is a looseness of definition and lack of clarity which must, it seems, go back to the original Korean. It is more important than ever to recall that it is the technical understanding of the skilled person, rather than the patent lawyer or grammarian, which one is seeking to extract from the document. [para. 35]

The first leg of Apple's argument was that the European patents were not sufficiently closely related to their Korean precursors to qualify for protection. As any mobile-phone user will be aware, the pace of development in the field is rapid and it was conceded by Samsung that if they could not claim priority, their European patents would be invalid on the ground that the technologies they described were not novel. Apple's second claim was to the effect that the European patents (and by implication the Korean ones) were invalid because the technologies described failed to meet the key requirement of patentability that there be an inventive step. Samsung's patent applications had, as is required, listed what it considered to be the current state of the art. Apple argued that, taking the state of the art into account, a person reasonably skilled in the field would have regarded Samsung's patented technology as an obvious next step.

Issues of priority

The Patents Act 1977 provides that an invention is entitled to priority if it is supported by matter disclosed in the priority document. Article 87(1) adopts rather different terminology providing that priority may be derived from an earlier application in respect of the 'same invention'.

The Patents Act provides that it is framed to have the same effect as the Convention and reference was made to the decision of the Enlarged Board of Appeal of the EPO in G02/98 *Same Invention* [2001] OJ EPO 413. Here it was stated that priority:

> is to be acknowledged only if the skilled person can derive the subject-matter of the claim directly and unambiguously, using common general knowledge, from the previous application as a whole.

As laid down by the Court of appeal in *Unilin Beheer v Berry Floor*[101] the test is effectively whether a skilled person could read the prior patent and know how to apply the invention described in the first patent.

What we see here is a nice illustration of the difference between novelty and obviousness. It is not enough that the notional skilled person could read the prior patent and see an obvious way to develop it in a different way. It has to be the same way. Where (linguistic

---

[101] [2004] EWCA (Civ) 1021.

issues apart) patents are the same there is no significant problem. Here though, as in many cases, there were differences. In an example which has been used in the courts, there might be a prior patent which claims elements A+B+C. Can a later patent which claims elements A+B only claim priority. The less than completely helpful answer, as so often, was that it all depends. Patents can be very different in their nature. They may describe new technology in which case omitting one item from a later application may not be significant. Alternatively, a patent may relate to the combination of existing items in a novel manner. Omitting one may take it outside the scope of the prior patent. To give a very trivial example, mixing red, yellow, and blue paints will produce (depending on the combinations) shades of grey or brown. Mixing only blue and yellow will produce green. Quite a different thing.

In construing the terms and scope of a prior patent it is well established that the task facing a court is to consider what a person 'skilled in the art' would have understood the patent to mean. This involves consideration of the specification and also of the claims listed in the document. The latter, as emphasised by Mr Justice Floyd, are more important:

> the exercise is one of construing the language of the claims in the context of the specification. The meaning of that language is informed by the technical understanding gained from reading the specification. Thus the specification has an important role in understanding the meaning of the language used. It is not, however, a proper approach to construction to start with the specification and ask what a patentee who has made that disclosure might be intending to claim, and then to shoe-horn the meaning of the language of the claim to fit with that understanding, whatever language he has actually used. To do so would be to afford supremacy to the description over the claims, contrary to the guidance given by Article 69 EPC and its protocol. [para. 67]

He continued at paragraph 106:

> If I may summarise, the task for the court is therefore:
>
> (a) to read and understand, through the eyes of the skilled person, the disclosure of the priority document as a whole;
>
> (b) to determine the subject matter of the relevant claim;
>
> (c) to decide whether, as a matter of substance not of form, the subject matter of the claim can be derived directly and unambiguously from the disclosure of the priority document.

After considering the evidence of expert witnesses for both parties the judge concluded that the European patent could not claim priority from the earlier Korean patent. In essence this conclusion would have been sufficient to dispose of the case. It was conceded by Samsung that developments in technology between the dates would have meant that the European patent application would have been struck down for lack of novelty. To cover the possibility that this element of the judgment might be struck down on appeal he continued to deal with Apple's second challenge. As was stated:

> Apple contend that the 726 patent is obvious over two prior art citations. The first is an article by Bömer and others entitled 'A CDMA Radio Link with "Turbo-Decoding": Concept and Performance Evaluation' ('Bömer'). The second is an article by Valenti and Woerner entitled 'Variable Latency Turbo Codes for Wireless Multimedia Communications' ('Valenti').

The Bömer article was published in 1995 and the Valenti article in 1997. As indicated above, both were cited in the Korean and European patent applications as evidencing the existing state of the art. Samsung claimed that their patents marked a sufficient advance over the state of the art. Counsel for Apple argued that a skilled person reading the cited articles would consider the subsequent patent specification to have been an obvious development from them.

Inevitably much of the material in the judgment is very technical in nature. The legal approach to be followed was specified by the Court of Appeal in *Pozzoli v BDMO*[102] in the form of a four-step test. As summarised at paragraph 148 in the present case, this requires the court to:

(1) (a) Identify the notional 'person skilled in the art'

    (b) Identify the relevant common general knowledge of that person;

(2) Identify the inventive concept of the claim in question or if that cannot readily be done, construe it;

(3) Identify what, if any, differences exist between the matter cited as forming part of the 'state of the art' and the inventive concept of the claim or the claim as construed;

(4) Viewed without any knowledge of the alleged invention as claimed, do those differences constitute steps which would have been obvious to the person skilled in the art or do they require any degree of invention?

Most judicial attention in the present case focused on the Bömer article. This described a concept for transmitting speech and data on 3G mobile networks. Samsung had implemented this in practice but the question was whether a skilled person reading the Bömer article and then the Samsung patent would say that the latter was an obvious step. The court accepted that the article and the patent had significant differences. The latter was certainly novel in patent terms but as the judge concluded:

154. … Neither side's expert suggested that this would present any difficulty. Both experts also expressed the view that it was obvious in the light of Bömer to specify different bit error rates, and thus different super frame sizes for the same service.

155. I have therefore come to the very clear conclusion that claims 1 and 14 are obvious in the light of Bömer.

In total the Samsung patent had twenty-five claims. In a course of action that attracted judicial displeasure, Samsung argued that each claim stood by itself. This is contrary to normal practice and the judge was of the view that claims 1 and 14 were vital to the whole patent as all the other claims were dependent upon them and, like a pile of dominoes, their fall would inevitably follow the major claims.

The judge did conclude that, if the Samsung patents had been valid, Apple's implementation in its iPhone and iPad would have constituted infringement. Given his previous findings, this was, at best, a pyrrhic victory for Samsung. It is only one battle in a protracted war (and it remains unclear whether Samsung will appeal) but this was a decisive victory for Apple.

Conclusions

It was suggested at the beginning of this chapter that the patent system was based largely on the notion of national patents. This is likely to remain the case, and even the proposed Community patent would exist alongside, rather than replace, national patents. The increasingly global nature of commerce and industry is serving to bring about an increasing degree of harmonisation and, as shown in the discussion earlier of the most recent European Patent Office case law, the TRIPS Agreement is providing a legal basis for

---

[102] [2007] EWCA Civ 588.

harmonising initiatives. The trend throughout the world is clearly to accept that software should be brought within the ambit of the patent system. In some senses, there is almost an element of competition between states as to who can provide the strongest protection. As was said in the United States case of *Lotus v Paperback*:

> It is no accident that the world's strongest software industry is found in the United States, rather than in some other jurisdiction which provides weaker protection for computer programs.[103]

It is now over thirty years since patent law was reformed by the Patents Act 1977. At that time, although the status of computer programs was certainly discussed in the preceding report of the Banks Committee,[104] it was not a matter of massive importance. In the intervening years, not only has the technology permeated into every aspect of life, the development of microprocessors has rendered almost redundant distinctions between hardware and software—to the extent that the term 'computer program' is seldom used today. From a situation of existing as a rather small adjunct to the industrial society, information technology has become pivotal to the information society. Software development has changed from a craft to an industry. The turnover and profits of software companies such as Microsoft dwarf those of the vast majority of industrial enterprises. The development of satisfactory forms of protection is a matter of great importance.

As will be discussed in the following chapters, one of the legislative trends of the 1980s was to provide that computer programs are protected under the law of copyright. Certainly copyright provides an acceptable and appropriate form of protection for most computer programs which do not possess significant elements of novelty or originality. Copyright, however, particularly given precedents in the United States and the United Kingdom placing limits on the scope of protection against non-literal copying, is less suitable as a vehicle for protecting innovative works. Competitors can readily discern the underlying— and unprotected—ideas and replicate these without the necessity to engage in literal copying of any of the code used in the original. In such situations, the attractions of the patent system are apparent. In return for disclosing details of the techniques employed, the patent holder secures monopoly protection against reproduction of the novel ideas.

When the topic of the patentability of computer programs was discussed by the Banks Committee in the 1970s, the issue was agreed to be finely balanced. Ultimately, the Committee recommended against eligibility on grounds both of principle and practice. In terms of principle, it was argued that no significant distinction existed between programs and methods of mathematical calculation, which had always been excluded from protection.

These arguments cannot be discounted. It may have been preferable had the relatively hard line against patentability advocated by Banks been enforced by the courts. Once the dam had been broken by the EPC decisions in *Vicom*[105] and *Genentech*,[106] the line has proved impossible to hold. In *Fujitsu*,[107] Mr Justice Laddie commented that the distinction between the prohibition against programs and that relating to methods for performing a mental act was 'a matter of semantics'. In respect of many of the decisions and distinctions drawn, it may be suggested that the issue of patentability has been submerged in a semantic sea. Whilst accepting that there may be reasons of principle why no software patents should be issued, it is more difficult to accept at this level that an image-processing system should qualify whilst a virtual reality system would not.

The Schleswig-Holstein Question refers to a series of disputes which arose in the nineteenth century concerning the relationship of the Duchies of Schleswig and Holstein and

---

[103] 740 F Supp 37 (1990).   [104] Cmnd 4407 (1970).
[105] *Vicom Systems Inc's Application* [1987] 2 EPOR 74.   [106] *Genentech Inc's Patent* [1989] RPC 147.
[107] *Fujitsu Ltd's Application* [1996] RPC 511.

Denmark and the Confederation of German States.[108] The origins of the dispute dated back to the twelfth century and, as with many such disputes, matters became ever more complex as time passed. The Schleswig-Holstein Question has become a byword for insoluble problems and the then British Foreign Secretary famously commented that the question was of such a level of complexity that only three people had ever understood it:

> The first was Albert, the Prince Consort and he is dead; the second is a German professor, and he is in an asylum: and the third was myself—and I have forgotten it.

In many respects, the issue of software patents, at least in Europe, is fast approaching the dimensions of the Schleswig-Holstein Question. As attitudes harden on both sides of the divide, so the attempt to rationalise the treatment of applications becomes more and more complex. When leading and eminent judges can accuse each other of a failure to understand basic concepts, there is little hope for the rest of us to make sense of the situation. In many respects, the European situation contrasts unfavourably with that applying in the United States where, although the topic is certainly not without its controversies, the basics are relatively clear.

One of the issues that has been raised periodically throughout this book has been whether computer-related matters should be regulated by the general law or whether the need could be identified for the enactment of technology-specific measures. The European Patent Convention, and statutes such as the United Kingdom's Patents Act which are based on its provisions, have perhaps attained the worst of all possible worlds. Like the Schleswig-Holstein Question, the origins of the decision to include a prohibition against the grant of patents to computer programs is lost in history, although, as indicated earlier, the finger of suspicion may point at the United Kingdom.

The point has also been made throughout this book that computer technology has advanced with incredible speed. Computers and computer programs in the late 1960s and early 1970s bore no resemblance to the modern industries. Indeed, the fact that it is universal practice to talk about the 'software industry' indicates how far events have moved on. It is perhaps unlikely that had the drafters of the European Patent Convention been gifted with the power of prophecy the same approach would have been adopted, but such a guess does not provide any form of resolution to the present problems. Attempts have been made. In 2000, a diplomatic conference considered a proposal to remove the exclusion of computer programs from the European Patent Convention. The attempt failed, principally for the valid reason that it would be wrong to treat the computer program exclusion in isolation from the other grounds, such as schemes or methods for performing a mental act laid down as bars to patentability. A further attempt was made by the European Commission to introduce a Directive on software patents which would have required the Member States to adopt a liberal approach towards the award of patents for software-related inventions. This was rejected by the European Parliament in 2005 and no moves have been brought to bring forward new proposals. By way of contrast, United States patent law remains based on a 1952 statute which, as was the case with the previous United Kingdom legislation, restricts itself to providing that:

> Whoever invents or discovers any new and useful process, machine, manufacture, or composition of matter, or any new and useful improvement thereof, may obtain a patent therefore, subject to the conditions and requirements of this title.[109]

Although the statute lays down requirements of novelty[110] and non-obviousness,[111] there is no list of prohibited subject matter.

---

[108] Cited in <http://thinkexist.com>.   [109] Title 35 United States Code, s. 101.   [110] s. 102.
[111] s. 103.

There is no doubt that the United States Patent and Trademark Office, largely driven by case law from the Court of Appeals for the Federal Circuit, has the highest United States judicial authority other than the Supreme Court, and has been a leading proponent of the application of patents for software-related inventions. The value of the solution remains largely unproven. In *Aerotel v Telco*, it was commented:

> despite the fact that such patents have been granted for some time in the United States, it is far from certain that they have been what Sellars and Yeatman would have called a 'Good Thing'. The patent system is there to provide a research and investment incentive but it has a price. That price (what economists call 'transaction costs') is paid in a host of ways: the costs of patenting, the impediment to competition, the compliance cost of ensuring non-infringement, the cost of uncertainty, litigation costs and so on. There is, so far as we know, no really hard empirical data showing that the liberalisation of what is patentable in the USA has resulted in a greater [*sic*] rate of innovation or investment in the excluded categories. Innovation in computer programs, for instance, proceeded at an immense speed for years before anyone thought of granting patents for them as such.[112]

Statistics produced by the United States Patent and Trademark Office indicate a steady increase in the number of challenges made to patents in the form of a request that the office re-examines their validity. Such an approach, it is suggested, is quicker and cheaper than instituting legal proceedings seeking the same effect. Although the percentage of patents that are challenged represents a small proportion of the numbers awarded each year, the statistics indicate that in a large majority of cases, the result of the re-examination is either the removal or at least the weakening of the patent. The key problem remains, as was identified in the Report of the Committee on Patents as far back as 1970, for patent examiners to be able adequately to identify and assess the state of the art in order to determine whether an application is truly novel and sufficiently inventive to qualify for the award of a patent.

It would be facile to suggest that patent law—which involves an amalgam of legal and technical requirements—can ever be simple. Its application to software arouses strong passions on both sides of the argument. There is a well-known tale of a motorist stopping to ask a passer-by directions to a particular location, only to be told after many attempts to describe a route, 'If I were you I wouldn't have started from here in the first place.' In many respects, this perhaps sums up where software patents are now. Radical reform of the patent system could be a massive undertaking and securing the necessary international consensus would be a Herculean task. Providing to some extent a mirror-image of developments in patent law, significant changes have taken place in the law of copyright, which has been seen as the most appropriate form of protection for the majority of computer programs.

---

[112] [2006] EWCA Civ 1371 at para. 20.

16

Copyright protection

Introduction

Although there appears globally to be an increasing willingness to bring software-related inventions within the ambit of the patent system, only a small proportion of computer programs will display the necessary degree of novelty and inventiveness to qualify for that form of protection. Virtually every program, however, will obtain a measure of protection under the law of copyright. In addition to software being protected by copyright, information recorded in electronic format such as email messages, multimedia packages, and web pages will also be protected by copyright.

It is difficult to open a newspaper or view a news website without seeing reports of Internet piracy and legal attempts to limit its scope. Copyright is a hot topic today.

Copyright basics

The essence of copyright can be deduced from the name itself. The owner of copyright in a work possesses the right to copy and, by inference, the right to prevent others from copying. Until the invention of moveable-type printing by Gutenberg in 1450, the issue of copying was of little legal importance. The beginning of mass publishing of literary works brought with it new forms of regulation and control, although these were concerned initially with issues of censorship rather than with the allocation and protection of rights in information. In England, use of the new technology was controlled by a requirement that printing be restricted to authorised printers and that the publication of individual books be licensed by the Crown. This scheme continued until 1695. With its abolition, petitions were presented to Parliament at the behest of the Stationers' Company, which had enjoyed an effective monopoly of publishing but which would now be subjected to competition. Responding to these representations, the first copyright Act, the Statute of Anne, was enacted in 1709. This Act granted the author (or assignee) the exclusive right to reproduce the work. In respect of existing works, this right would subsist for twenty-one years, with new works being protected for up to twenty-eight years, subject to these being registered with the Stationers' Company. The registration scheme was a comparatively short-lived component of the United Kingdom copyright regime, although it continues to be a feature of the United States system.

The copyright system has developed over the centuries, largely following changes in recording technology. As it became possible to record different forms of work in permanent form, so copyright law has tended to be extended to regulate the sector. In 1734, engravings became the first form of artistic work to be protected under the terms of the Engraving Copyright Act. In 1814, sculptures were brought within the copyright system by the Sculpture Copyright Act, and the Dramatic Copyright Act 1833 extended protection still further to encompass the public performance of musical and dramatical compositions.

The Fine Art Copyright Act 1862 marked a significant recognition of the intervention of technology, with protection being extended to photographs. Study of the various copyright statutes enacted in the twentieth century indicates a steady expansion in the range of subject matter covered, normally following close on the heels of technological developments. In the Copyright Act 1911, reference is made to:

> any record, perforated roll, cinematography film or other contrivance by which the work may be mechanically performed or delivered.[1]

The Copyright Act 1956 extended protection to television and radio broadcasts made by the BBC or the Independent Television Authority.[2] During the 1980s, albeit motivated as much by the desire to introduce significant criminal sanctions as by uncertainty on whether the subject matter was protected under existing provisions of copyright law, the Copyright (Computer Software) (Amendment) Act 1985 brought this subject matter unequivocally within the ambit of copyright law.[3] The current United Kingdom copyright law is to be found principally in the Copyright, Designs and Patents Act 1988. As was the case with the Patents Act 1977, a variety of motives prompted the introduction of the new legislation. The previous statute, the Copyright Act 1956, had been subjected to piecemeal amendment and a need could be identified for a consolidating piece of legislation, coupled with a measure of reform to take account of specific problems which had been encountered concerning the extent to which protection might be extended towards functional works such as the design of product components. These problems were manifested in the decision of the House of Lords in the case of *British Leyland Motor Corpn Ltd v Armstrong Patents Co Ltd*,[4] where it was held that a motor-car manufacturer could not rely upon copyright law to prevent competitors from producing spare parts, such as exhaust systems which owners might wish to purchase when the original components required to be replaced. An IT-related area where the issue remains topical relates to the market for replacement ink cartridges and toner for printers. Finally, reform of the United Kingdom's copyright system, in the shape of the introduction of a system of 'moral rights', was required to permit ratification of the 1971 and 1979 revisions to the Berne Convention. In contrast to the situation with patent law where protection is offered on a national basis, the Berne Convention, which has been signed by all the world's major countries, provides for the recognition of copyright in all signatory states.

Although the Copyright, Designs and Patents Act 1988 remains the major statute in the copyright field, further reform has been introduced pursuant to the requirements of the European Directive on the Legal Protection of Computer Programs.[5] Effect has been given to the Directive's requirements by the Copyright (Computer Programs) Regulations 1992,[6] which make a number of amendments to the text of the 1988 Act. A further European Directive, 'On the Legal Protection of Databases', introducing a *sui generis* form of protection for the contents of electronic databases, was adopted in 1996 and required to be adopted within the Member States by 1 January 1998.[7] The Copyright and Rights in Databases Regulations implemented the Directive within the United Kingdom.[8] Further changes to domestic law have also been made by the Copyright and Related Rights Regulations 2003[9] in order to satisfy the requirements of the Directive 'On the Harmonisation of Certain Aspects of Copyright and Related Rights in the Information Society'.[10] Also relevant are the

---

[1] s. 1(2)(d).   [2] s. 14.   [3] s. 1.   [4] [1986] AC 577.

[5] Directive 91/250/EC, OJ 1991 L 122/42.

[6] SI 1992/3233. Despite their title, these regulations were introduced under the authority of the European Communities Act 1972, as opposed to the Copyright, Designs and Patents Act 1998.

[7] Directive 96/9/EC, OJ 1996 L 77/20.   [8] SI 1997/3032.   [9] SI 2003/2498.

[10] Directive 2001/29/EC, OJ 2001 L 167/10.

provisions of the 2004 Directive on the Enforcement of Intellectual Property Rights (the Enforcement Directive).[11] This was implemented in the United Kingdom by the Intellectual Property (Enforcement etc.) Regulations of 2006[12]

The provisions of these Directives and their implementation within the United Kingdom are discussed in the following two chapters.

This chapter will initially outline the key features of the copyright system and will then continue to analyse the manner in which these have been applied within a software context. In many respects, the development of copyright protection for software displays almost a mirror image of the situation described in the previous chapter in respect of patents. Starting with a denial of patentability, the application of the patent system has grown over time. With copyright, early cases accepted a very high level of protection but with the passage of time this has been steadily weakened.

Obtaining copyright

In contrast to the patent system, the copyright regime is noteworthy for a near complete lack of procedural formalities. The substantive requirements will be considered in more detail later, but at the outset it may be stated that protection begins at the moment that a work is recorded in some material form. Copyright lasts during the lifetime of the author and continues for a period of up to seventy years after the author's death. During this time, civil and criminal penalties may be imposed upon a party who, without the consent of the copyright owner, reproduces all or a substantial part of the work or engages in one or more of a list of other prohibited acts.

Forms of protected work

The Copyright, Designs and Patents Act provides that:

1. Copyright is a property right which subsists in accordance with this Part in the following descriptions of work—

   (a) original literary, dramatic, musical or artistic works,

   (b) sound recordings, films, broadcasts or cable programmes, and

   (c) the typographical arrangement of published editions.[13]

   Although the Act refers to copyright constituting a 'property right', it is accepted that it is a specialised and limited right, the scope of which is to be found exclusively in the copyright legislation.[14] Although it is commonplace to talk about software theft and, indeed, the leading organisation set up to protect the interests of copyright owners is the Federation Against Software Theft (FAST),[15] dealings in copyright material cannot be the subject of a charge of theft—although the legislation does provide significant criminal penalties for incidents of breach of copyright.

   The provisions relating to copyright in typographical arrangements does not require further consideration in this book. All of the other headings can impact upon software,

---

[11] 2004/48/EC, OJ L195/16
[12] SI 2006 No. 1028.   [13] s. 1.
[14] See *CBS Songs Ltd and ors v Amstrad Consumer Electronics Plc and anor* [1988] AC 1013 [1988].
[15] <http://www.fast.org.uk/>.

however, although, as will be discussed later, the most significant category has been that of a literary work.

The requirement of originality

The Act provides that only 'original' works are to be protected. Semantically, the word might be equated with the requirement of novelty applying under the patents regime. In reality, the requirement of originality has been construed as requiring only that the work is that of the author—that is, it has not been copied from any other source. In *University of London Press Ltd v University Tutorial Press Ltd*,[16] Petersen J held that:

> The word 'original' does not mean that the work must be an expression of original or inventive thought. Copyright Acts are not concerned with the originality of ideas, but with the expression of thought, and, in the case of 'literary work', with the expression of thought in print or writing. The originality which is required relates to the expression of the thought. But the Act does not require that the expression must be in an original or novel form but that the work must not be copied from another work—that it should originate from the author.[17]

Under the United Kingdom's copyright system, the most crass and unedifying piece of prose (or the most error-ridden computer program) is as entitled to the benefit of copyright protection as the most illustrious example of the species (although it may fare less well in the marketplace). In the case of *Shetland Times v Willis*,[18] it was accepted without debate that the headlines of newspaper reports could qualify for protection, and the case of *Exxon Corpn v Exxon Insurance Consultants International Ltd*[19] provides a very rare illustration of a situation in which the requirement of originality was not met. Here, it was held that copyright could not subsist in the single word, Exxon, albeit that it had been selected after lengthy and expensive public research to find a name to replace the well-known brand Esso. This was a requirement of United States anti-trust litigation, although the name Esso continues to be used in the United Kingdom.

This approach is to be contrasted with that applying in Germany, where the application of strict qualitative criteria resulted, prior to the EC Directive 'On the Legal Protection of Computer Programs',[20] in an estimated 95 per cent of computer programs being denied protection on the ground that they were not original. The Directive would appear to endorse the United Kingdom position on the legal protection of computer programs, stating in its Preamble that 'no tests as to the qualitative or aesthetic merits of the program should be applied' and providing subsequently that:

> A computer program shall be protected if it is the author's own intellectual creation. No other criteria shall be applied to determine its eligibility for protection.[21]

The phrase 'intellectual creation' is more reflective of the civil law's system of authors' rights than the common law notion of copyright, and it might prove sufficiently vague to allow a measure of discretion in this area. It remains uncertain, therefore, whether the Directive on the Legal Protection of Computer Programs will secure its objective of eliminating 'differences in the legal protection of computer programs offered by the laws of the Member States (which) have direct and negative effects on the functioning of the common market as regards computer programs'.[22]

---

[16] [1916] 2 Ch. 601.   [17] At 608–9.   [18] (1997) SC 316.   [19] [1982] Ch. 119.
[20] Directive 91/250/EC.   [21] Art. 1(3).   [22] Directive 91/250/EC, Preamble.

Ownership of copyright

The author of a work will, subject to one exception, be the first owner of any copyright which may subsist in it.[23] Where a work is the product of two or more authors, any copyright arising will be the joint property of the authors.[24] The criterion for determining the existence of joint authorship is whether the individual contributions of the authors can be distinguished.[25] In this case, each author will possess individual copyright in his or her portion of the work. This may be a matter of some significance in the software field, where in the case of a program intended for use in a specific area of business, production may require both programming skills and knowledge of the subject area. Unless suitable contractual arrangements are negotiated, the result could be the existence of two separate copyrights, each useless without the other.

Employee-created works

The exception to the principle that the author is the first owner of copyright in a work applies where the work is created in the course of the author's employment. In this event, copyright will, subject to any contractual provision to the contrary, vest in the employer.[26] This approach marks a change from the position under previous copyright statutes, where the employer's rights in respect of employee-created works were limited in the situation where the work was created for publication in a newspaper, magazine, or other periodical.[27] Although the employer would possess copyright in the publication containing the work, all other rights in respect of it would remain with the author. Thus, the inclusion of the work in a database would require the author's permission. Today, many newspapers make copies of previous issues available in the form of an electronic database. Under the provision described above, the consent of the author of every piece of information appearing in the database would have been required. Responding to lobbying on the part of media interests, the Copyright, Designs and Patents Act 1988 eschews any exceptions to the general rule conferring unrestricted copyright on the employer.

Computer-generated works

Computers are frequently used to assist in the production of a work. In many instances, this will not affect copyright in the work at all. This book, for example, was typed on an Apple MacBook™ computer, using Microsoft Word™ software. In this, and in many other situations, the computer is merely a tool and the author of the text acquires full copyright in the completed work—which is then assigned to the publisher. In *Express Newspapers plc v Liverpool Daily Post and Echo plc*,[28] another case determined at interlocutory level, the plaintiff ran a competition 'Millionaire of the Month' in its newspaper. A number of other national newspapers operated similar competitions. In each case, the key feature was that competitors would have to check the newspaper each day to see whether numbers allocated to them matched winning numbers. The defendant republished all the winning numbers with the obvious intention that readers could participate in the competitions run by other publishers without having to purchase copies of the newspaper. In defence to an action alleging copyright infringement, the defendant claimed that as the numbers were selected

---

[23] Copyright, Designs and Patents Act 1988, s. 11(1).

[24] s. 10(3).   [25] s. 10(1).   [26] Copyright, Designs and Patents Act 1988, s. 11(2).

[27] Copyright Act 1956, s. 4(2).   [28] [1985] 1 WLR 1089.

by a computer program, they were not entitled to protection. Dismissing this defence, Whitford J (as he then was) held that a great deal of skill and labour had been required to develop the computer program (not least to ensure that too many winning numbers were not selected). As with the word-processing example cited above, the computer was no more than a tool giving effect to the intentions of its human controller.

In other instances, the role of the computer may move beyond that of recording a user's work and may serve to embellish the creation. An example concerns the practice of digital sampling. Other applications in the musical field might concern the use of electronic synthesisers. Without delving into the technical details concerning the manner in which these products function, it is sufficient to note that the involvement of the computer is at a qualitatively greater level than that occurring in word-processing applications.

A further situation which may raise questions of the ownership of copyright might apply where a database or expert system program is acquired. The program will require the addition of data by the user and the combination of the program and the user-supplied data will produce a new product in the form of the processed output. Again, this finished product will owe a considerable amount to the underlying program.

The Copyright, Designs and Patents Act 1988 contains a provision which appears to be unique in copyright statutes. It introduces a specific category of computer-generated work and provides:

> In the case of a literary, dramatic, musical or artistic work which is computer-generated, the author shall be taken to be the person by whom the arrangements necessary for the creation of the work are undertaken.[29]

The concept of a computer-generated work is defined as one where 'the work is generated by computer in circumstances such that there is no human author of the work'.[30]

It is unclear when this provision might be applicable. Few, if any, works will be created by a computer in the absence of any human involvement. In circumstances such as those identified here, human involvement will be required. The question which may have to be determined by a court in the event of any dispute is whether the input of any of the parties is sufficiently substantial to qualify them for sole ownership of copyright (as will almost certainly be the case with a piece of text produced on a word processor) or whether there might be joint ownership of copyright. In many instances, the enabling computer programs may be sold under the terms of a contract which prescribes the use to which a completed work may be put. Typically, the purchaser of the program will be entitled to use it for his or her own purposes but prohibited from selling or disposing of any work thereby created without the further agreement of the supplier.

In determining whether there is no human author of a work, two issues may be relevant. The first would be whether there is no human involvement of any kind in the production of the work. It is difficult to conceive of situations where the computer will act entirely on its own initiative. Once the possibility of some human intervention is accepted, the statutory provision might appear otiose. The general criterion for a literary or other work to be protected requires that it be the author's 'original' work. Although the requirement of originality has little application in the general field, the concept of computer-generated works can have meaning only if this is interpreted so as to exclude a human computer operator from qualifying for authorship where they make no intellectual contribution to the work. An example of such a situation might be where a computer program operates to produce a drawing on a completely random basis, with the operator's only contribution being to

---

[29] s. 9(3).   [30] s. 178.

initiate its operation. In this case, the operator, or a person who instructed that person to carry out the task, will become owner of the computer-generated work.

The duration of copyright will depend upon the particular form of the work. In the case of a literary, dramatic, or musical work, copyright will subsist during the lifetime of the author and for a period of seventy years after the author's death.[31] In the event that the work is computer-generated, copyright will last for fifty years from the end of the calendar year in which the work is produced.[32] The same period of protection extends to films, sound recordings, and broadcasts,[33] whilst a shorter period of twenty-five years is applicable to the typographical arrangements of a published work.[34]

The lifespan of copyright is clearly much greater than that of a patent, although it must be doubted whether a period of protection which, depending upon the age and longevity of the author, may subsist for a century or longer is of any practical significance in the information technology field. Given the pace of technological development, it is unlikely that any piece of software will retain commercial value for more than a few years, although, as the publicity surrounding the Millennium Bug evidenced, many programs have enjoyed a longer lifespan than originally expected. Even in the case of the author's own word-processing package, the copyright notice refers to versions of the program dating back to 1983, although it is not clear how much original code remains.

Infringement of copyright

As discussed in the preceding chapters, the award of a patent serves to confer upon the successful applicant a monopoly in respect of the exploitation of its subject matter. Although judicial references have been made to copyright conferring a monopoly—in the case of *Green v Broadcasting Council of New Zealand*,[35] Lord Bridge, delivering the judgment of the Privy Council, stated that '[t]he protection which copyright gives creates a monopoly'—it is generally accepted that the copyright owner possesses only the exclusive right to perform certain acts in respect of the work. These comprise the rights:

- to copy the work or any substantial part of it[36]
- to issue copies of the work to the public[37]
- to perform, show, or play the work in public[38]
- to broadcast the work or include it in a cable programme service[39]
- to make an adaptation of the work or do any of the above in relation to an adaptation.[40]

The nature of copying

The act of copying is defined as involving the reproduction of the work, or a substantial part of the work in any material form.[41] This is to include 'storing the work in any medium by

---

[31] Copyright, Designs and Patents Act 1988, s. 12(1). The only exception to this rule applies in favour of the work, *Peter Pan*. Copyright in this work was bequeathed upon the author's death to the Great Ormond Street Children's Hospital, with the revenue accruing from royalty payments, etc. constituting a significant portion of the hospital's income. The author, J. M. Barrie having died in 1937, copyright would normally have expired at the end of 1987. In what may be a unique provision, s. 301 and Sch. 6 of the Act provide, not inappropriately given the nature of the work's main character, that elements of the copyright in Peter Pan will never die.

[32] s. 12(3).   [33] s. 13.   [34] s. 15.   [35] [1989] 2 All ER 1056.
[36] Copyright, Designs and Patents Act 1988, s. 16(1)(a).   [37] s. 16(1)(b).   [38] s. 16(1)(c).
[39] s. 16(1)(d).   [40] s. 16(1)(e).   [41] s. 17(2).

electronic means'.[42] Thus, for example, the use of some form of scanning device to transform text into electronic format will constitute an infringement of copyright in the original text.

A popular saying is to the effect that if enough monkeys are given enough typewriters, eventually one monkey will hit the keys in such an order as to reproduce the works of Shakespeare. Discounting the inconvenient fact that the works of Shakespeare are out of copyright, and the considerable uncertainty as to whether a monkey could own copyright, the end-product would not infringe copyright for the reason that it represents an independent composition.

The question of whether one work infringes copyright in an earlier work is determined on the basis of objective criteria. It is not necessary that the act should have been deliberate. A number of cases have been brought in which the allegation has been made (and sometimes established) that a musical work was derived from an earlier composition which might well have been heard by the second composer, who retained a subconscious memory of the melody. The fact that the copying or plagiarism was unintentional will not serve as a defence. The key factors which will have to be established by a party alleging copyright infringement are that the alleged copyist would have had access to the work and that there are substantial similarities between the works which are not explicable by factors other than copying.

In situations where two or more people are working on the same topic, for example, a history of the Second World War, it is likely that similarities will exist between the finished works. In a non-fictional work, the ending must be the same and there is likely to be consensus regarding the key events of the conflict. Greater levels of similarity may raise suspicions that one author has relied too heavily on the work of the other.

In the United States' copyright system, a distinction is drawn between ideas—which are not protected by copyright—and particular forms of expression. In similar manner, the European Directive on the Legal Protection of Software provides that:

> Protection in accordance with this Directive shall apply to the expression in any form of a computer program. Ideas and principles which underlie any element of a computer program, including those which underlie its interfaces, are not protected by copyright under this Directive.[43]

Often referred to as the 'idea/expression dichotomy' this element has featured in many cases concerned with copyright infringement in software. Generally, however, although providing a useful sound bite, the idea/expression dichotomy can offer only limited assistance in determining whether copyright infringement has occurred.

How temporary is temporary?

One of the aspects of digital technology is that every act of use tends to require elements of copying. Copyright law gives rights owners a wide range of rights but in the analogue world there has been a distinction between what might be classed as active and passive acts of infringement. A party making an infringing copy of a work will commit an unlawful act but a person who reads or views such an article will not be considered guilty. As with many aspects of life, the Internet and digital technologies challenge established practice. The vulnerabilities of copyright owners have been well documented. It is also the case that users' rights are not clear-cut.

Consideration was given to the question when temporary acts of reproduction might constitute copyright infringement in the case of *Public Relations Consultants Association v*

---

[42] s. 17(3).   [43] Art. 1(2).

The Newspaper Licensing Agency Ltd and ors.[44] As was explained in the leading judgment of the case, every act of viewing a page on the Internet causes a copy of the contents to be stored in the cache memory of the browser. At issue was the question of whether such temporary reproductions breached the rights of copyright owners.

The particular dispute concerned the business of the appellants who offered its customers a service whereby they would be notified of any Internet publications of interest to them. Typically, a company might want to be notified of any media mention of its activities or those of its competitor. The appellants had obtained a licence from the relevant copyright owners to provide this service. Initially customers would be sent an email giving hypertext links to the relevant materials. It was accepted by all parties that emails constituted a form of permanent storage and that customers would also be required to obtain a licence. A subsequent development which constituted the genesis of the litigation saw customers able to access the data on the appellant's website. The question for the Supreme Court was whether the customers would be required to obtain a licence for use of material in this format. It was recognised, however that the issue had wider implications. As was stated:

> The issue has reached this court because it affects the operation of a service which is being made available on a commercial basis. But the same question potentially affects millions of non-commercial users of the internet who may, no doubt unwittingly, be incurring civil liability by viewing copyright material on the internet without the authority of the rights owner, for example because it has been unlawfully uploaded by a third party. Similar issues arise when viewers watch a broadcast on a digital television or a subscription television programme via a set-top box.[45]

At the heart of the dispute was the Directive on Copyright in the Information Society (Directive 2001/29/EC). This proclaims the intention to secure a 'high level of protection for copyright' but also to secure a harmonised approach across the Union towards the implementation of Article 9(2) of the Berne Convention which states that:

> It shall be a matter for legislation in the countries of the Union to permit the reproduction of such works in certain special cases, provided that such reproduction does not conflict with a normal exploitation of the work and does not unreasonably prejudice the legitimate interests of the author.

The balance between the legitimate interests of rights owners and users has proved to be very difficult to define. The Copyright in the Information Society Directive establishes in Article 5.1 a list of permitted activities. These encompass:

1. Temporary acts of reproduction referred to in Article 2, which are transient or incidental [and] an integral and essential part of a technological process and whose sole purpose is to enable:

   (a) a transmission in a network between third parties by an intermediary, or

   (b) a lawful use

   of a work or other subject-matter to be made, and which have no independent economic significance, shall be exempted from the reproduction right provided for in Article 2.

---

[44] [2013] UKSC 18.

[45] *Public Relations Consultants Association v The Newspaper Licensing Agency Ltd and ors* [2013] UKSC 18 at para. 4.

These exceptions are subject to the provisions of Article 5(5) which requires that activities must not conflict with a normal exploitation of the work or other subject matter and should not unreasonably prejudice the legitimate interests of the right holder.

These requirements were paraphrased by the Court of Justice for the European Union (CJEU) in the case of *Infopaq International A/S v Danske Dagblades Forening* as requiring that:

The act is temporary;

it is transient or incidental;

it is an integral and essential part of a technological process;

the sole purpose of that process is to enable a transmission in a network between third parties by an intermediary of a lawful use of a work or protected subject-matter; and

the act has no independent economic significance.[46]

The Supreme Court understands these criteria as cumulative rather than individual in nature:

They are overlapping and repetitive, and each of them colours the meaning of the others. They have to be read together so as to achieve the combined purpose of all of them.[47]

The Supreme Court made extensive reference to further cases before the CJEU.[48] Its judgment provides a useful summary and compilation of the CJEU's reasoning.

In many ways at the heart of the debate was the submission by counsel for the copyright owners that Article 5(1) of the Information Society Directive applied only to acts committed in the course of transmitting Internet content to end-users. It did not, it was suggested, confer any rights on end-users themselves. The Supreme Court rejected this contention. Delivering the leading judgment, Lord Sumption stated:

In my opinion, this is an impossible contention. In the first place, it is clear from the Directive's recitals, and in particular from recital 33, that it was intended that the exception should 'include acts which enable browsing as well as acts of caching to take place.' Browsing is not part of the process of transmission. It is the use of an internet browser by an end-user to view web pages. It is by its very nature an end-user function.[49]

and continued:

Once it is accepted that part of the purpose of article 5.1 is to authorise the making of copies to enable the end-user to view copyright material on the internet, the various conditions laid down by that article must be construed so far as possible in a manner consistent with that purpose. It must, if the exception is to be coherent, apply to the ordinary technical processes associated with internet browsing.[50]

The ordinary technical purposes, it was held, included the use of caches to store records of sites visited by users. Although it was recognised that the extent and duration of the data held in caches could be influenced by actions of users, this did not impact significantly

---

[46] Case 5/08 at para. 54. Available from <http://curia.europa.eu/juris/liste.jsf?&num=C-5/08>.

[47] *Public Relations Consultants Association v The Newspaper Licensing Agency Ltd and ors* [2013] UKSC 18 at para. 11.

[48] In particular Case C-5/08 *Infopaq International A/S v Danske Dagblades Forening* ('*Infopaq I*') [2010] FSR 495; Case C-403/08 *Football Association Premier League Ltd v QC Leisure and ors*; Case C-429/08 *Karen Murphy v Media ProtectionServices Ltd* (2012) 1CMLR 769; and Case C302-10 *Infopaq International A/S v Danske Dagblades Forening.*

[49] *Public Relations Consultants Association v The Newspaper Licensing Agency Ltd and ors* [2013] UKSC 18 at para. 27.   [50] para. 28.

on the provisions of Article 5(1) of the Information Society Directive. Lord Sumption continued:

> All that article 5.1 of the Directive achieves is to treat the viewing of copyright material on the internet in the same way as its viewing in physical form, notwithstanding that the technical processes involved incidentally include the making of temporary copies within the electronic equipment employed…if it is an infringement merely to view copyright material, without downloading or printing out, then those who browse the internet are likely unintentionally to incur civil liability, at least in principle, by merely coming upon a web-page containing copyright material in the course of browsing. This seems an unacceptable result, which would make infringers of many millions of ordinary users of the internet across the EU who use browsers and search engines for private as well as commercial purposes.[51]

It may not come as a surprise that the Supreme Court was very much in favour of ruling in a manner that legitimised normal Internet browsing activities. The need for a pan-European harmonised approach to these important questions was recognised and the Supreme Court decided that the CJEU should be asked to rule on the question whether:

> having regard in particular to the fact that a copy of protected material may in the ordinary course of internet usage remain in the cache for a period of time after the browsing session which has generated that copy is completed until it is overlaid by other material, and a screen copy will remain on screen until the browsing session is terminated by the user.[52]

This case is of interest at several levels. It provides a clear description and summation of the evolving jurisprudence of the CJEU in the field. More importantly, it provides a clear signpost as to the direction that the law should take in balancing the interests of rights owners and the public who may wish to access the works. It is too early to say that we have a definitive ruling but based on its past precedents it would be surprising if the CJEU were to rule other than in accordance with the suggestions of the Supreme Court. It is perhaps unfortunate that more than a decade after the enactment of the Copyright in the Information Society Directive we are still awaiting a definite answer to the question of what activities are legitimate for Internet users. The Supreme Court ruling does seem to suggest a viable way forward and it is to be hoped that the decision of the CJEU will be delivered in the not too distant future.

Fair and unfair use of an earlier work

Beyond those situations in which it may be apparent that a protected work has been copied, translated, or adapted, situations may arise in which it is clear that the work has been used in the course of producing another work, but where the conduct cannot equivocally be regarded as involving any of the acts prohibited in the legislation. In a variety of cases concerned with literary works, the courts have adopted a broad view as to the scope of copyright protection, extending it to conduct which is regarded as involving the inequitable exploitation of the work of another—what might in everyday language be referred to as 'plagiarism'.

In the case of *Harman Pictures NV v Osborne*,[53] the plaintiff owned the screen rights in respect of a book dealing with the Charge of the Light Brigade. Negotiations had taken place with a view to the defendants acquiring the rights. The negotiations came to nothing, but some time later, the defendants indicated their intention to produce a film on the same theme. The screenplay for the film was written by the first defendant. The plaintiff sought

---

[51] para. 36.   [52] para. 38.   [53] [1967] 2 All ER 324.

an injunction to prevent the film's distribution, alleging that the screenplay infringed its copyright.

Comparison of the screenplay with the book revealed points both of similarity and dissimilarity. The defendant did not deny having knowledge of the plaintiff's work, but argued that their screenplay had been based upon a much wider variety of sources.

> Whilst accepting that it was permissible for a later author to make use of an existing work, it was held that this could not be utilised as a substitute for the expenditure of independent effort. As was stated by Sir William Page Wood V-C in the case of *Jarrold v Houlston*:[54]I take the illegitimate use, as opposed to the legitimate use, of another person's work on subject matters of this description to be this: If, knowing that a person whose work is protected by copyright has, with considerable labour, compiled from various sources a work in itself not original, but which he has digested and arranged, instead of taking the pains of searching into all the common sources and obtaining your subject matter from them, you avail yourself of the labour of your predecessor, adopt his arrangements, adopt moreover the very questions he has asked or adopt them with but a slight degree of colourable variation, and thus save yourself pains and labour by availing yourself of the pains and labour which he has employed, that I take to be an illegitimate use.

In the present case, the issue was whether the defendant had worked independently to:

> produce a script which from the nature of things has much in common with the book, or did he proceed the other way round and use the book as a basis, taking his selection of incidents and quotations therefrom, albeit omitting a number and making some alterations and additions by reference to the common sources and by some reference to other sources?[55]

Considering these matters, Goff J determined that the similarities between the two works were sufficient to justify the grant of an interlocutory injunction, with terms preventing the defendants from 'exhibiting, releasing or distributing any film of or based on [the screenplay]'.[56]

The question of the use which can be made of an earlier work was again at issue in the case of *Elanco Products Ltd v Mandops Agricultural Specialists Ltd*.[57] Elanco had invented and secured patent protection for a herbicidal product. During the currency of the patent's validity, both the plaintiff and independent research institutions had made extensive studies of the herbicide's application. Some of the information derived from these studies was incorporated in the form of instructions which were supplied with the product.

Upon the expiry of the patent, the defendant commenced production and marketing of the herbicide. Initially, they produced an accompanying instructional leaflet that was a virtual copy of the plaintiff's. The plaintiff objected to this action, alleging that it infringed copyright in its compilation of instructions, and the leaflet was withdrawn. A revised version was produced which also brought objections. When a third version was still considered objectionable, the plaintiff sought an injunction. Although the final version of the defendant's leaflet used terminology different from that of the plaintiff's, it was alleged that it remained based upon their material, thereby constituting an infringement of their copyright.

Holding in favour of the plaintiff, Goff LJ agreed that there was an arguable case of copyright infringement:

> It may well be that if the respondents had in fact at the start simply looked at the available information...and from that decided what they would put in their literature and how they

---

[54] (1857) 3 K&J 708 at 716–17.   [55] *Harman Pictures NV v Osborne* [1967] 2 All ER 324 at 334.
[56] At 337.   [57] [1980] RPC 213.

would express it, the appellants would at least have had considerable difficulty in bringing home any charge of infringement, even, having regard to the evidence, if the results had been extremely similar and the selection of items had been the same. But they chose, on the evidence as it stands at the moment, to proceed by making a simple...copy, and then they proceeded to revise it. It may well be that the result produced that way is an infringement.[58]

Concurring, Buckley LJ ruled:

As I understand the law in this case, the defendants were fully entitled to make use of any information, of a technical or any other kind which was in the public domain, for the purpose of compiling their label and their trade literature, but they were not entitled to copy the plaintiffs' label or trade literature thereby making use of the plaintiffs' skill and judgement and saving themselves the trouble, and very possibly the cost, of assembling their own information, either from their own researches or from sources available in documents in the public domain, and thereby making their own selection of information to put into that literature and producing their own label and trade literature.[59]

In one significant respect, the decision in *Elanco*[60] must be approached with a measure of caution. The fact that the defendant had originally produced a near total copy of the plaintiff's work must have cast a shadow over its subsequent conduct. One aspect of the case would, however, appear apposite in a software context. As is the case with much software, the literary works were functional in nature. Unlike the situation where works are created with a view to the reader's entertainment, their purpose was to provide instruction. In the situation where a user has become familiar with the instructions issued by one producer, the use of semantic variations may result in unnecessary confusion. Whereas diversity of expression may be a valuable attribute in literature, its virtues are less obvious in a more technical arena.[61]

Other rights belonging to the copyright owner

As it was introduced, copyright protected only against literal copying of a work. As it has evolved, more extensive rights have been conferred on the right holder and a number of these are relevant in the IT context.

To issue copies of the work to the public

The owner of copyright in a work has the right to determine whether copies of that work might be made available to the public. This right extends only to the first occasion upon which the work is made available and not to any subsequent dealings in the work by way of importation, distribution, sale, hire, or loan.

In most cases, a person who has lawfully come into possession of a copy of a protected work will have the right, either to resell the copy or to make it available to members of the

---

[58] At 228.   [59] At 231.

[60] *Elanco Products Ltd v Mandops Agricultural Specialists Ltd* [1980] RPC 213.

[61] Some recognition of the different status of product instructions can be seen in the case of *Wormell v RHM Agriculture (East) Ltd* [1987] 3 All ER 75. Once again, a pesticide product was at issue, with the purchaser alleging that its failure to eradicate weeds rendered it unmerchantable in terms of s. 14 of the Sale of Goods Act 1979. Although this action failed, the court accepted that the adequacy or otherwise of instructions constituted a relevant factor in determining questions of merchantability. This approach may be contrasted with the general refusal of the courts to consider claims that the quality of a written work is unacceptably low quality.

public on a rental basis. The Copyright, Designs and Patents Act 1988 provides an exception to this rule in the case of the rental of computer programs, sound recordings, and films.[62] Essentially, such works may be hired only under the terms either of an order made by the Secretary of State or according to the provisions of a licensing scheme devised by the copyright owners and approved by the Copyright Tribunal. Either procedure will prescribe terms upon which the rental may occur and the royalty that will be payable to the copyright owner. The justification for this provision lies with the ease with which copies of software may be made. To this extent, the provisions for royalty payments can be seen as offering some compensation for losses which may result from such activities.

To perform, show, or play the work in public

The acts of performing or showing the protected work in public are reserved to the copyright owner. The issue of what is a public performance is not defined in the legislation. It would seem clear, however, that the operation of a computer game program within, for example, a public house or an amusement arcade would constitute an infringing act if committed without the consent of the copyright owner.

To broadcast the work or include it in a cable programme service

Although this may appear unlikely to be of great application in a software context, the case of *Shetland Times v Willis*[63] provides some authority for the proposition that a website is to be classed as a cable programme service, with individual pages being classed as cable programmes. The Act defines a cable programme service as:

> a service which consists wholly or mainly in sending visual images, sounds or other information by means of a telecommunications system, otherwise than by wireless telegraphy, for reception—
>
> (a) at two or more places (whether for simultaneous reception or at different times in response to requests by different users), or
>
> (b) for presentation to members of the public[64]

with any item included in such a service being classed as a cable programme. The case concerned two websites, the *Shetland Times*, which was the electronic form of an established newspaper, and the *Shetland News*, which existed only in electronic form. The *Shetland News* website copied headlines from the *Shetland Times* site (something which in itself was held to be a breach of copyright) and placed hypertext links allowing users to go to the appropriate section of the *Shetland Times* website. The case did not proceed to the stage of a full hearing, the judge accepting that there was a prima facie case that the *Shetland News* was in breach of the *Shetland Times*' rights in this regard.

To make an adaptation of the work

In respect of computer programs, it is provided that adaptation 'means an arrangement or altered version of the program or a translation of it'.[65] Producing, for example, a version

---

[62] s. 66.   [63] (1997) SC 316.

[64] Copyright, Designs and Patents Act 1988, s. 7. The Copyright and Related Rights Regulations 2003, SI 2003 No. 2498 repealed the specific definition of a cable programme service and subsumed its scope into the general definition of broadcasting.

[65] Copyright, Designs and Patents Act 1988, s. 21(4).

of a program originally designed to run under Microsoft Windows to operate on Apple computers will, in the absence of authorisation from the copyright owner, constitute unlawful adaptation.

The development of software copyright

Questions about the eligibility of computer programs for copyright protection began to emerge in the 1960s. Prior to this time, hardware and software tended to be supplied by the same party and generally equipment was rented by the customer (often with the manufacturer supplying staff to maintain the machine), rather than bought. In such an environment, there was little interest in issues of ownership of intellectual property rights. In 1969, prompted by anti-trust investigations by the United States competition authorities, IBM, then the dominant player in the computer market, announced that it was to separate its hardware and software operations. This has been seen as a pivotal move in the development of a distinct software industry and today there is little doubt that companies such as Microsoft and Google are more significant players than hardware producers. Indeed, IBM itself has sold off most of its hardware production businesses and is focusing on consulting and re-engineering services.

Once a distinct market began to develop in software, issues of legal protection were not far behind. One of the striking features of software is that it can be massively expensive to develop but can be reproduced quickly and at very low cost. Although there were debates in the 1970s and 1980s as to whether computer programs were a proper subject for protection under the copyright system, the fact that the underlying source code was written in a form of English meant that there was—at least from the perspective of the United Kingdom system, which imposes almost no qualitative requirements for the grant of copyright—little dispute that software should be protected as a form of literary work. The Copyright, Designs and Patents Act 1988, the EC Directive on the Legal Protection of Computer Programs,[66] the Berne and World Intellectual Property Organization (WIPO) Copyright Conventions, and the World Trade Organization's Agreement on Trade Related Aspects of Intellectual Property Rights (TRIPS) now all provide that computer programs are to be protected on this basis.

As enacted, the Copyright, Designs and Patents Act 1988 provided simply that the term 'literary work':

> means any work, other than a dramatic or musical work, which is written, spoken or sung, and accordingly includes—
>
> (a) a table or compilation; and
>
> (b) a computer program.[67]

In common with many other aspects of the subject, the term 'computer program' is not defined in the legislation. This may have been a matter of limited importance in 1988, but is becoming more significant in our digital age. A computer program may be developed which will itself cause images to be displayed on screen. Many computer games will fall into this category and the technique is increasingly used to create or enhance images in feature films. Recent examples include the films *Titanic* and *Gladiator*, whilst the film *Toy Story 2* is reported to be the first production which exists entirely in digital format. No actors were involved, with all the images being produced within a computer environment. Copies of the film are recorded on computer storage media and projected directly from this. As will

---

[66] Directive 91/250/EC.   [67] s. 3(1).

be discussed in more detail later, in such instances, it is difficult to tell where the computer program ends and the film begins.

In the course of producing a computer program, a good deal of other material may be developed. The process may begin with a general formulation of the intended purpose of the program. Subsequently, a detailed specification may be written down, describing all the functions and manner of operation to be provided in the completed work. This may take the form of a flow chart depicting the structure and sequence of the operations to be carried out. Drawings may also be made depicting various aspects of the screen displays to be produced.

It is almost certain that such preparatory works would have been protected under the original formulation of the Copyright, Designs and Patents Act 1988. As will be discussed at various stages later, the United Kingdom requires a very low degree of originality or literary merit in order to award copyright protection, and there is little doubt that even a few scribbles on a piece of paper would be protected. The situation was less clear in other EU Member States, and the Directive on the Legal Protection of Computer Programs made special provision for the protection of such materials.[68] In implementing the measure, the Copyright (Computer Programs) Regulations 1992[69] added a new section 3(1)(c) to the 1988 Act, referring to:

(c) preparatory design material for a computer program.

In some respects, the amendment may create more problems than it solves. Where the preparatory work is in the form of lines of code and written descriptions of the intended functions, there will be no problem in offering protection on this basis. The preparatory material may also take the form of flow charts or drawings of possible screen displays. In the Copyright, Designs and Patents Act 1988, the term 'artistic work' is defined as including 'any painting, drawing, map, chart or plan'.[70] Whilst it may be that artistic copyright will continue to exist in these elements, the rationale for protecting plans and drawings as something which they clearly are not appears somewhat obscure.

Applying copyright principles to software

In discussing the extent to which activities relating to software might contravene copyright law, three categories of potential infringement can be considered. The first two relate to what is called literal copying of software. In the first instance, this involves the making of a direct copy of software. This may be done for commercial gain, and will be discussed under the heading of software piracy. Also involving direct reproduction is the act of using software. Every time a program is used, a copy of its contents is required to be taken from its storage location on the computer to the machine's active processing memory. This creates problems for the relationship between copyright owner and user, and has led in part to the emergence of software licences. These documents, which are an almost inevitable companion to mass-produced software packages, typically confer use rights, but at the expense of seeking to oblige the user to accept other provisions limiting or excluding liabilities in the event that the software fails to operate in a satisfactory manner and thereby causes some form of injury or damage to the user. Although the Copyright, Designs and Patents Act 1988 as enacted was silent on all questions concerned with users' rights other than the somewhat nebulous concept of fair dealing, implementation of the EC Directive on the Legal Protection of Computer Programs[71] has brought about significant changes. Although the extent of some of the rights remains unclear, lawful users of software acquire a number

---

[68] Directive 91/250/EC, Art. 1(1).   [69] SI 1992/3233.   [70] s. 4(2).
[71] Directive 91/250/EC.

of entitlements, ranging from a right to use software to the ability to reverse engineer and decompile, albeit in limited circumstances.

The third category of infringement raises the most interesting legal issues. It concerns the situation whereby two programs exhibit similarities at the level of screen displays but not at the level of code. Although the phrase has rather fallen out of legal favour, the argument might be put in terms that one program has copied the 'look and feel' of another. This topic might also be considered at two levels. In the first—and more common—case, the alleged infringer will have had some access to the original program's code. Typically, a programmer will have worked on the development of one package, moved to another employer and been involved with the development of a competing program. In the second category, the parties will act much more at arm's length, with the only access obtained by the alleged infringer being to the working copy of the program.

Software piracy

The term 'software piracy' encompasses a range of forms of conduct. The Business Software Alliance (BSA), an organisation which includes most of the major Western software producers amongst its membership, has identified a range of forms of conduct:

- *multiple installation*

  This is where you install more copies of a software program than you have licences. For example, if you buy ten single-user licences for a product yet install it onto twenty machines, you are using ten illegal copies.

- *end-user piracy*

  Similar to multiple installation, this involves an end user (or company employee) copying programs illegally or using unlicensed software in the workplace.

- *client/server piracy*

  This occurs when a program is run off a server (rather than from individual PCs) and is accessed by more end users than the company has bought licences for.

- *online piracy*

  This happens when software is downloaded from the web and installed but not paid for. There are other types of software piracy (grey software, counterfeit software, etc.).[72]

Essentially, any conduct which can be considered an infringement of copyright will come within these definitions. As the term 'piracy' would suggest, there is little doubt that the conduct at issue is unlawful. A considerable number of studies have sought to assess the scale of the problem. Most have been conducted by or on behalf of organisations such as the Business Software Alliance (BSA). The fourteenth piracy study conducted by the BSA and IDA was published in May 2010[73] and gives statistics up to 2009.

The study indicated that the global piracy rate in 2009 was around 43 per cent indicating a reversal of a trend found in previous studies showing a reduction in the level of privacy. This, it is suggested, is due to a sharp increase in the number of personal computers in regions associated with a high level of piracy. The 'distinction' of topping the piracy charts falls to Zimbabwe, with a 92 per cent rate. Other significant offenders are China and Nigeria, with 77 and 82 per cent rates. At the other end of the spectrum, the United States

---

[72] <http://www.bsa.org/uk/types>.   [73] <http://www.bsa.org/idcstudy.aspx>.

posts a rate of 19 per cent, the United Kingdom stands only slightly higher at 26 per cent, with Western Europe generally averaging at 32 per cent.

In economic terms, the total loss is estimated at $39.5 billion. Given the scale of software use within North America and Europe, it is not surprising that the regions with the highest financial losses were North America and Western Europe, although a worrying trend identified is that the biggest increases in software use is now coming from areas which have much higher piracy. A further estimate of the impact of piracy can be taken from a further study produced for the BSA by Price Waterhouse in 1998.[74] This calculated that:

> Reducing software piracy rates by realistic levels from the 1996 Western European average of 43 per cent for PC business software to the corresponding U.S. average of 27 per cent, and equivalent reductions in other software categories would generate as many as 258,651 more job and $13.9bn additional tax revenues by the year 2001, in addition to forecast market growth.

User rights in respect of software

Whilst the application of provisions of copyright law to software-based products is less contentious than is the case with the application of the patent system, the principles of the copyright system were designed for application in the literary and artistic fields. Information technology products operate in the practical arena, and it may be argued that fundamental concepts such as reproduction or adaptation require to be applied in a modified form in such circumstances. Two particular difficulties can be identified.

The essence of copyright is that it prohibits the copying of a work without the consent of the copyright owner. In the case of most works, this does not impinge upon a third party's normal use of the work. The purchaser of a book can read it without requiring to make any form of copy. Likewise, a television broadcast can be watched and an audio cassette listened to without the need for any form of copying. Software (and indeed other digital products, such as CDs) operates in a different manner. Any form of use requires that the contents of the work be copied from a storage location to be processed within the equipment. Normal use requires copying, a fact which creates complications, not just in the field of copyright but also—through the widespread use of software licences—in the area of liability.

Fair dealing

Much is written and spoken concerning the right of a user to copy a work to such an extent as is justified under the heading of 'fair dealing' for the purposes of research or private study.[75] Few of these expressions receive any form of definition in the legislation. The concept of fair dealing will undoubtedly permit a degree of copying of a protected work, but the supplementary question 'how much?' cannot definitively be answered. At one time, the United Kingdom publishing industry suggested that the copying of up to 10 per cent of a book might be regarded as fair dealing. This was, however, an informal indication which was subsequently withdrawn. It would not appear that the extent of copying permitted under this heading has been at issue in any case.

Whilst the concept of private study is not one which will be of great practical significance in the software field, that of research is potentially much more so. It is to be noted that the word 'research' precedes the phrase 'private study' in the Copyright, Designs, and Patents

---

[74] Available from <http://globalstudy.bsa.org/2011/downloads/study_pdf/2011_BSA_Piracy_Study-Standard.pdf>.

[75] Copyright, Designs and Patents Act 1988, s. 29.

Act 1988. It would appear to follow, therefore, that its application is not restricted to the area of individual research, but will extend into the commercial sphere.

In the case of a traditional literary work, such as a book or article, the acts which encompass fair dealing can readily be identified. Clearly, researchers must be able to read the work and to quote small portions of it in any work which they themselves might compile. In the course of this task, they may copy portions of the work, perhaps by means of a photocopier, although infringement may occur equally well if the work is copied by hand. It must be accepted that the concept of fair dealing in a literary work cannot extend to the making of a copy of the complete work. Different considerations may apply in respect of software.

Two arguments can be put forward in support of such a proposition. First, whilst it is a very simple task to copy portions of a book—indeed it is much easier to copy a part than the whole—the reverse is the case with respect to a computer program. A second argument operates at a utilitarian level. The user of a book would generally be considered as having no legitimate need to take a second copy of the work in case the original suffers damage. This view would be justified on the basis that although the cosmetic appearance of a book may easily be harmed, for example through the spillage of a cup of coffee, the damage will seldom be such as to prevent its continued use. Software is a much more fragile creation and, terminal damage may easily result. In such an event, the making of a back-up copy might appear a reasonable precaution.

In concluding the examination of the fair dealing exception, the point must be stressed that any of the actions referred to above will be sanctioned only to the extent that they are carried out in connection with research. It is specifically provided that decompilation of a program will not be permitted under the fair-use provisions.[76] Assuming that a copy of software may legitimately be made for research purposes, its status will change in the event that the research ends and the copy is put to operational use.

A use right for software?

Reference has previously been made to the fact that copying or adapting a protected work constitutes an infringement of copyright. This raises one significant issue in relation to software. Whenever a computer program is operated, the process requires that its contents be copied from the storage disk upon which it normally resides into the hardware's memory. The act of using software in its normal manner is capable, therefore, of constituting a breach of copyright.

Prior to 1992, this was arguably the case, although it is submitted that a persuasive case could have been made out for implying at least a basic use right. Substantial precedent exists for such judicial creativity under patent law, where it has been held that the purchaser of a patented product may exercise all the normal rights of an owner, including the right to resell, unless specific notice has been given of restrictions.[77] With most software products, the response of producers to the uncertain state of the law was to seek to incorporate the terms of a licence into the contract with the end-user. The status of software licences will be considered in more detail in the context of liability issues. Essentially, the licence would grant permission for the use of software in specified circumstances, but would frequently couple this with clauses limiting or excluding liability in the event the performance of the software was defective. In 1992, the provisions of the Copyright Designs and Patents Act

---

[76] Copyright, Designs and Patents Act 1988, s. 29(4).
[77] See e.g. *National Phonograph Co of Australia v Menck* (1911) 28 RPC 229.

1988 were amended in order to implement the provisions of the EC Directive on the Legal Protection of Computer Programs.[78] The Copyright (Computer Programs) Regulations 1992[79] add a new section 50C to the 1988 Act, providing that:

> It is not an infringement of copyright for a lawful user of a copy of a computer program to copy or adapt it, providing that the copying or adapting—
>
> (a) is necessary for his lawful use; and
>
> (b) is not prohibited under any term or condition of an agreement regarding the circumstances under which his use is lawful.

In the European Commission's explanatory memorandum to the 1989 proposal for the Directive, it was argued that it was not clear:

> whether the practice of so-called, 'shrink wrap licensing' where use conditions are attached to a product which is, to all intents and purposes 'sold' to the user, constitutes a valid licence in all circumstances and in all jurisdictions.
>
> It is therefore proposed that... [w]here 'sale', in the normal sense of the word occurs, certain rights to use the program must be taken to pass to the purchaser along with the physical copy of the program.[80]

whilst the Preamble to the Directive on the Legal Protection of Computer Programs[81] states that:

> Whereas the exclusive rights of the author to prevent the unauthorized reproduction of the work have to be subject to a limited exception in the case of a computer program to allow the reproduction technically necessary for the use of the program by the lawful acquirer.
>
> Whereas this means that the acts of loading and running necessary for the use of a copy of a program which has been lawfully acquired... may not be prohibited by contract.

It may be queried how far the text of the Directive implements this. Article 4 makes it clear that the copyright owner retains the right to authorise:

> [the] permanent or temporary reproduction of a computer program by any means and in any form, in part or in whole. Insofar as loading, displaying, running, transmission or storage of the computer program necessitates such reproduction, such acts shall be subject to authorization by the rightholder.

Article 5 provides for an exception to this provision, stating that:

> In the absence of specific contractual provisions, the acts referred to in Article 4... shall not require authorization by the rightholder where they are necessary for the use of the computer program by the lawful acquirer in accordance with its intended purpose.

In implementing the Directive on the Legal Protection of Computer Programs,[82] the United Kingdom government substituted the term 'lawful user'[83] for the original 'lawful acquirer'. Another change was to substitute reference to 'lawful use'[84] for the Directive's 'intended use'. These changes undoubtedly complicate matters. The concept of 'lawful use', in particular, is defined as applying where a person has '(whether under a licence to do any act restricted by the copyright in the program or otherwise)... a right to use the program'.[85] This formulation relates to the status of the user as much as to the nature of the

---

[78] Directive 91/250/EC.   [79] SI 1992/3233.

[80] COM (88) 816 final—SYN 183, paras. 3.4–3.5.   [81] Directive 91/250/EC.

[82] Directive 91/250/EC.   [83] Copyright, Designs and Patents Act 1988, s. 50A.   [84] s. 50A.

[85] s. 50A(2).

application, thereby producing a somewhat circular effect. Although there seems no doubt that the Directive sought to confer a use right, it is less clear whether the United Kingdom implementing legislation secures this and it is possible that the issue may some day have to be resolved before the courts.

Although a basic use right will now be implied, difficulties may arise in a number of areas. Increasingly, computers are being networked. The communications facilities provided by such a development means that one copy of a program may be used by a considerable number of different people. Depending upon the nature of the program and the network, use may be either simultaneous or successive. A further difficulty arises in the situation where a user has two computers, typically one at home and one at work. In this case, the user may well wish to use the same software (perhaps a word-processing program) on both computers. In these situations, the need and justification for licences will continue.

Error correction

It is received wisdom that every computer program contains errors or 'bugs'. In accordance with the requirements of the EC Directive on the Legal Protection of Computer Programs,[86] it is provided that an authorised user may copy or adapt a program 'for the purpose of correcting errors in it'.[87] This provision might appear to give a user carte blanche to copy a program in the quest to discover errors. An alternative, and perhaps preferable, view is that the right will extend only in respect of particular errors which have been discovered by the user in the course of running the program in a normal manner.

Even on this basis, uncertainties remain as to the extent of the user's rights. Computer programs are not like other literary works. A typing or grammatical error occurring in a book may be corrected without the act having any impact upon the remainder of the work. The relationship between the various elements of a computer program is much more complex. If an error is discovered in the course of running a program, its cause may lie almost anywhere in the program. If the source of a particular error is detected and a correction made, it cannot be certain that the effects of the change will not manifest themselves in an unexpected and undesirable fashion elsewhere in the program. There is, indeed, a school of thought in software engineering that suggests that when errors are detected, rather than amending the program, operating procedures should be changed to avoid the conditions which it is known cause the specific error to occur.

Back-up copies

Computer programs are frequently supplied, and invariably held, on some storage device, such as a disk or tape. Such storage media are notoriously fragile and it is all too possible that their contents might be accidentally corrupted or erased. In such circumstances, it might not appear unreasonable for a user to seek to take a second, or back-up, copy of the work, with the intention that this will be stored in a safe location and brought into use in the event that the original copy of the software is destroyed.

As enacted, the United Kingdom Copyright, Designs and Patents Act 1988 (in contrast to several other copyright statutes) made no mention of the possibility that a user might make a back-up copy of a program which had been lawfully acquired. Although, once again, it is possible to argue that such a term must be implied into any relevant contract, the argument is more tenuous than that relating to the implication of a basic use right.

---

[86] Directive 91/250/EC. [87] Copyright, Designs and Patents Act 1988, s. 50C(2).

Implementation of the provisions of the Directive on the Legal Protection of Computer Programs[88] has brought about a measure of reform with the Copyright, Designs and Patents Act 1988 providing that a back-up copy may be made by a user where this is 'necessary... for the purposes of his lawful use'.[89] It is unclear how useful this provision might be. The making of a back-up copy will invariably be a wise precaution, but it is difficult to envisage any situation where the presence of a second copy is 'necessary' for the functioning of the original.

Some small measure of consolation may be offered to a user by the fact that the copyright owner may not validly restrict or exclude the operation of the provisions regarding the making of back-up copies.[90] It is doubted, however, whether the new provisions will alter significantly either the law or the practice in this area.

Reverse engineering and decompilation

When software is supplied to a customer, it will be in a form known as object or machine-readable code. If this were to be viewed by a user, it would appear as a series (a very long series) of zeros and ones. Obtaining sight of these digits will give little indication as to the manner in which the program is structured. Although it is possible for a program to be written in object code, much more programmer-friendly techniques are available and almost universally utilised. A number of what are referred to as 'high level' languages exist—examples are BASIC and FORTRAN. These allow programmers to write their instructions in a language which more closely resembles English, although the functional nature of computer programs limits the variations in expression which are a hallmark of more traditional literary works.

Most users, of course, will be concerned only with what a program does rather than the manner in which this is accomplished. Some, however, may have different motives. The practice of reverse engineering has a lengthy history in more traditional industries and, typically, involves the purchase and dismantling of the products of a competitor. In the computer context, reverse engineering may involve the study of the operation of a computer program in order to discover its specifications. This is essentially a process of testing and observation and might involve pressing various keys or combinations of keys in order to discover their effects. The technique known as decompilation may be used as part of this process. Normally involving the use of other computer programs to analyse the object code, the technique seeks to reproduce the original source code.

The two leading English authorities on the topic of reverse engineering point are *LB (Plastics) Ltd v Swish Products Ltd*[91] and *British Leyland Motor Corpn v Armstrong Patents Co Ltd*.[92] Although in the *LB Plastics* case, the alleged infringers had obtained a degree of access to the product drawings, in neither case was it argued that these had been reproduced directly. Instead, the case was based on the contention that by reproducing the finished object, respectively furniture drawers and a vehicle exhaust system, the provisions of section 48(1) of the Copyright Act 1956 had been breached. This provided inter alia: 'that copyright in a two-dimensional work, the product drawings, will be infringed by converting these into a three-dimensional form'.[93]

In *LB (Plastics)*,[94] the plaintiff designed and produced a drawer system. The key feature was that the drawers could be supplied to customers (generally, furniture manufacturers) in what was referred to as 'knock-down' form. This offered considerable benefits at the

---

[88] Directive 91/250/EC.   [89] Copyright, Designs and Patents Act 1988, s. 50A(1).
[90] Copyright, Designs and Patents Act 1988, s. 296A(1)(b).
[91] [1979] RPC 551.   [92] [1986] RPC 279.   [93] s. 48 (1) Copyright Act 1956.
[94] *LB (Plastics) Ltd v Swish Products Ltd* [1979] RPC 551.

transportation and storage stages, whilst the design facilitated swift and easy assembly of the drawers by the final producer. The concept proved commercially successful and some time later, the defendant introduced a similar range of products. It was alleged that this was achieved by copying one of the plaintiff's drawers.

In the High Court, Whitford J accepted that the resulting product infringed the plaintiff's copyright in two of the original product drawings. Although this ruling was reversed by the Court of Appeal, which held that an insufficient causal link existed between the drawings in question and the defendant's product, it was reinstated by the House of Lords.[95] A significant factor underpinning the judgment would appear to have been the recognition that although the defendant was required by commercial dictates to ensure that their drawers were functionally compatible with those produced by the plaintiff, this could have been attained in ways which required less in the way of replication of the original design.

The decision in *LB Plastics* was approved in the subsequent case of *British Leyland Motor Corpn v Armstrong Patents*.[96] Here, the plaintiff manufactured motor vehicles. The multitude of parts which make up each vehicle were produced in accordance with detailed designs drawn up by the plaintiffs. The defendant specialised in the manufacture of spare parts, in the particular case an exhaust system, which would be offered for sale to motor-vehicle owners. In order to allow the replacement systems to be fitted to the plaintiff's vehicles, their design required to be virtually identical to that of the original component. This was achieved by taking an example of the plaintiff's exhaust system and examining its shape and dimensions.

The plaintiff's exhaust system was not itself eligible for copyright protection; neither was protection available under the law of patents or of registered designs.[97] The court's attention was directed, therefore, to the question of whether copyright subsisted in the original engineering designs and, if so, whether the defendant's conduct constituted an infringement.[98] Holding in favour of the plaintiff on the issue of copyright infringement, the court (Lord Griffiths dissenting on the basis that, although the majority's opinion was in line with precedent, the case was one which justified the application of the 1966 Practice Direction) held that the defendant's conduct amounted to indirect copying of the designs, constituting a breach of section 48(1) of the Copyright Act 1956. This provides that the conversion of a two-dimensional work into one of three dimensions will constitute reproduction.

A further relevant case on this point is that of *Plix Products Ltd v Frank M Winstone*,[99] a case heard before the High Court of New Zealand, whose decision was upheld on appeal to the Privy Council. This case concerned the design of containers for the transport of kiwi fruits. During the 1960s and 1970s, the plaintiff designed and produced a number of containers which offered significant advantages in respect of the safe storage and transportation of the fruit. The New Zealand kiwi fruit industry is subject to tight regulation,

---

[95] *LB (Plastics) Ltd v Swish Products Ltd* [1979] RPC 551.   [96] [1986] RPC 279.

[97] The Copyright, Designs and Patents Act 1988 introduced the concept of a design right which will apply to drawings such as those at issue in *British Leyland Motor Corpn v Armstrong Patents* [1986] RPC 279. This right will substitute for copyright but, significantly, does not extend to any aspects of the design which enable the finished article to be 'connected to, or placed in or around or against, another article so that either article may perform its function' (s. 213(3)).

[98] The plaintiff's action ultimately failed on a second ground, the House of Lords holding that its claim to copyright was defeated by the right of a purchaser of their vehicle to obtain spare parts as economically as possible. The relationship between the provisions of intellectual property and competition law is assuming some significance in EU law. Recent dicta would suggest that, whilst a refusal to grant competitors licences in respect of the use of intellectual property rights will not constitute an abuse of Art. 102 of the Treaty on the Functioning of the European Union (formerly Art. 82 of the Treaty of Rome), any element of discrimination may render the conduct an abuse of a dominant position.

[99] [1986] FSR 63.

with the New Zealand Kiwi Fruit Authority having power to prescribe, inter alia, standards of packing. This power was exercised, with the standards being based on the plaintiff's designs. The defendants wished to penetrate this potentially lucrative market. Being aware of the potential intellectual property pitfalls, they sought to avoid infringement by engaging a designer who had no knowledge of the plaintiff's product. The designer was given the Fruit Authority's standards, together with samples of kiwi fruit and instructed to produce an appropriate design. Strict instructions were given that the project was not to be discussed with any other party and that no examination should be made of any existing product. Effectively, therefore, the designer was given a set of written specifications and instructed to begin work on a clean sheet of paper. Perhaps not surprisingly, the end result was a series of designs which, when put into production, resulted in a container extremely similar in appearance to the plaintiff's.

Holding that the plaintiff's copyright had been infringed, the High Court of New Zealand ruled that copyright in an artistic design could be infringed by a party who had been provided with a written or verbal description of the work in the event that the description provided was sufficiently detailed to convey the form (expression) of the work, as opposed to outlining the concept.[100] An illustration of the latter situation can be taken from the case of *Gleeson and Gleeson Shirt Co Ltd v H R Denne Ltd*.[101] Here, the plaintiff had designed a novel form of clerical shirt. The design proved commercially successful. A competing firm was asked by one of its clients whether it could produce a similar product. To this end, a general description of the shirt was given to one of its employees who had previously produced shirts containing similar features (although not in a single specimen). The resulting product was alleged to infringe the plaintiff's copyright in the artistic designs relating to its shirt. Dismissing this claim, it was held that the instructions given related only to the underlying ideas and that the application of the employee's own skill and knowledge had resulted in the creation of an independent piece of work. A second factor which appeared to influence the Court of Appeal in reaching this conclusion was the fact that the drawings upon which the plaintiff's copyright was founded were more in the nature of sketches than designs intended to serve as the blueprint for production. To this extent, the notion of an 'idea' and its distinction from 'expression' becomes blurred. As was stated in *Plix Products*:

> There are in fact two kinds of 'ideas' involved in the making of any work which is susceptible of being the subject of copyright. In the first place there is the general idea or basic concept of the work. This idea is formed (or implanted) in the mind of the author. He sets out to write a poem or a novel about unrequited love or to draw a dog listening to a gramophone... Then there is a second phase—a second kind of 'idea'. The author of the work will scarcely be able to transform the basic concept into a concrete form—i.e. 'express' the idea—without furnishing it with details of form and shape. The novelist will think of characters, dialogue, details of plot and so forth. All these modes of expression have their genesis in the author's mind—these too are 'ideas'. When these ideas...are reduced to concrete form, the forms they take are where the copyright resides.[102]

Even so, the distinction between protected and unprotected aspects of a work remains obscure. A significant factor relates to what might be termed the 'added value' element introduced by the author. Where the idea is expressed in simplistic or general terms (as with the sketches in *Gleeson*), a considerable degree of reproduction may be considered legitimate. In the event, however, that the expression is 'ornate, complex or detailed', the

---

[100] *Plix Products Ltd v Frank M Winstone* [1986] FSR 63.   [101] [1975] RPC 471.
[102] [1986] FSR 63 at 93.

would-be plagiariser must beware, as 'the only product he can then make without infringing may bear little resemblance to the copyright work'.[103]

Although the cases of reverse engineering are of considerable relevance to the present topic, one major point of distinction may be identified. It will be recalled that the legislation specifically provides that computer programs are to be protected as a species of literary work. Although no criterion of literary merit is applied, the protection must extend to a particular combination of letters and numbers. As stated, in the situation where access is obtained to these, it is arguable that a claim for breach of copyright will succeed, even though the literary aspects of the second work bear little resemblance to the original. Where there is no question of access, merely the assertion that the operation of the second program replicates the 'look and feel' of the original, and where there is little evidence of literal similarity, it is difficult to argue that the traditional reverse engineering cases referred to earlier have any applicability. In each case, the cornerstone of the copyright owner's claim has been that, albeit indirectly, protected drawings have been reproduced. In the event that the operation of a computer program is studied and the attempt made to replicate its functions, there may be no substantial similarity between the two sets of code which make up the programs.

A closer analogy with computer software may be found with the case of *Green v Broadcasting Corpn of New Zealand*.[104] The plaintiff, Green, had been author, producer, and presenter of a popular British television show, *Opportunity Knocks*. The show operated according to a specific format and considerable use was made of catchphrases. Some years later, a programme with the same title was produced in New Zealand, making use of the same formats and catchphrases. With the interpolation of a new presenter, the programme, it might be stated, mimicked the 'look and feel' of the original. Upon discovering this, Mr Green instituted proceedings alleging, inter alia, that the later programme infringed his copyright in the original production. This action was rejected in the High Court of New Zealand, which held that, in the absence of evidence that scripts for the programmes had been reduced to writing, details of the dialogue could not be regarded as protected. An alternative head of claim concerned the dramatic format of the original programme, the various items which were included, and the order in which they appeared. This claim was also rejected, the court referring to the views of a United States commentator to the effect that:

> Formats are thus an unusual sort of literary creation. Unlike books, they are not meant for reading. Unlike plays, they are not capable of being performed. Unlike synopses, their use entails more than the expansion of a story outline into a script. Their unique function is to provide the unifying element which makes a series attractive—if not addictive—to its viewer.[105]

With minimal substitution of terminology, these sentences would seem to describe exactly the nature and role of many items of computer software. Whilst the case would not provide authority for the proposition that the reproduction of every aspect of a user interface will be sanctioned, it does suggest that a considerable degree of commonality may be permitted.

Reverse engineering and computer programs

Computer programs can be divided into two broad categories—operating systems and application programs. An operating system—the best-known examples are perhaps Microsoft Windows or its Apple equivalent OSX—contains the basic instructions necessary for a

---

[103] [1986] FSR 63 at 94.   [104] [1989] RPC 469.
[105] R. Meadow, 'Television Formats: The Search for Protection', *Californian Law Review* 58 (1970), p. 1169 at 1170.

computer to operate. A very simple analogy might be made with a railway system. The gauge of the track and the height and width of tunnels and bridges might be regarded as equivalent to an operating system. They set down basic parameters which must be respected by anyone wishing to build a train to operate on the system. If the track gauge is 4ft 8ins, no matter how technologically advanced an engine might be, it will be quite useless if its wheels are set seven feet apart. In the computer field, programs such as word-processing and spreadsheet packages constitute the equivalents of railway engines. They work with the operating system to perform specific applications and must respect its particular requirements.

A producer intending to develop an applications package for use on a particular operating system must be aware of its functional requirements. In most instances, the information necessary will be made available by the producer of the operating system, whose own commercial interests will be best served by the widest possible availability of applications to run on the system. In the event that the information is not readily available—or that it is suspected that only partial information has been made available—the attempt may be made to reverse engineer the operating system.

A second occasion for the use of reverse engineering occurs at the level of applications packages. Programs such as word processors and spreadsheets store data in a particular format. In the case of basic text, a widely used standard exists—ASCII (American Standard Code for Information Interchange). The text of most word-processed documents is a much more complex creature. Particular fonts, type size, and line spacing will be used. Portions of the text may be printed in italics or may be emboldened or underlined. These matters are not standardised. A producer intent on developing a new word-processing program may wish to discover the codes used by rival producers so that conversion facilities may be built into the new product. From a commercial perspective, existing users are more likely to change to a new program if they can still use documents created using their existing program.

The final form of reverse engineering is the most controversial. Here, the object of the reverse engineering is to discover information about the user interface of an applications package, which may then be used as the basis for the attempt to produce a substantially similar package. In early court cases on the point in the United States, it was often asserted that the intent was to reproduce the 'look and feel' of the original package.

Given that a lawful user cannot be prevented from using a program for its normal purpose, some aspects of reverse engineering must be considered legitimate. A user who operates the program in a normal fashion in order to study its various aspects will not infringe copyright. Subject to strict conditions, a user will also be given the right to attempt to decompile a program's object code when this is done in order to produce a further program which will be interoperable with the copyright owner's. This would apply with respect to the first and second forms of reverse engineering discussed earlier. The right cannot be excluded by contract, but will apply only where the information required has not been made 'readily available' by the copyright owner. The term 'readily available' appears imprecise, and indeed was a key issue in anti-trust action brought by the European Commission against Microsoft. It would not seem to require that the information be supplied free of charge. The levying of excessive charges would obviously be incompatible with the provision, but the question will arise of what level is to be so considered. In most cases where interchange information is used, for example in the word-processing programs referred to earlier, it would appear that this is done under the terms of cross-licensing agreements between the parties involved.

A second issue raises more technical questions. Producers of operating systems will normally find it in their own commercial interest to make the information available to those who wish to produce applications to run on the system. In some cases, the producer of an operating system will also produce applications packages. The best-known example is Microsoft. Although sufficient information concerning its operating systems is made available to other producers, the systems have a number of what are referred to as 'undocu-mented calls' and it is frequently asserted that these are used by Microsoft's own applications packages. The situation might be compared with producing a road map of the British Isles which omitted all reference to motorways. A motorist who relied totally on the map would certainly be able find a route between Glasgow and London, although the journey might take considerably longer than one making use of the motorway network. Returning to the computer context, it may be queried whether the provision of incomplete information will resurrect the decompilation right. Against this, it may be noted that the legislation makes no mention of the quality of the interconnection which is to be enabled. If comparison is made with the patent system, which requires that an inventor disclose details of the man-ner in which the invention functions, the duty here is to disclose an effective manner of performing the invention, and not necessarily the optimum method. Any claim relating to the sufficiency of disclosure above and beyond that necessary to achieve interoperability might more reasonably lie under the heading of competition law.

The activities carried out in reliance on the decompilation right are to be restricted to the minimum necessary to obtain the information.[106] Again, this may be a difficult matter to determine. It might be that the user can determine which elements are essential to their legitimate goals only after the entire program has been decompiled. A further restriction imposed upon the user provides that information derived from the decompilation may not be passed on to any third party, except where this is done in order to produce the new interoperable program.[107]

The final restriction concerns the format of the finished program. This, it is provided, is not to be substantially similar in its expression to the original.[108] This is not to be implied as meaning that the program may not compete with the original. The producer of a word-processing program may decompile existing programs to discover details of their format so as to permit the new program to accept text files produced using the earlier pro-gram. What is not permitted is the production of a program which infringes copyright in the original. The question of how far copyright extends to the appearance and manner of functioning of computer programs is discussed in the next section.

Literal and non-literal copying

The question of when a basic idea is refined sufficiently to become a protected work is one of the most difficult issues in the field of copyright law. In the United States, what is invari-ably referred to as the 'idea/expression dichotomy' has assumed statutory form, with the United States Code providing that:

> In no case does copyright protection for an original work of authorship extend to any idea, procedure, process, system, method of operation, concept, principle or discovery, regardless of the form in which it is described, explained, illustrated or embodied in such work.[109]

The EC Directive on the Legal Protection of Computer Programs[110] applies this principle in the specific context of computer programs, providing that:

> protection...shall apply to the expression in any form of a computer program. Ideas and principles which underlie any element of a computer program...are not protected by copyright.[111]

---

[106] Copyright, Designs and Patents Act 1998, s. 50B(3)(b).   [107] s. 50B(3)(c).
[108] s. 50B(4).   [109] Title 17 USC at 102(b) (1982).
[110] Directive 91/250/EC.   [111] Art. 1(2).

For the United Kingdom, although Lord Hailsham indicated in *LB (Plastics) Ltd v Swish Products Ltd* that 'it is trite law that there is no copyright in ideas', he continued, 'But, of course, as the late Professor Joad used to observe, it all depends on what you mean by "ideas".[112] The notion of a formal separation between ideas and expressions is found nowhere in United Kingdom copyright law. Indeed, although the United Kingdom has incorporated most aspects of the Directive into national law—even where, as in the case of the application of protection to preparatory material, it is arguable that no specific provisions were required—no attempt was made to include this formulation in the implementing regulations.

The main justification for refusing protection to an idea lies in the belief that ideas as such are too intangible, too ethereal, to be protected. It is only when a thought or an idea is committed to paper or some other form of recording device, or even spoken in a public forum, that any evidence becomes available of the existence of what might be a protected interest. Even where this occurs, policy considerations operate to limit the scope of protection. Many legal journals (and academic CVs) would be much thinner if the first person to conceive of the notion of writing a learned article on the idea/expression dichotomy in copyright law had been granted a monopoly concerning the subject. The approach adopted under the law, both of patent and of copyright, has been to regard ideas as an unprotected step along the road to the protection of some concrete or practical manifestation of the concept. The grant of a patent requires a description of a practical application of the idea, whilst copyright law serves to protect a particular sequence of letters, words, figures, or symbols which constitute the application or expression of the underlying idea.

A second area of difficulty concerns the extent of the protection offered under copyright. There is no doubt that direct or literal copying of the work will constitute infringement. A less certain matter concerns the extent of the protection in respect of what is sometimes referred to as 'non-literal copying'. As discussed in more detail in the following sections, in the 1980s and early 1990s, this was regarded as the most critical issue in intellectual property law. From a high-water point of perceived protection around 1990, the effect of subsequent decisions in the United Kingdom and the United States has been to reduce the scope of protection. The increasing use of graphical interfaces and the application of text and graphic-rich applications such as multimedia products and, indeed, the Internet has brought with it a switch in emphasis from indirect protection of the underlying code to direct protection of the end-product. Given the ease with which material held in electronic format may be copied, attention has also tended to switch from the exercise of the exclusive rights which are pivotal to the copyright regime, to the issue of how copyright may be managed in the interests of both owners and users. An indication of the scale of the issue and the problems can be taken from a WIPO estimate presented to the European Commission's Legal Advisory Board that some 90 per cent of the costs incurred in producing a multimedia product made up of existing materials were related to the management of the intellectual property interests involved.

From a legal perspective, there is no doubt that the complete reproduction of software packages will constitute infringement of copyright. In other cases, elements of an earlier work may be reproduced. A typical scenario will see an employee changing jobs and subsequently producing software which incorporates routines from earlier works, the copyright in which will, of course, vest in the original employer. The issues involved here essentially concern the questions of whether a substantial amount of the previous work has been reproduced and whether any similarities can be explained by reasons other than that of deliberate copying. Particularly in the case of computer programs, a variety of producers

---

[112] [1979] RPC 551 at 629.

may be operating in the same field. In such a situation, and especially given the technical constraints which may operate, close similarities between two works may occur in the absence of deliberate copying or plagiarism. Similarities in the educational background of different programmers might also result in the production of substantially similar portions of program.

The rise and fall of look-and-feel protection

With the emergence of the PC, the possibilities for copyright infringement increased dramatically. As has been discussed earlier, in the situation where one party makes a complete or literal copy of a program, there is no doubt that infringement has occurred. A more difficult issue arises where there is an element of independent creative activity on the part of the second producer.

Starting in the late 1970s, a number of cases of this nature were raised in courts in the United Kingdom and the United States. The disputes can reasonably be placed into two categories. In the first, a person or persons would have been employed to work on the development of a particular computer program. The employment would come to an end and the individual, either in his or her own right or as an employee of another company, would be involved in the development of a similar program. The program might well be written in a different computer language, providing limited evidence of literal similarities, and would often incorporate additional features or refinements not found in the original. The contention on the part of the original copyright owner would be that a substantial part of the original program had been copied into the new version.

A second category of case involves parties acting very much at arm's length. The alleged infringer will have had the opportunity to see a copy of the original program in operation and will have set out to create from scratch a competing product which will replicate all or part of the on-screen appearance of the original.

The computerised pharmacist

In the first category of disputes, there is no doubt that the individual responsible for the development of the allegedly infringing product will have had access to all significant elements of the original program. The English case of *Richardson v Flanders*,[113] which was the first case concerned with software copyright to reach the stage of trial in the High Court, might be considered as a typical example of the species.

At issue in this case was a computer program designed for use by pharmacists. The program, which was developed to run on the then popular BBC microcomputers, performed a number of tasks. Principally, when the computer was attached to a printer it would automate and simplify the task of preparing dosage instructions to be supplied with medicines. The program's other major function was to assist in stock-keeping by keeping a record of the drugs dispensed. The program was marketed by the plaintiff, who had also performed a significant amount of work on the original program. Subsequently, the first defendant was employed to work on the project. It was accepted that all relevant copyrights in the work belonged to the plaintiff.

The program achieved considerable commercial success. Relationships between the plaintiff and the defendant were not so happy. The defendant resigned from his position, although he continued to perform some work for the plaintiff as an independent contractor

---

[113] [1993] FSR 497.

for a further period of time. With the advent of the IBM PC, one of the plaintiff's major customers expressed interest in a version of the program capable of running on this machine and which could be sold on the Irish market. Following discussions, the plaintiff decided not to proceed with the project but suggested that the defendant might be willing to perform the work. The program was completed and was sold in Ireland. The defendant subsequently contacted the plaintiff offering him the rights to market the product in the United Kingdom. These discussions proved fruitless and the defendant proceeded to market a modified version of the program in the United Kingdom. At that stage, the plaintiff initiated proceedings alleging that the new product infringed copyright in his original program.

Because of the fact that the programs had been developed to run on different computers, examination of the code used would have revealed few evidences of similarities. The programs did perform the same functions and had very similar appearances when operating on their respective hardware.

In the absence of any relevant United Kingdom precedent, the judge placed considerable reliance on United States authority, notably the case of *Computer Associates v Altai*.[114] The court, it was held, should conduct a four-stage test designed to answer the questions.[115] This would seek to answer the following questions:

1. whether the plaintiff's work was protected by copyright
2. whether similarities existed between the plaintiff's and the defendant's programs
3. whether these were caused by copying or whether other explanations were possible
4. in the event that copying was established, whether the elements copied constituted a significant part of the original work.

Given what has been said regarding the willingness of United Kingdom courts to confer copyright protection on a work, it is not at all surprising that the first question could be answered quickly and definitively in the affirmative. Consideration of the other issues was a more difficult task.

Examining the operation of the original program, the judge identified thirteen aspects of the functioning of the original program leading to the printing of the label for a drug container. This program also offered a stock-control function and some seventeen other features allowing a pharmacist to customise the program in accordance with any particular requirements. When the same analysis was applied to the revised program, seventeen points of similarity were identified between the two programs which would require further investigation to determine whether they were the product of copying.

These similarities were identified from an examination of the screen displays and key sequences. The judge did not attempt to compare the underlying codes. Although an expert witness for the plaintiff had presented an analysis of alleged similarities between the source codes of the two programs, the judge indicated that he found this 'extremely difficult to understand'. Counsel for the plaintiff failed to pursue an invitation to attempt further explanation, and the analysis formed no part of the final decision.

One obvious cause of similarities, that of deliberate copying, was rejected by the judge. It was accepted, however, that the defendant must have retained considerable knowledge of the plaintiff's program and that if similarities resulted from the unconscious use of this material, infringement might be established.

Examining the similarities between the two programs, most were considered explicable by reasons other than copying. The two programs, for example, presented dates in a similar format. Conventions for the presentations of dates are well established and the fact that

---

[114] 982 F 2d 693 (1992).   [115] *Richardson v Flanders* [1993] FSR 497.

two works utilise a similar format is more likely to be caused through adherence to such conventions rather than by copying.

In a second aspect, the original program had presented the pharmacist with the option of placing a date other than the current date on a label. This feature was reproduced in the revised program. Although the judge held that it was likely that this had been copied from the original, he held that, given there were a very limited number of ways in which the idea could be expressed, the fact that the two programs utilised very similar approaches did not establish infringement.

In total, six of the seventeen similarities identified by the judge were considered explicable by reasons other than copying. The remaining eleven items it was considered, with varying degrees of conviction, might have been copied from the original program. Eight of these, however, referred to matters which in the opinion of the judge did not amount to a substantial part of the program. One element found in both programs gave users an indication that their instructions have been accepted. In both programs, the message 'operation successful' would appear on the screen and the computer would emanate a double-beep sound. This aspect of the original program, it was held, 'lacks originality and cannot have required any significant skill or effort to devise it'.

Ultimately, infringement was established in respect of only three of the points of similarity, comprising editing and amendment functions and the use of dose codes. The similarities in respect of the editing function were perhaps especially noticeable as it operated in the same idiosyncratic (and probably erroneous) manner in both programs. The dose code facility allowed the user to abbreviate certain instructions regarding the dosage and the manner in which the medication was to be taken. Thus, in both programs, use of the abbreviation AC (*ante cibum*) would cause the instruction 'before food' to be printed on the label. Although a number of the abbreviations were held to be obvious, the fact that eighty-four out of ninety-one codes found in the original program were reproduced in an identical format in the later version, with only minor changes in another five, was held to raise an inference of copying.

Although copyright infringement was ultimately established, the plaintiff's victory was heavily qualified.[116] The copying was described as constituting 'a fairly minor infringement in a few limited respects and certainly not…slavish copying'. Although some of the processes adopted clearly differ from those in *Computer Associates*,[117] the effect of the judgment is similar in recognising that for functional works, external forces may well be the cause of similarities, thereby excusing conduct that might otherwise appear to constitute a breach of copyright.

Agricultural software

Allegations of copyright were again before the High Court in the case of *Ibcos Computers v Barclays Mercantile Highland Finance*.[118] Again, there was a background of the major defendant having worked for the plaintiff on the development of a software product intended for use by agricultural dealers, which was marketed under the name ADS. On leaving its employment, he developed a further and competing product which was marketed under the name of Unicorn. The plaintiff alleged that sufficient features of this were copied from the original to constitute an infringement of copyright.

In determining the criteria which would be applied in answering the question of whether infringement had occurred,[119] Jacob J was somewhat critical of the extensive references to

---

[116] *Richardson v Flanders* [1993] FSR 497.   [117] *Computer Associates v Altai*, 982 F 2d 693 (1992).
[118] [1994] FSR 275.   [119] *Ibcos Computers v Barclays Mercantile Highland Finance* [1994] FSR 275.

the United States decision in *Computer Associates*,[120] and warned against 'overcitation of United States authority based on a statute different from ours'. The approach to be adopted was for the court to determine whether there was a sufficient degree of similarity between the two works which, coupled with evidence of access to the original work, would establish an inference of copying. The onus would then switch to the defendant to establish that the similarities were explicable by causes other than copying. Evidence that 'functional necessity' served to narrow the range of options open to the defendant would be relevant. Trivial items may well provide the most eloquent testimony. As was said in *Bilhofer v Dixon*:

> It is the resemblances in inessentials, the small, redundant, even mistaken elements of the copyright work which carry the greatest weight. This is because they are the least likely to have been the result of independent design.[121]

In *Ibcos*, evidence was presented that the same words were misspelled in the same manner, the same headings were used in the two programs, and both shared the same bit of code which served no useful purpose for the functioning of the program. Beyond this, there were considerable similarities at the level of the code itself. In respect of one element of the programs, it was held that:

> there are 22 identical variables, 8 identical labels, 1 identical remark, 31 identical code lines and one identical redundant variable. This to my mind plainly indicates copying and enough in itself to constitute a significant part.[122]

The court recognised in *Ibcos* that copyright protection must extend beyond the literal aspects of the program code to aspects of 'program structure' and 'design features'. In the case of the former element, it was held that copyright subsisted in the compilation of individual programs which made up the ADS system. Although some differences existed between ADS and Unicorn, it was held that the defendant had taken 'as his starting point the ADS set and that set remains substantially in Unicorn'. Although the two programs had a different visual appearance and it was recognised that 'Unicorn is undoubtedly to the user a much friendlier program than ADS was at the time', the defendant, it was held, had taken 'shortcuts by starting with ADS and making considerable additions and modifications'.

Financial markets

A further significant decision was delivered by the High Court in April 1999, in the case of *Cantor Fitzgerald International v Tradition United Kingdom Ltd*.[123] Both companies involved in the case operated in the financial services market. The plaintiff had developed a computer package which was used in the course of its bond-broking activities. Much of the work in respect of this had been carried out by its Managing Director, a Mr Howard, and a team of programmers appointed by him. The Managing Director was dismissed in 1991. He subsequently secured employment with the defendant, in large part because of his suggestion that he could develop a similar system for it. On taking up employment, he secured the recruitment of three other members of the plaintiff's programming team.

The defendant obtained computers of the same type as those used by the plaintiff, and the employees (who were also defendants in the litigation) began work. In a period of less than three months, a working system was produced. Action alleging copyright infringement and breach of confidence was initiated by the plaintiffs, who argued that it would

---

[120] *Computer Associates v Altai*, 982 F 2d 693 (1992).   [121] [1990] FSR 105 at 123.
[122] *Ibcos Computers v Barclays Mercantile Highland Finance* [1994] FSR 275 at 308.
[123] [2000] RPC 95.

have been impossible for the programs involved to have been written from scratch in the time available.

Initially, the programmers denied that they had had access to any of the plaintiff's other source code. When the process of discovery highlighted evidence suggesting copying of certain modules, the truth emerged that the programmers had taken a copy of the plaintiff's source code with them. The defendant dropped its initial denial of any copyright infringement and the case proceeded on the basis of how extensive the copying had been.

Expert witnesses were appointed by both parties. The witness for the plaintiff was subjected to severe criticism by the trial judge, Pumphrey J, who opined that the witness had held back relevant information and had acted as an advocate for the plaintiff rather than as an objective and impartial expert. The defendant's witness, on the other hand, was regarded as 'an admirable expert'. His conclusions were perhaps surprising, and were summarised by the judge:

> The Tradition system comprises some 77,000 lines of source code divided into some 363 'modules'. A total of 2,952 lines of code are admitted to have been copied, of which some are repeated copies of a single block of code. In addition Dr McKenzie has identified some 1,964 lines of code which he says are questionable, although he says that the majority of the questionable code was probably not copied. This means that if the admissions are exhaustive, the copied code represents 2 per cent of the system by number of lines. If all the questionable code is included as well, the figure is about 3.3 per cent.[124]

Faced with this report, the plaintiff restricted its claim of copying to thrity-five of the systems modules. The question, therefore, was whether what was copied constituted a substantial part of the original program. It also made two claims alleging breach of confidence in respect of the techniques used for developing programs of the kind at issue and also in respect of the code itself, arguing that if the programmers had used their access to the plaintiff's code to 'increase their confidence' in the accuracy of their new work, that would of itself constitute misuse of confidential information regardless of whether the code was subsequently copied.

Initial reference was made to the decision of Jacob J in *Ibcos Computers v Barclays Mercantile Highland Finance*,[125] laying down the steps to be followed in deciding an action for infringement of copyright:

1. What are the work or works in which the plaintiff claims copyright?
2. Is each such work 'original'?
3. Was there copying from that work?
4. If there was copying has a substantial portion of that work been reproduced?

The situation in *Cantor*[126] was in many respects more complex than in *Ibcos*. Although the start point may have been the same, it was more questionable both of whether the end-product could be regarded as the product of copying of a substantial part of the original programs and, indeed, of whether what had been copied satisfied the criterion of originality required for copyright to come into existence. Pumphrey J expressed some doubt as to whether the application of criteria developed in a literary context was a proper approach when dealing with a functional product such as software:

> A program expressed in a computer language must not contain errors of syntax (or it will not compile) and it must contain no semantic errors. Computers do not have the capacity

---

[124] *Cantor Fitzgerald International v Tradition United Kingdom Ltd* [2000] RPC 95 at 102.
[125] [1994] FSR 275.   [126] [2000] RPC 95 at 102.

to deduce what the author meant when they encounter errors in the kind of software with which this action is concerned. If the software contains semantic errors it will produce the wrong answer or no answer at all: it may merely fail to run. The only opportunity that the programmer gets to express himself in a more relaxed way is provided by the comments in the code, which are for the benefit of the human reader and are ignored when the code comes to be compiled.[127]

It might be suggested from this that every line of code in a program should be considered essential for its operation and, therefore, that any copying would involve reproduction of a substantial part of the original. The Australian case of *Autodesk v Dyson*[128] was cited as authority for this proposition. For the United Kingdom, however, the court was not willing to follow such a line of argument. Whilst it was accepted that every line of a program was essential in order for it to function, the view of the court was that the determination of whether a substantial part of the work had been copied required to be made by reference to qualitative rather than to quantitative criteria:

> In the general case it is well established that a substantial part of the author's skill and labour may reside in the plot of a novel or play; and to take that plot without taking any particular part of the particular manner of its expression may be sufficient to amount to copyright infringement.[129]

For software, it was suggested:

> It seems to be generally accepted that the 'architecture' of a computer program is capable of protection if a substantial part of the programmer's skill, labour and judgment went into it. In this context, 'architecture' is a vague and ambiguous term.[130]

Two possible meanings were identified for the term, the first relating to the overall description of the system at a high level of abstraction. It could also mean, as was at issue, the overall program structure. Here, functions which it was agreed between the parties were essential elements of the particular software package were grouped into programs, with copyright being recognised in the 'compilation of the programs'.

In spite of the somewhat reprehensible nature of the programmer's work in *Cantor*[131] (which included documenting plans to alter code so as to disguise the fact that it had originated in the plaintiff's program), only a very limited degree of copyright infringement was established. The defendant had accepted liability for the points of similarity identified by its expert witness and in all other respects the finding of the court was that there was no infringement. Similarities were considered either to relate to insubstantial pieces of work or to be explicable by reasons other than copying.

The judgment in respect of the claims of breach of copyright follows what appears to be a general trend to limit the scope of copyright protection to little more than direct or literal copying. As such, it might appear to leave a copyright owner with limited protection. The alternative claim relating to breach of confidence fared better. Although it was held that the techniques used in the development of the original programs were not sufficiently novel or unusual to be regarded as trade secrets and entitled to protection on this basis, it was found, albeit without any detailed explanation, that the use of the original code as an aide-memoire constituted breach of confidence.

---

[127] [2000] RPC 95 at 130.   [128] [1992] RPC 575.
[129] *Cantor Fitzgerald International v Tradition United Kingdom Ltd* [2000] RPC 95 at 134.
[130] [2000] RPC 95 at 134.   [131] [2000] RPC 95.

Arm's length reproduction

In all of the cases cited here there had been some prior relationship between the parties which had given the alleged copyist access to the underlying source code of the original software packages. This eliminates any issue of whether the alleged copyist had had access to the protected work. Although there was a history of dealings between the parties, the High Court decision in *Navitaire Inc v easyJet Airline Company and Bulletproof Technologies Inc*[132] provided the first occasion where a copyright infringement case arose from a situation where the alleged infringers had enjoyed no significant access to the source code of the original program, but had based their work upon analysis of the operation of the program. The claimant, Navitaire had developed a computerised reservation system, 'OpenRes', designed for use in the airline environment. The defendant, easyJet, one of the United Kingdom's biggest airlines, had licensed this program for use in the course of its operations. After a period of time, it decided to develop its own system and employed the second defendant, a California-based software development company, to develop the programs which were completed and put into use under the name of 'eRes'. It was common ground between the parties that 'easyJet wanted a new system that was substantially indistinguishable from the OpenRes system, as easyJet used it, in respect of its "user interface" '. The claimant alleged that 'eRes' infringed its copyright in 'OpenRes'.

The infringement proceedings were prolonged and complex. In the final analysis, although some small elements of infringement were established, the great preponderance of the judgment was in favour of easyJet. The judge, Mr Justice Pumphrey commented:

> I consider that the better approach is to take the view that it is not possible to infringe the copyright that subsists either in the source code for a parser or in the source code for a parser generator by observing the behaviour of the final program and constructing another program to do the same thing. In expressing this view, I am verging on drawing a distinction between the 'idea' of the program and its 'expression'.

Such an approach had not previously been a feature of United Kingdom copyright law but support was taken from the provisions of Article 1(2) of the European Software Protection Directive stating that:

> Protection in accordance with this Directive shall apply to the expression in any form of a computer program. Ideas and principles which underlie any element of a computer program, including those which underlie its interfaces, are not protected by copyright under this Directive.

Much legal ink and judicial time has been spent on discussion of the question of when an unprotected idea becomes sufficiently detailed and specific to be classed as a protected form of expression. Counsel for the claimant placed reliance upon a number of authorities concerned with the topic of non-literal copying. In the case of *Harman Pictures v Osborne*,[133] for example, the owner of copyright in a book about the Crimean War was successful in a claim of copyright infringement against the producers of a film which depicted the same incidents as those described in the book. In all the cases cited, the critical difference from the present case was that the alleged infringer had enjoyed access to the copyright work.

Computer programs, it was suggested by the judge, could not easily be analogised with other forms of work. The difficulty, it was stated, was that, unlike any other form of literary work, there was limited linkage between the letters and words used in the original code and the end-product as displayed and operating on a computer screen. Two completely

---

[132] [2004] EWHC 1725 (Ch).   [133] [1967] 1WLR 723.

different sets of code could produce virtually identically functioning computer programs, even though the creator of the second had not had any form of access to the code of the first program.[134]

In the final analysis, the decision was reached that:

> Navitaire's computer program invites input in a manner excluded from copyright protection, outputs its results in a form excluded from copyright protection and creates a record of a reservation in the name of a particular passenger on a particular flight. What is left when the interface aspects of the case are disregarded is the business function of carrying out the transaction and creating the record, because none of the code was read or copied by the defendants. It is right that those responsible for devising OpenRes envisaged this as the end result for their program: but that is not relevant skill and labour. In my judgment, this claim for non-textual copying should fail.

Such a conclusion, it was stated, was not reached with any form of regret. It was the stated policy of the European Software Directive that computer languages and the ideas underlying computer programs should not qualify for copyright protection. It would be wrong for these exclusions to be circumvented by seeking to identify some overall function behind the program when this was a direct consequence of the operation of the unprotected elements. Additionally, it was held:

> As a matter of policy also, it seems to me that to permit the 'business logic' of a program to attract protection through the literary copyright afforded to the program itself is an unjustifiable extension of copyright protection into a field where I am far from satisfied that it is appropriate.[135]

Initially, it was indicated that an appeal would be lodged against this decision. The parties, however, reached an out-of-court settlement. Similar issues did reach the Court of Appeal in the subsequent case of *Nova Productions Ltd v Mazoooma Games Ltd and ors*.[136] The appellant in this case was a software game developer who had produced a computer game, based upon the game of pool, for use in arcade machines. A player would be presented with the image of balls on a pool table and using an electronic cue would attempt to strike the cue ball in such a manner as to cause it to knock one of the object balls into a pocket. Cash prizes would be paid depending upon the player's degree of success. The various defendants were responsible for the development of another game of pool and its use in arcade gaming machines. Although it was not alleged that the defendants had had any form of access to the original code, it was argued that they had seen the original and appropriated elements of its manner of operation sufficient to constitute infringement of copyright. These claims were rejected in the High Court, where the judge held that no features had been copied from the original game. Although a number had been 'inspired' or 'affected' by the study of the original this was not sufficient to establish breach of copyright. An appeal was lodged with the Court of Appeal with an initial request, which was rejected, that a number of questions be referred to the European Court of Justice for a preliminary ruling.[137]

Delivering the judgment of the court, Lord Justice Jacob reviewed the law relating to the protection of computer programs. In similar manner to his comments on the Patents Act and the European Patent Convention cited earlier, he lamented the fact that the drafts of the statutory instrument which implemented the Software Directive into the United Kingdom had strayed from its exact wording thereby adding additional levels of complexity to the task of interpreting its meaning. In particular, although not of major importance

---

[134] para. 125.   [135] paras. 129–30.   [136] [2007] EWCA Civ 219.
[137] [2006] EWCA Civ 1044.

to the case, the United Kingdom Regulations appeared to treat computer programs and their preparatory materials as the objects of two different forms of copyright, whereas the Directive envisaged only a single copyright in the program, including any preparatory materials.[138]

The key question related to whether what had been taken (if anything) was restricted to unprotected ideas or whether it formed elements of the expression of the software. For the appellant, it was suggested that elements of its game, such as the feature where the appearance of the cue 'pulsed' in proportion to the level of force which the player intended to put into a shot, was sufficiently detailed to merit protection. This claim was rejected. Although the original program may have been inventive, this was a criterion which was applicable in patent law rather than copyright. The claim for infringement of the program as a literary work failed on the ground that what was found to have inspired some aspects of the defendants' game was just too general to amount to a substantial part of the claimant's game.[139]

Although the issue was not analysed in great detail, it was also stated that the appeal would fail through the application of the principles laid down in *Navitaire v easyJet*. This, it was stated, was a stronger case, 'yet the claimants lost'.[140] The judge in *Navitaire*, it was held, 'was quite right to say that merely making a program which will emulate another but which in no way involves copying the program code or any of the program's graphics is legitimate'.[141]

Lord Justice Jacob's concluding remarks perhaps mark the final nail in the coffin of look-and-feel protection for software although a referral has been made to the European Court of Justice in the recent case of *SAS Institute v World Programming Ltd*.[142] Noting that it was agreed by all parties that the case had significance for the whole computer games industry, he acknowledged that counsel for the claimant had suggested that if the trial judge's decision was upheld, the consequence would be that computer games would be denied any effective form of protection in respect of conduct involving anything other than literal reproduction of the program code. Whilst this might be the case, consideration had to be given to the original nature and purpose of copyright and the concept of a balance being struck between protecting the work of an author and encouraging the creative works of others. The famous scientist, Sir Isaac Newton, once wrote, 'If I have seen further, it is because I stood on the shoulders of giants.'[143] In like manner, Lord Justice Jacob recognised that almost all literary work was derivative to some extent and acknowledged the importance of the fact that copyright law should not stifle the creation of new works, concluding:

> If protection for such general ideas as are relied on here were conferred by the law, copyright would become an instrument of oppression rather than the incentive for creation which it is intended to be. Protection would have moved to cover works merely inspired by others, to ideas themselves.[144]

---

[138] para. 28.   [139] para. 44.   [140] para. 46.   [141] para. 52.

[142] [2010] EWHC 3012 (Ch).

[143] Letter to Robert Hooke (a rival scientist), 15 February 1676, cited in the *Concise Oxford Dictionary of Quotations*.

[144] [2006] EWCA Civ 1044 at para. 55. In *SAS Institute v World Programming Ltd* [2010] EWHC 1829 (Ch) a referral was made to the European Court of Justice seeking a preliminary ruling on a number of questions concerning the extent of protection conferred under the Directive. The judge, Mr Justice Arnold, did indicate on a number of occasions that whilst making the reference, he was not persuaded that the previous decisions were in error.

Computer programs as visual works

In addition to protecting literary works, copyright has steadily been extended to cover other forms of recorded work, closely following developments in technology. The 1988 Act provides that:

Copyright is a property right which subsists in accordance with this Part in the following descriptions of work—

(a) original literary, dramatic, musical or artistic works,

(b) sound recordings, films, broadcasts or cable programmes.

In the early days of computers, very little was provided in the way of visual content. The first computers were effectively calculating machines with no form of visual display unit. Even when these became commonplace, and even with the move to applications such as word processing, the small amounts of memory and limited processing capacity of computers meant that there was little interest in the aesthetic appearance of a computer program. The world today, of course, is very different with many computer games utilising sophisticated graphics.

Two issues are of relevance in this context: first, the question of whether an image generated through the operation of a computer program might be classed as an artistic work and, secondly, whether moving images might be classed as films.

The issue of artistic copyright in software was discussed by the Court of Appeal in the case of *Nova Productions Ltd v Mazooma Games Ltd and ors*.[145] The facts of the case have been described earlier. The games, although not identical, shared a number of elements and it was the claimant's contention, inter alia, that the defendants' games infringed its artistic copyright in 'Pocket Money'. The case hinged upon the subset of artistic work referred to as 'graphic works',[146] and centred upon the individual screen frames. It was accepted that comparison of individual frames did not demonstrate any substantial degree of similarity but it was argued that 'there was in effect a further kind of artistic work, something beyond individual freeze-frame graphics'.[147] What the defendants had done, it was argued, was to 'create a 'dynamic reposing' of the original game, changing some of the level of details but retaining 'an essential artistic element of the original'.[148] At trial, the judge was prepared to accept that this was an arguable point, although he went on to hold that there had been no infringement in the particular case. Delivering the judgment of the Court of Appeal, Lord Justice Jacob disagreed:

'Graphic work' is defined as including all the types of thing specified in s. 4(2) which all have this in common, namely that they are static, non-moving. A series of drawings is a series of graphic works, not a single graphic work in itself. No-one would say that the copyright in a single drawing of Felix the Cat is infringed by a drawing of Donald Duck. A series of cartoon frames showing Felix running over a cliff edge into space, looking down and only then falling would not be infringed by a similar set of frames depicting Donald doing the same thing. That is in effect what is alleged here.

This reasoning is supported by the fact that Parliament has specifically created copyright in moving images by way of copyright in films. If (the claimant's argument was accepted), the series of still images which provides the illusion of movement would itself create a further kind of copyright work protecting moving images. It is unlikely that Parliament intended this.[149]

There would be no doubt that reproduction of the individual frames would have constituted infringement.

[145] [2007] EWCA Civ 219.   [146] s. 4(1).   [147] para. 13.   [148] para. 13.   [149] paras. 16–17.

To date, there have not been any cases involving the claim that a computer program is classed as a film. Many modern films make very extensive use of computer-generated images, to the extent that some characters, such as Gollum in the *Lord of the Rings*, are entirely computer-generated.[150] There appears to be little doubt that the programs responsible would qualify for protection as a film. Films, of course, enjoy copyright protection in their own right and there might be little benefit in bringing a claim for infringement on the basis of the software rather than the end-product. There is a further factor to be taken into consideration which perhaps influences much of what will be discussed in Chapter 17. Discounting the concept of piracy, whereby all of a work is copied and passed off as an original, there is limited value for a later party to slavishly copy elements of an earlier work of entertainment. Copying the appearance and actions of the character of Gollum from the *Lord of the Rings* and inserting this in a film on a different topic would not be likely to increase the appeal of the later film; rather the reverse as audiences who had seen Gollum would prefer to view a novel character. Different considerations apply with software products which are functional in nature and a user who has acquired familiarity with one form of interface will not unnaturally want to be able easily to transfer skills to another package produced by a different developer.

Conclusions

In many respects, developments in the field of software copyright provide a mirror image to the situation with software patents. In the latter case, at least at the level of decisions in the European Patent Office and even more so in the United States, there has been a move from an initial denial of patentability to a much more liberal approach. With copyright, whilst there has never been any significant doubt that software is eligible for protection, recent judicial decisions have significantly limited the scope of protection so that it will extend to little more than direct copying. As cases such as *Navitaire v easyJet* illustrate, a complex balancing act often requires to be performed, considering the interests of software developers, users, and in many instances, end-consumers.

Whilst copyright may no longer extend to cover the 'look and feel' of a program, there is no doubt that it does prohibit direct copying of the underlying code. Although at first sight unobjectionable, this does create problems for users. Unlike any other form of literary work, use of software requires copying. In this respect, software, which in the case of application packages such as word-processing or spreadsheet programs is effectively a tool, sits rather uneasily in the context of a form of protection designed for literary or artistic works. As the *Gowers Report* on the future of intellectual property law points out, for a user to burn the contents of a CD which he or she has bought onto an MP3 player constitutes a breach of copyright. Few users, it may be assumed, are aware of this and it may be doubted whether (m)any of those who do, care. A situation where conduct which almost everyone would regard as acceptable is in breach of the law can serve only to bring the law into discredit. Conversely, of course, software, given its digital format, is massively vulnerable to large-scale copying at little or no cost to the copyist. There is a need to rethink some of the basic tenets of copyright law and the following chapter will consider the provisions of the rather grandly named 'Copyright in the Information Society' Directive.

---

[150] For an account of developments in the field see <http://en.wikipedia.org/wiki/Computer-generated_imagery>.

17

Copyright in the information society

Introduction

Just as in the nineteenth century industry replaced agriculture as the dominant economic sector in advanced economies so the late twentieth and twenty-first centuries have seen the service sector adopting a position of pre-eminence. Information is very much the driving force behind the service-based economy whether in the form of raw data—as used in the financial services sector—or software or creative data in the form of audio or video productions.

In the *Gowers Report on Intellectual Property*, which was commissioned by the Treasury[1] to make recommendations on possible reforms to the United Kingdom's system of Intellectual property rights it was indicated that:

> Knowledge based industries have become central to the UK economy—in 2004 the Creative Industries contributed 7.3 per cent of UK Gross Value Added, and from 1997 to 2004 they grew significantly quicker than the average rate across the whole economy.[2]

One of the more contentious statutes of recent years has been the Digital Economy Act of 2010. The provisions of this measure will be discussed throughout this chapter. The statute is concerned in large part with the enforcement of copyright and it is noteworthy that it was sponsored by two government departments. The Department of Culture, Media and Sport might be seen as an obvious candidate but in many respects the impetus behind the legislation came from the then Department of Business, Enterprise and Regulatory Reform (BERR). Speaking during the Bill's second reading in the House of Lords, the then Secretary of State Lord Mandelson placed considerable emphasis on the economic interests involved:

> At the heart of what we are discussing today are the British creative and communications industries, which produce £125 billion a year and employ just fewer than 2 million people.

Continuing he noted that:

> Our copyright regime is 300 years old this year, which means that our copyright infringement problem is also 300 years old. But the dimensions of the problem have been exponentially changed by digital technology. The ease with which data can be transferred and shared is the most powerful transformative force in the digital economy. For creative businesses, it is also its Achilles heel.[3]

As has been discussed previously, copyright has proved a flexible and adaptable legal tool. The emergence of the digital world is bringing a new set of challenges, some concerned with the scope and the extent of copyright protection and, perhaps more significantly, others with issues related to its enforcement. As the information society becomes more and more entrenched,

---

[1] Text available from <http://www.official-documents.gov.uk/document/other/0118404830/0118404830. asp>.
[2] *Gowers Report*, para. E2.
[3] <http://www.publications.parliament.uk/pa/ld200910/ldhansrd/text/91202–0002.htm#0912023 80003 26>.

so the relevance of the system, especially with its notion of exclusive rights, becomes open to challenge. This chapter will look at some of the emerging issues in the attempt to consider whether, and to what extent, copyright principles have a future in this information society.

The fundamental principles of the law of copyright are laid down in the Berne Convention. Whilst the near universal acceptance of these is a major advantage for the system, lacunae have been perceived by actors operating within developed countries. In many respects issues with the application of copyright have been more significant in those countries which have followed the civil law tradition and based copyright largely on notions of artistic integrity than has been the case for the United Kingdom where copyright has almost from its beginnings been rooted in economic soil.

This chapter will consider two main topics. Examination will first be made of the provisions of the European Union's Copyright in the Information Society Directive. This sets out to amend some provisions of copyright law better to fit the realities of an online world. In the older, what we might call analogue, world, for example, a user could read a book or play music on a cassette tape without infringing the rights of the copyright owner. With digital works, any use involves copying—at least on a temporary basis. As has been discussed, copying a work is a right reserved to the copyright owner.

The second topic in the chapter will look at some of the issues associated with enforcement of copyright considering the extent to which intermediaries such as Internet Service Providers (ISPs) might be held liable for infringing acts committed by their users. Increasingly also, attention is being paid to the possibility that rights owners might proceed against the (possibly tens of thousands) of users whose actions infringe their rights. In many cases this will require the cooperation of ISPs and a major component of the Digital Economy Act is concerned with the manner in which this process might be managed.

The Directive on Copyright in the Information Society

As has been noted in the context of data protection, law-making in the European Union can be a lengthy process. A Green Paper entitled *Copyright and Related Rights in the Information Society* was published by the Commission in July 1995 but it was not until 2001 that the Directive on the Harmonisation of Certain Aspects of Copyright and Related Rights in the Information Society was finally adopted and implemented in the United Kingdom in 2003 by the Copyright and Related Rights Regulations.[4]

The Explanatory Memorandum to the original proposal[5] identified discrepancies in the level of protection offered within the Member States, not so much at the level of fundamental principle, but in respect of detailed implementation and the provision of exceptions. Thus, all Member States accept that a right holder possesses the exclusive right to reproduce material, but differ in respect of issues such as whether a temporary reproduction will constitute infringement. Variations occur also in respect of concepts such as fair dealing and the provision of special regimes for the educational sector. Again, some states make provision for a levy to be imposed upon the sales of recording media. The proceeds of this will be distributed between right holders with users being granted a right in return to make copies of works for private purposes.

Beyond the issue of reproduction, significant issues concern the extent of rights to distribute a work or to communicate its contents to the public. With the development of 'on

---

[4] SI 2003/2498.

[5] European Commission, Explanatory Memorandum on the Proposal for a Directive on the Harmonisation of Certain Aspects of Copyright and Related Rights in the Information Society, Brussels, 10 December 1997.

demand' services for the delivery of digital information in the form of audio or video material, lacunae exist between provisions relating to private communications and broadcasting. The Directive on Copyright in the Information Society[6] sets out to make provision for these matters and to harmonise existing national provisions, keeping in line with the provisions of the Berne Convention and the 1996 World Intellectual Property Organization (WIPO) Treaty on Copyright and Performances and Phonograms. In essence, the Directive is evolutionary rather than revolutionary in its contents. As Recital 5 indicates:

> Technological development has multiplied and diversified the vectors for creation, production and exploitation. While no new concepts for the protection of intellectual property are needed, the current law on copyright and related rights should be adapted and supplemented to respond adequately to economic realities such as new forms of exploitation.

Reflecting this approach, the initial articles of the Directive do little more than confirm existing principles of copyright law. Article 2 provides authors, performers, producers, and broadcasters with the exclusive right to prohibit direct or indirect, temporary or permanent reproduction of the protected work by any means or in any form. Article 3 provides for similar exclusive rights in respect of the communication of all or part of a work to the public by wire or wireless means. It is specifically provided that the provision is to extend to the situation where the works are communicated in such a way that 'members of the public may access them from a place and at a time individually chosen by them', for example over the Internet. Article 4 provides for authors to enjoy the exclusive right to control the distribution of works to the public by sale or otherwise.

Caching

Perhaps the most controversial section of the Directive is contained in Article 5, which provides an exception from the prohibitions against reproduction where data is stored, or cached, on a temporary basis as part of normal Internet activities. The essence of caching is that an ISP, faced with what are likely to be numerous requests for access to a particular web page, will maintain a copy on its own machines rather than having to send each request off in search of the original page. Caching raises a number of technical and logistical issues. Popular websites such as the BBC news pages, will be updated on a minute-by-minute basis and there may be issues of how current a cached copy might be. Apart from these issues, the main legal problem relates to the fact that copyright law prohibits reproduction of material without the consent of the right owner. The Directive sanctions:

1. Temporary acts of reproduction…which are transient or incidental [and] an integral and essential part of a technological process and whose sole purpose is to enable:

    (a) a transmission in a network between third parties by an intermediary, or

    (b) a lawful use of a work or other subject-matter to be made, and which have no independent economic significance, shall be exempted from the reproduction right provided for in Article 2.

Recital 33 indicates the intent behind this provision:

> The exclusive right of reproduction should be subject to an exception to allow certain acts of temporary reproduction, which are transient or incidental reproductions, forming an integral and essential part of a technological process and carried out for the sole purpose of enabling either efficient transmission in a network between third parties by an intermediary, or a lawful use of a work or other subject-matter to be made.

---

[6] Directive 2001/29/EC.

A range of situations might be envisaged in which this provision will be applicable. The act of viewing information on a web page will involve the making of a temporary copy of that data on the user's own equipment. The nature of the Internet, again, will mean that transient copies of email messages will be made at various stages of the message's journey from sender to recipient. Such copying clearly falls within the criteria of 'integral' and 'essential' used in Article 5 and poses no legal difficulty. The practice of caching, which is specifically referred to in the Recital, raises more difficult issues, and the inclusion of the phrase 'an integral and essential part' might be seen as robbing the provision of much of its meaning. The problem that may be faced under the Directive's provisions is that although the use of caching may be advantageous, it cannot be considered essential. The Internet could function without it although access speeds might be somewhat slower.

Copy protection and Digital Rights Management (DRM)

The use of copy-protection devices was a feature of many early software products. A wide range of techniques were utilised in the attempt to ensure that only an authorised user could make use of software. In some cases, anti-copying techniques would have been embedded in the software itself, in other cases physical devices were used. The absence of a uniform approach between producers meant that there was almost invariably a non-protected version of software available on the market and, given that the use of such devices normally made software more difficult to use, market forces compelled most producers to abandon such tactics.

Following a period when protection devices almost disappeared from the market, with devices such as digital video disks (DVDs) there are signs that the technique is returning to favour, although again there are questions as to how effective these might be. Here, manufacturers of disks embed a code corresponding to the region of the world in which the disk is marketed. DVD players are also coded in a similar manner, so the effect is intended to be that only disks marketed in one region can be played on equipment marketed in that area. A variety of techniques can be used to overcome this form of protection and the Directive sets out to provide legal sanctions against such acts. Article 6 provides that right holders be provided with legal remedies against those seeking to avoid or 'circumvent' 'effective' technical protection measures which utilise 'an access control or protection process, such as encryption, scrambling or other transformation of the work or other subject-matter or a copy control mechanism'.

Section 296 of the Copyright, Designs and Patents Act 1988 already provided a copyright holder who publishes work in a copy-protected electronic format with a right of action against a person who:

(a) makes, imports, sells or lets for hire, offers or exposes for sale or hire, or advertises for sale or hire, any device or means specifically designed or adapted to circumvent the form of copy-protection employed, or

(b) publishes information intended to enable or assist persons to circumvent that form of copy-protection

This provision with its limitation to devices 'specifically designed or adapted' is rather more restrictive than the Directive's provisions, which refer to an article's primary purpose.[7]

---

[7] Albeit, in a slightly different context, see the discussion of *CBS Songs Ltd v Amstrad Consumer Electronics plc* later, where the fact that a twin cassette deck had some legitimate uses provided a defence to a claim of copyright infringement, even though it might be argued that most purchasers would use the equipment for unlawful purposes.

Accordingly, whilst retaining the original formula in respect of computer programs (which are outside the scope of the Directive) the regulations introduce a number of somewhat complex provisions—new sections 296ZA (circumvention of technological measures), 296ZD (rights and remedies in respect of devices and services designed to circumvent technological measures), and 296ZE (remedy where effective technological measures prevent permitted acts).[8]

With traditional forms of literary work, it is customary to embed copyright details into the printed text. Where work is distributed in electronic format, the use of rights-management information would see details identifying copyright owners being embedded in the work, and a facility included to record the use made of the work. This would facilitate the tasks of establishing copyright and the extent of any infringing use of the work. As the Directive's Recitals indicate:

> (55) Technological development will facilitate the distribution of works, notably on networks, and this will entail the need for rightholders to identify better the work or other subject-matter, the author or any other rightholder.

We will return to this issue in more detail later. The Directive provides in Article 7 that:

Member States shall provide for adequate legal protection against any person performing without authority any of the following acts:

(a) the removal or alteration of any electronic rights-management information; or

(b) the distribution, importation for distribution, broadcasting, communication or making available to the public, of copies of works or other subject matter protected under this Directive[9] or under [the Database Directive[10]] from which electronic rights-management information has been removed or altered without authority, if such person knows, or has reasonable grounds to know, that by so doing he is inducing, enabling or facilitating an infringement of any copyright or any rights related to copyright as provided by law, or of the *sui generis* right provided for in [the Database Directive].

In order to implement this provision, the regulations add a further new section (296ZG) to the Copyright, Designs and Patents Act 1988. This provides that an offence will be committed by:

a person (D) who knowingly and without authority, removes or alters electronic rights management information which—

(a) is associated with a copy of a copyright work, or

(b) appears in connection with the communication to the public of a copyright work, and

(c) where D knows, or has reason to believe, that by so doing he is inducing, enabling, facilitating or concealing an infringement of copyright.[11]

Offences will also be committed by parties concerned with the importation, distribution, or communication to the public of copies from which electronic rights information has been removed.

---

[8] SI 2003/2498, Reg. 24.

[9] Directive on Copyright in the Information Society, Directive 2001/29/EC.

[10] Directive on the Legal Protection of Databases, Directive 96/9/EC, OJ 1996 L 77/20 (the Databases Directive).   [11] SI 2003/2498, Reg. 25.

Private copying in the digital age

In many jurisdictions, a measure of tolerance has traditionally been extended in respect of copying activities carried out by private individuals. In some European jurisdictions, such conduct is specifically authorised, often in parallel with the imposition of some form of levy on the costs of recording devices such as cassette tapes, the proceeds of which will go to authors' rights organisations to be distributed or used for the benefit of copyright owners, thereby providing at least some compensation for losses caused by copying.

Although at one stage it was proposed to introduce a similar scheme in the United Kingdom, the objection has always been that the devices can be used for lawful as well as for infringing purposes. An individual might, for example, use a cassette recorder and tape to record his or her own compositions, rather than to make a copy of a third party's work. In such a situation, it is difficult to identify equitable grounds for requiring payment to be made to copyright owners. The *Gowers Report* comments:

> Downloading music and films from the Internet is now the most common legal offence committed by young people aged between 10 and 25 in the United Kingdom. Up to 80 per cent of music downloads are not paid for, even though most consumers recognise it to be illegal. According to a report commissioned by the British Phonographic Industry (BPI), file-sharing cost the music industry £414 million in lost sales in 2005, on total retail sales of £1.87 billion. These losses have risen steeply from £278 million in 2003.[12]

Even though the United Kingdom does not legitimise domestic copying,[13] a measure of tolerance is shown by the fact that the criminal penalties applicable in the event of copying for commercial purposes do not extend where copying is carried out for social and domestic purposes. Such an approach can be justified in the context of analogue copying. It would be a rare student who has not infringed copyright at some stage through over-zealous use of a photocopier. Most readers will be familiar with the limitations of this copying technology. A photocopy of an article in a journal or a chapter of a book will invariably be of lower quality than the original. Slight movement of the page as the copy is being made will cause blurring of lines, the size of the book being copied and the paper being used in the photocopier may differ, again with adverse consequences for the appearance of the copy. Problems will be exacerbated if a photocopy is itself copied and by the time the process is repeated over a few generations of copies, the final version will be virtually indecipherable. Similar factors will apply when a cassette copy is made of a musical recording or television or film production. In general, with equipment normally available to the domestic copyist, the copying process is a laborious one and the results inferior in quality to the original work.

Where information is recorded in digital format, the task of the copier is very much easier. A copy of a digital work will be identical in terms of quality to the original, and the same result will apply no matter how many generations of copies are produced. The speed with which copies may be made is also generally increased, whilst the emergence of the Internet makes it possible for a program to be placed on a website and copied by tens or even hundreds of thousands of users around the world. The popular encryption program PGP was released to the world in this manner in order to pre-empt attempts by the United States authorities to prevent its distribution. Not even the might of the United States could put the technological genie back in that particular bottle. Today, much debate focuses on

---

[12] para. 217.

[13] Save in the case of use of a video recorder to record a television broadcast 'solely' in order to allow it to be viewed at a more convenient time (Copyright, Designs and Patents Act 1988, s. 70).

the availability of copyright protected material over the Internet through the medium of file sharing websites. As will be discussed later, one legal response to the problem has been to seek to impose liability on commercial third parties whose equipment or facilities are regarded as facilitating the infringing acts of private individuals. The question arises also as to what should be the level of liability imposed on the individual's concerned?

Regulation 26 of the Copyright and Related Rights Regulations 2003[14] provides for an extension of the scope of criminal offences. Previously, an offence was committed only when a copyright infringer acted in the course of a business. The Copyright, Designs and Patents Act 1988 is now amended to provide that:

(2A) A person who infringes copyright in a work by communicating the work to the public—

(a) in the course of a business, or

(b) otherwise than in the course of a business to such an extent as to affect prejudicially the owner of the copyright, commits an offence if he knows or has reason to believe that, by doing so, he is infringing copyright in that work.[15]

As the *Gowers Report* comments, however:

The fact that the letter of the law is rarely enforced only adds to the public sense of illegitimacy surrounding copyright law. Yet copyright is essential for protecting the investment that UK creative industries make in artists, performers and designers. If uses such as transferring music from CDs to an MP3 player for personal use are seen to be illegal, it becomes more difficult to justify sanctions against copyright infringement that genuinely cost industry sales, such as from freely downloading music and films using the Internet.[16]

A problem facing right holders seeking to take action against individuals is to identify those concerned. As has been discussed in the context of privacy, true anonymity is an elusive commodity where the Internet is concerned. It is feasible for right holders to acquire the details of the Internet Protocol (IP) addresses used by computers which are identified as uploading or downloading copyright-protected material. IP addresses are allocated to end-users by ISPs and these organisations are in a position to match names with IP addresses.

Attempts by aggrieved parties to seek court orders, commonly known as *Norwich Pharmacal* orders after the House of Lords' decision in the case of that name, have been a feature of a number of actions in the field of defamation and the principles described in that chapter of this book will also be relevant in the copyright field. Specific, albeit controversial, legislative action has now been adopted in the form of the Digital Economy Act 2010 and this chapter will continue to give consideration to the scope of this statute.

Copyright enforcement

Copyright is a property right and, as with any other form of property, owners may wish to take steps to protect and enforce their rights. Historically in the UK, enforcement has comprised of a mix of civil and criminal measures. The base measures for protection of rights owners is laid down in Directive 2004/48/EC on the Enforcement of Intellectual Property Rights[17] which refers also to the Trade Related Aspects of Intellectual Property Rights agreement which forms part of the General Agreement on Trade in Services which

---

[14] SI 2003/2498.   [15] s. 107.   [16] para. 327.   [17] OJ 2004 L 195/16.

operates under the auspices of the World Trade Organization. The Directive's key provision is in Article 3 that provides:

1. Member States shall ensure that, on application by a party which has presented reasonably available evidence sufficient to support its claims, and has, in substantiating those claims, specified evidence which lies in the control of the opposing party, the competent judicial authorities may order that such evidence be presented by the opposing party, subject to the protection of confidential information. For the purposes of this paragraph, Member States may provide that a reasonable sample of a substantial number of copies of a work or any other protected object be considered by the competent judicial authorities to constitute reasonable evidence.

2. Under the same conditions, in the case of an infringement committed on a commercial scale Member States shall take such measures as are necessary to enable the competent judicial authorities to order, where appropriate, on application by a party, the communication of banking, financial or commercial documents under the control of the opposing party, subject to the protection of confidential information.

A variety of remedies have been made available to copyright owners in the UK. These range from actions brought directly against alleged infringers (or those facilitating infringement) under either civil or criminal law to actions brought with a view to compelling intermediaries such as ISPs to intervene to restrict access to sites or users shown to be likely to commit infringing acts. A recent and very controversial statutory intervention has been in the form of the Digital Economy Act 2010 which follows a model adopted in a number of other European states, generally referred to as 'three strikes and you're out'. Effectively the statute provides a basis for preventing or restricting Internet access for persons who persistently engage in acts of copyright infringement.

Norwich Pharmacal orders and threats of litigation

Enforcement measures have been a source of considerable controversy in the intellectual property field. As discussed elsewhere, one of the features of the Internet is that it gives individuals access to technology to make copies of a work on a large scale. The Copyright, Designs and Patents Act 1988 (as amended by the Copyright and Related Rights Regulations 2003[18]) moves away from the traditional legislative approach which limited criminal liability to instances where copyright infringement was carried out with a view to commercial gain to focus on the impact that conduct has on the right owner. Section 107 provides:

A person who infringes copyright in a work by communicating the work to the public—

(a) in the course of a business, or

(b) otherwise than in the course of a business to such an extent as to affect prejudicially the owner of the copyright,

commits an offence if he knows or has reason to believe that, by doing so, he is infringing copyright in that work.

In addition to facing prosecution under copyright legislation (with a maximum penalty of three months' imprisonment) there have been a number of high-profile prosecutions against the administrators of alleged file-sharing websites on a charge of conspiracy (with other users of the site) to defraud (copyright owners). In one case heard at Newcastle Crown Court, the administrator of a file-sharing website that had reportedly received an income of

---

[18] SI 2003 No. 2498.

£300,000 per annum from advertising was sentenced to a four-year term of imprisonment. As a report[19] on the case indicates:

> At its peak the site attracted more than 400,000 visitors a day and was ranked as one of the top 500 websites in the world.

Beyond those who facilitate copying on a large scale there is no doubt that an individual who makes a single infringing copy of a work will be liable to an action for damages. There has been some increased emphasis on such activities. The case of *Media CAT v Adams and ors*[20] provides an example of conduct that appears to have occurred in a number of countries. In this case, lawyers claiming to act on behalf of copyright societies had obtained (largely through the use of *Norwich Pharmacal* orders) lists of names and addresses of thousands of individuals who had been allocated IP addresses that were suspected of having been used to commit copyright infringement – in the particular case by downloading copies of pornographic movies. Letters were sent to tens of thousands of individuals threatening to commence legal proceedings for infringement of copyright unless a specified sum (£495) was offered by way of settlement.

The approach of seeking to act against persons alleged to have downloaded pornographic material appears to have been a common feature of these campaigns on an international basis—perhaps relying on an embarrassment factor to persuade recipients of the letters to make payment. The procedural aspects of the case were complex and involved a number of hearings and judgments. Essentially when some individuals rejected the 'offer' and legal proceedings were initiated the claimants faced with extensive and generally adverse publicity sought to discontinue proceedings. This led to Mr Justice Birss sitting in the Patents County Court to delve deeply into the background to the litigation. The end result was that the cases were dropped, the law firm involved became bankrupt, and the solicitor with prime responsibility was struck off the register of solicitors.

It might be a brave claimant who will try to pursue similar tactics in the future. One of the major issues debated concerned the difficulty in identifying with any degree of certainly the particular individual responsible for online conduct. This will be considered in more detail later, but with households having multiple devices connected to the Internet and the near ubiquitous presence of wireless connections outside a work environment it can be very difficult to establish with any degree of precision which person in a multi-occupancy household engaged in any particular form of conduct.

The Digital Economy Act 2010

This Act has been one of the most controversial pieces of legislation adopted in the United Kingdom in recent years. The basic premise is perhaps generally accepted. Unauthorised copying, whether of computer programs or literary or audio visual material causes substantial losses to copyright owners. In some instances action can be taken directly against intermediaries such as ISPs or the operators of bulletin boards or websites considered to participate in infringing acts. In most instances, such operators may facilitate infringing conduct but will not be regarded as purporting to authorise it.

In these respects, the Act establishes the basis for procedures whereby copyright owners can take action against individuals whose allocated IP addresses have been identified by rights owners or bodies acting on their behalf as being associated with copying in breach

---

[19] <http://www.out-law.com/en/articles/2012/august/website-operator-jailed-for-four-years-for-conspiring-to-defraud-copyright-owners/>.   [20] [2011] EWPCC 6.

of the rights conferred under the Copyright, Designs and Patents Act 1988. General procedures are defined which will require to be supplemented by the provisions of codes of practice either approved or made by the Office of Communications (OFCOM). Further provisions are made for the imposition of sanctions against individuals who have been identified as infringers on a number (to be specified) of occasions. These may include the imposition of technical measures designed to limit or prevent Internet access. These provisions will not be introduced until twelve months after an order is made by the Secretary of State.

Online infringement of copyright

The Act establishes procedures which may be invoked by a copyright owner who has evidence indicating that a subscriber to an Internet access service has infringed the owner's copyright by means of the service or has allowed another person to use the service, and that other person has infringed the owner's copyright by means of the service The owner may make a copyright infringement report to the ISP who provided the Internet access service. This will come into force when an initial obligations code is approved by the Office of Communications—something that has still to take place.

An ISP who receives a copyright infringement report must notify the subscriber of the report if the initial obligations code requires the provider to do so. Notification must be sent to the subscriber within the period of one month beginning with the day on which the provider receives the report. The notification must include a statement that the notification is sent in response to a copyright infringement report; the name of the copyright owner who made the report; a description of the apparent infringement; evidence of the apparent infringement that shows the subscriber's IP address and the time at which the evidence was gathered; information about subscriber appeals and the grounds on which they may be made; information about copyright and its purpose; advice, or information enabling the subscriber to obtain advice, about how to obtain lawful access to copyright works; advice, or information enabling the subscriber to obtain advice, about steps that a subscriber can take to protect an Internet access service from unauthorised use; and anything else that the initial obligations code requires the notification to include. In particular this may include: a statement that information about the apparent infringement may be kept by the ISP; a statement that the copyright owner may require the provider to disclose which copyright infringement reports made by the owner to the provider relate to the subscriber; a statement that, following such a disclosure, the copyright owner may apply to a court to learn the subscriber's identity and may bring proceedings against the subscriber for copyright infringement; and, where the requirement for the provider to send the notification arises partly because of a report that has already been the subject of a notification, a statement that the number of copyright infringement reports relating to the subscriber may be taken into account for the purposes of any technical measures that may be imposed against the subscriber.

The initial obligations code

A draft Initial Obligations Code specifying the obligations which will be imposed on ISPs may be submitted to OFCOM by any interested parties or organisations. If it appears to OFCOM that it would be appropriate for them to approve the code for that purpose, they may by order approve it, with effect from the date given in the order. It is open to any interested party to submit a draft code to OFCOM but only one code may be in force at any given time.

An approved code must specify conditions that must be met for rights and obligations under the copyright infringement provisions or the code to apply in a particular case. In particular, these may specify that a right or obligation does not apply in relation to a copyright owner unless the owner has made arrangements with an ISP regarding the number of copyright infringement reports that the owner may make to the provider within a particular period. It may also require that the right holder make payment in advance of a contribution towards meeting costs incurred by the provider.

In order to be approved, a draft code must:

- specify the required provision about copyright infringement reports
- make the required provision about the notification of subscribers
- set the threshold applying for the purposes of determining who is a relevant subscriber[21]
- make provision about how ISPs are to keep information about subscribers
- limit the time for which they may keep that information
- make any provision about contributions towards meeting costs
- satisfy OFCOM that the requirements concerning administration and enforcement are met in relation to the code
- meet the requirements concerning subscriber appeals
- ensure that the provisions of the code are objectively justifiable in relation to the matters to which it relates and that those provisions are not such as to discriminate unduly against particular persons or against a particular description of persons and are proportionate to what they are intended to achieve and that, in relation to what those provisions are intended to achieve, they are transparent.

Initial obligations code by OFCOM in the absence of an approved code

It was the stated preference of government ministers that the initial obligations code should be drafted by representatives of the industries involved. In the event, however, that no satisfactory code should be produced, responsibility switches to OFCOM. In the six months following the entry into force of the relevant provisions of the Act,[22] OFCOM may produce such a code. At the end of this period, it must produce an initial obligations code on its own initiative unless a contrary order is made by the Secretary of State.[23]

A code produced by OFCOM may confer jurisdiction with respect to any matter (other than jurisdiction to determine appeals by subscribers) on OFCOM themselves and provide for OFCOM, in exercising such jurisdiction, to make awards of compensation or to direct the reimbursement of costs, or to do both. The code may provide for OFCOM to enforce, or to participate in the enforcement of, any awards or directions made under the code or make other provision for the enforcement of such awards and directions. The code may establish a body corporate, with the capacity to make its own rules and establish its own procedures, for the purpose of determining subscriber appeals, or may provide for a person with the function of determining subscriber appeals to enforce, or to participate in the enforcement of, any awards or directions made by the person. It may make other provision for the enforcement of such awards and directions and make other provision for the purpose of regulating the initial obligations.

---

[21]   See s. 124(3)(B).

[22]   At the time of writing, no dates have been specified.

[23]   s. 124D(2). The Secretary of State may give such notice only if it appears to the Secretary of State that it is not practicable for OFCOM to make a code with effect from the end of the period.

Notification reports

Any notification report[24] must include a statement that the notification is sent in response to a copyright infringement report from a named copyright owner. It must also include a description of the apparent infringement and evidence of the apparent infringement that shows the subscriber's IP address and the time at which the evidence was gathered. Information must also be given about subscriber appeals and the grounds on which they may be made and about copyright and its purpose. The subscriber must also be given advice, or information enabling the subscriber to obtain advice about how to obtain lawful access to copyright works and steps that a subscriber can take to protect an Internet access service from unauthorised use. The initial obligations code may also require the provision of other items of information with specific reference made to the provision of statements that information about the apparent infringement may be kept by the ISP; that the copyright owner may require the provider to disclose which copyright infringement reports made by the owner to the provider relate to the subscriber; that, following such a disclosure, the copyright owner may apply to a court to learn the subscriber's identity and may bring proceedings against the subscriber for copyright infringement; and where the requirement for the provider to send the notification arises partly because of a report that has already been the subject of a notification, a statement that the number of copyright infringement reports relating to the subscriber may be taken into account for the purposes of any technical measures.

Copyright infringement lists

An ISP must provide a copyright owner with a copyright infringement list[25] for a period if requested and where required by the initial obligations code.

Progress reports

OFCOM must prepare a number of reports for the Secretary of State about the infringement of copyright by subscribers to Internet access services. A full report must be provided for the period of twelve months beginning with the first day on which there is an initial obligations code in force and for each successive period of twelve months.

A full report under this section must include:

- an assessment of the current level of subscribers' use of Internet access services to infringe copyright
- a description of the steps taken by copyright owners to enable subscribers to obtain lawful access to copyright works
- a description of the steps taken by copyright owners to inform, and change the attitude of, members of the public in relation to the infringement of copyright.

The report must include an assessment of the extent of the steps mentioned above and also of the extent to which copyright owners have made copyright infringement reports and of the extent to which they have brought legal proceedings against subscribers in relation to whom such reports have been made. It must include also an assessment of the extent to

---

[24] Notification will be satisfied by sending a message to a registered email or postal address (s. 124A (9)).

[25] A 'copyright infringement list' is a list that sets out, in relation to each relevant subscriber, which of the copyright infringement reports made by the owner to the provider relate to the subscriber, but does not enable any subscriber to be identified.

which any such proceedings have been against subscribers in relation to whom a substantial number of reports have been made; and anything else that the Secretary of State directs OFCOM to include in the report.

OFCOM must prepare an interim report for the period of three months beginning with the first day on which there is an initial obligations code in force and for each successive period of three months, other than one ending at the same time as a period of twelve months where a full report is required to be published. This obligation will cease to have effect when the Secretary of State directs that it is no longer to apply.

An interim report under this section must include an assessment of the current level of subscribers' use of Internet access services to infringe copyright, an assessment of the extent to which copyright owners have made copyright infringement reports, and an assessment of the extent to which they have brought legal proceedings against subscribers in relation to whom such reports have been made. It must also include anything else that the Secretary of State directs OFCOM to include in the report.

Obligations to limit Internet access

The Secretary of State may by order impose a technical obligation on ISPs if OFCOM have assessed whether one or more technical obligations should be imposed on ISPs and, taking into account that assessment and any other matter that appears to the Secretary of State to be relevant, the Secretary of State considers it appropriate to make the order. No order may be made within the period of twelve months beginning with the first day on which there is an initial obligations code in force.

An order must specify the date from which the technical obligation is to have effect, or provide for it to be specified. The order may also specify the criteria for taking the technical measure concerned against a subscriber, the steps to be taken as part of the measure, and when they are to be taken.

Prior to making such an order, the Secretary of State must lay a draft of the order and a document which explains the order before Parliament, such draft to be approved by a resolution of each House. No further draft order setting a date for implementing the obligations may be laid during the period of sixty days beginning with the day on which the document was laid.

Following the expiry of this period, in preparing a draft order under this section to give effect to the proposal, the Secretary of State must have regard to any representations, and any recommendations of a committee of either House of Parliament charged with reporting on the draft order. When laying before Parliament a draft order to give effect to the proposal (with or without modifications), the Secretary of State must also lay a document that explains any changes made to the proposal contained in the document laid before Parliament.

Code by OFCOM about obligations to limit Internet access

For any period during which there are one or more technical obligations in force, OFCOM must by order make a technical obligations code for the purpose of regulating those obligations. This code may be made separately from, or in combination with, any initial obligations code. A maximum set of conditions are laid down in the Digital Economy Act relating to procedural and jurisdictional matters.

In making any such code OFCOM are required to ensure that:

- it meets criteria laid down in the Act requiring that requirements concerning administration and enforcement are met in relation to the code

- meets the requirements concerning subscriber appeals
- ensures that the provisions of the code are objectively justifiable in relation to the matters to which it relates and that those provisions are not such as to discriminate unduly against particular persons or against a particular description of persons and are proportionate to what they are intended to achieve and that, in relation to what those provisions are intended to achieve, they are transparent.

The code may specify conditions that must be met for rights and obligations under the copyright infringement provisions or the code to apply in a particular case, and require copyright owners or ISPs to provide any information or assistance that is reasonably required to determine whether such conditions are met. In this regard, the code may in particular specify that a right or obligation does not apply in relation to a copyright owner unless the owner has made arrangements with an ISP regarding the number of copyright infringement reports that the owner may make to the provider within a particular period and provide for payment in advance of a contribution towards meeting costs incurred by the provider. It may in particular be provided that, except as set out in the code, rights and obligations do not apply in relation to an ISP unless the number of copyright infringement reports the provider receives within a particular period reaches a threshold set in the code. If the threshold is reached, rights or obligations apply with effect from the date when it is reached or from such later time as may be specified in the code.

The code may confer jurisdiction with respect to any matter (other than jurisdiction to determine appeals by subscribers) on OFCOM themselves and provide for OFCOM, in exercising such jurisdiction, to make awards of compensation or to direct the reimbursement of costs, or to do both. The code may provide for OFCOM to enforce, or to participate in the enforcement of, any awards or directions made under the code or make other provision for the enforcement of such awards and directions. The code may establish a body corporate, with the capacity to make its own rules and establish its own procedures, for the purpose of determining subscriber appeals or may provide for a person with the function of determining subscriber appeals to enforce, or to participate in the enforcement of, any awards or directions made by the person. It may make other provision for the enforcement of such awards and directions and make other provision for the purpose of regulating the initial obligations.

Any code made by OFCOM will come into effect only with the consent of the Secretary of State and is subject to annulment in pursuance of a resolution of either House of Parliament. OFCOM is required to keep the contents of any code under review and, subject to the consent of the Secretary of State, make any amendment that is necessary to ensure that while it is in force it continues to meet the statutory criteria set out here.

Contents of code about obligations to limit Internet access

Any code must meet statutory requirements concerning enforcement, related matters, and subscriber appeals. It must also make any provision about contributions towards meeting costs that is required to be included by an order and any other provision that the Secretary of State requires it to make. The provisions of the code must be objectively justifiable in relation to the matters to which it relates, ensure that its provisions are not such as to discriminate unduly against particular persons or against a particular description of persons, are proportionate to what they are intended to achieve, and are transparent.

The specific requirements concerning enforcement and related matters are that OFCOM have, under the code, the functions of administering and enforcing it, including the function of resolving owner–provider disputes;[26] that there are adequate arrangements under the code for OFCOM to obtain any information or assistance from ISPs or copyright owners that OFCOM reasonably require for the purposes of administering and enforcing the code; and that there are adequate arrangements under the code for the costs incurred by OFCOM in administering and enforcing it to be met by ISPs and copyright owners.

The provisions made concerning enforcement and related matters may also (unless the Secretary of State requires otherwise) include, in particular, provision for the payment, to a person specified in the code, of a penalty not exceeding the maximum penalty for the time being specified in section 124L(2), and provision requiring a copyright owner to indemnify an ISP for any loss or damage resulting from the owner's infringement or error in relation to the code or the copyright infringement provisions.

Legal challenges to the Digital Economy Act

Unusually for a UK statute, a legal challenge to its validity was raised by BT and a number of other telecommunications networks. In R (on the application of British Telecommunications and others) v BPI (British Recorded Music Industry) Ltd and ors[27] challenges to the legality of the Act were raised and in very large part rejected by the High Court and the Court of Appeal. The key issues related to the questions of whether the Act conflicted with the requirements of the E-Commerce Directive and also whether the requirement to supply personal data about users breached the provisions of the Data Protection Act.

The E-Commerce Directive

Objections to the provisions of the Digital Economy Act centred on the immunities which are conferred on Information Society Service Providers by the E-Commerce Directive, in particular where they act as a mere conduit, as a host, or provide caching services.

Under the Digital Economy Act, ISPs will be required to cooperate with copyright owners in the service of copyright infringement reports and lists and face a range of legal sanctions in the event that they fail to act. As was noted in paragraph 48 of Lord Justice Richard's judgment:

> The appellants contend that the set of responsibilities imposed on them by the contested provisions with regard to notification of copyright infringement reports and the provision of copyright infringement lists, together with the related financial burden and exposure to liability for costs, compensation and penalties, renders them 'liable for the information transmitted' within the meaning of Article 12(1) (the 'mere conduit' defence) and is therefore incompatible with the article.

This contention was rejected. Lord Justice Richards quoted with approval the works of Mr Justice Parker in the High Court:

> Without the underlying infringement, there would be no CIR or CIL: but the legal test is not whether a liability has arisen because there was an initial infringement of copyright; the liability must arise in respect of that underlying infringement, so that the liability is for the information transmitted.

---

[26] 'owner–provider dispute' means a dispute that:

   (a) is between persons who are copyright owners or internet service providers and
   (b) relates to an act or omission in relation to a technical obligation or a technical obligations code.

[27] [2012] EWCA Civ 232.

Essentially, ISPs would face legal sanctions not in respect of the transmission by users of information over their networks but as a result of their failure to comply with legal requirements imposed directly on themselves.

A further argument advanced for the claimants was that, in contrast to the position under Articles 13 and 14 dealing with the caching and hosting immunities, there was no mechanism requiring ISPs to receive complaints from right owners and remove infringing material. The lack of such a provision in Article 12 was seen as giving a wider level of protection. This contention was also rejected on the ground that a 'mere conduit' has less direct control over information than a party who hosts material or maintains cached copies although the issue is perhaps related to the other major legal issue regarding the extent to which ISPs might be required to use filtering software to block access to specific websites.

A further challenge to the legitimacy of the Digital Economy Act was based on the provisions of Article 3 of the E-Commerce Directive. This provides in part that:

(1) Each Member State shall ensure that the information society services provided by a Service Provider established on its territory comply with the national provisions applicable in the Member State in question which fall within the coordinated field.

(2) Member States may not, for reasons falling within the coordinated field, restrict the freedom to provide information society services from another Member State.

The appellants' contention here was that the provisions of the Digital Economy Act might restrict the freedom of ISPs from other Member States from offering their services to UK users. The prime difficulty for the appellants was that Article 3(3) provided that the paragraphs quoted above do not apply in respect of categories services listed in the Annex to the Directive. The Annex makes specific reference to copyright and neighbouring rights.

For the appellants it argued that this exclusion was restricted to substantive issues of copyright law—the nature of the works which might be protected and the extent of protection. At the time the E-Commerce Directive was adopted, there was little in the way of harmonisation across the Member States. The Directive on Copyright in the Information Society which was adopted a year later had brought about a good measure of harmonisation and therefore the exclusion was no longer necessary or valid at least in respect of measures for copyright infringement.

Again, upholding the High Court ruling, Lord Justice Richards disagreed. Copyright, as referred to in the E-Commerce Directive should be given its normal meaning, 'encompassing all aspects of the law of copyright under national laws, and cannot have had the elaborate meaning attributed to it by the appellants'. If it had been the intention of the Copyright in the Information Society Directive to change the scope of the E-Commerce Directive, it would have required specifically the amendment of the earlier measure.

Data protection issues

The appellants' arguments in respect of data protection law related both to the general Data Protection Directive[28] and also to the Directive on Privacy in Electronic Communications.[29]

In respect of the general Directive, attention focused on the provisions of Article 8 which prohibits the processing of sensitive personal data unless strict conditions are complied with. This might be seen as pushing a case too far although the fault may lie more with the concept of sensitive data than with the appellants' arguments. It may certainly be the case that the materials we download unlawfully may say something about our political or religious views etc., but the connection appears a little tenuous.

[28] Directive 95/46   [29] OJ 2002, L201/37 as amended by Directive 2009/136, OJ 2009 L 337/11.

One of the conditions laid down in the Directive for justifying processing is where this 'relates to data which are manifestly made public by the data subject or is necessary for the establishment, exercise or defence of legal claims'. The appellants pointed to the government impact assessment statement produced during the Digital Economy Act's passage to the effect that the new procedures would persuade 70 per cent of infringers to stop infringement without the need for further legal proceedings. How then could the provisions meet the conditions for legitimate processing?

The communications privacy Directive refers, inter alia, to the processing of traffic data—relating to the source and origins of communications. It authorises processing of such data where the processing is:

> a necessary, appropriate and proportionate measure within a democratic society to safeguard national security (i.e. State security), defence, public security, and the prevention, investigation, detection and prosecution of criminal offences or of unauthorised use of the electronic communication system.

Here the complaint was that processing of data would be in connection with the institution of civil (rather than criminal) proceedings. The answer to the challenge came principally from decisions of the European Court of Justice in file-sharing cases such as Case C-275/06, *Productores de Musica de España (Promusicae) v Telefonica de España SAU*.[30] The Court of Justice drew a link between the general and electronic communications data protection Directives and ruled that:

> It is clear, however, that Article 15(1) of Directive 2002/58 ends the list of the above exceptions with an express reference to Article 13(1) of Directive 95/46. That provision also authorises the Member States to adopt legislative measures to restrict the obligation of confidentiality of personal data where that restriction is necessary inter alia for the protection of the rights and freedoms of others. As they do not specify the rights and freedoms concerned, those provisions of Article 15(1) of Directive 2002/58 must be interpreted as expressing the Community legislature's intention not to exclude from their scope the protection of the right to property or situations in which authors seek to obtain that protection in civil proceedings.

It might be asked why, if it was so clearly the legislature's intention to allow disclosure for the purposes of civil proceedings it did not make the effort to add a two-word phrase to the provision?

Where now for the Digital Economy Act?

We are now past the fourth anniversary of the Digital Economy Act receiving Royal Assent but in spite of an OFCOM consultation period on the contents of the initial obligations code expiring in July 2010, we await even a draft instrument. There seems to be serious doubt whether these provisions of the Act will ever be brought into force.

In some important respects it seems that the emphasis of right owners is switching to seeking to act directly against ISPs to compel the blocking (or attempted blocking) of access to specified sites. More recently we have also seen major activities by law enforcement agencies in a range of countries, including the United Kingdom, seeking to disrupt the activities of sites associated with large-scale copyright infringement.

A number of European countries have sought to implement legislation along the lines adopted in the Digital Economy Act. It is perhaps fair to say that success has been limited. And perhaps it is time to recognise that the model may be lawful but is flawed.

---

[30] [2008] ECR I-271.

Blocking orders

Part of the reason why the Digital Economy Act has not yet entered into force is that right owners have found an alternative mechanism to seek to block access to allegedly infringing sites involving obtaining a court order requiring ISPs to block user search requests (generally using the same software as is used to block access to sites identified as hosting child pornography. The first case to apply this concept was *Twentieth Century Film Corpn and ors v BT* which was decided in July 2012. The judgment, which concerned the actions of an Internet site Newzbin2 has potentially important implications for network providers, websites, and perhaps also the future of the somewhat controversial Digital Economy Act.

The site Newzbin is no stranger to the courts. Operating as a form of online members' club with users being required to pay subscription fees in return for access, it provides information and technology which could be (and by all the evidence is) used to make unlawful copies of copyright protected works. In 2010 a High Court ruling[31] held that it was liable jointly with users for their acts of copyright infringement on the basis that the site owners knew full well what activities were going on but turned blind eyes that Admiral Nelson would have been proud of.

The issue of awareness was, of course, also an issue in the case of *L'Oreal v eBay*.[32] There is a clear distinction between a party such as eBay who knows that their facilities or products are likely to be used for unlawful purposes against their wishes and those who seek actively to facilitate it. An older analogy may be apposite. Any car manufacturer must be aware that burglars and robbers use motor cars to facilitate their crimes and getaways. It would be inconceivable however that liability would follow save in the situation where there was direct awareness of the criminal intents of a particular buyer.

The initial High Court ruling effectively put Newzbin out of business. Websites are not geographically dependent however and in a short period of time Newzbin2 was established and commenced operations from Sweden. Proceedings were initiated by a range of copyright owners asking the High Court to order BT, the United Kingdom's largest ISP, to use the same forms of filter which it already applied to block access to sites identified as containing child pornography to block access from the United Kingdom to Newzbin2.[33]

In many respects the case followed a pattern which was established in cases such as *Bunt v Tilley*[34] discussed previously where claimants sought information from a third party such as an ISP to identify a party against whom they wished to commence legal proceedings. The typical response has been for the third party to indicate that they will supply the data but only if required so to do by a court. In the present case, BT's approach was similar. It was represented in court and although it challenged aspects of the claimants' case it did not appear to do so with enormous vigour and is on record as describing the judgment as being 'helpful' in that it has clarified the law and will make it easier for the company to comply with its obligations in future.

Three questions were identified by Mr Justice Arnold as being of critical importance:

First, what must the Service Provider have 'actual knowledge' of? Secondly, in what manner may a Service Provider be given 'actual knowledge' of something which it did not know before? Thirdly, if some actual knowledge is proved, what is the scope of the injunction that may be granted?

The first question has been important in a number of cases and the judgment provides a helpful summary of the relevant case and statute law. The issue and debate has centered in

---

[31]   [2010] EWHC 608.   [32]   [2009] EWHC 1094.
[33]   Subsequently a considerable number of similar cases have been raised against other ISPs and file-sharing websites.   [34]   [2006] EWHC 407.

the past on the question whether a party such as an ISP might, out of fear of being joined as a defendant in litigation, act too readily and hastily when presented with a complaint. In defamation cases the concern has been that an ISP might block access to a posting which is allegedly defamatory thereby setting up a clear conflict with the rights of freedom of expression guaranteed under Article 10 of the European Convention on Human Rights. Matters are perhaps a little simpler in the copyright context where issues of infringement may be more clear-cut and where there is less of an issue regarding freedom of expression. Mr Justice Arnold concluded:

> I consider that what must be shown is that the Service Provider has actual knowledge of one or more persons using its service to infringe copyright. The more information the Service Provider has about the infringing activity, the more likely it is that the Service Provider will have actual knowledge. Thus it may well be relevant to consider whether or to what extent the Service Provider has knowledge of particular copyright works (or at least classes of copyright works) being involved, of particular restricted acts (or at least types of restricted act) being committed and of particular persons (or at least groups of persons) committing those acts; but it is not essential to prove actual knowledge of a specific infringement of a specific copyright work by a specific individual.

A wide range of legal measures and provisions were debated in court. The most significant was section 97A of the Copyright, Designs and Patents Act of 1998 which was added to the statute in the course of the UK's implementation of the Copyright in the Information Society Directive. This provides that a court may issue an injunction against a Service Provider in respect of conduct by a third party where the provider has 'actual knowledge' that the third party is using its facilities to infringe copyright. In determining whether the provider has actual knowledge, the Act identifies a number of factors to be taken into account. These include whether the provider has been notified by a right owner of the conduct which has allegedly been perpetrated.

In the present case it was accepted that BT had not been expressly notified of a specific infringement by a specifically identified individual but, it was held, the broader picture had to be considered. BT must be assumed to have been aware of the information set out in the High Court's judgment of 2010. It must have known that copyright infringement was rife on the Newzbin2 site. As Mr Justice Arnold commented

> It appears to be quite hard to find any content on Newzbin2 that is not protected by copyright.

The unequivocal conclusion was that the statutory criteria were satisfied and BT were ordered to use specified forms of technology to block access to Newzbin2. Others are far better qualified than me to comment on whether the blocking technology is likely to be effective but it does seem to me that the approach adopted by the High Court has much more merit than the Digital Economy Act's proposals to inhibit individual Internet access in total.

There are many ISPs in the United Kingdom and, as is also an issue under the Digital Economy Act, economies of scale may mean that responsibilities and remedies may be imposed on or sought from only large-scale players such as BT. This may itself have legal implications. In competitive markets, it cannot be fair that some players are subject to more extensive requirements than others.

Finally, it is noteworthy to see the extensive references to the Hargreaves Report on Intellectual Property by Mr Justice Arnold. We have a copyright system which, if not broken, is struggling to live up to its original ideals. Court decisions—or statutes such as the Digital Economy Act—may supply sticking plasters but, faced with what is increasingly seen as a gaping wound, they can provide only limited assistance to a patient who needs to be taken into intensive care and subjected to more radical medical and surgical intervention.

New directions in UK copyright law

It is sometimes a feature of the United Kingdom legislative process that changes to one area of legislation are quietly introduced within a statute primarily directed at other areas of activity. This has been the case with the enactment of the Enterprise and Regulatory Reform Act 2013, a measure that makes some significant changes to United Kingdom copyright law. In large part the provisions relate to topics that were dropped from the Digital Economy Bill (now Act) 2010 in order to enable it to complete its parliamentary passage before the legislature was dissolved prior to the 2010 general election.

In common with many other statutes, the copyright provisions in the Enterprise and Regulatory Reform Act establish a framework which may be filled in by Regulations to be introduced by government ministers. This has been the cause of some controversy as, given that secondary legislation is subject to a significantly reduced level of parliamentary scrutiny than is the case with primary legislation, a potentially broad discretion has been given to the government concerning the definition of the final legal regime.

A further reform was introduced in the Legal Deposit Libraries (Non-Print Work) Regulations 2013. For many years, the law (most recently in the form of the Legal Deposit Library Act 2003) has required that a copy of every published printed material is to be supplied by the publisher to the British Library. A number of other, so-called deposit libraries in England, Scotland, and Ireland are entitled to request a copy (free of charge) of every printed work. In reality requests are made as a matter of course. The 2013 Regulations extend this provision to cover works such as blogs and even Twitter postings published in electronic form. As we rely more and more on electronic communications, Internet-based activity is no longer of merely ethereal significance. The British Library has commented:

> If you want a picture of what life is like today in the UK you have to look at the web...
>
> We have already lost a lot of material, particularly around events such as the 7/7 London bombings or the 2008 financial crisis.
>
> That material has fallen into the digital black hole of the 21st century because we haven't been able to capture it.
>
> Most of that material has already been lost or taken down. The social media reaction has gone.[35]

Orphan works

The emergence of the Internet has seen a massive increase in the amount of data in existence. It is estimated that more data has been created in the past few years than in the whole of previous human history. More data is available online than has ever been the case in printed form.

The proliferation of data and the new publications opportunities established by the Internet create many issues for copyright law. A particular issue addressed by the new Act is that it is not always easy for a party wishing to use data to discover who the copyright owner is in order to seek their permission to reuse the work in another publication. A simple example can be seen in the search engine Google Images which will generally link to images but often give limited information as to who owns the copyright in them. At a further level, given the length and uncertain duration of copyright protection—the life of an author and up to seventy year's after death—there are many literary works for which it will be difficult to trace the owner of copyright. Although much remains to be defined, that Act

---

[35] <http://www.huffingtonpost.co.uk/2013/04/05/british-library-to-harvest-web_n_3018784.html>.

provides that the Secretary of State may by regulations provide for the grant of licences in respect of works that qualify as orphan works under the regulations.

The regulations may specify a person or a description of persons authorised to grant licences, or provide for a person designated in the regulations to specify a person or a description of persons authorised to grant licences.

The regulations must provide that, for a work to qualify as an orphan work, it is a requirement that the owner of copyright in it has not been found after a diligent search made in accordance with the regulations.

The regulations may provide for the granting of licences to do, or authorise the doing of, any act restricted by copyright that would otherwise require the consent of the missing owner.

The regulations must provide for any licence:

- to have effect as if granted by the missing owner
- not to give exclusive rights
- not to be granted to a person authorised to grant licences.

The regulations may apply to a work although it is not known whether copyright subsists in it, and references to a missing owner and a right or interest of a missing owner are to be read as including references to a supposed owner and a supposed right or interest.

Perhaps surprisingly, the Act does not define the concept of 'orphan works' but the term is generally interpreted to refer to works where the copyright owner cannot be identified. There is also, of course, the question of who should be allowed to grant licences for orphan works. The Act provides that anybody may approach the Secretary of State (the government minister responsible for operating the legislation). The likelihood is that a licence to grant licences will be granted to the Copyright Licensing Association which is the major body acting on behalf of authors in respect of granting licences in respect of the use of works.

There is much, perhaps too much, that remains uncertain concerning the scope of the new provisions. The general approach is to be commended. The Internet offers significant new opportunities to disseminate data. Books that may have been out of print for decades may enjoy a new lease of life when published electronically—although a cynical author might suggest that it is difficult to think of many examples. We have seen in recent years the emergence of, and litigation surrounding, the attempts by Google to digitise copies of as many books as it can get its electronic scanners close to. The issues are important and perhaps the major point that will almost certainly arise concerns the treatment that should be given to a long-forgotten work—by a long-forgotten author and possibly deceased—that becomes a major commercial success thanks to the Internet.

Harvesting the Internet

As mentioned earlier, the British Library has started to compile a record of the contents of the Internet, or at least those parts which are published in the United Kingdom. Given the global nature of the Internet this may not always be an easy issue to determine. The Regulations provide that:

(a) it is made available to the public from a website with a domain name which relates to the United Kingdom or to a place within the United Kingdom; or

(b) it is made available to the public by a person and any of that person's activities relating to the creation or the publication of the work take place within the United Kingdom.[36]

---

[36] Reg. 18.

The sum of £3 million (around €3.6 million) has been invested in the project. Two techniques may be utilised. Agreement may be reached between the Library and major content providers (such as online newspapers) for the latter to provide copies of works. The Regulations mandate also the use of web harvesters, defined in Regulation 2 as 'a computer program which is used to search the Internet in order to request delivery of online work on behalf of a deposit library'. The software will search all publicly available websites within the.uk country domain. The initial search is estimated to take three months.

Preservation of its cultural heritage has long been seen as an important task for any country. Extension of existing library holdings to include works available only in electronic form is to be welcomed at least in principle. There are, however, concerns about some elements of the project. Collecting and preserving for posterity copies of individual's Facebook pages and Twitter postings does raise concerns about the protection of personal privacy. Much has been written and said about the problems individuals have had of restricting access to their social-networking publications—particularly if their circumstances have changed.

Conclusions

Copyright was born in turbulent times, when the invention of the printing press served as a catalyst for radical political and religious reforms. Although the nature of the controversies may have changed, with disputes predominantly between copyright owners and users, the role of the state as an enforcement agency through the application of criminal law sanctions remains significant and, certainly, the scope and extent of copyright protection and enforcement remain matters of considerable controversy.

Prior to considering where and how intellectual property should develop, it is perhaps useful to look back to consider how and why the systems developed. The first intellectual property statutes were motivated very much by economic and trade considerations. In the English patent system, for example, invention took second place to the need to overcome by force of law the obstacles placed by local tradesmen against those seeking to apply techniques and technologies, established in other countries but novel in England. In order to encourage foreigners to ply their trade in the country, a monopoly in respect of the particular technology would be conferred. As the system developed, the monopoly element became increasingly abused. Exclusive rights were conferred in respect of the manufacture and sale of well-established goods. A particularly unpopular patent related to the manufacture of playing cards. The abuses of the patent system played a part in the enactment of the Statute of Monopolies in 1623, which limited the grant of patents to the situation where a new product or process was invented. From there the patent system developed along well-known lines, with the national dimension of the system remaining very much applicable today.

A similar trend can be mapped in respect of the copyright system. Essentially a product of the invention of the printing press, this seeks to protect a range of interests associated with the creation and publication of literary, musical, and dramatic works. If we look back to the world's first copyright statute, the Statute of Anne of 1709, we see that its scope is limited to the direct and complete reproduction of books. The statute is a very short instrument but one which repays examination. Its Preamble recites the reasons behind the statute's introduction:

> Whereas Printers Booksellers and other Persons have of late frequently taken the Liberty of printing reprinting and publishing or causing to be printed, reprinted or published Books and other Writings without the consent of authors or proprietors of such Books and Writings to their very great Detriment and too often to the ruin of them and their Families.

For preventing therefore such Practices for the future and for the Encouragement of learned Men to compose and write useful Books...[37]

A number of other features of the legislation deserve brief comment. In the event of infringement, although any infringing copies were to be handed over to the copyright owner for destruction, the financial penalties imposed on the infringer took the form of a penalty payable to the Crown. The copyright owner, also, was not free to demand such price as was thought fit for the book. The Statute of Anne 1709 allowed any person to make complaint to one or more high officials (including the Archbishop of Canterbury and the Lord Chief Justice) that the price demanded by a bookseller or printer was 'too high and unreasonable'. In the event that the complaint was upheld, the price would be reduced to a specified amount. Any subsequent attempt to charge a higher price would be punishable by a fine. It is interesting to speculate how such a provision might be applied in the context of today's software and information products.

In general, it may be stated that the approach in the Statute of Anne 1709 is more consistent with the attempt to balance competing interests rather than to confer exclusive rights. It seeks specifically to promote learning. Over the centuries, the range of works protected by copyright has expanded steadily, as has the protection afforded to copyright owners and the extent of their remedies. Less and less emphasis is placed on the educative goals of the system or on the rights of those who seek to use the protected works.

Whilst the basic notion that a work should not be copied for commercial gain remains valid, the application of copyright law is hindered by the fact that digital technology operates in a different manner than its analogue equivalent. Although one motive behind statutes such as the United States Digital Millennium Copyright Act and the Directive on Copyright in the Information Society[38] is to confer a measure of legal immunity on users and ISPs, it is difficult to see why a user's freedom to act in a reasonable manner should depend upon exceptional provisions.

The problem may not be one only for users. Another aspect of digital technology is that it puts extensive copying facilities in the hands of private individuals. The existence of systems such as Napster and MP3 provides eloquent testimony to this. In the Council of Europe's Cybercrime Convention, when providing for the imposition of criminal sanctions for various forms of copyright infringement, the instrument eschews the traditional formula that copying take place for commercial purposes with the requirement that copying take place on a commercial scale. This undoubtedly reflects the fact that a single individual with an Internet connection can, without seeking to secure any direct financial gain, cause significant loss to copyright owners.

Whilst there will always be those users who wish to obtain something for nothing, a perception of imbalance between the rights afforded to producers and users can only encourage disregard of the law. It may be that just as software companies have reduced levels of piracy in part through offering added value in the form of upgrades and customer support services to legitimate users of software packages, so the wider information industries might have to make use of similar techniques. The purchaser of a music CD might, for example, qualify for reduced price admission or preferential access to concerts performed by the artist(s) involved.

At a more legalistic level, in the English case of *R v Gold*,[39] the House of Lords had to consider the question of whether the transitory holding of data in part of the memory of

---

[37] Capitalisation and (lack of) punctuation as in original. [38] Directive 2001/29/EC.
[39] [1988] 1 AC 1063.

a computer system satisfied a requirement that data be 'recorded or stored'. Holding that this was not the case, the court ruled that the process required 'a degree of continuance'. It may be that the implementation of a similar approach could resolve at least some of the issues arising in respect of digital information. In general terms, there needs to be recognition that whilst an author or other inventor may choose to keep a work out of the public domain, once the decision has been taken to make it available, rights have to be balanced against those of other parties, especially those who invest time or money in order to use the work. As is often noted in the context of human rights law, rights are accompanied by responsibilities. It is difficult either in law or in practice to see that these are currently in balance in the intellectual property field.

18

Protection of databases

Introduction

United Kingdom law has long protected compilations of information under copyright law, with very (very) limited exceptions.[1] Most other jurisdictions have adopted a more restrictive policy although where effort and money has been expended in producing compilations of information such as directories or catalogues, protection may well be offered under the law of unfair competition. Rather like privacy, this is not a concept that is recognised as such in the UK although as with privacy, similar results may be obtained through the operation of a number of other legal principles.

During the 1980s and 1990s we saw the beginnings of markets in electronic databases. The capability of computers to store and process large amounts of data opened up new commercial markets. The United States was quick to expoit these possibilities and companies based there acquired a major share of the global database market.

Within Europe a perceived discrepancy in the legal protection was afforded to databases across the Member States. As the Commission noted:

> While droit d'auteur Member States protected only 'original' databases that required an element of 'intellectual creation', the common law Member States also protected 'non-original' databases involving considerable skill, labour or judgment in gathering together and/or checking a compilation ('sweat of the brow' copyright).
>
> – In practice, the higher standard of 'originality' that applied in droit d'auteur countries had the effect of protecting fewer databases by copyright (protection was limited to so called 'original' databases).[2]

The solution adopted took the form of the EC Directive of 11 March 1996 on 'The Legal Protection of Databases'.[3] This is implemented in the UK by the Copyright and Rights in Databases Regulations 1997.[4]

The database Directive creates a new form of intellectual property right—the database right. Its scope and extent will be considered in this chapter but at the outset a note of scepticism may be sounded. Both before and after the implementation of the Directive, UK-based companies have consistently produced more databases than any other Member State (around double the number produced by the next-largest country, Germany). It is almost certainly the case that linguistic issues are a greater factor in market access and success

---

[1] In the case of *Exxon Corpn v Exxon Insurance Consultants International Ltd* [1982] Ch. 119 the High Court held that the single word 'Exxon' was not protected by copyright. This is perhaps the only case in which protection has been denied. In the Scottish case of *Shetland Times Ltd. v Jonathan Wills and anor*, (1997) FSR the court had no difficulty in accepting that the headlines of newspaper stories were protected by copyright.

[2] First evaluation of Directive 96/9/EC on the legal protection of databases. Available from <http://ec.europa.eu/internal_market/copyright/docs/databases/evaluation_report_en.pdf>.

[3] Directive 96/9/EC, OJ 1996 L 77/20 (the Database Directive).   [4] SI 1997/3032.

than legal factors. More generally, as the Commission noted in 2005, the concept of a *sui generis* database right (which is not found in any other major country) may have proved counter-productive:

> According to the Gale Directory of Databases, the number of EU-based database 'entries' was 3095 in 2004 as compared to 3092 in 1998 when the first Member States had implemented the 'sui generis' protection into national laws.
>
> It is noteworthy that the number of database 'entries' dropped just as most of the EU-15 had implemented the Directive into national laws in 2001. In 2001, there were 4085 EU-based 'entries' while in 2004 there were only 3095.[5]

Not the most impressive track record and there is no later evidence of improvement.

What is a database?

The concept of a database is one which does not receive specific mention in the United Kingdom's copyright legislation. The term tends to be used with specific reference to computers; the *Concise Oxford Dictionary* defines it as a '[l]arge body of information stored in a computer which can process it and from which particular bits of information can be retrieved as required'. The initial draft of the EC's Database Directive adopted a similar approach, limiting its application to:

> a collection of work or materials arranged, stored and accessed by electronic means, and the electronic materials necessary for the operation of the data base such as its thesaurus, index or system for obtaining and presenting information.[6]

Although there might be pragmatic reasons for limiting the scope of legislation, there is no reason in principle why more traditional forms of data storage, such as a card-index file, should not also be classed as a database. In the final version of the Database Directive,[7] and in the Copyright and Rights in Databases Regulations 1997, which implement the provisions of the Directive for the United Kingdom, a broader definition applies, referring to:

> a collection of independent works, data or other materials which:
>
> (a) are arranged in a systematic or methodical way; and
>
> (b) are individually accessible by electronic or other means.[8]

The Preamble to the Database Directive expands on this definition somewhat, stating that:

> Whereas the term 'database' should be understood to include literary, artistic, musical or other collections of works or collections of other material such as texts, sound, images, numbers, facts, and data; whereas it should cover collections of independent works, data or other materials which are systematically or methodically arranged and can be individually accessed; whereas this means that a recording or an audio-visual, cinematographic, literary or musical work as such does not fall within the scope of this Directive.[9]

Examples of databases

Starting with non-automated systems, a paper telephone directory can be classed as a database. Here, data in the form of names, addresses, and telephone numbers are arranged in

---

[5] First evaluation of Directive 96/9/EC on the legal protection of databases.
[6] COM (92) 393 final, Art. 1.   [7] Directive 96/9/EC.   [8] SI 1997/3032, Reg. 3.
[9] Directive 96/9/EC, Recital 17.

alphabetical order, and may be retrieved by users through opening the directory at the appropriate page. Card-index systems, such as those catalogue systems which used to occupy significant areas of floor space within libraries, also function in a similar manner. On the basis of the definition cited earlier, one might even class the contents of the library itself as a database.

With the dawning of the digital revolution and the ability to record and store any form of information in electronic format, the range and commercial value of databases has increased dramatically. Introducing the proposed regulations in Parliament, the Minister of State stated that:

> The database sector is a major United Kingdom industry. Estimates of the size of the UK database market range up to £10 billion but even that may be an underestimate. It is growing at more than 11% a year. About 350 firms are believed to be active in the sector, 30 of which are large suppliers and the rest small and medium-sized enterprises. UK suppliers have a share of the wider European Union market which has been put at more than 50%.[10]

Many electronic databases are accessible on an online basis. Most lawyers will, for example, be familiar with the 'Lexis' database. Located in Dayton, Ohio, this represents the world's largest collection of case law and statutory material. The parallel 'Nexis' service provides access to electronic copies of the contents of a vast range of newspapers and journals. Also on the market is a wide range of CDs. Such capacity devices typically have a storage capacity of around 650MB of data. A 500-page book would occupy somewhere in the region of 2.5MB. A single CD could, therefore, contain the text of some 300 volumes, although this figure would drop if pictures and illustrations were to be embedded in the text.

Databases and new technology

Traditionally, one of the basic requirements for a functional database has been that its contents are stored in accordance with a predetermined structure. A similar requirement applies to many automated databases, where data is stored in predetermined fields. With developments in retrieval software and what are referred to as relational databases, it is less and less necessary for information to be stored in accordance with a predetermined structure. In general, the tendency is to allow users maximum flexibility in using a database rather than requiring searches to be formulated in accordance with predetermined structures. Once again, the telephone directory may provide an apposite example. With a paper directory, a user can search effectively only by means of the structure devised by the publisher—effectively in alphabetical order by reference to subscribers' surnames. CD directories typically allow searches by reference to any item of data—or to a combination of items. Reverse searching is a popular feature which allows names to be identified from telephone numbers or a listing produced of all subscribers resident in a particular street.[11]

Where a database comprises an amalgam of data and retrieval software, it will be necessary for the software to compile indexes of words used in the data, such indexes being used in subsequent acts of retrieval. Such a system is likely to come within the definition. More problematic issues will arise where the retrieval software is separate from the data being searched. The WWW, for example, consists of tens of millions of individual items of data controlled by millions of users. It is difficult to think of a less structured network than the

---

[10] Fourth Standing Committee on Delegated Legislation, 3 December 1997.

[11] See e.g. British Telecom's (BT) online directory at <http://www.bt.com/phonenetuk/> and the more extensive service at <http://www.192.com/>.

WWW, yet search engines such as Google provide increasingly sophisticated searching facilities. Whilst it must be likely that many items on the WWW will qualify for copyright protection in their own right, others may not, for example law reports or copies of statutes from countries which regard such materials as being in the public domain. It may be that the list of materials identified by a search engine as meeting the user's request will itself constitute a database. In this instance, there might be a further issue, discussed later—who is to be considered owner of any resulting database right?

Traditional forms of protection for databases

The rationale behind the Database Directive lies in the belief that 'databases are at present not sufficiently protected in all Member States by existing legislation'.[12] This may certainly have been the case in some other Member States, notably Germany, which have required strict qualitative criteria for the award of copyright, but it is less applicable in a United Kingdom context. The basis for the legal protection of databases lies in the copyright system. As we have seen, section 3 of the Copyright, Designs and Patents Act 1988 defines a literary work so as to include 'a table or compilation'. Although there is little precedent on the point, there seems little doubt that a database would fall within the latter category.

Copyright in respect of the contents of a database may arise in two ways. First of all, the individual pieces of work located therein may qualify for copyright protection in their own right. An example might be of a database consisting of a collection of poems. Each poem, it may be assumed, will be protected by copyright. Additionally, the database may qualify for protection in its own right, a matter which may acquire particular importance if portions of the subject material are not so protected, for example, because the author has been dead for more than seventy years or, in the case of collections of factual material, because the nature of the data excludes copyright protection. The names of individual companies, for example, will be unlikely to be protected by copyright, but a compilation such as the FTSE 100 will enjoy protection as a compilation. Again, as was at issue in the case of *Ladbroke (Football) Ltd v William Hill (Football) Ltd*,[13] although the names of individual football teams will not be protected by copyright, a compiled fixture list will be eligible for protection.

Discounting the issue of whether the contents of a database might qualify for protection in their own right, the issue arises of whether the degree of effort which accompanies the compilation of a database is sufficient to qualify for such a grant. Traditionally, a major element of the task facing the compiler of a database has been to determine the order in which the material is to appear and subsequently give effect to this concept. Using modern technology, text can be scanned and converted into digital format. Whereas traditional compilations such as directories will require to be carefully structured to make it easy for users to find particular items of information, the utilisation of appropriate software will mean that the entire contents of a database may be scanned with reference to a particular word or phrase. In such a case, there is less need for the database compiler to expend effort in arranging the layout of the database.

It is also one of the features of many computerised services that they seek to take advantage of the processing and storage capabilities of computers in order to present a comprehensive collection of materials. The goal of a legal database such as Lexis is to provide a transcript of every High Court decision delivered in the English courts. Similarly, the website of the Scottish Courts Administration[14] provides the text of every High Court and Court of Session judgment. This is to be contrasted with the more traditional law reports, which

---

[12] Recital 1.   [13] [1964] 1 WLR 273.   [14] <http://www.scotcourts.gov.uk/>.

contain only a comparatively small number of decisions, and where some skill and labour will be expended by the publishers to determine which cases are of sufficient importance to warrant a place in a particular volume.

The 'sweat of the brow' doctrine

In the event that a database seeks to provide a comprehensive coverage of its chosen subject area, it may be difficult to evidence any originality in the selection process. It is here that a significant divergence exists between the United Kingdom approach and that adopted in almost every other copyright system. As has been stated, the United Kingdom system imposes minimal qualitative requirements relating to originality. In the case of a compilation, the traditional justification for extending protection has been the effort that has gone into selecting the works to be incorporated therein—what has been referred to in the United States as the 'sweat of the brow' doctrine. This approach is well illustrated in the case of *Waterlow Publishers v Rose*.[15] The plaintiff, under contract to the Law Society, had published listings, arranged geographically, of English solicitors and barristers in a publication known as the *Solicitors' Diary and Directory*. A listing of all solicitors was supplied to the plaintiff by the Law Society, and this was used to send out forms seeking further information about areas of specific expertise.

Prior to 1984, a company owned by the defendant had been contracted to print copies of the directory. Following a takeover of the plaintiff, this work was transferred to another firm. The defendant thereupon determined to publish a similar work, the *Lawyers' Diary*, which would compete with the plaintiff's publication. The defendant's manner of work was to commence with the *Solicitors' Diary*, which constituted the only comprehensive public listing of the names and addresses of solicitors. A copy of the entry in the *Solicitors' Diary* would be sent out to the individuals concerned and they would be asked to reply, either confirming the accuracy of the information or making any changes that were felt desirable. The plaintiff alleged that this method of work meant that the resultant publication infringed its copyright.

In deciding the case, the court had to consider, first, the question of whether copyright subsisted in the compilation of names, addresses, and other information published in the *Solicitors' Diary* and, secondly, whether the defendant's conduct constituted infringement. Although it was recognised that the nature of compilations was such that it might be difficult to identify a single person as author, the fact that the plaintiff was identified as publisher established a presumption that copyright was owned by it. Regarding the issue of infringement, the Court of Appeal held that:

> Mr Rose argued that he only used the existing directory to get in touch with the solicitors and that his work was then based upon the forms returned to him...There were something like 50,000 forms and the names and addresses to which they were sent were all obtained from the Solicitors' Diary 1984...In my judgement that goes beyond lawful use of an existing publication and amounted to an infringement of the plaintiff's copyright.[16]

The effect of this and of similar decisions is that extensive copyright protection is afforded to databases compiled in the United Kingdom. A similar approach had been followed in the United States, until the landmark Supreme Court case of *Feist Publications Inc v Rural Telephone Service Co Inc*[17] signalled a significant change of direction.

The case concerned the extent of copyright protection in a telephone directory. The respondent, Rural, was a telephone service provider which was required under the terms

---

[15] [1995] FSR 207.   [16] *Waterlow Publishers v Rose* [1995] FSR 207 at 221.
[17] 111 S Ct 1282 (1991).

of its operating licence to publish a directory of its subscribers. A substantial number of service providers operate in the United States, each publishing directories covering a small geographical area. The appellant, Feist, was a publishing company which specialised in publishing directories which covered a wider geographical area than that of a typical small-scale provider such as Rural. It entered into negotiations seeking licences to publish from eleven different telephone utilities. Only Rural refused permission.

Despite Rural's refusal, Feist went ahead with the publication, extracting the necessary information from Rural's directory. Although it added some items of information and attempted to verify other items independently, 1,309 entries in the Feist directory were identical to their Rural counterparts. More damningly, four of these were fictitious entries inserted by Rural in order to provide a means of detecting unauthorised copying.

Rural's action alleging copyright infringement succeeded before the lower courts. The Supreme Court took a different view.[18] Infringement, it was held, could occur only when what was copied was protected under the copyright regime. Although the level of originality required as the basis for protection was low, there was 'a narrow category of works in which the creative spark is utterly lacking or so trivial as to be virtually non-existent'. Rural's telephone directory, it was held, fell into this category. Its selection of listing 'could not be more obvious'. Rural, it was held, 'expended sufficient effort to make the . . . directory useful, but insufficient creativity to make it original'.

The decision in *Feist* produced considerable comment and controversy within the United States and prompted a significant tightening up of the criteria for the award of copyright generally. Certain aspects of the court's reasoning are potentially significant for the United Kingdom system. In particular, the court explicitly rejected the notion that the expenditure of effort, the 'sweat of the brow', could suffice for the grant of copyright. Even so, the court makes it clear that only a modicum of creativity is required. Although copyright does not subsist in an alphabetical listing of subscribers, subsequent cases have held that 'yellow pages'-type listings, where subscribers are grouped according to the nature of their business or profession, will attract protection.

A further illustration of the new United States approach can be found in the case of *ProCD v Zeidenberg*.[19] As was stated in the case report:

> Plaintiff spent millions of dollars creating a comprehensive, national directory of residential and business listings. Plaintiff compiled over 95,000,000 residential and commercial listings from approximately 3,000 publicly available telephone books. The listings include full names, street addresses, telephone numbers, zip codes and industry or 'SIC' codes where appropriate. Plaintiff sells these listings on CD-ROM discs under the trademark 'Select Phone TM', as well as under other trade names and trademarks.[20]

The plaintiff's pricing strategy was to sell copies of the CD at a low price for consumer use, but levy higher rates for those seeking to make commercial use of the product. The defendant purchased a copy of the consumer CD, which retailed for less than $100. Using its own retrieval software, it placed a copy of the plaintiff's listings on an Internet site, from where it allowed users to extract up to 1,000 listings free of charge. More extensive access, typically for commercial purposes, could be obtained at a cost less than that charged by the plaintiff. The site was soon attracting up to 20,000 visitors a day and, fearing significant adverse effects on sales of its CD, the plaintiff sought an injunction preventing its continued operation. Although at first instance the injunction was refused, the Court of Appeals eventually found in favour of the plaintiff on the ground that the defendant was bound

---

[18] *Feist Publications Inc v Rural Telephone Service Co Inc* 111 S Ct 1282 (1991).
[19] 86 F 3d 1447 (1996).   [20] 86 F 3d 1447 (1996) at 1447.

by the terms of a licence accompanying the CD which prohibited its use for commercial purposes; it was common ground that no copyright subsisted in the data itself.

More recently, litigation was initiated by the legal database supplier, Lexis, against an Internet-based company, Jurisline. In the United States, Lexis markets compilations of law reports in CD format. Jurisline admittedly copied the contents of these CDs and placed the material on a website. Access to the site is free of charge, with the intention being that the site's costs will be met by advertising. As in the *ProCD* case,[21] the CDs in question are supplied subject to the terms of a licence which restricts the use to which the materials may be put. It appears, however, that the terms of the licence are not made accessible to the user until after the CD is purchased. An additional argument advanced on behalf of Jurisline is to the effect that Law Reports in the United States are regarded as being in the public domain so that:

> the limitations built into Lexis' licensing agreement attempt to control an 'essential facility' in violation of federal antitrust law.
>
> Lexis may not use a contract to take public domain material such as court opinions—which are explicitly not covered by the federal copyright law—and create a level of protection that is tantamount to a federal copyright.[22]

The litigation was settled prior to trial but the case does serve to indicate the complexity of some of the issues involved. Whilst there is little scope for originality in the production of a comprehensive collection of law reports, denial of protection for the efforts and investment required to gather the material together might dissuade commercial publishers from making the initial effort. Such a decision would deny copyists their raw material, but would also produce the same effect for the public.

As indicated in *ProCD*,[23] one of the consequences of the *Feist*[24] decision has been the emergence of a new market in the United States for CD and Internet-based compilations of telephone directories. Selling for a few dollars, these will contain hundreds of millions of names and numbers, often providing additional facilities such as a reverse-search option allowing a person's address to be identified from a telephone number. In the United Kingdom, BT has continued to assert copyright in telephone directories and has threatened copyright actions against parties planning to introduce competing products. This situation has now changed, not through the operation of copyright law but as a result of the actions of the Director General of Telecommunications, who inserted a clause in BT's licence requiring it to make directory information available to third parties.

A major goal of the Database Directive[25] is to eliminate obstacles to the creation of a single market by harmonising the level of protection afforded to databases. Although not explicitly stated in the Preamble, there was undoubtedly the feeling that the United Kingdom's 50 per cent share of the EU database market was due in part to the fact that strong legal protection provided an incentive for database producers to locate their businesses in the United Kingdom. An alternative explanation might refer to the advantages of working in the English language and the larger market available to such databases.

The database regime

The provisions of the Database Directive can be grouped into three categories. First, it makes provision regarding the application of copyright to the contents of databases.

---

[21] *ProCD v Zeidenberg*, 86 F 3d 1447 (1996).
[22] Cited in D. Wise, 'Lexis Battles Web Upstart', *New York Law Journal*, 8 February 2000.
[23] 86 F 3d 1447 (1996).   [24] 111 S Ct 1282 (1991).   [25] Directive 96/9/EC.

Secondly, it provides for the extent of and exceptions to such copyrights. Finally, a new *sui generis* right is established to benefit some databases that are excluded from the copyright regime.

Copyright and databases

Article 1 of the Database Directive[26] provides that:

databases which, by reason of the selection or arrangement of their contents, constitute the author's own intellectual creation shall be protected as such by copyright.

The key phrase in this provision refers to work being 'the author's own intellectual creation'. This term is not defined further. In the implementing United Kingdom regulations, it is provided that:

For the purposes of this Part, a literary work consisting of a database is original if, and only if, by reason of the selection or arrangements of the contents of the database the database constitutes the author's own intellectual creation.[27]

The formula that work will be protected when it is the author's 'own intellectual creation' is also used in the EC Directive on the Legal Protection of Computer Programs,[28] which provides that these are to be protected as literary works. When the Directive was implemented into United Kingdom law, this phrase was not included. Introducing the regulations in Parliament, however, the Minister of State commented that:

Some people felt that no amendment of the [Copyright, Designs and Patents Act 1988] was needed to introduce the test and that the current test for the originality of literary works was enough.

The government do not share that view. The Directive is clear. It requires copyright protection for databases 'which by reason of selection or arrangement of their contents, constitute the author's own intellectual creations'.

This is intended to exclude so-called sweat of the brow databases—that is, ones that involve time, money or effort but no intellectual creation, such as the white pages telephone directory.[29]

Assuming this view is correct, it gives rise to the suggestion that the United Kingdom has failed to implement the Database Directive[30] adequately. If the view is incorrect, the effect of the regulations has been to introduce unnecessary complexity into copyright law. Prior to implementation of the Directive, section 3(1) of the Copyright, Designs and Patents Act 1988 provided that the term 'literary work' was to encompass:

any work, other than a dramatic or musical work, which is written, spoken or sung, and accordingly includes:

(a) a table or compilation;

(b) a computer program; and

(c) preparatory design material for a computer program.[31]

---

[26] Directive 96/9/EC.
[27] SI 1997/3032, Reg. 6 introducing a new s 3A(2) into the Copyright, Designs and Patents Act 1988.
[28] Directive 91/250/EC, OJ 1991 L122/42 (the Software Protection Directive).
[29] Fourth Standing Committee on Delegated Legislation, 3 December 1997.   [30] Directive 96/9/EC.
[31] s. 3, as amended by the Copyright (Computer Programs) Regulations 1992, SI 1992/3233.

This is now amended to read:

> any work, other than a dramatic or musical work, which is written, spoken or sung, and accordingly includes:
>
> (a) a table or compilation other than a database;
>
> (b) a computer program;
>
> (c) preparatory design material for a computer program; and
>
> (d) a database.[32]

For the purposes of this Part of the Act, a literary work consisting of a database is original if, and only if, by reason of the selection or arrangements of the contents of the database the database constitutes the author's own intellectual creation.[33]

Given that databases were hitherto regarded as a form of compilation, this approach might not be considered entirely satisfactory, and it is unclear where the division between the two categories lies. The Preamble to the Database Directive recites that:

> as a rule, the compilation of several recordings of musical performances on a CD does not come within the scope of this Directive, both because as a compilation, it does not meet the requirements for copyright protection and because it does not represent a substantial enough investment to be eligible under the *sui generis* right.[34]

Under previous United Kingdom law, there is little doubt that such a work would benefit from protection as a compilation. The question discussed later in this chapter is whether implementation of the Directive will alter this situation.

Licensing and databases

In the first draft of the Database Directive,[35] provision was made for database owners to be required to grant licences to users in certain circumstances:

> If the works or materials contained in a database which is made publicly available cannot be independently created, collected or obtained from any other source, the right to extract and re-utilize, in whole or substantial part, works or materials from that database for commercial purposes shall be licensed on fair and non-discriminatory terms.[36]

It was also provided that licences should require to be issued:

> if the database is made publicly available by a public body which is either established to assemble or disclose information pursuant to legislation or is under a general duty to do so.[37]

At least in respect of the first category, compulsory licences would only be available in very limited circumstances. It might be commented, in particular, that in most cases where only one party could obtain data, this might fall into the category of confidential information or be regarded as a trade secret, and would certainly not be made available to the public. In the event, the proposal was dropped following objections from Parliament, although it is provided that the issue is to be kept under review by the Commission, which

[32] Copyright, Designs and Patents Act 1988, s. 3(1).
[33] SI 1997/3032, Reg. 6, introducing a new s. 3A into the Copyright, Designs and Patents Act 1988.
[34] Directive 96/9/EC, Recital 19.   [35] Directive 96/9/EC.
[36] COM (92) 393 final, Art. 8(1).   [37] Art. 8(2).

had to report to the Council and Parliament within the first three years of the Database Directive's[38] operation, indicating whether the operation of the new regime:

> has led to abuse of a dominant position or other interference with free competition which would justify appropriate measures being taken including the establishment of non-voluntary licensing arrangements.[39]

Extensive provisions are made in the Copyright, Designs and Patents Act 1988[40] for the handling of licensing agreements between copyright owners and those wishing to make use of their materials. The Copyright Tribunal is established to determine disputes as to the nature and extent of such schemes. The regulations extend the scope of the statutory provisions and of the Tribunal's jurisdiction to matters relating to database licences.[41]

Other copyright changes

A number of other changes were made to the provisions of the Copyright, Designs and Patents Act 1988. In order to implement the provisions of the Software Protection Directive,[42] amendments were made by the Copyright (Computer Programs) Regulations 1992,[43] which had the effect of allowing the lawful user of a program to perform acts which might otherwise be restricted by copyright. In particular, this would sanction such copying of the program as was necessary for its use. Similar considerations will apply with electronic databases (whether online or held on disk) and the regulations add equivalent authorising provisions to the 1988 Act. Any attempt contractually to restrict or exclude the operation of these rights is now declared void.[44]

The database right

Implementation of the Database Directive[45] will have the effect of removing the protection of copyright from certain databases. Balancing this, a new database right is created which will arise when:

> there has been a substantial investment in obtaining, verifying or presenting the contents of the database.[46]

The maker of the database will be the first owner of the database right except in the case where the work is created by an employee, in which event the employer will own the right.[47]

It is not clear how much investment will be required to justify application of the adjective 'substantial'. The Database Directive's[48] assertion that a musical compilation will not require substantial investment has been cited earlier. Dependent upon the popularity of the music involved, it may be, however, that a high price will need to be paid to obtain the necessary copyright licences.

The database right is not presently found in any international agreements, although World Intellectual Property Organization (WIPO) has proposed a draft treaty which would establish such a right. Pending the adoption of this instrument (which has been the subject of considerable hostility from certain quarters in the United States, where it is seen as marking a retreat from the principles of free access to data enshrined in the

---

[38] Directive 96/9/EC.
[39] COM (92) 393 final, Art. 16(3).   [40] See Chs. VII and VIII.   [41] SI 1997/3032, Reg. 25.
[42] Directive 91/250/EC.   [43] SI 1992/3233.
[44] Reg. 9, inserting a new s. 50D into the Copyright, Designs and Patents Act 1988.
[45] Directive 96/9/EC.   [46] SI 1997/3032, Reg. 13.   [47] Reg. 14.   [48] Directive 91/250/EC.

Feist[49] decision, protection is limited to individuals or undertakings who are nationals of, or incorporated in a state within, the European Economic Area (EEA).[50] Assuming that the effect of the changes to the Copyright, Designs and Patents Act 1988 discussed earlier do have the effect of taking databases outwith the scope of copyright protection, the effect will be to reduce the level of protection afforded to databases owned by non-EEA nationals or undertakings, without conferring the compensatory benefit of the new database right. To this extent, non-EEA database owners may be significant losers under the new regime. This may cause difficulties where databases are maintained on the WWW. Implementation of the Database Directive[51] in the United Kingdom might have the effect of removing some such databases from the copyright regime, but where the database is controlled by a non-EEA national, the compensatory database right will not be available. The effect of the new regime will be, therefore, to reduce the level of protection afforded within the United Kingdom to, for example, United States-based database providers.

It is immaterial for the existence of this right, which is stated to be a 'property right' whether the database or its contents are protected by the law of copyright. The right will be infringed by a person who:

> without the consent of the owner...extracts or reutilises all or a substantial part of the contents of the database.[52]

This may take the form either of a single act or of a succession of smaller extractions. Where conduct by a lawful user would not infringe the database right, it is provided that any term or condition which seeks to restrict this will be null and void. The traditional copyright exemption permitting such use as comes under the heading of fair dealing is restated in modified form for the new right. This provides that:

> Database right in a database which has been made available to the public in any manner is not infringed by fair dealing with a substantial part of the database for the purposes of illustration for teaching or research, other than teaching or research for a commercial purpose, provided that the source is indicated.[53]

Infringement of the database right will expose the perpetrator to actions for damages, injunctions, or accounting of profits as specified in section 96 of the Copyright, Designs and Patents Act 1988.[54] Significantly, however, although the Database Directive[55] confers considerable discretion on Member States as to the nature of the rights and remedies adopted in respect of the new right, the 1988 Act's provisions relating to criminal penalties do not extend to infringements of the database. Also unavailable are the rights of seizure of infringing copies and the right to demand delivery up. It may be that such rights are of limited relevance to online databases but, as has been discussed, the right extends to a wide range of electronic and manual products.

Duration of the right

The right will come into existence when a database is made available to the public and will subsist for a period of fifteen years. It is provided, however, that:

> Any substantial change to the contents of a database, including a substantial change resulting from the accumulation of successive additions, deletions or alterations, which would result

---

[49] *Feist Publications Inc v Rural Telephone Service Co Inc*, 111 S Ct 1282 (1991).
[50] SI 1997/3032, Reg. 18.   [51] Directive 96/9/EC.   [52] SI 1997/3032, Reg. 16.
[53] Directive 96/9/EC, Art. 9, as implemented by SI 1997/3032, Reg. 20.   [54] SI 1997/3032, Reg. 23.
[55] Directive 96/9/EC.

in the database being considered to be a substantial new investment shall qualify the database resulting from that investment for its own term of protection.[56]

The application of this provision should be non-problematic where databases (perhaps a telephone directory) are issued on an annual basis. Its application to online databases may be more contentious, and the provision cited above was amended from earlier proposals to try to cover the situation where a database was subject to continual minor amendment. The example might be taken of an online database of law reports such as Lexis. In most areas, cases are stored for a period of fifty years. If reports are added on a daily basis, each day will see a database which is very slightly different from the earlier one. On a rough-and-ready calculation, the change from one day to another will be in the region of 0.0001 per cent of the total database. This can surely not be considered substantial. As additions accumulate and are accompanied, perhaps, by changes to the structure of the database itself, it must be likely that the criteria will be satisfied before the expiry of the fifteen-year period. Assuming continuing development of the database, it will obtain perpetual protection.

In practice, it must be likely that the issue of whether the contents of a database remain protected by the database right will be significant only when legal proceedings are brought alleging infringement. A database might, for example, be made available to the public in the year 2000 and subjected to continual minor amendments. In 2020, the database owner might institute proceedings against a third party, alleging breach of the database right. In this event, evidence could be submitted to the court of the state of the database in 2000 compared with its 2015 incarnation. In the event this indicated substantial additional investment, the court would have to conclude that a new period of protection began in 2015 and that infringement had occurred.

The database right in the courts

The extent of the database right was at issue before the English Courts in the case of *British Horseracing Board Ltd, the Jockey Club and Weatherbys Group Ltd v William Hill Organization Ltd.*[57] The claimant in this case is the body responsible for the operation of the horse-racing industry in the United Kingdom. The defendants are a major firm of bookmakers. As part of its activities, the claimants compiled and maintained databases of horses and jockeys scheduled to participate in horse races. The databases were extremely large and subject to a process of continual updating. It was estimated that some 800,000 entries were added or revised each year. The cost of the work was put at some £4 million annually.

The database had been used by the defendant and other betting operators for a number of years. No complaint had been made regarding this. As with so many other aspects of life, the emergence of the Internet—in the particular case as a medium for betting—changed circumstances. William Hill published information concerning horses and riders competing in particular races taken from the database on its website, only for the claimants to allege that this constituted unauthorised extraction and reutilisation of a substantial part of the database. Each day's use of the data, it was argued constituted extraction and reutilisation of a substantial part of the database. Alternatively, it was argued that even if the individual extracts were not to be considered substantial, the totality of the defendant's practices amounted to repeated and systematic extraction or reutilisation of insubstantial elements of the database, a practice which was prohibited by Article 7(5) of the Database Directive.

---

[56] Directive 96/9/EC, Art. 10(3), as implemented by SI 1997/3032, Reg. 17.   [57] [2001] 2 CMLR 12.

For the defendant, it was argued that a distinction had to be drawn between the protected elements of the database, a concept which was described as its 'database-ness', and the underlying information which was not protected. Factual information such as the names of horses and riders and the races in which they were registered to compete could not be the subject of protection under the Directive.

Expanding upon the definition of the concept, it was suggested that:

> Since no right is created in the works, data or other materials, the 'database-ness' of a database must lie in the fact that the independent materials are arranged in a systematic or methodical way, and are individually accessible... the acts amounting to infringement of a database must in some way take unfair advantage of this 'database-ness'. Any acts which do not make any use of the arrangement of the contents of the database, nor take advantage of the way in which the maker has rendered the contents individually accessible, cannot infringe the database right.[58]

This is perhaps the crux of the debate. Whilst early database software packages required that great attention be paid to the structure and layout of the database, modern techniques permit searching to be carried out independently of structure. The idea that a predetermined structure was necessary for the establishment of protection was rejected by Mr Justice Laddie, who ruled that there was nothing in the Directive to support the existence of a concept of 'databases-ness' which, he held, converged two distinct concepts:

> the feature of form which have to exist before a database will be recognised as existing and the features of content or investment which are protected once a database is held to exist. Thus a database consists of a collection of data brought together in a systematic or methodical way so as to be individually accessible by electronic or other means.

The form of the database, might be protected by copyright rather than the database right. As regards the contents of the database, he stated, it was made clear in the Recitals to the Directive that a user was not entitled to take the contents and rearrange them. As was provided in Recital 40:

> the object of this *sui generis* right is to ensure protection of any investment in obtaining, verifying or presenting the contents of a database for the limited duration of the right; whereas such investment may consist in the deployment of financial resources and/or the expending of time, effort and energy.

In the particular case, the claimant had expended considerable effort in taking details of horses and riders from its existing database, placing them in the context of a specific race, and verifying the accuracy of the resulting lists of horses and riders. The essential reason why the defendant's conduct infringed the database right was not that they had copied details of horses and riders but that they had relied upon the investment made by the claimant to ensure that the data was accurate.

The claimants also succeeded in their second contention that the defendant's conduct amounted to repeated and systematic extraction and/or reutilisation of insubstantial parts of the database. For the defendants, it was argued that there was not one single database but that as it was continually updated, there was in effect a whole series of works. Each act of extraction and reutilisation had to be considered as occurring in respect of a novel database. The judge was not convinced. The Directive, it was held:

> has to be construed to make sense... There is nothing in the Directive which suggests that it was not to apply to dynamic databases in just the same way as it applies to ones which are

---

[58] [2001] 2 CMLR 12 at para. 45.

built and modified in discrete, well defined steps. Many of the most valuable databases are those which are under constant revision…

The claimant's database, it was ruled, was a single database which was constantly being refined. This, of course, raises the spectre of continuous protection for databases. If protection were to begin anew each time new items of data were included, the consequence would be that for at least some forms of database—and the one at issue in the present case would furnish a prime example—protection might be eternal, at least for so long as the database was maintained:

> In my view the BHB Database is a single database which is in a constant state of refinement. It seems to have been so regarded by all the witnesses. An attempt to split it into a series of discrete databases, besides being impossible to do, would not reflect reality. Its contents change with time and without any obvious break. So too, the term of protection changes. As new data are added, so the database's term of protection is constantly being renewed. However, an unlicensed third party who takes only older data from it only faces a database right which runs from the date when all of that older data was present in the database at the same time. This does not render Article 10(3) meaningless. First, it emphasises that the term keeps being renewed as the database is renewed. Secondly, it makes clear that if someone takes an existing database and adds significantly to it, he obtains protection for the database incorporating his additions. This would be so even if the new author is not the same as the author of the original database…[59]

Repeated references in the judgment make it clear that the purpose of the new right is to protect investment rather than creativity. In determining whether a substantial part of the database had been extracted, account was to be taken of qualitative and quantitative aspects. No hard-and-fast rule could or should be laid down for the task of balancing quantitative and qualitative aspects. As was stated:

> No useful purpose would be served by trying to assess this issue first on a quantitative basis and then, separately, on a qualitative basis. They should be looked at together.

The importance of the information to the alleged infringer is not irrelevant. In some cases, of which this is an example, 'the significance of the information to the alleged infringer may throw light on whether it is an important or significant part of the database'.[60]

Following the decision in the High Court, the defendants appealed to the Court of Appeal which stayed proceedings[61] to request the European Court of Justice to issue a preliminary ruling on a set of eleven questions relating to the scope of the Database Directive. The court delivered its opinion in November 2004.[62] Largely disregarding the opinion of the Advocate General, the court adopted a very restrictive view as to the scope of the database right.

Initial consideration was given to the second and third questions posed by the Court of Appeal. These asked:

(2) What is meant by 'obtaining' in Article 7(1) of the Directive? In particular, are the facts and matters (at issue in the case) capable of amounting to such obtaining?

(3) Is 'verification' in Article 7(1) of the Directive limited to ensuring from time to time that information contained in a database is or remains correct?

The court referred to the Directive's Recitals which referred to the intention to promote investment in systems which contribute to the development of the information market.

---

[59] *British Horseracing Board Ltd, the Jockey Club and Weatherbys Group Ltd v William Hill Organization Ltd* [2001] 2 CMLR 12 at 244.

[60] At 235.   [61] [2001] EWCA Civ 1268.   [62] [2004] EUECJ C–203/02.

A distinction was drawn between the expenditure of resources to compile and verify existing material which it compiled into a new database, and the use of resources for the creation and verification of new materials. In the present case, the activity fell into the latter category.

The court was also asked to consider where the distinction should lie between substantial and insubstantial acts of reproduction and when repeated acts of extraction could be taken to unreasonably prejudice the rights of the database owner as laid down in Article 7(5) of the Directive. Again, the court's interpretation was restrictive. The prohibition against repeated acts of extraction, it was held, applied only where the end result would be the recreation of the whole or a substantial part of the database. Although William Hill's acts were systematic and repeated, there was not, it was held, any:

> possibility that, through the cumulative effects of its acts, William Hill might reconstitute and make available to the public the whole or a substantial part of the contents of the BHB database.

Following the decision of the European Court of Justice, the Court of Appeal overturned the ruling of the High Court,[63] albeit with a measure of reluctance, Lord Justice Clarke commenting:

> I am conscious that in doing so I have agreed to allow an appeal against a decision which I was inclined to think was correct when the case was last before the Court of Appeal in July 2001.[64]

The claimant's case, it was stated, rested on the approach that the Directive covered all aspects of the process of compiling the databases. The European Court ruling, however, in the words of Lord Justice Jacobs:

> implicitly rejected that approach. It focussed on the final database—that which is eventually published. What marks that out from anything that has gone before is the BHB's stamp of authority on it. Only the BHB can provide such an official list. Only from that list can you know the accepted declared entries. Only the BHB can provide such a list. No one else could go through a similar process to produce the official list.
>
> ...So if one asks whether the BHB published database is one consisting of 'existing independent materials' the answer is no. The database contains unique information—the official list of riders and runners. The nature of the information changes with the stamp of official approval. It becomes something different from a mere database of existing material.[65]

The Directive, it was held, did not protect the claimant's database.

Football fixture lists

The decision in the *BHB* case constituted a blow to the scope of the database right. The extent of this was again at issue in the High Court in the case of *Football Dataco Ltd and ors v Brittens Pools and ors*.[66] At issue in the case were rights in respect of fixture lists prepared for the major football associations in England and Scotland. The defendants, it was claimed, were making unauthorised use of the fixture lists in breach of the database right. It was also claimed that their conduct infringed the claimant's copyright in the fixture lists.

Extensive evidence was provided as to the manner in which the fixture lists were compiled, a process which it was claimed was 'a mixture of art and science'.[67] A range of factors had to be taken into account to ensure, for example, that two clubs in the same city would

---

[63] [2005] EWCA Civ 863.   [64] para. 37.   [65] paras. 129–30.   [66] [2010] EWHC 841 (Ch).
[67] para. 15.

not play at home at the same time. Clashes with other large-scale events were also to be avoided so that, for example, Chelsea would not be scheduled to play at home during the period of the Notting Hill Carnival which is held close to their stadium. It was accepted by the judge, Mr Justice Floyd, that the process involved significant skill and labour. The work, he concluded:

> is not mere 'sweat of the brow', by which I mean the application of rigid criteria to the pro-
> cessing of data. It is quite unlike the compiling of a telephone directory, in that at each stage
> there is scope for the application of judgment and skill. Unlike a 'sweat of the brow' compila-
> tion, there are some solutions which will simply not work, and others which will be better.[68]

Following the decision in *Football League Ltd v Littlewoods Pools*[69] in 1959, it had been accepted that fixture lists were protected by copyright as a literary work under domestic law. The question arose whether the introduction of the database right had altered the situation. It was recalled that one of the aims of the Directive was to eliminate discrepancies in the level of protection across the Member States. A broadly similar case to the present had been referred by other national courts to the European Court of Justice as *Fixtures Marketing v Oy Weikus AB and ors*.[70] Giving a preliminary ruling, the European Court of Justice gave consideration to the scope of Article 7 of the Directive, which provides that:

> Member States shall provide for a right for the maker of a database which shows that there
> has been qualitatively or quantitatively a substantial investment in either the obtaining,
> verification or presentation of the contents to prevent extraction and/or re-utilization of the
> whole or a substantial part, evaluated qualitatively and/or quantitatively, of the contents of
> that database.

The Court ruled that fixture lists were not protected under Article 7. Echoing its judg-ment in the *BHB* case it held that in determining whether there was investment in obtaining the contents of a database, account had to be taken only of the effort expended in obtaining the data used to make up the database and did not extend to effort spent in manipulating existing data. With fixture lists, whether involving horse races or football matches, the data was there and there could not, therefore, be a claim to database protection.

This conclusion was followed in the present case. Unlike in the *BHB* case, however, there was a secondary and successful claim under copyright law. There was, it was accepted, no element of individual identifiability in the work. Unlike, for example, crosswords where regular users can identify the individual styles of the problem setters, no one looking at a particular sequence of fixtures would be able to identify a particular creator. This, it was held, was not required and the true test was whether sufficient judgment and discretion was required to reach the threshold for protection under database copyright. The work involved here satisfied the test and the fixture lists were deemed to be protected under copyright.

How much is too much?

The Database Directive and the *sui generis* right it establishes has not featured extensively before the courts in the United Kingdom. The decision in the leading case of *British Horse Racing Board v William Hill* was widely seen as limiting the value of the right although the decision in Dataco demonstrated the continuing application of the more general data-base copyright. In the case of *Beechwood House Publishing v Guardian Products Ltd and Precision Direct Marketing Ltd*,[71] heard before Judge Birss QC in the Patents County Court,

---

[68] para. 43.   [69] [1959] 1 Ch 637.   [70] Case C-46/02.
[71] <http://www.bailii.org/ew/cases/EWPCC/2011/22.html>.

there was no dispute that the claimants owned the database right but the court had to consider a range of issues relating to the acquisition and extent of the database right.

The facts of the case are relatively straightforward. The claimant company publishes a database listing contact details of a large number of health professionals working in GP practices. The database was first created in 1994 and was subject to a continuing process of updating. In 1997, another party, Bespoke Database Organisation Ltd, purchased a licence for a single use of that part of the database (then referred to as edition 5) which listed nurses working in medical practices. At that time there were 8,363 nurses identified on the database. In breach of contractual obligations the data was not deleted after its single use (for a mailing exercise) but a copy was retained and formed part of a larger database which was eventually sold to the second defendants in 2006 and used in 2007 to conduct a mailing to practice nurses on behalf of the first defendants (both companies were owned by the same person although legally were distinct entities). It was accepted that at that stage 6,901 of the practice nurse details were identical (others may have been modified over the years to reflect changes in personnel). The database was used to send a mailing to, inter alia, 6,000 practice nurses. Of these, 4,783 records were identical to those found in the original 1997 database.

As with many database producers, the claimants had seeded their database with a small number of false entries, in one case using the name and address of its managing director. Such tactics can assist in proving infringement. It would be possible for another party to compile a database covering the same subject matter—all of the data is in the public domain—and produce an identical product through their own work. It would be implausible beyond belief, however, that independent work could produce the same false entries. In the event, a copy of the mailing arrived at a seeded address and the parties were on their way to the courts.

The copying was not an issue but the case focused on the question whether what had been taken represented a substantial part of the original database. There was also a claim by the defendants that the data which originated from 1997 was out of date and possessed no commercial value.

In respect of the issue of substantiality, the Database Directive requires that there should be extraction and or reutilisation of a substantial part of a protected database. The Directive provides:

> 'substantial', in relation to any investment, extraction or re-utilisation, means substantial in terms of quantity or quality or a combination of both.

It will be seen that there are a number of elements here. A database will be protected only if there has been substantial investment in its creation and the database right will be infringed only if what is extracted or reutilised represents a substantial part of the work.

Counsel for the defendants pleaded first that there had been no evidence led to show that the claimants had made a substantial investment in the database. This claim was rejected. Evidence submitted to the court by the claimant had indicated that in 2009 maintaining the database cost the claimant around £110,000 per annum. This was largely made up of staff time spent telephoning around 11,500 GP practices to confirm or update the details associated with them. Although there was no direct evidence regarding costs incurred in 1997, the figures were considered to be scaleable. The judge ruled:

> 37.... if one wanted numbers for edition 5, a simple pro-rata calculation would give them. Edition 5 was 43,000 records, whereas in 2009 evidence, the database was about 150,000 odd records. Thus edition 5 is about 30% of the size of the database today.
>
> 38. Accordingly, considering the number of phone calls made per year, the figures are as follows: Instead of 52,000 phone calls per year, pro-rata about 15000 phone calls per

year will have been made at the relevant time. Thus 8,000 practice nurses in edition 5 will represent 8/43rds of the total, which is just under 3,000 phone calls per year. 6,000 records would represent about 2,200 phone calls per year. The lowest number of all, 4,783 identical records present in the mailing list, would correspond to about 1,800 phone calls. One can do the same with the figures for the man weeks' worth of telephone research. 80 man weeks today...pro-rata would represent about 24 man weeks at the time of edition 5 and 6,000 practice nurses from edition 5 would represent 3 man weeks per year for telephone research.

This, it was ruled, was sufficient evidence to justify a conclusion that there had been substantial investment in the original database.

On the question of whether what had been extracted or reutilised was a substantial part of the original database, reference was made to the decision of the European Court of Justice in the *BHB* case:

27. How does one assess what is substantial? The answer is provided by *The British Horseracing Board v. William Hill...*:

...

(71) The expression substantial part, evaluated qualitatively, of the contents of a database refers to the scale of the investment in the obtaining, verification, or presentation of the contents of the subject of the act of extraction and/or reutilisation, regardless of whether that subject represents a quantitatively substantial part of the general contents of the protected database. A quantitatively negligible part of the contents of a database may in fact represent, in terms of obtaining, verification, or presentation, significant human, technical, or financial investment.

...

44. In terms of the quantitative question, we are comparing 6,000 records out of 43,000 records, i.e. about 14%. Even if one considers the 4,783 identical records, the fraction is about 11%...In my judgment...'quantitatively substantial' cannot require the numerical majority of the records. It must refer to a part having substance. In terms of volume, 11 or 14% of the data must be at the lower end of what could be regarded as quantitatively substantial. It seems to me, however, that even 11% represents a significant part of the volume of the database whose creation required substantial resources...

45. Alternatively, regardless of my conclusion from a quantitative point of view, I find that the 6,000 records or the 4,783 identical records are qualitatively a substantial part of the edition 5 database. It seems to me that the scale of the investment that these records represent, (as I have found, thousands of phone calls and staff working for weeks to compile and validate the data) is a significant human and financial investment. On that basis, regardless of whether the volume is or is not quantitatively substantial, it is qualitatively a substantial part of edition 5.

A further claim made on behalf of the defendants was that the passage of time between the compilation of the 1997 database and the use made of its contents by the defendants in 2007 meant that the data was likely to be inaccurate (the defendants suggested that only 20 per cent of the records would remain completely accurate) and of no commercial value.

The obvious retort to this argument is clearly along the lines that if the data was inaccurate why did the defendants use it? This point was made by the judge, but at a more legalistic level he ruled that:

The fact that the commercial value of what was taken may be low when it was taken ten years later, cannot be relevant. The point may or may not be relevant to quantum, but, in my judgment, it cannot be relevant to substantiality. The database rights last for 15 years. It seems to me that if the part extracted would have represented a substantial part in 1997, when it was current data, it would still be a substantial part of that 1997 database 10 years later. It does not stop being substantial just because time has passed and the world has moved on.

Conclusions

Since the United States Supreme Court moved away from the 'sweat of the brow' doctrine in its decision in *Feist*,[72] the United Kingdom (and to an extent, Commonwealth jurisdictions) have been isolated in terms of the extent of copyright protection. Copyright has been held to extend to subjects such as a football fixture list, whilst the threat of copyright litigation was used by BT during the latter years of the twentieth century to deter parties who were planning to publish competing telephone directories in CD format. There is perhaps little doubt that the British Horse Racing Board could have succeeded in an action for copyright infringement under the old United Kingdom regime. The fact that the case was litigated to the extent that it was may be indicative of a point made by Mr Justice Laddie:

> These propositions dovetail with a more general point, namely that database right is to be construed so as to be narrower than the protection which used to be afforded to compilations under English copyright law.[73]

Given the increasing economic importance of the informational content of databases, this is a rather paradoxical conclusion. As has been the case in other areas, there is a degree of tension between the common and civil law legal traditions. It is arguable that if the United Kingdom afforded too much protection to works possessing little or no literary worth, other Member States afforded too little protection. The result, in the form of the Database Directive, has been a compromise. Only time will tell whether the compromise will be a successful one. In 2005, the Commission published a review of the working of the Database Directive.[74] This accepted that the scope of the *sui generis* right had been 'severely curtailed' by the decision of the Court of Justice in the *William Hill* and similar cases. The basic purpose of the Directive was to promote the development of the European database market and the evaluation aimed to determine:

> whether the European database industry's rate of growth increased after the introduction of the new right; whether the beneficiaries of the new right produced more databases than they would have produced in the absence of this right; and whether the scope of the right was drafted in a way that targets those areas where Europe needs to encourage innovation.[75]

The evidence for the success of the Directive was limited. Although a majority of those expressing views felt that databases were more strongly protected under the Directive than previously (presumably excluding the United Kingdom), the report stated:

> The economic impact of the '*sui generis*' right on database production is unproven. Introduced to stimulate the production of databases in Europe, the new instrument has had no proven impact on the production of databases. Data taken from the GDD (Gale Directory of Databases)…show that the EU database production in 2004 has fallen back to pre-Directive levels: the number of EU-based database 'entries' into the GDD was 3095 in 2004 as compared to 3092 in 1998. In 2001, there were 4085 EU-based 'entries' while in 2004 there were only 3095.[76]

---

[72] *Feist Publications Inc v Rural Telephone Service Co Inc*, 111 S Ct 1282 (1991).

[73] *British Horseracing Board Ltd, the Jockey Club and Weatherbys Group Ltd v William Hill Organization Ltd* [2001] 2 CMLR 12 at 232.

[74] Available from <http://ec.europa.eu/internal_market/copyright/docs/databases/evaluation_report_en.pdf>.

[75] At Section 1.2.   [76] At Section 1.4.

Views were sought on four options for change. These involved: the repeal of the Directive, the repeal of the *sui generis* right, the modification of the *sui generis* right, or the maintenance of the status quo. Fifty-five comments were received, with the Commission reporting in 2006 that:

> 8 contributions support Option 1, 3 contributions support Option 2, 26 support Option 3 and 26 support Option 4.[77]

To date, there has been no indication from the Commission that anything other than maintenance of the status quo is under active consideration.

---

[77] <http://ec.europa.eu/internal_market/copyright/prot-databases/prot-databases_en.htm>.

19

Design rights

Introduction

Whilst the patent system can offer protection in respect of the manner in which an object functions, the system of registered designs protects elements of its appearance. In some respects the regime can be seen as similar to the copyright system. Section 17(3) of the Copyright, Designs and Patents Act 1988 provides that copyright is infringed by a person who makes 'a copy in three dimensions of a two-dimensional work (or)...a copy in two dimensions of a three-dimensional work'. The limitation of copyright protection is that it extends only to end-works that satisfy the statutory requirements relating to artistic creativity. Section 51 of the 1988 Act provides that:

> It is not an infringement of any copyright in a design document or model recording or embodying a design for anything other than an artistic work or a typeface to make an article to the design or to copy an article made to the design.

Especially with the heavy involvement of systems of computer-assisted design in modern manufacturing it will be doubtful whether many designs will qualify for copyright protection. The system of design rights provides potential protection in such a situation.

The development of design right and key legislative instruments

Two forms of design right are available in the United Kingdom: registered and unregistered design rights. The former is the older concept and can trace its origins back several centuries. Initially applicable to designs intended to be imprinted on linen, the system was extended to other forms of product by the Copyright and Design Act of 1839. This offered protection for 'the ornamentation and for the shape and configuration of any article of manufacture'.[1]

There has been a close linkage between the administration of the system of registered designs and that of patents. The Registered Designs Act of 1949 provides that applications for the grant of a registered design are to be submitted to the Comptroller General of Patents, Designs and Trademarks.[2] The 1949 Act is still in force although its provisions have been amended substantially by the Copyright, Designs and Patents Act 1988 and by the Registered Designs Regulations 2001[3] which was introduced in order to implement the European Directive 987/71 on the legal protection of designs.[4] A further minor change was made by the Regulatory Reform (Registered Designs) Order 2006.[5]

Also relevant is Council Regulation (EC) No. 6/2002 of 12 December 2001 on Community Design.[6] This Regulation establishes the notion of a 'registered Community design' which

---

[1] <http://www.ipo.gov.uk/types/design/d-about/d-whatis/d-history.htm>.   [2] s. 44.
[3] SI 2001 No. 3949.   [4] OJ 1998 L289/28.   [5] SI 2006 No. 1974.   [6] OJ 2002 L3/1.

may be awarded by the Office for Harmonisation in the Internal Market—the same office that is responsible for the Community Trademark. The provisions of the Regulation will be considered in more detail later within the context of litigation between Apple and Samsung concerning the question whether the design of Samsung's Galaxy tablet computer infringed Apple's design right in respect of its iPad.

The notion of unregistered design right was introduced to the United Kingdom in the Copyright, Designs and Patents Act 1988. This was brought about in large part because of a confused trail of judicial precedent concerning the relationship between registered designs and copyright which culminated in the decision of the House of Lords in the case of *British Leyland v Armstrong Patents*.[7] The case concerned the design of exhaust systems for cars produced by British Leyland. As with many other elements of motor vehicles, exhaust systems require to be replaced at periodic intervals and a number of third-party companies, including the defendant sought to produce replacement systems which could be purchased by car owners rather than obtaining these from the original manufacturer. We see the same situation arising in many areas of economic activity; a significant example today is the acquisition by customers of replacement ink supplies for printers and copiers.[8] The designs did not qualify for registered design protection because their shape and dimensions were dictated by the design of the original vehicle but the House of Lords ruled that they were entitled to protection under the law of copyright.[9] The somewhat paradoxical result was that a design which could not qualify for registered design right (which then gave protection for a maximum period of fifty-five years) would benefit from the (at that time) copyright protection of life plus fifty years.

The 1988 Act amended the copyright definition of artistic works to reduce the scope of protection for industrial designs. Section 51 provides that:

> It is not an infringement of any copyright in a design document or model recording or embodying a design for anything other than an artistic work or a typeface to make an article to the design or to copy an article made to the design.

As a form of compensation for industrial designers the maximum duration of registered design protection was extended from fifteen to twenty-five years and a new form of right— the unregistered design right—was introduced.

---

[7] [1986] RPC 279.

[8] See *Canon v Green Cartridge* [1997] UKPC 19 where the Privy Council held that a Hong Kong manufacturer who manufactured printer cartridges designed to be compatible with the appellant's laser printers had infringed copyright. The decision in British Leyland was distinguished on the basis that printer cartridges require to be replaced on a more regular basis than do motor-vehicle spare parts such as exhaust systems. The Privy Council cited data relating to the cost of running a printer that suggested that:

> The aftermarket (as it is called) in cartridges contributes a significant part to the plaintiff's profits. The defendant's business plan, prepared when it decided to enter the market in 1990, analysed the lifetime cost of one of the plaintiff's typical desktop laser printers as follows. The initial cost was US$1,700. During a projected life of 5 years or 200,000 copies, the owner would need about 62 cartridges at $120 each, involving a further expenditure of $7,500. [para. 4]

[9] In some respects the decision was a pyrrhic victory for British Leyland as the House of Lords proceeded to rule that the company must be considered to have impliedly given customers a licence to obtain replacement parts for their vehicles and, by implication to permit third party manufacturers to produce and market such components. The issue whether this approach is compatible with human rights legislation has been doubted. Copyright is stated to be a 'property right' and the first protocol to the European Convention on Human Rights provides that:

> Every natural or legal person is entitled to the peaceful enjoyment of his possessions. No one shall be deprived of his possessions except in the public interest and subject to the conditions provided for by law and by the general principles of international law. [Art. 1]

It is difficult to see how a requirement to grant a licence can be compatible with this provision and the Privy Council in *Canon v Green Cartridge* explicitly refused to adopt their Lordships' dicta on this point.

Registered design right protection

Within the United Kingdom, the 1949 Act (as amended) sanctions the registration and protection of designs that relate 'the appearance of the whole or a part of a product resulting from the features of, in particular, the lines, contours, colours, shape, texture or materials of the product or its ornamentation'.[10] The term product is defined to encompass 'any industrial or handicraft item other than a computer program; and, in particular, includes packaging, get-up, graphic symbols, typographic type-faces and parts intended to be assembled into a complex product'.[11] A 'complex product' is any product 'which is composed of at least two replaceable component parts permitting disassembly and reassembly of the product'.[12]

A product will be eligible for registration if it satisfies the criteria that it is 'new and has individual character'.[13] Novelty is established if the design has not been previously published within the European Economic Area.[14] The concept of 'individual character' refers to the fact that:

> a design has individual character if the overall impression it produces on the informed user differs from the overall impression produced on such a user by any design which has been made available to the public before the relevant date.[15]

This requirement has been contentious in the IT field and will be considered in more detail later. Design rights are not available in respect of any 'features of appearance of a product which are solely dictated by the product's technical function'.[16]

Applications for registration are to be made to the Intellectual Property Office. Unlike the patent system where the onus of establishing issues of eligibility rests with the applicant, in cases where an application is made for a registered design right it is provided that an application shall not be refused unless the Registrar can show due cause.[17] The grounds upon which the Registrar may refuse an application are limited and effectively refer designs which may offend public morality or which seek to make unauthorised use of protected symbols such as national flags or symbols relating to the Olympic Games (introduced in the context of the London 2012 Games).

At the stage of dealing with an application for registration, the possibility for examination is limited. The details of the application will be made public and the Intellectual Property Office indicates that a decision should be reached within a month of the receipt of the application. As with patents, it is more likely that the validity of the award will be challenged in the context of subsequent legal proceedings brought by a party claiming that the design is not truly eligible for protection.

A successful application gives a monopoly right to use of the design for a period of up to twenty-five years. As with the patent system this represents the maximum period of protection. An award will be granted for an initial period of five years and this may be renewed at similar intervals up to the maximum period of protection.

Unregistered design right

As its title would indicate, the Copyright, Designs and Patents Act provides the statutory basis for design right. In similar manner to the provisions relating to copyright and to patents it provides that:

> Design right is a property right which subsists in accordance with this Part in an original design.[18]

---

[10] Reg. 2 of the Design Right Regulations 2001.   [11] Reg. 2.   [12] Reg. 2.   [13] Reg. 2.
[14] Reg. 2.   [15] Reg. 2.
[16] Reg. 2. See also the discussion of the case of *British Leyland v Armstrong Patents* at Ch. 20.   [17] Reg. 4.
[18] s. 213.

By comparison, design right gives you automatic protection for the internal or external shape or configuration of an original design, namely its three-dimensional shape. Design right allows you to stop anyone from copying the shape or configuration of the article, but does not give you protection for any of the two-dimensional aspects, for example surface patterns. Protection is limited to the United Kingdom, and lasts either ten years after the first marketing of articles that use the design, or fifteen years after creation of the design—whichever is earlier. For the last five years of that period the design is subject to a licence of right. This means that anyone is entitled to a licence to make and sell products copying the design commencing from the date when the design is first made available to the public.

As with copyright, design right comes into existence with its creation with no procedural requirements. In addition to the general design right there is a system of registered design right.

Design rights in tablet computers

Recent years and months have seen a plethora of intellectual property lawsuits between technology companies as each tries to use its portfolio of intellectual property rights to secure a competitive advantage over its rivals. Most of these cases have led either to a settlement between the parties or have yet to reach the higher levels of the judicial exception. The case of *Samsung Electronics (UK) Ltd v Apple Inc* is a notable precedent with the English Court of Appeal delivering final rulings in October and November 2012.

In 2004 Apple (under the name of, inter alia, Steve Jobs) was granted a Community Registered Design[19] in respect of features of what we now know as tablet computers. The first iPad was introduced in 2010 and a number of other manufacturers, including Samsung sought to market competing products.

Apple's response to the emergence of competition from Samsung was to claim that the design of its Galaxy tablet infringed its design right. In the present litigation, Samsung's lawyers reached the court first and sought an order to the effect that it had not infringed Apple's design right. An additional claim was that the design right should not have been granted and should be declared invalid. Proceedings to that effect had been initiated by Samsung before the Office of Harmonisation for the Internal Market (OHIM) which is responsible for the administration of the system of Community Design Rights.

In parallel with the English litigation, actions alleging infringement were brought before the German, Dutch, and Spanish courts. In both jurisdictions, Apple lost its case although it secured an injunction against Samsung's sale of its tablet computers under German unfair competition law. As was stated, however in the English High Court:

> It was not disputed that Apple has the right to start full infringement proceedings in those countries and that the preliminary decisions are not binding. This action is the first substantive hearing in the Community of the issue of infringement.[20]

Six (or, by the time proceedings came to court, eight) years is a long time in the development of computer technology and the court made it clear that the issue was not whether Samsung's Galaxy Tablet copied Apple's iPad (that might be the subject for a future copyright case). The question was a narrower one of whether the Galaxy design infringed Apple's 2004 design right.

---

[19] No. 000181607-0001.   [20] [2012] EWHC 1882 (Pat) at para. 6

Article 3 of the European Regulation provides that:

'design' means the appearance of the whole or a part of a product resulting from the features of, in particular, the lines, contours, colours, shape, texture and/or materials of the product itself and/or its ornamentation;

Under Article 4, designs might be protected to the extent that they are 'new and (have) individual character'. These terms are defined further in Articles 5 and 6 respectively:

A design shall be considered to be new if no identical design has been made available to the public

A design shall be considered to have individual character if the overall impression it produces on the informed user differs from the overall impression produced on such a user by any design which has been made available to the public.

The scope of Community design right protection is defined in Article 10:

The scope of the protection conferred by a Community design shall include any design which does not produce on the informed user a different overall impression.

Effectively a later design will infringe if an 'informed user'—a criterion analogous to the patent system's 'person skilled in the art'—regards it as equivalent. Apple, as is well known, were early market leaders in the field of tablet computers. Samsung and other manufacturers were seeking to compete in the market.

Judge Birss gave detailed consideration to the features in Apple's design right specification and to those found in the Samsung product. In respect of the Apple design he concluded:

The extreme simplicity of the Apple design is striking. Overall it has undecorated flat surfaces with a plate of glass on the front all the way out to a very thin rim and a blank back. There is a crisp edge around the rim and a combination of curves, both at the corners and the sides. The design looks like an object the informed user would want to pick up and hold. It is an understated, smooth and simple product. It is a *cool* design.[21]

The adjective 'cool' is not one which is frequently found in judicial decisions. It appears again in the judge's final conclusion:

The informed user's overall impression of each of the Samsung Galaxy Tablets is the following. From the front they belong to the family which includes the Apple design; but the Samsung products are very thin, almost insubstantial members of that family with unusual details on the back. They do not have the same understated and extreme simplicity which is possessed by the Apple design. They are not as *cool*. The overall impression produced is different.[22]

An uncool product clearly could not infringe a 'cool' design and the judge found in favour of Samsung.

The next stage was to consider the question of remedies. A declaration of non-infringement was non-controversial but Samsung sought more. It asked for an injunction restraining Apple from continuing to argue that the Samsung design infringed its right. The judge rejected this but did accept a further and rather unusual request that Apple should arrange (and pay) for the publication of a notice in a number of UK publications (including the *Financial Times* and *Guardian* newspapers) and on its own website to the effect that:

On 9th July 2012 the High Court of Justice of England & Wales ruled that Samsung Electronic (UK) Limited's Galaxy Tablet Computers, namely the Galaxy Tab 10.1, Tab 8.9

---

[21] para. 182, emphasis added.   [22] para. 190, emphasis added.

and Tab 7.7 do not infringe Apple's registered design No. 00181607-0001. A copy of the full judgment of the High Court is available via the following link: [2012] EWHC 1882 (Pat).

The ruling went into considerable detail concerning the prominence to be given to the notice. It was to appear not later than page 6 of the newspapers and for the website was to appear on the home page 'in a font size no smaller than Arial 11pt'. There should also be a hyperlink to the judgment both of which should remain displayed for a period of six months.

Apple subsequently brought an appeal to the Court of Appeal both on the substantive aspects of the judgment and regarding the nature of the remedy proposed. In July 2012, the Court of Appeal agreed to postpone the publication requirement pending its final deliberations.[23] This came with the publication of a judgment in October 2012.[24] In essence this confirmed the decision of Judge Birss in the High Court. In the intervening period, however, a German court had delivered an interim judgment which contradicted the findings of the English High Court and found in favour of Apple. This attracted the wrath of Lord Justice Jacob in the Court of Appeal and it is appropriate to quote this section of the judgment at some length as it has wide significance for the operation of intellectual property law within the European Union:

> 56. Firstly I cannot understand on what basis the Court thought it had jurisdiction to grant interim relief...
>
> 57.... It is true that Samsung applied for declarations of non-infringement on the same day, 8th September 2011 in Spain, the Netherlands and England and Wales and there could be (but I think rather overtaken by events given that the trial and appeal are over here) a dispute about which case started first in point of time. After all there is now a Community-wide decision on the point, now affirmed on appeal. One would think that ought to put an end to all other litigation about it.
>
> 58. Secondly I cannot see any basis for an interim injunction. The UK court had already granted a final declaration...
>
> ...
>
> 61. Finally I regret to say that I find the Oberlandesgericht's reasoning on the merits sparse in the extreme...
>
> 62. What the Oberlandesgericht did not do was to consider Judge Birss's decision in detail. It gave only meagre reasons for saying 'The Court cannot concur with the interpretation of the High Court'. I regret that. In Grimme v Scott [2010] EWCA Civ 1110, this Court said:
>
> > 'Broadly we think the principle in our courts—and indeed that in the courts of other member states—should be to try to follow the reasoning of an important decision in another country. Only if the court of one state is convinced that the reasoning of a court in another member state is erroneous should it depart from a point that has been authoritatively decided there. Increasingly that has become the practice in a number of countries, particularly in the important patent countries of France, Germany, Holland and England and Wales. Nowadays we refer to each other's decisions with a frequency which would have been hardly imaginable even twenty years ago. And we do try to be consistent where possible.'
> >
> > 'The Judges of the patent courts of the various countries of Europe have thereby been able to create some degree of uniformity even though the European Commission and the politicians continue to struggle on the long, long road which one day will give Europe a common patent court.'

---

[23] [2012] EWCA Civ 1223.   [24] [2012] EWCA Civ 1339.

63. That principle was not followed by the Oberlandesgericht. If courts around Europe simply say they do not agree with each other and give inconsistent decisions, Europe will be the poorer.

Different legal systems and courts have different traditions but the basic thrust of the argument seems to be irrefutable. If the notion of a single market is to have any meaning, there does need to be a high degree of cooperation between national courts.

A final element to the case relates to the requirement that Apple publish information about the litigation. In an interim hearing before the Court of Appeal in July 2012, the judges agreed to postpone the implementation of this part of the ruling until the full hearing in October. At this time Lord Justice Jacobs indicated that he would, in isolation, have concluded that the 'massive publicity of HHJ Birss's "not as *cool*" judgment had made it unnecessary' (at para. 82, emphasis added). He continued:

83. But I have come to the firm conclusion that such an order is necessary now. The decision of the Oberlandesgericht received much publicity. What was the ordinary consumer, or the marketing department of a potential Samsung customer to make of it? On the one hand, the media said Samsung had won, on the other the media were saying that Apple had a German Europe-wide injunction. Real commercial uncertainty was thereby created. A consumer might well think 'I had better not buy a Samsung—maybe it's illegal and if I buy one it may not be supported'. A customer (and I include its legal department) might well wonder whether, if it bought Samsung's 7.7 it might be in trouble before the German courts. Safest thing to do either way is not to buy.

Although it was recognised that the decision of the Court of Appeal would also attract publicity, the court was critical of Apple's behaviour in the months between the High Court ruling and the appeal proceedings. It had given extensive publicity to the interdict issued by the German court and had taken steps to have it enforced. Ultimately, Apple undertook before the Court of Appeal that it would take steps to have the German interdict withdrawn. Nonetheless, the court ruled that the publicity requirements should be upheld. The purpose, it was stated, was not to expose Apple to 'public humiliation' but to recognise that Apple's conduct in Germany had prompted a fall in Samsung's market share in the UK tablet market from 10 per cent to 1 per cent.

That should have been the end of the matter but the parties were to return to the Court of Appeal in November 2012[25] with Samsung claiming that Apple had failed to comply with the publicity order. It had delayed unreasonably the publication of adverts in newspapers and journals. In respect of its web page (Apple.com/uk), whilst this did provide a link (in the most minimalist way compatible with compliance with the Court order) to a copy of the judgment, it followed this by several paragraphs of text which gave a partial and prejudiced summary of the judgment. These sections began:

In the ruling, the judge made several important points comparing the designs of the Apple and Samsung products:

'The extreme simplicity of the Apple design is striking. Overall it has undecorated flat surfaces with a plate of glass on the front all the way out to a very thin rim and a blank back. There is a crisp edge around the rim and a combination of curves, both at the corners and the sides. The design looks like an object the informed user would want to pick up and hold. It is an understated, smooth and simple product. It is a *cool* design.' [para. 11, emphasis added]

---

[25] [2012] EWCA Civ 1430.

The Court of Appeal was singularly unimpressed. Apple, it was held, had engaged in misleading and deceptive practices. Statements were either factually inaccurate or were taken out of context in such a way as to render them misleading. It must publish the order as issued by the court without modification or addition.

Conclusions

The *Apple v Samsung* litigation shows some of the difficulties that exist in trying to apply EU-wide rights (the Community Design Right) when enforcement remains the province of national courts. Whilst it is apparent that English courts are increasingly citing decisions from other jurisdictions and the practice is presumably reciprocated, linguistic differences must be an issue and it does seem that the results may differ across national borders.

Although it has occupied a fair amount of judicial time in the UK—and in other EU Member States, it is not apparent what has been the point of the exercise. In many respects the case can be seen as a skirmish within a wider Internet Protocol (IP) war but it is not clear if there can ever be winners and losers, at least in the legal sense. In the present case, Samsung won but its market share in the UK has plummeted. The case was, perhaps, on a relatively obscure branch of IP law and there is a massive gap between public (and journalistic) perceptions of the outcome and the rather narrower legal findings. Apple had registered a design in 2004. The iPad it eventually put onto the market was certainly not identical to that design. A major fact was that developments in processing power and designs meant that the 2010 production model could be thinner and lighter than anything that could have been produced in 2004. It was not alleged (at least in this case), that Samsung had copied the iPad.

Samsung won the case but, aided by Apple's publicity machinery, one may suspect that the message most non-legal people will take from the litigation, is that the Galaxy is not as 'cool' as the iPad!

It is always dangerous to try to take too many messages from a single case. What we can see, perhaps, is how fluid IP law is. We have seen the expansion of the topic of software patents and the decline of the relevance of copyright law—at least at the level of non-literal copying. The battleground continually changes and what we have in the design-right litigation is something that sounds a bit like copyright, but is not. It is something that sounds a bit like patent litigation, but is not. At the end of the day, property is about money, and what we see in the intellectual property sphere are disputes between commercial undertakings all of whom are seeking to secure some form of financial advantage.

20

Trade mark and domain-name issues

Introduction

Along with patents and copyright, trade marks constitute a key component of the system of intellectual property rights. In the United Kingdom, the system originated in the Trade Marks Registration Act 1875. The present law is to be found in the Trade Marks Act 1994, which was introduced in order to enable the United Kingdom to comply with its obligations under the 1988 EC Directive to Approximate the Laws of the Member States Relating to Trade Marks.[1] The 1993 Council Regulation on the Community Trade Mark[2] established a Community Trade Mark to operate in parallel with national systems. At the international level, the Madrid Agreement Concerning the International Registration of Marks provides for a system of international registration of trade marks.[3]

As defined in the Trade Marks Act 1994, a trade mark is:

> any sign capable of being represented graphically which is capable of distinguishing goods or services of one undertaking from those of other undertakings.
>
> A trade mark may in particular, consist of words (including personal names), designs, letters, numerals or the sale of goods or their packaging.[4]

Details of trade marks are recorded in the Register of Trade Marks, a document which is open to public inspection.

The scope of this definition is broader than might initially appear to be the case. In our digital age, virtually everything is capable of being represented in graphical form. The process of 'sampling', for example, would allow any sound to be depicted in graphical format. A trade mark has been awarded for the distinctive sound of the telephone which features in advertising for the Direct Line Insurance company. In similar vein, the Chanel No. 5 perfume smell has been trade marked under the description:

> The scent of aldehydic-floral fragrance product, with an aldehydic top note from aldehydes, bergamot, lemon and neroli; an elegant floral middle note, from jasmine, rose, lily of the valley, orris and ylang-ylang; and a sensual feminine base note from sandal, cedar, vanilla, amber, civet and musk. The scent also being known by the written brand name No 5.

This latter description illustrates a difficulty with the system. Although the description may identify the ingredients used, it makes no reference to the relative proportions of the ingredients or to the manner of manufacture. It would be possible to perform a

---

[1] Directive 89/104/EC, OJ 1989 L 40/1 (the European Trade Mark Directive).
[2] Regulation 40/94/EC, OJ 1994 L 11/1. Although dated '94' the Regulation was adopted on 20 December 1993.
[3] The text of the Agreement is available from <http://www.wipo.int/madrid/en/legal_texts/trtdocs_wo015.html>.   [4] s. 1(1).

chromatographic analysis and provide a much more detailed and specific description of the product. This might also prove useful to would-be counterfeiters. In the particular instance cited, inspection of the Register of Trade Marks would be of little assistance to anyone wishing to determine whether a product infringed the Chanel trade mark. This could only be determined by an inspection of samples of the perfumes involved. What is protected may not be apparent from scrutiny of the register.

In terms of their manner of issuance, trade marks fall somewhere between patents and copyright. Registration of the trade mark (in the United Kingdom, responsibility for the system vests in the Patent Office) is an essential requirement. This distinguishes the system from the copyright regime, where the right arises as soon as work is recorded in some manner. Although there are provisions relating to what form of marks may or may not be used, these requirements fall short of the exacting requirements of novelty and inventiveness applied under the patent system. The Register of Trade Marks is divided into forty-two categories and an applicant will be required to specify those in respect of which he or she would wish the trade mark to apply. A sliding scale of fees will apply, depending on the number of categories applied for.

Once accepted for registration, a trade mark will be valid indefinitely. The first trade mark was issued in 1876 in respect of the red triangle symbol found on containers of Bass beer and remains valid to this day. The two main threats to trade mark owners are that the mark will fall into disuse or, at the other end of the spectrum, will become so widely used on account of the proprietor's failure or inability to take action against infringers that it takes on a generic meaning rather than 'distinguishing goods or services of one undertaking from those of other undertakings'. The word 'aspirin', for example, was once a registered trade mark (and remains so in France) owned by the German Bayer company. The trade mark rights in the United Kingdom were lost in the First World War, and the term may now be used to describe any painkiller containing the drug aspirin.

At the international level, the Madrid Agreement Concerning the International Registration of Marks provides for a system of international registration of trade marks. The Agreement provides that the owner of a trade mark in one signatory state may request the national authority to present an application for international registration to the International Bureau of the World Intellectual Property Organization (WIPO), indicating those countries in which recognition of the mark is sought. In turn, the International Bureau notifies each state referred to which must give notice of a refusal to accept the trade mark, generally within a period of twelve months. The effectiveness of the international system is limited by the fact that many significant countries, including the United States, are not signatory to its various constituent agreements and protocols.[5]

Effect of trade marks

As with other forms of intellectual property, trade marks constitute 'property rights', conferring upon the proprietor the exclusive right to certain forms of use of the mark.[6] A trade mark will be infringed in two main situations:

1. where an identical or similar mark is used in respect of goods or services which are identical or similar to those forming the subject of the trade mark and where there is a consequential likelihood of confusion on the part of the public

---

[5] The text of the Agreement (as amended on a number of occasions), is available from: <http://www.wipo.int/madrid/en/legal_texts/trtdocs_wo015.html>.   [6] Trade Marks Act 1994, s. 2.

2. where the identical or similar mark is used and the goods or services are not identical or similar to those forming the subject of the trade mark but where the trade mark has a reputation in the United Kingdom and where its reproduction 'takes unfair advantage of, or is detrimental to the distinctive character or repute of the trade mark'.[7]

In the first situation, dispute is likely to centre upon the issue of whether an allegedly infringing mark is sufficiently similar to confuse members of the public. Thus the name 'OXOT' has been held to infringe the trade mark 'OXO'. In most cases, the fact that the mark is used in respect of different categories of goods or services will defeat a claim of infringement. Where the trade mark has widespread recognition, infringement may occur when the use of the name (or a similar name) is regarded as seeking to benefit unfairly from association with the brand name or is likely to reduce its standing. In one United States case, use of the name 'Dogiva' for dog biscuits was held actionable on the first of these grounds by the proprietors of the trade mark 'Godiva', representing the well-known Belgian chocolates.

Passing off

By no means every name or indication of origin can be protected under the law of trade marks. Although United States practice appears to be somewhat more liberal, in the United Kingdom popular names and geographic indicators cannot be protected as trade marks as these are considered insufficiently descriptive of the origin of goods or services. Thus, a name such as McDonald cannot be protected by trade mark, although, as is the case with regard to the well-known fast-food supplier of that name, trade marks encompass almost every other aspect of the business, from the 'Golden Arches' symbol through styles of writing and design to the names of individual dishes, for example 'BigMac'. On occasion, in deciding on the eligibility of a name submitted for trade mark registration, the Patent Office has had recourse to documents such as telephone directories in order to determine whether a name is in common usage.

A trader finding that it is unable to register its name as a trade mark will not be deprived of legal protection. The doctrine of 'passing off' is a common law creation located in the law of tort and is based on the premise that 'nobody has any right to represent his goods as the goods of somebody else'. The action is effectively one of unfair competition and will lie where a competitor markets goods or services in such a manner that the public are likely to be confused as to their origins. In the case of *Erven Warnink v Townend*,[8] Lord Diplock identified five requirements for a successful action:

(1) a misrepresentation

(2) made by a trader in the course of trade,

(3) to prospective customers of his or ultimate consumers of goods or services supplied by him,

(4) which is calculated to injure the business or goodwill of another trader (in the sense that this is a reasonably foreseeable consequence) and

(5) which causes actual damage to a business or goodwill of the trader by whom the action is brought or...will probably do so.

Although the doctrine of passing off is limited to use of a name in a manner which will harm commercial interests, recent decisions under the Internet domain-name dispute

---

[7] s. 10.   [8] [1979] FSR 39.

resolution procedures indicate that protection may extend to private interests in respect of the practice sometimes described as 'cybersquatting'.

Trade marks and information technology

As with many other forms of products and services, information technology products are likely to seek the protection of trade mark law. Many product names are trade marked—Apple and Microsoft, for example, are both registered trade marks, together with symbols such as the famous Apple logo. In these situations, the application of trade mark law raises no novel issues.

With the emergence and increasing commercialisation of the Internet, many businesses have sought to establish a presence in cyberspace. Typically, they will seek to register a domain name which incorporates their real-life identity. British Airways, for example, can be found at <http://www.britishairways.com>. In some cases, businesses which exist wholly or primarily on the Internet have sought to register aspects of the domain-name structure as a trade mark, an example being Amazon.com, where the.com element is part of the registered mark. The United Kingdom Patent Office has published notices on 'Practice on Trade Marks Incorporating the Word Net'[9] and on 'Registration of Internet Domain Names as Trade Marks'.[10] The notices indicate that in deciding whether a mark should be registered, elements such as http, www, .com, .co.uk are to be discounted in determining the eligibility of the mark. The term will then fall to be judged on normal criteria. Initially, applicants should show that the mark is distinctive of their business or that goods or services have been supplied under the name in such a manner as to show factual distinctiveness.

Where novel issues have arisen is in the relationship between trade mark rights and the allocation of Internet domain names. As the systems of allocating domain names developed, the responsible agencies adopted a first come, first served policy. As the commercial attractiveness of the WWW has increased, so more and more commercial organisations have sought to develop a presence. The impact of a web presence will obviously be enhanced by use of the organisation's trading name, something which may well be protected by trade marks. What many have discovered is that, whether by accident or design, the name is already in use. In such instances, consideration may well be given to the possibility of raising an action alleging infringement of the trade mark. Unfortunately, the application of trade mark law to the operation of the Internet is not without its difficulties.

Problems are exacerbated by a number of features of the system of Internet domain names. In many instances, the names of undertakings may be shared by many individuals. There are in excess of 2,000 Macdonalds listed in the Glasgow telephone directory alone. Although the existence of sub-domains such as.co and.ltd means that the same name might be used in these various sectors, there may not be enough sub-domains to go around. Even where domain names identical to a trade mark have been obtained by another commercial undertaking, there may be no question of infringement when this undertaking's activities are conducted in different sectors. Again, domain names cannot incorporate a distinctive type font or style of presentation of a name or identifying badges or signs.

Additional problems exist in respect of the generic top-level domain names such as.com. These may be obtained by anyone from anywhere in the world. This global system sits uneasily with the trade mark system which, albeit with mechanisms for international cooperation, is still based on the notion of national rights. It may well be the case that the same

---

[9] Available from <http://www.ipo.gov.uk/tmmanual-chap3-add.pdf>.
[10] Available from <http://www.ipo.gov.uk/types/tm/t-about/t-whatis/t-domain.htm>.

trade mark is owned by different persons or undertakings in different states. An example is Budweiser beer. Although this has been the subject of a dispute between United States and Czech-based brewers, for historical reasons, the name has been used by two distinct parties.

In considering the relationship between trade marks (and other legal rights such as passing off) and domain names, consideration will first be given to a number of cases which have been brought before the courts in the United Kingdom. Following this, reference will be made to the dispute resolution procedure adopted by Internet regulatory agencies.

Internet-related trade mark disputes

Most of the disputes which have reached the courts have concerned the question of whether use or possession of a domain name including a trade mark constitutes infringement. Two situations might arise, the first concerned with cases of domain-name hijacking as discussed earlier, and the second with the more problematic case of honest concurrent usage.

Domain-name hijacking

As indicated, domain registries have operated (and to a considerable extent, continue to do so) on the basis of accepting the first application for registration of a particular domain name. This has been open to exploitation by street- (or Internet-) wise users, who have sought to register large numbers of popular names. Names such as Macdonalds, Hertz, and Rolex were issued to applicants with no connection with the well-known firms. The practice of seeking a domain name corresponding with a well-known organisation is generally referred to as 'domain-name hijacking'. As the commercial usage of the Internet has increased, so the benefits of obtaining a domain name which is readily identifiable with the owner's business has become recognised. It is reported that one domain name (pizza.com) has been sold for no less than £1.3 million,[11] with a number of firms conducting online auctions for the sale of attractive domain names.[12]

In the case of a number of the names mentioned above, the return of these to their 'rightful' owners has been accompanied by the making of payments to charity. Other 'hijackers' have acted from less altruistic motives. The first Internet-related dispute to come before an English court provides an illustration. In *Harrods v Lawrie*,[13] the plaintiff successfully asked the High Court to order the defendant to give up all claim to the domain names Harrods.com and Harrods.co.uk. It was noted that the defendant had also registered the names ladbrokes.com and cadburys.com. A spokesman for Harrods suggested:

> There can be only two purposes in him registering the name. One is to demand money from us to relinquish it, and the other to stop us using it. Either purpose is, we think, illegal and we believe that the existing laws of this country should be sufficient to establish that a company may protect its name and reputation on the Internet.

The decision in this case was handed down in the absence of the defendant and is of very limited precedential value. A non-Internet-related case which may be of relevance in illustrating the issues involved is that of *Glaxo plc v Glaxowellcome Ltd*.[14] Here, a merger had been proposed between two pharmaceutical companies, Glaxo and Wellcome. The news was announced in a press release on 23 January 1995, which stated that the new company

---

[11] <http://news.bbc.co.uk/1/hi/7331042.stm>.   [12] See e.g. <http://www.domdeal.com/>.
[13] *Daily Telegraph*, 14 January 1997.   [14] [1996] FSR 388.

would trade under the name Glaxo-Wellcome plc. The following day, one of the defendants, who acted as a company registration agent registered a company under the name Glaxowellcome Ltd. The defendants' normal business was to create 'shell' companies which would be sold for a fee of £1,000. The plaintiffs discovered the details of the registration which would have prevented their own use of the name. The defendants refused to sell the rights in the name for their standard fee, but indicated 'without prejudice' that this might be arranged for a fee of £100,000. The plaintiffs alleged that the defendants were guilty of the tort of 'passing off' and sought an order requiring the defendants to change the name of their company to something 'which did not contain the names "Glaxo" or "Wellcome" or any other confusingly similar words'.

This order was granted in the High Court, Lightman J holding that the plaintiffs were not obliged to follow the statutory procedures for challenging the registration of a company name with the Registrar of Companies, proceedings which could well be lengthy. The court, he stated:

> will not countenance any such pre-emptive strike of registering companies with names where others have the goodwill in those names, and the registering party then demanding a price for changing the names. It is an abuse of the system of registration of companies' names[15]

and granted an injunction 'specifically requiring the company and subscribers to take all such steps as lie within their power to change or facilitate the change of name'.

A more significant and directly relevant decision is that of the Court of Appeal in *British Telecommunications plc, Virgin Enterprises Ltd, J Sainsbury plc, Marks & Spencer plc and Ladbroke Group plc v One in a Million*.[16] The defendant, One in a Million, together with four other companies, acted as dealers in Internet domain names. Included in the names registered by them were:

ladbrokes.com	bt.org
sainsbury.com	virgin.org
sainsburys.com	marksandspencer.co.uk
j-sainsbury.com	britishtelecom.co.uk
marksandspencer.com	britishtelecom.net
cellnet.net	britishtelecom.com

The plaintiff companies alleged that the defendant's conduct constituted both threats to engage in and completed acts of passing off and trade mark infringement. Judgment was granted in their favour in the High Court, with the judge accepting that the defendant's conduct demonstrated a consistent and deliberate pattern of registering domain names which were either identical or confusingly similar to names and marks owned and used by other persons. In the absence of any evidence justifying acquisition of the names, the plaintiffs were awarded a permanent injunction.[17]

The defendants lodged an appeal but the Court of Appeal upheld the initial judgment in all respects. In respect of the allegation that the defendant had engaged in passing off, it was argued that the mere act of registering names was not sufficient. Although the defendant had in the past registered and sold domain names, there had been no attempt to offer the

---

[15] *Glaxo plc v Glaxowellcome Ltd* [1996] FSR 388 at 391.
[16] [1999] FSR 1. The decision at first instance is reported at [1998] FSR 265.   [17] [1998] FSR 265 at 273.

present names for sale—perhaps because the plaintiffs were so quick to seek an injunction. For the defence, it was argued that until some attempt was made to use or sell the names, there could be no element of threatened trade mark infringement or risk of deception to the public. This contention was rejected. Delivering the judgment of the court, Lord Justice Walker identified the criteria that should be applied by a court in deciding whether to grant relief:

> The court should consider the similarity of the names, the intention of the defendant, the type of trade and all the surrounding circumstances...If, taking all the circumstances into account the court should conclude that the name was produced to enable passing-off, is adapted to be used for passing-off and, if used, is likely to be fraudulently used, an injunction will be appropriate.[18]

The judge proceeded to examine the activities of the defendant in some detail. As indicated, a considerable number of instances were identified when names of well-known companies had been registered and subsequently offered for sale. British Telecommunications had been offered the domain bt.org for about £5,000. This had itself resulted in threats of legal action by BT, which culminated in the defendants agreeing to the transfer of the domain name. Burger King was also reported to have been offered the domain burgerking.org for a 'mere' £25,000. After considering a number of similar cases where he considered there was an express or implicit threat to sell the domain names to a third party, Walker LJ described the defendants' conduct as evidencing 'systematic registration' of well-known brands names with the intention of 'extracting money from the owners of the brands'.

In respect of a number of the domain names, the defendant argued that there could be other legitimate holders of the name:

> there are people called Sainsbury and Ladbroke and companies, other than Virgin Enterprises Ltd, who have as part of their name the word Virgin and also people or firms whose initials would be BT.[19]

Even the defendant had to concede that this argument could not apply in respect of the name marksandspencer.co.uk. The court was also unimpressed with the arguments relating to the other companies. Once again, the pattern of the defendants' behaviour was damning.

A number of the plaintiffs also brought action alleging trade mark infringement. Section 10(4) of the Trade Marks Act 1994 defines what constitutes use of a trade mark:

> For the purposes of this section, a person uses a sign if, in particular, he—
>
> (a) affixes it to goods or the packaging thereof;
>
> (b) offers or exposes goods for sale, puts them on the market or stocks them for those purposes under the sign, or offers or supplies them under the sign, or offers or supplies services under the sign;
>
> (c) imports or exports goods under the sign; or
>
> (d) uses the sign on business papers or in advertising.

In *One in a Million*, Walker LJ took the view that the use was in connection with the defendant's business of supplying services. Counsel for the defendant argued that in order to constitute infringement there had to:

> be a trade mark use in relation to goods or services, in the sense that it had to denote origin. He also submitted that the use had to be confusing use.[20]

---

[18] *British Telecommunications plc, Virgin Enterprises Ltd, J Sainsbury plc, Marks & Spencer plc and Ladbroke Group plc v One in a Million* [1999] FSR 1 at 8. [19] At 23. [20] At 25.

These issues are potentially significant in the Internet context. In the present case, the defendant's conduct again told against them, it being held that:

> I am not satisfied that Section 10(3) [of the Trade Marks Act 1994] does require the use to be trade mark use nor that it must be confusing use, but I am prepared to assume that it does. Upon that basis I am of the view that threats to infringe have been established . . . The domain names were registered to take advantage of the distinctive character and reputation of the marks. That is unfair and detrimental.[21]

The issue of 'trade mark use' and the possibility of confusion were discussed in more detail in the Scottish case of *Bravado Merchandising Services Ltd v Mainstream Publishing (Edinburgh) Ltd*.[22] An author had written a book about the pop group, 'Wet Wet Wet'. The group had trade marked its name in categories relating to printed matter. The book's title was *A Sweet Little Mystery—Wet Wet Wet—The Inside Story*. It was alleged that this constituted trade mark infringement.

Delivering judgment, Lord McCluskey made frequent reference to the criterion of whether the name was used 'in a trade mark sense'. He pointed out that:

> a travel writer who wrote an article about a fortnight's hill walking in the Lake District might well, if he had been unlucky enough, give it the title 'Wet Wet Wet'.

Such usage would be descriptive of the topic and would not constitute use in a trade mark sense. In the present case, however:

> The repeated reference to 'Wet' has nothing to do with moisture or political timidity. On the contrary, the use of 'Wet Wet Wet' is avowedly and obviously a use of the name which the group has registered. Accordingly, even if the use is appropriate to indicate the subject matter of the book on whose cover it appears that use does not thereby cease to be used in a trade mark sense.[23]

If use of a trade mark as the title of a book constitutes trade mark use, there can be little doubt that use as a domain name would be similarly regarded. Lord McCluskey went on, however, to consider the defence provided by section 11(2) of the Trade Marks Act 1994. This sanctions:

> the use of indications concerning the . . . intended purpose of goods or services . . . provided the use is in accordance with honest practice in industrial or commercial matters.

In the present case, the use of the trade mark was to indicate the subject matter of the book. The judge commented that:

> In the course of the discussion, as I noted earlier, such names as Ford, Disney and Guinness were discussed. It would be a bizarre result of trade marks legislation, the primary purpose of which is to 'guarantee the trade mark as an indication of origin', if it could be used to prevent publishers from using the protected name in the title of a book about the company or product. If that had been the intention of Parliament, I would have expected it to be made plain.[24]

Accordingly, the claim of trade mark infringement was dismissed. It is perhaps unlikely that a defendant such as One in a Million could satisfy the Trade Marks Act 1994, section 11(2) defence, but the issue may be more open in the case where a site contains material about a trade mark owner. If the author's book could legitimately use the group's name as its title,

---

[21] At 25.   [22] [1996] FSR 205.
[23] *Bravado Merchandising Services Ltd v Mainstream Publishing (Edinburgh) Ltd* [1996] FSR 205 at 213.
[24] At 216.

the same might be said of a website containing information or comment about the group. On the same basis, someone establishing a website to discuss the current United States antitrust litigation involving Microsoft might well wish to include reference to the company in the domain name.

Honest concurrent use

In the cases discussed so far, there appears little doubt that the parties seeking to register the domain names were acting, at the least, in bad faith and without possessing any colourable title to use of the name. Other circumstances may be less clear-cut, with two or more parties possessing rights in respect of a name. The problem may arise in a number of ways. With forty-two categories of goods and services in the Trade Mark Register, the same name may have been allocated to a number of persons. The existence of many national trade mark regimes is likely to result in further duplication, whilst in the case of trade marks which can be used as human surnames, tens of thousands of persons may have an entitlement to the name.

A number of actions have reached the courts involving disputes between parties as to the right to a particular Internet domain name. Many of the disputes have also involved the organisations responsible for the administration of the system of domain names and these have devised a bewildering range of policies in the attempt to limit their exposure in trade mark disputes. If a name is retained following a challenge from a trade mark owner, there is the possibility that the registered owner may regard them as jointly liable with the name holder. If the name is withdrawn following a complaint, an action may be brought by the registered owner alleging breach of contract. The case of *Pitman Training Ltd v Nominet United Kingdom*[25] is illustrative of the situations that are likely to arise.

The Pitman publishing company was established in 1849 and expanded to cover a range of publishing and training activities. In 1985, the various divisions of the business were sold, the publishing business being acquired by Pearsons, the second defendant in the present case, and the training business by the plaintiff. An agreement was reached at that time providing for the continued use of the Pitman name by the new owners.

In February 1996, a request was submitted to Nominet United Kingdom, the organisation which administers much of the.uk domain-name system, by an Internet Service Provider (ISP), Netnames, acting on behalf of the publishing company and seeking registration of the names 'pitman.co.uk' and 'pitman.com'. The application was accepted. Although the publishers had plans to establish a website and reference to its new domain names was used in some of their advertising, it does not appear that any significant use was made of the Internet.

In March 1996, another ISP acting on behalf of the plaintiff, Pitman Training, made a totally independent request for the allocation of the domain name 'pitman.co.uk'. Under the allocation rules operated by Nominet, a system of 'first come, first served' applied. Under this provision, the plaintiff's request should have been rejected. Owing to some administrative mishap, however, the request was accepted and the original registration was removed and reallocated to the plaintiff, who promptly made extensive use of the name, sending out significant mailings and publishing adverts inviting email responses to the 'pitman.co.uk' address. From a commercial perspective, the exercise was not successful. Only two replies had been received by the date of the trial.

It was not until December 1996 that the second defendant discovered that its domain name had been withdrawn. It made a complaint to its ISP, requiring reinstatement of its

---

[25] [1997] FSR 797.

name. Prolonged negotiations followed, involving all of the parties to the case but without an acceptable solution being reached. Finally, on 4 April 1997, Nominet, applying its 'first come, first served' rule, indicated that the domain name would be removed from the plaintiff and reallocated it to the second defendant. Matters then switched to the High Court.

On 11 April, a consent order was made restraining Nominet from transferring the domain name pending a full hearing or further order. In May 1997, the matter returned to the High Court, where the Vice-Chancellor held that the injunction should be withdrawn on the basis that the plaintiff had not demonstrated a reasonable prospect of succeeding in its action. As was stated:

> It is trite law and, of course, common ground that interlocutory relief in an action can only be granted in support of some viable cause of action. If a plaintiff cannot show a reasonably arguable cause of action against a defendant the plaintiff cannot obtain any interlocutory relief against that defendant however convenient the grant of that relief might appear to be.[26]

In terms of intellectual property, the plaintiff's main ground of action was that the defendant had committed the tort of passing off. This contention was not accepted by the judge. The name Pitman had been used for publishing for almost 150 years. The agreement at the time of the break-up of the original company provided for its continued use in this context. Indeed, it was suggested, given the terms of the agreement, if any party was guilty of passing off it was more likely to be the plaintiff. He concluded:

> That there may be some confusion experienced by some members of the public is undoubtedly so. But that confusion results from the use by both companies, PTC and Pitman Publishing, of the style Pitman for their respective trading purposes. No viable passing off claim against Pitman Publishing arising out of the future or past use by Pitman Publishing of the 'pitman.co.uk' domain name has, in my judgment, been shown.[27]

In many respects, it may be considered that the problems of trying to apply national trade mark law in the context of the Internet are intractable. Final reference may be made to the case of *Prince plc v Prince Sports Group*.[28] The plaintiff was a United Kingdom company providing a range of computer consultancy and training services. The defendant was a major United States-based sports goods manufacturer which possessed United States and United Kingdom trade marks in respect of the use of the name Prince for sports goods.

In 1995, the plaintiff applied for and was awarded an Internet domain name as Prince.com. In 1997, the defendant became aware of this fact and its attorneys wrote a letter to the plaintiff, indicating that a failure on its part to relinquish rights in the name would constitute trade mark infringement and impliedly threatening legal proceedings:

> Dear Sirs:
>
> We represent Prince Sports Group, Inc, with respect to trademark and other intellectual property matters. Prince is the owner of the famous PRINCE trademark, which has been used in connection with tennis rackets, squash rackets, other sporting items and clothing for at least the past 20 years in the United States. Prince is the owner of several US registrations for the PRINCE mark, many of which are incontestable, e.g., Registration Nos 1,049,720; 1,074,654; 1,111,008; 1,103,956; 1,233,680; 1,284,452; 1,290,202; and 1,290,217. Our client has also registered the PRINCE mark in many other countries throughout the world, including the United Kingdom.

---

[26] *Pitman Training Ltd v Nominet United Kingdom* [1997] FSR 797 at 806. [27] At 807.
[28] [1998] FSR 22.

Through extensive sales and advertising under the PRINCE mark and the excellent quality of our client's products, the PRINCE mark has become an asset of immeasurable goodwill and value to our client.

It has come to our client's attention that you have registered 'PRINCE.COM' as a domain name with Network Solutions Inc, (NSI) thereby preventing our client from registering its house mark and trade name as a domain name. We are writing to advise you that your company's use and registration of PRINCE as a domain name constitutes infringement and dilution of our client's trademark rights in PRINCE, as well as unfair competition, under the Lanham Act, 15 USC 1051 *et seq*.

This matter can be amicably resolved by an assignment of the PRINCE.COM domain name to Prince Sports Group, Inc, in accordance with the procedures of NSI and an agreement not to use PRINCE as part of any new domain name you may select. While we are willing to wait for your orderly transition to a new domain name, we must have your immediate written agreement to assign the PRINCE.COM domain name to Prince Sports to avoid litigation.

We look forward to hearing from you or your attorneys in the very near future.[29]

The plaintiff considered that the letter related to proceedings in the United Kingdom. Under United Kingdom trade mark law, an unjustified threat to institute infringement proceedings is actionable, section 21 of the Trade Marks Act 1994 providing that:

1. Where a person threatens another with proceedings for infringement of a registered trade mark other than—

   (a) the application of the mark to goods or their packaging;

   (b) the importation of goods to which, or to the packaging of which, the mark has been applied; or

   (c) the supply of services under the mark any person aggrieved may bring proceedings for relief under this section.

2. The relief which may be applied for is any of the following—

   (a) a declaration that the threats are unjustifiable;

   (b) an injunction against the continuance of the threats; or

   (c) damages in respect of any loss he has sustained by the threats.

The plaintiff sought all three remedies plus a further declaration that its conduct did not constitute trade mark infringement. It achieved significant but not total success. Although the plaintiff's letter made extensive reference to United States trade marks and to provisions of United States law, it was considered that it could also reasonably be understood as relating to proceedings in the United Kingdom. The threat of action did not come under the headings in section 24(1) of the Trade Marks Act 1994. Although the plaintiff's business involved the supply of services, the threat of action was general in its terms. The court therefore awarded the remedies under section 24(2)(a) and (b). It rejected the request for a more extensive declaration of non-infringement, holding that such a determination was not appropriate for interim proceedings. As regards damages, the court was of the view that the plaintiff had not suffered any financial loss sufficient to sustain a claim for damages.

Reverse domain-name hijacking

Whilst there is little doubt that the attempt wrongfully to utilise a trade mark or similar identifier as a domain name will be struck down, the practice referred to as reverse domain-name

---

[29] *Prince plc v Prince Sports Group* [1998] FSR 21 at 24–5.

hijacking has acquired some publicity, albeit without any significant legal authority. The practice has been defined by the Internet Corporation for Assigned Names and Numbers (ICANN) as the attempt to use procedures 'in bad faith to attempt to deprive a registered domain-name holder of a domain name'.[30] An example of the application of this doctrine can be seen in a dispute between the Driver and Vehicle Licensing Agency (DVLA) in the United Kingdom and a United States-based company, DVL Automation. Although it owned the domain name DVLA.gov.uk, the DVLA objected to the registration of the domain DVLA.com by the United States company and instituted arbitration procedures before WIPO under the Uniform Dispute Resolution Rules (discussed in more detail later). It was argued that:

> Ignoring the '.com' domain name extension, is identical to the Complainant's famous DVLA name and trademarks. There is no difference between the Respondent's chosen domain name and the Complainant's trade name and trademarks. The impression given to web users is that the Respondent's domain name and the Complainant's marks are one and the same, that is, that any associated goods or services are sponsored by, endorsed by, or affiliated with the Complainant.

It was further argued that as the respondent traded under the name DVL Automation it would have a legitimate interest in the name DVL.com but not DVLA.com. It was also asserted that the respondent had no trade mark registered in the name DVLA and no legitimate interest in its use. These arguments were unequivocally rejected by the arbiter:

> The Complainant claims that the Respondent cannot have a legitimate interest in the domain name since it does not have a trademark in 'DVLA'. However, the Policy does not require, and has never required, that the Respondent have a registered mark for it to have a legitimate interest in a domain name. Alternatively the Complainant argues that the Respondent's trading name is 'DVL Automation' rather than 'DVLA', and therefore there is 'no reason why the Respondent should have any interest in a domain name incorporating "DVLA"'. It is hard to know how to respond to this sort of assertion, except to say that if this were the standard by which a Respondent's legitimate interest was assessed then almost no Respondent could ever hope to retain its domain name. It is an unsupportable statement, on a par with the Complainant's assertion that the Respondent has no legitimate interest in the domain name 'since the Respondent trades as DVL Automation and not as DVLA'.
>
> The Complainant's final assertion, that there 'is no evidence that the Respondent is making a legitimate non-commercial or fair use of the Domain Name' is dangerously close to an outright lie. The Complaint specifically discloses that the Complainant has seen the website at 'dvla.com', which the Respondent is using for its clearly bona fide business purposes, and which is utterly removed from vehicle licensing or any other usage which might be characterized as illegitimate. The Respondent is a registered company, doing business at a domain name which has an obvious connection with its company name. The Complainant notes as much in its Complaint, and yet it maintains this position. It cannot do so in good faith.

The conclusion was damning:

> I consider that the Complainant has brought this action in bad faith...the Complaint discloses that the Complainant is aware of the business and corporate status of the Respondent, and has examined the website available at the domain name. The domain name was registered over 6 years ago, and is being used for a legitimate business.

The DVLA case is in some respects a typical example of the issues which have arisen when a party seeks to stretch the level of protection conferred by trade marks. An alternative form of

---

[30] <http://www.icann.org/dndr/udrp/uniform-rules.htm>.

the practice has occurred in several cases where the target of the complaint is what is generally referred to as a.sucks website. These are typically established by dissatisfied customers of an organisation and, prefixed with the name of a company, provide a forum for the ventilation of complaints against the company. The basic purpose of trade mark law is to prevent confusion in the minds of the public about the origin of goods or services and increasingly of a website. Perhaps reflecting the early and evolving nature of the cases, decisions have been contradictory and, as with the DVLA case, have been brought in the course of dispute resolution procedures established by ICANN or by national domain-name registries. Consideration will next be given to the manner in which these procedures have been operated.

The Uniform Dispute Resolution Rules

A feature of early disputes concerned with rights relating to domain names was the attempt by domain-name registries such as Network Solutions and Nominet to devise policies designed to render them immune from legal action. In many respects, the agencies were put in difficult legal positions. In the *Pitman* case[31] discussed earlier, for example, the domain-name registry, Nominet, was threatened with legal action by one party unless the name was reassigned and with action by the other in the event that it was reassigned. A classic example of a 'no win' situation.

With the emergence of ICANN as the coordinating body for the system of domain names, a new approach has been adopted to the problem of trying to resolve domain-name disputes without invoking national courts. Any organisation wishing to act as a registry in respect of the generic domain names is obliged to conduct business according to the 'Uniform Domain Name Dispute Resolution Policy'.[32] This requires applicants for domain names to submit to mandatory dispute resolution procedures before approved dispute resolution service providers in the event of any claim that:

(i) your domain name is identical or confusingly similar to a trademark or service mark in which the complainant has rights;

(ii) you have no rights or legitimate interests in respect of the domain name; and

(iii) your domain name has been registered and is being used in bad faith.

The onus is on a complainant to establish all of these heads of claim.[33]

Originally, four organisations were recognised as offering dispute resolution services under the ICANN rules:

1. the Asian Domain Name Dispute Resolution Centre[34]

2. International Institute for Conflict Prevention and Resolution (CPR)

3. the National Arbitration Forum

4. WIPO.[35]

The CPR Institute and the National Arbitration Forum—which described itself as the 'largest provider of domain name dispute resolution in North America'—are no longer active in the field. Throughout, the major player has been the WIPO, which as of 2007 had received almost 12,000 complaints concerning the use of domain names.

---

[31] *Pitman Training Ltd v Nominet United Kingdom* [1997] FSR 797.
[32] Available from <http://www.icann.org/udrp/udrp.htm>.
[33] Uniform Dispute Resolution Rules, r. 4a.   [34] <https://www.adndrc.org>.
[35] <http://arbiter.wipo.int/domains/>.

An early decision of the WIPO dispute resolution panel in the case of *Jeanette Winterson v Mark Hogarth* illustrates how these requirements might be applied. In this case, the complainant, a well-known author, objected to the registration of the domain names:

jeanettewinterson.com

jeanettewinterson.net

jeanettewinterson.org

by the respondent, a Cambridge University academic.[36]

In circumstances similar to those at issue in the *One in a Million* case,[37] the registrant had registered a range of domains, making use of the names of well-known authors. Contact had been made with a number of these; in the case of one, Joanna Trollope, a letter was sent to her literary agent indicating the intent to auction the names to third parties, but giving the author a right of 'first refusal' to acquire the names for a fee of 3 per cent of her 1999 gross book sales. Similar communications were made to the complainant.

In answering to complaints, the respondent wrote to the effect that:

> The Complainant also contends that the Respondent has no rights to or legitimate interests in respect of the domain names in issue, that the Complainant has not consented to use of the Mark by the Respondent and that the Respondent has registered and is using the domain names in bad faith.

The respondent stated that:

> he registered the domain names in issue in the belief that JEANETTE WINTERSON was not a trade mark or a service mark and that the domain names in issue were registered with a view to developing a website devoted to the work of the Complainant.

It was held by the panel that the Uniform Domain Name Dispute Resolution Policy required that a complainant establish all three grounds specified—namely, use of an identical or confusingly similar mark, in breach of a trade or service mark in which the respondent has no rights, and in circumstances evidencing bad faith.

It is clear that the name used is effectively identical to the complainant's name. More significant was the finding of the panel in respect of the next ground. Here, it was ruled that:

> The Rules do *not* require that the Complainant's trademark be registered by a government authority or agency for such a right to exist.

The complainant being resident in England, it was ruled, English law had to be applied to determine the extent of rights. The doctrine of passing off, it was held could also be invoked:

> 6.11 There are a number of English cases dealing with passing-off the names of well-known individuals and personalities, which all—as may be expected—turn on the facts. These include, the Uncle MAC case [*McCulloch v Lewis A May (Produce Distributors) Ltd* [1947] 2 All ER 845]; the KOJAK case [*Taverner Rutledge v Trexpalm* (1975) FSR 479]; the WOMBLES case [*Wombles Ltd v Wombles Skips Ltd* [1977] RPC 99]; the ABBA case [*Lyngstad v Anabas Products* [1977] FSR 62]; and the Teenage Mutant Ninja Turtles case [*Mirage Studios v Counter Feat Clothing Co Ltd* [1991] FSR 145]. The case for decision here does not concern whether or not passing-off has occurred *but* whether the Complainant (Jeanette Winterson)

---

[36] A copy of the decision can be obtained from <http://arbiter.wipo.int/domains/decisions/index.html>.

[37] *British Telecommunications plc, Virgin Enterprises Ltd, J Sainsbury plc, Marks & Spencer plc and Ladbroke Group plc v One in a Million* [1999] FSR 1.

has rights in her name sufficient to constitute a trade mark for the purposes of para. 4a of the Policy.

6.12 In the Panel's view, *trademarks* where used in para. 4a of the Policy is not to be construed by reference to the criteria of registrability under English law [the ELVIS PRESLEY case] but more broadly in terms of the distinctive features of a person's activities, in other words, akin to the common law right to prevent unauthorised use of a name. Thus, applying English law the Complainant clearly would have a cause of action to prevent unauthorized use of the Mark JEANETTE WINTERSON in passing-off.

The other tests being satisfied, the panel ordered that the registrations should be transferred to the complainant.

The decision in this case appears in line with the authorities cited. The complainant was a well-known and successful author and the effect of the registrations complained of would satisfy the criteria for the award of a remedy by the English courts. The English courts have never, however, accepted that any general right to personality exists which can be infringed by use of a name or other indications of identity.[38] It must remain an open question whether any action would lie against registrations such as those reported to have been made in the name of the recent Prime Minister Tony Blair's youngest son ('leoblair.com' and 'leoblair.co.uk').

Some time after the development of dispute resolution schemes for WWW sites within the generic top-level domains, a similar scheme was adopted to deal with disputes within the.uk top-level domain. Operated by the domain-name registry Nominet, a panel of around thirty experts act as adjudicators with individual cases being heard by a single person.[39] The basis for any complaint is that there has been 'abusive registration of a domain name'. This encompasses a domain name which either:

i.   was registered or otherwise acquired in a manner which, at the time when the registration or acquisition took place, took unfair advantage of or was unfairly detrimental to the Complainant's Rights; or

ii. has been used in a manner which took unfair advantage of or was unfairly detrimental to the Complainant's Rights.[40]

Beyond substituting the perhaps more pejorative term 'abusive registration' for the ICANN criterion of 'bad faith', the substance of the policy is broadly similar.

The first decision under the new procedure was delivered in 2001. The pharmaceutical company, Eli Lilly, was successful in its application to have rights in the domain xigris.ci.uk transferred to it. Eli Lilly had obtained a European Community Trade Mark in the name Xigris in 1999. The domain name had been registered by an ex-employee in June 2001. No representations were made by the employee in response to Eli Lilly's complaint and, although there was no evidence available as to the purpose for which the registration might have been made, the expert held that the circumstances surrounding the case were such that a prima facie case of abuse had been made out and that, in the absence of any attempt at explanation, the request for transfer should be granted.[41]

In total, more than 6,000 disputes have been referred to the United Kingdom dispute resolution service, although around 25 per cent of these have been declared invalid on procedural grounds and did not therefore proceed to any form of dispute resolution. Following receipt of a valid complaint, the first step in the process is to attempt mediation and more

---

[38] See discussion in W. Cornish and D. Llewelyn, *Intellectual Property: Patents, Copyrights, Trademarks and Allied Rights* (London, 2007), paras. 16.33–16.34.   [39] <http://www.nominet.org.uk/disputes/drs/>.

[40] <http://www.nominet.org.uk/disputes/when-use-drs/policy-and-procedure/drs-policy>.

[41] DRS 0001 (2001).

than half of the cases are resolved at this stage. As of September 2007, 728 cases had proceeded to the stage of a hearing before an expert. In almost 80 per cent of cases the decision was in favour of the complainant but in three cases, as well as finding for the respondent, the expert made the determination that reverse domain-name hijacking had taken place. Appeals may be made against the decision of an individual expert. These will be heard before a panel of three experts. To date, twenty appeals have been made, half being determined in favour of the appellant and half sustaining the original decision. The roll-call of complainants includes some of the best-known names in the United Kingdom's commercial and public life, featuring organisations such as Harrods, Vodaphone, Barclays Bank, Nokia, the Royal Marines, and Interflora. It appears almost to be the case that an incident of cybersquatting is an integral consequence of commercial success.

Trade marks and Internet search engines

During the initial days of the Internet there was substantial litigation concerning the use of trade marks as a component of an Internet domain name. Thanks to the adoption of ICANN's domain-name dispute resolution policy and its national equivalents, these issues have largely disappeared from the law courts. As one source of litigation has dried up, however, others have surfaced in respect of the use of trademarks to influence the manner in which search engines present users with the results of search requests and also the responsibility of online market places such as eBay where counterfeit goods are offered for sale on their virtual premises.

The workings of search engines are complex and different engines utilise different algorithms to determine the order in which results are presented. This raises some interesting legal issues and the case of *Interflora v Marks and Spencer*[42] illustrates well some of the problems in the field.

The claimant Interflora is the accepted market leader in the sector consisting of the remote delivery of flowers. In the United Kingdom it delivers some 3.2 million flower orders every year accounting for about 18 per cent of the total market for cut flowers (around 65 per cent is represented by direct sales in supermarkets and other retailers). When Interflora was established, in 1908, customers would visit a local outlet and a telephone or telegraph order would be placed with the franchisee closest to the recipient's address. As with many other businesses much of the activity is now carried out online and more than half of orders are now placed that way.

Interflora is essentially a network operation involving cooperation between thousands of independent florist companies. It has some 40,000 members in 140 countries. Traditionally, members have been small operators with only one or two sales outlets. More recently Interflora has entered into marketing agreements with some larger suppliers including the major UK supermarket chain Sainsbury's. As was noted in court:

> From 1995 to about 2000 IBU had a relationship with Sainsbury's that involved co-branded Sainsbury's/Interflora leaflets being placed in selected Sainsbury's stores. These invited customers to place an order with Interflora via a dedicated telephone number. Calls on that number were answered 'Interflora Sainsbury's'.

Essentially, the operation was a virtual one. Orders placed via the Sainsbury promotion would be passed on for fulfillment by local Interflora members and the flowers delivered would carry only the Interflora branding. A further and continuing relationship exists

---

[42] [2013] EWHC 1291.

between Interflora and the Cooperative funeral care service under which the availability of Interflora funeral wreaths is advertised on the Cooperative website.

The Interflora brand is widely recognised and, as was noted in court, the term is widely used in web searches by users wishing to arrange for the delivery of flowers:

> According to a United Kingdom newsletter...in February 2008 **interflora** was the most searched for term in the flower sector and accounted for one in five visits to the top 25 flower websites, followed by the generic term "flowers". At that time M & S was not listed in the top 10 flower delivery websites. **Interflora** was searched for 30 times more frequently than 'marks and spencer flowers'.

The name 'Interflora' is protected under trade mark law and there was no suggestion that the trade mark is not fully valid. Search engines such as Google earn almost all of their income from advertising and a major component of this income comes from companies who are willing to pay in return for their goods or services being given a high ranking in what have been referred to at various times as 'sponsored links' or 'Ads' (advertisements).

A company wishing to advertise in this manner will seek to register a number of words with Google. When a user types the word the relevant sponsored link box will appear. Many companies make extensive use of this service. In respect of the first defendant, evidence was given to the effect that:

> Over time, M & S has built up a large number of keywords it bids on. As at 21 December 2012, there were approximately 4.2 million keywords spread across 80,556 ad groups, 2,659 campaigns and 32 accounts. The vast majority of these keywords are generic terms, such as 'suits'. Many of them are selected on exact match, but M & S also use phrase match, broad match and negative matching. Mr Lemon's evidence was that about 92.5% of M & S's keyword advertising budget was now spent on generic terms, about 5% supporting M & S's own brands and about 2.5% on competitive brand bidding.[43]

Google UK (unlike many of its other European affiliates) allows advertisers to pay to register third-party trade marks as search terms. More than one company may register the same terms and indeed a sort of auction can occur whereby the company that offers the highest payment will receive the highest ranking in the sponsored links. A user entering a search request will receive on the first results page a list of sponsored links clearly marked as such within a shaded box. This will be followed by a ranking of results in accordance with the normal operation of the search engine's algorithms. Payment by the advertiser to Google is triggered when a user clicks on the sponsored link and is taken to the relevant home page.

The claimants alleged that the actions of Marks and Spencer constituted unlawful use of their trade mark. Following an initial hearing before the High Court in 2009,[44] a number of questions relating to the scope and extent of trade mark law were referred to the European Court of Justice[45] which delivered its ruling in 2011.[46] Following a series of domestic procedural issues, the case returned to the High Court which delivered its ruling in May 2013.

Initial consideration was given to Article 16 of the Trade Related Aspects of Intellectual Property Rights Agreement which provides that:

> The owner of a registered trademark shall have the exclusive right to prevent all third parties not having the owner's consent from using in the course of trade identical or similar signs for goods or services which are identical or similar to those in respect of which the trademark is registered where such use would result in a likelihood of confusion. In case of the use of an identical sign for identical goods or services, a likelihood of confusion shall be presumed...

---

[43] At para. 133   [44] [2009] EWHC 1095 (Ch).   [45] [2010] EWHC 925 (Ch).
[46] [2011] ECR I-0000.

Whilst Article 5 of the European Trademark Directive states that:

> The registered trade mark shall confer on the proprietor exclusive rights therein. The proprietor shall be entitled to prevent all third parties not having his consent from using in the course of trade:
>
> (a) any sign which is identical with the trade mark in relation to goods or services which are identical with those for which the trade mark is registered;
>
> (b) any sign where, because of its identity with, or similarity to, the trade mark and the identity or similarity of goods or services covered by the trade mark and the sign, there exists a likelihood of confusion on the part of the public, which includes the likelihood of association between the sign and the trade mark

In a classic case of trade mark infringement the infringer will place names or logos belonging to the right holder on what are effectively counterfeit goods. The situation in the present case is somewhat different in that there was no visible use by the defendants of the Interflora trade mark. As Mr Justice Arnold noted:

> The case law of the CJEU establishes that the proprietor of a trade mark can only succeed in a claim under Article 5(1)(a) of the Directive...if six conditions are satisfied: (i) there must be use of a sign by a third party within the relevant territory; (ii) the use must be in the course of trade; (iii) it must be without the consent of the proprietor of the trade mark; (iv) it must be of a sign which is identical to the trade mark; (v) it must be in relation to goods or services which are identical to those for which the trade mark is registered; and (vi) it must affect or be liable to affect the functions of the trade mark.

It was accepted that the first five conditions had been established by the claimants and the discussion focused on the final condition: had the defendants' conduct affected the functioning of the Interflora trade mark? In order to determine this it was necessary to consider other authorities, in particular the decision of the European Court in the further trade mark case of *L'Oreal and ors v eBay and ors*,[47] following a further reference made by Mr Justice Arnold in July 2009.[48]

In this case a series of ten questions were referred to the European Court concerning the legality under trade mark law of the offering for sale on eBay of a range of cosmetic products in respect of which trade mark rights were unquestionably owned by L'Oreal. Some of the questions referred to the conduct of the sellers but probably the major issues of principle related to the extent to which eBay, which provided the online marketplace for sales, would be liable in its own right for trade mark infringement on the part of its users or whether it might benefit from the protection of the defence provided under the E-Commerce Directive to the effect that it acted merely as a host for material provided by its users. This states that:

> 1. Where an information society service is provided that consists of the storage of information provided by a recipient of the service, Member States shall ensure that the service provider is not liable for the information stored at the request of a recipient of the service, on condition that:
>
>   (a) the provider does not have actual knowledge of illegal activity or information and, as regards claims for damages, is not aware of facts or circumstances from which the illegal activity or information is apparent; or
>
>   (b) the provider, upon obtaining such knowledge or awareness, acts expeditiously to remove or to disable access to the information.

---

[47] Case C-324/09.   [48] [2009] EWHC 1094.

Although there is to be no liability in damages (or also under criminal law), the Directive makes it clear that there is to be no immunity from the grant of a court order 'requiring the service provider to terminate or prevent an infringement' (injunctive relief).

In respect of the liability of the individual sellers the Court made the important observation that trade mark rights can be enforced only against a party who acts in the course of trade—'in the context of a commercial activity'. The emergence of sites such as eBay does undoubtedly create some issues in determining whether sellers are acting in the course of a business. In the real world the status of a seller may be readily apparent from the nature of the premises used for transactions. This is less apparent on sites such as eBay and the distinction between private sellers, those acting in the course of a hobby, and outright commercial sellers is not always easy to make.

As with most aspects of life, the operations of eBay are not entirely simple and straightforward and a number of issues are discussed. Three are of particular importance. Does the fact that eBay processes its user's data in order, for example, to allow online auctions to be conducted take it outside the scope of the 'hosting' defence? Secondly, assuming the defence is potentially available, what level of awareness might be ascribed to eBay regarding the presence of materials on its site in circumstances that would suffice to take it outside its protection? Finally, the Court considered the nature of the injunctive relief which might be available against eBay to claimants such as those in the present case.

In common with many aspects of the legislation, the E-Commerce Directive offers little guidance as to the scope of the activity of hosting, although Recital 42 of the Directive indicates that:

> The exemptions from liability established in this Directive cover only cases where the activity of the information society service provider is limited to the technical process of operating and giving access to a communication network over which information made available by third parties is transmitted or temporarily stored, for the sole purpose of making the transmission more efficient; this activity is of a mere technical, automatic and passive nature, which implies that the information society service provider has neither knowledge of nor control over the information which is transmitted or stored.

There is no doubt that eBay acts as more than a passive host in respect of its customers' data. The Court provides a synopsis of its *modus operandi* in paragraphs 28–30 of its judgment:

> eBay operates an electronic marketplace on which are displayed listings of goods offered for sale by persons who have registered for that purpose with eBay and have created a seller's account with it. eBay charges a percentage fee on completed transactions.
>
> eBay enables prospective buyers to bid for items offered by sellers. It also allows items to be sold without an auction, and thus for a fixed price, by means of a system known as 'Buy It Now'. Sellers can also set up online shops on eBay sites. An online shop lists all the items offered for sale by one seller at a given time.
>
> Sellers and buyers must accept eBay's online-market user agreement. One of the terms of that agreement is a prohibition on selling counterfeit items and on infringing trade marks.

In spite of this, the Court ruled that:

> the mere fact that the operator of an online marketplace stores offers for sale on its server, sets the terms of its service, is remunerated for that service and provides general information to its customers cannot have the effect of denying it the exemptions from liability provided for by Directive 2000/31.

This, however, is not the end of the matter. The issue of when eBay might be assumed to be aware of illegal actions by its users is of great significance. In the case of ordinary (typically non-commercial users), the Court ruled that:

In situations in which that provider has confined itself to a merely technical and automatic processing of data and in which, as a consequence, the rule stated in Article 14(1) of Directive 2000/31 applies to it, it may none the less only be exempt, under paragraph 1, from any liability for unlawful data that it has stored on condition that it has not had 'actual knowledge of illegal activity or information' and, as regards claims for damages, has not been 'aware of facts or circumstances from which the illegal activity or information is apparent' or that, having obtained such knowledge or awareness, it has acted expeditiously to remove, or disable access to, the information.

For ordinary users the Court indicated that to benefit from the exemption a site owner would have to publish contact details in a sufficiently prominent manner to facilitate the making of complaints by right owners. This is itself a requirement of the Electronic Commerce Directive.

All users, however, are not the same and in some cases eBay will seek to develop a closer relationship with commercial sellers. eBay's documentation refers to the concept of 'power sellers' who have generated significant sales over a period of time. The site also embodies the concepts of anchor sites. As the Court noted:

In some cases eBay assists sellers in order to enhance their offers for sale, to set up online shops, to promote and increase their sales. It also advertises some of the products sold on its marketplace using search engine operators such as Google to trigger the display of advertisements.

In such a situation a higher degree of responsibility would lie with eBay. In words perhaps analogous to Mr Justice Arnold's comments in the High Court suggesting that eBay should stand behind its sellers as an insurer in the event of any claim of infringement of intellectual property rights, the European Court ruled that:

Where ... the operator has provided assistance which entails, in particular, optimising the presentation of the offers for sale in question or promoting those offers, it must be considered not to have taken a neutral position between the customer-seller concerned and potential buyers but to have played an active role of such a kind as to give it knowledge of, or control over, the data relating to those offers for sale. It cannot then rely, in the case of those data, on the exemption from liability referred to in Article 14(1) of Directive 2000/31.

The European Court considered the extent to which right owners might be entitled to seek injunctive relief against information society service providers. Although not explicitly stated in the E-Commerce Directive, such remedies are certainly not excluded as is the case with other forms of civil and criminal liability.

The key issue which the Court was asked to address concerned the range of parties against whom injunctive relief might be sought and, quite recently in the UK in the light of the recent controversy about super-injunctions, the breadth of the coverage of injunctions. In this context the European Court's pronouncements have also to take account of the provisions of the Copyright Enforcement Directive.[49] Under this, Member States are required to ensure 'that rightholders are in a position to apply for an injunction against intermediaries whose services are used by a third party to infringe an intellectual property right...'

---

[49] Directive 2004/48/EC of 29 April 2004 on the enforcement of intellectual property rights. OJ 2004 L 195/16.

A key issue for the Court was to determine whether:

> that provision requires the Member States to ensure that the operator of an online market-place may, regardless of any liability of its own in relation to the facts at issue, be ordered to take, in addition to measures aimed at bringing to an end infringements of intellectual property rights brought about by users of its services, measures aimed at preventing further infringements of that kind.

It was argued on behalf of eBay that an injunction could only be issued to prevent the continuance of 'specific and clearly identified infringements'. The Court, following the opinion of the Advocate General, rejected such a restrictive interpretation holding that the objectives of the Enforcement Directive required the possibility that an injunction might:

> order an online service provider, such as a provider making an online marketplace available to internet users, to take measures that contribute not only to bringing to an end infringements committed through that marketplace, but also to preventing further infringements.

Whilst the E-Commerce Directive specifically excludes the imposition of any general or specific duty on the part of an Information Society Service Provider to monitor activities by its users, the grant of injunctive relief must be available not only for past actions but also to prevent 'further infringements of that kind. Those injunctions must be effective, proportionate, dissuasive and must not create barriers to legitimate trade.'

The key issue is that of proportionality. Here the words of the Advocate General are worth repeating:

> The requirement of proportionality would in my opinion exclude an injunction against the intermediary to prevent any further infringements of a trade mark. However, I do not see anything in Directive 2004/48 which would prohibit injunctions against the intermediary requiring not only the prevention of the continuation of a specific act of infringement but also the prevention of repetition of the same or a similar infringement in the future, if such injunctions are available under national law. What is crucial, of course, is that the intermediary can know with certainty what is required from him, and that the injunction does not impose impossible, disproportionate or illegal duties like a general obligation of monitoring.
>
> An appropriate limit for the scope of injunctions may be that of a double requirement of identity. This means that the infringing third party should be the same . . . and that the trade mark infringed should be the same in the cases concerned. Hence, an injunction could be given against an intermediary to prevent the continuation or repetition of an infringement of a certain trade mark by a certain user. Such an injunction could be followed by an information society service provider by simply closing the client account of the user in question.

Issues relating to trade marks and the Internet have been before the European Court on a number of occasions. In cases such as L'Oreal the focus has been on the appearance of counterfeit items on sites such as eBay and the extent to which intermediaries such as eBay should be held liable. The present case is somewhat different in that it related to the question of whether the defendants' conduct was lawful or unlawful.

Following initial proceedings before the High Court, Mr Justice Arnold referred four questions to the European Court for a preliminary ruling. As seems to be commonly the case, the Court conflated these into a single issue, whether the use of a trade mark for the purpose of what is generally referred to as comparative advertising could constitute infringement. As was stated at paragraph 43 of the judgment:

> It is therefore appropriate to provide the referring court with guidance on interpretation in relation to the trade mark's function of indicating origin, its advertising function and its 'investment' function.

The Court continued:

> 51. In carrying out its examination of the facts, the referring court may choose to assess, first, whether the reasonably well-informed and reasonably observant internet user is deemed to be aware, on the basis of general knowledge of the market, that M & S's flower-delivery service is not part of the Interflora network but is, on the contrary, in competition with it and, second, should it become apparent that that is not generally known, whether M & S's advertisement enabled that internet user to tell that the service concerned does not belong to the Interflora network.

> 52. In particular, the referring court may take into account that, in the present case, the commercial network of the trade mark proprietor is composed of a large number of retailers which vary greatly in terms of size and commercial profile. The Court considers that, in such circumstances, it may be particularly difficult for the reasonably well-informed and reasonably observant internet user to determine, in the absence of any indication from the advertiser, whether or not the advertiser—whose advertisement is displayed in response to a search using that trade mark as a search term—is part of that network.

The European Court ruling is perhaps somewhat less Delphic in its pronouncements than is often the case and did send a fairly clear signal to the High Court.

After presenting an extensive analysis both of the jurisprudence of the European Court and cases from the national courts of other Member States, Mr Justice Arnold ruled in favour of Interflora. The early European jurisprudence, he indicated laid emphasis on whether informed consumers might be misled by the use made of the trade mark. Most of the cases to date have concerned comparative advertising regarding prices—with, for example, one shop claiming that it was offering an item for sale at a lower price than a named (and trade marked) competitor. The requirement is that care has to be taken to ensure that like is being compared to like. In the present case the key question to be answered was whether a reasonably informed consumer might gain the false impression from seeing the Marks and Spencer sponsored link after entering the word 'Interflora' as a search term that there was a commercial connection between the two undertakings? Mr Justice Arnold answered the question in the affirmative. The reasonably informed consumer would, he ruled, have been aware that Interflora was the trade mark for a network of independent flower suppliers. Reference was made to further guidance supplied by the European Court in its preliminary ruling. This was to the effect that:

> The function of indicating the origin of the mark is adversely affected if the ad does not enable normally informed and reasonably attentive internet users, or enables them only with difficulty, to ascertain whether the goods or services referred to by the ad originate from the proprietor of the trade mark or an undertaking economically connected to it or, on the contrary, originate from a third party. [para. 84]

It continued at paragraph 89:

> In the case where a third party's ad suggests that there is an economic link between that third party and the proprietor of the trade mark, the conclusion must be that there is an adverse effect on the function of indicating origin. [para. 136]

Effectively, Mr Justice Arnold ruled, the Court was saying that, if the theoretical possibility of confusion was established, the onus of proof lay with the defendant to establish that this had not occurred. Whilst comparative advertising was not per se unlawful and indeed had been supported by the European Court as a means for promoting competition, in the particular case Marks and Spencer had not led any evidence to challenge Interflora's contention that consumers had been misled and that there had been an adverse effect on the functioning of its trade mark.

This is an interesting case but, as with all interesting cases, perhaps creates more questions than answers. There have been many cases of trademark owners losing their protection because they have allowed the mark to become a generic term. 'Hoover' is perhaps the classic case where the trademark became widely used to refer to vacuum cleaners. With any form of intellectual property right there is a fine line between legitimate and excessive use of the right. Comparative advertising and the attempt to persuade a consumer to modify their initial preference are well established. 'Are you sure that you want to buy a BMW. Maybe an Audi would be a better purchase.' As e-commerce expands, these issues are going to arise increasingly in an Internet context.

The situation with Interflora is somewhat unusual in that the organisation is made up of a network, mainly of very small members but with linkages to much larger organisations. There were certainly grounds for the judge to conclude that informed users might be misled whether Marks and Spencer were associated with Interflora. I might be inclined to differ with his conclusion, but the judge is the sole determinant on questions of fact and it seems very unlikely that his decision can be challenged on this ground.

There is perhaps a final twist to the tale. In March 2013, at almost the same time as the High Court ruled in favour of Interflora it was reported that Google had imposed sanctions on Interflora in respect of alleged attempts by them to manipulate their search rankings in ways prohibited under Google's own rules. According to one report in March 2013:

> Interflora, the popular online florist, had been kicked into the long grass by Google for breaching the search engine's rules, or Webmaster Guidelines as it calls them, has triggered a fair bit of talk across the search engine optimisation (SEO) and marketing community.[50]

The timing was bad for Interflora coming in the period just before Mothers' Day which is one of the busiest times for floral deliveries. The effect of Google's action was effectively to blacklist the company so that searches for the name 'Interflora' would not provide any links to its services. There is no suggestion that the blacklisting (which was for only a limited period of time and has now been removed) was linked in any way to the court case. It is perhaps, however, another piece of evidence to suggest that law and Internet technology are uneasy companions.

Conclusions

With the emergence of global and national dispute resolution procedures, trade mark disputes involving the use of domain names appear to have largely vanished from the legal system. Although most disputes are settled, statistics from the dispute resolution organisations do show that the majority of decisions reached are in favour of the complainant. Given the nature of many of the incidents above which involve blatant hijacking of the name of a business, this rate is not in itself a source of surprise. What may be a greater cause for concern is the fact that the law applied in a number of instances appears to be almost, but not quite, trade mark law. In one sense, disputes are being hijacked from the courts to tribunals which are strongly supported by commercial pressures. The approach, especially concerning the allocation of generic domain names, may represent a way forward for dispute resolution in what is an increasingly globalised society, but great care needs to be taken to ensure that it acquires a considerable measure of legitimacy and is not seen as the captive of particular interest groups.

---

[50] <http://blogs.independent.co.uk/2013/03/01/interflora-suffers-seo-setback-as-mothers-day-approaches/>.

PART IV

E-Commerce

Introduction

It is difficult today to open a newspaper or view a website without seeing some story relating to e-commerce. Lauded in some quarters, it is vilified in others as contributing (along with out-of-town superstores) to the demise of the traditional High Street. This book will focus on the legal implications of e-commerce but it is useful to take some time at the outset to set the scene.

The notion of transactions between sellers and buyers located hundreds of miles apart is not at all novel. With the development of efficient railway and postal networks in the nineteenth century we saw the emergence of catalogue or mail order selling. Just as the emergence of the electric telegraph in the nineteenth century had societal impacts similar to those brought about by the Internet and modern notions of e-commerce. Although statistics are scarce, it does appear that catalogue selling in the late nineteenth and early to mid twentieth centuries accounted for levels of sales comparable to those reported today for consumer e-commerce transactions.

It is always tempting to look at the past through rose-tinted spectacles, but whilst the traditional High Street would provide butchers and bakers (perhaps not so many candle-stick makers) the range of goods available to shoppers was rather limited and catalogues provided access to items that would otherwise be difficult to obtain or provided competition to what would otherwise have been monopolistic suppliers. At a personal level, I grew up in the 1960s in a medium-sized town in Scotland (about 20,000 people) and recall that there was only one shop that sold electrical appliances such as TVs and washing machines.

The catalogue selling industry was particularly prominent in the United States with the catalogue issued by the Sears corporation acquiring almost mythical status. In an era where people living in rural areas had very limited access to retail facilities, catalogue selling provided an opportunity to access current designs for clothing and household objects.

Moving on, the modern notion of e-commerce dates back to the 1960s when businesses began to set up arrangements with customers and suppliers for the electronic ordering and supply of goods. The initial arrangements, generally known as electronic data interchange (EDI) agreements, were closed networks. Only the contracting parties could operate under their provisions. A very simplistic example might see a contract between a supermarket and a producer of baked beans. When the supermarket's check-out systems recorded the sale of a can of beans, it would place an order with the producer for the delivery of another can. The essential legal feature is that a valid contract can be created without any direct human involvement. Today we are starting to hear a great deal about machine-to-machine communications and EDI systems are one of the pioneers in the field.

More recently there have been moves to open up supply contracts with public- and private-sector organisations establishing web portals that invite tenders for the supply of goods and, increasingly, services. The Government Procurement Service (GPS) is an executive office of the Cabinet Office and has the remit to encourage widespread participation by small and medium enterprises in public procurement and to centralise procurement across the sector. This might be by, for example concluding a model contract for the supply of paper clips that might be utilised by any public-sector body and obviate the need for each department and agency to conduct its own procurement exercise, The GPS website indicates that its procurement contracts cover energy, travel, fleet, office solutions, communications services, print, professional services, ICT, e-commerce, and property and facilities management.

In the late 1990s the United Kingdom (and many other developed countries) experienced what was referred to as the dot com boom. Like many booms it was followed by the dot com crash around the beginning of this millennium. The reasons were many and various but a major factor was that physical delivery networks struggled to cope with orders resulting in a loss of consumer confidence as presents intended to be opened on Christmas Day failed to materialise until the New Year. Recent years have seen a resurgence within the sector.

The latest statistics from the Office for National Statistics indicate a continuing growth in e-commerce. It now accounts for around 19 per cent of all sales. It should be noted, however, that around 14 per cent of sales (around two-thirds of e-commerce transactions) fall into the category of EDI and represent sales between businesses or similar organisations. So-called B–C (business to consumer) transactions, that attract the main share of media publicity concerning e-commerce, make up a minority share in terms of value.

In the context of B–C e-commerce sales OFCOM's Communications Market report published in August 2013 indicated that '(a)verage weekly internet retail sales grew 10.3% year on year to May 2013, up from £528m to £582m'. Perhaps not surprisingly, sales peaked in the December 2012 where sales amounted to £847 million, itself an increase of nearly 18 per cent on the figures for December 2011. A particular growth sector, especially in the developing world, is in mobile commerce, where transactions are concluded using a mobile phone. In the United Kingdom, mobile advertising revenue increased nearly twentyfold in the period 2008–12 (from £29 million to £526 million). Research suggests that quite a high percentage of mobile browsing of e-commerce sites stops at the payments page, perhaps because the prospect of keying in long credit card numbers on a mobile phone screen is challenging. Some systems have been introduced to simplify the process such as 'Pingit'. Operated by Barclays Bank, it allows users to enter a pre-arranged five-digit code to authorise transactions.

A more recent category of e-commerce sees transactions between consumers (C–C) on electronic marketplaces such as eBay. According to OFCOM more than half of the UK's online population visited eBay on an average month. Sites such as eBay facilitate sales between consumers, effectively operating as a giant street market or car-boot saleroom. Within the UK eBay sales have reached around £1 billion a year with a profit of around £250 million. Although it is increasingly common for businesses to use eBay and similar sites as a portal for their online sales a substantial portion of eBay sales are between consumers.

The legal dimension

We will discuss legal issues in significantly more detail in the following chapters but it may be helpful at this stage to give an overview of the key topics. One will be very familiar to anyone who has read this far in the book. We live in a global society with globalised businesses. Perhaps not a purely legal issue, but there has been considerable publicity about the ability of online businesses (and multinational companies generally) to minimise their exposure to national taxes. It is reported, for example, that eBay paid UK taxes of £1.2 million in 2010 on the back of profits of around £250 million. That represents a tax rate of 0.48 per cent. The distinction between tax avoidance (legal) and tax evasion (unlawful) is hard to draw but it is, I think, fair comment that national states are struggling to regulate companies operating in cyberspace.

As indicated, distance selling is not a new phenomenon. Purchasing goods or services on this basis does mean that it is difficult for the customer to examine them prior to concluding a contract. There are some moves towards the use of 3D holograms and augmented reality technologies to allow, for example, a customer to get a sense of how a particular clothing outfit might look when superimposed on their own image. Even with such technologies it is difficult to recreate fully the look and feel of objects. One of the ways that distance-selling legislation has developed has been to provide consumers with a period within which they can cancel the contract if they discover that goods or services do not meet their expectations.

What we see in this respect is perhaps another area where the law is struggling to come to terms with technology and also good business practice. Just as in the real world some companies—Marks and Spencer comes to mind—have improved consumer confidence and brand awareness by offering returns policies that are more generous than required by law, so some Internet retailers have secured recognition for their returns policy. The retailer Amazon typically scores highly in consumer surveys in this respect.

Services such as airline tickets raise some complex issues. There is not the same question whether the customer will like they way an item of clothing looks or feels on them. I may simply book a flight from Glasgow to London on 24 March 2015. Obviously there may be legal issues after the flight if it is heavily delayed or my baggage is lost but I know from personal experience that online booking is not always an infallible process. It does appear that most airline booking systems are different. It is all too easy, and I write from personal experience, to make a booking for the wrong date. How and whether this can be corrected is uncertain as a matter of law. Some airlines allow online bookers a period, typically twenty-four hours, to correct any mistakes free of charge. Others do not!

One of the inconveniences for most of us wishing to acquire goods or services is that we have to pay for them. Payment mechanisms play a vital role in driving e-commerce. We have established systems such as credit and debit cards but they are predicated on formal banking systems. Especially in the developing world, relatively few people have bank accounts and there have been significant developments—now reaching to the developed world in respect of transferring funds using mobile phones. Especially with the growth in the number of people using 'smart phones', now more than half of the UK population, mobile commerce and payment is becoming a major issue.

I've mentioned eBay and one of the most profitable parts of the company is its payment system 'PayPal'. There are more than 20 million UK PayPal accounts. PayPal is registered as a bank in Luxembourg so at one level the comment might be that a third of the United Kingdom's population has an offshore bank account. On another level we might consider the appropriate level of regulation for what is often referred to as microfinance. Again this is a concept which is established in developing countries—with a Nobel Peace Prize being awarded to its 'inventor', Mohammad Yunus, in 2006. As is so often the case, authoritative statistics are lacking but it appears that the average PayPal account balance is around £30. Whilst a failure of the system might be annoying, the consequences would not compare to the worst-case scenarios arising from the banking crisis of 2007–8 when, we have been told, the British Prime Minister considered putting the army on the streets to prevent a breakdown of law and order should banks have closed their doors and cash machines stopped dispensing money.

The global reach of the Internet raises other issues, not least that of jurisdiction and choice of law. International commerce has, of course been in existence for many millennia but has tended to be specialised in its nature. When I studied my law degree, commercial law was studied under the name Mercantile Law which itself traces its origins to the body of rules devised by merchants to regulate international transactions. Until the emergence of the Internet, consumer international trade was essentially limited to the purchase of tacky souvenirs from Majorca or Benidorm. Everyone would accept that caveat emptor was the rule of the day and if the goods fell apart on their return to the UK matters would be written off to experience. If consumers purchased more expensive items such as the holiday itself, it would generally be done by means of a contract with some United Kingdom-based intermediary, typically a travel agent. One of the features of the Internet is that intermediaries play a much diminished role in consumer life and increasingly we contract directly with foreign suppliers. The question arises, of course, what happens when things go wrong? Three issues will be of critical importance. Which legal system will govern the transaction, which country's courts will have jurisdiction to try any case, and what are the procedures and possibilities for enforcing any judgment in another country? From the consumers' standpoint, if we are based in the United Kingdom and have a complaint about the service provided by a Greek hotel we would clearly want to bring a case before the domestic courts. Equally of course, the Greek hotel will almost certainly want to have the case heard in Greece. One of the key factors for the courts in making a decision will be whether the Greek hotel actively solicited business from the United Kingdom. If it has a website in English, the answer may well be yes; if the site is only in the Greek language, the conclusion will probably be different.

Conclusions

There are lots of questions, and in many cases we are waiting for definitive answers. In the age of the Internet it is difficult to think of anything that we cannot buy online. Its largely outside the scope of this book but electronic conveyancing means that we can buy and sell houses without using a single piece of paper. One of the major issues in this kind of situation is how we can replicate electronically traditional requirements that documents be signed. Cryptography and notions of digital signatures provides a major part of the answer.

With electronic commerce, many of the issues that we have considered in previous sections arise again. We are seeing global markets. Online delivery of items such as software, MP3 files, and e-books makes location entirely irrelevant. Improvements in logistic delivery systems, themselves largely a by-product of e-commerce, make the transfer of physical objects such as books and laptop computers a much simpler and cheaper prospect than was the case a decade ago. One of the issues that has arisen concerns individuals using the Internet to order goods from a foreign supplier. Traditionally, individuals travelling abroad have been allowed to bring goods to a certain value into the United Kingdom without being liable to pay import taxes or VAT (duty-free allowance). How can this translate into an e-commerce context? Some specific issues have arisen in the context of the Channel Islands. Connected in some respects with the United Kingdom which has responsibility for their defence and foreign affairs, in other respects they are independent and are not considered part of the European Union. Significantly, the Channel Islands do not have a system of VAT. This encouraged many e-commerce operators to set up a warehouse in the Channel Islands to fulfil orders from United Kingdom customers, effectively being able to undercut domestic suppliers by 20 per cent (the rate of VAT at the time of writing this book). The loophole—if it was one—has now been closed but it illustrates both the legal issues that can arise and also the practicalities (or impracticalities) for customs forces to examine millions of individual letters and packages arriving in the United Kingdom.

21

International and European initiatives in e-commerce

Introduction

The growth of e-commerce has been one of the most notable developments of the Internet age. Following a stutter at the time of the so-called dot com crash around the turn of the century, the sector has resumed what appears to be a remorseless rise. Any statistics are perhaps of fleeting value but the following data may indicate the qualitative and quantitative scale of e-commerce in today's Britain. Seventy per cent of UK households and 62 per cent of the population, it is estimated by the office of National Statistics, make use of the Internet for buying goods or services. The value of online sales was estimated to be £4.4 billion in June 2010 with increases in value of more than 20 per cent in the past year. By 2012 around 10 per cent of all national expenditure took place online. Significantly in societal terms, a third of individuals have indicated that when shopping for goods or services which can be obtained either online or in the High Street, they would actively prefer to deal online. Perhaps marking a return to earlier days when, especially in more rural areas, catalogue shopping was a popular activity, online sales figures in fields such as clothing are increasing faster than the average with 2010 figures marking a 32 per cent increase on the previous year.

Although in the e-commerce sector it is frequently difficult to distinguish hype from reality, there is no doubt that an increasing range of contracts will be concluded using some form of electronic communication. In many cases concerned with services, delivery, and perhaps performance, will also take place within an electronic environment.

In the context of traditional business activities, it is often stated that the three attributes most critical to commercial success are 'location, location, and location'. It is regarded as one of the hallmarks of e-commerce that issues of location, at least at the physical level, are of no significance. Paradoxically, however, when consideration is given to legal issues, location returns very much to the forefront. The most important questions concern the determination of when and where a contract is made and which laws and tax regimes will govern the transaction.

International initiatives

Given the international nature of the topic, it is not surprising that many of the activities in the field of e-commerce have been initiated by international organisations. The UN Commission on International Trade Law (UNCITRAL) adopted a model law on e-commerce in 1996 whilst, in December 1999, the Organisation for Economic Co-operation and Development (OECD) agreed Guidelines on Electronic Commerce.[1] The goal of the guidelines, it is stated:

> is that consumers shopping on-line should enjoy transparent and effective protection that is not less than the level of protection that they have in other areas of commerce.

---

[1] Available from <http://www.oecd.org/dataoecd/18/13/34023235.pdf>.

Among other things, they stress the importance of transparency and information disclosure.

The model law and the guidelines have no binding force. In focusing on regulatory activity, attention must concentrate on the activities of the EU and of national legislatures. EU involvement in the field of e-commerce can be traced primarily to a Commission Communication, 'A European Initiative in Electronic Commerce', published in April 1997.[2] Itself building on earlier information society initiatives, this outlined a programme for regulatory action across a range of topics. In what might be considered chronological order, action was required in order to ensure that organisations were enabled to establish electronic businesses in any of the Member States, that legal barriers to electronic trade should be removed, and that provision should be made for the manner in which contracts should be negotiated and concluded. Finally, legislation might be required in the field of electronic payments.

The mechanics of e-commerce constitute one aspect of the regulatory task. It was also recognised that other more general principles would require to be applied in the context of commercial applications. Issues such as data protection arise whenever personal data is transmitted and received. Again, as will be discussed in the following chapter, the use of cryptographic techniques as a means for enhancing security, both to preserve privacy and to enhance consumer and business confidence in the integrity of electronic communications, raises significant and controversial regulatory questions.

Although it is tempting to regard e-commerce as a new phenomenon, this is to neglect a significant existing market sector—that dealing with mail-order or catalogue selling. Especially in the United States, there is a substantial tradition of sales being conducted on this basis—dating back to the Wild West days beloved of cyberspace analogists. Given the federal nature of the United States Constitution, such sales also occurred across state boundaries. The oft-cited Uniform Commercial Code was first promulgated in 1940 to provide means to overcome jurisdictional and substantive problems arising when a supplier located in one jurisdiction contracted with a customer in another. Subject to some variations, it provides a common body of rules applicable throughout the fifty states. Recent (and highly controversial) developments in the United States have resulted in proposals to amend the venerable provisions of the Uniform Commercial Code to take account of the special nature of software sales.[3] Most initiatives seeking to amend the Code are the joint product of two bodies, the American Law Institute (ALI) and the National Conference of Commissioners on Uniform State Laws (NCCUSL). Originally, it was proposed to table an amendment to Article 2 of the Code. This provision deals with the law relating to the sale of goods. During 1999, a division occurred between the two drafting bodies, with the ALI taking the view that the proposal as drafted was too heavily weighted in favour of the interests of software developers and suppliers. The NCCUSL proceeded with the proposal, which was changed into a stand-alone statute, the Uniform Computer Information Transactions Act. The measure has been passed to the fifty states, although it has been enacted in only two (Maryland and Virginia).

Key legal instruments

A number of measures adopted or proposed by the EU are relevant to any discussion of e-commerce. Three are of particular relevance. The Distance Selling Directive[4] and

---

[2] Available from <http://www.cordis.lu/esprit/src/ecomcom.htm>.

[3] For a vast range of materials and comments on the proposed new law, see <http://www.2bguide.com/legart.html>.

[4] Directive 97/7/EC.

substantive law elements of the Electronic Commerce Directive[5] will be discussed in the present chapter. The Electronic Commerce Directive also contains provisions relating to the legal recognition of electronic contracts in cases where national laws require that contracts be concluded in a particular form. These matters, which are also covered in the Directive on 'A Community Framework for Electronic Signatures',[6] will be discussed in the next chapter.

The Distance Selling Directive

The market for distance selling through catalogues is a well-established one, especially in remote areas where retail outlets are few and far between. The sector is particularly well estab-lished in the United States, and it is anticipated that businesses with experience of these forms of transactions will be well placed to benefit from the move to e-commerce. Over the past decade, the telephone, fax machine, and, most recently, email and the WWW have been used to solicit consumer contracts. One of the most important European legal instruments is the Directive on the Protection of Consumers in Respect of Distance Contracts.[7] The Directive applies to all forms of distance selling, but contains some provisions relating specifically to the use of electronic communications. A number of these have been supplemented by the terms of the Electronic Commerce Directive.[8] The Distance Selling Directive was required to be implemented within the Member States by June 2000. The Preamble makes its rationale clear:

> Whereas the introduction of new technologies is increasing the number of ways for con-sumers to obtain information about offers anywhere in the Community and to place orders; whereas some Member States have already taken different or diverging measures to protect consumers in respect of distance selling, which has had a detrimental effect on competition between businesses in the internal market; whereas it is therefore necessary to introduce at Community level a minimum set of common rules in this area.[9]

The Distance Selling Directive defines the term 'distance contract' as:

> Any contract concerning goods or services concluded between a supplier and a consumer under an organized distance sales or service-provision scheme run by the supplier, who, for the purpose of the contract, makes exclusive use of one or more means of distance communication up to and including the moment at which the contract is concluded.[10]

Annex 1 contains an illustrative list of communication technologies. In addition to tra-ditional categories, such as letters and press advertisements, reference is made to the use of systems of videotext, email, and facsimile transmission.

The Distance Selling Directive's provisions commence at the stage where the consumer's entry into a contract is solicited, the principal requirement here being that promotional techniques must pay due regard to the consumer's privacy, conform to the 'principles of good faith', and provide 'clear and unambiguous information' regarding the nature of any product or service, its price, and the identity of its supplier.[11] In the case of telephone communication, the supplier is obliged to make its identity, and the fact that the call is commercial in nature, clear at the commencement of a call.[12]

The Distance Selling Directive also provides that two forms of technology, automated calling systems and fax machines, may be used only with the prior consent of the con-sumer—what might be referred to as an 'opt in' system.[13] Automated calling systems involve

---

[5] Directive 2000/31/EC.   [6] Directive 99/93/EC, OJ 2000 L 13/12.
[7] Directive 97/7/EC, OJ 1997 L 144 (the Distance Selling Directive). A further proposal for a Directive concerns the distance selling of financial services, COM (98) 468 final of 14 October 1998.
[8] Directive 2000/31/EC.   [9] Recital 4.   [10] Directive 97/7/EC, Art. 2(1).
[11] Art. 4(2).   [12] Art. 4(3).   [13] Directive 97/7/EC, Art. 10(1).

the use of a computer system to call numbers and on answering, play a pre-recorded message to the recipient. Such technologies are effectively prohibited in the United Kingdom as their use would require a licence from OFTEL, which has indicated objections to the practice. In the case of other forms of communication, it is provided that these are to be made only when the consumer has not indicated a clear objection to receipt of solicitations.[14] The operation of an 'opt out' system would be compatible with this requirement.

The rationale behind the selection of specific prohibited technologies is not clear. Recital 17 of the Distance Selling Directive[15] asserts that the consumer's right to privacy should extend to 'freedom from certain particularly intrusive means of communication'. It is difficult to argue, however, that a pre-recorded telephone message is intrinsically more intrusive than other forms of telephone canvassing. Unsolicited faxes also are unlikely to be seen as invasive of privacy, and perhaps a more persuasive basis for restricting these lies in the fact that the recipient of a fax incurs cost in terms of the paper and ink used for its reproduction. This was, perhaps, more of a factor with previous generations of fax machines, which required the use of special (and expensive) paper.

Assuming that discussions between supplier and consumer extend beyond the initial contact, there is a clear need to ensure that the latter is made aware of the terms and conditions associated with a particular contract. The Distance Selling Directive provides for two approaches, the first of which is outwith the scope of the present study, requiring the grant of a 'cooling off' period following the conclusion of the contract.[16] More relevant are provisions requiring that the consumer be given information as to terms. Article 4 specifies the items of information which must be given. These relate primarily to the identity of the supplier, the nature and cost of the goods or services, and any arrangements for delivery. These are relatively easily satisfied in traditional mail order or catalogue sales, but in respect of electronic communications, Recital 13 states that:

> Whereas information disseminated by certain electronic technologies is often ephemeral in nature insofar as it is not received on a permanent medium; whereas the consumer must therefore receive written notice in good time of the information necessary for proper performance of the contract.

Whilst the comment regarding the transient nature of information displayed on a website, for example, is basically true, the text of an email message can be as locatable as any written message. It would seem somewhat Luddite were a party engaging in e-commerce to be required to supply confirmation details on paper. The Distance Selling Directive requires that confirmation be supplied in writing or:

> in another durable medium available and accessible to him.[17]

It may be that the transmission of an email which may be stored on the consumer's computer would satisfy this requirement. This is the view which has been adopted by the then Department of Trade and Industry, which commented in its second consultation paper:

> We consider that confirmation by electronic mail would meet the definition of confirmation in 'another durable medium available and accessible to [the consumer]', where the order has been made by means of e-mail. We have not however specified this in the Draft Regulations since the Directive is not specific on the point, and only a court can determine the meaning of the wording.[18]

---

[14] Art. 10(2).   [15] Directive 97/7/EC.   [16] Art. 6.   [17] Art. 5.   [18] para. 3.9.

The Electronic Commerce Directive and Regulations

A proposal for a Directive on 'Legal Aspects of Electronic Commerce' was introduced in November 1998.[19] The proposal was debated in the European Parliament[20] and following its comments, an amended proposal was introduced in September 1999,[21] becoming law on its adoption by the Council of Ministers in May 2000.[22] It is implemented in the United Kingdom by the Electronic Commerce (EC Directive) Regulations 2002,[23] which follow very closely the wording and format of the Directive. Following a lengthy period when the measures were not at issue before the courts, there have recently been a number of cases concerning aspects of the legislation. These will be considered later but in many respects it might be doubted whether the Directive would have been adopted in the same form had the law-makers been able to predict the ways in which technology would develop.

The Directive was drafted at a relatively early stage of the development of the Internet at a time where the majority of domestic users were accessing services via dial-up or narrowband connections. In 2000 the UK telecommunications regulator OFTEL, estimated that less than 1 per cent of UK domestic users had broadband connections. Although the bulk of the Directive's provisions which relate to consumers' rights in respect of contracts concluded or performed over the Internet are technologically neutral and have stood the passage of time quite well, the specific provisions dealing with the liability of intermediaries have been relatively seldom tested in the courts and when this has occurred their application in the modern Internet context has been difficult.

The scope of the measure is broad-ranging. It applies to what are referred to as 'Information Society Services' which are supplied by 'Information Society Service Providers'. Although the E-Commerce Directive refers to information society services, the definition of these is to be found in Directive 98/48/EC which relates to issues of standardisation within the EU. This provides that the term encompasses:

> any service normally provided for remuneration, at a distance, by electronic means and at the individual request of a recipient of services.

For the purposes of this definition:

> 'at a distance' means that the service is provided without the parties being simultaneously present,
>
> 'by electronic means' means that the service is sent initially and received at its destination by means of electronic equipment for the processing (including digital compression) and storage of data, and entirely transmitted, conveyed and received by wire, by radio, by optical means or by other electromagnetic means,
>
> 'at the individual request of a recipient of services' means that the service is provided through the transmission of data on individual request.

The rationale for the requirement that services should be provided with a view to some remuneration is explained in the Recitals to the Directive. Recital 19 states:

> Whereas, under Article 60 of the Treaty as interpreted by the case-law of the Court of Justice, 'services' means those normally provided for remuneration; whereas that characteristic is absent in the case of activities which a State carries out without economic consideration in the context of its duties in particular in the social, cultural, educational and judicial fields;

---

[19] OJ 1999 C 30.

[20] Material relating to all stages of the Directive's passage can be found at <http://ec.europa.eu/internal_market/e-commerce/directive_en.htm#preparatory>.   [21] COM (99) 427 final.

[22] Directive 2000/31/EC, OJ 2000 L 178/1.   [23] SI 2002/2013.

Effectively, the European Union has limited legislative competence in the situations where services are provided other than for commercial purposes. If a service is provided without there being any intention to make some form of profit, the Electronic Commerce Directive and the implementing United Kingdom regulations can have no application. Given the high rate of failure among e-commerce operations, it is clear that the quest for profit need not be successful but the aspiration must be present.

The Recitals to the Electronic Commerce Directive envisage the possibility that commercial benefit for the service provider might not come about in a direct manner:

(18) Information society services span a wide range of economic activities which take place online; these activities can, in particular, consist of selling goods online; activities such as the delivery of goods as such or the provision of services off-line are not covered; information society services are not solely restricted to services giving rise to online contracting but also, in so far as they represent an economic activity, extend to services which are not remunerated by those who receive them, such as those offering online information or commercial communications, or those providing tools allowing for search, access and retrieval of data; information society services also include services consisting of the transmission of information via a communication network, in providing access to a communication network or in hosting information provided by a recipient of the service.

In the case of search engines such as Google, for example, although the service is provided free of charge to end-users, the service provider seeks (and obtains) significant profit from selling advertising services to other providers. As stated above, however, if there is no commercial motive underpinning the provision of services, the legislation does not apply. In the case of *Metropolitan International Schools Ltd v Designtechnica Corporation and Google UK and Google Inc*,[24] a case concerned in part with the liability of a search engine provider for defamatory comments accessible via links provided by it, the judge, Mr Justice Eady, quoted from the leading textbook on the topic *Gatley on Libel and Slander* (11th edn) at paragraph 6.28, to the effect that that:

Many internet service providers charge no fee to users and derive their revenue from advertising or commission on telephone charges but the remuneration presumably does not have to be provided by the user so the vast majority will be covered, though a business organisation operating an internal network would not.

He concluded:

Although the matter is by no means free from doubt, it would appear on balance that the provisions of the 2002 Regulations are apt to cover those providing search engine services.

Defences provided to Information Service Providers

One of the key purposes of the E-Commerce Directive is to harmonise the level of liability applying across the EU Member States and to provide re-assurance to those acting or contemplating entering into the sector that they will not be subject to excessive levels of liability greater than those applying to more traditional operators. Three specific defences are provided in the legislation applying where the Information Society Service Provider acts only in the capacity of hosting material generated by its customers, holds data merely for caching purposes to facilitate access and onward transmission, or provides a 'mere conduit' through which customers data flows.

---

[24] [2009] EWHC 1765 (QB).

The provisions of the caching and hosting defences have been considered in more detail in Chapter 17 in the context of Internet Service Provider (ISP) liability for copyright infringement. The 'mere conduit' defence has been perhaps the most contentious provision of the legislation and has been at issue in a number of cases brought against website administrators whose facilities have been, it was alleged, used to perpetrate acts of copyright infringement. Analogies are frequently drawn with the operation of postal or telecommunications networks where the network provider will have no knowledge of the contents of messages sent using its facilities. The Directive provides in Article 12 that:

1. Where an information society service is provided that consists of the transmission in a communication network of information provided by a recipient of the service, or the provision of access to a communication network, Member States shall ensure that the service provider is not liable for the information transmitted, on condition that the provider:

    (a) does not initiate the transmission;

    (b) does not select the receiver of the transmission; and

    (c) does not select or modify the information contained in the transmission.

2. The acts of transmission and of provision of access referred to in paragraph 1 include the automatic, intermediate and transient storage of the information transmitted in so far as this takes place for the sole purpose of carrying out the transmission in the communication network, and provided that the information is not stored for any period longer than is reasonably necessary for the transmission.

3. This Article shall not affect the possibility for a court or administrative authority, in accordance with Member States' legal systems, of requiring the service provider to terminate or prevent an infringement.

The Electronic Commerce (EC Directive) Regulations provide similarly:

(1) Where an information society service is provided which consists of the transmission in a communication network of information provided by a recipient of the service or the provision of access to a communication network, the service provider (if he otherwise would) shall not be liable for damages or for any other pecuniary remedy or for any criminal sanction as a result of that transmission where the service provider—

    (a) did not initiate the transmission;

    (b) did not select the receiver of the transmission; and

    (c) did not select or modify the information contained in the transmission.

(2) The acts of transmission and of provision of access referred to in paragraph (1) include the automatic, intermediate and transient storage of the information transmitted where:

    (a) this takes place for the sole purpose of carrying out the transmission in the communication network, and

    (b) the information is not stored for any period longer than is reasonably necessary for the transmission.

There do not appear to be any significant variations between the two sets of provisions.

The operation of these terms has been discussed in two English cases in the context of actions for defamation. In the case of *Bunt v Tilley and ors*,[25] the claimant alleged that a

---

[25] [2006] EWHC 407.

number of statements posted on websites were defamatory of him. Among the defendants were three ISPs—AOL, Tiscali, and BT—who had provided services to three individual defendants who were the authors of the postings. Although the point was somewhat peripheral to the main argument which concerned the nature of the definition of a publisher of defamatory information as laid down in the Defamation Act 1996, the court appeared to accept the proposition that ISPs should be regarded as playing a role analogous to that of the operators of a telephone network in that they had no actual knowledge or control over the contents of communications.

The issue was discussed more extensively in the case of *Metropolitan International Schools Ltd v Designtechnica Corporation and Google UK and Google Inc.*[26] In this case, the claimant alleged that the second and third defendants, who operated the well-known search engine Google.com and provided access from within the UK domain-name system (Google.co.uk), made available links to a website operated by the first defendant which contained material which was defamatory in nature. Evidence was led as to the scale of Google's operations with the search engine indexing around 39 billion publicly available web pages. The index was compiled entirely automatically. Search requests were also met entirely by automatic means with no element of human intervention.

The second and third defendants applied to have the action dismissed on a number of grounds, including, most relevantly, that Google could benefit from the 'mere conduit' defence. In this context the judge, Mr Justice Eady (who delivered also the judgment in *Bunt v Tilley*) held that:

> When a search is carried out by a web user via the Google search engine it is clear, from what I have said already about its function, that there is no human input from the Third Defendant. None of its officers or employees takes any part in the search. It is performed automatically in accordance with computer programmes.
>
> When a snippet is thrown up on the user's screen in response to his search, it points him in the direction of an entry somewhere on the Web that corresponds, to a greater or lesser extent, to the search terms he has typed in. It is for him to access or not, as he chooses. It is fundamentally important to have in mind that the Third Defendant has no role to play in formulating the search terms. Accordingly, it could not prevent the snippet appearing in response to the user's request unless it has taken some positive step in advance. There being no input from the Third Defendant, therefore, on the scenario I have so far posited, it cannot be characterised as a publisher at common law. It has not authorised or caused the snippet to appear on the user's screen in any meaningful sense. It has merely, by the provision of its search service, played the role of a facilitator.
>
> Analogies are not always helpful, but there will often be resorted to when the common law has to be applied to new and unfamiliar concepts. Here, an analogy may be drawn with a search carried out in a large conventional library. If a scholar wishes to check for references to his research topic, he may well consult the library catalogue. On doing so, he may find that there are some potentially relevant books on one of the shelves and make his way there to see whether he can make use of the content. It is hardly realistic to attribute responsibility for the content of those books to the compiler(s) of the catalogue. On the other hand, if the compilers have made an effort to be more informative, by quoting brief snippets from the book, the position may be different. Suppose the catalogue records that a particular book contains allegations of corruption against a living politician, or perhaps it goes further and spells out a particular activity, such as 'flipping' homes to avoid capital gains tax, then there could be legal liability on the part of the compiler under the 'repetition rule': see e.g. *Gatley on Libel and Slander* (11th edn) at paras 11.4 and 32.8.

---

[26] [2009] EWHC 1765 (QB).

It was noted that in a number of jurisdictions specific legislative provision had been made to confer immunity on the operators of search engines. In some jurisdictions this took place in connection with the 'mere conduit' defence and in others in relation to a further defence provided in the directive relating to 'hosting' of material. The possibility of adopting a similar approach for the United Kingdom was discussed in a Consultation Paper published by the then Department of Trade and Industry in 2005 but the matter was not progressed. In the event, the judge did not feel it necessary to give a definitive ruling on the application of the defence as it was found that Google had not published the material under the terms of the Defamation Act 1996.

To date, therefore, there has been no English authority directly concerned with the application of the 'mere conduit' defence either generally or in the specific context of intellectual property rights. A recent Swedish authority appears to have been involved with similar issues. In the so-called 'Pirates Bay' case the Stockholm District Court tried a number of defendants who were responsible for the operation of a website, 'The Pirates Bay'. This website provided a facility for users to upload and download torrent files but an important distinction lies in the fact that on the basis of the findings of the Swedish court, the Pirates Bay website provided storage facilities for its users to upload and download material. The case therefore proceeded on the basis of other provisions of the E-Commerce Directive relating to the caching and hosting of material.

One of the defence claims was to the effect that the service provided only a search-engine facility and that there was no knowledge of the contents of files exchanged between users. This was rejected by the court which ruled that it must have been obvious to the defendants that the site contained torrent files which infringed copyright and that they took no active steps to remove these. The conclusion reached by the court was that even if it could not be said that there was precise knowledge of each infringing file, there was a general culture of indifference towards copyright infringement which was sufficient to remove the immunity from liability offered under the E-Commerce Directive.

Substantive provisions in the Directive

When and where is a contract made?

In order for a contract to be concluded, there must be an unconditional offer and acceptance. In many instances, of course, there may be several iterations of offer and counter-offer before the parties reach agreement on all important matters concerned with the contract.

In the situation where a customer purchases goods in a shop, there is little problem in determining the question where a contract is made. The question when the contract is concluded is a little more problematic. In the situation where goods are displayed in retail premises, it is normally the case that the display constitutes an invitation to treat. An offer to purchase will be made by the customer, which may be accepted (or rejected) by the seller. There are sound reasons for such an approach, not least due to the possibility that goods might be out of stock or that the wrong price tag may have been placed on an item by mistake (or through the action of some third party). In practical terms, it can be said that a contract will typically be concluded when the customer's offer of payment is accepted by the seller.

Subject to any other mechanism agreed between the parties, it is generally the case that acceptance becomes effective when it is communicated to the offeror. Clearly, in the case of a face-to-face transaction, this occurs at the point where the acceptor indicates—whether by words or actions—that the offer is acceptable. Matters become rather more complex when the parties to the transaction are at a distance. Here, two sets of rules have been developed, depending on the nature of the communications technology employed. The rule relating to postal contracts form a well-established feature of the legal system. Here, it is provided that the contract is deemed to have been concluded at the moment the acceptance is placed into the postal system. The main rationale for such an approach is that once the message has been posted, it moves out of the control of the sender. The effect of this is, of course, that a contract will be concluded before the offeror is aware of the fact of acceptance. It is also the case that having been posted, an acceptance cannot be withdrawn, even though this may have been brought to the attention of the offeror prior to delivery of the acceptance.

The postal rule is to be contrasted with another rule relating to the use of forms of technology which might be classed as involving 'instantaneous communication'. In *Entores Ltd v Miles Far East Corpn*,[27] the question at issue was where a contract made following communications by telex should be regarded as having been concluded. The plaintiffs, who were located in London, had made an offer which had been accepted by the defendants in Amsterdam. Holding that the contract was made when the acceptance was received by the plaintiffs in London, Parker LJ held that where:

> parties are in each other's presence or, though separated in space, communication between them is in effect instantaneous, there is no need for any such rule of convenience. To hold otherwise would leave no room for the operation of the general rule that notification of the acceptance must be received. An acceptor could say: 'I spoke the words of acceptance in your presence, albeit softly, and you did not hear me'; or 'I telephoned to you and accepted, and it matters not that the telephone went dead and you did not get my message'... So far as Telex messages are concerned, though the despatch and receipt of a message is not completely instantaneous, the parties are to all intents and purposes in each other's presence just as if they were in telephonic communication, and I can see no reason for departing from the general rule that there is no binding contract until notice of the acceptance was received by the offeror.[28]

This view was endorsed by the House of Lords in the case of *Brinkibon Ltd v Stahag Stahl und Stahlwarenhandel GMBH*,[29] although it was recognised by Lord Wilberforce that the result might have to be reviewed in the event that it could be established that there was:

> some error or default at the recipient's end which prevents receipt at the time contemplated and believed in by the sender... No universal rule can cover all such cases; they must be resolved by reference to the intentions of the parties, by sound business practice and in some cases a judgement where the risks should lie.[30]

In the context of the present work, the key question is whether emails and other forms of message transmitted over the Internet will be classed as coming under the postal rule, or whether the provisions relating to instantaneous communications will apply. Although the issue of determining when an email contract is concluded might appear to be of the 'number of angels on a pinhead' category, this is not always the case, especially when—as in the *Entores*[31] and *Brinkibon*[32] cases—transactions possess an international dimension. In such cases, the questions will arise of which law will govern the transaction and which courts will have jurisdiction in the event of a dispute. In the event that a contract is silent on the point, the location where a contract is concluded will be a major factor in determining the choice-of-law question.

---

[27] [1955] 2 All ER 493.   [28] [1955] 2 All ER 493 at 498.   [29] [1982] 1 All ER 293.
[30] [1982] 1 All ER 293 at 296.   [31] *Entores Ltd v Miles Far East Corpn* [1955] 2 All ER 493.
[32] *Brinkibon Ltd v Stahag Stahl and Stahlwarenhandel GMBH* [1982] 1 All ER 293.

In terms of speed of transmission, email might generally be equated with fax or telex transmission. In the event of problems or congestion on the networks, messages may be delayed by hours or even days and, in terms of the nature of transmission, the more accurate parallel may be with the postal system. An email message will be passed on from point to point across the network, with its contents being copied and forwarded a number of times before being delivered to the ultimate recipient. There is no single direct link or connection between sender and receiver.

The Electronic Commerce Directive provides a somewhat complex mechanism for determining the moment at which a contract is concluded. It is stated that:

> Member States shall lay down in their legislation that, save where otherwise agreed by professional persons, in cases where a recipient, in accepting a service provider's offer, is required to give his consent through technological means, such as clicking on an icon, the contract is concluded when the recipient of the service has received from the service provider, electronically, an acknowledgment of receipt of the recipient's acceptance.[33]

Such an approach posed problems for the United Kingdom system which, as stated earlier, sees offers emanating from the customer rather than the supplier. There appears also to be an element of unnecessary complication by adding the requirement of acknowledgement of receipt of acceptance as a condition for the conclusion of a contract. The original proposal was even more prolonged, stating that the contract would not be concluded until acknowledgement was made of receipt of the acknowledgement! Receipt of acceptance would seem quite sufficient for this legal purpose. An alternative, and perhaps preferable, approach is advocated by the International Chamber of Commerce, whose draft Uniform Rules for Electronic Trade and Settlement propose that:

> An electronic offer and/or acceptance becomes effective when it enters the information system of the recipient in a form capable of being processed by that system.[34]

Albeit intended primarily for business-to-business contracts rather than the EU's consumer contract focus, this approach seems to achieve the legal requirements in a rather simpler fashion. Simplest of all, however, would be the United Kingdom approach, which would allow the seller to combine acceptance of the customer's offer with acknowledgement of the terms of the transaction.

A further obligation is proposed in the EC Electronic Commerce Directive. Member States are required to ensure that national laws require that:

> the service provider shall make available to the recipient of the service appropriate means that are effective and accessible allowing him to identify and correct handling errors and accidental transactions before the conclusion of the contract. Contract terms and general conditions provided to the consumer must be made available in a way that allows him to store and reproduce them.[35]

Whilst the provision is well meaning, it is difficult to identify how the result might be achieved. The provisions relating to the moment of formation of contract discussed earlier require that 'the service provider is obliged to immediately send the acknowledgement of receipt'. We can assume that in most cases this will be transmitted automatically. This affords very little time for the customer to identify and seek to correct any mistakes which have been made.

An alternative approach would be to provide consumers with a 'cooling off' period within which a contract might be terminated. The Distance Selling Directive provides for

---

[33] Directive 2000/31/EC, Art. 11.   [34] Art. 2.1.1.   [35] Directive 2000/31/EC, Art. 11(2).

a seven-day period, beginning with the date upon which goods supplied under the contract were received by the consumer.[36] The provision does not, however, apply to contracts for the provision of services where 'performance has begun with the consumer's agreement, before the end of the seven-day working period'. This will exclude contracts for the electronic delivery of software. Exemption is also provided in respect of contracts 'for the supply of audio or video recordings or computer software which were unsealed by the consumer'. The legitimate concern in all these cases is that the consumer would have the ability to copy the material before returning the originals to the supplier and seeking a refund of the purchase price.

Choice-of-law issues

As has been stated frequently, location is irrelevant in e-commerce. It is also the case that the largest body of sites offering to supply goods or services is in the United States. A consumer located in the United Kingdom and wishing to engage in e-commerce is almost inevitably going to have to deal with United States-based companies. International trade, which hitherto has been almost exclusively the preserve of large commercial operators, is assuming a significant consumer dimension.

In any situation where buyer and seller are located in different jurisdictions, two key legal issues will arise. The first is to determine which legal system will govern the transaction and the second to determine which courts will be competent to hear disputes arising from the transaction. In many instances, it will be the case that the parties make explicit contractual provision for both matters. In a contract between parties in Scotland and France, for example, it might be provided that French law will govern the transaction but that disputes may be raised in the French or the Scottish courts, the latter being required to decide the case according to the relevant principles of French law.

In general, parties have (subject to the legal systems chosen having some connection with the subject matter of the contract) complete freedom to determine choice-of-law issues. Different rules apply where consumers are involved. Problems also arise where the parties fail to make explicit provision for issues of jurisdiction. In this case, the matter may fall to be decided by the courts.

As discussed in the context of contract formation, the question of when and where a contract is concluded is a major factor in determining which legal system is to govern the transaction. Where transactions are conducted over the Internet, the question is not always easy to answer. The global top-level domain name.com gives no indication where a business is located. Even where the name uses a country code such as.de or.uk there is no guarantee that the undertaking is established in that country. It is relatively common practice, based in part upon security concerns, to keep web servers geographically separate from the physical undertaking. A website might, for example, have an address in the German (.de) domain. Its owner, however, might be a United Kingdom-registered company.

The question of whether an Internet-based business can be regarded as having a 'branch, agency or establishment' in all the countries from which its facilities may be accessed is uncertain. The OECD has pointed out in the context of tax harmonisation that the notion of permanent establishment, which is of major importance in determining whether an undertaking is liable to national taxes, may not be appropriate for e-commerce.

Within Europe, the Brussels[37] and Rome[38] Conventions make special provision for consumer contracts. The latter provides that a supplier with a 'branch, agency or establishment' in the consumer's country of residence is to be considered as domiciled there. Further, consumers may choose to bring actions in either their country of domicile or that of the

---

[36] Directive 97/7/EC, Art. 6.   [37] C 189 of 28 July 1990.   [38] OJ 1980 L 266/1.

supplier, whilst actions against the consumer may be brought only in the consumer's country of domicile.

The Brussels Convention builds on the Rome Convention's provisions and provides that an international contract may not deprive the consumer of 'mandatory rights' operating in the consumer's country of domicile. The scope of mandatory rights is not clear-cut but, given the emphasis placed on the human rights dimension in many international instruments dealing with data protection, it is argued that any attempt contractually to deprive consumers of rights conferred under the Council of Europe Convention and the EC Electronic Commerce Directive[39] would be declared ineffective on this basis.

More recent developments may complicate matters. The Electronic Commerce Directive provides that transactions entered into by electronic means should be regulated by the law of the state in which the supplier is established. This approach is justified on the basis of supporting the development of the new industries, Recital 22 stating that:

> in order to effectively guarantee freedom to provide services and legal certainty for suppliers and recipients of services, such Information Society services should only be subject to the law of the Member State in which the service provider is established.

At the same time, however, the Commission has adopted, by the Regulation on Jurisdiction and the Recognition and Enforcement of Judgments in Civil and Commercial Matters,[40] amendments to the Brussels and Rome Conventions which have the effect of subjecting all consumer contracts to the law of the consumer's domicile.[41] This approach is justified on the basis that the consumer is regarded as the weaker party in any contract with a business organisation.

There appears to be an inescapable conflict between choice-of-law provisions designed to favour the development of e-commerce by making more predictable the nature of the liabilities incurred by service providers, and giving priority to the interests of consumers by maximising their access to local courts and tribunals. The Explanatory Memorandum to the draft Regulation stated that:

> The Commission has noted that the wording of Article 15 has given rise to certain anxieties among part of the industry looking to develop electronic commerce. These concerns relate primarily to the fact that companies engaging in electronic commerce will have to contend with potential litigation in every Member State, or will have to specify that their products or services are not intended for consumers domiciled in certain Member States.

The intention was announced to review the operation of Article 15 two years after the Regulation's entry into force. In the shorter term, public hearings on the subject were announced and were held in Brussels in November 1999. The hearings attracted an audience of several hundred persons and produced several hundred pages of comments and suggestions. No consensus was—or perhaps could be—reached and the position remains one where different Commission Directorates appear to be promoting different policies.

Alternative dispute resolution

One palliative for jurisdictional problems is to try to obviate the need for formal legal proceedings. Two provisions in the Electronic Commerce Directive[42] seek to facilitate this. Article 16 requires Member States and the Commission to encourage the drawing up at Community level of codes of conduct designed to contribute to the implementation of

---

[39] Directive 2000/31/EC.   [40] Regulation 44/2001/EC, OJ 2001 L 12/1.   [41] Art. 15.
[42] Directive 2000/31/EC.

the substantive provisions of the Directive. Such codes, which will be examined by the Commission to ensure their compatibility with Community law, might provide a valuable unifying force throughout the EU. Article 17 obliges Member States to:

> ensure that, in the event of disagreement between an Information Society service provider and its recipient, their legislation allows the effective use of out of court schemes for dispute settlement, including appropriate electronic means.

Although a number of online dispute resolution services have been established, these have mainly been in the United States and do not appear to have attracted significant custom. In the United Kingdom, the 'Which Web Trader' scheme operated by the Consumers Association was introduced in 1999 and required participating traders to observe a code of practice. The scheme closed on the ground that it was not economically viable in 2003.[43]

In 1998, the Commission adopted a 'Communication on the out-of-court settlement of consumer disputes'.[44] A Commission Working Document on the creation of a European Extra-Judicial Network (EEJ-NET)[45] was published in March 2000. This notes that:

> The continuing expansion of economic activity within of [sic] the internal market inevitably means that consumers' activities are not only confined to their own country. Greater cross border consumption has arisen due to an increase in consumer travel and the emergence of new distance selling technologies like the Internet. This increase in cross border consumption, especially with the ever-increasing expansion of electronic commerce and the introduction of the Euro, is invariably likely to lead to an increase in cross border disputes. It is, therefore, necessary and desirable to create a network of general application which will cover any kind of dispute over goods and services.

The Commission is now proposing the establishment of a network of National 'Clearing Houses'. These organisations will give consumers wishing to pursue complaints against suppliers located in their jurisdiction information about available facilities for dispute resolution. The Clearing Houses will also assist their own national consumers who are in dispute with a supplier in another Member State by liaising with the relevant Clearing House to provide information about dispute resolution procedures. A further Green Paper on alternative dispute resolution in civil and criminal law was published by the Commission in 2002.[46]

Conclusions

The scope of the Electronic Commerce Directive[47] is broad-ranging and is generally non-controversial. Even matters such as the procedure for concluding a contract may cause theoretical rather than practical problems. The major criticism that might be made of the EU's activity in the field of e-commerce is that initiatives are dispersed across a range of measures. As well as complicating the task of determining what the law is in a particular respect, there is the potential for internal conflict, as has been discussed in relation to the issue of choice of law.

Perhaps the key message which can be taken from the initiatives discussed in this chapter is that in most cases, the application of traditional legal provisions will be quite adequate in order to regulate e-commerce. The key issue is perhaps the negative one that legal

---

[43] <http://www.out-law.com/page-3223>.   [44] COM (98) 198 Final.

[45] Available from <http://europa.eu/legislation_summaries/consumers/protection_of_consumers/l32031_en.htm>.

[46] COM (2002) 196 Final.   [47] Directive 2000/31/EC.

requirements should not impede the operation of e-commerce. This issue primarily arises in the context of formal or procedural requirements that a contract be concluded or evidenced in writing. The issue as to what extent such requirements might be satisfied in an electronic environment has become entangled with the topic of encryption. Both topics will be considered in the following chapter.

22

Cryptography, electronic signatures, and the Electronic Communications Act 2000

Introduction

As has been discussed throughout this book, we rely upon electronic communications and services for almost every aspect of our lives. As with any essential service there are obvious risks arising from any loss or corruption of the facility. As considered in the context of computer crime, the Internet is fertile territory for those with criminal inclinations. The dangers of identity theft have been described and, even more directly, loss of data relating to credit cards or bank accounts can be used very quickly as part of a criminal scheme.

One technique which has been employed for centuries by persons wishing to conceal matters from the gaze of third parties is to use some form of encryption. With this, even should data be seen by an unauthorised person it would be of little value. As was considered in connection with the new 'Citizens' Rights' Directive, an exception to the breach notification requirements will apply where data which may have been lost or mislaid is in encrypted form.

Encryption, traditionally used to protect the meaning of a message from unauthorised parties, in the Internet age is playing two further roles. A factor which is intrinsic to many human and business relationships is to know who a party is dealing with. As has again been considered in different contexts, on the Internet it can be difficult to verify identity. An adult male can, in the context of a social-networking website, adopt the persona of a female child. Encryption linked to the operation of certification schemes can provide assurance that a person (or company) is who they claim to be. Finally, the law has traditionally required that some forms of contract should be concluded in writing and authenticated by the signatures of the parties. Modern encryption techniques afford the possibility of developing an electronic signature that can not only replicate but also enhance the trust that might be placed in the scrawl of ink that typically represents a human signature.

Although, to an extent, encryption may seem a somewhat esoteric topic and relatively few individuals may make direct use of encryption when communicating by email, it is in many ways pivotal to the success of electronic commerce with many websites making use of encryption to protect communications to and from their customers. Any time a person uses a website which claims to use SSL (secure socket layer) software or whose URL has the prefix 'https', they will, perhaps unknowingly, be using encryption. In the wake of the NSA/GCHQ electronic eavesdropping revelations, a number of major Internet players such as Google, Microsoft, and Yahoo have announced that they will encrypt all data passing between their data centres. Given further reports that the current standards for encryption have been weakened through the involvement of the national security agencies, there may be some doubt about how effective this will be in protecting the integrity of individual communications.

Prior to considering some of the legal issues associated with encryption, this chapter will provide a brief account of the nature of encryption. Attention will then be paid to the provisions of the European Directive on a Community Framework for Electronic Signatures[1] and the United Kingdom's Electronic Communications Act 2000.

The nature of encryption

Although certainly not the first, one of the most famous early users of encryption was Julius Caesar, who wrote and transmitted his dispatches from Gaul in what is now referred to as the Caesar code. This involves placing two lines of the alphabet above each other and shifting one by a pre-arranged number of letters. For example, placing two alphabets above each other with a shift of three would give the result:

ABCDEFGHIJKLMNOPQRSTUVWXYZ
DEFGHIJKLMNOPQRSTUVWXYZABC

Thus the letter C would become F; A become D; and T become W. So the word CAT would be written as FDW.

The Caesar code is an example of what is referred to as a substitution cipher. The other main form of encryption has involved a process of transposition. Effectively, this involves taking a phrase, such as:

WET DAY IN GLASGOW

omitting spaces, and placing the letters into blocks of five letters each, producing:

WETDA YINGL ASGOW

The letters in each block are then shuffled in a predetermined manner. If the first letter is moved to the fourth space, second to fifth, third to first, fourth to second, and fifth to third, we arrive at:

TDAWE NGLYI GOWAS

Obviously, a real-life example would require to be more complex if the code were to be reasonably secure but the key point is that, until recent times, all codes were based on substitution or transposition techniques. Throughout history, there has been a constant battle between those seeking to use encryption to preserve secrecy and those wishing to break the codes. In his book, *The Code Book*, Simon Singh recounts how a critical factor in the decision to execute Mary, Queen of Scots was the successful attempt by Francis Walsingham, Queen Elizabeth's chief secretary, in deciphering coded messages exchanged between Mary and others conspiring to overthrow the English monarch.[2]

In the pre-computer age, the battle between code makers and breakers was often regarded as an intellectual pursuit akin to solving a crossword puzzle.[3] The advent of the computer has revolutionised the situation. Much has been written concerning the British and United States cryptographic operations during the Second World War. These led to the development of the world's first practical computing machines. Although limited by

---

[1] Directive 1999/93/EC, OJ 2000 L013/12.

[2] S. Singh, *The Code Book* (London, 1999). This book provides an excellent account of the history and nature of cryptography and has been drawn on heavily in the preparation of this chapter.

[3] A contest to solve *The Times* crossword puzzle in less than 12 minutes was used by the security service as a front for the quest to find suitable people to work on its attempt to break the German Enigma code.

today's standards, the processing power of these computers transformed code breaking from what had been an intellectual pursuit into an exercise in number crunching. The analogy might be made with a combination lock on a safe and the contrast between the stereotypical image of a skilled safe-breaker using a stethoscope to detect the correct combination and the random selection of numbers continued until the correct combination is achieved. Whilst the effort of trying several million possible combinations would be too great for humans, the task is comparatively simple for a computer.

In response to the vulnerability of traditional forms of encryption, modern systems place reliance upon mathematical techniques. One of the first of a new generation of cryptographic techniques was implemented in the United States Data Encryption Standard, or DES, which has been a source of some controversy since its inception in 1977, with allegations, most recently from Edward Snowden, that its effectiveness was deliberately reduced at the behest of the United States' National Security Agency (NSA). The level of security is basically as great as the complexity of the encryption software. The analogy might be made with a combination lock. A lock with three dials provides some security, but one with five considerably more so. The original version of DES used what is described as a 56-bit key. This has some 70 quadrillion combinations—a massive figure for human calculators, but one which provides a more manageable challenge to modern computers. The selection of a 56-bit key is rumoured to have been influenced by the NSA, which is reported to possess the world's most powerful computers, machines capable of decoding messages encoded using a 56-bit key within a matter of hours. As computer technology develops, it has become possible for other organisations to acquire the processing power required. In 1998, the Electronic Frontier Foundation, a civil liberties pressure group, claimed to have built a 'DES cracker' for $250,000 whilst, in yet another significant demonstration of the power of the Internet, it has been reported that messages have been successfully decoded using several thousand computers linked together over the Internet and operating throughout the night whilst their normal users slept.[4]

DES—and other forms of substitution and transposition codes—are examples of single-key or symmetric encryption systems. In the same way that the same key is used to open and lock a door, a message is encoded and decoded using the same key. Apart from the vulnerability of codes to attack by code breakers, the most significant point of weakness has concerned the fact that a single key is used to encode and to decode the message. If a sender wishes the recipient to be able to decipher his or her messages, it is necessary to deliver a copy of the key. Just as homeowners may be wary of allowing a person they are not familiar with to obtain access to their keys, so a code user will be wary about divulging it to someone they do not have reason to trust. Whilst systems such as DES might be used within closed networks of trusted parties—Electronic Data Interchange (EDI) agreements would be an obvious example—it can be of limited value in the wider world of e-commerce. Here, just as is the case in the High Street, the intention is that customers and suppliers who have no prior knowledge of or relationship with each other can conduct business.

A solution to this problem emerged with the development of public-key or asymmetric cryptography. The concept was initially devised in 1976 by two mathematicians, Whitfield Diffie and Martin Hellman, and was brought to practical fruition by three further mathematicians, Ron Rivest, Adi Shamir, and Leonard Adleman, after whom the RSA system is named. It has recently been reported that similar work had been conducted in the United Kingdom at the Government Communications Headquarters (GCHQ), although details were withheld on grounds of national security.[5]

---

[4] There were 3,500 computers linked over the Internet, searching possible key combinations at a rate of 1.5 trillion keys per hour. In total, 312 hours of processing were required to find the correct key.

[5] See <http://www.wired.com/wired/archive/7.04/crypto.html>.

The RSA system has proved controversial in a number of respects. Although the system was developed using public funds, the algorithms were patented (the patents expired in the year 2000) by a private company which marketed the software on a commercial basis. The system was first marketed in 1977, and required levels of processing power which effectively limited its use to large organisations and government departments. A modified form of public-key encryption, still based on the RSA algorithms but suitable for use on personal computers, was developed by Phil Zimmerman and is generally referred to by the acronym PGP (Pretty Good Privacy). Zimmerman's original intention was reportedly to offer the system on a commercial basis. In 1991, however, he became concerned at legislative proposals being discussed in the United States Congress which, if enacted, would have restricted the availability of encryption software. Zimmerman's response was to persuade a friend to place a copy of PGP on the Internet. From that date, the cryptographic genie has been well and truly out of the bottle and copies of PGP can be downloaded free of charge from a wide range of Internet sites.

For a number of years, Zimmerman faced threats of patent infringement action by RSA, but eventually the parties concluded a licence allowing the use of the RSA algorithms in non-commercial copies of PGP. This has been dropped. The United States government also places restrictions on the strength of RSA software which may lawfully be exported from the United States and threatened action against Zimmerman. Doubts were raised, however, as to whether causing a copy of PGP to be placed on the Internet constituted an act of exporting as defined in the relevant legislation and, given that the system could not be uninvented, the decision was taken to drop proceedings.

A user of either PGP or RSA software will generate two keys, a public and a private key. The act of generating the keys typically requires nothing more than random movements of the computer mouse. Messages can be encrypted using either key, but possession of the other key will be required in order to decrypt them. Although the mathematics are beyond the comprehension of mere lawyers, the system is claimed to be significantly more secure than single-key systems, although it also operates considerably more slowly.

If consideration is given to the nature of the public-key system, strengths and weaknesses can be identified. The scenario might be postulated whereby A receives a message which purports to have been sent by B and encrypted using the latter's private key. Assuming A had details of the public key, the message can be decrypted and A can be certain that the message has not been tampered with following its encryption. A cannot, however, be certain that B has not let the private key fall into a third party's hands. Again, given the ease with which PGP software and email accounts can be acquired or forged, if A and B have not dealt previously, A cannot be confident that B is who he or she claims to be. A final weakness may be most relevant in the commercial context. B may be a company and its encryption key used to encrypt a message ordering 100,000 widgets to be supplied by A, the well-known widget manufacturer. A will have no means of knowing that the person sending the message on B's behalf is authorised to engage in such transactions.

The same issues will apply in the event that A replies to B, encrypting the message with A's public key. Again, there can be confidence that the message has not been intercepted and amended in transit but less reliance upon the identity of the claimed sender. Indeed, given that the essence of the public key is that it is public, it might be a foolhardy person who would place too much credence on the origin of a message. From the point of view of the sender, he or she may be given details of a public key and told that it belongs to Ian Lloyd, a well-known supplier of memorabilia of Glasgow Celtic Football Club. Encouraged by the prospect of secure communications, credit card details may be transmitted with a view to acquiring a selection of materials. Unfortunately, the key may have been generated by a criminal seeking to acquire valid credit card numbers.

Enter trusted third parties

If the aim of encryption is to authenticate the accuracy of a transmission and to identify its sender, systems of public-key cryptography score one out of two. To provide mechanisms for promoting trust in the identity and status of the parties involved, the involvement of trusted third parties (TTPs), also referred to as certification agencies, has emerged. The TTP will seek evidence that the party sending a message is who he or she claims to be and will cause a certificate to that effect to be attached to a message. For the United Kingdom, banks, some solicitors and accountancy firms, and even the Post Office, have expressed interest in acting as TTPs.

The basic operation of TTPs is non-controversial and can be equated with traditional professions such as that of notary, or even with the role of a witness to a document. TTPs will almost inevitably obtain information about their customers' keys and some offer what is referred to as a key recovery service. This effectively involves them keeping secure a copy of a private key. In the event that the user forgets the key or—perhaps more likely—details are destroyed by a disaffected or departing employee, the loss can be made good.

As with many issues concerned with the Internet, initial moves in the field came from the United States. Here, enormous controversy followed proposals to introduce a new system of encryption, the Escrowed Encryption Standard, more commonly referred to as the 'Clipper Chip'. The attraction of this system, which would be based on public-key cryptography, would be that any form of digitised data would be encrypted in such a way as to ensure a high level of security. The less welcome aspect of the system was that its structure would enable keys to be made available to government agencies, enabling messages to be readily deciphered. Concerns were expressed as to whether the legal controls envisaged concerning release of the keys would provide adequate safeguards. Although legislation implementing the Clipper proposals did not pass through Congress, it was announced in Autumn 1996 that export controls on encryption software would be reduced in return for an industry commitment to the introduction of a key recovery system requiring that copies of all keys be held by a TTP. It would appear in this case that the prime motive was that the third party should be trusted by the government rather than by the contracting parties.

Much of the legislative debate in the late 1990s has concerned the role of TTPs and systems of key recovery and escrow. In March 1997, the Council of the Organisation for Economic Co-operation and Development (OECD) adopted 'Guidelines for Cryptography Policy'.[6] In a manner similar to that adopted in the field of data protection, the guidelines identify eight principles which should inform national legislation in this field:

1. Cryptographic methods should be trustworthy in order to generate confidence in the use of information and communications systems.

2. Users should have a right to choose any cryptographic method, subject to applicable law.

3. Cryptographic methods should be developed in response to the needs, demands, and responsibilities of individuals, businesses, and governments.

4. Technical standards, criteria, and protocols for cryptographic methods should be developed and promulgated at the national and international level.

5. The fundamental rights of individuals to privacy, including secrecy of communications and protection of personal data, should be respected in national cryptographic policies and in the implementation and use of cryptographic methods.

---

[6] Available from <http://www.oecd.org/document/34/0,3746,en_2649_34255_1814690_1_1_1_1,00.html>.

6. National cryptographic policies may allow lawful access to plain text, or crypto-graphic keys, of encrypted data. These policies must respect the other principles contained in the guidelines to the greatest extent possible.

7. Whether established by contract or legislation, the liability of individuals and entities that offer cryptographic services or hold or access to cryptographic keys should be clearly stated.

8. Governments should cooperate to coordinate cryptographic policies. As part of this effort, governments should remove, or avoid creating in the name of cryptography policy, unjustified obstacles to trade.

A strong relationship can be identified between these principles and a number of those applying in the data protection field. Although the guidelines recognise the need for some legal controls over the use of cryptography, it is stressed throughout that these must 'respect user choice to the greatest extent'. To this extent, the guidelines are seen as moving away from the United States-sponsored notion of mandatory key escrow, a move which is also followed in recent EU and United Kingdom legislation and proposals.

It is not the purpose of this chapter to discuss in detail the political aspects of encryption policy. It is suggested, however, that both sides are failing to come to terms with the reality of modern life. Those advocating extensive powers for law enforcement agencies are, in many respects, looking back to a form of golden age when governments could exercise genuine control over communications. Terrestrial broadcasting was largely a state-controlled monopoly, and the limits of transmitter power meant that foreign broadcasts could be received only in regions close to national borders. Postal and telecommunication services were also state-controlled, and international communications were conducted only on a small scale. The world has moved on and attempts to exert control again are likely to be doomed to failure.

Those opposed to the interception of encrypted messages may suffer from a similarly dated view of the world, harking back to a golden era of individual anonymity. In many Western countries, this can be considered to have reached its apogee in the 1960s. The past thirty years have seen a massive increase in the amount of personal data recorded and processed. Privacy in the traditional sense has largely vanished. In part, this is as a result of public-sector activity, but a large and growing threat comes from the private sector. There has never been a situation in which all communications receive immunity from interception. Whilst there is certainly need for controls to be introduced concerning interception and decryption of encoded messages, the notion that individuals should be assured of absolute privacy for their communications has never been a feature of societal life.

Legal approaches

The key European legal instrument in the field of cryptography is the 1999 Directive on a Community Framework for Electronic Signatures.[7] With the enactment of the Electronic Communications Act 2000 in May 2000, the United Kingdom would appear to have met all its obligations under the Directive.

The main purpose of the Electronic Signatures[8] and Electronic Commerce[9] Directives and the Electronic Communications Act 2000 is to encourage the development of electronic

---

[7] Directive 99/93/EC, OJ 2000 L 13/12 (the Electronic Signatures Directive).   [8] Directive 99/93/EC.

[9] Directive 2000/31/EC.

equivalents to written documents and manual signatures. In considering the impact of the Directives and the Act, consideration might usefully be divided into three sections. First, a brief account will be given of the background to the Electronic Communications Act 2000, a measure which will be pivotal to many of the developments described in this chapter. Next, an examination will be made of provisions relating to requirements for writing. This may relate both to the contractual situation and to other cases, such as the submission of tax returns. Finally, consideration will be given to requirements for signature. The notion of electronic or digital signatures has become inextricably linked with the use of cryptographic techniques and this section will commence with a brief description of this somewhat complex topic.

Background to the Electronic Communications Act 2000 and E-Commerce Directive

After a number of false dawns and extensive consultation exercises, an Electronic Communications Bill was introduced in the House of Commons in November 1999. The Bill, it was stated in the Second Reading debate:

> will be Britain's first 21st century law. It was the first Bill referred to in the Queen's Speech, it was the first to be introduced; and, tonight, it will become the first to receive Second Reading. It will bring our statute book into the 21st century, provide a sound legal basis for electronic commerce and electronic government, and help to build consumer and business confidence in trading on the Internet.[10]

In the event, the need to introduce emergency legislation to suspend the operation of Northern Ireland's power-sharing executive meant that the measure was not to be the first statute of the twenty-first century. Once this prospect had been removed, some of the sense of urgency which had accompanied the early stages of the Bill seemed to be dissipated and it was not until 25 May 2000 that the measure received the Royal Assent.

The genesis of the measure can be traced to a Consultation Paper published by the previous administration, in March 1997, on the 'Licensing of Trusted Third Parties for the Provision of Encryption Services'. In April 1998, the then Department of Trade and Industry published a statement on 'Secure Electronic Commerce'. This marked the first occasion when the term 'electronic commerce' was used in an official statement. It was indicated that:

2. The Government places considerable importance on the successful development of electronic commerce. It will, if successfully promoted, allow us to exploit fully the advantages of the information age for the benefit of the whole community.

3. The Government is committed to the successful development and promotion of a framework within which electronic commerce can thrive. Electronic commerce, as indicated below, is crucial to the future growth and prosperity of both the national economy and our businesses. Although the prime economic driver for electronic commerce may currently lie with business-to-business transactions, it is clear that consumers (whether ordering books or arranging pensions) will also directly benefit.

---

[10] Patricia Hewitt, Minister for Small Business and E-Commerce, 340 HC Official Report (6th series), col. 4, 29 November 1999.

Although the statement used the term electronic commerce, its contents were almost exclusively concerned with security issues. The statement continued:

> To achieve our goals, however, electronic commerce, and the electronic networks on which it relies, have to be secure and trusted. Whether it be the entrepreneur E-mailing his sales information to a potential supplier or the citizen receiving private advice from their doctor; the communications need to be secure. In a recent DTI survey 69% of UK companies cited security as a major inhibitor to purchasing across the Internet.[11]

Security can have a number of components and the statement referred approvingly to BS7799, which was referred to as the 'national standard on information security'. As well as organisational and technical measures, however, the statement focused on encryption policy. As discussed, this has been, and remains, a contentious political issue and the paper was criticised widely as appearing to promote a scheme of mandatory key escrow.

The next significant event occurred in March 1999, when a Consultation Paper, 'Building Confidence in Electronic Commerce', was published.[12] This indicated that 'The Government is committed to introducing legislation in the current Parliamentary session.' Comments were sought within a three-week period. Although cryptography policy again featured prominently in the document, significant provisions were also introduced concerning procedural issues of e-commerce, specifically relating to the removal of requirements that contracts be concluded in writing or be accompanied by a signature.

The Electronic Communications Act 2000 contains three parts. Part I contains provisions relating to the use of encryption and the provision of certification schemes which have now been repealed and replaced by a voluntary industry-led scheme; Part II is designed to facilitate e-commerce by removing requirements that contracts or other forms of transaction be reduced to writing and/or authenticated by the signatures of the parties involved; whilst Part III contains miscellaneous provisions, mainly concerned with a change to the telecommunications licensing regime.

The basis of requirements for writing

In a 1990 report, 'Preliminary Study of Legal Issues Related to the Formation of Contracts by Electronic Means', UNCITRAL identified four reasons which had historically prompted a requirement that contracts be concluded in writing. These were the desire to reduce disputes; to make the parties aware of the consequences of their dealings; to provide evidence upon which third parties might rely upon the agreement; and to facilitate tax, accounting, and regulatory purposes.

A wide range of statutory provisions make provision for information to be supplied 'in writing', for example, company accounts. In a number of instances, specific statutory provision has been made for the acceptance of computer-generated information. In the taxation field, for example, electronic copies of invoices will be accepted for purposes connected with Value Added Tax. As will be discussed, the Electronic Communications Act seeks to pave the way for greater acceptance of electronic information as satisfying requirements for writing. At present, however, statutory requirements will be subject to the terms of the Interpretation Act 1978, which defines writing as including:

> typing, printing, lithography, photography and other modes of representing or reproducing words in a visible form, and expressions referring to writing are construed accordingly.[13]

---

[11] Available from <http://www.fipr.org/polarch/secst.html>.
[12] Available from <http://www.cyber-rights.org/crypto/consfn1.pdf>.   [13] Sch. 1.

A document which exists solely in digital form, for example an email message stored on the hard disk of the recipient's computer, will not be capable of coming within this definition, as the electronic impulses representing its contents are not visible.

It seems clear that the 1978 definition was introduced at a time when communication between computers was limited and, as with other statutory definitions of that era relating to concepts of recording and storage, is ill-suited to the modern age. The UN Model Law on Electronic Commerce introduces the concept of 'a data message', which is defined as:

> information generated, sent, received or stored by electronic, optical or similar means including, but not limited to, electronic document interchange (EDI), electronic mail, telegram, telex or telecopy.[14]

The UN Model Law goes on to provide that:

> Where the law requires information to be in writing, that requirement is met by a data message if the information contained therein is accessible so as to be usable for subsequent reference.[15]

The desire to reduce requirements for paper-based documents is a feature of the Electronic Commerce Directive.[16] This provides that:

1. Member States shall ensure that their legislation allows contracts to be concluded electronically. Member States shall in particular ensure that the legal requirements applicable to the contractual process neither prevent the effective use of electronic contracts nor result in such contracts being deprived of legal effect and validity on account of their having been made electronically.

2. Member States may lay down that paragraph 1 shall not apply to the following contracts:

   (a) contracts requiring the involvement of a notary;

   (b) contracts which, in order to be valid, are required to be registered with a public authority;

   (c) contracts governed by family law; and

   (d) contracts governed by the law of succession.[17]

The effect of this provision would be to ensure that most forms of e-commerce can be conducted without requiring to comply with any additional requirements relating to form. This general rule may, at the option of a Member State, be subject to exceptions. The situations specified in the proposed Directive relate to contracts which are regarded as being of special importance. In respect of these, national laws typically require that the terms of the contract be recorded in writing and signed by the contracting parties.

The Electronic Communications Act 2000, which sought to implement the European Directive on Electronic Signatures provides, in section 7, definitions of the concept of electronic signatures and, by section 8, confers power upon the government to modify existing legislative requirements which would inhibit the use of electronic communications by, for example, requiring the use of traditional paper-based signatures. Relatively little use has been made of this regulatory power, something which is perhaps explained by the fact that rather few restrictions were in force prior to the enactment of the legislation. The Companies Act 1985 (Electronic Communications) Order 2000 is perhaps the most relevant piece of legislation and provides for the submission of company records and accounts to be made in electronic rather than the previously required paper format.

---

[14] Art. 2.   [15] Art. 6.   [16] Directive 2000/31/EC.   [17] Art. 9.

In addition to a lack of barriers preventing the use of electronic communications to and from government, incentives are sometimes offered to individuals and to undertakings to transact electronically with government agencies. These may, for example, take the form of extended deadlines for submission of tax returns or a reduction in the fees payable to reflect the economies secured through the use of electronic communications. In a recent initiative by the Driver and Vehicle Licensing Agency, motorists who opt to renew their car tax online will have their names entered into a prize draw with the possibility of winning an (environmentally friendly) motor car. Although some transactions may be conducted entirely electronically, others, such as the issuance of vehicle taxation documents, result in the issuance of a paper licence document. Again, in cases such as this, as an alternative to the customer supplying physical or electronic evidence such as their possession of vehicle insurance or a permit certifying that the vehicle is in a satisfactory mechanical condition (MOT certificate), data will be exchanged either between government departments or with trusted private sector agencies such as the Motor Insurers Bureau which maintains a data-base of all car insurance policies. A number of other data exchange agreements are also in force allowing, for example, photographs supplied in connection with driving licence applications to be accessed also in connection with a subsequent passport application. Following the publication of the Varney Report, *Service Transformation: A Better Service for Citizens and Business' in 2006, a Better Deal for the Taxpayer*, an initiative, generally referred to as 'Tell us once', has been launched which seeks to minimise the need for citizens or businesses to provide the same piece of information several times to different government departments.

In respect of electronic communications between government departments and agencies, use is made of the Government Secure Intranet (GSI). With infrastructure provided by Energis and data centres and applications supplied by Fujitsu, this was relaunched in 2004 linking over 140 local and central government departments with over 280,000 users on a:

> United Kingdom secure IP managed network, and (a) exchange and share Restricted (and Confidential) information with other GSi community customers and other networks such as the CJX, MoD, NHS and EU networks and (b) more safely access the public Internet. Standard GSi services include wide area connections to customer sites, directory, mail relay, firewalls and anti-virus scanning. Other GSi services include anti-spam and anti-image scanning, application development and hosting, closed user groups, remote access for home or mobile workers and VOIP. Appropriately sponsored private sector companies may order GSi GSE services.[18]

In conclusion, electronic documents are not normally either issued to or required from end-users. More critical is the exchange of information in electronic form either between government and end-users or within government itself. In the latter context it is relevant to note the recent publication of the Data Sharing Review although the thrust of this is on the data protection implications of the sharing of personal data rather than the exchange of business-related data. As indicated earlier, only a few legal requirements relating to the production of documents in specified paper format existed and the introduction of new requirements for electronic documents would in many respects mark a retrograde step.

In 'Transformational Government',[19] the United Kingdom's policies for modernising government services were laid down. Traditional structures, it was stated:

> are still paper-based and staff-intensive. The underlying assumption is that customers will fill in forms and that staff will process them by routine rather than by risk-managed

---

[18] <http://www.ogc.gov.uk/contractsdatabase/list_all_contracts_375.asp>.
[19] <http://www.paisdigital.org/documentos/docsinnovacion/2005/Transformational_government.pdf>.

exception. Telephone access, customer access over the web and other improvements have sometimes been grafted onto this base. This locks in high costs and difficulty in meeting changing customer or policy requirements. Choice is costly and slow to implement.

Historically government services depended almost entirely on form-filling and face to face meetings. Over the next decade, the principal preferred channels for the delivery of information and transactional services will be the telephone, internet and mobile channels—as well as the increasingly important channels within the digital home. Using customer insight, government will drive take-up of the best new digital channels and exploit mobile technologies; and it will innovate its services to take swift advantage of new technologies as they emerge.

One area highlighted for improvement concerned the number of government websites. In 2005, there were over 2,500 such websites with each department having its own web presence. The quality of these sites was variable and had been the subject of criticism by the National Audit Office, which monitors public expenditure in terms, inter alia, of its value for money. A significant process of rationalisation saw a number of sites closed and the remainder moved under the auspices of two web portals: Direct.gov,[20] concerned primarily with the provision of information and advice to individuals, and Businesslink.gov,[21] which, as the name suggests, is aimed at the business community and is the focus of most attention in the context of the United Kingdom's implementation of the Services Directive, in particular in connection with the establishment of points of single contact. In its most recent review of government services offered over the Internet, published in July 2007,[22] the National Audit Office identified signs of progress:

> There are indications that government web provision became more comparable with the best private sector websites in the period around 2003–04, and the vast majority of government sites have quite similar and effective levels of functionality and design. In our survey they are rated reasonably well.

In addition to the two web portals, or in the Audit Office's terminology 'supersites', the Government Gateway[23] provides a means for individuals and businesses to register to communicate with government agencies. Registration is largely designed to provide a vehicle to allow the identity of the individual or business to be verified. Once this has been done, use of the Gateway will facilitate access to services such as, for example, payment of personal or business taxes. Considerable emphasis is placed on the levels of security associated with the Gateway site with the statement made that:

> The Government Gateway is a secure site. All information that you send and receive is transmitted through a 128-bit Secure Socket Layer connection (SSL). SSL creates a secure link between your browser and our server. You will always know when you are using a secure connection because a padlock icon is displayed on the status bar of your browser. SSL also encrypts data and guarantees that it is not altered between your computer and our server.
>
> . . .
>
> All information that you send and receive through the Government Gateway is encrypted to the highest industry standards.

The site also supports the use of digital certificates. In general, however, relatively little use is made of digital certificates in the United Kingdom. In many respects, the jurisdiction has tended to take a relatively lenient approach towards issues of identity management. Even where traditional forms of signatures have been required it has always been accepted

---

[20] <http://www.direct.gov.uk/>.   [21] <http://www.businesslink.gov.uk/>.
[22] <http://www.publictechnology.net/sector/uk-e-government-national-audit-office-report-situation-analysis>.   [23] <http://www.gateway.gov.uk/>.

that the use of mechanical forms of writing or even rubber stamps will suffice to comply with legal requirements.

Electronic documents and the requirements for writing

The basis for much of the Electronic Communications Act's provisions on this field lies in the European Directive on Electronic Signatures.[24] Although much of the work relating to the legal status of such signatures has concerned the use of public-key encryption, the Directive and the Act seek to be technologically neutral. Its implementation would have the effect of providing for electronic equivalents to writing and signature to be accepted within the Member States. The Directive is expressly stated to be unconcerned with contractual and other procedural requirements.[25] Its purpose is stated to be:

> to facilitate the use of electronic signatures and to contribute to their legal recognition. It establishes a legal framework for electronic signatures and certain certification-services in order to ensure the proper functioning of the internal market.[26]

The Electronic Signatures Directive identifies two forms of signature: electronic signatures and advanced electronic signatures. These are defined as:

1. 'electronic signature' means data in electronic form which are attached to or logically associated with other electronic data and which serve as a method of authentication; and

2. 'advanced electronic signature' means an electronic signature which meets the following requirements:

   (a) it is uniquely linked to the signatory;

   (b) it is capable of identifying the signatory;

   (c) it is created using means that the signatory can maintain under his sole control; and

   (d) it is linked to the data to which it relates in such a manner that any subsequent change of the data is detectable.[27]

The term 'electronic signature' is very broad. It would encompass, for example, the use of scanning equipment to create a digital image of a person's signature, with this image being reproduced at the end of a word-processed letter. Advanced forms of signature will require the use of some form of encryption. The Electronic Signatures Directive refers to this under the heading of 'Secure-Signature-Creation Device'. The technical attributes to be possessed by such devices are specified in Annex 3, whilst the Directive provides that Member States may, acting in accordance with criteria to be specified by the Commission, establish mechanisms to verify the conformity of particular systems of encryption.[28]

In terms of the legal status to be afforded to electronic signatures, the Electronic Signatures Directive provides that:

1. Member States shall ensure that advanced electronic signatures which are based on a qualified certificate and which are created by a secure-signature-creation device:

   (a) satisfy the legal requirements of a signature in relation to data in electronic form in the same manner as a hand-written signature satisfies those requirements in relation to paper-based data; and

   (b) are admissible as evidence in legal proceedings.

---

[24] Directive 99/93/EC.
[25] See also the provisions of the Electronic Commerce Directive, Directive 2000/31/EC.
[26] Directive 99/93/EC, Art. 1.   [27] Art. 2(1).   [28] Art. 3(4).

2. Member States shall ensure that an electronic signature is not denied legal effectiveness and admissibility as evidence in legal proceedings solely on the grounds that it is:

- in electronic form; or

- not based upon a qualified certificate; or

- not based upon a qualified certificate issued by an accredited certification-service-provider; or

- not created by a secure signature-creation device.[29]

An advanced electronic signature will give a considerable degree of assurance that the signature is that of a particular person. There cannot be assurance that its use has been authorised by the owner, either generally or in the context of a particular transaction. It might be, for example, that an unauthorised third party has obtained a copy of a private key. Alternatively, a company may have a private key which is used by an employee to place an order for goods but where the employee is acting in excess of his or her authority. To overcome these difficulties, the notion has been advanced that the use of a signature should be certified by an independent agency. The Electronic Signatures Directive identifies criteria which must be met in what is called a 'qualified certificate':

(a) an indication that the certificate is issued as a qualified certificate;

(b) the identification of the certification-service-provider and the State in which it is established;

(c) the name of the signatory or a pseudonym, which shall be identified as such;

(d) provision for a specific attribute of the signatory to be included if relevant, depending on the purpose for which the certificate is intended;

(e) signature-verification data which correspond to signature-creation data under the control of the signatory;

(f) an indication of the beginning and end of the period of validity of the certificate;

(g) the identity code of the certificate;

(h) the advanced electronic signature of the certification-service-provider issuing it;

(i) limitations on the scope of use of the certificate, if applicable; and

(j) limits on the value of transactions for which the certificate can be used, if applicable.[30]

This is, in effect, creating a role for the TTPs, now known as certification-service-providers, discussed earlier. Annex 2 of the Directive specifies a wide range of technical and organisational attributes which must be demonstrated in order for a certificate issued by a service provider to be recognised as a qualified certificate.

The Electronic Signatures Directive makes it clear that no limitations are to be imposed upon the freedom of anyone to engage in the activity of a certification-service-provider. It is provided, however, that:

Member States may introduce or maintain voluntary accreditation schemes aiming at enhanced levels of certification-service provision. All conditions related to such schemes must be objective, transparent, proportionate and non-discriminatory. Member States may not limit the number of accredited certification-service-providers for reasons which fall within the scope of this Directive.[31]

---

[29] Art. 5.   [30] Annex 1.   [31] Art. 3(2).

It may well prove, of course, that a person wishing to engage in the business of certification-service-provider may find that commercial pressure dictates that accreditation is sought.

Electronic signatures and the Electronic Communications Act 2000

The Electronic Signatures Directive[32] was required to be implemented in the Member States by July 2001. The United Kingdom met this timetable with the enactment of the Electronic Communications Act, which received Royal Assent on 25 May 2000. Reference has previously been made to the role of this statute in providing for electronic communications to be taken as satisfying requirements for writing. The Act also provides for recognition of electronic signatures and for the activities of what are referred to as cryptography service providers.

Electronic signatures

The Electronic Communications Act 2000's provisions relating to the recognition of electronic signatures are rather more simple than those found in the Directive. The Act eschews the distinction between 'electronic' and 'advanced electronic signatures', instead providing that:

In any legal proceeding–

(a) an electronic signature incorporated or logically associated with a particular electronic communication or with particular electronic data, and

(b) the certification by any person of such a signature,

shall each be admissible in evidence in relation to any question as to the authenticity of the communication or data or as to the integrity of the communication or data.[33]

The term 'electronic signature' is defined in terms similar to those found in the Directive:

For the purposes of this section an electronic signature is so much of anything in electronic form as—

(a) is incorporated into or otherwise logically associated with any electronic communication or electronic data; and

(b) purports to be so incorporated or associated for the purpose of being used in establishing the authenticity of the communication or data, the integrity of the communication or data, or both.[34]

Effectively, the decision will be left to a court what weight to attach to any particular signature.

In the situation where a signature is required to validate a contract, the provisions of section 8 of the Electronic Communications Act 2000 will again be relevant. As is the case with requirements for writing generally, rather than providing for blanket recognition of electronic signatures, the Act provides that secondary legislation may be made in order to provide for:

the doing of anything which under any such provisions is required to be or may be authorised by a person's signature or seal, or is required to be delivered as a deed or witnessed by electronic means.[35]

---

[32] Directive 99/93/EC.　　　[33] s. 7(1).　　　[34] s. 7(2).　　　[35] s. 8(2)(c).

Cryptography service providers

The final, and most controversial, element of the Electronic Communications Act 2000 concerns the provisions made for cryptographic service providers. This term is defined as encompassing:

> any service which is provided to the senders or recipients of electronic communications, or to those storing electronic data, and is designed to facilitate the use of cryptographic techniques for the purpose of—
>
> (a) securing that such communications or data can be accessed, or can be put into an intelligible form, only by certain persons; or
>
> (b) securing that the authenticity or integrity of such communications or data is capable of being ascertained.[36]

The service must either be provided from premises within the United Kingdom or be provided to persons carrying on a business in the United Kingdom. A German service provider marketing services to United Kingdom-based companies would come within the second element of this definition.

Anyone is entitled to establish a cryptography support service. Equally, there is no obligation imposed on users of encryption to involve such a service in their transactions. Especially in cases where parties have a background of previous dealings or operate as part of an EDI network, such third-party involvement may well be rendered otiose.

At present, no restrictions—and virtually no legislation—apply to the use of encryption or cryptography services. Maintenance of the status quo would not justify such flagship legislation. What was envisaged in Part I of the Electronic Communications Act 2000 was the establishment of a voluntary register of accredited cryptography service providers along the lines provided for in the Electronic Signatures Directive.[37] Whilst the decision to seek registration will be a voluntary one, the intention is that the existence of such a scheme will promote public confidence in what must be regarded as an embryonic profession.

The Electronic Communications Act 2000 provided in sections 2 and 3 that responsibility for the establishment of such a register is to vest in the Secretary of State (or such other body to whom performance of the task may be delegated). As indicated, however, the intention was that the register should be operated on a voluntary basis. Section 16 provided that the provisions would come into force on such day as may be fixed by order, but that if no order were made within five years from the date of Royal Assent, the order-making power would lapse. This indeed happened. Discussions with the Alliance for Electronic Business resulted in the establishment of a 'non-statutory self-regulating scheme (tScheme) for Trust services'.[38] The scope of the proposal is described as being 'to operate and enforce a voluntary approval scheme for trust services'. The overall objective is stated to be to provide a mechanism that will:

- set minimum criteria for trust and confidence
- be responsible for:
  - the approval of electronic trust services against those criteria
  - the monitoring of approved services
  - provide a means of redress where services fall below those criteria
- and thereby promote the benefits of using an approved electronic trust service.

---

[36] s. 6.   [37] Directive 99/93/EC.   [38] Available from <http://www.tscheme.org/>.

Five organisations are currently approved for the provision of services. An indication of the nature of the likely requirements can be found in Annex 2 of the Electronic Signatures Directive[39] (with which the Electronic Communications Act 2000 is designed to be compatible). This refers to the need for demonstrable reliability of the systems, technologies, and personnel involved in the provision of the service; the acceptance of liability for losses caused through errors in the service provision; and the observance of a proper degree of confidentiality regarding details of the customer's business. Further indication regarding the criteria which might be applied can again be taken from the Alliance for Electronic Business Scheme, which states that:

> It is anticipated that the criteria will address business, management, operational and technical issues necessary for approval. Criteria will relate to both the services offered and the organisations offering them and will be based as far as possible on existing criteria in the marketplace.
>
> The actual criteria used for assessment will be a selection of elements from publicly available, and wherever possible international, technical or management standards (e.g. ISO 9000, BS 7799, X.509, FIPS 140; and from other appropriate criteria published by bodies such as FSA and OFTEL).
>
> In addition to adopting previously defined standards the organisation will, when necessary, create criteria not already existing in the marketplace. It is vital to the success of [the] scheme, and its take up by providers, that it does not duplicate existing approval and regulatory structures, but builds on their foundations.
>
> The selection of criteria, termed an Approval Profile, will be unique for each different type of service. Criteria will be selected by reference to specific versions of standards, and reviewed periodically to ensure that the most relevant and appropriate criteria are applied, as the standardisation process and services develop. A list of the criteria selected, including any necessary identifying publication information (e.g. dates, versions, etc.) will be maintained and publicly available.

It is clear from the above that there can be no single scheme of certification. Given the vast range of transactions that may be carried out electronically, such an approach is necessary and desirable. It is to be expected and hoped that standards will emerge over time to give appropriate guidance to the courts and other agencies on what reliance might reasonably be placed upon a particular form of certificate. One thing does seem certain: accreditation will not be a cheap process for service providers. The Minister for Small Business and E-Commerce stated in Committee that:

> An estimate of the possible costs involved for a medium-sized company that is seeking approval for the issue of certificates would be between £10,000 and £30,000.[40]

Conclusions

There seems little doubt that e-commerce will continue to expand significantly in the coming years. It is the author's view that this will take place in spite of concerns regarding lack of security. Consumers run the risk of falling victim to fraud in every aspect of life. The Internet is no better and no worse in this respect. Encryption is frequently used by service providers to enhance security. This is typically done in a manner which makes no demands on the consumer. The complexities of public-key cryptography are such that its use is likely to remain restricted to the commercial sector and to techno-freaks.

[39] Directive 99/93/EC.
[40] HC Official Report, SC B (Electronic Communications Bill), col. 37, 9 December 1999.

A further development which may enhance consumer confidence in e-commerce relates to the acceptance by credit card providers of the risk of loss due to fraud on the Internet. Under section 75 of the Consumer Credit Act 1974, credit card providers incur joint and several liability with merchants in respect of any claim which a consumer may have in respect of misrepresentation or breach of contract relating to a transaction valued at between £100 and £30,000. In the event that the consumer's details are intercepted by a third party and subsequently misused, section 83 of the Act may be of assistance. This provides that the card holder is not liable for loss arising from third-party use of the credit facility by 'another person not acting as the debtor's agent'. Section 84 does provide that the consumer may be liable (up to a maximum of £50) for misuse of a 'credit token' during the period when it leaves the consumer's control until its loss is reported to the creditor. The term 'credit token' is defined as a 'card, check voucher, coupon, stamp, form, booklet or other document or thing'. This can clearly relate to the physical card rather than the numbers contained thereon.

If the Internet creates the problem, it may also provide the solution. A growing number of credit card suppliers conduct business over the Internet. As described previously, this can result in very considerable cost savings. One card provider, Egg.com,[41] offers its customers a guarantee against the risk of loss through fraud in respect of activities carried out within the card company's own network of approved dealers. Again, the impression is given that the credit card company will be liable only after redress has been sought and refused by the supplier. Section 75 of the Consumer Credit Act 1974 gives the consumer the option of which party to proceed against in the first instance and the case of *Office of Fair Trading v Lloyds TSB Bank plc and ors*[42] confirmed that this right applies in respect of all transactions, regardless of where the supplier might be located. In the event that loss follows from a transaction concluded over the Internet with a supplier based in China and using a credit card supplied by a United Kingdom-based financier, the credit card company will incur joint and several liability.

The Commission and United Kingdom legislative provisions regarding electronic signatures may be of greater relevance in the commercial sector, where many requirements of form currently restrict the extent to which companies can maximise the use of electronic communications. However, this may relate more to undertakings' relations with the state than to between themselves. The unanswered question in this—as in many other areas of IT law—is whether legal provisions will be relevant in the face of seemingly remorseless advances in technology.

---

[41] <http://www.egg.com>.   [42] [2007] UKHL 48.

23

Electronic money and online gambling

Introduction

We are fast moving towards, indeed it is fair to say we live in, societies where paper (or as is suggested for the UK, plastic) currency notes and coins are being used less and less. There is much talk of a 'cashless society'. Recent estimates indicate that retail transactions made using credit or debit cards account for almost 80 per cent of all sales.[1] The advent of contactless cards allows for the very speedy payment of small transactions (typically less than £20) and makes their use much more attractive than previously for transactions such as the purchase of a cup of coffee or a newspaper. In many situations such as e-commerce it is effectively impossible to pay for transactions with cash and even in the physical world, businesses such as 24-hour garages are often reluctant to accept cash late at night.

The use of established systems of credit and debit cards to finance transactions raises few issues at domestic level although as discussed elsewhere, this has been contentious in the context of international e-commerce where there have been questions whether credit institutions are obliged to compensate consumers in respect of transactions with businesses located outside the UK. Increasing use is also being made of other forms of electronic payment mechanisms where the linkage with traditional banking institutions is more limited. Although perhaps still at the evolving stage in Europe, we are seeing the emergence of 'mobile wallets'. A component of mobile devices, these allow users to pay for a range of goods and services using credit previously stored in the wallet.

Generally referred to as electronic or e-money applications, they may be either hardware- or software-based. Store gift cards are an example of the former category as would be a transport card such as London Transport's 'Oyster card', whilst e-money stored on an account in the Internet, such as PayPal, is software-based. The gift card market in the United Kingdom has been valued at some £5 billion per annum.[2] In some cases, stores offer their own gift card facility—Amazon for example—but most of the serried ranks of cards displayed in supermarkets and other retail outlets are produced by third-party e-money issuers under contract to the particular retailer.[3] As has been extensively publicised, individuals holding such cards may be financially vulnerable in the event that the company promoting the card becomes insolvent.

Two more recent developments also merit consideration. Linked in some respect to the notion of e-money has been the introduction of systems of virtual currencies of which Bitcoins is perhaps the best-known (and controversial) example. In essence, virtual

---

[1] See <http://www.bbc.co.uk/news/business-24029785>.

[2] <http://www.ukgcva.co.uk/>. A perhaps unpublicised benefit to retailers is that it is estimated that some £250 million worth of gift cards are not redeemed each year: <http://www.bbc.co.uk/news/uk-17644528>.

[3] See e.g. <http://www.svmeurope.co.uk/Products/GiftCardcodes.aspx>.

currencies offer an alternative to traditional financial systems. The value of any currency depends in part on its legal status and also on its acceptance in the market. A good example can be seen in the situation in the United Kingdom where the legally approved currency is issued by the Bank of England but where banknotes issued by banks in Scotland and Northern Ireland are generally accepted as equivalent in terms of their face value—essentially because the banks that issue the notes are perceived as financially reliable. The technology behind virtual currencies will be considered in more detail later, but virtual currencies will succeed or fail depending on their linkage with real-world currencies. As with all currencies, relative values may rise and fall. The case has been widely recorded of an individual who invested $27 in Bitcoins around the time the system was established in 2009 and found in 2013 that they were worth nearly $900,000.[4] More recently, following raids by US law enforcement agencies against organisations suspected of using Bitcoins to facilitate money laundering, their value has declined with reference to other established currencies.

A further evolving trend, particularly since the global banking crisis and the reduction of credit facilities available from these institutions, has been the practice of 'peer to peer' lending. Essentially responding to a climate of low interest rates for savers and the lack of traditional credit, a number of firms have established themselves as facilitators between the parties. In some respects the model follows the well-publicised system of micro-finance for the developing world that earned its inventor the Nobel Peace prize.

E-money

Considerable attention has been given over the past decade as to how the issuance and use of such forms of electronic money should be regulated. Whilst the interests of consumers require that operators be regulated, there is a general recognition that the application of the full panoply of regulation associated with traditional banking and credit card operations may be excessive in the context of what are often fairly small-scale operations and where the consumers' level of exposure is generally quite limited.

National and European legislation

Initial sector-specific legislation was introduced by the European Union in the form of the Directive on the taking up, pursuit of and prudential supervision of the business of electronic money institutions.[5] In the United Kingdom, the Financial Services and Markets Act 2000 designated the issue of e-money as a 'regulated activity'[6] and particular provision to implement the Directive was made in the Electronic Money (Miscellaneous Amendments Regulations 2002.[7]

The 2000 Directive was criticised in many quarters[8] as being too demanding of small e-money providers and a simplified and revised version was adopted in the 2009 Directive

---

[4] <http://www.theguardian.com/technology/2013/oct/29/bitcoin-forgotten-currency-norway-oslo-home>. The headline figure is a little misleading. Any attempt to realise the value of all the Bitcoins would have had the effect of depressing the value of the currency very significantly.

[5] Directive 2000/46/EC L275/39.

[6] s. 19. More detailed provision was made in the Financial Services and Markets Act 2000 (Regulated Activities) Order 2001, SI 2001 No. 544.   [7] SI 2002 No. 765.

[8] See the 2005 Evaluation Report on the Working of the Directive, available from <http://ec.europa.eu/internal_market/payments/docs/emoney/evaluation_en.pdf>.

of the same name.[9] This had to be implemented in the Member States by May 2011. For the United Kingdom, this took the form of the Electronic Money Regulations 2011.[10]

A range of forms of electronic money can be identified with the major variants relating to identified e-money and anonymous e-money (also known as digital cash). Identified e-money contains information revealing the identity of the person who originally withdrew the money from the bank. Also, in much the same manner as credit cards, identified e-money enables the bank to track the money as it moves through the economy. Anonymous e-money works just like real paper cash. Once anonymous e-money is withdrawn from an account, it can be spent or given away without leaving a transaction trail.

The nature of e-money

The term 'electronic money', as defined, means electronically (including magnetically) stored monetary value as represented by a claim on the electronic money issuer[11] which is issued on receipt of funds for the purpose of making payment transactions and is accepted by a person other than the electronic money issuer; 'electronic money' does not, however, include:

(1) monetary value stored on instruments that can be used to acquire goods or services only in or on the electronic money issuer's premises or under a commercial agreement with the electronic money issuer, either within a limited network of service providers or for a limited range of goods or services; or

(2) monetary value that is used to make payment transactions executed by means of any telecommunication, digital or IT device, where the goods or services purchased are delivered to and are to be used through a telecommunication, digital or IT device, provided that the telecommunication, digital or IT operator does not act only as an intermediary between the payment service user and the supplier of the goods and services.[12]

The last paragraph above was drafted to remove uncertainties whether mobile-phone service providers might be caught under the legislation in respect of pre-pay customers. The first paragraph does perhaps create a loophole in respect of gift cards. Where these can, as is usually the case, be used only in one store, the safeguards introduced by the e-money Directives and Regulations will not apply—as has been seen in a number of business failures in the UK where consumers have been left with gift cards of limited or no value.

In some instances electronic money will be associated with traditional financial service providers and will be regulated in the same manner. A number of other players, sometimes quite small in size are entering the market. The best known is perhaps PayPal which provides payment mechanisms for services such as eBay. Their modus operandi is for customers to transfer funds to them which they may then use to purchase goods or services online with PayPal acting as an intermediary to transfer payment to the seller. An alternative model sees the use of stored credit on payment cards. A well-known example is the Oyster card which is extensively used for public transport services in the London area. Here customers make payment to the provider and in return have credit stored on their card which can be used.

---

[9] Directive 2009/110/EC, OJ 2009 L 267/7.   [10] SI 2011 No. 99.
[11] The scope of the term 'electronic money issuer' is defined in Reg. 2 of the Electronic Money Regulations 2011 to include, banks, credit institutions, the post Office, and authorised electronic-money institutions.
[12] Reg. 2(1).

E-money issuers and small e-money issuers

Anyone issuing e-money requires to be authorised by the Financial Conduct Authority (the successor to the Financial Services Authority). The authority is required to maintain a register[13] of authorised electronic money institutions and small electronic-money institutions. Small electronic-money institutions are defined as organisations which do not have more than €5 million worth of e-money in circulation at any time.

In addition to commercial electronic-money issuers it is specifically provided that the Authority may include on the register any European Economic Area (EEA)-authorised electronic-money institutions—the Post Office Limited; the Bank of England, the European Central Bank, and the national central banks of EEA states other than the United Kingdom, when not acting in their capacity as a monetary authority; or other public authority or government departments and local authorities when acting in their capacity as public authorities—where such persons issue electronic money.

Criteria for admission to the register

The Regulations specify detailed criteria that must be satisfied for an application for authorisation as an e-money issuer (or registration as a small e-money issuer to be accepted). Essentially evidence must be submitted relating both to the financial stability of the organisation and the suitability (in respect in particular of the lack of criminal convictions or insolvency incidents amongst the directors and senior management).[14] An authorisation will lapse if e-money is not issued within twelve months of its grant.

Safeguarding arrangements

The Regulations make extensive provision both regarding the capital requirements that must be satisfied by a prospective e-money issuer and also as to the internal financial procedures that must be put in place, effectively to ring-fence money received in order to obtain e-money from other aspects of the provider's business.

Passport rights

The Directive and the Regulations make extensive reference to so called 'passport rights'. This refers to the ability of a company which has been authorised as an electronic-money issuer in one EU country to commence operations in other states. One of the most high-profile examples is PayPal which began its European life with authorisation from the UK and expanded to other states on the basis of this. It is now regulated under Luxembourg law.

Virtual currency

The notion of a currency other than one issued by banks under legislative authority is not new. In many respects notions of currency and money have become conflated but it is perhaps fair to suggest that money is anything that can be used to purchase goods or services. It may be represented in terms of a value related to currencies but this is not always an accurate reflection of intention.

---

[13] The Register is accessible at <http://www.fsa.gov.uk/register/2EMD/2EMD_MasterRegister.html>.

[14] Regs. 6 and 13.

An early, but relatively recent, example of an alternative form of currency could be the system of 'Green Shield' stamps that were issued by many businesses from the 1950s. Customers would receive stamps (similar in appearance to postal stamps) in quantities dependant on the value of their purchase. These could be redeemed for other goods. The Trading Stamps Act 1964[15] required that all such stamps display a cash amount for which they could be exchanged. This tended to be set at a derisory level so that perhaps 1,000 stamps (equivalent to around £50 of purchases) would be needed to exchange for around 1 penny in cash.

Trading stamps have effectively disappeared from the market place[16] and been replaced by loyalty cards but they do provide an early example of an alternative form of currency (the notion of trading stamps dates back in some respects to the nineteenth century), albeit one linked to an established financial system.

More modern examples of alternative currencies might be seen in frequent-flier schemes operated by many airlines. There is a secondary market for air miles. A quick search on a system such as eBay will show many offers to sell air miles. Air miles have value although it is difficult to quantify these. Flights booked with air miles tend to require the customer to pay taxes and (unspecified) charges. These charges can be so high that it is not uncommon to find that a flight booked with air miles is actually more expensive than one bought for cash. The system is effectively a closed one, however, in that the miles can be redeemed only with the airline or with nominated partners.

Moving into the Internet era we start to see the emergence of virtual currencies.[17] Perhaps more popular a decade ago than today we saw the development of alternative online worlds. The site Second Life is a prominent example which sought to replicate many of the attributes of the real world. Users could buy virtual property and furnish it with assets. In part, Second Life works on the basis of traditional currencies but users can also purchase what are referred to as Linden Dollars—a virtual currency that could be used to buy and sell assets with other users. The site's terms and conditions state that:

> 4.5 'Linden Dollars' are virtual tokens that we license. Each Linden Dollar is a virtual token representing contractual permission from Linden Lab to access features of the Service. Linden Dollars are available for Purchase or distribution at Linden Lab's discretion, and are not redeemable for monetary value from Linden Lab.
>
> ...
>
> You acknowledge that Linden Dollars are not real currency or any type of financial instrument and are not redeemable for any sum of money from Linden Lab at any time. You agree that Linden Lab has the right to manage, regulate, control, and/or modify the license rights underlying such Linden Dollars as it sees fit and that Linden Lab will have no liability to you based on its exercise of this right. Linden Lab makes no guarantee as to the nature, quality or value of the features of the Service that will be accessible through the use of Linden Dollars, or the availability or supply of Linden Dollars.

Although, as with air miles, Linden dollars can be bought or sold on sites such as eBay and there are some procedures for them to be converted back into physical currencies, they have primary value only in the context of Second Life—just as air miles can ultimately be redeemed only in the context of the airline's programme.

---

[15] Now repealed by the Regulatory Reform (Trading Stamps) Order 2005 SI 2005 No. 871.

[16] Green Shield stamps had set up a chain of shops where customers could redeem their stamps. The name has disappeared but the stores continue having been re-branded in 1973 as Argos.

[17] For an interesting study on the nature of virtual currencies see the Research Paper published by the Bank of Canada at <http://www.bankofcanada.ca/wp-content/uploads/2013/11/wp2013-38.pdf>.

Systems such as Bitcoin mark another stage in the development of virtual currencies and attempts to tie the virtual more closely to the physical financial world. Bitcoin's origins can be traced to a research paper published in 2009 by an author writing (apparently) under the pseudonym Sakoshi Nakomato. The paper,[18] entitled 'Bitcoin: A Peer-to-Peer Electronic Cash System', described a system of virtual currency based upon the application of cryptography. Bitcoins are created, or 'mined', by individuals using dedicated software to identify appropriate cryptographic identifiers and can be bought by users via currency-exchange sites. As its website states:

> Bitcoins have value because they are useful as a form of money. Bitcoin has the characteristics of money (durability, portability, fungibility, scarcity, divisibility, and recognizability) based on the properties of mathematics rather than relying on physical properties (like gold and silver) or trust in central authorities (like fiat currencies). In short, Bitcoin is backed by mathematics. With these attributes, all that is required for a form of money to hold value is trust and adoption. In the case of Bitcoin, this can be measured by its growing base of users, merchants, and startups. As with all currency, Bitcoin's value comes only and directly from people willing to accept them as payment.[19]

Bitcoins provide an alternative to established forms of currency transfer. As the original paper indicated, it operates on a peer-to-peer or user-to-user basis and thereby eliminates many of the transaction costs associated with other forms of fund transfers. As a paper published by the European Central Bank indicates:

> Users have several incentives to use Bitcoins. Firstly, transactions are anonymous, as accounts are not registered and Bitcoins are sent directly from one computer to another. Also, users have the possibility of generating multiple Bitcoin addresses to differentiate or isolate transactions. Secondly, transactions are carried out faster and more cheaply than with traditional means of payment. Transactions fees, if any, are very low and no bank account fee is charged.[20]

Because of the mathematics involved in the mining of Bitcoins, it is stated that there cannot be more than 21 million in existence. The value of the currency is established in relation to physical currencies. One of the notable features of the system is that there have been extensive fluctuations in conversion rates. These are often associated with external events. One of the concerns that has been raised about the virtual currency is that it is susceptible to being used by criminals—as, of course, is any other form of currency. In October 2013 a website, 'Silk Road', that was implicated in drug dealing, was shut down by the FBI and Bitcoins valued at some $3.6 million were seized from its operator. It had been estimated that 5 per cent of Bitcoin usage was related to that site. In the immediate aftermath of the FBI action, the value of the currency plummeted but very quickly recovered. The incident is interesting. Publicity linking the virtual currency with criminal conduct caused its value to drop but a perception that the problem had been eliminated created a sense of respectability—although it now appears that the website in question has reappeared in much the same form.

The future of virtual currencies remains unclear. With respect to Bitcoin, some states such as Germany and Austria are trying to bring them within the general taxation system. Thailand has attempted to prohibit use of the currency.[21] The problems within the Eurozone and also the currency crisis in countries such as Argentina indicate the limitations of national states. It may be that systems such as Bitcoin will come and go but there is perhaps an argument that a Bank of Google might carry as much credibility as the Bank of England.

---

[18] <http://bitcoin.org/bitcoin.pdf>.   [19] <http://bitcoin.org/en/faq>.
[20] <http://www.ecb.europa.eu/pub/pdf/other/virtualcurrencyschemes201210en.pdf>.
[21] <http://www.telegraph.co.uk/finance/currency/10210022/Bitcoins-banned-in-Thailand.html>.

Peer-to-peer lending

A recent development has seen a number of companies providing, so-called peer-to-peer lending facilities. It is reported that at least one major retail bank is considering entering the market, which at the latest estimate provides around £380 million of credit annually. In large part, peer-to-peer lending is a product of the Internet age and also of the credit shortage resulting from the banking crisis which continues to affect most countries.

In essence the scheme is simple. The companies involved act as online intermediaries between individuals who want to invest money and companies (and in some cases individuals) who wish to borrow. The company will carry out credit checks on potential borrowers and will award a credit rating. This will determine the rate of interest that will be charged for any loan. Investors can determine how much they wish to invest and identify the companies they wish to lend to. The amount will generally start at a small sum, around £20, and the advice is normally that loans should be spread across as wide a range of borrowers as possible. The peer-to-peer company will receive and transfer the money (via a ring-fenced account with a High Street bank) and take responsibility for seeking to obtain repayment in due course.

The peer-to-peer system is claimed to offer benefits to all concerned. Even allowing for the perhaps inevitable bad debts, it is claimed that the average investor will receive a return of around 6 per cent, significantly more than can be obtained from most other forms of investment. Borrowers receive access to credit which would otherwise be unobtainable and, even where other sources might be available, pay a relatively low rate of interest. The peer-to-peer facilitating company receives a commission on all transactions.

A considerable measure of government support has been given to the system. In December 2012, the Department for Business, Industry and Skills announced public funding of £55 million to match an equivalent amount from private sector sources would be made available to a number of peer-to-peer companies.[22]

At the moment there is limited regulation of the sector. The Financial Conduct Authority, replacing the Office of Fair Trading in the role, is responsible for issuing licences to organisations involved in the credit field. Any peer-to-peer company will have to obtain a licence although this is in respect of a relatively minor field of debt administration. Effectively this requires that they demonstrate only that they have appropriate procedures in place to manage repayment of loans.

Concerns have been expressed about the basic structure of the industry with the *Financial Times* commenting that the 'hands off' nature of the peer-to-peer company's involvement raises echoes of one of the major causes of the financial crisis: that institutions sought to offload responsibility for the repayment of loans and so had no incentive to act responsibly.[23] Whilst this is currently a relatively minor risk, it could become more significant as the sector expands, perhaps paradoxically with financial support from the public sector.

In 2013, the Financial Conduct Authority was established as a new agency to take over responsibility for the financial services sector from the Office of Fair Trading and the Financial Services Authority. The latter agency had been widely criticised for a failure to exercise appropriate regulatory oversight at the time of the banking crisis. In a consultation paper published in March 2013, views were sought on how future regulation might evolve. Specific reference was made to peer-to-peer lending with the proposal made that it should

---

[22] <http://news.bis.gov.uk/Press-Releases/Small-businesses-offered-110-million-of-new-finance-684c2.aspx>

[23] <http://www.ft.com/cms/s/0/04d6bdce-f2ee-11e2-802f-00144feabdc0.html#axzz2b5NoOzSb>

be considered a 'bespoke regulated credit activity' with enhanced protection provided to both borrowers and lenders. The consultation paper commented:

> We envisage the lending aspect of a peer-to-peer platform's activities being treated as an investment activity and that lenders providing the finance should be appropriately protected regardless of the status of the borrower (for example whether the borrower is a consumer, sole trader, partnership or company).
>
> …Among the rules that we are considering applying primarily to protect consumer borrowers are:
>
> - a requirement for the platform to provide borrowers with adequate explanations of the key features of the credit agreement (including identifying the key risks) before the agreement is made;
>
> - a requirement for the platform to assess the creditworthiness of borrowers before the credit agreement is made;

In seeking to implement these recommendations, a statutory instrument has been laid before Parliament. The Financial Services and Markets Act 2000 (Regulated Activities) (Amendment) (No. 2) Order 2013 makes a number of significant changes to existing regulation. It introduces the concept of 'Operating an Electronic System in Relation to Lending'.

Online gambling

Introduction

Online gambling[24] represents a significant and growing share of the UK gambling market. In statistics published in March 2013[25] the Gambling Commission—the statutory body charged with overseeing the industry within the United Kingdom—indicated that gambling revenues from this sector had reached more than £2 billion per annum, which is some 10 per cent of the global market in this sector. Possession of a licence is necessary for gambling to take place on a legal basis and in September 2013, 275 licences were in force. The United Kingdom market for online gambling is the largest, by a factor of almost three, of any of the EU Member States.[26] These figure undoubtedly understate the amount of money spent within the sector with many operators, including some of the largest betting organisations switching their online operations to jurisdictions outside the United Kingdom.[27]

Under the Gambling Act 2005, licences were required by operators who had equipment located in the UK. In response to the move to locate businesses outside the jurisdiction, the Gambling (Licensing and Amendment) Act 2014 will require operators that transact with or advertise to British consumers to obtain an operating licence from the Gambling

---

[24] Sometimes also referred to as Internet gambling, the term can encompass a wide range of forms of gambling. By a significant margin, the largest market is in the form of betting on the outcome of sporting or other events. Other significant activities take the form of casino operations or the operation of online games of Bingo.

[25] Available from <http://www.gamblingcommission.gov.uk/gambling_sectors/remote/about_the_remote_gambling_indu/about_remote_gambling.aspx>.

[26] European Commission Green Paper on Online Gambling in the Internal Market. The second-largest market is in Germany in spite of a legal prohibition against the marketing of such forms of gambling.

[27] One of the leading operators, William Hill, reported online revenues in 2010 of £251.5 million with a more than 50 per cent increase in income over the preceding year. Formerly regulated in the United Kingdom, the company's online operations are now conducted from and regulated in Gibraltar: <http://www.william-hillplc.com/>.

Commission. It remains to be seen how effective enforcement might be although many of the major online operators also have a significant High Street presence and will therefore have assets which can be attacked in the course of any litigation.

The UK approach is much more permissive than is the case in many other countries. The United States, for example, maintains a prohibition against any form of online gambling.[28] This led to a major dispute between the United States and Antigua which, as with other Caribbean countries has promoted itself as a base for gambling operations. Following proceedings lasting for a decade, the World Trade Organization ruled in January 2013 that by prohibiting its citizens from lawfully accessing gambling services hosted in Antigua, the United States was in breach of its free trade obligations under the terms of the General Agreement on Trade in Services (GATS).[29] As with many issues relating to Internet-based activities, enforcement of prohibitions such as those adopted by the United States can be problematic although in the case of gambling, there is the possibility of taking action against necessary intermediaries, in this case financial institutions that provide the facilities necessary for the gambling activities.

The Gambling Act 2005

The Gambling Act 2005 provides that any significant form of gambling activity is to be unlawful in the absence of a licence and establishes the Gambling Commission as a licensing and regulatory body. There is at present no specific European legislation in the field of gambling although a Commission Green Paper on Online Gambling in the Internal Market was published in March 2011[30] and the European Parliament adopted a resolution on the topic in November 2013.[31] The provisions of more general items of European legislation, in particular the Directive on Electronic Commerce, may be of considerable relevance with much online gambling falling within the category of Information Society Services.

Licencing of remote gambling activities

The Gambling Act defines the term 'remote gambling' as gambling[32] in which persons participate by the use of remote communication using the Internet, telephone, television, radio, or 'any other kind of electronic or other technology for facilitating communication.'[33]

The Gambling Act provides that the Gambling Commission may issue licences for a wide range of activities and players within the gambling spectrum. A remote operating licence must be sought where remote gambling equipment used by the licensee in connection with the licensed activities is situated in Great Britain.[34]

---

[28] The state of New Jersey authorised online gambling in 2013 (see <http://www.bbc.co.uk/news/technology-25051312>although this is available only to persons resident in the state.

[29] For an account of the case see <http://www.antiguawto.com/WTODispPg.html>.

[30] Com (2011) 128 Final.

[31] Available from <http://www.europarl.europa.eu/sides/getDoc.do?pubRef=-//EP//TEXT+TA+P7-TA-2013-0348+0+DOC+XML+V0// EN>.

[32] Gambling is defined in s. 2 as gaming (further defined in s. 6(1) as involving playing a game of chance for a prize), betting (further defined as making or accepting a bet on the outcome of a race, competition, or other event or process, the likelihood of anything occurring or not occurring, or whether anything is or is not true), and participating in a lottery (further defined in s. 14 and the emphasis of which lies in the fact that winning or losing is a matter of chance rather than involving the exercise of any skill or judgment).   [33] s. 4.

[34] s. 89.

Licences fall into a range of categories. Operating licences may be issued to parties providing betting, bingo, casino, or lottery facilities. In respect of any of these activities, the Act provides for the issuance of remote operating licences.[35] Licences are also required to be obtained by a person who manufactures, adapts, supplies, or installs gambling software.[36]

In addition to operating licences issued to the business per se, the Gambling Act requires that personal licences be obtained by individuals performing specified management functions within an organisation or performing specified roles in relating to the control of gambling operations. These provisions apply regardless of the nature of the business.

Technical standards

In addition to issuing operating licences, the Gambling Commission may establish, or provide for, the establishment of standards in respect of the hardware and software used in the course of online gambling. It may provide also for the manner in which compliance with the standards can be determined.[37]

The Remote Gambling and Software Technical Standards were first adopted by the Gambling Commission in June 2007. These were replaced by a revised version in August 2009. The purpose of the standards is to detail 'the specific technical standards and the security requirements that licensed remote gambling operators and gambling software operators need to meet'.[38]

Conclusions

As with so many aspects of information technology law, what we see in these fields is a complex mix of problems and opportunities. The success of e-commerce is completely dependent upon the availability of payment mechanisms. Paper notes and metallic coins cannot be transmitted electronically. We have, of course, long had alternatives that might be classed as working within the system. Credit cards have existed in the United Kingdom for around half a century and are inextricably linked to 'real' currencies. It is perhaps too soon to say what the future might be for alternative forms of virtual currency. As we have seen in the ongoing Euro crisis, confidence and credibility is critical to any unit of currency. Would a future 'Bank of Apple' (or Samsung or Google) carry less confidence than many national money issuers? Barring the most major currencies, I suspect the answer would be 'no'.

Online gambling raises the same issues in respect of payment mechanisms but also others in respect of control questions. As with other policy issues, such as the control of alcohol and drugs, different countries have differing approaches, based perhaps on strongly held convictions. Enforcing these in the context of a global communications network is difficult but, as has been seen in the example of the United States and online gambling, can be reasonably effective when efforts are directed at financial intermediaries such as banks and credit card companies. Even alternative payment mechanisms such as PayPal seem to have decided that tangling with the United States authorities would not be a wise commercial move. Whether virtual currencies would have the same concern is more doubtful given that one of their major claimed benefits is the degree of anonymity associated with their usage.

---

[35] s. 68.   [36] s. 66.   [37] s. 97.
[38] Available from <http://www.gamblingcommission.gov.uk/pdf/Testing % 20 strategy %20for%20compliance%20 with%20remote%20gambling%20and%20software%20technical%20standards%20-%20August%202009. pdf>.

24

Contractual liability for defective software

Introduction

Software is undoubtedly the driving force of the information society. By any standards, the sector is a major contributor to national economies and employment and it should be borne in mind that these figures relate to only one part of the information technology industry. The traditional notion of a computer is that it consists of a monitor, processing unit, keyboard, and sundry peripherals such as the ubiquitous mouse. Most people will recognise such a device when they see one. It is less easy to recognise a motor car or video recorder as a computer, yet a modern motor car is in many respects a sophisticated computer system, to the extent it has been calculated that the 'chip cost of a new car is now greater than the metal cost'.[1] A vast range of objects, from domestic appliances to nuclear power stations, is dependent on microprocessors. In many cases, these are, quite literally, built into a structure. Worldwide, it is estimated that there are some 20 billion embedded chips in use, a fact which caused great concern in the context of the Millennium Bug. It has been reported that:

> All buildings built between 1984 (the year when building services started to computerise) and 1996/7 (the period when most new buildings were fitted with systems that were millennium compliant) are likely to be affected by the millennium bug. Bovis Construction Group, one of the biggest building contractors has written to the owners of 870 buildings it has built since 1984 warning them integral systems ranging from ventilation and heating to intruder alarms and connections to the electricity supply network may fail. This is because many building systems use microchips to identify dates for switching machinery on and off and to alert maintenance staff of the need for servicing.[2]

As the importance of software increases, so does the level of societal vulnerability in the event of any failure. In purely economic terms, losses are potentially massive. Although it is tempting to take the example of the Millennium Bug as a case where the degree of risk was exaggerated, even what might be regarded as a false alarm proved an extremely costly exercise. The British Bankers Association estimated that United Kingdom banks spent £1 billion checking and repairing systems. British Telecom budgeted for expenditure of £300 million. Worldwide, costs were estimated at some £400 billion. To put these figures into perspective, these figures exceed the total financial cost of the Vietnam War.[3]

Matters could, of course, have been significantly worse in the event of extensive problems materialising. One estimate suggested that the effect of the bug would cause 8 per cent

---

[1] <http://www.scl.org/members/emagazine/vol9/iss3/vol9-iss3-peter-cochrane-art.htm>.
[2] Cited in evidence to the House of Commons Select Committee on Science and Technology.
[3] *Sunday Times*, 10 August 1997. The cost of the Vietnam War has been estimated at some £370 billion.

of Western European companies to fail. The prospect of global recession was frequently raised in reports. Additionally, as indicated, the application of information technology in a vast range of applications conjured up the spectre of hospital patients dying because of failures of medical devices; trains, planes, and automobiles crashing; massive power cuts; and shortage of food and drink due to failures in retailers' distribution systems. Fortunately, the predictions of computer doom proved unfounded, but the incident may have served a useful, albeit expensive, purpose in bringing home the extent of our society's dependence on information technology. What the incident also achieved was to highlight the fact that where losses arise through the improper operation of systems and equipment, considerations of legal liability will not be far behind.

To date, comparatively few cases concerned specifically with issues of software quality have reached the stage of court proceedings. A variety of explanations may be proposed for this state of affairs. Although parties may not wish to litigate when the answer is certain, excessive uncertainty as to the very basis upon which a court may decide will itself inhibit litigation. Some of the most basic questions concerning the application of provisions of contractual and non-contractual liability in the information technology field admit of no easy or certain solution. With one exception, all of the cases which have reached the stage of High Court proceedings have concerned relatively high-value contracts for software which has either been developed under the terms of a specific contract (bespoke software) for one or a small number of clients or has been modified extensively to suit the needs of a particular customer (customised software). To date, there have been no cases concerned with the extent of the liabilities which will apply to mass-produced or standard software packages such as word-processing or spreadsheet programs. A further factor complicating such cases is the invariable presence of a software licence. The role of these documents in respect of intellectual property issues has been discussed previously. In respect of liability considerations, the terms of the licence inevitably seek to limit or exclude the producer's liabilities in the event that the performance of the software does not match the user's expectations.

Forms of liability

Two main strands of liability run through the field of private law. The law of contract confers rights and imposes duties upon contracting parties. Whilst the nature and extent of these may be determined in large part by the expressed wishes of the parties, these may be constrained by the provisions of statutes such as the Sale of Goods Act 1979 and the Unfair Contract Terms Act 1977. It is, of course, a basic tenet of the common law that contractual rights can be enforced only by those who are a party to the contract. In the situation where no contract exists, attention must turn to non-contractual remedies. Until recently, the basis of these has rested in the law of tort/delict. The prerequisite for a successful action in tort is evidence of negligence on the part of the defendant (absent exceptional circumstances where strict liability has attached to this party's actions). The passage of the Consumer Protection Act 1987 has radically transformed the non-contractual position. Based on the provisions of an EC Directive on the Approximation of the Laws, Regulations and Administrative Provisions of the Member States Concerning Liability for Defective Products,[4] this serves to impose a strict-liability regime, whereby the producer of a product is held liable for personal injury or damage to non-commercial property resulting from the presence of a defect within the product, irrespective of any fault on their part.

---

[4] Council Directive 85/374/EEC, OJ 1985 L 210/29.

The nature of software defects

Prior to considering issues of legal liability, it might be helpful to attempt a brief analysis of the nature of the differences which exist between software and the tangible products with which society and the law are more familiar. Defects in a traditional product such as a motor car may originate in one of two ways. Design defects relate to some failure at the design stage, with the consequence that the failure node will be exhibited in every species of the product. A more commonplace form of defect is introduced during the production stage. It might be, for example, as happened in the case of *Smedleys v Breed*,[5] that a caterpillar found its way into a can of peas somewhere within the canning process. Such defects will be restricted to one or to a limited number of examples of the product. In the *Smedleys* case, for example, only four caterpillars or other foreign bodies had been reported from an annual production of 3.5 million cans.

If a party is trying to establish that a product fails to comply with relevant quality requirements, the task is almost invariably simpler where defects arise in production. In most cases, what a claimant will seek to establish is that compared with other examples of a product, the one at issue is of inferior quality. The case might be put, for example, that 3,499,996 cans of peas did not contain foreign bodies. The four that did should, therefore, be considered exceptional (or exceptionally bad). Evidential burdens are more extensive when all examples of the product exhibit the same properties. A prime example is in the pharmaceutical field, where adverse reactions to a product are generally caused because of the properties of the drug, rather than through contamination of a particular tablet or bottle of medicine.

Where software is concerned, the nature of the digital copying process is such that there can be a high degree of confidence that every copy of software will be identical. If particular copies are corrupted, the likelihood is that they will not work at all, so that any defect becomes apparent before any damage is caused. If a customer should wish to establish that a copy of a word-processing program which has been purchased is not of satisfactory quality, argument will have to proceed by reference to word-processing programs produced by other producers and to general standards. Although the task can be accomplished, it is a significantly more onerous burden than that faced by a person claiming the existence of a production defect.

A more general difference may be identified at the level of the testing which may be carried out in respect of a product. With a product such as a motor car, it is possible to test every component so as to provide definitive information about its properties. Often, however, testing entails destruction of the item involved and, even where this is not the case, it will seldom be commercially feasible to test every specimen of the product. In production, it is possible that some components will be of inferior quality to those tested. Only a portion of products will possess any particular defect and these may not be the ones which are selected for inspection. The conclusion from this analysis is that it is possible to test one item exhaustively, but that the results have limited applicability regarding other items of the same type.

The situation is radically different where software is concerned. It is impossible to test even the simplest program in an exhaustive fashion. This is because of the myriad possibilities for interaction (whether desired or not) between the various elements of the program. In the world of popular science, much publicity has been given in recent years to what is

---

[5] [1974] AC 839.

known as the chaos theory. This suggests that every event influences every other event; that the beating of a butterfly's wings has an impact upon the development of a hurricane. On such an analysis, totally accurate weather forecasting will never be practicable because of the impossibility of taking account of all the variables affecting the climate. The theory's hypothesis is reality in a software context. Although software can and should be tested, it has to be accepted that every piece of software will contain errors which may not materialise until a particular and perhaps unrepeatable set of circumstances occurs. It is commonplace for software to be placed on the market in the knowledge that it contains errors. Early users, in effect, act as unpaid testers. As faults are reported to the producer, fixes will be developed and incorporated into new versions of the software.[6]

Especially where software is used in safety-critical functions, it is sometimes advocated that where an error is discovered, it is preferable to devise procedures to prevent the circumstances recurring than to attempt to modify the software. The argument is that any change to the software may have unanticipated consequences, resulting in another error manifesting itself at some time in the future. The cause of a massive failure which paralysed sections of the United States telecommunications system in 1991 was ultimately traced to changes which had been made in the call-routing software.[7] The software contained several million lines of code. Three apparently insignificant lines were changed and chaos ensued. By way of contrast, the operators of London's Docklands Light Railway, whose trains are driven under computer control, took the decision that they would not make any changes to the software after it had passed its acceptance tests. The result was that for several years, trains stopped on an open stretch of line, paused for a few seconds and then continued with their journey. It had been intended to build a station at the site. After the software was accepted, the plans were abandoned, but the trains remained ignorant of this fact.

Forms of software

As indicated, software is supplied in a variety of situations and under a range of conditions. Viewed across the spectrum, at one end we can identify bespoke or made-to-measure software products. The cost of these may run into many millions of pounds, with the essential feature being that the supplier agrees to design and develop software to suit the needs of a particular customer, or a comparatively small number of identified customers. The software will be supplied under the terms of a written agreement negotiated between the parties. Perhaps not surprisingly, given the costs involved, almost all of the software-related disputes which have reached the courts have been concerned with such forms of contract.

At the far end of the software spectrum are standard software packages. In this category, identical copies will be supplied to users—perhaps tens or even hundreds of thousands in number—often via a substantial distribution chain and at a cost ranging from tens to thousands of pounds. There will seldom be any written agreement negotiated in advance between the parties, with the producer attempting to introduce a set of terms and conditions through the device of a licence. As will be discussed later, the validity of software licences is open to challenge on a number of grounds.

---

[6] See the discussion of the case of *Saphena v Allied Collection Agencies* [1995] FSR 616.

[7] Most of the examples of software failure cited in this chapter have been culled from the columns of comp. risks, an Internet-based newsgroup which chronicles the failures of safety-critical systems and the risks they pose to the public.

A final and more nebulous category of software is referred to as having been 'customised'. This involves the supplier modifying existing software, developed either by themselves or by a third party, better to suit the requirements of a particular customer. The degree of customisation may vary from making very minor adjustments to a single package to developing a unique system based on a combination of a number of existing packages. With developments in 'object oriented engineering' it may be expected that the range of customised products will increase substantially as developers base their operations on a 'pick-and-mix' philosophy.

The legal status of software and software contracts

Throughout this book, use has been made of terms such as 'software industry' and of software being 'produced'. Such terms are in common use. The pages on the Microsoft website describing its software packages are titled 'products',[8] whilst the Price Waterhouse study discussed in the context of copyright law is titled *The Contribution of the Packaged Software Industry to the European Economies*. The fact that terms are in popular usage does not, of course, mean that their legal interpretation will be the same, and over the years, much legal ink has been spilled in discussion of the question of whether contracts for the supply of software should be regarded as a species of goods or as a form of services.

Much of the discussion regarding status has focused on two decisions of the Court of Appeal. In *Lee v Griffin*,[9] the Court of Appeal was faced with a contract under which a dentist undertook to make a set of dentures for a patient. A dispute subsequently arising, the court was faced with the question of the contract's proper categorisation. Holding the contract to be one of sale, the court held that the essential test was whether anything that could be the subject matter of a sale had come into existence. In the event, for example, that an attorney was engaged to draw up a deed for a client, it was held that the contract would be one for services. In other situations, however:

> I do not think that the test to apply to these cases is whether the value of the work exceeds that of the materials used in its execution; for, if a sculptor were employed to execute a work of art, greatly as his skill and labour, assuming it to be of the highest description, might exceed the value of the marble on which he worked, the contract would in my opinion, nevertheless be a contract for the sale of a chattel.[10]

On this basis, it would appear that the supply of software on some storage device such as a disk or CD would be classed as involving goods. The increasingly common situation where software is supplied electronically, typically being downloaded from a website, could not, of course, come within the definition.

The distinction between goods and services was again at issue before the Court of Appeal in the case of *Robinson v Graves*.[11] The contract here was one whereby an artist agreed to paint a portrait of his client's wife. On the basis of the situation hypothesised in *Lee v Griffin*,[12] it would appear that such a transaction should be regarded as one of sale. In the event, however, it was held that it should be regarded as one for services. In reaching this conclusion, the court sought to identify the prime purpose of the contract. In the oft-quoted words of Greer LJ:

> If the substance of the contract...is that skill and labour have to be exercised for the production of the article and...it is only ancillary to that that there will pass from the artist

---

[8] <http://www.microsoft.com/en/us/default.aspx>. [9] (1861) 1 B&S 272. [10] At 278.
[11] [1935] 1 KB 579. [12] (1861) 1 B&S 272.

to his client or customer some materials in addition to the skill involved in the production of the portrait, that does not make any difference to the result, because the substance of the contract is the skill and experience of the artist in producing the picture.[13]

Although the court in *Robinson*[14] did not overrule, or even distinguish, the earlier authority, it must be doubted how far the two approaches can truly be considered compatible. It would appear that the decision in *Robinson* has been the more influential in recent years but, even so, its application in a software context has not been without its difficulties. Whilst it would seem to suggest that contracts for the development of bespoke software should be regarded as services, standard software exhibits many of the attributes associated with goods.

In the final analysis, the precise categorisation of software contracts may be a matter of limited practical significance. In most of the cases which have come before the courts, the dispute has centred on the interpretation of a specific contract between the parties. The court's task is to determine what the contract said, rather than concern itself unduly with categorisations. Even where no detailed contract exists, there is little difference between the relevant statutory provisions. The Sale of Goods Act 1979 implies terms relating to title, description, and quality. The Supply of Goods and Services Act 1982 implies requirements that the supplier should exercise reasonable skill and care and that any goods ultimately supplied will comply with identical requirements relating to title, description, and quality as those required under the Sale of Goods Act 1979. Faced with this convergence between the statutory provisions, it is not surprising that Staughton LJ, delivering judgment in the case of *Saphena Computing Ltd v Allied Collection Agencies Ltd*, was able to state:

> It was, we are told, common ground that the law governing these contracts was precisely the same whether they were contracts for the sale of goods or for the supply of services. It is therefore unnecessary to consider into which category they might come.[15]

In the case of *St Albans District Council v ICL*,[16] the Court of Appeal was braver—or more foolhardy. Here, Sir Iain Glidewell posed the question, 'Is software goods?' He continued:

> If a disc carrying the program is transferred, by way of sale or hire, and the program is in some way defective, so that it will not instruct or enable the computer to achieve the intended purpose, is this a defect in the disc? Put more precisely, would the seller or hirer of the disc be in breach of the terms of quality or fitness implied by s. 14 of the Sale of Goods Act [1979].[17]

There was, he recognised, no English or indeed any common law precedent on this point. An analogy was drawn, however, with another form of informational product:

> Suppose I buy an instruction manual on the maintenance and repair of a particular make of car. The instructions are wrong in an important respect. Anybody who follows them is likely to cause serious damage to the engine of his car. In my view the instructions are an integral part of the manual. The manual including the instructions, whether in a book or a video cassette, would in my opinion be 'goods' within the meaning of the Sale of Goods Act and the defective instructions would result in breach of the implied terms.
>
> If this is correct, I can see no logical reason why it should not also be correct in relation to a computer disc onto which a program designed and intended to instruct or enable a computer to achieve particular functions has been encoded. If the disc is sold or hired by the computer manufacturer, but the program is defective, in my opinion there would prima

---

[13] [1935] 1 KB 579 at 587.   [14] *Robinson v Graves* [1935] 1 KB 579.
[15] [1995] FSR 616 at 652.   [16] [1996] 4 All ER 481. Reported at first instance at [1995] FSR 686.
[17] At 492.

facie be a breach of the terms as to quality and fitness for purpose implied by the Sale of Goods Act.[18]

As will be discussed, this statement will have implications for all of those involved in the information market. In the case of *Wormell v RHM Agriculture Ltd*,[19] the Court of Appeal recognised that where instructions for use were supplied along with a product, the sufficiency and adequacy of these should be taken into account in considering questions of the product's merchantability. *St Albans District Council v ICL*[20] appears, however, to be the first occasion in which instructions per se were subjected to the qualitative requirements of the Sale of Goods Act 1979. It remains uncertain, however, how extensive liability will be. The analogy drawn with a motor instruction book may be appropriate. In the circumstances described, where following the instructions will result in serious damage, there could be little argument that the book is not fit for its purpose. The decision becomes much closer if the complaint is that the book describes an inefficient method for performing work. Another problematic case might be where an instruction is so obviously wrong that no reasonable person would follow it. Equivalents in a software context might be inefficient methods of saving word-processed documents or defects which require a user to 'work around' them. Further cases will be required before we can attempt a plausible answer to the question of what these qualitative requirements mean in a software context.

There is, of course, the increasing possibility that software might be downloaded over the Internet so that no tangible objects change hands. Indeed, in the present case, the practice for installing software was that an ICL engineer would visit, load the software from disk, and retain the disk. In such cases, there could be no transfer of goods. In such situations, it was indicated, in determining the extent of the parties' obligations:

> The answer must be sought in the Common Law. The terms implied by the Sale of Goods Act . . . were originally evolved by the Courts of Common Law and have since by analogy been implied by the courts into other types of contract.
>
> . . .
>
> In the absence of any express term as to quality or fitness for purpose, or of any term to the contrary, such a contract is subject to an implied term that the program will be reasonably fit for, i.e. reasonably capable of achieving the intended purpose.[21]

Given the existence of a specific contract between the parties, these comments must be regarded as *obiter dicta* rather than as binding precedent. They do appear, however, to be in line with a judicial trend to imply requirements that software be fit for its purpose into contracts unless the terms make clear provision to the contrary. Any ambiguities will be interpreted *contra proferentem*, with the case of *Salvage Association v CAP Financial Services*[22] providing a good illustration of how restrictive this doctrine may be. The key issue, therefore, must be to determine what concepts, such as fitness and the newly introduced requirement that goods be of 'satisfactory quality', might mean in an informational context.

Implied terms in software contracts

The Sale of Goods Act 1979 provides for three conditions to be implied into a contract of sale. Although there is room for argument whether software is generally sold by virtue of the fact

---

[18] At 493.   [19] [1987] 3 All ER 75.   [20] [1996] 4 All ER 481.
[21] *St Albans District Council v ICL* [1996] 4 All ER 481 at 494.
[22] (9 July 1993, unreported), CA. The case is reported at first instance at [1995] FSR 654.

that intellectual property rights will remain with the original owner, the Supply of Goods and Services Act 1982 provides that the implied terms will extend to any other contract for the supply of goods. Although interpretative problems may remain in the situation discussed in the previous section, where software is supplied over the Internet, for example, the categorisation of contracts as forms of sale or rental or loan is of no significance. Reference throughout this section will be to the provisions of the Sale of Goods Act 1979, as amended by the Sale and Supply of Goods Act 1994.

One of the cornerstones of English commercial law has been the doctrine of *caveat emptor* ('let the buyer beware'). Traditionally, no provisions relating to the quality of goods has been implied into contracts of sale. In previous eras, this approach was not as inequitable as it might appear in the twenty-first century. Goods were simple in nature and composition, and it was a feasible task for a buyer to make an assessment of their condition and suitability. As goods became more sophisticated, it became increasingly difficult for an inexpert customer to examine them. Even if a potential buyer were to wish to do this, the reaction of the seller of a computer could well be predicted in the event that a customer was to produce a screwdriver and seek to disassemble the equipment. The notion of the implied term has been developed, first by the courts and now enshrined in statute, as a means for protecting the interests of the consumer. In general law, of course, an implied term is overridden by any contrary express agreement made between the parties. Often such an express term will seek to reduce or exclude the liability of the seller in the event that the performance of the goods is inadequate. Again, the first attempts to control these contractual tactics were made by the courts, with Parliament intervening in 1977 with the passage of the Unfair Contract Terms Act 1977. The following sections will consider the extent of the obligations implied by law into contracts for the supply of software. Attention will then be paid to the extent to which these might validly or lawfully be reduced by the application of devices such as licences or contractual terms.

Title in software

By virtue of section 12 of the Sale of Goods Act 1979, a seller must guarantee that he or she possesses the right to sell the goods and that full title to the goods will be transferred to the buyer, except for such limitations as are brought to the buyer's attention prior to the contract of sale. In terms of the usage of the goods, it is provided that the buyer is to enjoy 'quiet possession'. This entails that the buyer's freedom to deal with the goods in such manner as might be desired is not to be restricted by virtue of any rights retained by the seller or by some third party. In many cases concerned with software, the sale will be made by a retailer, with the producer retaining ownership of copyright in the work and remaining an interested third party.

The major limitations imposed upon the buyer's freedom to deal with software are found in the copyright legislation. As has been seen, the mere use of software might constitute a breach of copyright. The buyer's right under section 12 of the Sale of Goods Act 1979 is always subject to the caveat that the use proposed is lawful. The terms of the European Directive on the Legal Protection of Computer Programs[23] might have implications for the operation of section 12. Under the Directive, a number of forms of behaviour concerned with software, for example modification for the purpose of error correction, will be permitted unless the terms of a contract or licence provide otherwise. Where the copyright owner intends to exercise this option and seeks to do so by means of a licence document whose

---

[23] Directive 91/250/EC, OJ 1991 L 122/42.

contents are not disclosed to the buyer until after the contract of sale is concluded, the failure to give prior notice might place the seller in breach of section 12.

Description

Section 13 of the Sale of Goods Act 1979 provides that where a sale is by description, there is to be an implied condition that the goods will correspond with this description. In the course of many contracts of sale, a variety of claims may be made concerning the attributes of the product involved. Not all such elements will be incorporated into the final contract. Many laudatory phrases, typically used in promotional materials, will be regarded as too general. A claim that a product is 'user-friendly' might, for example, be regarded as insufficiently precise to be considered as a description, although in such cases it may be that an action will lie on the ground of misrepresentation.

Claims of compatibility with other products, typically that a piece of software will operate on a specified piece of hardware, might be regarded as descriptive. Equally, lists of the features possessed by a product will be considered as part of its description, although even here the matter may not be beyond doubt. In the case of a popular laser printer, for example, the product specification made reference to a printing speed of four pages per minute. The statement appears true, but what is not made clear is that the printer can only print four copies of the same page in any given minute. The printing process requires that data regarding the contents of any page be transmitted from the computer to the printer. This process takes some time, with the result that the speed for printing a multi-page document slows to little more than a single page per minute. One factor which is relevant throughout all the discussion of liability is the absence of clearly defined industry standards and conventions. In the absence of these in respect of speed of printing or many other attributes concerned with the functioning of information technology systems, it may be difficult to establish liability in respect of claims that are accurate but potentially misleading.

Quality

The Sale of Goods Act 1979 requirements relating to product quality are so well known that little exposition is required. Two partially overlapping conditions will be implied into a contract of sale. Goods must be of satisfactory quality and reasonably fit for any particular purpose for which they are supplied.[24] The requirement that goods supplied be of satisfactory quality was introduced in 1995 in substitution for the concept of merchantable quality. The notion of merchantable quality can be traced back to the Middle Ages. It assumed statutory form for the first time in the Sale of Goods Act 1893 and was retained in the Sale of Goods Act 1979. The latter statute also introduced a new definition, providing that goods would be of merchantable quality if they are:

> as fit for the purpose or purposes for which goods of that kind are commonly bought as it was reasonable to expect having regard to any description applied to them, the price (if relevant) and all the other relevant circumstances.[25]

The law relating to sale of goods was the subject of a report by the Law Commissions in 1987.[26] This expressed concerns at the suitability of the venerable concept of merchantability to deal with the complexities inherent in many modern products. Beyond the issue of whether the terminology itself was not unduly archaic, the notion of a general requirement

---

[24] s. 14.   [25] s. 14(6).

[26] A Joint Report was published: Law Commission No. 160, Scots Law Commission No. 104, Cm. 137.

of fitness for purpose (as opposed to the more specific instantiation in the second implied term) was developed in an era of comparatively simple products, which would either work or fail to work. With a modern product, such as a motor car or a software product, the manner or quality of performance is of at least as much importance.

Acting on the Law Commissions' recommendations, the requirement that goods be of satisfactory quality was substituted in the Sale and Supply of Goods Act 1994. The definition of the new requirement retains echoes of its predecessor. It is now provided that:

> goods are of satisfactory quality if they meet the standard that a reasonable person would regard as satisfactory, taking account of any description of the goods, the price (if relevant) and all the other relevant circumstances.[27]

The statute goes on, however, to list a number of specific factors which are to be taken into account in determining whether goods are of satisfactory quality:

> the following (among others) are in appropriate cases aspects of the quality of goods:
>
> (a) fitness for all the purposes for which goods of the kind in question are commonly supplied;
>
> (b) appearance and finish;
>
> (c) freedom from minor defects;
>
> (d) safety; and
>
> (e) durability.

A number of points from this new definition may be of considerable significance in a software context. Problems have arisen in the past where an object is fit for only some of its normal purposes.[28] An integrated spreadsheet/word-processing/database package, for example, might perform satisfactorily in two modes but be unworkable in the third. A design package may be satisfactory for external designs but unsuited for internal design. It is now clearly stated that products must be fit for all the purposes for which they are commonly supplied. Products of the kind mentioned above will fail to meet the statutory requirement. Producers will be well advised to give greater care to the descriptions of their products and, at the risk of blunting their marketing strategy, make clear any design limitations applying to the product.

A number of the other features of the definition of satisfactory quality will also be relevant in a computer context. The criteria relating to appearance and finish might be invoked in respect of the user interface and screen displays of a software product. Perhaps the biggest source of problems may arise with the specific mention of 'freedom from minor defects'. Given that all software products contain defects, this may be of considerable significance. It must be stressed, however, that the Sale of Goods Act 1979 does not require that goods be perfect. The standard relates to the expectations of a 'reasonable person'. The major impact may lie in the fact that the specific mention of minor defects may be expected to draw a court's attention to this aspect of an allegedly defective product. Assessment of software products causes particular difficulties. With most products, defects are likely to be introduced at the production stage. If a complaint relates to the allegedly defective performance of a television set, the item at issue can normally be compared with other examples of the same model produced by the same manufacturer. Given the fact that all copies of a software product are likely to be identical, the only basis for comparison will be with the products of competitors. This creates problems in comparing like with like.

---

[27] Sale of Goods Act 1979, s. 14.   [28] *Aswan Engineering v Lupdine* [1987] 1 WLR 1.

The decision as to whether a product is satisfactory is a factual one. A variety of factors may be taken into account. The question of price is one which is of considerable weight in many cases. In *Rogers v Parish*, Mustill LJ stated that '[t]he buyer was entitled to value for his money'.[29] In the vast majority of cases, one might reasonably expect that a more expensive product will be of better quality than a lower-priced alternative. This approach may break down to some extent in the context of software. The physical components make up such a small part of the value of a package that it is unlikely that any significant variation might be expected here. The point can also be made that it is easier and cheaper to emulate than to innovate. On this basis, and ignoring possible intellectual property complications, it might not be unreasonable to expect a lower-priced derivative package to attain a similar level of quality to that of the original. The speed of development in the entire information technology field also makes difficult the task of determining issues of quality and value for money. A product which might have been regarded as of acceptable quality if sold for £500 on 1 January might be regarded much less favourably if sold for the same amount (or even at a lower price) on the following 31 December.

Further problems may arise in determining the proper purpose of an item of software. Difficulties may be exacerbated by a lack of customer knowledge, as epitomised in the first software disputes to reach the courts, *MacKenzie Patten v British Olivetti*.[30] In this case, the plaintiff, a small firm of solicitors, entered into an agreement for the supply of a computer in the apparent belief that this would be able to access court schedules held on a computer at the Old Bailey. This was notwithstanding the fact that neither computer possessed any form of communications capability. It is also the case, of course, that design limitations are not as apparent in software products as may normally be the case. Under the provisions of the Sale of Goods Act 1979, a customer wishing to receive the benefit of the fitness-for-purpose condition is obliged to inform the seller if it is intended to put the product to some unusual purpose. No specific mention need be made if the product is intended to be put to its normal use. 'Normal' in this sense may be interpreted in two ways. First, consideration must be given to the normal uses of a product of the type in question. Thus, a screwdriver is to be used to insert and remove screws. Use as a crowbar would not be classed as normal. A second element might relate to the scale of the intended use. Most products might be intended for a specific sector of a market. A low-cost and low-powered electric drill might be suitable for occasional use in domestic circumstances, but would not be fit for intensive use by a professional builder or joiner. With most products of this kind, design limitations will be apparent. A customer putting a product to excessive use might not receive the court's sympathy in the event of a claim that the product was not fit for its purpose. With software products, design limitations will be much less transparent. A disk retailing at £10,000 will look no different from a blank disk worth a few pence. The development of cheap personal computers has led to the marketing of 'cut-down' versions of computer programs originally designed for the commercial market. Intended for domestic use, these may be marketed on the back of the original but may lack some of its features and capabilities. This may render the program unfit for use at a commercial level of activity. The limitations will not be as apparent as with the electric drill, and sellers may be faced with a dilemma. If they do not make them clear to potential buyers, they may run the risk that a naïve and inexperienced business user may purchase the product and find it unsuitable, whilst drawing excessive attention to the limitations of the product might not be advisable in marketing terms.

---

[29] [1987] 2 All ER 232 at 237.   [30] (1985) 48 MLR 344.

Remedies for breach of the implied terms

In the event of a breach of any of the implied terms, the buyer's claim may be to reject the goods supplied as failing to conform with the contractual requirements. It follows that if the goods are validly rejected, the buyer will be released from any obligation to pay for them. If the seller's breach of contract has resulted in the buyer suffering any further loss, the rejection of the goods may be accompanied by a claim for damages.

The right to reject will be lost where the buyer's conduct indicates acceptance of the goods. The Sale of Goods Act 1979 provides that the buyer is to be given a reasonable opportunity of examining them. This may occur before or after the sale.[31] One factor which may arise in software contracts, given the near certainty that every copy of a particular package will be identical, concerns the problem of whether the opportunity to examine a copy in the seller's premises will debar the right of rejection, even though a different copy is supplied to the customer.

The Sale of Goods Act 1979 provides further that the right to reject will cease when the buyer does any act which is inconsistent with the seller's continuing ownership or by the lapse of a 'reasonable time'.[32] In respect of the first of these elements, it might be queried whether the act of completing and returning a licence agreement accompanying the software might be regarded as an act inconsistent with the seller's ownership. In the case of many popular software programs, the disks are contained in an envelope inside the packaging. The envelope bears a legend to the effect that opening it signifies acceptance of a licence agreement. The validity of such techniques will be explored in more detail later, but the buyer may be put in the position whereby taking the steps that are physically necessary to use the software might involve an act which is inconsistent with the seller's title. Given that the buyer's right to use the software will otherwise be severely restricted, such a view would appear harsh but by no means illogical.

More difficult still is the question of what will be considered a reasonable time to examine the goods. In the case of *Bernstein v Pamsons Motors (Golders Green) Ltd*,[33] a new motor car was sold to the plaintiff. Some three weeks after delivery, the car suffered a major and potentially dangerous breakdown on a motorway. Examination revealed that a blob of sealing compound had somehow found its way into the vehicle's lubrication system during the course of manufacture. During the course of the engine's short life, the object floated around the system until the occasion when it caused an obstruction, blocking the flow of oil, to the severe detriment of the engine.

Under the terms of the Sale of Goods Act 1979, goods are accepted when the buyer retains them beyond a reasonable length of time without intimating any complaint to the seller. In this case, it was held that the passage of three weeks sufficed to prevent the buyer from rejecting the vehicle. A purchaser, it was held, was entitled to such time as was required to make a general examination of the goods. Although this time would vary depending upon the complexity of the goods, no account would be taken of the nature of the particular defect in question.

The implications of this case for software purchasers are not positive. Although particular defects may not manifest themselves for a considerable period of time, it seems unlikely that a general examination of software, of the kind sanctioned in *Bernstein*, would occupy a substantial period of time. It must be stressed, however, that the fact that the right to reject is lost does not imply that the buyer possesses no remedies. In the event that goods are unmerchantable or are not fit for their purpose, a remedy will remain in damages. The

---

[31] s. 34(1).   [32] s. 35(1).   [33] [1987] 2 All ER 220.

situation at issue in *Bernstein* is again relevant in a software context. The engine of the motor car suffered significant damage in the incident. The seller was willing to repair those components which had identifiably been affected. The customer, however, expressed the fear that the stresses incurred during the incident might have affected other components, rendering them more likely to fail in the future. This fear served to reduce significantly the customer's confidence in the vehicle. Although the judge accepted that the vehicle was not of merchantable quality and an award of damages was made, it is arguable that this provided an inadequate remedy. In the software context, it might be argued that a customer who discovered significant defects in a software product might justifiably fear that efforts on the supplier's part to correct these might create further problems or, alternatively, that other defects might be lying in wait. The fact that software is not susceptible of exhaustive testing, coupled with its intangible nature, makes the issue of customer confidence a significant one.

The fact that a buyer no longer possesses the right to reject goods for non-conformity with contractual obligations does not mean that no remedies are available. An action for damages will always be competent. In respect of the product itself, the measure of damages will reflect the difference between the value of the goods as supplied and the cost of acquiring goods which will conform with the contractual obligations. The implications of this may be significant. An example might be taken of a seller who, having been informed of the buyer's requirements, supplies a system for £4,000. In the event that the system proved not to be fit for that purpose and evidence indicated that a sum of £10,000 might be required in order to meet the requirements, the measure of damages would reflect this difference. This may not be an unlikely scenario in the information technology field. One of the criticisms made in the inquiry into the failures of the London Ambulance Service's computer system was that the cost of the system was approximately half of that which might have been expected for such a significant project.

Software quality and the courts

Having outlined the general principles applicable in any contractual action relating to the quality of goods supplied, attention will be paid in the remainder of this chapter to the approach adopted by the courts in the limited number of cases which have reached the High Court or Court of Appeal. Initially, examination will be made of the application of the quality requirements. It is a feature of software contracts that the attempt is normally made to limit or even to exclude liabilities which would normally arise under the application of the law of contract. Such provisions are subject to judicial scrutiny under the provisions of the Unfair Contract Terms Act 1977. In respect both of quality requirements and of the validity of exclusion clauses, a variety of judicial approaches can be identified and even nearly twenty years after the first case reached the Court of Appeal, it remains difficult to lay down precise guidelines concerning the nature and extent of liability. In some respects, the situation may be characterised as similar to that applying in respect of the categorisation of contracts as involving goods and services where two precedents exist rather uneasily in the cases of *Lee v Griffin*[34] and *Robinson v Graves*.[35]

Questions of time

The inclusion of the word 'reasonable' or 'reasonably' in the statutory requirement indicates that a customer may not be entitled to expect perfection. This may be relevant in two

---

[34] (1861) 1 B&S 272.   [35] [1935] 1 KB 579.

respects. The first concerns the condition in which the goods are delivered, and the second, the broader question of the level of quality ultimately attained by the product. In the case of *Eurodynamic Systems v General Automation Ltd*,[36] the High Court was faced with a dispute concerning, inter alia, the quality of an operating system for a computer. Steyn J stated that:

> The expert evidence convincingly showed that it is regarded as acceptable practice to supply computer programmes [*sic*] (including system software) that contain errors and bugs. The basis of the practice is that, pursuant to his support obligation (free or chargeable as the case may be), the supplier will correct errors and bugs that prevent the product from being properly used. Not every bug or error in a computer programme can therefore be categorised as a breach of contract.

It is not, of course, only with software that a product may originally be supplied suffering from minor defects. Although the continued presence of these after the supplier has been offered the opportunity of repair will eventually lead to a finding that the product is not of satisfactory quality, the courts have tended to require that this opportunity be given. In the Scottish case of *Millars of Falkirk Ltd v Turpie*,[37] a new car was sold to the defendant. Immediately upon taking delivery, he discovered an oil leak emanating from the power-assisted steering unit. Upon being notified, the sellers attempted to repair the defect. This attempt proving unsuccessful, the defendant refused to pay for the vehicle and purported to reject it. Holding that he was not entitled so to do, the Court of Session ruled that although the car as supplied was not of merchantable quality, the seller must be granted a reasonable opportunity to repair the defect. 'Many new cars', it was stated, 'have on delivery to a purchaser, some defects, and it was not exceptional that a car should come from the manufacturer in the condition of the defendant's new car on delivery.'[38] As the buyer had failed to allow this, the breach of contract was on his part.

Given the received wisdom that all software contains defects, it would appear that a customer will have to extend reasonable tolerance towards their supplier if or when minor defects manifest themselves. This is well illustrated by the case of *Saphena Computing v Allied Collection Agencies Ltd*,[39] the first software dispute to reach the Court of Appeal. The appellant, Saphena Computing, was a small firm specialising in the supply of third-party hardware and software, either produced or customised by itself. The respondent was engaged in the business of debt collection. Under an initial contract between the parties, it was agreed that Saphena would supply a quantity of software. The software was ordered in January 1985 and installed between February and April. Despite initial teething problems, it was functioning satisfactorily by May 1985. In August 1985, a second contract was made for the supply of further software. It was intended that this would upgrade the defendant's system. Upon installation of the system, a degree of modification was required as a result of difficulties in attaining compatibility with the existing system and through changes in the defendant's requirements.

Although attempts were made to remedy the problems, it was common ground between the parties that the system was not operating in a satisfactory manner by February 1986. On 11 February, a telephone conversation took place between representatives of the parties. In the course of this, it was agreed that the relationship should be terminated. Unfortunately, untangling the legal consequences was to prove no simple matter, and when the dispute went to trial, proceedings before the High Court lasted for seventeen days.

Subsequent to the termination of the contract, another programmer was contracted to work on the system. In the course of this work, the source code of the programs produced

---

[36] (6 September 1988, unreported), QBD.   [37] 1976 SLT (Notes) 66.   [38] At 67.
[39] [1995] FSR 616.

by the plaintiff was copied. Responding to this action, the plaintiff instituted proceedings alleging breach of copyright in its programs. It was further claimed that the defendant had acted wrongfully in terminating the contract and that the plaintiff was entitled to the price of the goods or services supplied under the contract. This latter contention was challenged by the defendant, who counterclaimed for damages, alleging that the software supplied was not to be considered fit for its purpose. The plaintiff succeeding in all significant aspects of its claim, the defendant appealed to the Court of Appeal which unanimously affirmed the findings of the lower court. In particular, it was held, there was an implied term as to the fitness for the purpose for which the software was required. It had to be reasonably fit for such purposes as had been notified to the supplier before the orders were placed or were notified subsequently and accepted by the supplier. These obligations had not been fulfilled by the supplier at 11 February when the relationship was terminated. Although the software was usable at this stage, it was not entirely fit for the defendant's purposes. There remained faults which required correction. However, the defendant was not entitled, at that stage, to terminate the agreement on this basis. Software, it was held by Staughton LJ:

> is not a commodity which is delivered once, only once, and once and for all, but one which will necessarily be accompanied by a degree of testing and modification.[40]

Thus, it would not be a breach of contract to deliver software in the first instance with a defect in it. In this respect, software must be distinguished from other products, in that the concept of delivery is a much more fluid one. In part, this is due to the necessary interaction between supplier and customer:

> Just as no software developer can reasonably expect a buyer to tell him what is required without a process of feedback and reassessment, so no buyer should expect a supplier to get his programs right first time.[41]

The eradication of defects may be a lengthy and laborious process. In the absence of specific provisions relating to acceptance tests and procedures, it is debatable as to how long the buyer must allow this process to continue. Certainly, the message from *Saphena* would indicate that the buyer must exercise caution and restraint before seeking to terminate a contractual relationship. In this instance, the effect of termination was that:

> the defendant thereby agreed to accept the software in the condition in which it then was and, by agreement, put it out of the plaintiff's power to render the software fit for its purpose. The original agreements were thereby varied by deleting the fitness term.[42]

In the event, the plaintiff was held entitled to payment of a reasonable sum in respect of its work on the software and was freed from the requirement to conduct any further work on the system. The defendant's counterclaim for damages in respect of losses caused by the alleged unfitness of the software was dismissed.

The final question before the court concerned the extent of the defendant's right to seek to rectify the defects. To affect this process, it would require access to the programs' source code. Although the plaintiff's contractual conditions made it clear that the source code remained its property, in view of the circumstances under which the agreement had been cancelled, the court held that the defendant must be allowed such access to this as would enable it to cure the defects in the software. In so far as the defendant had gone beyond this by copying portions of the code, it was acting in breach of copyright.

---

[40] *Saphena Computing v Allied Collection Agencies Ltd* [1995] FSR 616 at 652.   [41] At 652.
[42] At 618.

The principal lesson which might be taken from the *Saphena* case[43] is that there is need for precision in the drafting of contractual provisions. In this case, the court had to find its way through a number of written agreements, coupled with evidence of verbal negotiations and promises which were considered to have also constituted part of the agreement. In spite of these factors, the parties do not appear to have addressed the basic question of what level of quality was to be expected, how conformity with this was to be established, and what periods of time would be appropriate for testing and the rectification of errors.

Problems with the Community Charge

Although it was held in *Saphena* that the customer could not expect software to work perfectly from the moment it was supplied, the next case to be considered, *St Albans District Council v ICL*,[44] illustrates that this cannot provide a defence in a situation where software proves incapable of meeting its basic purposes.

The background to the case began with the introduction of a new form of local taxation, the Community Charge. This tax, more commonly known as the poll tax, proved one of the less popular forms of taxation in recent British history. In fiscal terms, the tax is no longer operative but, thanks to the litigation in *St Albans*, it has made a significant contribution to information technology law. The case was concerned with the acceptability of hardware and software supplied to the plaintiff for the purpose of administering the operation of the tax. The case is undoubtedly the most significant precedent in the field of information technology law and deserves detailed consideration.

The key element of the poll tax was that, subject to a very limited number of exceptions, all those aged eighteen or above living in a local government district were required to pay an identical sum. No account was taken of a taxpayer's income, so that a person earning £100,000 would pay the same as a person earning £10,000. In administrative terms, this approach simplified the task of the local authorities. Effectively, all that was required was to calculate the income required, the number of persons liable to pay the tax, and divide the one by the other.

If ever a task could be seen as made for the computer, this was surely it, and apparently without exception, local authorities invested heavily in IT systems to administer the tax. Many of the authorities, St Albans included, entered into contracts with the computer supplier ICL, who promoted an IT system referred to as 'The ICL Solution'. At the time the contract was signed, the elements of the system required to cope with the specific demands of the Community Charge had not been completed or tested. This fact was promoted as a positive benefit to the authority. The developers would use a seventy-strong development team to produce the necessary software and by entering into the contract, the Council would be able 'to input into the development process in order to be sure that this product meets your specific requirements'.[45]

The contract, valued at some £1.3 million, was concluded subject to ICL's standard terms and conditions, which excluded all liability for consequential loss and limited liability for other losses to a maximum of £100,000. The system was delivered to the council timeously but, as envisaged in the contract, the software required was to be delivered and installed in stages as various elements were completed and in line with legislative requirements relating to the introduction of the new tax. Initial elements were to be completed in Autumn 1988, with the full system being operable by February 1990.

[43] At 652.   [44] [1996] 4 All ER 481. Reported at first instance at [1995] FSR 686.
[45] At 483.

One of the first tasks which needed to be conducted by local authorities was to calculate the number of persons in their area liable to pay the tax. Many local authorities were politically opposed to the new system, and in order to prevent them delaying its introduction, the legislation provided a rigid timetable for the various actions required, with penalties being imposed upon recalcitrant authorities. St Albans Council was, therefore, faced with the requirement to complete its count by a certain date. Once the figure had been calculated, the legislation provided that it could not be altered.

The calculation was carried out using the ICL system in early December 1989 and a figure of 97,384.7 was produced. Unfortunately, the version of the software used had a bug and, for some unknown reason, a new release which would have cured the problem was not installed on the Council's computers prior to the calculation. The correct figure, it was subsequently discovered, was almost 3,000 lower at 94,418.7. The financial effects were significant. The council was effectively caught in a double-edged trap. Their income was reduced because the 3,000 phantom taxpayers would clearly not produce any income. To compound matters, part of the Community Charge income was destined to be transferred to the larger Hertfordshire County Council and this figure was also calculated on the basis that St Albans' taxpaying population was greater than it actually was. When the accounts were finally completed, it was calculated that the loss to St Albans was over £1.3 million.[46]

Although the defendant did not dispute the fact that the software involved in the calculation had been defective, it argued that its obligation was merely to supply a system which would be fully operative at the end of February 1990. Until then, as was recognised in the contract, the system would be in the course of development. Save where it could be shown that the supplier had acted negligently, it was argued, the case of *Saphena v Allied Collection Agencies*[47] provided authority for the proposition that 'the plaintiffs had impliedly agreed to accept the software supplied, bugs and all'. This contention was rejected, with Nourse LJ stating in the Court of Appeal that:

> Parties who respectively agree to supply and acquire a system recognising that it is still in the course of development cannot be taken, merely by virtue of that recognition, to intend that the supplier shall be at liberty to supply software which cannot perform the function expected of it at the stage of development at which it is supplied.[48]

In the particular case, it was of critical importance that the system should have been able to provide an accurate population count in December 1989.

The defendant's arguments relating to the protection conferred by its exclusion clause will be considered in more detail later. Although it might be argued that the defect in *St Albans* was considerably more serious than the failures in *Saphena*, the tenor of the judgment does seem to be much more 'user-friendly' than was the case in the earlier judgment.

Water privatisation

ICL was also the defendant in the most recent case concerned with software quality, *South West Water Services Ltd v International Computers Ltd*.[49] Once again, the origins of the case lay in politics, on this occasion the privatisation of the English water companies. Following the establishment of the Office of the Water Regulator, a formula was devised which would limit the ability of the companies to increase charges to customers. The intention was that

---

[46] In the event, ICL was held liable for only some two-thirds of the amount, it being held that the remainder could be recouped from taxpayers by increasing the rate of tax in the next financial year.

[47] [1995] FSR 616. [48] *St Albans District Council v ICL* [1996] 4 All ER 481 at 487.

[49] [1999] Masons CLR 400.

the companies would only be able to maintain their profits through efficiency gains. The plaintiff identified its billing system as a candidate for such savings. The introduction of a new IT system, it was considered, would allow forty-six employees to be made redundant.

A prolonged contractual process then followed, although, as was the case in St Albans,[50] external factors, in the form of scheduled reviews to be conducted by the Regulator, imposed immutable deadlines for the accomplishment of a working system and its associated cost savings. One false start ensued, with a contract being entered into with a major supplier who quickly discovered that the project could not be completed on time. The contract was cancelled by South West Water (SWW).

A new call for tenders was initiated on the basis of a User Requirements Specification (URS) drawn up by SWW. The defendant entered into negotiations on the basis of customising a package (Custima) developed by a third party, Creative Computer Systems (CCS), in which it held a 30 per cent stake. The Custima package would require to be customised to meet the user's requirements. The extent of customisation required was at the heart of the subsequent legal dispute. In his findings of fact, the judge held that:

> In my view the problem started here. Although SWW never agreed with ICL or CCSL any specification other than in conformity with the URS, ICL proceeded on the basis that in the end it would be able to persuade SWW that it did not need to provide what was specified in the URS.[51]

Essentially, it would appear, the supplier was very keen to obtain the contract, not least because with the existence of a considerable number of privatised utilities, it saw prospects of a lucrative market in selling further versions of the system. The customer's specifications were seen as being unnecessarily rigorous and it was hoped that it could be persuaded to accept a more realistic approach, one which would involve significantly less work in customising the Custima software.

Following extensive discussions, a contract was awarded to ICL in September 1994, with the completed system being scheduled for delivery on 31 October 1995. The contract was costed at some £3.6 million. Expert evidence before the court was of the view that the time-table was a tight one. Progress was poor, with several deadlines for delivery of component parts being missed. Even though a delay in completion until the end of March 1996 was agreed between the parties, by early in that month it was clear that the timetable would not be met and the customer served notice terminating the contract. An action was brought seeking recovery of sums paid under the contract plus compensation for additional losses. The claims were based on allegations both of misrepresentation and of breach of contract. These contentions were rejected by the supplier, who argued that its entry into the contract had followed misrepresentations from the customer regarding the amount of work that would be required in order to customise the software to suit its needs. It was also contended that exclusion clauses in the contract served to limit the extent of its liability.

In the event, the customer succeeded on all counts. A key factor in the failure of the contract was identified as lying in the lack of a properly structured agreement between ICL and CCS. The need for what was described as a 'seamless relationship' between these parties had been identified as critical by the customer. In its absence, there could be no guarantee that the effort required to customise the software would be forthcoming. It was argued on behalf of ICL that there could be no representation as, at the time relevant statements were made, there had been the intention to conclude such a contract. The judge disagreed, holding that there was no evidence to support such an assertion. Records of discussions

---

[50] St Albans District Council v ICL [1996] 4 All ER 481.   [51] [1999] Masons CLR 400 at 402.

between ICL and CCS indicated clearly that the latter would not have been willing to enter into a contract on the basis of the arrangements proposed by ICL. Even if the representation had originally been made in the belief it was warranted, there was ample evidence to show that ICL must have been aware before the conclusion of the contract that it did not continue to be valid.

In respect of ICL's claim that the customer had misled them as to the amount of work required, the judge was not able to accept that the evidence supported this. In any event, it was clear that:

> Not only were ICL not misled but ICL were in fact the experts whose duty it was to evaluate the project and use their skill, with the assistance from (CCS) in making proposals as to how the project was to be carried out.[52]

Whilst this falls short of imposing duties to advise, counsel, or warn customers regarding the merits and suitability of their wares, it does suggest that suppliers cannot, as was indicated in this case, remain silent concerning what are considered to be unrealistic expectations on the part of the customer in the belief that it could subsequently be persuaded to adopt a more realistic view as to its requirements.

The Monday software package

In *SAM Business Systems Ltd v Hedley & Co*,[53] the claimant supplied the defendants, a small firm of stockbrokers, with a software package called Interset. The software was intended to replace an existing system called ANTAR, which it was feared (perhaps wrongly) was not 'year 2000 compliant'. Following some negotiations, the contract was signed in October 1999 and it was estimated that a period of twelve weeks would be required to install the software and transfer the defendant's processing operations from its old system.

In pre-contractual negotiations, the customer alleged, the sellers stated that the system would cost no more than £180,000, with a money-back guarantee in the event it failed to work in a satisfactory manner. Although no particular figures were specified in any of the contractual documents, the case proceeded on the basis that this was the appropriate figure relating to the supply and installation of the software and some items of associated hardware. The licence for supply and use of the software was costed at £116,000. Half of this sum was to be paid at the time the contract was entered into, with two further payments to be made when the software was installed and finally when it had been accepted. Under the terms of the contract, the customer was given a period of thirty days to test the software to ensure conformity with specification. In the event that defects were discovered, these were to be reported. If they were not rectified within ninety days, the customer would have the option to reject the software and obtain a refund of all sums paid. This, it was stated, represented the full extent of the supplier's liability.

The migration to the new system proved an unhappy experience for all concerned. The salient facts will be considered in more detail but in February 2001, some seventeen months later, the defendants decided to abandon their efforts to make the new system work and had decided instead to outsource their processing operations to another company. By this stage, the defendants had paid a total of £183,000, reflecting payments in respect of the licence, the purchase of some items of hardware, and a sum of approximately £14,000 in respect of a separate maintenance contract. The final licence installment had not been paid. Further negotiations took place between the parties, but in June 2001, the claimant commenced

---

[52] At 402.   [53] [2002] EWHC 2733 (TCC), [2003] 1 All ER (Comm) 465.

proceedings claiming some £310,000 partly in respect of the outstanding licence fee but principally for what was described as 'post-installation maintenance'. A total of 785 hours of work was alleged to have been expended in this manner. The defendant counterclaimed, seeking nearly £790,000, reflecting a total refund of all sums paid for Interset, plus damages reflecting 'increased cost of working, write-offs, fines and additional charges, mitigation costs, and loss of profits'.

As has been typical in cases involving liability for software, the judgment can be split into two components concerning the questions of whether the software supplied complied with contractual and legal requirements relating to quality and, in the event that the answer to this question was in the negative, whether clauses limiting or excluding the supplier's liability complied with the requirements of unfair contract terms legislation. In respect of the quality requirements, the court accepted that terms must be implied into the contract to the effect that the software would be developed and installed with 'all professional skill and care' and that it would be 'reasonably fit' for the purposes required by the customer and, more specifically, would perform in such a way as to allow the customer to meet its own obligations as required by the Financial Services Authority.[54]

From the early stages, the attempts to introduce Interset proved difficult and doubtless frustrating for both parties. The judgment charts a familiar if depressing path through the detritus of a failed commercial relationship lasting for some eighteen months. The software was supplied timeously but errors continually manifested themselves, to the extent that the defendant was warned by the financial services regulator for failing to comply with its requirements regarding record keeping and accounting and was also fined by the Inland Revenue for late payment of stamp duty taxes arising from transactions. Although the suppliers acknowledged that there were some bugs in the software which required to be corrected, it was also argued that the defendant's staff were largely to blame for failures. The system did mark a substantial change from the defendant's existing package which operated under the DOS operating system, making use solely of keystrokes for command and control purposes. Interset operated under Microsoft Windows and provided the now ubiquitous graphical user interface. As was concluded by the judge:

> what was being presented to Hedleys was a system with a very high degree of automation, a system that was going to be operable by ordinary people, and not technically qualified people.[55]

This was to be a matter of some importance, as one of the claimant's chief arguments was to the effect that the system had been installed and was working effectively in a considerable number of other business environments. A prime cause of any failure to operate in a satisfactory manner for the defendant was allegedly 'because the staff at Hedley's were not trained for the work or were otherwise incompetent'. Although it was acknowledged that the staff's IT knowledge was limited and somewhat dated to the extent that they were not familiar with the use of a mouse,[56] it was accepted that they were committed to attempting to make the new system work. It was the supplier's responsibility to provide training and blame for failures in this respect was placed upon the trainer supplied by them, whose evidence left the judge rather unimpressed. She, he commented, 'gave her evidence in a curiously deadpan manner. Perhaps it was due to nervousness, but if she taught in that manner I can understand that she might have difficulty in communicating computer skills'.[57]

---

[54] [2002] EWHC 2733 (TCC), [2003] 1 All ER (Comm) 465 at [50].   [55] At [21].
[56] *SAM Business Systems Ltd v Hedley & Co* [2002] EWHC 2733 (TCC), [2003] 1 All ER (Comm) 465 at [5].
[57] [2002] EWHC 2733 (TCC) at [83].

The fact that Interset was used successfully elsewhere was considered to be a matter of limited significance:

> I am no more impressed by it than if I were told by a garage that there were 1,000 other cars of the same type as the one I had bought where there was no complaint of the defect that I was complaining of so why should I be complaining of a defect? We have all heard of Monday cars, so maybe this was a Monday software programme.[58]

Given that it is received wisdom that all copies of software are identical, this is at first sight a rather puzzling comment. Certainly, there should be few if any instances of what can be classed as production defects in copies of software. Linked with the issue of training, however, indication can be seen of some of the complex interactions which impact upon the user's ability to use software effectively. Many of the applications of Interset software were in larger organisations. At the time of the case, the evidence was that only one other stockbroking firm was using the system and in general it appears that most users had staff with greater IT skills than those possessed by the defendant's.

A litany of complaints is reported in the judgment[59] and the claimant expended very significant amounts of staff time in seeking either to rectify problems or establish work-around procedures to allow operators to avoid undesirable results. The decision of the Court of Appeal in the case of *Saphena v Allied Collection Agencies*[60] was cited as authority for the proposition 'that in a bespoke system bugs were inevitable'. The later decision of the court in the case of *St Albans District Council v ICL* was also referred to, Lord Justice Nourse here ruling that:

> Parties who respectively agree to supply and acquire a system recognising that it is still in the course of development cannot be taken, merely by virtue of that recognition, to intend that the supplier shall be at liberty to supply software which cannot perform the function expected of it at the stage of the development at which it is supplied.[61]

The systems involved in both *Saphena*[62] and *St Albans*[63] were referred to as 'bespoke' systems and therefore distinguishable from the customised system supplied to the present defendant. This is perhaps putting matters too strongly. In *Saphena*, the supplier's business was described as consisting of providing 'hardware obtained from others, and software comprising some standard items and others specially written'. In *St Albans*, the tax collection system at issue had also been supplied to a number of other local authorities. Where a better distinction perhaps lay was in the state of development of the system. In *St Albans*, the software was being developed in parallel with the enactment of the legislation establishing the tax which it was designed to help collect. Upgrades and revisions were continually being supplied to the users and, indeed, the fluid nature of the software posed serious problems in trying to replicate and explain the nature of the error which gave rise to the litigation. Interset, however, had been promoted as a 'developed system'. Such a system, it was held, should not have any bugs in it. This is perhaps a counsel of perfection but the judge did accept that if defects were speedily rectified without cost to the customer there may well be no liability on the part of the supplier. This seems an eminently correct ruling, although as was recognised in the judgment:

> SAM, like some others in the computer industry seem to be set in the mindset that when there is a 'bug' the customer must pay for putting it right. Bugs in computer programmes

---

[58] *SAM Business Systems Ltd v Hedley & Co* [2002] EWHC 2733 (TCC), [2003] 1 All ER (Comm) 465 at [103].   [59] Ibid., (Comm) 465.

[60] [1995] FSR 616.   [61] [1996] 4 All ER 481 at 487.

[62] *Saphena Computing v Allied Collection Agencies Ltd* [1995] FSR 616.

[63] *St Albans District Council v ICL* [1996] 4 All ER 481 at 487.

are still inevitable, but they are defects and it is the supplier who has the responsibility for putting them right at the supplier's expense.[64]

In line with these arguments, the sums claimed by the claimant in respect of the time and effort incurred in seeking to modify the software was rejected. The defendant was held to have been entitled to take the view that the software contract had not been completed in a satisfactory manner and the claimant's claim for additional payments was rejected. However, from its perspective, it was unfortunately also necessary to consider the effectiveness of the claimant's exclusion clauses, which effectively limited its liability to providing a refund of sums paid in the situation that the customer followed the contractual procedures regarding rejection. As will be discussed later, the defendant failed in this task, rendering victory in respect of the claim of defectiveness pyrrhic.

The dog with an MBA

It is sometimes said that 'whilst to err is human, to really foul it up requires a computer'. The recent English case of *BSkyB v EDS and ors*[65] perhaps provides evidence suggesting that the age of human frailty is not yet past.

As with many software disputes, the case began with lofty aspirations. BSkyB (better known as Sky) is the UK's leading satellite TV broadcaster. The market for providing access to television (and increasingly also telephone and Internet services) is a competitive one and the efficient handling of customer enquiries, requests, and complaints is vitally important. In many respects, customer retention has become a more important issue than customer acquisition and the case report makes extensive reference to the phenomenon known as 'consumer churn'—the proportion of customers who switch suppliers in any given year and the desirability of reducing this as much as possible. Sky decided that a solution lay in the development of a new customer-relationship management system to create a 'world class customer experience' and, following a competitive tender process, the contract was awarded to a consortium including the lead defendant in the present case. The value of the contract was initially £47 million and it was provided that the new system should be developed and made operational within a nine-month period.

As with many software projects, initial optimism soon faded and it was recognised that the original schedule and costings were unsustainable. The agreement was modified between the parties but it took an additional four years of work before the new system was functioning in an acceptable manner and the costs had risen to £265 million. Inevitably, perhaps, the lawyers were not far behind with Sky instituting legal proceedings seeking damages of around £709 million in respect of losses which it claimed to have suffered in its business activities because of the late completion of the contract. In large part this was on the basis that customers who should have received a 'world class customer service' had incurred a poorer experience and had as a consequence taken their custom elsewhere. In logistical terms the case is undoubtedly massive. The trial occupied 109 days of court time with legal costs estimated at around £70 million. The judgment which was handed down in December 2009 runs to almost 500 pages.

Whilst the case is likely to go down as one of the most expensive in legal history, its legal dimensions are perhaps less significant. The agreement between the parties provided, as is fairly standard procedure, for limitations on liability in respect of any contractual breaches. There was no doubt that the clauses had been validly incorporated into the agreement which, if effective, would have limited EDS's liability to around £30 million. The contract

---

[64] *SAM Business Systems v Hedley* [2002] EWHC 2733 (TCC) at [19].   [65] [2010] EWHC 86 (TCC).

had a further provision—generally referred to as an 'entire agreement' clause. Again, this is commonplace in commercial contracts. In a case such as the present, there will have been extensive negotiations and discussions between the parties prior to the conclusion of the contract. The effect of the clause is to affirm that every matter related to the contract is contained in the final agreement and that prior statements—referred to as representations—are to be disregarded.

At this stage, things might appear bleak for Sky. Its basic argument was that it had been led into concluding the contract on the basis of false representations made by an employee of EDS. In most cases, this would have been covered by the 'entire agreement' clause but the argument put forward on behalf of Sky was that these had been made not by accident or even through negligence but as part of a deliberate policy of deceit. As such, the statements would be classed as fraudulent misrepresentations. For perhaps obvious reasons, it was held, a party who has procured the making of a contract through fraud cannot rely on any contractual clauses limiting the extent of liability.

Essentially the case turned upon the judge's assessment of the character of the key witness for EDS. This individual claimed to have been awarded the degree of MBA (Master of Business Administration) from an institution, Concordia College, located on the Caribbean island of St John. The nature of this qualification was tested extensively in court. The witness claimed that he had attended lectures and seminars at the institution over a period of many months. Unfortunately, the evidence established that the 'college' did not actually have any teaching premises. It was effectively what is referred to as a 'degree mill'—an organisation that will offer a purported degree certificate to an individual subject to no other criterion than an ability to pay for it. Although the witness presented what appeared to be a transcript of his class marks and a (glowing) letter of recommendation from the college principal, counsel for Sky was able to demonstrate to the court that an application made on behalf of his dog produced an MBA, an identically worded letter of recommendation, and a rather better set of class marks.

It is not uncommon for individuals to exaggerate the nature and extent of their qualifications. A considerable number of well-known individuals have been caught claiming to possess qualifications of doubtful value. It is an old maxim that if a person finds himself in a hole, the first thing to do is stop digging. This the witness signally failed to do. More and more elaborate tales regarding the degree were presented in the witness box only to be demonstrated to be false. Ultimately, the judge concluded regarding the witness:

> This is not a case where there was merely a lie as to the MBA degree. Such a lie might have had a limited effect on credibility and might be explicable on the basis that (the witness) wished to bolster his academic qualifications and was embarrassed about the way he did it. However his dishonesty did not stop at that. He then gave perjured evidence about the MBA, including repeatedly giving dishonest answers about the circumstances in which he gained his MBA...In doing so, he gave his evidence with the same confident manner which he adopted in relation to his other evidence about his involvement in the Sky CRM Project. He therefore demonstrated an astounding ability to be dishonest, making up a whole story about being in St John, working there and studying at Concordia College. EDS properly distance themselves from his evidence and realistically accept that his evidence should be treated with caution.
>
> ...In my judgment, (the witness's) credibility was completely destroyed by his perjured evidence over a prolonged period. It is simply not possible to distinguish between evidence which he gave on this aspect and on other aspects of the case. My general approach to his evidence has therefore to be that I cannot rely on the truth of his evidence unless it is supported by other evidence or there is some other reason to accept it, such as it being inherently liable to be true.[66]

[66] paras. 194–5.

Essentially, it was argued that the witness had engaged in a course of deliberately deceitful behaviour, including the forging of emails designed to conceal a mistake in financial calculations made by the witness. Counter-evidence existed in respect of the allegations but, given the comments quoted above, it is not surprising that the judge concluded that:

> Having come to the conclusion that I have about his conduct in relation to the Concordia MBA and the evidence that he gave in court, I have no hesitation in finding that (the witness) simply created the 12 July email to cover his error in the hope that he could convince everyone that he had spotted the error at the time and dealt with it.

In English civil cases, the decision has to be made by a judge on the basis of an assessment of the balance of probabilities. Where the credibility of a witness has been destroyed in one context, it must be at least damaged in others and in a number of instances throughout the case the judge accepted the evidence of witnesses for Sky as being more likely to be accurate.

The legal victory for Sky was by no means complete. Save for the issue of fraud, the judge held that the contractual provisions and limitation clauses were effective in protecting EDS against the full financial consequences of its failure to meet its contractual requirements. Nonetheless, although the final award of damages remains to be fixed it appears to be generally accepted that the award will be in the region of £200 million. Initially it was indicated that an appeal would be lodged against the decision at first instance. Perhaps driven in part by changes in ownership of EDS, this was not pursued and an agreed damages payment was fixed at just over £300 million.

Exclusion or limitation of liability

In the previous sections in this chapter, consideration was given to the nature and extent of the liabilities which may arise pursuant to the production, supply, and use of software. Although the argument that software should be treated in the same manner as any other product is a weighty one, it must also be conceded that software producers may be exposed to a greater degree of risk than their more traditional counterparts. First, if one copy of a software product exhibits defects, it must be extremely likely that all copies will be so tainted. With manufactured products generally, most defects are introduced at the production stage and affect only a portion of the products in question. A finding that one copy of a software package is unmerchantable might, by way of contrast, leave its producer liable to every purchaser. A further problem is that many losses resulting from software defects will be economic in nature. Such losses may not only be extensive but are also extremely difficult to quantify and, accordingly, to insure against. A spreadsheet program, for example, may be used for domestic accounting purposes, where the degree of financial exposure in the event of error may be minimal, or in the course of preparing a multi-million pound construction contract, where any error might threaten the financial viability of a contracting party.

Few would argue that the state of the law relating to software liability is satisfactory. Uncertainty feeds upon uncertainty and perception appears more significant than reality. The producer's fear that it may be exposed to crippling legal actions has resulted in an almost universal practice of seeking to exclude some and place limits on the extent of their liabilities in respect of other forms of loss resulting from the operation (or non-operation) of their software. The validity of such clauses[67] has been at issue in most of the disputes which have reached the courts.

---

[67] In this section, the term 'exclusion clause' will be used to refer both to clauses which seek to exclude and to those which limit the extent of liability. Most terms under discussion fall into the latter category.

An initial point to note is that in order to be effective, a clause must be incorporated into the contract. The rules relating to this are to be found in common law rather than statute, and require that reasonable steps be taken to bring the existence of the clause to the notice of the other contracting party. This may be accomplished in a number of ways, with a major factor being whether the software is supplied pursuant to a written contract signed by both parties. In such cases, there will generally be little doubt that the exclusion clause forms part of the contract, and discussion will focus on the effect of the provisions of the Unfair Contract Terms Act 1977 and the Unfair Terms in Consumer Contracts Regulations 1999.[68]

More difficult issues arise when software (typically standard) is supplied through less structured channels. Such software is typically supplied subject to what is generally referred to as a 'shrink-wrap licence'. The term appears to date from early forms of consumer software, mainly computer games. These were typically supplied on an audio cassette, with the terms of a very basic licence printed on the cellophane wrapping of the cassette. Today, licences tend to be printed on substantial booklets (often making separate provisions to accommodate the legal requirements of a range of countries in which the software is sold) included inside packaging. The validity of these is subject to some debate.

Enforceability of shrink-wrap licences

Many contracts, of course, are made other than by means of a signed document; a typical example might relate to the purchase of a piece of standard software from a shop. In this situation, the legal requirement will be that reasonable steps should be taken to bring the existence of any contractual provisions to the notice of the other party prior to the conclusion of the agreement.[69] It is not required that he or she should be aware of all of the details or of the legal implications arising from the contract. An example can be taken from a railway ticket. The ticket will contain reference to the carrier's conditions of carriage but will not itself contain details of these. The presence on the ticket of a notice referring the customer to the conditions will suffice to incorporate them into the contract. Returning to the software context, the display of a clause on the outside of the packaging (or perhaps on a notice displayed in the seller's premises) will serve to give the customer notice of its existence. It is increasingly the case that software is supplied over the Internet. The practice has implications in respect of a number of areas of the law, not least, as will be discussed later, in the field of taxation. From a licensing perspective, use of the Internet may simplify the supplier's task of establishing customer awareness of and agreement to the licence terms. It is a simple matter to cause either a set of the terms or at least reference to their existence to be displayed, with the customer required to 'click' on a button marked 'I accept' before the transaction can proceed.

Assuming that the terms of the licence—including its provisions restricting liability—become incorporated into the contract, attention must again turn to the effect of the Unfair Contract Terms Act 1977 and the Unfair Terms in Consumer Contracts Regulations 1999.[70] To date, all litigation concerned with the effectiveness of exclusion or limitation clauses in software contracts has occurred in the context of commercial transactions. The increasing use of software within the home must increase the importance of the consumer sector and

---

[68] SI 1999/2083.

[69] See *Thornton v Shoe Lane Parking Ltd* [1971] 2 QB 163, where the display of exclusion clauses inside a car park was held to be ineffective, the contract having been concluded at the point when the customer entered into the premises.   [70] SI 1999/2083.

initially, therefore, consideration will be given to the potential application of the legislation in this regard.

Consumer contracts

Somewhat confusingly, different definitions of the term 'consumer' are found in the Unfair Contract Terms Act 1977 and 1999 Regulations. The Act provides that a person deals as a consumer if:

(a) he neither makes the contract in the course of a business nor holds himself out as doing so; and

(b) the other party does make the contract in the course of a business.[71]

Additionally, where goods are supplied under the contract, these must be of a kind ordinarily used for private use or consumption. It would seem that computer games must satisfy this requirement. Although the status of other forms of software, such as word-processing or accounting packages or Internet access software, may at one stage have been debatable, it would seem that they are now sufficiently widely used to be classed as consumer products. This issue may not arise under the Regulations, which make no reference to the nature of goods, requiring only that they be obtained for non-business purposes.[72]

In respect of statutory requirements relating to title, description, or quality, the Unfair Contract Terms Act 1977 provides that exclusion or limitation will not be permitted.[73] In the case of consumer contracts falling under the ambit of the Sale of Goods Act 1979, the prohibition is even more extensive. Here, the Consumer Protection from Unfair Trading Regulations[74] (previously the Consumer Transactions (Restrictions on Statements) Order 1976)[75] provides that any attempt at restriction or exclusion will constitute a criminal offence. An offence will also be committed when any form of guarantee is offered other than those provided for in the Sale of Goods Act 1979, unless it is made clear that this is offered in addition to, rather than in substitution for, the consumer's rights under the legislation. It appears common practice amongst the suppliers of computer games to display notices restricting the buyer's rights to the supply of a replacement game in the event that the original is defective. In the event that the contract is regarded as one involving the sale or supply of goods, the display of such notices will render the supplier involved liable to criminal prosecution.

In terms of their scope, the 1999 Regulations are broader,[76] applying to any term in a non-negotiated contract for goods or services other than those defining the main subject matter or relating to the adequacy of the price. Such terms will not be binding on the consumer if they are determined to be unfair. An unfair term is one which:

contrary to the requirements of good faith causes a significant imbalance in the parties' rights and obligations under the contract to the imbalance of the consumer.[77]

This is a somewhat nebulous criterion. Schedule 2 to the Regulations contains an 'indicative and non-exclusive list of the terms which might be considered unfair'. These include clauses purporting to limit the legal rights of consumers in the event of unsatisfactory performance. A further illustration stigmatises clauses:

making an agreement binding on the consumer whereas provision of services by the supplier or seller is subject to a condition whose realisation depends on his own will alone.

---

[71] s. 12(1). [72] s. 2. [73] s. 6. [74] SI 2008/1277 [75] SI 1976/1813.
[76] SI 1999/2083. [77] Unfair Contract Terms Act 1977, s. 4(1).

It might be that this provision could be invoked in the event that a software producer seeks to link a right to use software to the acceptance of restrictive terms within a licence.

A further aspect of the 1999 Regulations[78] may be of considerable significance. Although many forms of exclusion clause have long been regarded as of dubious quality, the difficulties facing individual litigants have prevented these being challenged before the courts. The Regulations establish a role for the Director General of Fair Trading providing that the Director is to consider any complaint that a contract term is unfair and may then seek an injunction preventing the continued use of the term (or any similar term) in consumer contracts.[79]

Non-consumer contracts

In the case of non-consumer contracts for supply of goods, as well as any contracts where standard form contracts are used, limitation or exclusion clauses will be valid only in so far as they satisfy the statutory requirement of reasonableness.[80] The Unfair Contract Terms Act 1977 lists a number of factors that are to be taken into account in deciding any such question.[81] These include the strength of the parties' respective bargaining positions, the practice of the trade or profession involved, and whether the customer was given the option of contracting on terms which did not seek to exclude liability.

The term 'standard form contract' is not defined in the Unfair Contract Terms Act 1977. In the Scottish case of *McCrone v Boots Farm Sales*,[82] it was held that a standard form contract existed where a party invariably sought to do business on terms which did not differ to any material extent. It was immaterial whether these were reduced to writing or were, at least in part, agreed orally. Such an approach has been upheld in subsequent cases, with the courts being willing to overlook minor variations where it can be shown that a party will generally do business only on the basis of a substantially identical set of terms and conditions.

The definition of standard form contracts in a software context was considered in the case of *Salvage Association v CAP Financial Services Ltd*.[83] At issue here was a contract for the computerisation of the plaintiff's accounting system. The project proved unsuccessful, and, after a number of broken completion dates, the plaintiff terminated its agreement with the defendant and sought damages. Much of the dispute centred on the applicability and enforceability of clauses limiting the defendant's liability in the event of breach of contract. In respect of the question of whether the clauses were to be classed as standard form contracts, Thayne Forbes J analysed the history of the contract, pointing to the fact that extensive negotiations had taken place between the parties prior to its conclusion. Although the terms of the agreement 'closely followed CAP's standard terms of contract', this fact was not to be taken to mean that the contract was one of a standard form. Six factors were identified as relevant to the determination:

(i) the degree to which the 'standard terms' are considered by the other party as part of the process of agreeing the terms of the contract;

(ii) the degree to which the 'standard terms' are imposed on the other party by the party putting them forward;

(iii) the relative bargaining power of the parties;

---

[78] SI 1999/2083.   [79] Reg. 10.   [80] s. 8.
[81] s. 11 for England and Wales, s. 24 for Scotland, and Sch. 2 applying throughout the United Kingdom.
[82] 1981 SLT 103.
[83] (9 July 1993, unreported), CA. The case is reported at first instance at [1995] FSR 654.

(iv) the degree to which the party putting forward the 'standard terms' is prepared to entertain negotiations with regard to the terms of the contract generally and the 'standard terms' in particular;

(v) the extent and nature of any agreed alterations to the 'standard terms' made as a result of the negotiations between the parties; and

(vi) the extent and duration of the negotiations.

Applying these criteria he concluded that:

In this case SA had considered the various drafts of the contract that had been sent by CAP and had taken legal and other advice on all the proposed terms in order to decide what alterations it wished to make. To the extent that SA sought changes and additions to the draft terms, CAP largely agreed them. I am satisfied that the terms of the second contract were not imposed on SA by CAP, but were fully negotiable between parties of equal bargaining power and that CAP was prepared to engage in a meaningful process of negotiation with SA as to those terms. The process of negotiation between the parties took place over a considerable period of time.

The contract was not, therefore, a standard form contract, although, as will be discussed, its terms were struck down on the basis that they constituted an unreasonable attempt to evade liability for negligence.

A different conclusion was reached in *St Albans District Council v ICL*.[84] Here, the Council published a call for tenders, negotiated—albeit fairly incompetently—with a number of potential suppliers, engaged in further negotiations with ICL, and concluded a contract, one clause of which stated that it was subject to ICL's standard terms and conditions. As was stated by Nourse LJ in the Court of Appeal:

Scott Baker J [the judge at first instance] dealt with this question as one of fact, finding that the defendant's general conditions remained effectively untouched in the negotiations and that the plaintiffs accordingly dealt on the defendant's written standard terms for the purposes of s 3(1) (see [1995] FSR 686 at 706). I respectfully agree with him.

A similar decision was reached in *South West Water v ICL*.[85] Once again, the customer had initially argued that the agreement should be made on the basis of its own standard terms and conditions. The defendant countered by submitting a contract governing a previous agreement between the parties. This was subject to some negotiation, but it was agreed that the limitation clauses in the contract were taken from ICL's standard terms. Considering the nature of the agreement, Toulmin J made reference to the leading textbook, *Chitty on Contracts*. This stated that:

Since in any event, no two contracts are likely to be completely identical, but will at least differ as to subject-matter and price, the question arises whether variations or omissions from or additions to standard terms thereby render them 'non-standard' and they do not whether all the terms become standard terms.[86]

Referring to the decision in *St Albans*,[87] it was held that the contract was a standard form contract.

In some respects, the conclusion may be seen as a surprising one. A water authority is a substantial party and the decision makes several references to the fact that discussions

---

[84] [1996] 4 All ER 481.   [85] [1999] Masons CLR 400.
[86] J. Chitty, *Chitty on Contracts*, 27th edn (London, 1994), para. 14–056.
[87] *St Albans District Council v ICL* [1996] 4 All ER 481.

between the parties were extensive. Evidence from ICL concerning one meeting was to the effect that:

> It was a take it or leave it session. They [SWW] were very hard negotiators but we took the decision to proceed as it was too good a long term opportunity to walk away from.

Perhaps the most significant factor was the fact that the contract signed between the parties was silent on what was described as the 'very obvious circumstance' of what should happen in the event of a total failure to deliver a workable system. The judge concluded:

> The reason it was not covered is because the parties used a standard ICL contract which was only slightly adapted. Those standard ICL terms were not appropriate where substantial development work was required to adapt the basic system, as in this case.[88]

The requirement of reasonableness

In determining whether clauses limiting or excluding liability can be considered fair and reasonable, the Unfair Contract Terms Act 1977 provides initially that regard is to be had to 'the circumstances which were or ought reasonably to have been, known to or in the contemplation of the parties when the contract was made'.[89] It provides further that account is to be taken of:

(a) the resources which he could expect to be available to him for the purpose of meeting the liability should it arise; and

(b) how far it was open to him to cover himself by insurance.

Schedule 2 to the Act continues to provide a set of 'Guidelines' to be taken into account. These include:

- the strength of the parties' respective bargaining positions
- the general practice of a particular trade or profession
- whether the goods are made, processed, or adapted to the special order of the customer.

In the case of *Photo Production Ltd v Securicor Transport Ltd*, Lord Wilberforce stated with reference to the Unfair Contract Terms Act 1977:

> in commercial matters generally, when the parties are not of unequal bargaining power, and when risks are normally borne by insurance, not only is the case for judicial intervention undemonstrated, but there is everything to be said, and this seems to have been Parliament's intention, for leaving the parties free to apportion the risks as they think fit and for respecting their decisions.[90]

In *Salvage Association v CAP Financial Services Ltd*,[91] it was accepted that the parties were of equal bargaining power. There had been genuine negotiations and the plaintiff had at all relevant times the realistic option of giving its business to another producer. A number of factors, however, operated to justify a finding that the limitation clause was unfair. First, reference was made to the discrepancy between the contractual limit of £25,000 and the defendant's general acceptance of liability up to £1 million. Additionally, whilst the losses claimed by the plaintiff were covered under an insurance policy taken out by the

---

[88] *South West Water v ICL* [1999] Masons CLR 400. [89] s. 11.
[90] [1980] AC 827 at 843. [91] (9 July 1993, unreported), CA.

defendant, albeit one which was subject to a £500,000 excess, it was accepted by the court that the plaintiff would have been unable to obtain insurance cover against losses of the kind incurred at other than a prohibitive price.

The decision of the Court of Appeal in *St Albans District Council v ICL*[92] provides further evidence of a judicial willingness to scrutinise the terms of contracts entered into by large organisations. Following the introduction of the Community Charge legislation, the plaintiff, in common with all other local authorities, was under considerable pressure to introduce new computer systems capable of coping with the administrative demands of the new tax. After an initial call for tenders, the choice of supplier was effectively between the defendant and IBM. Assessing various elements of the competing bids, including the terms and conditions associated with each, the decision was made to accept the defendant's tender and Council officers were instructed to negotiate with ICL to secure the best possible deal.

The negotiations do not appear to have been conducted by the Council with great expertise. Following submission of a draft contract based upon a Council official's previous employment with London Transport, everything proceeded on the basis of ICL's standard terms and conditions (again, out of date in respect of the level of liability accepted). As the deadline for the introduction of the new tax approached, the Council was under some pressure to conclude the agreement. When concerns were raised concerning the limitation on liability clause, the defendant's response was to indicate that unless the contract was concluded by the following Monday, there could be no guarantee that the system would be delivered in time for the introduction of the tax, a consequence which could have dire financial consequences for the authority. A letter from the defendant stated:

> With regard to ICL's contractual terms and conditions...our offer is based on these standard terms and conditions, and given the tight time-scale, I would advise you to make use of them.
>
> These standard ICL conditions are accepted by over 250 local authorities, and in no way detracts from the business partnerships.[93]

The plaintiff promptly signed the contract. Given these circumstances, it is not surprising that the court held that the contract was a standard form contract and that it did not satisfy the statutory criterion of reasonableness. In reaching this decision, the Court of Appeal approved the judgment of Scott Baker J at first instance, where he identified as determining factors, the points that:

(1) the parties were of unequal bargaining power;

(2) the defendants have not justified the figure of £100,000, which was small, both in relation to the potential risk and the actual loss;

(3) the defendants were insured; and

(4) the practical consequences.

I make the following observations on the fourth point, which follows on in a sense from the third. On whom is it better that a loss of this size should fall, a local authority or an international computer company. The latter is well able to insure (and in this case was insured) and pass on the premium cost to the customers. If the loss is to fall the other way it will ultimately be borne by the local population either by increased taxation or reduced services. I do not think it unreasonable that he who stands to make the profit (ICL) should carry the risk.[94]

---

[92] [1996] 4 All ER 481.   [93] *St Albans District Council v ICL* [1995] FSR 686 at 695.
[94] At 711.

The decisions of the Court of Appeal in the cases of *St Albans District Council v ICL*[95] and *South West Water v ICL*[96] cast significant doubt on the effectiveness of contractual provisions whereby software suppliers sought to limit the extent of their liabilities in the event that software failed to operate in a proper manner. A further decision of the court in the case of *Watford Electronics Ltd v Sanderson CFL Ltd*[97] may signal a less interventionist policy on the part of the judiciary. Albeit of less precedential value, the decision of the High Court in *SAM Business Systems Ltd v Hedley & Co*,[98] discussed earlier, also provides useful guidance concerning the application of the statutory criteria.

In *Watford Electronics v Sanderson CFL Ltd*,[99] the supplier, Sanderson, undertook to provide an integrated software system to control all aspects of the customer's business. Unfortunately, the project was not completed to the satisfaction of the customer and legal proceedings were initiated seeking damages of some £5.5 million. At trial, the judge found that the supplier was in breach of its obligations to supply a system of reasonable quality. The supplier's conditions of contract limited its liability to the cost of any defective goods supplied. The bulk of the customer's claim related to losses of profit resulting from the failure of the system to operate in a satisfactory manner. The trial judge ruled that this clause was invalid under the provisions of the Unfair Contract Terms Act 1977, which provide that exclusion clauses found in standard form contracts will be valid only in so far as they can be considered fair and reasonable. The present clause, it was held, could not be so regarded.

The Court of Appeal took a different view. The customer, it was held, was an experienced and established business. There had been extensive negotiations between the parties. It was noted that the customer used a very similar form of exclusion clause in contracts with its own customers. The conclusion reached was that:

> Where experienced businessmen representing substantial companies of equal bargaining power negotiate an agreement, they may be taken to have had regard to the matters known to them. They should, in my view be taken to be the best judge of the commercial fairness of the agreement which they have made; including the fairness of each of the terms in that agreement. They should be taken to be the best judge on the question whether the terms of the agreement are reasonable.[100]

The exclusion clause was therefore upheld and the supplier's appeal was upheld.

The judgments in *Watford v Sanderson* do not refer to the decisions in *St Albans*[101] and *South West Water*[102] and the tone does differ markedly. It may be noted that especially in the *St Albans* case, negotiations between the parties appear to have been conducted in a rather ineffective manner. Owing to an error, indeed, the contract limited liability to a sum less than that which the supplier would normally have accepted. External factors also placed the customer under considerable pressure to conclude the agreement. It may be that in these circumstances, the present court would also have declared the exclusion clause to be unfair. *Watford v Sanderson* does indicate, however, that where it appears that genuine negotiations have taken place and where it is clear that the customer has freely determined to enter into a contract in awareness of the nature and significance of exclusion clauses, the courts will be slow to interfere.

---

[95] At 711.   [96] [1999] Masons CLR 400.   [97] [2001] EWCA Civ 317, [2001] 1 All ER (Comm) 696.

[98] [2002] EWHC 2733 (TCC), [2003] 1 All ER (Comm) 465.

[99] [2001] EWCA Civ 317, [2001] 1 All ER (Comm) 696.   [100] At [55]–[56].

[101] *St Albans District Council v ICL* [1995] FSR 686 at 695.

[102] *South West Water v ICL* [1999] Masons CLR 400.

A similar approach was taken by the High Court in the case of *SAM Business Systems Ltd v Hedley & Co*[103] discussed earlier. Here, the contract provided in part that the customer would have a period of thirty days following installation in which to test the software and report defects. It was only if defects continued for more than ninety days from the date of installation that the contract provided for the customer's right to initiate proceedings for rejection. This, effectively obtaining a refund of the purchase price, was stated to be the sole remedy available to the customer. The customer in the present case had suffered a significant loss of business and, whilst the computer system cost around £185,000, it sought damages of almost £800,000. The supplier sought to rely upon the contractual limitation provisions but the customer contended that these were not fair and reasonable.

Given that the terms were part of the supplier's written terms of business there was little doubt that the Unfair Contract Terms Act 1977 should apply. The judgment gives extensive and helpful consideration to the extent to which the various criteria identified as components of the requirement of reasonableness may be relevant in cases such as the present. A key factor to be taken into account was whether it would have been feasible for the customer to have obtained similar software without the accompaniment of exclusion clauses. The evidence before the court was to the effect that '[t]he only way to get the software they needed was by contracting on terms that made rigorous exclusions of liability because those were the terms on which all suppliers were contracting'.[104] The fact that similar terms were commonplace in the field is a relevant factor in determining issues of reasonableness.

Ultimately, considering the contract as a whole, the judge concluded that its terms were fair and reasonable. The customer was buying under constraints of time as the year 2000 was fast approaching and its existing system was not capable of coping with the change to the third millennium as required by its sector regulator, the Financial Services Authority. To a considerable extent, it was accepted, the customer was the cause of its own misfortunes. Whilst an attempt totally to exclude liability would have been considered unreasonable, in the circumstances of the case, the judge concluded:

> Not forgetting my duty to look at each term individually, it is important to look at each in relation to the whole contract. Before contract, SAM says, 'We think our system is marvellous and will do everything you need, but if you are not satisfied you can ask for your money back'...Having regard to the enormous potential liabilities, that seems to me to be a reasonable arrangement in the circumstances existing between the two parties.[105]

The end result of the litigation might be considered as a draw. The supplier was not able to recover additional costs incurred in seeking to place the software into a satisfactory state and the customer was similarly unsuccessful in securing reimbursement of losses caused through the failure of the software to operate in a satisfactory manner.

Conclusions

In the early days of software, it was commonplace for suppliers to seek totally to exclude all liabilities relating to their products. A 1993 version of the standard licence used by a major software producer stated that:

Limited Warranty and Disclaimer of Liability

> The software and accompanying written materials (including instructions for use) are provided 'as is' without warranty of any kind. Further, [Producer] does not warrant, guarantee or make any representations regarding the use of, or the results of use, of the software or

---

[103] [2002] EWHC 2733 (TCC), [2003] 1 All ER (Comm) 465.   [104] At [70].   [105] At [71]–[72].

written materials in terms of correctness, accuracy, reliability, currentness, or otherwise. The entire risk as to the results and performance of the software is assumed by you. If the software or written materials are defective you, and not [Producer] or its dealers, distributors, agents or employees, assume the entire cost of all necessary servicing, repair or correction.

The above is the only warranty of any kind, either express or implied, including but not limited to the implied warranties of merchantability and fitness for a particular purpose, that is made by [Producer] on this...product.

The world has moved on and more recent versions are somewhat more 'generous', guaranteeing that the software will perform 'substantially in accordance with the accompanying Product Manual(s) for a period of 90 days'. In general, as was indicated at the outset of the chapter, clauses excluding liability have largely been replaced by those seeking to limit the extent of liability. In a number of cases, it has been accepted that it is easier and more cost-effective for a software producer to obtain insurance cover in respect of claims which might be made by customers, than it is for customers to obtain cover against more speculative risks associated with the failure of an automation project intended to bring future gains in efficiency and productivity. There may be cases where exclusion clauses will be upheld, but the range of these may be diminishing. In *South West Water v ICL*, in rejecting the defendant's attempts to limit liability to a partial refund in the case of a total failure of the project, it was held that:

> In some cases such a clause might be reasonable to reflect the balance of risk in a developing project, but there is no evidence that this is the case here.[106]

Given the vital role played by software in the modern world, it must be right that issues of liability should be assessed by the standards and criteria applied to industrial products rather than to those of a niche market within the services sector. Whilst the cases of *Watford Electronics Ltd v Sanderson CFL Ltd*[107] and *SAM v Hedley*[108] produce results which are more favourable to the producer than was the case in the *ICL* cases, the emphasis remains on the criterion of fairness. Especially in situations in which its functioning is critical to the survival of the customer's business it is not unreasonable that every effort should be made to ensure both that the software itself is suitable and that arrangements—in the form of contractual safeguards or the acquisition of insurance cover—are in place to guard against the risk of failure. *Caveat emptor* has not returned to business contracts but neither is a supplier expected to act as nanny to its customers.

---

[106] [1999] Masons CLR 400.   [107] [2001] EWCA Civ 317.
[108] [2002] EWHC 2733 (TCC), [2003] 1 All ER (Comm) 465.

PART V

Internet–Specific Issues

In some respects this Part is possibly superfluous. The Internet and its implications have underpinned most of what has been considered in the previous Parts of this book. It is perhaps helpful, however, in this concluding Part to reflect more directly on the Internet and its impact on us all.

It is perhaps easy to under-emphasise the speed with which the Internet has developed. Television services for example began in the United Kingdom in the 1930s. Admittedly with an interruption in services during the Second World War, it took thirty years before 90 per cent of the population had a receiver. The telephone took even longer to become established. In 1965, almost a century after its invention, only 22 per cent of UK households had a network connection.

In part it is the speed of Internet take-up that is impressive, but more so the manner in which it has revolutionised communications. If we look at events such as the downfall of Communist regimes and the more recent 'Arab Spring' it is almost inconceivable that events could have occurred at such speed in the pre-Internet era. Yet there is always a 'but'. One of the classical political mantras is that there should not be power without responsibility. Is this always the case with the Internet? As with many questions, the answer is a mixture of 'perhaps' and 'sometimes'. Social-networking sites and email communications often eschew the control tactics applied by more traditional media outlets. Newspapers and broadcasters employ a small army of lawyers to vet content to guard against the appearance of defamatory material. Broadcasts of events such as the Leveson Inquiry (and many 'live' broadcasts) come with a short built-in transmission delay to ensure that unsuitable material does not reach a mass audience.

It is not the case that those publishing on the Internet are immune from the law. In the following chapter there is mention of the case of *McAlpine v Bercow* in which a senior Conservative politician obtained damages from the wife of the Speaker of the House of Commons who had made Twitter postings which were seen as alleging illegal conduct on his part. Pursuing such actions in the courts does, of course, require the claimant to have access to significant resources and there is also frequently the issue whether a defendant might have the resources to satisfy any award of compensation (and legal costs) that may be made.

In some respects, the major change that the Internet has made is to give anyone and everyone a global pulpit. It is always tempting to exaggerate possibilities. I have a blog associated with this book—but fear that not that many people follow it. It is perhaps a trivial example but on my calculations only a small percentage of people who have bought copies of the book ever view the updating blog. It is clearly not a major force for change in the field. There is, however evidence that younger generations are turning to Internet sites as a first port of call for news rather than newspapers or broadcasting. It is certainly also the case, as has been discussed earlier, that national injunctions against the dissemination of information are essentially unworkable in the Internet context. Again, the inevitable 'but'. Individuals may find themselves liable in defamation actions in countries where they might never have intended to publish material. A global soapbox has perils as well as benefits.

This section seeks also to consider issues of Internet governance. As the network developed it was essentially managed by technical people. Most of the original work originated in the United States (although the work of the UK scientist Sir Tim Berners Lee was largely responsible for the technology underpinning the World Wide Web). Concerns have been expressed in other parts of the world at what is seen as excessive US control over current regulatory agencies, specifically the Internet Corporation for Assigned Names and Numbers (ICANN). A problem is to find alternative global alternatives. For many decades, telecommunications markets tended to be monopolistic and (with the notable exception of the United States) controlled by national governments. The International Telecommunications Union (ITU) was established in the nineteenth century to provide a forum within which governments could negotiate policy issues. The ITU continues to be influential but very much of the telecommunications infrastructure is now operated within the private sector with notions of competition very much entrenched, especially in the mobile sector.

As always, many questions and fewer answers, which is, of course, why the topic is such a fascinating one.

25

Social networking, defamation, and the Internet

Introduction

The legal notion of defamation is a long-established one, dating back at least as far as Roman law. Essentially it consists in the dissemination of false information about an individual (or an organisation) with the intention that it damages the subject's reputation. This can be as serious a matter as more physical injuries or damage. As Shakespeare wrote:

> Who steals my purse steals trash; 'tis something, nothing; 'Twas mine, 'tis his, and has been slave to thousands; But he that filches from me my good name Robs me of that which not enriches him, And makes me poor indeed.[1]

In recent decades, the High Court in London has come to be regarded as the libel capital of the world. A variety of reasons lie behind this. Although levels of compensation have been reduced from the high-water mark in the late 1980s and 1990s, when in a number of cases juries awarded damages in excess of £1 million, damages awards are still higher than in many other European states. The English defamation system is also very claimant-friendly. The claimant must establish that words are capable of having a defamatory meaning and the burden of establishing innocence lies with the defendant. The question of whether words are capable of having a defamatory meaning is very context-dependent and a seemingly innocuous phrase may be considered defamatory.

In recent years it has been recognised that although defamation actions provide a lucrative source of income for many English lawyers, the spectre of what is referred to as libel tourism is not entirely an edifying one. This has been coupled with a perception that the defamation system was tilted too heavily in favour of claimants and there has been pressure for reform. The end-product is the Defamation Act of 2013 which became law in April 2013 after a somewhat fraught parliamentary passage during which the measure became caught up in the wider debate about privacy and press freedom.

The Internet era has created many new situations in which the law of defamation might be invoked. One of the features of the Internet in recent years has been the emergence of social-networking sites such as Facebook and Twitter. Persons posting on these sites can attract a large audience. The company Peerindex publish an annual survey[2] of the most-followed Twitter posters. Perhaps unsurprisingly, the top six places are occupied by celebreties with the Prime Minister slipping in at number 7 with 400,000 followers. (The person with the largest number of Twitter followers was Harry Styles from the band One Direction with 15.4 million followers. The five members of the band indeed occupy the top five places on the list.)[3]

---

[1] *Othello*, Act 3, Scene 3.

[2] The most recent is available from <http://www.peerindex.com/pi-uktwitter140.html>.

[3] Much the same comment mig1ht be made about many 'blogs'. Postings by well-regarded individuals can attract audiences equal to those of many established publishers.

The ability to access large numbers of readers almost simultaneously has historically been the preserve of the mass media. Times are changing and to put some of the figures cited above into perspective, the UK's top selling newspaper, *The Sun* sells slightly more than 2 million copies a day. More heavyweight papers such as *The Guardian* and *The Times* have sales figures of around 200,000 and 400,000 respectively. For regional newspapers, data published by the Press Gazette indicates that most of the 450 publications have a circulation of less than 20,000.[4]

Statistics are often misleading and it must be acknowledged that most national newspapers also have an online presence. The *Daily Mail* newspaper averages around 5 million online visitors a day[5] but it seems clear that new online sources—whether blogs or social-networking sites are taking audiences away from more established outlets. As mentioned in the introduction to this section, the recent case of *McAlpine v Bercow*[6] provides an interesting example.

In this case the plaintiff was a prominent Conservative politician and the defendant was the Labour-supporting wife of the Speaker of the House of Commons. A BBC news programme had reported the false allegation that an unnamed Conservative had engaged in paedophilic behaviour. There was much media speculation about this person's identity—especially on social-media sites—and the defendant posted a message on her Twitter feed 'Why is Lord McAlpine trending?'[7] The defendant's Twitter postings had attracted some 50,000 followers. The text message was accompanied by an emoticon depicting what was referred to as an innocent face. The High Court held that the post was defamatory. Given the publicity afforded to the allegations, a reasonable interpretation of the words was that the claimant was the individual involved. In respect of the emoticon, the court ruled:

> In my judgment the reasonable reader would understand the words 'innocent face' as being insincere and ironical. There is no sensible reason for including those words in the Tweet if they are to be taken as meaning that the Defendant simply wants to know the answer to a factual question.[8]

The tweet, it was held, pointed 'the finger of blame'.

The defendant agreed to pay £15,000 by way of compensation and subsequently tweeted:

> I have apologised sincerely to Lord McAlpine in court—I hope others have learned tweeting can inflict real harm on people's lives.

An expensive lesson.

Although not of great legal significance the case is interesting in a number of respects. The defendant's followers were much more numerous than the readers of most regional papers. As has more recently been noted by the Attorney General (whose tweets attract only 4,000 followers), the range of dissemination of many tweets falls into the range previously associated with traditional media outlets—yet posters do not have the training or access to legal advice associated with more traditional outlets. Inappropriate use of social-media sites has been a cause of concern in a number of areas of the legal process. In a recent case in the English Crown Court, the defendant was charged with a number of offences relating to child abduction and sexual assault. One juror placed the following message on her Facebook page, 'I don't know which way to go, so I'm holding a poll', and asked for views whether she should vote for the defendant's guilt or innocence.

---

[4] <http://www.pressgazette.co.uk/regional-abcs-paid-local-press-circulation-drops-64-cent-full-breakdown>.

[5] Figures are collated by the Audit Bureau of Circulation (ABC). The full reports are vailable only to purchase but details are widely reported in the media. See e.g. <http://www.theguardian.com/media/abcs>.

[6] [2013] EWHC 1342 (QB).

[7] 'Trending' generally means that a person is attracting considerable attention on social-media sites.

[8] para. 84.

Such an action is in complete breach of the rules that prohibit jurors discussing a case with anyone other than other members of the jury. To make matters worse, the juror failed to enable any of Facebook's privacy settings so that the message could be seen not only by her contacts but also by anyone logging into Facebook. A message was sent anonymously to the court informing it of the posting and the juror was dismissed. The case was investigated as possibly constituting the serious criminal offence of contempt of court but it was finally decided not to take matters any further. In other cases, however, jurors have been convicted and imprisoned for using the Internet to conduct searches relating to cases that they were involved in. In one case,[9] prior to the commencement of a trial for alleged sex abuse, the judge directed the jury as to their rights and responsibilities. In respect of the Internet he stated:

> There have been problems. Jurors have become detectives in their own court. And here is the sort of problem. Last week, at Kingston Crown Court, a seven-week trial had to be aborted because the jurors started on the Internet and Googling people, and the judge found out because the other jurors reported the errant juror. Seven weeks—I dread to think what it cost, in a country which will ill afford the waste of, say, half-a-million pounds.

After indicating that it would be unacceptable to attempt to 'Google' himself, the lawyers involved in the case, or the defendant he commented:

> If you said to me, 'What is the biggest threat to trial by jury in this country?' I would say to you, 'No question: improper use of the Internet by jurors. No question'.[10]

In the case of the first defendant, the conduct complained of was the making of a Facebook posting (subsequently reported to the trial judge by a Facebook 'friend'):

> Woooow I wasn't expecting to be in a jury Deciding a paedophile's fate, I've always wanted to **** up a paedophile & now I'm within the law.

In the case of the second defendant, apparently because of frustration at the slow pace at which the case appeared to be proceeding, Google searches were made into the background of the case and reported to fellow jurors (who in turn reported the communication to the judge).

It was announced in December 2013 that the Attorney General who has traditionally published advice to newspapers and other media organisations will now:

> be publishing court advisory notes that have previously only been available to mainstream media outlets. The notes will be published on the gov.uk website and via the Twitter feed of the Attorney General's Office, @AGO_UK...[11]

In the case of *HMA v Davey and Beard*, the court noted that:

> In the case relating to Mr Davey, after he had been discharged as a juror, the judge told the jury in very sweeping terms that they should not use the internet. We can quite understand why he did this, but as Lord Carlile QC pointed out what he said went beyond what would be permissible under Articles 8 and 10 (of the European Convention on Human Rights), quite apart from imposing restrictions on jurors properly carrying out day to day tasks which cannot be easily done without use of the internet.[12]

Also in December 2013, the Law Commission published its report[13] on juror misconduct and Internet publications. This provides an extensive analysis of current case and statute law and also provisions legislated specifically to criminalise conduct of the nature referred to.

---

[9] *HMA v Davey and Beard* [2013] EWHC 2317.   [10] para. 14.
[11] <http://techcrunch.com/2013/12/04/the-fine-blue-line/>.   [12] para.60   [13] Law Com No 340.

In the remainder of this chapter we will focus on the law of defamation and consider its operation in an Internet context from two angles. First, we will look at the liability of the individuals who make comments that are alleged to be defamatory and, secondly, at the responsibilities of intermediaries. In this chapter we will focus on the position of Internet Service Providers (ISPs) and search engines.

The nature of defamation

The term 'defamation' tends to be used as a generic descriptor for actions in which it is alleged that the making of untrue and unwarranted comments about an individual have tended to lower that person's standing in the eyes of right-thinking members of society. The question of what sorts of comments would produce this effect is not easy to answer and will vary with changing social attitudes. Until the Second World War, it was not considered defamatory to accuse someone of being anti-Semitic. The term 'computer hacker' was orig-inally used to describe someone who was particularly skilled in operating computers and finding solutions to problems. In this context, the phrase could not be considered defama-tory. Today, of course, the generally accepted meaning has changed and the accusation that someone is a computer hacker might have legal consequences.

In English law, a distinction exists between libel and slander. The law of libel applies to comments which are recorded in some permanent form—in print or on tape, whilst slan-der is reserved for comments which are more transient in nature. In general, the law of libel operates on a stricter basis than that of slander, based in part on the assessment that state-ments that are recorded are likely to be more damaging to the subject than those which are not. Developments in recording and broadcasting technology have served to blur both the distinction between libel and slander and the rationale for distinct treatment. A statement on a live television broadcast might be heard by tens of millions of viewers and be far more damaging to the reputation of the subject than would be the case with a letter published in a local newspaper. In the case of broadcasting, the Defamation Act 1952 provided that the law of libel was to apply in respect of any statements made.

The law on defamation

The body of current defamation law has a range of sources and many actions involve an amalgam of these. Common law principles remain of considerable significance, particu-larly in determining the extent of the liabilities that may be incurred by the person directly responsible for a defamatory statement.

It is an easy matter for a person to make and disseminate a defamatory comment about another. A case which is still cited in Internet-related cases is that of *Bryson v Deane*.[14] Here the offending material was posted on a golf-club notice board. Clearly in such a situation only a relatively small number of people would have the opportunity to see the posting. In order to reach a wider audience some form of access to the mass media has generally been required. It is certainly possible that a media organisation may itself publish defamatory material and be subject to common law rules, but it may also serve as a conduit for the dissemination of the words of others. A stereotypical example might see a newspaper publishing a letter from a reader. The Defamation Act 1996 provides defences for publishers who unwittingly disseminate defamatory material produced by third parties.

---

[14] [1937] 1 KB 818.

Most recently, and still to be tested before the courts, the Defamation Act 2013 seeks to update the law of defamation for the Internet age. Traditional intermediary publishers such as newspapers have been joined by Internet sites hosting blogs whilst, as referred to earlier, social-networking sites facilitate a wide dissemination of information. Beyond the attraction of postings from major or minor celebrities we have the phenomonen of postings from ordinary individuals going 'viral' and attracting massive public interest. Effectively with the Internet we have a whole new range of intermediaries who might be seen as facilitating the dissemination of defamatory material. With a publisher such as a newspaper there is the real possibility for the publisher to assess a letter or similar submission before allowing it to be published. In the Internet context, ISPs and blog-hosting sites may perform a similar role in terms of facilitating dissemination but there is little or no possibility for material to be assessed prior to publication.

Over the years, there have been repeated criticisms that the English law on defamation is weighted too heavily in favour of the claimant. Once it is established that the statement is capable of having a defamatory meaning, the onus switches to the defendant to show that it was not defamatory of the claimant. Such an approach does perhaps sit uneasily with the provisions of Article 10 of the European Convention on Human Rights which guarantees the right to receive and impart information. Although the article goes on to sanction derogatation where this is necessary to protect the reputation of others, the proportionality threshold required under the Convention is a high one.

In part because of the above factors, a number of cases have been brought before the High Court in circumstances where the claimant appeared to have only a tenuous connection with the English legal system. The global reach of the Internet poses significant jurisdictional challenges. In the era of the printed word, the vast majority of a newspaper's circulation would be restricted to its country and jurisdiction of publication.[15] Similarly, most television and radio broadcasts have been received only in one national territory—although satellite broadcasting is changing this situation. With the Internet, the place of publication becomes a matter of little practical significance so that it is as easy for a United Kingdom-based browser to view the web version of the *New York Times* as its London equivalent. Questions of where and when a defamatory comment is published have assumed considerable importance and the Defamation Act 2013 and the Defamation (Operators of Websites) Regulations make a number of significant changes to both aspects of substantive law and to jurisdictional issues.

Who is liable for defamatory comments?

It may be stated without qualification that a person who makes a defamatory comment is potentially exposed to an action for defamation and examples have been cited earlier. The poster of a defamatory message runs the risk of legal action though the task of identifying the party responsible may not be an easy one. Even if a message appears to originate from a particular individual, it may be necessary to establish that it is genuine. In the United States case of *Stratton Oakmont v Prodigy*,[16] a message appeared to have been sent from a particular user's account. The user, however, denied that the message had been sent by him or from his equipment. In this particular case, the issue was not of great significance as the action

---

[15] The existence of separate legal systems in Scotland and England has posed some difficulties in the past in respect of the law of defamation.

[16] (1995) 195 NY Misc LEXIS 229.

proceeded against the service provider, who, it appears, had always been the major target of the litigation. In other cases, it may be necessary for a claimant to establish that a message was sent by the party whose identifiers appear. It appears that it is possible for a user's identity to be impersonated. Instances have been reported of forged email messages purporting to have originated from the White House. Another technical facility which may complicate any legal proceedings is the use of anonymous remailing services. These services, which may be based anywhere in the world, accept messages from users, strip out the details of the original poster, and forward them to the addressee, with no indication of the identity of the original sender. Such a technique makes it impossible to identify the author without the cooperation of the operator of the remailing service. Such cooperation may not readily be forthcoming, and considerable controversy surrounded attempts by the Church of Scientology to discover the identity of a user who posted documents relating to the organisation, allegedly in breach of copyright. On this occasion, the remailing service involved was based in Finland.[17]

Even in the event that a service provider does not actively refuse to cooperate with a complainant, legal complexities may arise. The decision of the Court of Appeal in the case of *Totalise v Motley Fool Ltd*[18] raises a number of interesting issues concerning the interaction between the requirements of data protection and other elements of law. Interactive Investor operated a business providing financial information to individual investors. The information was made available via a website. Included on the website was a bulletin-board facility allowing users to post views and comments.

In order to access the website, users had to register and indicate acceptance of the operator's terms and conditions. These contained a data protection notice to the effect that the provider was:

> registered under the Data Protection Act 1998. All personal information you supply to us will be treated in accordance with that Act. We will collect and use your personal information in order to operate, enhance and provide to you the Information Services you request.
>
> We will not pass your personal information on to any other person except to our Service Providers, where it is necessary, to enable us to provide you with the Information Services you request from us.

One user, operating under the pseudonym 'Zeddust' posted comments which were defamatory of the claimant company. The claimant company complained to Interactive, who removed the posting and suspended the user. Totalise then requested provision of information identifying the poster in order that it might initiate proceedings for defamation. This was refused by Interactive, who stated that the supply of personal data would place it in breach of its terms and conditions and also of the requirements of the Data Protection Act 1998.

Totalise instituted proceedings seeking a court order requiring disclosure of the data. This was granted by a High Court judge, who also made an order holding Interactive liable for the costs incurred by Totalise. An appeal was made on the issue of costs, the key question being whether Interactive had acted unreasonably in refusing to hand over the data without subjecting Totalise to the expense of obtaining a court order (costs were assessed at just under £5,000).

The Court of Appeal held that the behaviour was not unreasonable. The issues involved, it was ruled, were complex, especially with the addition of the Human Rights Act 1998 to the United Kingdom statute book. A balance had to be struck between the interests of the claimant in being able to secure a remedy and the right of the individual to respect for private life. Such a task was one for the courts and, it was held:

> It is difficult to see how the court can carry out this task if what it is refereeing is a contest between two parties, neither of whom is the person most concerned, the data subject; one

---

[17] *The Independent*, 4 March 1995.   [18] [2001] EWCA Civ 1897, [2002] 1 WLR 1233.

of whom is the data subject's prospective antagonist; and the other of whom knows the data subject's identity, has undertaken to keep it confidential so far as the law permits, and would like to get out of the cross-fire as rapidly and as cheaply as possible. However the website operator can, where appropriate, tell the user what is going on and to offer to pass on in writing to the claimant and the court any worthwhile reason the user wants to put forward for not having his or her identity disclosed. Further, the Court could require that to be done before making an order. Doing so will enable the Court to do what is required of it with slightly more confidence that it is respecting the law laid down in more than one statute by Parliament and doing no injustice to a third party, in particular not violating his convention rights.[19]

It is important to keep in mind that there was no appeal against the initial ruling that in this case the identifying data should be handed over to the claimant. The decision, therefore, gives no sort of green light for the posting of defamatory comments under the shield of anonymity. It does, however, provide welcome recognition of the fact that privacy issues are important and are not to be discarded lightly in the face of competing claims.

The issue was discussed more extensively in the case of *Metropolitan International Schools Ltd v Designtechnica Corporation and Google UK and Google Inc.*[20] In this case, the claimant alleged that the second and third defendants, who operated the well-known search engine Google.com and provided access from within the UK domain-name system (Google.co.uk), made available links to a website operated by the first defendant which contained material which was defamatory in nature. Evidence was led as to the scale of Google's operations with the search engine indexing around 39 billion publicly available web pages. The index was compiled entirely automatically. Search requests were also met entirely by automatic means with no element of human intervention.

The second and third defendants applied to have the action dismissed on a number of grounds, including, most relevantly, that Google could benefit from the 'mere conduit' defence. In this context the judge, Mr Justice Eady held that:

50. When a search is carried out by a web user via the Google search engine it is clear, from what I have said already about its function, that there is no human input from the Third Defendant. None of its officers or employees takes any part in the search. It is performed automatically in accordance with computer programmes.

51. When a snippet is thrown up on the user's screen in response to his search, it points him in the direction of an entry somewhere on the Web that corresponds, to a greater or lesser extent, to the search terms he has typed in. It is for him to access or not, as he chooses. It is fundamentally important to have in mind that the Third Defendant has no role to play in formulating the search terms. Accordingly, it could not prevent the snippet appearing in response to the user's request unless it has taken some positive step in advance. There being no input from the Third Defendant, therefore, on the scenario I have so far posited, it cannot be characterised as a publisher at common law. It has not authorised or caused the snippet to appear on the user's screen in any meaningful sense. It has merely, by the provision of its search service, played the role of a facilitator.

52. Analogies are not always helpful, but there will often be resort to analogy when the common law has to be applied to new and unfamiliar concepts. Here, an analogy may be drawn perhaps with a search carried out in a large conventional library. If a scholar wishes to check for references to his research topic, he may well consult the

---

[19] At [26].   [20] [2009] EWHC 1765.

library catalogue. On doing so, he may find that there are some potentially relevant books in one of the bays and make his way there to see whether he can make use of the content. It is hardly realistic to attribute responsibility for the content of those books to the compiler(s) of the catalogue. On the other hand, if the compilers have made an effort to be more informative, by quoting brief snippets from the book, the position may be different. Suppose the catalogue records that a particular book contains allegations of corruption against a living politician, or perhaps it goes further and spells out a particular activity, such as 'flipping' homes to avoid capital gains tax, then there could be legal liability on the part of the compiler under the 'repetition rule': see e.g. *Gatley on Libel and Slander* (11th edn) at paras 11.4 and 32.8.

Further consideration was given to these issues in the case of *Sheffield Wednesday Football Club Ltd and ors v Hargreaves*.[21] The claimants here were parties connected with the management of a less-than-triumphant English football club. The defendant operated a supporters' website which allowed for the posting of comments on matters concerned with the club. A number of comments (published pseudonymously) were considered to have been defamatory of the claimants who brought an action before the courts seeking an order that the website owner identify the individuals responsible (users were required to register with the site owner before being allowed to post comments).

The basis for the action (as was also the case under *Totalise v Motley Fool*) lay under doctrine laid down by the House of Lords in the case of *Norwich Pharmacal Co v Commissioners of Customs and Excise*.[22] This established the doctrine that a party to potential litigation could seek disclosure of information held by a third party which might identify others against whom a claim could be made if three conditions could be satisfied:

- a wrong had arguably been committed against the claimant by a third party whose identity was not known to the claimant
- identification of the third party must be necessary to allow proceedings to be instituted
- the party against whom the action is brought must be in a position to identify the wrongdoer.

Although these conditions will normally be met in cases involving Internet bulletin boards, it was emphasised that the court retained a discretion whether to make such an order. As is common in discussion groups devoted to participants' enthusiasms, many of the postings complained of, although technically defamatory, were insulting rather than damaging. The judge described several of the comments as being 'trivial' or amounting to no more than 'saloon-bar moaning about the way in which the club is managed'. In these cases, the court declined to order the identification of the posters. In other instances, complaints centred on allegations of financial impropriety and in these cases it was held that disclosure should be made.

Once again, a balancing act has to be performed between notions of free speech and the interests of the subject of material not to have their reputation or financial interests damaged. The approach of the court in *Sheffield Wednesday* is to be welcomed in recognising that the full might of the law should not be used against those who engage in what might be regarded as robust criticism in a forum where this can cause little genuine harm to the subject. In other cases, matters may take a different aspect. In 2008 an agreed award of £100,000 damages, possibly the largest award in a case of Internet defamation, was made in respect of the activities of a website, 'Dads Place'. In a statement to the court it was recounted that:

this group were responsible for the publication of a seriously defamatory, abusive and scurrilous anonymous website at www.dadsplace.co.uk...Over a period of two years from April

---

[21] [2007] EWHC (QB) 2375.   [22] [1973] 2 All ER 943.

2004 to about mid-July 2006, from behind their cloak of anonymity, Dads Place used their publications and in particular the Website to conduct a malicious, unpleasant and relentless campaign of libel and harassment.[23]

It appears that the website was established by one of the defendants, a property developer, to pursue a personal and professional vendetta against a rival company and its managing director. Few could argue in support of a right to anonymity when conduct is so malign in nature and, as indicated in court, had such damaging consequences for the personal and professional lives of those targeted.

Employer's liability

As more and more companies make use of email as a method of communication between staff, so there will be increasing exposure to action on the basis of vicarious liability in respect of the use or misuse made of the communications network. In 1997, the Norwich Union insurance company reached a settlement in a libel action brought by a health insurance company, Western Provident Association. Under the terms of the agreement, Norwich Union agreed to pay £450,000 in damages and costs in respect of libellous messages concerning the association's financial stability which had been contained in email messages exchanged between members of the Norwich Union's staff.[24]

The fact that a settlement was reached prior to trial means that the case is of no value as a legal precedent. The lesson for those engaging in email discussions is obvious: that although communications may be approached as a form of conversation, everything is recorded almost without limit of time and can be retrieved at a later date. A similar example of this phenomenon can be seen in the discovery of internal Microsoft emails during the legal investigations into its commercial practices conducted by the United States Department of Justice. One significant factor limiting the extent of liability for defamatory communications made by employees may be that the vicarious liability applies only in respect of acts committed in the course of employment. In the Norwich Union case, the communications were clearly work-related but it is unlikely that an employer would be held liable in the event, for example, that employees used email facilities to exchange defamatory comments on subjects unconnected with work. To minimise the risks of liability, it would be advisable for employers to indicate clearly in contracts of employment or staff handbooks what uses may or may not be made of electronic communications.

Faced with concern at their potential liabilities for misuse of electronic communications, it is commonplace for employers to monitor use of the facilities. In the United States, a number of actions have been reported of corporations being sued 'for millions of dollars' by employees alleging that fellow workers have been engaging in some form of electronic harassment involving the posting of abusive or offensive messages.[25]

Faced with such exposure, employers may well be tempted to use packages to monitor email communications within the workplace. One such package, it is reported:

> may be programmed to suit the offensiveness threshold of each particular firm. Thus it might be that a message between two secretaries that contained the words 'sex' or 'black'—or something profane—would immediately appear on their boss's computer screen for inspection.[26]

Under present United Kingdom law, it would appear that use of such a system would not be unlawful. Although the provisions of the Regulation of Investigatory Powers Act 2000 will govern the interception of email messages passing through a public telecommunications network,

---

[23] http://www.theguardian.com/media/2008/apr/03/medialaw.digitalmedia>.
[24] *The Times*, 18 July 1997.   [25] *The Independent*, 20 July 1997.   [26] *The Independent*, 20 July 1997.

this statute does not apply to private networks. In the case of *Halford v United Kingdom*,[27] however, the European Court of Human Rights held that the Convention's requirements relating to protection of privacy had been breached where telephone calls made from work premises by a senior police officer had been 'bugged' on the authority of her Chief Constable. Argument on behalf of the United Kingdom to the effect that the telephones in question belonged to the employer, in this case the government, did not sway the court. It would appear that any monitoring of email might be challenged on this basis, although it is not clear whether the giving of notice to employees that phone calls or email messages might be monitored would remove their 'reasonable expectation' of privacy in their communications.

Liability of ISPs as publishers

With the exception of the issue of whether a defence should be available for those who post defamatory messages in the heat of a flame war, there can be little dispute that the author of such a posting should face the legal consequences. More controversial is the question of how far the operators of an online service should incur liabilities akin to those of traditional publishers in respect of messages appearing on their systems.

The Defamation Act 1996 sought to update the law relating to defamation. It followed a study conducted by the Law Commission which recommended the introduction of a new defence of 'innocent dissemination'. The Act accordingly provides that:

1. In defamation proceedings a person has a defence if he shows that—

   (a) he was not the author, editor or publisher of the statement complained of;

   (b) he took reasonable care in relation to its publication; and

   (c) he did not know, and had no reason to believe, that what he did caused or contributed to the publication of a defamatory statement.[28]

It is further provided that:

In determining for the purposes of this section of whether a person took reasonable care, or had reason to believe that what he did caused or contributed to the publication of a defamatory statement, regard shall be had to—

   (a) the extent of his responsibility for the content of the statement or the decision to publish it;

   (b) the nature or circumstances of the publication; and

   (c) the previous conduct or character of the author, editor or publisher.

The section proceeds to define the terms 'author', 'editor', and 'publisher'. It is important to note that these definitions apply only for the purposes of the section. A publisher is defined as:

a commercial publisher, that is, a person whose business is issuing material to the public, or a section of the public, who issues material containing the statement in the course of that business.[29]

It is further provided that for the purposes of the section a person will not be classed as an author, editor, or publisher if the involvement with the work is 'only' in specified capacities. The relevant categories relate to involvement:

   (a) in printing, producing, distributing or selling printed material containing the statement;

---

[27] [1997] IRLR 471.   [28] s. 1.   [29] s. 1(2).

(b) in processing, making copies of, distributing or selling any electronic medium in or on which the statement is recorded, or in operating or providing any equipment, system or service by means of which the statement is retrieved, copied, distributed or made available in electronic form; or

(c) as the operator or provider of access to a communications system by means of which the statement is transmitted or made available, by a person over whom he had no effective control.[30]

The first United Kingdom case to reach the stage of High Court proceedings was that of *Godfrey v Demon*.[31] Although the case was settled prior to a full trial, preliminary hearings have raised a number of interesting and potentially significant issues concerned with the extent of an ISP's liability for defamatory postings carried on its services.

The plaintiff, Dr Laurence Godfrey, was a United Kingdom-based lecturer in computer science, mathematics, and physics. He appeared to be a keen poster to Usenet, with reference being made in the court proceedings to a posting record of more than 3,000 messages. A number of Dr Godfrey's postings, it was suggested by the defendant at a later stage in proceedings, were intended to provoke a violent response from other posters. As was stated in the judgment:

The words complained of were posted to a newsgroup. Newsgroup users have come to abide by an informal code of conduct known as 'netiquette', which is intended to introduce an element of restraint and moderation with regard to the content of postings. Those who persist in breaching netiquette are almost invariably exposed to irate (and sometimes offensive or aggressive) postings from aggrieved users: this practice is known as 'flaming'. As a regular newsgroup user, it is to be inferred that the Plaintiff would at all material times have known of the foregoing facts and matters.[32]

Rather than perpetuating a flame war, Dr Godfrey had, on at least seven occasions, instituted proceedings against both posters and ISPs alleging that comments defamed him. The defence alleged that:

the Plaintiff has cynically pursued the tactic of posting deliberately provocative, offensive, obnoxious and frequently puerile comments about other countries, their citizens and cultures; and has done so with a view to provoking others to trade insults which he can then claim are defamatory and seek to use as the basis for bringing vexatious libel actions against them and against access or service providers such as the Defendant.[33]

The conduct at issue in the *Demon* case was slightly different. A message purporting to come from Dr Godfrey had appeared in the Newsgroup 'soc.culture.thai'. The message was a forgery, and in its tone and content was described by the judge as being 'squalid, obscene and defamatory of the plaintiff'. The basis for the defamation would lie in the argument that the plaintiff's standing in the eyes of right-thinking members of society would be damaged if it was thought that he held the views attributed to him in the email. The defendant, Demon, is a well-known ISP. Messages in 'soc.culture.thai' could be accessed by its subscribers, the postings being held on Demon's servers for around fourteen days.

The posting at issue, which originated in the United States, appeared in the newsgroup on 13 January 1997. On 17 January, Dr Godfrey faxed the defendant's managing director with the demand that the posting be removed from Demon's servers. It was accepted by both sides that this could have been done. Although Demon acknowledged that the fax had been received, it appeared that it never reached its managing director's desk and the

---

[30] s. 1(3).   [31] [1999] EMLR 542.   [32] para. 7.   [33] para. 7.

message remained on its site until routinely deleted after a fortnight. The plaintiff subsequently brought proceedings seeking damages in respect of the damage to his reputation caused by the defendant's actions. The defendant denied liability on two grounds. First, it was argued, its conduct was covered by the defence of innocent dissemination established under the Defamation Act 1996. Secondly, it was denied that there had been any publication of the comment by it. The plaintiff brought action before Moreland J in the High Court, seeking as a preliminary step to strike out these defences as invalid.

It was held by Moreland J that Demon was not to be considered as acting as a publisher in respect of the postings and therefore satisfied the first requirement of the defence. The provisions, however, were cumulative, with Demon also being required to demonstrate that it had taken reasonable care and was unaware of the fact that its actions had caused the publication of a defamatory comment. From the recital of the facts presented here, it is clear that these elements constituted a much more substantial hurdle, and it is perhaps not surprising that the court held that the defence could not be sustained. The defamation action related only to the period after 17 January 1997, when the plaintiff's fax arrived and, as the defendant had taken no action to examine the matter, it was not in a position to demonstrate that reasonable care had been taken.

The judge's finding appears in line with the Law Commission's recommendation concerning reform of the law of defamation. In its Consultation Paper, the Law Commission had suggested:

> The defence of innocent dissemination has never provided an absolute immunity for distributors, however mechanical their contribution. It does not protect those who knew that the material they were handling was defamatory, or who ought to have known of its nature. Those safeguards are preserved, so that the defence is not available to a defendant who knew that his act involved or contributed to publication defamatory of the plaintiff. It is available only if, having taken all reasonable care, the defendant had no reason to suspect that his act had that effect.[34]

The fact that a faxed message of complaint attracted no response of any sort makes it difficult to see how Demon could have availed itself of the defence of innocent dissemination. The more interesting and controversial question might relate to what could have been expected of the defendant if its administrative procedures had been more effective. It is clear from the calendar of events described that the case concerned a period of about ten days. There would have been limited opportunity for the defendant to undertake in-depth inquiries. As noted, the offending message entered the Internet via a United States-based ISP. Without the active cooperation of this party, there may well have been little that the defendant could do to verify the true identity of the sender. Even with cooperation, with the proliferation of sites such as libraries and coffee shops offering access to the Internet with a minimum of registration procedures, which could themselves be falsified with minimal effort, the task of identifying individual users is a daunting one. Given the timescale and the technical constraints identified, it would appear that an ISP in receipt of a complaint regarding a posting would have little choice other than doing nothing or removing the posting from its servers. The first action obviously carries the risk of an action for defamation, but the automatic removal of messages upon receipt of a complaint is something which carries its own problems and dangers.

It would appear that following the decision, a number of ISPs have adopted a policy of automatically withdrawing access to material in respect of which any form of complaint

---

[34] Law Commission, *Reforming Defamation Law and Procedure* (1995), para. 2.4.

has been received. One case reported by the Campaign against Censorship of the Internet appeared to go even further:

> Outcast magazine hadn't even done anything wrong: the solicitors alleged that Outcast might commit a libel at some unspecified time in the future, and that if they did, they would hold Netbenefit responsible. The ISP demanded a lawyer's guarantee against any such future wrongdoing, and when Outcast was unable to provide it within 3 hours, deleted the entire web site.[35]

The case of *Tamiz v Google*[36] illustrates well some of the issues and complexities associated with the topic. Allegedly defamatory comments had been posted regarding the conduct of the claimant a one-time candidate for the Conservative Party in London. A London newspaper had published a story that he had referred to women as 'sluts'. This was picked up and reposted in a blog hosted on Google's Blogger system and attracted a number of comments. The claimant brought defamation proceedings against Google in respect of these postings.

At first instance[37] it was held that although some of the postings were defamatory (as in *Sheffield Wednesday v Hargreaves*) others fell into the category or 'mere verbal abuse'. The Court of Appeal did not dissent from this finding. A further finding had been made to the effect that Google should not be classed as publishers either on the basis of the common law of defamation or alternatively under the provisions of section 1 of the Defamation Act 1996. Of particular relevance, it was held, was the fact that Google took 'reasonable care in passing the complaint on to the blogger after it had been notified of it'. A period of slightly more than a month elapsed between Google notifying the blogger and the contested posts being removed.

An interesting element of the case which indicates some of the jurisdictional complexities in the Internet field is that the blogger system is operated by Google Inc. which is based in the United States and states in its terms and conditions that use by bloggers is subject to US law. Under US law, as the Court of Appeal noted:

> [Google Inc.] is not a publisher of third party content hosted on blogspot.com. US law works on the basis that claimants must raise their defamation issues directly with the author of the material, not third party service providers such as Blogger.com.

Consideration will be given later to jurisdictional issues but at a practical level, the appellant's contact was exclusively with Google UK.

The Court of Appeal disagreed with the trial judge (Mr Justice Eady who has delivered many of the significant rulings in the field of Internet defamation). The present case, it was held, should be distinguished from *Bunt v Tilley* where the publisher's role was purely passive. It was agreed that Google could not be held liable in respect of the initial postings. As Mr Justice Eady had noted, 'the aggregate contain more than half a trillion words, with 250,000 new words added every minute'. As in previous cases, attention focused on the time period between Google receiving a report alleging that content was defamatory and taking action. At first instance it was held that they had no case to answer. As summarised by the Court of Appeal, the view was taken that:

> Google Inc's 'take-down' procedure might not have operated as rapidly as the claimant would wish, but it did not follow as a matter of law that between notification and take-down Google Inc became liable as a publisher of the offending material. While efforts were being made to achieve a takedown in relation to a particular URL it was hardly possible to fix Google Inc

[35] <http://www.edri.org/>.   [36] [2013] EWCA Civ 68.   [37] [2012] EWHC 449.

with liability on the basis of authorisation, approval or acquiescence. On the facts of the case, he believed it unrealistic to attribute responsibility for publication to Google Inc.[38]

The Court of Appeal disagreed with this finding. Reference was made to the 1937 case of *Byrne v Deane*.[39] In this case an allegedly defamatory comment was posted onto the noticeboard of a golf club. Club rules made it clear that notices could be posted only with the prior consent of the club secretary. The fact that the club allowed the posting to remain on the board for several days rendered them potentially liable as, because of the provision in the rules, they had the legal entitlement to remove it. Google also had, because of the provisions in their terms and conditions of use, a legal right to remove any posting on a blog site. As was held:

> The provision of a platform for the blogs is equivalent to the provision of a notice board; and Google Inc goes further than this by providing tools to help a blogger design the layout of his part of the notice board and by providing a service that enables a blogger to display advertisements alongside the notices on his part of the notice board. Most importantly, it makes the notice board available to bloggers on terms of its own choice and it can readily remove or block access to any notice that does not comply with those terms.[40]

Although it was held that Google could not benefit from the 1996 Act's defences it did succeed on another ground. The original postings complained of had appeared in April, Google was informed in July, and they were removed in August. It was accepted that Google's liability could only extend to the period between when they were informed of the complaint regarding the postings and the time they were removed. It was in the nature of blog postings, it was held, that they attracted most attention and comments in the period after their initial publication. It was unlikely, therefore, that any significant additional damage would have been caused in the period following notification to Google. At trial it had been held that:

> the period between notification of the complaint and removal of the offending blog was so short as to give rise to any potential liability on the part of Google Inc only for a very limited period, such that the court should regard it as so trivial as not to justify the maintenance of the proceedings. The judge said that, to adopt the words in *Jameel (Yousef) v Dow Jones & Co*[41]...'the game would not be worth the candle'.

The Court of Appeal agreed:

> any damage to the appellant's reputation arising out of continued publication of the comments during that period will have been trivial;...I do not accept...that various other features of the claim, including the fact that the appellant's name is relatively uncommon and distinctive in this jurisdiction, undermined the judge's conclusion.[42]

The Defamation Act 2013 now provides in section 5 a defence to the operators of websites in respect of material posted on the website by other persons. The defence will apply regardless of whether postings are moderated or unmoderated. Beyond this, however the defence is not unqualified and the Act continues to provide that the defence will be defeated if a claimant can show that it was not possible for them to identify the poster (perhaps because messages were posted under a pseudonym), that the website operator had been served with a notice of complaint specifying the details of the posting and indicating why it is considered to be defamatory, and that the operator had failed to act on the notice and remove the posting.

---

[38] para. 20.   [39] [1937] 1 KB 818.   [40] para. 33.   [41] [2005] QB 946.   [42] para. 50.

The Defamation(Operators of Websites) Regulations 2013[43] specify more precisely the procedures that are to be followed. Regulation 3 specifies the manner in which the information listed above is to be provided. An indication must also be given whether the complainant is willing for their contact details to be provided to the poster.

The Schedule to the Regulations specifies the steps that the operator must take following receipt of a notice of complaint. A period of forty-eight hours (excluding weekends and public holidays) is allowed to contact the poster with details of the complaint (excluding the identity of the complainant if this has been requested). The notice must indicate that the posting may be removed if no valid response is received within five days. A valid response is one which indicates whether the poster consents to the removal of the material or, in the event this is not the case, provides details of the poster's name and postal address. The poster must indicate whether he is willing for the ilocation information to be passed on to the complainant but in any event this data will put the website operator in a position to comply with any *Norwich Pharmacal* order that might subsequently be sought by the complainant. In the event the poster fails to respond, if the website operator wishes to retain the benefit of the defence, the posting must be removed within forty-eight hours of the expiry of the deadline for a response.

The procedures established by the Regulations are somewhat complex. Their motives are laudable in attempting to strike a balance between promoting freedom of speech and protecting the reputation of individuals against defamatory attack. This is perhaps an impossible task. Just as with the debate on privacy, there is often the suspicion that access to the law is the preserve of the well-to-do. Effectively all that the Act and Regulations may do is to facilitate the task of a complainant in taking action against a poster. Defamation actions are notoriously expensive. Some measures have been taken to reduce costs and reference might be made to the Pre-action Protocol for Defamation[44] introduced as part of the civil justice reform package. The ongoing (at the time of writing) defamation litigation involving the former government Chief Whip and *The Sun* newspaper involving reporting of the so-called 'Pleb-gate affair' does provide an example of the operation of the new rules. Delay in submitting documents on the part of the former Whip led to the court holding that he could be awarded no more than £2,000 in costs (against an estimated £500,000) in the event his claim succeeded. Whether the purpose of the changes was to protect the media is perhaps a topic for debate.

Single or multiple publications?

With many traditional works, ascertaining the date of publication is a relatively straightforward matter. Different factors may apply in the case of online resources, as was at issue in the case of *Loutchansky v Times Newspapers Ltd*.[45] Here, the claimant sued the defendant newspaper in respect of a number of stories which suggested that he was linked to organised crime in Russia. In common with most other newspapers *The Times* publishes an 'online' edition with the added capability for readers to search an archive of previous editions. The stories relating to Mr Loutchansky appeared on the online edition.

Actions for defamation require to be commenced within one year of the publication of the material complained of.[46] The action relating to the online publication was not raised within a year of the initial publication but it was argued on behalf of the claimant that publication in the

---

43 SI 2013 No. 3028.
44 <http://www.justice.gov.uk/courts/procedure-rules/civil/protocol/prot_def>.
45 [2001] EWCA Civ 1805, [2002] QB 783.   46 Limitation Act 1980, s. 4A.

context of an online work occurred anew each time the material was accessed by a reader. This argument was accepted by the trial judge and endorsed by the Court of Appeal. By way of contrast, the courts in the United States apply what is referred to as the 'single publication' rule. The basis of this was explained in the case of *Ogden v Association of the United States Army*:

> it is the prevailing American doctrine that the publication of a book, periodical or newspaper containing defamatory matter gives rise to but one cause of action for libel, which accrues at the time of the original publication, and that the statute of limitations runs from that date. It is no longer the law that every sale or delivery of a copy of the publication creates a new cause of action.[47]

Counsel for the newspaper did not seek to argue that its case was sustainable under the established United Kingdom position but sought to persuade the Court of Appeal that it should adopt the single publication rule on the basis that the emergence of the Internet and the wide and long-lasting possibilities for accessing material raised the possibility of an excessive degree of liability for defamatory material. The ongoing nature of the liability, which would begin again whenever someone downloaded material, would, it was claimed, render meaningless the provisions of the Limitation Act 1980,[48] which require that legal proceedings be brought within a year from the date of publication. The availability of Internet-based databases of the contents of newspapers and magazines, it was argued, provided a valuable social function and the law of defamation should evolve to meet the needs of the Internet age. Reference was made to the European Convention of Human Rights, which in Article 8 guarantees the right to freedom of expression. The presence of a perpetual threat of defamatory actions would, it was argued, deter exercise of the right to an unreasonable extent.[49]

The Court of Appeal was not convinced, whilst accepting the argument that the maintenance of archives performed a valuable role, this was a relatively insignificant aspect of the right of freedom of expression:

> Archive material is stale news and its publication cannot rank in importance with the dissemination of contemporary material. Nor do we believe that the law of defamation need inhibit the responsible maintenance of archives. Where it is known that archive material is or may be defamatory, the attachment of an appropriate notice warning against treating it as the truth will normally remove any sting from the material.

It is certainly difficult to defend the deliberate retention on a database of material which is known to be defamatory. The situation is more complex where its status is unclear, especially, perhaps, in a situation where a challenge is made to the accuracy of a report several years after the date of original publication.

The defendants' argument for an evolutionary change in the nature of defamatory liability received rather perfunctory treatment, the court concluding to the effect that:

> The change in the law of defamation for which the appellants contend is a radical one. In our judgment they have failed to make out their case that such a change is required.[50]

Further and more extensive discussion regarding the desirability of adopting a 'single publication' rule took place in the Australian case of *Dow Jones & Co Inc v Gutnick*.[51] Here, a story had appeared in the appellant's journal and website which was allegedly defamatory of the defendant. Proceedings were raised in the Australian courts. The appellants sought to have these struck out on the basis that publication had occurred when the material was

---

[47] (1959) 177 Supp 498 at 502.   [48] s. 4A.   [49] [2001] EWCA Civ 1805 at [71].
[50] *Loutchansky v Times Newspapers Ltd* [2001] EWCA Civ 1805, [2002] QB 783 at [74]–[76].
[51] [2002] HCA 56, Aus HC.

loaded onto its servers in New Jersey in the United States. The Australian courts, it argued, were not therefore, the most appropriate forum for the action.

Once again, the defendant sought to persuade the court to change traditional practice. The argument was addressed with some sympathy by Mr Justice Kirby. In the course of a judgment which is replete with useful information and comment regarding the impact of the Internet on legal rules he stated that:

> The idea that this Court should solve the present problem by reference to judicial remarks in England in a case, decided more than a hundred and fifty years ago, involving the conduct of the manservant of a Duke, despatched to procure a back issue of a newspaper of minuscule circulation, is not immediately appealing to me. The genius of the common law derives from its capacity to adapt the principles of past decisions, by analogical reasoning, to the resolution of entirely new and unforeseen problems. When the new problem is as novel, complex and global as that presented by the Internet in this appeal, a greater sense of legal imagination may be required than is ordinarily called for. Yet the question remains whether it can be provided, conformably with established law and with the limited functions of a court under the Australian constitution to develop and re-express the law.[52]

Although he recognised that trenchant criticisms could be made of the existing state of the law he concluded, in line with the remainder of the High Court of Australia, that change of the nature and extent required was properly a matter for the legislature rather than the courts. Echoing comments of the Canadian Supreme Court in the case of *R v Stewart*,[53] he concluded:

> It would exceed the judicial function to re-express the common law on such a subject in such ways. This is a subject of law reform requiring the evaluation of many interests and considerations that a court could not be sure to cover.[54]

The Defamation Act 2013 does make significant changes to the single publication rule although these do still have to be tested before the courts. Section 8 of the Act entitled 'Single Publication Rule' provides that:

(1) This section applies if a person—

    (a) publishes a statement to the public ('the first publication'), and

    (b) subsequently publishes (whether or not to the public) that statement or a statement which is substantially the same.

    ...

(3) For the purposes of section 4A of the Limitation Act 1980 (time limit for actions for defamation etc) any cause of action against the person for defamation in respect of the subsequent publication is to be treated as having accrued on the date of the first publication.

The section goes on to provide that:

(4) This section does not apply in relation to the subsequent publication if the manner of that publication is materially different from the manner of the first publication.

(5) In determining whether the manner of a subsequent publication is materially different from the manner of the first publication, the matters to which the court may have regard include (amongst other matters)—

    (a) the level of prominence that a statement is given;

    (b) the extent of the subsequent publication.

---

[52] *Dow Jones & Co Inc v Gutnick* [2002] HCA 56 at 92.   [53] 50 DLR (4th) 1.   [54] [2002] HCA 56 at 138.

Effectively the clause repeals the multiple publication rule except in the situation where material is republished in different form or to a greater extent. This may give rise to some issues where, for example, a web posting attracts little interest when first published but subsequently, because of further events, attracts a much wider audience. A posting in 2012, for example, about the Archbishop of Buenos Aires might have attracted little attention but, if it is now picked up by a Google search for Pope Francis, the impact may be much greater.

Jurisdictional issues

Jurisdictional issues arise in virtually every aspect of information technology law and the topic of defamation is no exception. As indicated earlier, there has been evidence of the phenomonen of libel tourism with claimants seeking to bring their cases before the High Court in London even where they may have only a limited connection with the English legal system. The relatively high level of liability placed on defendants and the generous financial awards made by the courts have obvious allure. In the case of *Loutchansky v The Times*,[55] the Court of Appeal heard a case brought by:

> an international businessman of Russian and Israeli dual nationality. He was born in Tashkent and subsequently based in Latvia. Prior to December 1994 he was a regular visitor to England with numerous personal business contacts here. In that month, however, the Home Secretary personally directed his exclusion from the United Kingdom on the ground that his presence here would not be conducive to the public good.[56]

This is one aspect of the topic and the key issue would be whether a foreign claimant had a reputation that could be damaged in England. A second—which is linked to the single/ multiple publication issue—is where defamation claims are made against a party based outside the jurisdiction. The Australian case of *Gutnick v Dow Jones*[57] provides a good illustration. A US-based publishing company was sued in the Australian courts in respect of an article published by it even though the evidence was that the potential readership for the article in Australia was miniscule.

In the case of *Karpov v William Felix Browder and ors*,[58] a Russian policeman sought to raise defamation proceedings before the High Court in respect of comments published on an English-language website published from Russia. A video published on the website alleged that the claimant had been involved in criminal activities. A key issue was whether the claimant had sufficient standing to bring proceedings before the High Court. In terms of whether he had a reputation to protect, the court noted that:

> The Claimant has frankly and realistically acknowledged that, prior to the publications of which complaint is made, he had no real and substantial reputation in this jurisdiction...
>
> The Claimant accepts that prior to the campaign commenced by the Defendants...he had no significant reputation within the jurisdiction. Since the commencement of that campaign and by reason of the Defendants' publications the Claimant has acquired an appalling reputation, such that if he entered the jurisdiction—which he ordinarily would wish to do—he would be open to the severest public obloquy.[59]

Holding that the case should be struck out as disclosing no cause of action the court restated the traditional jurisdictional test that there should be evidence that a 'real and substantial tort' had been committed within England.

---

[55] [2001] EWCA 1805.   [56] para. 4.   [57] [2002] HCA 56.   [58] [2013] EWHC 3071.
[59] para. 63.

This decision is in line with the approach set out by Lord Goff in the case of *Spiliada Maritime Corpn v Consulex Ltd*:[60]

> The basic principle is that a stay will only be granted on the ground of *forum non conveniens* where the court is satisfied that there is some other available forum, having competent jurisdiction, which is the appropriate forum for the trial of the action, i.e. in which the case may be tried more suitably for the interests of all the parties and the ends of justice.

Effectively, the English courts would claim jurisdiction unless, as was the situation in the *Karpov* case where it was ruled that the Russian courts were the appropriate venue, some other legal system has clearly a stronger connection with the case. The Defamation Act 2013 adopts a different approach providing in section 9 that:

> A court does not have jurisdiction to hear and determine an action to which this section applies unless the court is satisfied that, of all the places in which the statement complained of has been published, England and Wales is clearly the most appropriate place in which to bring an action in respect of the statement.

ISPs and the Electronic Commerce Directive

Although it has not been the subject of litigation, provisions of the European Directive on Electronic Commerce[61] may provide some protection for ISPs.[62] It lays down in Article 12 what is generally referred to as the 'mere conduit' defence. This provides that an Information Society Service Provider will not be liable to any form of legal proceeding (other than ones seeking an injunction or otherwise relating to future activities) where it:

(a) does not initiate the transmission;

(b) does not select the receiver of the transmission; and

(c) does not select or modify the information contained in the transmission.

Essentially, the provider makes available a communications network and has no effective control over the use that is made of it by users. This is in many respects a long-established principle. The Royal Mail, for example would not incur any liability for a letter sent through its network that contained defamatory comments. Matters are perhaps more complex in the Internet context. ISPs have greater control over materials and, as has been discussed in the context of copyright enforcement, may be required to take steps to prevent users accessing specified sites.

The provisions of Article 12 would apply where an ISP provides the facility for sending an email message between users. In other cases, the provider may go further. An example can be seen in the case of a website or a bulletin board such as the one at issue in *Sheffield Wednesday v Hargreaves* discussed earlier. In this case the activity is classed as hosting and again the Directive provides a qualified defence with Article 14 stating that:

1. Where an information society service is provided that consists of the storage of information provided by a recipient of the service, Member States shall ensure that the service provider is not liable for the information stored at the request of a recipient of the service, on condition that:

    (a) the provider does not have actual knowledge of illegal activity or information and, as regards claims for damages, is not aware of facts or circumstances from which the illegal activity or information is apparent; or

---

[60] [1987] AC 460 at 476.   [61] Directive 2000/31/EC.
[62] For more detailed consideration of the Directive see Ch. 23.

(b) the provider, upon obtaining such knowledge or awareness, acts expeditiously to remove or to disable access to the information.

Finally in this context Article 15 provides further that:

Member States shall not impose a general obligation on providers, when providing the services covered by Articles 12 to 14, to monitor the information which they transmit or store, nor a general obligation actively to seek facts or circumstances indicating illegal activity.

The scope of protection extended under the provision is somewhat uncertain. In a scoping report on the law of defamation published in 2002,[63] the Law Commission comment:

There has been some debate on how far this test differs from the test under section 1 of the Defamation Act 1996. One view is that article 14 [of Directive 2000/31/EC] mirrors section 1 by providing that once an ISP is aware that material is defamatory and fails to act, the protection is lost. The other view is that it may provide wider protection: it is not enough for the ISP merely to know that the material is defamatory. They would also need to know that it was 'illegal' (or at least be aware of facts and circumstances from which the illegal activity was apparent). On this basis, the ISP would need to know that the material was not only defamatory but also libellous (i.e. that the potential defences of justification, fair comment or privilege were not available).[64]

The Commission's conclusion was to the effect that:

In order to resolve this question, one needs to ask what constitutes an 'unlawful activity' in defamation law. Under current English law, it is *prima facie* unlawful to publish a defamatory statement that refers to the claimant (though in some circumstances it may be open to a defendant to prove a defence, such as truth). On this basis, it would seem that an ISP has 'actual knowledge of unlawful activity' as soon as they become aware that a publication has taken place that would make reasonable people think less well of a third party. The provider does not need to be aware that the material is false.[65]

It seems doubtful that the Electronic Commerce Directive[66] and the Regulations[67] significantly clarify the previously uncertain state of the law and, as indicated, it appears that most ISPs adopt a 'safety first' policy whereby information is withdrawn. Whilst understandable, such a response and situation is not desirable and clarification of this area of the law would be beneficial.

Conclusions

The English law of defamation has been regarded as being considerably stricter than that applying in most other jurisdictions. Although there will often be considerable practical difficulties in pursuing and enforcing an action against a foreign-based party, the suggestion has been made by one lawyer that:

Plaintiffs will be able to choose countries with repressive libel laws, like Britain. Anyone with an international reputation will sue here, because, relatively speaking, it's like falling off a log.[68]

Pending implementation of reforms to the United Kingdom's defamation laws, this may indeed be the case but, as with so many aspects of the topic, we are once again brought

---

[63] CP5 (Special) Scoping Study No. 2.   [64] para. 2.18.   [65] para. 2.22.
[66] Directive 2000/31/EC.   [67] SI 2002/2013.   [68] *The Guardian*, 25 April 1995.

to the realisation that national boundaries may be of little effect in the era of the global information infrastructure. As always, however, there may be a significant gap between an individual considering himself or herself to be the victim of defamation finding a claimant-friendly jurisdiction and securing enforcement of any award made in other jurisdictions. It may be considered unlikely, for example, that a United States court would enforce an award of damages made against a United States citizen by an English court in respect of a defamatory comment posted on the Internet from the United States. In the case of *Telnikoff v Matusevitch*,[69] the claimant had obtained an award of damages in the English courts following publication of a newspaper article deemed to be defamatory. He took action to enforce the award in the United States, only for the Court of Appeals for the District of Columbia to rule that the 'cause of action on which the judgment is based is repugnant to the public policy of the State' and to refuse to order its enforcement.

---

[69] 702 A 2d 230 (1997).

26

Internet regulation and domain names

Introduction

The communications sector has always been subject to regulation and the Internet is no exception. In some respects, it may be argued that the Internet is the most heavily regulated electronic communications network in the world in that activities carried out over it are subject, in theory if not always in practice, to a regulation in every country in which its contents might be accessed. When it comes, however, to the issue of regulation of the overall network, specific legal provisions are more limited. Reference to the Internet is entirely lacking in the Communications Act 2003, which provides the basis for the regulation of electronic communications networks and services and, indeed, when the legislation was before Parliament, government ministers were at pains on numerous occasions to point out that the measure was not intended to regulate the Internet. The Digital Economy Act 2010 does contain some provisions relating to Internet regulation but only at a relatively minor level in connection with the operation of domain-name registries. Section 1 of the Act adds a new section 134C to the Communications Act 2003 requiring the Office of Communications to prepare, at the request of the Secretary of State, a report relating to the allocation of domain names and as to any potential misuses of the system.

Internet access is dependent on two major factors: Internet (generally referred to as IP) addresses, which are a functional equivalent to telephone numbers, and domain names. The former element raises a number of technical issues but is generally non-contentious. As will be discussed in more detail later, systems of domain names—which effectively serve as an alias for IP numbers—are much more controversial and raise major issues how the Internet should be regulated.

Beyond names and numbers, an issue of current discussion is the notion of 'net neutrality'. The underlying theory is simple. Access to the Internet should be available to all content providers on equal terms. The scope of the concept, however, is rather more limited. All Internet users will be aware that the speed of Internet access is dictated in part by technical factors—much is written and spoken about the broadband divide where urban networks are generally capable of carrying traffic at much higher speeds than their rural counterparts. Again, most Internet Service Providers (ISPs) will limit customers' access speeds depending on the amount that they pay for the service. Effectively, therefore, net neutrality is limited to networks with the key concept being that some content providers should not be able to pay in order for their traffic to obtain priority over that from other providers. Adoption of such a policy has been advocated by the European Commission although there appears to be disagreement between the Member States whether such an approach is justified. An alternative approach is to suggest that the market should be left to its own devices. One ISP might, for example, target its services at users who essentially want access to textual material and restrict the speed of video downloads. Other ISPs may adopt the opposite approach.

The emergence of Internet regulation

It is often stated that the person who controls access to files and records is the most powerful individual in any organisation or, indeed, country. The same can be said of the Internet. In order to function as a global communications network, global cooperation is needed and the key question is who is to perform this role?

In large part, Internet traffic is carried over communications networks owned and controlled by a range of public- and private-sector communications providers. As was noted in the decision of the European Commission prohibiting a proposed merger between the United States-based telecommunications companies, MCI/Sprint and Worldcom:

> The Internet is an interconnected 'networks of networks' that carries bits of data between two or more computers through thousands of interconnected networks. Approximately 300 networks providing Internet connectivity operate long distance transmission networks that, together, form the global Internet's international 'backbone'. A handful of these operate networks that connect to multiple countries in more than one region. It is estimated that the ten largest Internet connectivity providers control 70 percent of international Internet bandwidth. Below the top tier providers are a number of Internet connectivity providers that operate at regional level (Europe, USA and Asia).[1]

Whilst communications companies may carry traffic, for any form of two-way communication it is a basic necessity that the parties should be able to identify each other. Traditionally, this may take the form of indicators, both of individual identity and of geographical location. What we often have is a mixture of names and numbers.

From a human perspective, names offer many benefits, especially in the form of ease of recognition and recollection. Perhaps indicative of human limitations, the average person has a greater facility for remembering words than numbers. It is reported, for example, that the ubiquitous PIN code was set at four digits because its creator's wife told him that was the longest sequence that she could remember.[2] From an efficiency standpoint, however, numbers possess overwhelming advantages. Names may often be duplicated so that there are, for example, locations called Glasgow in Jamaica, South Africa, and Zimbabwe. In the United States, there are towns called Glasgow in Alabama, Minnesota, Delaware, Iowa, California, Georgia, Illinois, Missouri, Ohio, Oregon, West Virginia, Kentucky, Missouri, Montana, North Carolina, Virginia, and Pennsylvania. There is, however, only one city of Glasgow with the telephone dialling code of 44 (0)141.

Until the 1960s, most telephone exchanges were referred to using an abbreviated form of the area covered. Telephone numbers for the town of Kirkintilloch, for example, would use the code KIR.[3] In reality, of course, as those familiar with sending text messages on mobile phones will be aware, the letters matched to numbers on the telephone dial or keypad.[4]

---

[1] Case No. COMP/M. 1741-MCI at para. 16.

[2] See <https://www.schneier.com/blog/archives/2007/07/why_an_atm_pin.html>.

[3] For more information on old dialling codes, see <http://www.telephonesuk.co.uk/old_dialing_codes.htm#ODC>.

[4] Recently, a number of companies have sought to obtain telephone numbers which relate to letters in such a way as to promote their business. In evidence before the Select Committee on Trade and Industry in 1999, the Director General of Telecommunication cited the case of a travel agency called Boomerang Travel, whose telephone number translated to '4 Australia'. Two practical problems were identified with this technique. First, many fixed-line phones are marked solely with numbers. Secondly, even when letters are used, the Director reported that there are four different variations in the manner in which the letters ABCDEF are presented. Depending on the pattern used, the consequence might be a wrong number.

Given that each number typically occupies the space associated with three or four letters, the number of memorable combinations was severely limited, even at the national level. The *Oxford English Dictionary*, for example, references some 290,000 words and 615,000 word forms. As the telephone network expanded and as it became possible for users to dial directly on an international basis, so the complexity of numbers increased.

It was always the case, of course, that letters served as a translation of the numbers that underpinned the telephone network. This is also the case with the Internet. At a technical level the Internet functions through the processing of Internet protocol (IP) addresses. All devices connecting to the Internet need to have an IP address—effectively an equivalent to a telephone number.

In the telephone context there has been discussion concerning what are referred to as 'golden numbers'. Essentially these are numbers which might be easily remembered by listeners. The number 0800 000 000 is more memorable than 0800 514 7692. Generally, however, and especially in the Internet context, numbers are a neutral commodity. I certainly have an IP address for my Internet connection but do not have a clue what it is.

The nature and role of IP addresses differs depending on circumstances. A difference exists between static and dynamic addresses. Any device connecting to the Internet needs to have an IP address. In the case of a smart phone, for example, accessing the Internet over its communications network, a separate (dynamic) IP address will be allocated for each connection taken from a collection of addresses allocated to the network provider. For most home broadband connections, the IP address might be classed as semi-static. Connections tend to be left on continually and will retain their IP address. If the router is rebooted, however, the new connection will almost certainly have a new IP address.

Within a house, or in contact with a single router, a distinction exists between private and public IP addresses. Although not exact, an analogy might be made with telephone extensions. There may be multiple instruments but all will share the same telephone number. Much is written today about the concept of the 'Internet of things' and the key concept is that Internet connectivity will be built into the most basic devices. A fridge, for example, might be programmed to monitor its stock levels and order deliveries from a local supermarket when they diminish. The UK is engaging in a major (albeit delayed) programme to install 'smart' electricity meters in all homes. These will track consumption on a real-time basis and send readings automatically to the utility provider. Increasingly, of course, the world is mobile and more and more e-commerce is being fuelled by contracts made over phones or tablet computers.

The mushrooming demand for Internet connectivity has resulted in a shortage of IP addresses. Under the main system in use today, referred to as IP 4, IP addresses are thirty-two binary digits in length (normally in the region of eight or nine decimal numbers). There are potentially some 4.3 billion unique combinations of numbers. This has led to the introduction of a new numbering system known as IP V6. An increase in number length to 128-bit numbers is calculated to provide capacity for some 340 billion, billion, billion, billion computers. Even at the Internet's (and mobile-phone networks') current rates of expansion, this should be sufficient for the foreseeable future, although take-up of the new system remains slow and some respected commentators have issued warnings that the Internet may be entering what is described as 'turbulent times'.[5] The problem appears to be most significant in the United States which historically has held the largest number of IP addresses.

---

[5] See e.g. <http://www.guardian.co.uk/technology/2010/nov/11/google-vint-cerf-internet>.

Domain names

As indicated, the issuance of IP numbers is a relatively non-problematic task. As with phone numbers, although some combinations might be more memorable than others, this is a matter of limited importance. Initially, all Internet connections were referred to solely by an IP number. As the number of users increased, so pressure grew for a more memorable means of identification. In 1987, the system of domain names first came into effect. By 1992 there were around 15,000 domain names. Today there are some 250 million. It is reported that:

> The largest TLDs in order by zone size were .com, .de (Germany), .net, .tk (Tokelau), .uk (United Kingdom), .org, .cn (China), .info, .nl (Netherlands) and .ru (Russian Federation).[6]

Tokelau may seem a strange entry on the list. It is classed as a non self-governing territory of New Zealand and consists of three islands with a population of around 1,400. It offers free domain-name registration and is frequently used in connection with phishing attacks. Another small Pacific territory with an interesting tale is Tuvalu, a collection of nine small coral atolls in the Pacific Ocean close to Fiji. It is classed as a 'Least Developed Country', with a population of about 10,000 and a GDP of $11 million. Its only export is copra. It has one computer connected to the Internet. It also 'possesses' the ISO code of TV and, in 1998, entered into a deal worth $50 million with a Canadian company for licensing rights to the domain .tv. The company planned to sell domain names to television companies wishing to establish a web presence. Sadly for the Tuvaluans, the deal fell through when the company failed to make payments, although it has recently been announced that a similar, albeit less valuable, agreement has been concluded. Other locations which have proved popular 'homes' for websites are Tonga, whose ISO code is .to, and Italy, with the designator .it.

Typically, users will seek to obtain a name which either in full or by abbreviation matches their real-life existence. We might think of the British Broadcasting Corporation (BBC) whose website can be accessed via 'bbc.co.uk' or well-known sites such as amazon.co.uk. Whilst, as discussed, with the emergence of IP V6, the supply of IP numbers is potentially virtually inexhaustible, words are in rather shorter supply. A typical directory might contain in the region of 200,000 words. At the level of personal names, large numbers of individuals coexist happily under the same identifiers. The Glasgow telephone directory, for example, lists some twenty pages of McDonalds. Because each domain name has to be mapped with a specific IP number, the Internet is not nearly as flexible. Although, as will be discussed later, the domain-name structure offers a range of categories based both on national origin and nature of activity, the issue of allocation of, and rights to, particular domain names remains one of the most problematic aspects of the Internet and its regulation.

At the outset, it should be stressed that for the working of the Internet, it is a user's IP number which is critical. Typing an address such as www.bbc.co.uk in a web browser initiates a process of trying to match the name with the appropriate IP number. Initially, the attempt will be made by the ISP's own equipment. If it fails to make a match, the query will be passed on to more comprehensive name servers, a process known as domain-name resolution. The definitive tables of names and numbers are maintained on what are referred to as root servers. There are thirteen of these machines. Ten are located in the United States, with the remaining three being in England, Japan, and Sweden. The key root server is maintained by Verisign, with the other servers downloading information about new domains

---

[6] <http://techcrunch.com/2013/04/08/internet-passes-250m-registered-top-level-domain-names/>.

from this server on a daily basis. Although many ISPs will maintain their own domain-name server, the information on this will invariably have been copied, perhaps with a delay of a few days, from the root servers. In order to be accessible to the Internet world, therefore, it is imperative that a user be issued with an IP number and that the registered name and domain be accepted by the Network Solutions root server.

Regulation of the domain-name system

In the past, communications regulation has tended to operate at a national level, with international agencies such as the International Telecommunications Union operating at a functional rather than a policy level in respect of international communications. Almost from the outset, the Internet has operated on an international basis and the question of control has come to assume considerable political and legal importance. Regulatory structures have tended to evolve rather than develop in any structured way, and a baffling range of organisations and acronyms need to be confronted in any attempt to understand the manner in which the Internet operates and is controlled.

In its pioneering days in the 1980s and early 1990s, the Internet had limited impact upon the average person. Whilst its initial status as almost a form of private members' club continues to influence debate as to the shape and form of regulation, with some users calling for the law to provide the same freedom for internal self-regulation as is afforded to voluntary organisations, the prevailing view is that the Internet's effect on the wider world is such as to call for a greater degree of legal involvement. One of the major forces for change has undoubtedly been the increasing use of the Internet for commercial purposes. At the beginning of the twenty-first century there seemed to be no limits to the potential growth of commercial activities on the Internet. Investors rushed to take a stake in any and every form of business and share values soared to dizzying levels. Contemporaneously with a more general fall in worldwide share values, the dot com boom turned into a crash although recent evidence suggests the sector is rebounding strongly as organisations have come to realise where the strengths and weaknesses of this form of activity lie. It has been suggested that e-communications involve a switch from 'bricks and mortar' to 'clicks and mortar' and the true value of e-commerce lies in the facility to provide information-based products and services. This definition encompasses subjects such as airline tickets, where it is becoming more difficult and expensive to purchase tickets using any mechanism other than the Internet.

As the Internet has developed more and more political and economic significance, so issues of regulation have become more prominent. Until the second half of the 1990s Internet regulation was effectively the preserve of the United States government which would directly contract out domain-name and number allocation responsibilities. As Internet penetration moved beyond its originally US-centred borders, the involvement of the US government became—and to a considerable extent remains—contentious. In 1998 the United States Department of Commerce concluded a contract with a not-for-profit company, the Internet Corporation for Assigned Names and Numbers (ICANN). It is described as:

> a non-profit, private sector corporation formed by a broad coalition of the Internet's business, technical, and academic communities. ICANN has been designated by the U.S. government to serve as the global consensus entity to which the U.S. government is transferring the responsibility for coordinating four key functions for the Internet: the management of the domain name system, the allocation of IP address space, the assignment of protocol parameters, and the management of the root server system.[7]

[7] <http://www.icann.org/en/correspondence/roberts-testimony-28jul99.htm>.

Following this quite precise job description, there is a reversion to platitude with the comment that:

> ICANN is dedicated to preserve the operational stability of the Internet; to promote competition; to achieve broad representation of the global Internet community; and to coordinate policy through private-sector, bottom-up, consensus-based means.

Especially in the developing world, there has been concern that ICANN remains too closely associated with the United States government. In 2012 a major global meeting—the World Summit on the Information Society—was held under the auspices of the International Telecommunications Union (ITU) in Dubai. The ITU has the honour of being the world's oldest international organisation having been founded in 1865 to coordinate the international transmission of telegrams. The key item on the agenda was whether the ITU should take over more responsibility for Internet regulation. Essentially, the ITU, which is now a specialised agency of the United Nations, is governed by the governments of its Member States. A total of 193 states are members of the ITU. Calculating the number of nation states is always a difficult task but most estimates put the number at slightly more than 200. The only countries of any size or significance that are not members of the ITU are North Korea and Borneo.

The key item on the agenda in Dubai was whether the ITU should assume greater responsibility for Internet regulation. The obvious benefit is that it is effectively responsible to governments around the world. Less positively, telecommunications markets have largely been privatised. In the United Kingdom, for example, there is no state involvement in the sector at all. When the ITU was established, state monopolies in respect of the provision of services were dominant. In some respects it is an organisation that has lost its original *raison d'être* and is seeking to find a new one. In the event, largely because of resistance from the United States and European Union countries, the event ended without any form of agreement regarding the way forward and it appears likely that ICANN will continue to perform its coordinating role for the foreseeable future.

The domain-name structure

It is probably unnecessary to spend much time describing the core elements of the domain-name structure. Everyone who has used the Internet will be familiar with these. As the Internet emerged, we had the notion of generic names. Two initial categories of domain name can be identified—generic and country code. Initially there were only a few generic codes, perhaps the best known of which is .com, widely used by commercial entities.

Initially the range of generic domains was limited. Until 2012, only twenty-one domains were operational, some widely available such as the .com designation but others limited to narrower categories of users with, for example, .edu being limited to United States-based educational institutions. Technical support for each domain name is provided by an organisation known as a registry. Effectively, each registry will maintain the definitive database of all names allocated and their associated IP numbers.

These names carry no indication of country of origin. Although it is sometimes assumed that the names 'belong' to the United States,[8] this is not the case and many companies operating on an international basis see value in possessing a non-country-specific identifier. British Airways, for example, has a website at http://www.britishairways.com.

---

[8] Two other generic codes, .gov and .mil, are restricted to United States governmental and military organisations.

The limitation in the number of domains was always a political rather than a technical decision. Although they never achieved wide usage, a number of alternative naming structures were developed. The year 2012 marked a significant change in the approach of ICANN with a potentially massive increase in the number of domains. Any organisation could apply to operate its own domain and by May of that year, 1,930 organisations had applied. The application process is a somewhat expensive one costing around £150,000, in large part evaluating applications to ensure that they have the technical and administrative capability to operate a domain without impacting on the operation of the Internet as a whole. The application form is around 360 pages long.

Applications for new domains fall into a range of categories. Some, which have recently been introduced, allow names to be expressed in a range of non-Latin based scripts such as Arabic or Chinese. Four might be cited:

- شبكة: Arabic for 'web/network'
- онлайн: Cyrillic for 'online'
- сайт: Cyrillic for 'site'
- 游戏: Chinese for 'game'.[9]

Other applications have been made by companies. Google, for example, has applied to register (amongst others) the domains .google and .youtube. Others are geographical in nature such as .london whilst a further category is subject related such as .beer and .sex.

National domain names

In addition to the system of generic domain names administered by ICANN there also exists what are referred to as country-code domain names. These are controlled by national organisations. The situation with regard to the national domains is rather complex, with a mix of public- and private-sector organisations playing the role of domain-name registry. In the United Kingdom, this role is played by a non-profit-making company, Nominet.[10] As with much of the Internet, the legal basis for its actions is unclear, it being stated that:

> Nominet UK derives its authority from the Internet industry in the UK and is recognised as the UK registry by the Internet Assigned Numbers Authority (IANA) in the USA.[11]

Based on ISO standard 3166, national codes consist of a two-letter denominator for every country in the world. The United Kingdom, for example, is referred to as .uk, France as .fr, and Germany as .de. These are generally referred to as second-level domain names.

As with generic domain names there is a trend towards liberalisation of the system. Historically in the United Kingdom, country-level domain names have been linked to particular forms of use. Universities and colleges, for example, have been located in the domain '.ac.uk', whilst government websites have used '.gov.uk' and commercial organisations have had access to '.co.uk'. The additional descriptive element sees a name such as 'soton.ac.uk' referred to as a third-level domain name.

A new, more open policy was announced by Nominet in November 2013 with initial implementation scheduled for the summer of 2014. All existing third-level users will be given the opportunity to apply to transfer their registration to a simple.uk category. One of the first applicants has been the Supreme Court. Currently this can be accessed

---

[9] <http://www.icann.org/en/news/press/releases/release-23oct13-en>.   [10] <http://www.nic.uk/>.
[11] <http://www.docstoc.com/docs/28555913/INTERNET-DOMAIN-NAMES>.

as 'supremecourt.gov.uk' and concern had been expressed by some of the judges that this linkage with government gave the impression that they were connected with, rather than independent of, government. From 2014 their domain name will be 'supremecourt.uk'.

Conclusions

The Internet has developed to an extent which could never have been foreseen in the pioneering days of the 1970s. In little more than a quarter of a century, it has become an essential component of the global economy. However, even so, it continues to defy definition. We can identify individual attributes, but the overall picture remains elusive.

Index

access to computers, offences involving 202–10
  authorised users, unauthorised access by 207–10, 212–14
  illegal access 203–4
  obtaining or enabling access 204–6
  unauthorised access 206–7
accounts and records, data protection exemption for 69
accurate and up-to-date data 107–8
adequacy, relevant and not excessive data 103–8, 169–80
administration of justice and sensitive data 96, 99
advertising, marketing and public relations, data protection exemptions for 69
agricultural software 339–40
air passenger data 178–80
alternative dispute resolution (ADR) 439–40
American Law Institute (ALI) 428
anonymity 3–4, 12, 461
armed forces data 127
Asia-Pacific Privacy Charter (APEC) initiative 32
Attacks against Information Systems Directive 200, 243
automated calling systems 164, 429–30
automated decision-making 135–6, 141
automated exchanges 147
Automatic Number Plate Recognition (ANPR) 13
automatic processing 29, 54, 112, 419

back-up copies 327, 329–30
barcodes 14
binding corporate rules (BCRs) 185–6
biometric data 43–4
Bitcoins 459–60, 464
blocking orders 365–6
botnets 109, 211–12
British Library 367, 368–9
British Standard on Information Security Management (BS 7799) 71, 449, 457
broadcasts and copyright 346, 350, 352

bullying online 229, 239–42
cable programme services and copyright 322
caching 317–19, 350–1, 362–3, 432–3, 435
calling line identification 162–3
CCTV (closed circuit television camera) 3, 13, 43
Centre for the Protection of the National Infrastructure (CPNI) 194–5
child pornography 200, 202, 229–36, 365
choice-of-law 438–9
Citizens' Rights Directive 38, 150–3
closed circuit television camera (CCTV) 3, 13, 43
codes of practice
  data protection 78–9, 84, 95, 110, 141
  Digital Economy Act 2010 357–62, 364
  Information Commissioner 78–9, 110
  initial obligations 358, 360–2
  list of relevant codes 141
  trade associations 79
Committee on Data Protection (UK) 34–5
Committee on Privacy (UK), report of 33–4
communications data
  Communications Data Privacy Directive 150, 156–66
  interception of communications see interception of communications
  Internet see Internet
  location data 3, 10, 14, 21, 95, 148–9, 155–9, 162, 192
  retention of data 22, 158, 198
  terrorism 10–11
  traffic data 21, 95, 151–8, 166, 364
community charge 103–4, 484–5
comparative advertising 420–1
compensation see damages/compensation
computer fraud 221–8, 229
  deception of a machine 221, 224–7
  dishonestly obtaining services 227–8

jurisdiction 251–2
computer games 236, 259, 323, 345–6, 493–4
computer pornography
  child pornography 200, 202, 229, 231–5, 365
  Internet 200, 202, 229–36, 242, 365
  multi-media products 236–7
  pseudo-photographs 233–5
computer programs see software
computer-related crime 189–254
  access
    illegal 203–10
    obtaining or enabling 204–6
    unauthorised use by authorised users 207–10
    unauthorised, when access is 206–7
  availability of computer data and systems, offences against 202–10
  confidentiality 202–10
  cybercrime to cyberwarfare, from 193–5
  cyberdefences 193–4
  damage to data 212–14
  denial-of-service attacks 202, 214–16
  detection and prosecution 243–54
  EU law 194, 198, 200–3, 206, 230–1, 243–4, 253
  evidence 244–51, 253–4
  extradition 253–4
  forgery 221, 222–4
  forms of crime 189–95
  fraud 189–91, 202, 208–9, 212, 221–9, 251–2, 458
  hacking 191–3
  hearsay evidence 251
  illegal access 203–10
  integrity of computer data and systems, offences against 202–10
  interception of communications see interception of communications
  interference with data and systems 211–12
  international responses 197–201
  Internet 229–42

computer-related crime (*cont.*)
jurisdictional issues 221, 223,
230, 237–9, 242, 243, 251–3
legislation 202–20
malicious communica-
tions 217–19, 239–41
misuse of devices 216–17
money 460, 464
national responses 197–8
pornography *see* **computer
pornography**
pseudo-photographs 233–5
security measures 189–90
substantive provisions
202–20
user names/passwords, trade
in 216
confidentiality
computer-related
crime 202–10
electronic communications
151–2
professional secrecy 80
references 127
**connected line
information** 162–3
consumer contracts 494–5
contract
consumers 494–5
data protection 95–6
e-commerce 435–9
non-consumer 495–7
software *see* **software, contractual liability for defective**
transborder data flows 182–5
writing requirements 449–53
controllers *see* **data controllers**
cookies 12, 14, 148, 150, 153–5
copy protection devices 351–2
copyright 257–9, 309–47
adaptations 322–3
broadcasts 346, 350, 352
cable programme service 322
compensation 322, 353, 358,
361–2
computer-generated works
313–15
crime prevention and law
enforcement 364
database protection 379–80
design right 259, 392–3
employee-created works 313
enforcement 247–8, 354–7
Enterprise and Regulatory
Reform Act 2013 367
EU law 349–55
fair and unfair use of earlier
work 319–21
forms of protected work
311–12

freedom of expression 366
information society and *see*
**information society,
copyright in the**
infringement, definition
of 315
nature of copying 315–21
Norwich Pharmacal
orders 355–6
obtaining copyright 311
originality requirement 312
ownership 313–23
perform, show, play the work
in public 322
piracy 257–8
public domain, information in
the 321, 371, 375, 378
public, issues of copies to
the 321–2
remedies 355
Scottish law 260
Statute of Anne 258, 260, 309,
369–70
statutory provisions 258,
309–12
threats of litigation 355–6
**corporate finance, data
on** 127–8
Council of Europe
Cybercrime Convention *see*
**Cybercrime Convention
(Council of Europe)**
data protection 20, 28–31,
34–7, 58, 62, 79, 95, 139,
168, 439
European Convention on
Human Rights 28, 30
OECD 30–1
credit card fraud 2, 221, 226,
458
credit reference agencies 89–92,
137, 214
crime *see* **computer-related
crime; crime prevention and
law enforcement**
**crime prevention and law
enforcement**
Bitcoins 460
copyright 364
data protection 15, 23–7,
101–2, 115, 123, 149–51,
158, 166
encryption 447
interception of communications 2–3, 21, 157, 247–50
privacy 149, 187
retention of data 105–7, 149,
157–8
search warrants 10, 74,
248–50

surveillance 3, 9–10, 20–1,
248
transfer of communications
data 8, 25, 187
criminal records 99, 105, 132–3
**Crown employment/
appointments, data on** 127
cryptography *see* **encryption
and cryptography**
currency 462–4
**cyber bullying and
harassment** 229, 239–42
**Cybercrime Convention
(Council of Europe)**
child pornography 229,
232–3
criticism 198–9
data and system
interference 211–12
forgery 221–2
fraud 221–2
freedom of
expression 229–30
illegal access 203
implementation 198–9
interception of communications 202, 210–11, 244
misuse of devices 216–17
racism and xenophobia,
protocol on 229–30
signature and ratification 199
United States 229–30

damage to computer
data 212–14
encryption 213
hacking 192–3
timelock functions 213
unauthorised use 213–14
viruses 214
damages/compensation
copyright 322, 353, 356, 358,
361–2
data protection 107, 130–1,
136, 140–6, 161, 173–4,
184–5
defamation 503, 505–6,
512–13, 516, 522, 525
e-commerce 480–1
industrial designs 393
patents 277–8
software, contractual liability
for defective 483, 488,
490, 492, 495, 499–500
trade marks 410, 417–19
data controllers 56–7,
66–70
data security 109–10
definition 56–7
exemptions 67–8

legitimate interests of controller, processing for 96–7
negotiations 128
procedural
    requirements 66–70
registration to notification, from 66–7
staff administration 68–9
Data Encryption Standard (DES) 444
data protection 26–187
    access timetable 115
    Asia-Pacific Privacy Charter initiative 32
    assessment of processing, right to request an 131–2
    audits 75–6
    automated decision-making 135–6, 141
    codes of practice 78–9, 84, 95, 110
    compensation/damages 107, 130–1, 136, 140–6, 161, 173–4, 184–5
    Council of Europe 20, 28–31, 34–7, 58, 62, 79, 95, 139, 168, 439
    crime prevention and law enforcement 15, 23–7, 101–2, 115, 123, 149–51, 158, 166
    criticism of regime 39–40
    data controllers 56–7, 66–70, 96–7, 109–10, 128
    data processors 57–8
    Data Protection Act 1984 35–7
    Data Protection Act 1998 38–40
    Data Protection Directive see **Data Protection Directive**
    data protection principles see **data protection principles**
    Data Protection Register 72–3
    data subject, definition of 58
    defamation 510–11
    denial of access 129–30
    development in UK 33–41
    Digital Economy Act 2010 363–4
    direct marketing 133–5
    enforcement 73–7
    entry and inspection, powers of 73–4
    European Convention on Human Rights 33, 35, 39–40, 85, 92, 96, 116–17
    exceptions 115–29
    exemptions 69, 140–5

freedom of expression 139, 143–4
freedom of information 27, 30, 39–40, 48–50, 54, 56, 80, 139
identification, issues of 50–2
independent data protection supervisors 70–1
individual rights and remedies 112–37
Information Commissioner 64–6, 76–80
    codes of practice 78–9
    dissemination of information 77–8
    general duties 77–80
    international cooperation 79
    professional secrecy 80
information notices 74–5
information to be supplied on notification 71
Information Tribunal 65–6, 80–1
international initiatives 27–33, 79
Internet 147–8
jurisdiction 58–60, 79, 184
media 40, 138–45
monetary penalties 77
non-automated filing systems 53–6
object to processing, right to 133–6
OECD 28, 30–2
personal data
    concept 42–4
    data subject, relating to 46–50
    sensitive personal data 44–6
preliminary assessments 72
principles see data protection principles
private and family life, right to respect for 19–20, 40, 45–6, 85, 92, 117, 143, 363
processing, concept of 52–3
professional secrecy 80
rectification of inaccurate data 130
resist enforced access, right to resist 132–3
retention see **retention of data**
scope 42–61, 140–5
security 109–10, 151–2
sensitive personal data see **sensitive personal data**
subject access
    access timetable 115
    exceptions 115–29

information rights 112–14
resist enforced access, right to 132–3
supervisory agencies 62–5
    forms 62–4
    key functions 64–5
Telecoms Data Protection Directive 37–8, 149–50, 155–6, 161, 164
terrorism 23, 44, 149, 177–8
third-party data 116–19
transborder data flows see **transborder data flows**
undertakings 75
United Nations (UN) Guidelines 32–3
Data Protection Directive
adoption 28, 37–8
automatic processing 53
codes of practice 78, 110
consent 93
cookies 148
Council of Europe Convention 62
credit scoring 136
data controllers 57
Data Protection Act 1998 36–9, 48, 60
data protection principles 83
data security 109
direct marketing 134
employment-related processing 98
exemptions 99–100, 144
extraterritoriality 59
free movement of data 59
identification 50–1
implementation 38
independent data protection supervisors 70
Information Commissioner 79
knowledge 47
manual records 53
media 139, 144
object, right to 135
personal data, definition of 42–3, 53
preliminary assessments 72
privacy 56, 149
professional secrecy 80
record-keeping, duration of 108
relevance 103
subject access rights 86, 112, 115, 124, 130–2
supervisory agencies 64, 67, 76
Telecoms Data Protection Directive 37–8, 149–50
transborder data flows 169–73, 177–82, 186

data protection principles
83–111
accuracy 107–8
adequacy and relevance
issues 103–8
administration of justice,
necessity for 96, 99
codes of practice 110
consent
duration 95
explicit 97
subject consent 93–5, 97
sensitive data 97
contract with data subject,
necessity for concluding or
performing a 95–6
credit reference agency
cases 89–92
data security 109–10
duration of record
keeping 108–9
electronic communications
sector 146–9
enforcement notices 146
ethnic monitoring 99
exemptions 140–5
factors legitimising
processing 97–101
fair processing 85–92
credit reference agency
cases 89–92
information not obtained
from data subject 86–7
information obtained from
data subject 86
unfair processing
subsequent to obtaining
data 87–9
first principle, exceptions
to 101–2
general data 95–7
individual rights and
remedies 146
Information Commissioner,
granting of assistance
by 146
law enforcement, exceptions
for 101–2
lawful processing 85, 92–101
duration of consent 95
specific factors legitimising
processing 92–3
subject consent 93–5
legal obligations, necessity to
comply with 96
legitimate interests of
controller 96–7
media 138–40
medical purposes, processing
for 99

political data 101
Privacy and Electronic
Communications Directive
and Regulations 150–66
public domain, information
in 99
purpose limitation 102–3
revenue-gathering purposes,
exceptions for 101–2
sectoral aspects 138–66
sensitive personal data 83,
85, 93, 97
Secretary of State, orders
of 100–1
special information
notices 145
special purposes, processing
for 140–5
activities covered 140–1
procedural aspects 142–5
scope 141
specified bodies, processing
by 98
timeousness 107–8
vital interests of data subject,
protection of 96, 98
database protection 372–91
copyright 379–80
Database Directive 372–3,
378–91
database regime 378–90
database right 381–90
courts, in 383–6
duration 382–3
football fixture lists 386–90
'database-ness' 384
definition 373
duration of right 382–3
examples 373–4
expenditure of effort 376–8,
388–9
football fixture lists 386–90
freedom of expression 385
licensing 380–1
new technology 374–5
substantiality 388–90
sweat of the brow
doctrine 376–8
traditional protection 375–6
deception of a machine 221, 224–7
decompilation 330, 334–5
defamation 514–19
damages/compensation 503,
505–6, 512–13, 516, 522, 525
data protection 510–11
E-Commerce
Directive 523–4
employers' liability 513–14
freedom of expression 366,
509, 511, 520

identity issues 509–12
innocent dissemination
514–16
Internet 503, 505–24
Internet service providers,
liability of 509–17, 523–4
jurisdictional issues 509,
522–3, 525
liability 509–13
libel and slander, difference
between 508
libel tourism 505, 522
mere conduit 508, 511, 523–4
nature of defamation 508
public interest 509
single or multiple
publications 519–22
social networking sites 503,
505–6, 509
time limits 519–20
United States 509–10, 513,
517, 520–1, 525
defective software see **software,
contractual liability for
defective**
denial of access 129–30
denial-of-service attacks 202,
214–16
**DES (Data Encryption
Standard)** 444
**description, implied terms
relating to** 477
design rights 392–9
computer-assisted design 392
copyright 259, 392–3
development of right 392–3
EU law 392–3, 396–8
individual character 394
legislation 392–3
novelty 259, 394
patents 259
registered Community
Design 392–3
registered design
protection 392–5
tablet computers 395–9
term of protection 393, 394–5
unregistered design
right 392–5
digital cash 461
**Digital Economy Act
2010** 356–67
blocking orders 365–6
codes on initial obliga-
tions 357–62, 364
copyright infringement
lists 359
copyright infringement
reports 357
data protection 363–4

domain names 526
Electronic Commerce
  Directive 362–3
future of Act 364
initial obligations codes for
  ISPs 357–62, 364
Internet access, limits on 355,
  360, 361–2
Internet service
  providers 356–63
legal challenges to Act 362
notification reports 359
OFCOM 358, 360–2
online infringement of
  copyright 357
progress reports 359–60
**Digital Rights Management
(DRM)** 351–2
direct marketing 17, 88–9, 95,
  133–5, 161, 165
directory information 160–2
**dishonestly, obtaining
services** 227–8
**Distance Selling
Directive** 429–30
DNA 3, 10, 23, 100, 105–6, 260,
  269, 288
domain names 404–15, 529–33
  Digital Economy Act
    2010 526
  e-commerce 530
  generic domains 531
  hijacking 404–8, 526
  honest concurrent
    use 408–10
  ICANN 411–12, 414–15, 504,
    530–2
  national domain
    names 532–3
  Nominet 408–9, 412, 414,
    532
  regulation 530–3
  reverse hijacking 410–12
  structure of domain
    names 531–2
  trade marks 259, 404–15
  Uniform Dispute Resolution
    Rules 412–15
  United States 530–1
  withdrawal of names 408
**Driver and Vehicle Licensing
Agency (DVLA)** 13, 411–12
**DRM (Digital Rights
Management)** 351–2

eBay 365, 415, 417–20, 424–5,
  461, 463
e-commerce 423–68
  alternative dispute resolution
    439–40

choice-of-law 438–9
Citizens' Rights Directive
  150, 153
contract formation 435–9
cookies 12, 14, 148, 150,
  153–5
data protection 146–66
defences provided to ISPs
  432–5
Distance Selling Directive
  429–30
domain names 530
Electronic Communications
  Act 2000 448–57
electronic signatures 453–5
encryption and cryptog-
  raphy 442–8, 456–7
EU law 150–66, 417–20,
  428–41, 448–57, 523–4
gambling 467
growth in usage 424
interception of
  communications 246–7
international initiatives
  427–8
IP addresses 148
mere conduit 523–4
money 459–66, 468
OECD 427–8
Privacy and Electronic
  Communications Directive
  and Regulations 150–66
security 442–58
taxation 424–5, 426
unsolicited communications
  93–4, 148–9, 163–6, 430
VAT 426
writing, requirements
  for 449–53
education data 125–6
electoral registers 87–9
electronic commerce *see*
  e-commerce
**electronic communications
sector**
  data protection 146–9
  Electronic Communications
    Act 2000 448–57
  mobile-phone wars 302–3
  Privacy and Electronic
    Communications Directive
    and Regulations *see*
    **Privacy and Electronic
    Communications
    Directive and Regulations**
electronic money 459–66, 468
  admission to register, criteria
    for 462
  anonymous e-money
    (digital cash) 461

Bitcoins 459–60, 464
  definition 461
  EU law 460–1, 464
  national legislation 460–1
  issuers 462
  money laundering 460
  passport rights 462
  peer-to-peer lending 460,
    464, 465–6
  safeguarding arrangements
    462
  small issuers 462
  virtual currency 459–60,
    462–4, 468
electronic signatures 453–5
  advanced electronic
    signatures 453–5
  certification 454–5
  encryption 453, 455
  EU law 453–5
**electronic vehicle identification
(EVI)** 14
emails
  contract, formation of 436–7
  monitoring 7, 19, 151, 514
  unsolicited 164–6
  vicarious liability 513
employment
  copyright works created by
    employees 313
  data processing 98, 101
  defamation, employers'
    liability for 513–14
  monitoring employees 19,
    151–2, 514
  staff administration and data
    controllers 68–9
**encryption and
cryptography** 442–8, 456–7
  Bitcoins 464
  crime prevention and law
    enforcement 447
  damage to data 213
  electronic signatures 453, 455
  EU law 447–8
  interception of communica-
    tions 245, 247–8
  OECD 446
  trusted third parties 446–7
  United States 353, 442–7
enforcement notices 72, 74–5,
  146
**ENISA (EU Agency for
Network and Information
Security)** 194, 200–1
**entry and inspection,
powers of** 73–4
**equal opportunities
policies** 101
error correction 329

ethnic monitoring 99
EU law
  Attacks against Information
    Systems Directive 200, 243
  Charter of Fundamental
    Rights of the EU 30, 35
  child pornography 200
  Citizens' Rights Directive 38,
    150–3
  Communications Data Privacy
    Directive 150, 156–66
  competition 126, 381
  computer-related crime 194,
    198, 200–3, 206, 230–1,
    243–4, 253
  copyright 349–55
  cybersecurity 194
  data protection see Data
    Protection Directive
  database protection 372–3,
    378–91
  design right 392–3, 396–8
  e-commerce 150–66, 417–20,
    428–41, 448–57, 523–4
  electronic money 460–1, 464
  electronic signatures 453–5
  encryption 447–8
  ENISA (EU Agency for
    Network and Information
    Security) 200–1
  European Cybercrime Centre
    (EC3) 201
  gambling 467
  Information Society
    Directive 317–19, 349–52,
    363, 366
  patents 266–7
  Privacy and Electronic
    Communications Directive
    and Regulations 150–66
  sensitive personal data 44–5,
    49, 100, 178, 363
European Convention on
  Human Rights 18–19, 24
  Council of Europe 28, 30
  data protection 33, 35, 39–40,
    85, 92, 96, 116–17
  freedom of expression 28,
    64, 139, 143, 241, 366, 385,
    507, 509, 519–20
  Human Rights Act 1998 40,
    510, 520
  interception of
    communications 245
  private and family life, right
    to respect for see private
    and family life, right to
    respect for
European Cybercrime Centre
  (EC3) 201

European Network and
  Information Security Agency
  (ENISA) 194, 200–1
European Patent Convention
  (EPC) 264–7, 271–2, 281–4, 287
European Patent Office
  (EPO) 268, 273, 285–6, 289
evidence
  computer-related crime
    244–51, 253–4
  extradition 253–4
  hearsay 253–4
examination marks and scripts,
  data on 128
exclusion or limitation of
  liability 492–3
expression, freedom of see
  freedom of expression
extradition 253–4

Facebook 4, 8, 16, 229, 369, 505–7
fairness
  copyright 319–21
  data processing 85–92
  software copyright 326–7
Federal Trade Commission
  (FTC) 173, 175, 211
Federation Against Software
  Theft (FAST) 311
file-sharing 241, 353, 355, 364
film rental 322
Financial Conduct Authority
  (FCA) 81, 462, 465
financial markets decision
  340–2
Financial Services Authority
  (FSA) 46, 50, 56, 77, 81, 118,
    465
flame wars 514–15
football fixture lists 386–90
forgery 221, 222–4
fraud
  computers 189–91, 202,
    208–9, 212, 221–9, 251–2,
    458
  credit cards 2, 221, 226, 458
  misrepresentation 491–2
freedom of expression
  copyright 366
  data protection 139, 143–4
  database rights 385
  defamation 366, 509, 511,
    519–20
  European Convention on
    Human Rights 28, 64,
    139, 143, 241, 366, 385,
    507, 509, 519–20
  privacy 129, 143–4, 230, 241,
    520
  United States 229–30, 249

freedom of information
  data protection 27, 30, 39–40,
    48–50, 54, 56, 80, 139
  Information Commissioner
    65
  professional secrecy 80
  tax data 16–17

gambling see online gambling
games (computer) 236, 259,
  323, 345–6, 493–4
GATS (General Agreement
  on Trade in Services) 260,
  267–8, 354–5, 467
GATT (General Agreement on
  Tariffs and Trade) 260, 267–8
GCHQ (Government
  Communications
  Headquarters) 1, 3, 244–5,
  442, 444
golden numbers 528
Google
  data protection 56, 62, 112
  database protection 375
  defamation 435, 511, 517–18,
    522
  electronic money 464, 468
  encryption 442
  intellectual property 255,
    257, 302, 323, 367–8
  privacy 22, 28, 186
  security 8–9
  Street View 112
  surveillance 22
  trade marks 416, 419, 422

hacking 1, 138, 191–3
harassment 218–19, 239–42
health data 45–6, 99, 124–5
hearsay evidence 251
history data 126
honours, data on 127
human embryos, data on 128
human rights
  Charter of Fundamental
    Rights of the EU 30, 35
  European Convention
    on Human Rights see
    European Convention on
    Human Rights
  UN rapporteur 33
  Universal Declaration of
    Human Rights 18, 24

ICANN (Internet Corporation
  for Assigned Names and
  Numbers) 411–12, 414–15,
  504, 530–2
idea/expression dichotomy 316,
  335–6

identification issues 50–2
identity theft 81, 96, 109, 190,
  202, 442
illegal access to
  computers 203–4
implied terms 475–81
industrial designs 393
Information Commissioner
  audits 75–6
  codes of practice 78–9, 110
  cookies 153–5
  data protection 64–6, 76–80
    codes of practice 78–9
    dissemination of
      information 77–8
    general duties 77–80
    international
      cooperation 79
    professional secrecy 80
  disseminating
    information 77–8
  enforcement notices 72, 74–5
  enforcement powers 72–7
  entry and inspection, powers
    of 73–4
  establishment 65–6
  freedom of information 65
  general duties 77–80
  granting of assistance 146
  information notices 74–5
  international cooperation 79
  Leveson Inquiry 63–4
  list of relevant codes 141
  privacy 15
  professional secrecy 80
  undertakings 75
information notices 74–5
Information Security
  Management, British
  Standard on (BS
  7799) on 71, 449, 457
information society, copyright
  in the 348–54
  British Library 367, 368–9
  caching 350–1
  deposit libraries 367
  Digital Economy Act 2010 see
    **Digital Economy Act
    2010**
  digital rights
    management 351–2
  harvesting the Internet 368–9
  Information Society
    Directive 317–19, 349–52,
    363, 366
  Internet access, limits on 355,
    360, 361–2
  new directions 367–9
  orphan works 367–8
  private copying 353–4

temporary acts of
  reproduction 316–19
third-party liability for
  infringements 385–7
information technology see
  e-commerce; Internet;
  software
Information Tribunal 65–6, 80–1
innocent dissemination 514–16
insurance purposes, sensitive
  data for 100
intellectual property
  law 255–63
  copyright see **copyright**
  database protection see
    database protection
  design rights see **design rights**
  developing countries 260
  domain names see **domain
    names**
  GATS 260, 267–8, 354–5
  GATT 260, 267–8
  historical background 255–61
  patents see **patents**
  trade marks see **trade marks**
  TRIPs 260, 267–8, 293, 305,
    323, 354–5, 416
**interception of
  communications** 7–11,
  210–11, 244–50
  access by agencies 244
  content, interception
    of 245–6
  crime prevention and law
    enforcement 2–3, 21, 157,
    247–50
  Cybercrime Convention 202,
    210–11, 244
  e-commerce 246–7
  employees, monitoring 151–2
  encryption 245, 247–8
  European Convention on
    Human Rights 245
  financing interception 246–7
  national security 21, 244–6
  Office of Interceptions
    Commissioner 245
  Regulation of Investigatory
    Powers Act 2000 3, 8, 21,
    151, 157, 210–11, 244–7
  remote access issues 34
  search warrants 248–50
  surveillance see **surveillance**
  telephone tapping 3, 245
  warrants 210, 245–6, 248–50
international cooperation 79,
  194, 198, 201, 231, 243, 403–4
**International Tele-
  communications Union
  (ITU)** 167, 504, 530–1

Internet 503–33
  access, limits on 360, 361–2
  caching 317–19, 350–1,
    362–2, 432–3, 435
  categorisation of 230
  child pornography 200, 202,
    229, 231–5, 365
  commercialisation see
    e-commerce
  cookies 153–5
  copyright see **information
    society, copyright in the**
  criminality 229–42
  cyber bullying and
    harassment 229, 239–42
  data protection 147–8
  defamation 503, 505–24
  Digital Economy Act
    2010 355, 360, 361–2
  domain names see **domain
    names**
  e-commerce see **e-commerce**
  IP addresses 148, 528
  IP numbers 526, 529, 531
  jurisdictional issues 237–9,
    425–6, 428, 438, 509, 517,
    522–3, 525
  jurors, use by 506–7
  mere conduit defence 362–3,
    508, 523–4
  national security 193–5
  net neutrality 526
  piracy 325–6
  pornography 200, 202,
    229–36, 242, 365
  privacy 4, 12, 369
  regulation 526–33
  service providers and
    defamation 509–17,
    523–4
  social media see **social
    media**
  terrorism 193–5
  trade marks 404–22
**Internet Assigned Numbers
  Authority (IANA)** 532
**Internet Corporation for
  Assigned Names and
  Numbers (ICANN)** 411–12,
  414–15, 504, 530–2
**Internet Watch Foundation
  (IWF)** 230–1
inventive step and patents 257,
  267–72, 275, 287, 290–3,
  296–7, 303
investigative journalists 138–9
IP (Internet Protocol)
  numbers 526, 529, 531
IT see **software**
itemised billing 159–60

judicial appointments, data
  on 127
junk mail 88, 90, 134, 166
jurisdictional issues
  computer-related crime 221,
    223, 230, 237–9, 242, 243,
    251–3
  data protection 58–60, 79,
    184
  defamation 509, 522–3, 525
  Internet 237–9, 425–6, 428,
    438, 509, 517, 522–3, 525
  joint jurisdiction 252
  multiple jurisdiction 59
  residence 58
  significant link
    requirement 252–3
jurors and the Internet 506–7

knowledge and information,
  distinction between 4

lawful data processing 85, 92–101
legal obligations, data processing
  to comply with 96
legal proceedings, processing of
  sensitive data for 99
legal professional privilege, data
  subject to 129
Leveson Inquiry 1, 39, 63–4, 81,
  138–9, 141, 503
licensing
  database protection 380–1
  gambling 457–8
  shrink-wrap licences 493–7
limitation or exclusion of
  liability 492–3
Lindop Committee 34–5
literary works, definition of 312
location data 3, 10, 14, 21, 95,
  148–9, 155–9, 162, 192
look and feel protection 337

malicious communications
  217–19, 239–41
malware 211–12
management forecasts, data
  on 127
'Mandrake system' 13
manual records 53–6
marketing data 69
media
  anonymity 3
  data protection 40, 138–45
  freedom of expression 143
  hacking scandal 102
  Leveson Inquiry 1, 39, 63–4,
    81, 138–9, 141, 503
  private and family life, right to
    respect for 40

public interest 144
regulation 63
social media see social media
special purposes, data
  processing for 140–5
medical information 45–6, 99,
  124–5
mental acts, patents for schemes
  for performance of 301–2
merchantable quality 477,
  481–2
mere conduit defence 362–3,
  508, 511, 523–4
Microsoft litigation 286
Millennium Bug 315, 469
ministerial appointments, data
  on 127
misuse of (computer) devices
  216–17
misuse of information 23
mobile phones
  hacking 1, 138
  mobile-phone wars 302–3
  networks 147, 156, 247, 302,
    305
  privacy 4, 8
  retention of data 155, 157–9
  surveillance 8
money see electronic money
money laundering 14, 460
multi-media products and child
  pornography 236–7

National Conference of
  Commissioners on Uniform
  State Laws (NCCUSL) 428
national security
  agencies 1–2, 7–8, 41, 178–9,
    195, 245
  data 119–22
  ECHELON 7
  GCHQ 1, 3, 244–5, 442, 444
  interception of communica-
    tions 21, 244–6
  Internet 8–9, 193–5
  National Security
    Strategy 193–4
  retention of data 21, 157–8
  surveillance 7–8, 10, 41, 245
  terrorism 193–4
negligence 191, 470, 485, 491,
  496
negotiations, data on 128
Nominet 408–9, 412, 414, 532
non-automated filing
  systems 53–6
non-profit-making
  organisations (NPMs) 70
Norwich Pharmacal orders
  355–6, 512, 519

novelty requirement for patents
  definition 268–9
  mosaic test 268
  obviousness 303–4
  originality requirement for
    copyright, comparison
    with 312
  preliminary examination 274
  public domain, information
    in 268–9
  revocation 278
  software 257, 264, 281–2,
    286–7, 298, 303–7
  technical contribution 296

OECD see Organisation for
  Economic Co-operation and
  Development (OECD)
OFCOM 63, 358, 360–1, 424
online gambling 466–8
  E-Commerce Directive 467
  EU law 467
  Gambling Act 2005 467
  Gambling
    Commission 466–8
  licensing 466–8
  technical standards 468
  United States 467–8
Organisation for Economic
  Co-operation and
  Development (OECD)
  aims 30
  Council of Europe 30–1
  data protection 28, 30–2
  Declaration on Transborder
    Data Flows 31
  Guidelines for Cryptography
    Policy 446
  Guidelines on Electronic
    Commerce 427–8
  Guidelines on the Protection
    of Privacy and Transborder
    Data Flows 31, 168, 174
  Guidelines for the
    Security of Information
    Systems 199–200
  privacy 28, 31–2
  tax harmonisation 438
originality requirement for
  copyright 312
orphan works 367–8
Oyster cards 3, 10, 459, 461

passenger name records
  (PNRs) 178–80
passing off 259, 402–3
passport rights 462
passwords, trade in 216
patents 255–7
  applications 273, 274–5

award of a patent 275–6
compensation 277–8
economics of system 260
European Patent
    Convention 265–7, 271–2,
    281–4, 287
examination
    preliminary 274
    substantive 275
GATS 267–8
industrial application, capacity
    for 255–6, 267, 270–1, 275,
    282, 285, 293, 295
infringements 276–7
integers 276–7
international arena 264–79
inventive step 257, 267–72,
    275, 287, 290–3, 296–7, 303
matters excluded from
    protection 271–2
novelty *see* **novelty requirement
    for patents**
Patent Co-operation
    Treaty 265, 303
pharmaceuticals 256, 267,
    272, 276
preliminary examination 274
process of obtaining and
    enforcing a patent 273–7
public domain, information in
    the 260, 264, 268–9, 275
publication of
    applications 274–5
remedies 277
requirements 268–73
revocation 277
software *see* **software
    patents**
specification and statements
    of claim 273–4
substantive examination 275
third-party involvement 275
unitary patent 266–7
WTO 267–8
PayPal 425, 459, 461–2, 468
pension benefit programmes,
    patents for 294–5
personal data 19–20, 42–50
phishing 190, 529
photographs *see*
    pseudo-photographs
piracy 257–8, 325–6
policing and data protection
    Police National Computer
        (PNC) Weeding Rules 105
    subject access 122–4
political purposes, data
    processing for 98, 101
pornography *see* **computer
    pornography**

principles of data protection *see*
    data protection principles
priority and patents 303–5
privacy 2–5, 17–20
    anonymity 2–3
    Committee on Privacy 33–4
    confidentiality 40
    crime prevention and law
        enforcement 149, 187
    data protection *see* **data
        protection**
    freedom of expression 129,
        143–4, 230, 241, 520
    Information
        Commissioner 15
    informational privacy 12,
        20, 27
    Internet 4, 12, 369
    mobile phones 4, 8
    OECD 28, 31–2
    physical privacy 12
    post-WWII expansion of
        rights 17–20
    Privacy and Electronic
        Communications Directive
        and Regulations *see*
        **Privacy and Electronic
        Communications
        Directive and Regulations**
    retention of data 149, 155,
        186
    surveillance 2–3, 12, 14–18,
        22–4
    United States 2, 15, 17, 19,
        26, 29–32
Privacy and Electronic
    Communications Directive
    and Regulations 150–66
    breach notification 152–3
    calling line
        identification 162–3
    confidentiality 151–2
    connected line
        information 162–3
    cookies 153–5
    data protection 150–66
    directory information 160–2
    itemised billing 159–60
    network and service providers,
        obligations imposed on 150
    retention of data 157–9
    security 151–2
    traffic and location
        data 155–7
    unsolicited
        communications 163–6
**private and family life, right to
    respect for** 18–20
    data protection 19–20, 40,
        45–6, 85, 92, 117, 143, 363

employees, monitoring 19,
    514
freedom of expression 520
harassment 241
jurors and the Internet 507
media 40
private life, definition
    of 18–19
private investigators 2, 102–3,
    138–9
product liability *see* **software,
    contractual liability for
    defective**
professional secrecy 80
programs *see* **software**
pseudo-photographs 233–5
psychological
    surveillance 11–12
public domain, information
    in the
    copyright 321, 371, 375, 378
    data protection 27, 99, 140
    database protection 388
    patents 260, 264, 268–9, 275
public interest
    data protection 47, 65, 80, 91,
        96, 100–1, 123, 126, 140–5,
        181
    defamation 509
    media 144
    patents 264
public relations data 69

quality, implied terms relating
    to 477–9, 481–92

racism and xenophobia 229–30
radio frequency identification
    (RFID) tags 14
record-keeping, duration
    of 108–9
rectification
    inaccurate data 130
    software copyright 329
Register of Trade Marks 400–1
registered design
    protection 392–5
regulatory activity and data
    protection 126
relevant, data must be 103–8
research data 126
retention of data
    code of practice 157–9
    crime prevention and law
        enforcement 105–7, 149,
        157–8
    Cybercrime Convention 198
    data protection
        principles 108–9
    data security 109–10

retention of data (*cont.*)
 legal basis 157–8
 mobile phones 155, 157–9
 national security 21, 157–8
 privacy 149, 155, 186
 terrorism 149, 158
Revenge pornography 240–2
revenue-gathering and data
 protection 101–2, 122–4
reverse engineering 330–6
right to respect for private and
 family life *see* **private and**
 family life, right to respect for

'safe harbor' principles 172–5
safeguarding arrangements 462
search engines 22, 319, 375,
 415–22, 432–5 *see also* **Google**
search warrants 10, 74, 248–50
Secretary of State, data
 processing by order of 100–1
security
 computer-related
 crime 189–90
 cybersecurity 193–5
 data security 109–10, 151–2
 electronic
 communications 151–2
 encryption *see* **encryption**
 and cryptography
 Google 8–9
 national security data *see*
 national security
self-incrimination, data subject
 to 129
sensitive personal data 42, 44–6
 administration of justice
 and 99
 air passenger data 178
 consent 95, 97, 100–1, 143
 data protection principles 83,
 85, 93
 employment-related
 processing 98, 101
 equal opportunities
 policies 101
 ethnic monitoring 99
 EU law 44–5, 49, 100, 178,
 363
 factors legitimising
 processing 97–101, 145
 genetic research 100
 insurance purposes 100
 legal proceedings 99
 list of categories 44
 media 142–3
 medical information 45–6, 99
 political activities 98, 101
 private and family life, right to
 respect for 363

public domain, information
 in the 99
public interest 101
Secretary of State, processing
 by orders of the 100
specified bodies, processing
 by 98
traffic and location data 157
transborder data flows 167,
 173, 178, 183
vital interests 96, 98
whistleblowing 100
September 11, 2001,
 consequences of 20–1
shrink-wrap licences,
 enforceability of 493–7
signatures *see* electronic
 signatures
silence as not constituting
 acceptance 93
social media
 content, availability of 4
 cyber bullying and
 harassment 229, 239–42
 data controllers 5, 111
 defamation 503, 505–6, 509
 malicious communica-
 tions 217–19, 239–41
 online personas 12, 442
 prevalence of usage 10, 229
 privacy 16, 369
 terrorism 217–18
social work data 125–6
Society for Worldwide
 Interbank Financial
 Telecommunications
 (SWIFT) 176–8
software
 agriculture software 339–40
 bespoke products 472
 customised software 473
 defective *see* **software,**
 contractual liability for
 defective
 definition 323
 forms of software 472–3
 legal status 487–90
 rental 321–2
 standard packages 472
 theft 311
software, contractual liability
 for defective 469–501
 community charge 484–5
 consumer contracts 494–5
 courts and quality 481–92
 description 477
 exclusion or limitation of
 liability 492–3
 forms of liability 470
 forms of software 472–3

implied terms 475–81
 description 477
 quality 477–9
 remedies for breach 480–1
 title in software 476–7
 legal status of software and
 contracts 473–5
 nature of defects 471–2
 quality 477–9, 481–92
 reasonableness
 requirement 497–500
 remedies for breach 480–1
 shrink-wrap licences,
 enforceability of 493–7
 consumer contracts 494–5
 non-consumer
 contracts 495–7
 reasonableness 497–500
 time, questions of 481–4
 title in software 476–7
 water privatisation 485–7
software copyright 323–35
 agricultural software
 decision 339–40
 applying copyright
 principles 324–5
 arm's length
 reproduction 343–5
 back-up copies 329–30
 computerised pharmacist
 decision 337–9
 copy protection
 devices 351–2
 decompilation 330, 334–5
 development 323–4
 error correction 329
 fair dealing 326–7
 financial markets
 decision 340–2
 literal and non-literal
 copying 335–7
 literary works 258
 look/feel protection 337
 piracy 258–9, 325–6
 client/server 325
 end-user 325
 multiple installation 325
 online 325
 reverse engineering 330–6
 user rights 326, 327–9
 visual works, programs as
 346–7
software patents 272–3, 280–308
 'any hardware' approach
 297–8
 contribution approach 297
 European Patent Convention
 282–4
 failure rate of companies
 256–7

Hitachi decision 295–6
IBM's Application 292–4
jurisprudence, development
  of 289–92
mental acts, schemes for
  performance of 301–2
Microsoft decision 296
mobile-phone wars 302–3
novelty 257, 264, 281–2,
  286–7, 298, 303–7
obviousness 303–4
patentability issues 268,
  271–2, 278, 281–95, 301,
  306–7, 311, 347
Patents Act 1977 282–4
pension benefit
  programmes 294–5
priority 303–5
trolls 257
standard packages 256
technical contribution 284–9
technical effect approach 297
United States 307–8
sound recordings, rental of 322
special information notices 145
special purposes, data
  processing for 140–5
speech, freedom of *see* freedom
  of expression
staff administration 68–9
state security *see* national security
statistical data 126
subject access provisions and
  data protection
  access timetable 115
  exceptions 115–29
  information rights 112–14
  resist enforced access, right
    to 132–3
supervisory agencies
  (data protection) 62–5
surveillance 7–17
  CCTV 3, 13, 43
  communications data 10
  crime prevention and law
    enforcement 3, 9–10,
    20–1, 248
  data surveillance 12
  direct surveillance 12
  ECHELON 7
  employees, monitoring 13
  forms 11–12
  image-recognition systems
    3, 12
  interception of communica-
    tions *see* interception of
    communications
  legislation 20–2
  living in surveillance
    society 7, 12–14

location data 10
mobile phones 8
national security 7–8, 10,
  41, 245
privacy 2–3, 12, 14–18, 22–4
public and private
  surveillance 9–11
targeted surveillance 12
terrorism 20–1
United States security
  agencies 1, 7–8, 41
sweat of the brow
  doctrine 376–8
SWIFT (Society for Worldwide
  Interbank Financial
  Telecommunications) 176–8

tablet computers and design
  right 395–6
tax
  data protection 101–2, 122–4
  e-commerce 424–5, 426
  freedom of
    information 16–17
  OECD 438
  privacy in dealing with tax
    system 16–17
terrorism
  Centre for the Protection of
    the National Infrastructure
    (CPNI) 244
  communications data 10–11
  cyberwarfare 192–5
  data protection 23, 44, 149,
    177–8
  malicious communica-
    tions 218, 240
  national security 193–4
  privacy 149
  retention of data 149, 158
  social media 217–18
  surveillance 20, 110
  SWIFT 177–8
  Terrorist Financing Tracking
    Program (TFTP) 177–8
third-parties 116–19
  copyright 317–18, 326,
    353–4, 365–6, 419
  data 116–19
  database protection 378,
    383, 385
  encryption 446–7
  patents 275, 285
  trusted third parties
    (TTPs) 446–7
timelock functions 213
title in software 476–7
trade marks 400–22
  comparative advertising
    420–1

computer games 259
domain names 259, 404–15
E-Commerce Directive
  417–20
effect of trade marks 401–2
generic terms 422
information
  technology 403–4
Internet related
  disputes 404–22
passing off 259, 402–3
search engines 415–22
threats of litigation 406,
  409–10
Trade Mark Directive 259,
  400, 417
use of 417
traffic data 21, 95, 151–8, 166,
  364
transborder data flows 167–87
  adequacy of protection
    consequences of finding of
      adequacy 175–6
    definition 170–1
    determining adequacy,
      procedures for 169–76
  safe harbor
    agreement 172–5
  when not provided 180–6
  air passenger data 178–80
  binding corporate
    rules 185–6
  contract, role of 182–5
  regulation 168–9
  safe harbor agreement 172–5
  SWIFT case 176–8
TRIPS 260, 267–8, 293, 305,
  323, 354–5, 416
Trojan Horse attacks 215
trusted third parties
  (TTPs) 446–7
Twitter 217–18, 229, 367, 369,
  503, 505–7

ulterior intent offence 206–7
unauthorised access to
  computers 206–10, 212–14
UNCITRAL Model Law on
  E-Commerce 427, 449
Uniform Commercial Code
  (UCC) (US) 428
Uniform Dispute Resolution
  Rules (UDRR) 412–15
unitary patents 266–7
United Nations (UN)
  Guidelines Concerning
    Computerised Personal
    Data Files 32–3
  human rights, rapporteur
    on 33

United Nations (UN) (*cont.*)
International
Telecommunications
Union 167, 504, 530–1
organised crime 243
privacy 28, 186
United States
air passenger data 178–80
computer-relates crime 197,
208, 222, 230, 232, 237–9,
249
constitutionally guaranteed
rights 17
copyright 265, 312, 316, 323,
325–6, 334–40, 347, 370
Cybercrime Convention
229–30
Data Encryption
Standard 444
data protection and 396,
407
database protection 372,
376–8, 381–2, 390
defamation 509–10, 513, 517,
520–1, 525
domain names 530–1
e-commerce 423, 428–9, 438,
440, 443–7, 472
email 166, 513
encryption 353, 442–7
extradition 208, 222
freedom of expression

229–30, 249
gambling 467–8
IP addresses 528
Internet 527–31
law enforcement 10
online gambling 467–8
patents 257, 267, 273, 275,
278–81, 285, 293–4, 300,
306–9
personal information, use
of 24
privacy 2, 15, 17, 19, 26, 29–32
search warrants 249
security agencies 1, 7–8,
178–9, 195
terrorism 178
trade marks 259, 401–4,
408–11
transborder data flows 168,
172–8
**unregistered design
right** 392–5
unsolicited communications
88, 93–4, 148–9, 163–6,
430
**user names/passwords, trade
in** 216

VAT 426
video recordings 236, 438
virtual criminality 229–42
child pornography 232–5

cyber bullying and harassment 229, 239–42
jurisdictional issues 237–9
multimedia products 235–7
pornography 230–1
pseudo-photographs 233–6
racism and
xenophobia 229–30
virtual currency 459–60, 462–4,
468
virtual worlds 229, 463
viruses 195, 197, 199, 201, 202,
211–15, 451
**visual works, programs
as** 346–7
**vital interests of data
subjects** 96, 98
voice traffic 151, 168, 245

water privatisation 485–7
whistleblowing 1, 8, 100
Wikileaks 1
**World Trade Organization
(WTO)**
GATS 260, 267–8, 354–5,
467
GATT 260, 267–8
patents 267–8
TRIPS 260, 267–8, 293, 305,
323, 354–5, 416

Younger Report 33–4